D1521852

Advance Praise for *After Violence*

"*After Violence* does the unexpected—and does it consummately! Unlike most studies of mass violence, which focus on its 'upstream' causes, Javeline looks 'downstream'—at the reactions of the victims, their neighbors, and the authorities. The strategy pays off magnificently: in contrast to the common focus on escalation, she finds peaceful protest. This is a book that scholars of violence and of peaceful protest will want to read and reflect on." –**Sidney Tarrow**, Maxwell Upson Professor of Government Emeritus, Cornell University

"Javeline poses a 'murder mystery': why in spite of all theories and evidence pointing toward the Beslan school massacre generating interethnic warfare, did it result in a large-scale nonviolent social movement? In particular, what was it about the individuals involved that led to this outcome? A fascinating read." –**Gary Goertz**, Professor Emeritus of Political Science and Peace Studies, University of Notre Dame

"Over three days in early September 2004, some 1,200 students, teachers, and parents were taken hostage in School No. 1 in Beslan, North Ossetia, Russia. Over 330 would die in the school seizure, but nearly 900 would survive. How would the experience shape their subsequent attitudes and behavior? In this extraordinary book, Javeline draws on direct data from nearly all survivors to answer the question. Her findings are illuminating and surprising in equal measure. This is engaged social science at its very best." –**Doug McAdam**, Ray Lyman Wilbur Professor of Sociology Emeritus, Stanford University

"The hostage taking at School No. 1 in Beslan, in Russia's multinational North Caucasus, in 2004, was a horrendous act of terrorism, brought to an end by security forces with heavy casualties. Many expected the siege to be followed by a wave of intercommunal violence, but the wave did not materialize. Debra Javeline's exhaustively researched and elegantly written study explains why this was so and draws lessons for broader understandings of life and politics after conflict." –**Timothy Colton**, Morris and Anna Feldberg Professor of Government and Russian Studies, Harvard University

After Violence

*Russia's Beslan School Massacre and
the Peace That Followed*

DEBRA JAVELINE

OXFORD
UNIVERSITY PRESS

OXFORD
UNIVERSITY PRESS

Oxford University Press is a department of the University of Oxford. It furthers
the University's objective of excellence in research, scholarship, and education
by publishing worldwide. Oxford is a registered trade mark of Oxford University
Press in the UK and certain other countries.

Published in the United States of America by Oxford University Press
198 Madison Avenue, New York, NY 10016, United States of America.

© Oxford University Press 2023

All rights reserved. No part of this publication may be reproduced, stored in
a retrieval system, or transmitted, in any form or by any means, without the
prior permission in writing of Oxford University Press, or as expressly permitted
by law, by license, or under terms agreed with the appropriate reproduction
rights organization. Inquiries concerning reproduction outside the scope of the
above should be sent to the Rights Department, Oxford University Press, at the
address above.

You must not circulate this work in any other form
and you must impose this same condition on any acquirer.

Library of Congress Cataloging-in-Publication Data
Names: Javeline, Debra, 1967– author.
Title: After violence : Russia's Beslan school massacre and the peace that
followed / Debra Javeline.
Description: First Edition. | New York : Oxford University Press, [2023] |
Includes bibliographical references and index.
Identifiers: LCCN 2022058618 (print) | LCCN 2022058619 (ebook) |
ISBN 9780197683347 (Hardback) | ISBN 9780197683354 (epub) | ISBN 9780197683361
Subjects: LCSH: Beslan Massacre, Beslan, Russia, 2004. |
Terrorism—Russia—History—21st century. | Violence—Psychological aspects.
Classification: LCC HV6433.R9 J38 2023 (print) | LCC HV6433.R9 (ebook) |
DDC 363.3250947—dc23/eng/20221207
LC record available at https://lccn.loc.gov/2022058618
LC ebook record available at https://lccn.loc.gov/2022058619

DOI: 10.1093/oso/9780197683347.001.0001

Printed by Integrated Books International, United States of America

To the people of Beslan. Your pain is not forgotten. Your peaceful activism is admired and appreciated.

Contents

PART III. GENERALIZING FINDINGS
FROM BESLAN VICTIMS

Figures

Tables

Acknowledgments

This entire book is an acknowledgment, an expression of profound appreciation for the fortitude of the people of Beslan.

To those victims who agreed to participate in surveys and/or focus groups, thank you for sharing your stories. I hope I have treated these stories and the memories of your loved ones with the dignity and respect they deserve, and I hope my interpretations of events after the school hostage taking have done justice to your complex and difficult situations. I am grateful for the privilege of learning from you. Hearing your concerns and frustrations, I understand that you yourselves often see the ineffectiveness of your public actions after the terrorist attack that forever changed your lives. I hope that this narrative of your actions may slightly alter your perspective, for even if you were received poorly by the authorities and sometimes by each other, I see much in your overall reaction that could serve as a model for other communities. You did the best you could under extraordinarily horrible circumstances, and thanks to you, violence in your region did not spiral into greater violence. Given the interethnic violence plaguing other regions of the world, the peaceful outcome after violence in Beslan is worthy of global gratitude.

Thank you to the many Russian journalists who courageously covered the aftermath of the Beslan school hostage taking with incredible thoroughness, sensitivity, and insight. I am especially indebted to Elena Milashina and Marina Litvinovich, without whom I and the world would have a far weaker understanding of the terrorist attack and victim activism.

Thank you to Anna Andreenkova and her talented staff at the Institute for Comparative Social Research (CESSI) for collaborating and implementing the surveys and focus groups from which this book's findings are drawn. I cannot imagine a more fulfilling partnership. Thank you to Vanessa Baird who began this journey with me and contributed greatly to survey and focus group methodologies and data analysis. The book builds on Javeline and Baird (2011). Thank you to Betsy Brooks, one of the most impressive undergraduates I have ever taught, who collaborated on the chronology in the Appendix and helped puzzle through inconsistencies in the official and unofficial records of the hostage taking.

Several scholars read parts of this manuscript and offered thoughtful feedback that shaped the final product. Many thanks to Dave Campbell, Matt Evangelista, Evgeny Finkel, Jill Gerber, Sarah Lindemann-Komarova, Kim Marten, Jim

McAdams, and Roger Petersen. Mark Beissinger and Sid Tarrow went above the call of duty in providing detailed, highly critical but always constructive and helpful comments. Tim Colton has my special gratitude as advisor and friend throughout the years who helped usher the manuscript to ultimate publication. Ruth Abbey also has my special gratitude for friendship and insightful guidance along the way.

Funding for surveys, focus groups, and writing was generously provided by the National Council for Eurasian and East European Research, as well as Notre Dame's Nanovic Institute for European Studies, Institute for Scholarship in the Liberal Arts (ISLA), Kellogg Institute for International Studies, and Kroc Institute for International Peace Studies. ISLA also generously funded indexing and permissions to use the book's cover and interior images. Notre Dame colleagues Matthew Sisk and Monica Moore have my deep thanks for assistance with map creation and image searching, respectively, as do David McBride and his team at Oxford University Press for decisively steering the publication process.

Early versions of the manuscript were presented at Indiana University's Department of Political Science and Russian & East European Studies program and the University of Pennsylvania-Temple University European Studies Colloquium; conferences of the Southern Political Science Association, Midwest Political Science Association, American Political Science Association, Program on New Approaches to Russian Security (PONARS), and Association for Slavic, East European, and Eurasian Studies; and the University of Notre Dame's Rooney Center for the Study of American Democracy, Kellogg Institute for International Studies, Kroc Institute for International Peace Studies, and Social Movements and Politics workshop. I thank all participants for helpful feedback.

I have the good fortune and privilege to love and be loved by my cherished adult family, Tony Ciliberti, Barbara Javeline, Brian Javeline, Lucy Venegas, Jodi Simons, Clayton Simons, Jill Gerber, Cynthia Belis, Stephen Belis, Carol Rose, Sylvia Tesh, Carol Smith, and Philip Smith, and to enjoy the fond memories of Anna Goldberg, Lester Soloway, Ilene Singer, Don Singer, Elaine Rose, and Stanley Goldberg. I also have the good fortune and privilege to parent three amazing kids, Jake, Gabrielle, and Danielle, to be an aunt to my fantastic nieces, Taylor, Jennifer, Hailey, and Lindsey, and to be a special kind of aunt, Aunt Jav, to the fabulous Sam, Alex, and Jessie. During the writing of this book, these privileged roles allowed me to appreciate the gravity of the loss of a child, if one could even do so, because the mind fights a parent on daring to imagine the kind of loss faced by Beslan parents. I cried from imagining, I cried from fighting the imagination. I hope the writing that emerged was better for the struggle. I thank all these wonderful people with whom I am lucky enough to share my life.

Glossary of Individuals

Beslan activists

Bzarova, Emilia	Voice of Beslan
Diova, Zalina	Voice of Beslan
Dudiyeva, Susanna	Mothers of Beslan
Gadiyeva, Aneta	Mothers of Beslan
Guburova, Zalina	Mothers of Beslan
Karlov, Valery	Independent activist
Kesayeva, Ella	Voice of Beslan
Khamitseva, Alma	Voice of Beslan
Kochishvili, Mziya	Mothers of Beslan
Kokoity, Mziya	Mothers of Beslan
Margiyeva, Svetlana	Voice of Beslan
Melikova, Marina	Voice of Beslan
Nogayev, Elbrus	Retired lieutenant colonel of Beslan police investigations department
Pak, Marina	Mothers of Beslan
Sabanov, Azamat	Independent activist
Sidakova, Rita	Mothers of Beslan
Tagayeva, Emma	Voice of Beslan, wife of Ruslan Betrozov, sister of Ella Kesayeva
Tebiyev, Ruslan	Independent activist
Techiyeva, Rita	Mothers of Beslan
Tedtov, Elbrus	Editor-in-chief of local Beslan newspaper, *Zhizn Pravoberezhnya*, former police officer
Tuayeva, Elvira	Mothers of Beslan
Tuayev, Mairbek	Chairman of Beslan Public Council

Frequently referenced former hostages

Betrozov, Ruslan	Father, assassinated
Dudiyeva, Fatima	Police officer
Mamitova, Larisa	Doctor
Tsaliyeva, Lydia	Former principal of Beslan School No. 1

Officials of the Russian Federation

Anisimov, Vladimir — Deputy Director of Federal Security Service until 2006

Aslakhanov, Aslambek — Advisor to President Putin on the Caucasus 2004–2008

Chaika, Yuri — Prosecutor General 2006–2020

Fridinsky, Sergei — Deputy Prosecutor General for Southern Federal District until 2004

Khloponin, Alexander — Presidential Envoy to North Caucasus Federal District 2010–2014

Kolesnikov, Vladimir — Deputy Prosecutor General 2002–2006

Kozak, Dmitry — Presidential envoy to Southern Federal District 2004–2007

Krivorotov, Konstantin — Lead investigator for Prosecutor General's official investigation until 2005

Medvedev, Dmitry — President 2008–2012, Prime Minister 2012–2020

Nurgaliyev, Rashid — Minister of Internal Affairs 2003–2012

Patrushev, Nikolai — Federal Security Service Director 1999–2008

Peskov, Dmitry — Spokesperson for Vladimir Putin 2000–present

Pronichev, Vladimir — Deputy Director of Federal Security Service until retirement in 2013

Putin, Vladimir — President 2000–2008 and 2012–present, Prime Minister 1999–2000, 2008–2012

Savelyev, Yuri — Former Rector of St. Petersburg Institute of Military Mechanics, State Duma deputy and dissenting member of Torshin commission, conducted independent investigation

Shepel, Nikolai — Deputy Prosecutor General for Southern Federal District 2004–2006

Sobolev, Viktor — Lieutenant General and Commander of 58th Army 2003–2006

Sydoruk, Ivan — Deputy Prosecutor General for Southern Federal District 2006–2012

Tikhonov, Alexander — General and Special Forces Commander of Federal Security Service

Tkachov, Igor — Lead investigator for Prosecutor General's official investigation as of September 2005

Torshin, Alexander — Federation Council Deputy Speaker, head of parliamentary commission investigation

Ustinov, Vladimir — Prosecutor General 2000–2006, Presidential Envoy to Southern Federal District 2008–present

Officials of the Republic of North Ossetia

Aguzarov, Tamerlan — Chief Justice of North Ossetia's Supreme Court, 1999-2011

Andreyev, Valery — Director of Federal Security Service until 2004

Bigulov, Alexander — Prosecutor until 2006

Dzantiyev, Kazbek — Minister of Internal Affairs until 2004

Dzasokhov, Alexander — President 1998–2005, Federation Council member 2005–2010

Dzgoyev, Boris — Minister of Emergency Situations 1997–unknown

Dzugayev, Lev — Presidential Press Secretary until 2004, Minister of Culture and Mass Communications 2004–unknown

Gobuyev, Oleg — Mayor of Beslan

Kesayev, Stanislav — Deputy Speaker of Parliament, head of republic's independent investigation

Khalin, Alexei — Lead investigator for Prosecutor's Office 2009–unknown

Mamsurov, Taimuraz — President 2005–2015, Parliament leader 2000–2005

Solzhenitsyn, Alexander — Lead investigator for Prosecutor's Office until 2009

Zangionov, Vitaly — Officer of Federal Security Service, official negotiator during hostage taking

Other officials or public individuals

Aidarov, Miroslav — Director of Pravoberezhny District Department of North Ossetian Interior Ministry, tried for negligence and amnestied

Aushev, Ruslan — President of Ingushetia 1993–2001

Chedzhemov, Taimuraz — Attorney for Beslan victims until 2007

Dryayev, Georgy — Chief of Staff of Pravoberezhny District Department of North Ossetian Interior Ministry, tried for negligence and amnestied

Grabovoi, Grigorii — Tried and convicted self-declared messiah who claimed to resurrect the dead

Gurazhev, Sultan — Ingush police officer abducted and released by hostage takers on route to Beslan

Gutseriyev, Mikhail — Former Deputy Speaker of Russian State Duma, president of Rusneft oil company, unofficial negotiator during the siege

Kotiyev, Akhmed Former Deputy Director of Malgobek [Ingushetia]
District Division of Internal Affairs, tried for
negligence and acquitted

Martazov, Taimuraz Deputy Head of Public Security of Pravoberezhny
District Department of North Ossetian Interior
Ministry, tried for negligence and amnestied

Maskhadov, Aslan Former President of Chechnya and separatist leader

Roshal, Leonid Moscow pediatrician, unofficial negotiator during
the siege

Yevloyev, Mukhazhir Former Director of Malgobek [Ingushetia] District
Division of Internal Affairs, tried for negligence and
acquitted

Zyazikov, Murat President of Ingushetia 2002–2008

Journalists

Allenova, Olga *Kommersant*
Chivers, C. J. *The New York Times, Esquire*
Farniyev, Zaur *Kommersant*
Litvinovich, Marina *Pravda Beslana*
Marzoyeva, Emma *Caucasian Knot*
Meteleva, Svetlana *Moskovskii komsomolets*
Milashina, Elena *Novaya gazeta*
Politkovskaya, Anna *Novaya gazeta*, book author
Shavlokhova, Madina *Izvestia, Kommersant, Gazeta*
Tokhsyrov, Vadim *Kommersant*
Voitova, Yana *The Moscow Times*

Militants

Basayev, Shamil Chechen rebel leader and presumed mastermind of
the Beslan attack

Khodov, Vladimir Wanted terrorist, second-in-command of the hostage
takers, known as Abdul or Abdulla

Khuchbarov, Ruslan Wanted terrorist, leader of the hostage takers, known
as *Polkovnik* or "Colonel"

Kulayev, Khan-Pasha Brother of Nur-Pasha

Kulayev, Nur-Pasha Surviving hostage taker, captured, tried, and
presumably incarcerated for life

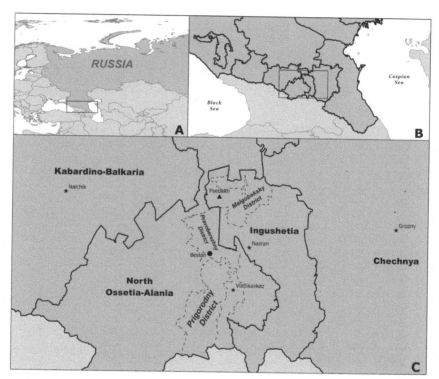

The town of Beslan (C) is located in the North Caucasus (B) of the Russian Federation (A).

Credit: Matthew Sisk.

Introduction

Peace after Violence in Beslan

The horrific act of violence that took place in 2004 was expected to incite retaliation. After all, it was considered to be the most appalling act of terrorism in Russia's history. On September 1, dozens of militants seized School No.1 in the little town of Beslan in Russia's North Ossetian Republic in the North Caucasus, west of Ingushetia and Chechnya and approximately 570 miles south of Moscow. Violence in the Caucasus was familiar and the casualties frequent, but this particular act seemed to cross a line even by Caucasian standards. Among some 1,200 hostages were hundreds of children who endured fifty-three grueling hours of grotesque mistreatment, culminating in hundreds of deaths, physical injuries, and mass psychological trauma. If the tragedy was a prelude, many observers predicted that the story of Beslan would soon involve a spiral of retaliatory ethnic violence in the North Caucasus. Victims of the school hostage taking were predominantly ethnic Ossetians who identified as Christians, and the perpetrators were predominantly ethnic Ingush and Chechens who identified as Muslims, so logically the Ossetians would seek vengeance against their Muslim neighbors.

This is instead the story of expectations unrealized, of retaliation that mostly did not happen but could have. It is a study of victims of unimaginable violence and why some choose retaliatory violence along ethnic lines while others react nonviolently. It is also the story of post-violence political activism and what motivates victims to choose this less destructive path.

Unrealized Expectations of Retaliatory Violence

In 2004, political officials and observers of the North Caucasus commonly predicted ethnically motivated revenge attacks in retaliation for the school siege (Dyupin 2004; Weir 2004). Some suggested the possibility of full-scale ethnic violence and war. Indeed, surviving and incarcerated hostage taker Nur-Pasha Kulayev claimed that the Beslan hostage taking was specifically designed to provoke Ossetians to conduct revenge attacks on Ingush and Chechens and thereby foster greater ethnic conflict, violence, and outright war throughout the North Caucasus. President Vladimir Putin too suggested that inciting conflict was

After Violence. Debra Javeline, Oxford University Press. © Oxford University Press 2023.
DOI: 10.1093/oso/9780197683347.003.0001

the aim of the hostage takers who hoped that their violent act would serve as a trigger and ignite fighting. In a national address, he said that the hostage takers and their bosses tried to provoke further conflict and "rupture the fragile balance" of ethnic and religious differences in the region (Mydans 2004b). "Those who have sent bandits to commit this heinous crime have aimed at setting our peoples against one another, intimidating the citizens of Russia and unleashing a bloody feud in the North Caucasus" (Sands 2004a).

Former president of Ingushetia, Ruslan Aushev, warned, "The Caucasus is on the threshold of a new ethnic war. The war in Chechnya might look like nothing in comparison with this possible war" (Mite 2004). Ruslan Khasbulatov, former speaker of the Russian parliament, commented, "One push, like a new Ossetian-Ingush war, and the entire Caucasus will be engulfed in one bloody, senseless and hopeless melee that Russia will not have enough troops to contain" (McAllister and Quinn-Judge 2004). A local policeman agreed, "It would take just one match and this whole place would go up in flames. . . . No one is going to forgive, that's certain. This is the Caucasus. That doesn't happen. . . . wait till the 40 days [of traditional mourning] are over," and the policeman made a cutting motion with one hand across the palm of the other (Mydans 2004b).

Adding fire to these expectations of retaliatory violence, local authorities were reported as saying that "a criminal has a nationality," and local newspapers published lists of terrorists' names and nationalities (Mite 2004), with "Chechen" and "Ingush" predominating. Deputies to Ingushetia's parliament, the National Assembly, were concerned enough about the possibility of retaliatory violence to adopt a formal appeal to their counterparts in North Ossetia. On October 6, 2004, the Ingushetian deputies warned of a concerted campaign to sow interethnic discord across the North Caucasus and called for measures to end rhetoric that might fuel mutual enmity, revenge, or branding an entire ethnic group as responsible for the crimes committed by a handful of its members (Fuller 2004).

The concerns and fears about retaliatory violence had foundation. Immediately after the hostage taking, anti-Ingush rallies were held by Ossetians in Prigorodny, a disputed district in North Ossetia that once was part of Ingushetia and had housed an Ingush majority. Police and Russian troops increased their presence to prevent the rallies from turning violent, and fearing retaliation, Ingush families began fleeing Prigorodny, and Ingush students left their North Ossetian universities (Sands 2004a; Weir 2004).

In a meeting in the gymnasium of the wrecked school, many victims insisted on vengeance:

"Let's gather up all of the men in the villages and fight!"

"The people who don't want to fight say, 'So many innocent lives will suffer if we take up arms.' Well, we've already suffered enough. It's time to fight."

"Of course, after the funerals our men will try to take matters into our hands. And of course, this is the right thing to do."

"[T]his is the time to take up arms, because the blood that was spilled was ours. Who among us can just go home and live calmly?" (Rodriguez 2004a)

Almost a year later, prominent Russians continued to assert that provocation of interethnic violence was a prime motive for the hostage taking and that the provocation could have worked. Noted pediatrician and negotiator during the hostage taking, Dr. Leonid Roshal, said, "What did [Chechen rebel leader Shamil] Basayev want to do? He wanted Ossetians to take spades and machine guns and move on to Ingushetia. If someone's child is taken hostage, he may do this" (Official Kremlin International News Broadcast 2005).

In a focus group of male Beslan victims over thirty-five years old, participants were asked whether people had been thinking about taking revenge on the Ingush.

VITALY: Yes, some people were [thinking this way].
BORIS: In the beginning, there was such an opinion.
VITALY: Yes, it was a stressful situation.
TAMERLAN: People had this idea. You could even say the overwhelming majority of people . . .
KAZBEK: To tell the truth, if I had seen a full bus with Ingush people right after the events and there had been children there, I would have shot all of them. All of them.
TOTRAZ: You are overreacting.
KAZBEK: I would have shot everybody there.
TOTRAZ: I don't think you would have shot children.
ALIK: I can easily believe him.
KAZBEK: I would have shot because I saw in the hall, in the morgue. . . . I mean, I am talking about the first days after the events.

In a separate focus group, female victims remembered the same discussions and expectations of retaliatory violence.

ANGELA: At that time it was true [that there were attempts at revenge].
VERA: Well, consider the state everyone was in at that time.
VALYA: This desire originated in rage.
VERA: These were men who buried their children. I think not only an Ossetian but a Russian would also avenge his child.
VALYA: Everyone went there, not only Ossetians. At that time, everyone was in such a rage that they were ready for anything.

In response to whether people in 2008 still thought they should take revenge and even look for such an opportunity, the men answered:

BORIS: No one will tell you openly about it. Probably they do.
ALIK: No person will say that it is unnecessary, that it is senseless. If a person slapped you in the face once and you didn't respond, the second time he will cut off your finger, and the third time your hand, and then in general . . .
KAZBEK: In the Bible it is one way, but in real life, it is another. Share your bread with your enemy. I will share dynamite with him.

Rumors circulated that at least some retaliatory violence materialized. Human rights activist Timur Aliyev claimed that only hours after the siege ended, Ossetians took a handful of Ingush hostages in the village of Chermen, twelve kilometers southeast of Beslan (McAllister and Quinn-Judge 2004), and some Beslan residents allegedly headed into Ingushetia and abducted ten Ingush men (Walsh 2004a). Later, in 2007, Suleiman Vagapov, deputy to presidential envoy to the Southern Federal District Dmitry Kozak, circulated a document describing a North Ossetian group that engaged in abductions as retaliation for the school hostage taking and claiming that 238 people went missing in North Ossetia, 26 of whom were Ingush. In 2006–2007, 25 Ossetians and 19 Chechens and Ingush were reportedly abducted (Fuller 2007). Also in 2007, Lieutenant Colonel Alikhan Kalimatov of the Russian Federal Security Service was shot dead on the Caucasus highway in Ingushetia where he was investigating the kidnappings of ethnic Ingush in North Ossetia ("High-Ranking Security Officer" 2007).

There may have been other incidents of retaliatory violence. However, the bigger story of the Beslan aftermath is in how little retaliatory violence actually occurred, especially relative to expectations and relative to historical patterns in the North Caucasus. The September 2004 hostage taking did not initiate a new ethnic war or significantly escalate the level of violence in an already tense region. Importantly, most Beslan victims and their relatives, neighbors, and other co-ethnics opposed the idea of responding to violence with further violence.

As participants in a focus group of female victims under thirty-five years old explained:

IRINA: There were people who wanted it [revenge]. They were not a majority, but if they had felt support, they would have gone.
BELA: No, better a thin peace than a war.

Participants in a focus group of female victims over thirty-five years old also dismissed revenge as a viable option:

DINA: And did you want us to attack our neighbors?

BERTA: And on whom to take revenge now?

TATIANA: There is nobody.

BERTA: And slaughter—what do you mean? Ossetia will now get together and attack Ingush, Georgians? This is senseless.

RAISA: We are used to a fair trial. That's all.

BERTA: And again there will be no result. And we need a result.

TATIANA: And we don't need war.

BERTA: War is just bloodshed with no result.

TATIANA: Like here. Our children again.

BERTA: Children, young boys will be left without parents.

The men over thirty-five provided some details on the decision to avoid retaliatory violence:

ALIK: Literally a few days later, I don't remember the date exactly, the most active young people gathered in our recreation center. And there was one question: What is to be done? Serious inter-republican problems may emerge. But as we have many clear heads, sensible ones—there were very many people there, and they decided that we would not take any active actions until we sorted out all our funerals, all this business. That is why it was quiet. I know what you mean: why didn't you all take machineguns?

KAZBEK: Everybody was very emotional. So one small spark, and it would have been bad. Everybody understood that.

ALIK: God, help us to avoid an explosion between the two republics.

KAZBEK: Everybody had a say. We listened to everybody there. But most people were saying that it does not pay to do anything for the time being.

Unexpected Political Activism in Beslan

Instead, starting in September 2004, the town of Beslan, with its population of only 36,000, became the site of some of the most politically active of Russia's 140 million citizens. Before the hostage taking, Beslan was unknown outside of Russia and rarely made the news even inside Russia. Beslan was far from any major power center, and its residents were not wealthy or powerful or more highly educated than other Russian citizens. There was little reason to predict the sustained activism that followed.

Virtually overnight, thousands of Beslan residents began engaging in politics, with dozens becoming full-fledged activists for years to come. They held rallies at their House of Culture, central square, and other sites. They set up websites and organizations. They attended town meetings, signed petitions, and met with local and national politicians and aggressively pursued them with demands. They blockaded a highway, staged a courtroom sit-in, went on a hunger strike, and carried out independent information-gathering in order to challenge the authorities. They traveled to Vladikavkaz, Rostov, and Moscow. They litigated, appealed to the international community, and filed a complaint in the European Court of Human Rights.

While observers and politicians in September 2004 and beyond were predicting retaliatory violence, few if any were predicting this outpouring of political activism. Certainly, no one was predicting the sheer size of the activist population, the diversity of the participatory acts, or the perseverance of many who continue to challenge the authorities even today. In the early aftermath, the number of participating individuals was remarkable: hundreds showed up for various rallies, and occasionally more than a thousand, in a town only thirty-six times as large. Victims describe these early events as spontaneous, with no clear leaders or official sources of information, just relatives and neighbors instinctively spreading the word to go. Even those who were just released from the hospital and who were, in the words of one victim, "half-dead, cut, and injured here and there and everywhere and could hardly move," went to the rallies. Funerals too became a kind of rally, and for some two months afterward while the entire town buried their loved ones, the politicized crowds retained their momentum.

By then, Beslan residents were emboldened, with many willing to vocalize their grievances in public settings where they could be individually identified by authorities. For example, at 3 p.m. on November 3, 2004, just two months after the hostage taking, more than a thousand residents gathered at the House of Culture to meet with an official delegation headed by Russian Deputy Prosecutor General for the Southern Federal District, Nikolai Shepel, and including the former mayor of Beslan and other officials. Shepel informed the crowd that there had been thirty-two terrorists, that the terrorists had been using drugs, that there were no weapons planted in the school in advance, that the terrorists brought the weapons with them, and that legal action had been taken against police officers in North Ossetia and Ingushetia for dereliction of duty. In response, the angry and at times explosive public challenges began by dozens of different speakers:

"Why do you keep saying there were 32 terrorists? We all saw that there were many more than that!"

"We all know that there were weapons in the school even before it was seized. Why are the authorities denying this?"

"There *were* weapons!"

"There were so many that they couldn't possibly have brought them all with them!"

"We don't like what you're saying. Maybe you're not authorized or allowed to disclose all the information, but at this point nobody has any use for half-truths or half-measures. The deputy prosecutor general says that they're investigating the causes and circumstances that made the terrorist act in Beslan possible. But all of us already know what those causes and circumstances are. And the main cause is all the corruption in the government and the internal affairs agencies, and the corrupt people that [North Ossetian] President Dzasokhov has surrounded himself with! Why punish the rank-and-file policemen who have been dismissed and put in jail. Forty ordinary policemen have been fired, but no top officials have lost their jobs."

"Tell us, who conducted the negotiations with the terrorists? Who's going to answer for the fact that nothing came of them?"

To Shepel's answer that professionals who specialize in conducting negotiations were called in from Moscow, the crowd exclaimed, "Who are these people? Tell us their names!"

Another official, a senior investigator in the Prosecutor General's Office, Konstantin Lyufi, declared that the terrorists didn't make any demands, and the Beslan residents shouted, "Why are you lying?"

"They began making demands in the first hour. We all knew about their demands! And the authorities knew about them too! [The terrorists] told us, 'Your government doesn't care about you. Your government isn't even saying how many of you there are here.'"

"People at the [task force] headquarters told us that the children were being given food and water, but they weren't being given anything!"

"What was [former president of Ingushetia Ruslan] Aushev doing there?"

"And since when is the ex-president of Ingushetia the top man in Russia? Where were the rest of them? While we were sitting in the gymnasium, the terrorists told us, 'The most important man in Russia is coming.' And we all thought that Putin was coming, and we expected him. But then Aushev arrived. So where was Putin?"

In response to Shepel's clarification that President Dzasokhov and head of the Federal Security Service (FSB) Administration in the North Caucasus Valery

Andreyev were in charge of the hostage release task force, the Beslan residents called out, "And why was one [Andreyev] dismissed but not the other?" Getting no answer, people shouted for the delegation to leave (Shavlokhova et al. 2004).

Two months later, on January 20, 2005, after other rallies and petitions and a preliminary report of the General Prosecutors that did not address the question of which political leaders deserved blame for the tragedy, victims' relatives and other Beslan residents began a blockade of the Rostov-Baku/Caucasus Federal Highway just outside of Beslan. Starting with 50 participants, the blockaders soon swelled to 200, and by evening, 400 people were blocking the highway, with others supplying sandwiches, tea-filled thermoses, bonfire wood, and other provisions. Some carried signs that read: "Why Were Our Children Killed?"; "We Demand an International Investigation"; and "Dzasokhov is a Puppet of Moscow." The protesters built tents across the highway, expressed dissatisfaction with the Russian parliamentary commission that was investigating the hostage taking and the government's response, and refused to leave until President Dzasokhov resigned, other officials faced criminal prosecution, the parliamentary commission suspended its work, a more objective investigative committee took its place, and the administrative border with Ingushetia was properly sealed by police and security forces (Bakhvalova 2005; Chivers 2005a; Tokhsyrov 2005). The blockade ended four days later when protesters were promised a meeting with Dmitry Kozak, then presidential envoy to the South Federal District (Bakhvalova 2005).

As the months and years progressed, political activities occasionally attracted the same high numbers of participants as these initial activities, especially for the annual events commemorating the hostage taking and for uniquely salient events like the trial of the captured hostage taker, Nur-Pasha Kulayev, but activities also suffered from the attrition and protest fatigue typical of rank-and-file participants. More noteworthy perhaps than the endurance of the rank and file were the actions of the sizable and energetic activist core that remained. Susanna Dudiyeva and Ella Kesayeva became the most well-known of these activists, chairing the support and advocacy groups, Mothers of Beslan and Voice of Beslan, respectively, and acting as tireless spokespeople and organizers of rallies, petitions, and meetings with officials. Beyond these full-time activists, many other victim-activists had a smaller media presence but devoted countless hours to political activities since 2004.

For example, in March of 2007, eighty victims filed a court complaint about violations of their rights to justice and demanded criminal investigations of Dzasokhov, Andreyev, and Russian Special Forces Commander General Aleksandr Tikhonov for their actions during the crisis. In May 2007, when three police officers accused of failing to stop militants from seizing the school were granted amnesty, approximately twenty-five women responded by smashing courtroom windows, overturning furniture, and tearing down blinds and a

Russian flag. In June 2007, eighty-nine relatives of victims filed a joint complaint in the European Court of Human Rights accusing the Russian government of failing to investigate the hostage taking properly. By June 2008, Voice of Beslan filed criminal charges against Putin for violations of eleven articles of the Russian Criminal Code, including negligence and murder.

Looking back on these astounding political activities, it is easy to take them for granted. The grievances may seem logical or even obvious, as may the decision to act politically on behalf of the grievances. However, back in 2004, none of the above activities or the dozens more discussed in this book seemed logical, let alone obvious.

Individual Variation in Responses to Violence

As impressive as the low aggregate level of retaliatory ethnic violence was, it reflected the behavior of only some percentage of Beslan victims and their families, friends, and neighbors. Most victims avoided violence, and some definitively supported nonviolence, but some chose otherwise. As impressive as the high aggregate amount of post-violence political participation was, it involved only some percentage of the possible participants. Many victims chose to be politically active, but many chose otherwise. The individual variation drives this book.

The study focuses on individuals, rather than the town of Beslan as an undifferentiated unit or the Ossetian people or some other group. The question about individual behavior after a violent episode is important because "survivors' psychological traumas exist at the individual level of analysis and are not amenable to aggregation to the units of analysis [such as] insurgent organizations, ethnic groups, states, etc." (Petersen and Zukerman 2009:567). The importance of group-level dynamics for both peaceful and violent action is not discounted. Rather, the inquiry holds these dynamics relatively constant by asking which members within an unambiguously aggrieved group take either type of action.

The study thus contributes to a literature that is dominated by studies at higher levels of aggregation (e.g., Demmers 2012). Prior emphasis on group dynamics makes sense, given the collective and interdependent nature of much violent and peaceful action. Studies show that individual decisions to support retaliatory violence and/or participate in politics are affected by other individuals and the community as a whole. Social norms, for example, may reward or punish violence (Elster 1998:51; Bhavnani 2006). When violence is legitimized and justified by group myths and symbols, framed to make sense, and rewarded with enhanced in-group status, the propensity for violence increases, and when violence is socially unacceptable and subject to in-group policing by co-ethnics, the propensity for violence is reduced (Horowitz

1985, 2001:267; Brass 1996; Fearon and Laitin 1996; Green et al. 2001:486; Kaufman 2001, 2006; Demmers 2012:132–136; McDoom 2013). Similarly, social networks and norms influence participation in politics (Hayes et al. 2006:259). When participation is perceived as valued or expected, and especially when evidence exists of participation by other community members, individuals feel encouraged to participate, and when participation or the cause that motivates it is scrutinized or criticized, individuals feel discouraged from participating (Klandermans 1984; Klandermans and Oegema 1987; Finkel et al. 1989; Muller et al. 1991; Chong 1991; Hayes et al. 2006:259). Indeed, one of the most robust correlates of institutional and extra-institutional political activism like protest is whether the individuals were ever asked to participate (Verba et al. 1995, chap. 5; Varese and Yaish 2000; Javeline 2003b). Violent and peaceful actions may be influenced not only by community networks and norms but also by community leaders. Political elites or "entrepreneurs" often provoke large-scale violence (Kuran 1998; Lake and Rothchild 1996, 1998; Fearon and Laitin 2000:846) and often "prospect for participants" in nonviolent political action (Brady et al. 1999).

This book analyzes varying individual responses in a relatively constant setting of community norms and pressures, including historical traditions of retaliatory violence that may have lost influence over time. It asks which individuals, after the violent episode in Beslan, were most receptive to retaliatory ethnic violence and "recruitable," should provocative elites have emerged and tried to manipulate the public (Kalyvas and Kocher 2007:182; also Horowitz 2001:50–51), and which individuals were mobilized politically.

Analysis of individual variation in responses to violence requires thoughtful consideration of which individuals to study, or case selection. Whose response matters? This study assumes that grievances define which populations are most relevant. Grievances like victimization by violence are the reason that retaliatory violence and political activism are possibilities. Rather than sample among the general population or use country-level indicators such as ethnic diversity or economic inequality as proxies for grievances (e.g., Collier 2000; Fearon and Laitin 2003), proxies that are often poor (Humphreys 2005; Cramer 2006), this study assumes that grievances should be observed and verified at the individual level by isolating and investigating a population of incontrovertibly aggrieved individuals. Such an approach maximizes the validity of measurements and findings. Importantly, grievances should be less significant for variability across individuals than as the defining component of the post-violence context. Within an aggrieved community, particularly one victimized by violence, grievances may be universally severe and not vary significantly enough to differentiate supporters of retaliatory violence from non-supporters, activists from nonactivists.

The Puzzle

What motivates different responses to violence? This question has endured because so often violence begets more violence. Violated individuals desire revenge, retaliation, retribution, an-eye-for-an-eye, tit-for-tat, or vengeance by some other name. They want to get even, settle scores, right wrongs, and make someone pay, and they engage in vendetta or blood feuds. The cycle of violence can seem inescapable because the motivation perpetuates itself: "An act of revenge results in a new offense to be righted, and when the act is perpetrated not against the same person who did the offense but against another who is part of the same family, tribe, or social group (the logic of 'vendetta'), the possibilities for escalation are endless" (Solomon 1994:308).

The vindictive drive is a natural human impulse (Jacoby 1983; Frijda 1994; Solomon 1994) that is especially prevalent in situations of ongoing ethnic conflict and civil war (Kalyvas 2006:58–61). Vengeance may serve to equalize power, restore self-esteem, deter recurrence of harm, or provide relief from the pain caused by harm or humiliation (Frijda 1994). The avenger is at times a celebrated member of society, particularly when the punishment would avenge harm to women and children, the proverbial innocents, and when successful retaliation conveys manliness and honor.

However, violence also inspires more normatively productive behavior, such as nonviolent political participation, that in turn may serve to reduce future violence. Understanding how to achieve the latter productive response is important to advancing knowledge and also to real-world concerns about how to maintain peace while redressing grievances. Indeed, it is one of the most fundamental questions about politics: Can there be peaceful solutions to violence? What makes victims of communal violence feel that their grievances are most appropriately expressed peacefully and politically?

Violence here is defined as "behavior designed to inflict injury on people or damage to property" (Graham and Gurr 1969:xxvii; della Porta 1995:2). Retaliatory violence involves injurious behavior that is motivated explicitly by previous physical injury or property damage and is directed at the perpetrator, his or her family, or community members. Retaliatory ethnic or communal violence involves injurious behavior directed at members of an ethnic, cultural, religious, or linguistic group. Political participation refers to "action by ordinary citizens directed toward influencing some political outcomes" (Brady 1999:737).

From a normative perspective, the ideal response is political participation without violence. Apolitical nonviolence may be an acceptable outcome and certainly preferable to retaliatory violence against perpetrators or members of their ethnic group, if the sole criterion is preventing further loss of human life, but it is less than ideal for the interest representation and health of the community that just experienced a violent episode. Absent political action, victims are likely to have grievances and interests that remain poorly addressed. Although political action in no way guarantees interest representation, the probability of grievance satisfaction is especially low if the grievances never get articulated in the political arena in the first place. Festering grievances are problematic in their own right and could also keep alive the possibility of future violence (Dollard et al. 1939; Gurr 1970; Berkowitz 1993; Anderson and Huesmann 2003). A nonviolent activist response to violence thus may do more to ameliorate future violence than a nonviolent docile response.

What factors encourage peaceful political responses to violence? What factors discourage retaliatory violence? Are the factors that encourage political responses the same as those that discourage further violence? Can we identify any factors that encourage victims and witnesses to violence to choose peaceful political responses instead of retaliatory violence?

These questions are especially important given the prevalence of terrorism and other horrific acts of violence in communities throughout the world. Individual victims and their relatives, friends, neighbors, and co-ethnics are understandably distraught and tempted to respond in kind. Much may be learned from those situations where restraint is exercised by many but not all, especially when restraint is accompanied by peaceful participation in public life.

Advantages of Studying Beslan

From a social science perspective, a study of Beslan victims has the virtue of allowing us to identify with accuracy a reasonably finite pool of aggrieved individuals.[1] Other studies of violent and peaceful individual behavior typically survey members of a relatively arbitrary group and ask probing questions about grievances in order to isolate aggrieved individuals from the rest and then study the behavior of that small subsample, or studies assess grievances superficially by asking about each group member's "most important problem" or dissatisfaction and then assume that these varying problems or dissatisfactions should motivate behavior in the same way (see Brady 1999:789 for a critique). Studies frequently rely on university students who have been coaxed to participate for course credit and then asked about potentially non-salient or salient but not especially weighty issues (e.g., van Zomeren et al. 2004; Becker et al. 2011; Jost et al. 2012). They are thus prone to measurement error from the mis-categorization of cases. For example, studies may seek to explain the nonviolence or political inaction of a

---

[1] See Javeline and Baird (2007) for a similar strategy of studying victims of the 2002 Moscow theater hostage taking.

presumably "aggrieved" or "dissatisfied" individual, when in fact that individual was not aggrieved in the first place, and inaction requires little if any explanation.

Brady (1999:794) describes the problem as follows: "Most people are not very good at articulating their problems and needs, and even after identifying them, most people may not find them very helpful in recounting instances of political participation." He recommends asking about political actions first and then about the problems, issues, or needs that motivated the actions.

This book offers an alternative and novel solution to human difficulties in recalling and articulating problems and actions: studying victims of violence like those in Beslan. Such individuals are part of a finite group who suffered some public and therefore objective, powerful, and easily validated grievance. There is no risk of mistakenly categorizing them as aggrieved or misidentifying their problem. They have suffered by any definition, and their violent and nonviolent responses could offer insights about the potential for retaliation among other violence victims.

The relative uniformity of the grievance is another virtue of studying Beslan victims. Participation studies typically lump together all aggrieved or dissatisfied individuals regardless of the source or nature of their grievance, with potentially misleading results if in reality different grievances elicit different political responses (but see Schlozman et al. 1995 for a notable exception). A study of responses to the Beslan hostage taking minimizes much of this potential error. Some respondents suffered more directly than others, but this variation falls within a known range, from loss of loved ones or severe bodily injury to posttraumatic stress or anxiety, and the variation can be measured, tested, and controlled in analysis.

Finally, participation studies often suffer from an insufficient number of participants and thus a sample so heavily skewed toward nonparticipation as to jeopardize the validity of results. Many studies try to compensate by substituting attitudinal questions for behavioral questions, such as asking whether the respondent would participate in a hypothetical scenario or whether the respondent approves of participation (e.g., Barnes et al. 1979). While the attempt to increase cases of participation is commendable, the approach is still suboptimal and prone to measurement error, since intentions to participate are not the same thing as actual participation (Klandermans and Oegema 1987; Brady 1999:752–753, 757). Victims of the Beslan hostage taking include a relatively large number of participants in politics, and this study thus avoids the pitfall of a heavily skewed dependent variable.

Table I.1 lists some recent examples from the literature on the role of emotions in collective action, a literature highly relevant to post-violence behavior. As described in future chapters, this literature offers many useful insights, but as the table shows, most studies rely on small and often nonrandom samples of

Table I.1. Examples of Study Samples

Study	Sample size	Selection method	Survey mode
Simon et al. (1998)	95	registered members of the German Senior Protection League Gray Panthers recruited at regular group meetings	paper-and-pencil questionnaires
	117	American gay men recruited at meetings of gay groups or in gay coffee houses	paper-and-pencil questionnaires
van Zomeren et al. (2004)	88	Dutch first year students recruited from psychology courses in exchange for partial course credit	experiments
	85	Dutch first year students recruited from psychology courses in exchange for partial course credit	experiments
	100	Dutch first year students recruited from psychology courses in exchange for partial course credit	experiments
Simon and Ruhs (2008)	333	Turkish Germans recruited via a snowball sample	paper-and-pencil questionnaires or online surveys
Becker et al. (2011)	71	German students recruited in exchange for partial course credit	web-based experiment
	101	German students recruited in public areas	lab experiment
Halperin et al. (2011)	262	Israeli Jewish citizens who were a subsample of a nationwide sample	phone surveys
	262	Israeli Jewish citizens who were a subsample of a different nationwide sample	phone surveys
Tausch et al. (2011)	332	German students recruited via email lists	online survey
	156	Indian Muslim students recruited during classes	paper-and-pencil questionnaire
	466	British Muslims recruited via Facebook	online survey

(continued)

Table I.1. Continued

Study	Sample size	Selection method	Survey mode
Jost et al. (2012)	108	New York University students recruited in exchange for partial course credit	paper-and-pencil questionnaire
	25	Greek protesters recruited at a premarch rally	experiment
	59	members of the United Kingdom's National Union of Teachers recruited via email	web-based experiment

individuals whose grievances are often manufactured in an experimental setting or simply are weaker than the real-world grievances that typically drive political or violent action. The study of 1,098 Beslan victims and their undeniable grievances can apply the insights from these prior studies to an important real-world setting and potentially validate or challenge the findings.

A study of Beslan victims also has the advantage of avoiding sampling error. The study is largely based on a census survey: instead of sampling from the population of 1,340 victims (described below), interviewers attempted to interview all 1,340 and came reasonably close to doing so. Identifying and locating individuals connected to a local school in a small town like Beslan is relatively easy. All Beslan victims live locally; most know other victims; and teachers and school administrators have lists of students and their families. Lists of victims, their addresses, and their injuries were even available on the Internet at www.beslan. ru, www.moscowhelp.org, and other websites, as well as from the humanitarian organization Caucasus Refugee Council and a committee of Beslan teachers (Vlasova 2004a, 2004b). Some bias or error in the findings may exist because the achieved response rate was 82 rather than 100 percent (described below), and it is plausible that the 18 percent of missing victims, or "nonrespondents," might share some common characteristics that are relevant for retaliatory violence or political participation. However, unlike most other studies of either political participation or support for violence, this study did not employ the methodological process of sampling from a population of interest and so is free from sampling error.

Perhaps the most compelling advantage of studying the aftermath of the hostage taking is that it represents a "negative case," or a situation where retaliatory ethnic violence realistically could have occurred but did not (Mahoney and Goertz 2004). It is a "near miss." A study of Beslan victims provides a critically necessary complement to the much more abundant studies of "positive cases," or violent outbreaks, and thus can help fill important knowledge gaps.

Goals of the Book

The mission of this book is threefold. First, the book aims to honor the survivors of the Beslan school hostage taking by telling their story, not just during the three tragic days, but during the grueling aftermath. The loss of loved ones is a traumatic experience, especially when those loved ones are children who suffered greatly, and lost lives are worthy of remembrance. Surviving, too, is worthy of remembrance, especially when the survivors have resisted a rather human urge for vengeance and instead pressed their cause with perseverance, intelligence, and dignity. The book should leave an accurate and respectful portrait of the survivors for posterity.

The second goal is to understand the Beslan aftermath. The school hostage taking was a transformative experience in the lives of most contemporary citizens of the Russian Federation. At the most basic level, it instilled or worsened fears about an anything-goes style of terrorism in Russia, committed mainly by Muslims from the North Caucasus, and a kill-the-enemy-at-all-costs style of counterterrorism. It meant that nothing and no one, not even the country's schools and its most youthful and vulnerable citizens, were safe from perverse atrocities. In terms of ethnic violence, it was a stark reminder that interethnic and interreligious conflict remained a prominent feature of contemporary political and social life in Russia. At the level of high politics, Vladimir Putin used the school hostage taking to consolidate and strengthen his powers as president by eliminating the election of governors and republican presidents in favor of direct presidential appointment; substituting party lists for single-member districts in parliamentary elections; raising the eligibility threshold for parties to win seats from 5 percent to 7 percent; and taking various measures to rein in the media and civil society. The school hostage taking marked the culmination of Putin's increasingly centralized control of the country and establishment of hierarchical authority, known as "the power vertical" (Lemaitre 2006).[2]

---

[2] In 2012, new legislation under then-President Dmitry Medvedev provided for the return of direct, albeit complicated, gubernatorial elections and simplified procedures for political parties to register and participate in elections. The measures, while in a liberal democratic direction, did little to challenge the power vertical. By 2013, President Putin began to roll back reforms by, for example, allowing regional legislatures to forgo elections and appoint governors from a list of candidates approved by the president.

The event is thus worthy of investigation from many angles. Other scholars have already made powerful contributions to our understanding of the hostage taking itself and Russia's counterterrorism operation in Beslan (Dunlop 2006, 2009; Tuathail 2009; Harding 2012) and of the backdrop of ethnic and political conflict in the North Caucasus (King 2008; Zurcher 2009; Schaefer 2011). No study has yet described and analyzed the important and surprisingly peaceful aftermath. Here readers will find this description and analysis based largely on the testimony of the vast majority of individuals who played a role in that aftermath.

The third goal is to learn from Beslan. From a social science perspective, Beslan victims are cases of individuals who have suffered from trauma and violence. More specifically, they are cases of survivors of ethnic violence. As such, their stories and their post-violence behaviors are relevant to the numerous other cases of victims of violence, and the book aims to generalize to these other cases and discover what, if anything, could be learned from Beslan victims and applied elsewhere.

An argument could be made that Beslan victims are unique and that any explanations of their post-violence behavior are not very generalizable. At the time, there were only 720,000 Ossetians in the world, 445,000 of them living in North Ossetia, and only 500,000 Ingush and 1,500,000 Chechens, most living in their titular republics but many living elsewhere. The population of North Ossetia was roughly 710,000, and the Beslan population was a mere 36,000. The Ossetians are a relatively unique Orthodox Christian people living on both the north and south sides of the Caucasus among Muslim and Georgian neighbors, respectively. It is therefore reasonable to ask whether findings from this small corner of the universe are relevant in other cultural and geopolitical contexts. It is also reasonable to ask whether findings from a post-communist context are relevant in other political contexts. Perhaps the findings in Beslan are influenced by the victims' socialization under Soviet rule and culture or recent experiences under the contemporary Russian government.

To some extent, the uniqueness of this particular conflict and these particular people should be acknowledged. However, while the details might be unique, the larger context of victimization by violence committed mostly by members of a rival ethnic group and met with a failed government response, has parallels in many other conflict settings. After the atrocities, victims usually contemplate their victimization and whether and how to deal with it. They respond with a range of emotions, attitudes, and behaviors that seem common across countries and cultures (e.g., Mikula et al. 1998:781). Relationships between these individual-level variables are not strongly influenced by supposedly unique contextual factors. Limits to generalizability will therefore be discussed, along with similarities between the Beslan context and other post-violence situations and how findings from Beslan apply broadly to these other situations.

The Evidence

This study represents the first attempt to document the behavioral aftermath of a large-scale violent episode for nearly all direct victims of that violence. It is a multi-method study, using systematic surveys, in-depth focus groups, journalistic accounts, nongovernmental organization (NGO) reports, and prior scholarly research. The most novel aspect of the study is its comprehensive coverage, in breadth and depth, of the victim population, combined with consideration of individuals who were geographically proximate to the victims. Details about methodology, including survey sampling, administration, translation, data processing, and weighting; focus group participant selection, recruitment, and administration; confidentiality procedures; and the difficulties encountered in this type of research, can be found in Appendix B.

Beslan Victim Survey

The main evidence for this study comes from a survey of victims of the Beslan school hostage taking. Victims were conceived not exclusively as hostages but also as the adult family members with closest ties to hostages, much as the term "victim" is used in instances of disappearances and other human rights violations for judicial and other purposes (Bassiouni 2006:255–256). One can be victimized by kidnapping or murder, and one could be victimized by losing a family member to kidnapping or murder.

Operationally, the goal was to identify a finite universe of people who could incontrovertibly be defined as victims and who were old enough to be interviewed on such a traumatizing topic and to participate in peaceful political activism or ethnic violence. A victim was thus defined as a surviving adult (18+) hostage, parent or guardian of an underage hostage, or next of kin of a deceased hostage. The definition omits teenagers who may be on the cusp of maturity and thus could participate peacefully or violently in public life, but ethical concerns about the children's mental well-being prevailed. The definition also omits relatives and friends of deceased or surviving hostages beyond parents and next of kin who were deeply affected by the event and thus may reasonably be labeled "victims." However, defining victim so broadly as to include all aunts, uncles, cousins, grandparents, friends, neighbors, and coworkers would run the risk of making the victim label so broad as to be meaningless. The narrow definition ensures that everyone who meets the above definition is truly a victim.

(As a counterweight to the definitional decision for the victim survey, questions were included in the nonvictim surveys, described below, about the respondents' relationships with former hostages, and thus the continuum between victims and nonvictims can be analyzed and whether social proximity to victims influences peaceful or violent behavioral outcomes.)

From a list of 1,226 hostages,[3] one victim respondent was assigned for each former hostage, or two in the case of parents of underage hostages. The difficulty of accomplishing this task is that many former hostages were related. Many families had more than one child and/or more than one adult in the school. In such cases, the principle for selection was still one target respondent per former hostage, with the exclusion of parents who would both be interviewed in all cases (one child or more in the school, one parent or both parents in the school).

If an adult was killed or a child was orphaned as a result of the Beslan tragedy, next of kin was determined in accordance with norms in North Ossetia. Most people in Beslan live with their extended families in a single dwelling, in one large community (two or three separate houses in one yard), or in nearby dwellings (two or three apartments in a single apartment building or neighboring buildings). In the absence of parents, children are cared for by either grandparents or aunts and uncles. In Ossetian families, the oldest couple is usually responsible for the whole extended family (Isaenko and Petschauer 1999:163). If a hostage was killed and had no surviving next of kin, as was the case for 24 of the 1,226 former hostages, no target respondent was assigned.

According to the above rules of one targeted respondent per former hostage or two in the case of parents, the total number of people labeled as victims and contacted to participate in the survey was 1,340. Importantly, and novel to this research, this victim population was not sampled, which could have introduced sampling bias. Instead, the entire population was targeted for inclusion in the study.

Only 192 victims refused to participate (44 former hostages and 148 parents or other relatives of former hostages), a remarkably low number given the

---

[3] Deciding which Beslan residents match the above definition was not straightforward. The exact number of hostages held in School No. 1 is still a matter of debate. Public officials, NGOs, and journalists reported different numbers of hostages ranging from 1,128 to 1,388 (Sidorov 2004; Walsh 2004a, 2004b; Lenta.ru 2005). To compose a list of hostages, information was combined from a variety of sources including the Procuracy, City Social Provision division that administers social aid to victims, Mothers of Beslan, and various journalists. For examples, see the lists available at http://www.utro.ru/articles/2004/09/17/beslan_spisok.html (1,380 names of former hostages), http://www.newsru.com/russia/17sep2004/spisok.html (1,345), http://www.pravdabeslana.ru/trigoda/spisok_z.htm (1,116), and http://student.km.ru/view.asp?id=9BDA5589D42048BB8BFBE329A3933EB9 (1,360). All names were put in a single, inflated list of 1,479 names. After consulting with neighbors and the City Information and City Registration lists, misspellings were corrected, and duplicates, nonhostages, and nonexistent individuals were identified and eliminated. Of the initial 1,479 people, some information such as age or other demographic was found on 38 (21 adults and 17 children) who could nevertheless not be located, while 215 had no information at all and were determined to be duplicates or nonexistent individuals. *The resulting list contained the names of 1,226 hostages,* which is close to the average number of published estimates. It is possible that the 38 individuals who were impossible to locate moved from Beslan with their entire families, removing the possibility of testing hypotheses about the effects of having an exit strategy on the propensity for peaceful political activism or retaliatory violence.

sensitivity of the topic.[4] Reasons for refusal for the most part involved victims not wanting to recall a painful event and live in the past and instead wanting to forget and move on.[5] Given the desire to forget among many nonrespondents, it is plausible that nonresponse in the survey is correlated with nonparticipation in politics and low support for retaliatory violence. However, it is less plausible that survey nonresponse influences relationships between variables. For example, the data show a powerful relationship between anger and political participation that would likely hold if the (likely) less angry and less participatory survey nonrespondents were included. Still, as with any survey-based research, the potential bias from potentially systematic nonresponse must be kept in mind.

Face-to-face interviews were conducted in respondent homes in May through August of 2007. *The resulting sample of 1,098 victims of the 1,340 initially contacted represents an 82 percent response rate* (Table I.2), exceptionally high for most survey research and especially for the finite and sensitive population of Beslan victims, which should maximize confidence in the validity of results.

Nonvictim Survey in Beslan and Vladikavkaz

The above definition of a victim of violence could be challenged and therefore leave readers unpersuaded by the findings. The individuals included are incontrovertibly victims: for example, if an individual loses a spouse in a terrorist attack, as happened to many in Beslan, there should be no argument against labeling that individual "victimized" or "aggrieved." However, what of the deceased person's parents, siblings, aunts, uncles, cousins, grandparents, friends, neighbors, and coworkers? Where do we draw an appropriate, uncontroversial line between the directly aggrieved and the indirectly aggrieved and decide which individuals are worthy of study for their post-violence responses? To place the question in a relevant context for American readers, if an individual was in the World Trade Center at the time of the September 11 bombing, that person is unquestionably labeled victimized or aggrieved, but what about residents of lower Manhattan, upper Manhattan, commuters to Manhattan, and those living in nearby New Jersey, Connecticut, and so on?

The literature on social movements does not offer much guidance on this question. For social movement scholars, individuals are categorized by issue position and level of mobilization but not by proximity to the grievance. For example, those not directly affected by a grievance are called "adherents" if they sympathize with the aggrieved without providing support, or "constituents" if they do provide support

---

[4] Thirty-eight were out of town or otherwise unavailable for the entire duration of the survey, 7 moved and had no forwarding address, and 5 did not participate for other reasons.

[5] A smaller number of victims thought that surveys were useless and would not help them personally.

Table I.2. Beslan Victim Survey

Respondent's relationship to hostage

	N	Total contacts	Response rate	% of sample
Parent or other relative of underage hostage	598	755	79	54
Self - Parent hostage or other adult hostage accompanying child to school	280	328	85	25
Next of kin of deceased hostage	171	198	86	15
Self - Teacher hostage or school administrator hostage	36	44	82	3
Relative of adult hostage (in cases where adult hostage was interviewed as parent of underage hostage)	13	15	87	1
Total	1,098	1,340	82	100

Response rate

	N	%
Interviews completed	1,098	82
Refused	192	14
Unavailable/out-of-town	38	3
Moved with no forwarding address	7	.5
Other reason for nonparticipation	5	.4
Total contacts	1,340	100

(McCarthy and Zald 1973, 1977; Ennis and Schreuer 1987; Cress and Snow 1996). However, adherents or constituents with personal or geographic connections, such as the white spouse of an African American, a male whose sister faced sex-based job discrimination, or a Pennsylvania resident who lived fifty miles from Three Mile Island, are not differentiated from other adherents or constituents. This omission is important because an individual's personal and geographic proximity to a grievance—how directly or indirectly a grievance is experienced—is probably a crucial factor in explaining political participation or support for retaliatory violence.

To fill this gap in the literature, the Beslan victim survey is supplemented with two city-wide random sample nonvictim surveys. The variation in proximity to the grievance among nonvictims was measured with survey questions such as the number of family members who were held hostage. The majority of the findings in this book are based on the Beslan victim survey and victim focus groups, but Chapter 12 relies heavily on the nonvictim survey to test for the effects of grievances on post-violence behavior and whether the factors that are so important for motivating the behavior of directly aggrieved individuals are also important for motivating the behavior of indirectly aggrieved individuals.

The nonvictim population was defined as the adult (18+) population of Beslan (26,100 adults and 36,000 total population as of January 1, 2008) and Vladikavkaz (240,600 adults and 312,700 total population), using data from the Russian census. Most residents of these cities knew some victims or were otherwise affected by the devastating tragedy that occurred in their backyards. They are labeled nonvictims only in a technical sense to differentiate them from the former hostages, parents of underage hostages, and next of kin of deceased hostages who comprised the study population in the victim survey.

Random samples were selected of the adult population of each city. Face-to-face interviews were conducted in respondent homes in December 2008 and January 2009. *The resulting samples of 1,023 Beslan residents and 1,020 Vladikavkaz residents of the 1,550 and 1,650 initially contacted in each city represent a 66 and 62 percent response rate, respectively* (Table I.3).

Table I.3. Nonvictim Surveys Response Rates

	Beslan		Vladikavkaz		Total	
	N	%	N	%	N	%
Interviews completed	1,023	66	1,020	61.8	2,043	63.8
Nonresponse, including the following:	527	34	630	38.2	1157	36.2
No one was home (at least five visits)	156	10	248	15	404	13
Household refused (no time, afraid of strangers, do not participate in surveys in general, etc)	169	11	113	7	282	9
Selected respondent refused	62	4	76	5	138	4
Selected respondent was unavailable (vacation, business trip)	49	3	69	4	118	4
Contact with household was not possible (locks, dogs, gates)	38	2	79	5	117	4
Respondent was ill or unable to talk	34	2	21	1	55	2
Interview interrupted	19	1	24	1	43	1
Total contacts	1,550	100	1,650	100	3,200	100

Focus Groups

In addition to the surveys, six focus groups were conducted in December 2008, with a total of 49 participants. The focus groups supplemented the survey data with free-flowing conversation and group interaction that elicited more detailed information and unprompted perspectives potentially missed by asking only closed-ended questions.

Six focus groups of 6–9 participants each were conducted in Beslan, with participants selected at random from the database of respondents to the victim survey, using sex, age, and level of activism as selection criteria (Table I.4). Groups were separated by these categories in order to maximize the participation of all focus group members and the openness of discussion. North Ossetian and Russian colleagues advised that women and men would speak more freely when separated and that young people would speak more frequently when not constrained by deference toward their elders, advice consistent with the historical record of traditional etiquette governing relations among people of different gender and age in the North Caucasus (Isaenko and Petschauer 1999:166–168). Activists and nonactivists might participate more comfortably and frequently if their behavior was the norm in their discussion group. Moreover, the precise questions asked in the focus groups differed slightly for activists versus nonactivists, with the activist groups focused more on explaining participation and the nonactivist groups focused more on explaining nonparticipation.

Activists were defined as those who participated in four or more public activities out of the thirty activities asked in question 23 of the 2004 victim survey. Two hundred and fifty-seven people, or 23.4% of victim respondents, met the activist definition. Nonactivists were defined as those who participated in zero of the thirty activities in question 23. Five hundred and forty-eight people, or 49.9% of victim respondents, met the nonactivist definition.

Table I.4. Focus Group Composition

Group	Sex	Political activism	Age	# of participants
1	Female	Activists	35 years and younger	9
2	Female	Activists	Older than 35 years	9
3	Male	Activists	35 years and younger	8
4	Male	Activists	Older than 35 years	6
5	Female	Nonactivists	Any	9
6	Male	Nonactivists	Any	8

Each focus group included people who experienced different types of traumatic effects from the Beslan hostage taking. Some focus group participants were the survivors of a dead child or other relative; some were caretakers for seriously injured relatives; and some were related to hostages who emerged alive and healthy. Since there was less reason to believe that the degree of trauma would be a main factor in the openness and frequency of focus group participation, sex, age, and level of activism were prioritized in dividing groups. Furthermore, dividing groups by the degree of trauma would have been subjective, forcing a rank ordering of death of a child, death of another relative, inability to locate and identify a relative's dead body, serious lifelong injury to a child, and other terrible outcomes.

All participants in the focus groups were eighteen years of age or older. In order to minimize self-censorship, the focus group methodological literature recommends not including family members and close friends in the same groups. Accordingly, each group comprised victims who were not relatives, close friends, neighbors, or even acquaintances, a difficult task in the small town of Beslan.

Limitations of this Study

As with any social science endeavor that involves studying humans in real times and places, the study of Beslan victims was subject to several constraints, such as the decision to avoid talking to victims younger than eighteen, discussed above. Critics of this study may point out that younger people, especially in their volatile teens, might experience different behavioral motivations than those of adults, and excluding them from analysis might bias any findings. All statistical analysis controls for age, but critics may have a point in wondering if the effects of age are not linear and if instead there is a specific behavioral effect of being a teenager that the study simply cannot capture.

This possibility is real but was a lesser concern than the ethical concerns of including children in the study. The trauma among Beslan victims was overwhelming, and many adult victims had difficulty being interviewed and broke down in tears. Re-traumatizing individuals who were probably the most emotionally fragile of the victim population was an unacceptable risk. Indeed, interviewing children probably would have been prohibited. In March 2006, at least one reporter discussed this prohibition, noting that "these kids have been smothered in ghoulish attention, and they must be allowed to merge back into the innocent world of childhood—if, after their unspeakable experiences, such a thing is possible" (Church 2006). On the second anniversary of the terrorist attack, children at the commemorative ceremonies told reporters that they were scared to sleep because they dreamed about terrorists and woke up with their hearts pounding. Plainclothes police officers approached the children and asked them not to talk with reporters and asked the reporters not to awaken traumatic memories in the children (Panyushkin 2006a).

The most likely effect of the decision to omit children from the study is to limit the generalizability of results to adults who are eighteen years of age or older.

Another limitation of the study is that it analyzes violent inclinations toward a rival ethnic group and peaceful action in the political arena. It does not analyze violent action in the political arena or peaceful reconciliation attempts with the rival ethnic group, mostly because neither was a serious possibility in the aftermath of Beslan. There was little to no talk among Beslan victims of attacking major public officials such as Putin, Dzasokhov, or Tikhonov, nor of reaching out to Ingush or Chechen neighbors and creating interethnic NGOs or other community groups or institutions that aimed to improve Ossetian-Ingush or Ossetian-Chechen relations. Asking questions about such actions would have wasted valuable interview time and potentially soured respondents on the study by making the interviewers seem ill-informed and the survey questions unworthy of serious consideration. Also, there were potential ethical and security issues in asking questions about violence toward government officials, if the survey served to provoke such violence or was seen as doing so. Had authorities learned about such questions, they could have forced the interviews to stop and the study to end or, worse, threatened respondents who revealed, or were assumed to reveal, preferences for attacking officials. As a result, this study provides no possibility to test directly why some victims of violence choose violent politics or peaceful ethnic reconciliation, although some inferences could be drawn from the discussion of generalizability in Chapter 13 and the Conclusion.

Still another limitation is that the measures of political participation are behavioral and actual, whereas the measure of violence is attitudinal and therefore hypothetical. As described above and in Chapter 4, a major advantage of studying Beslan victims is that so many individuals participated in concrete political actions, and interviewers asked about these concrete actions instead of substituting with traditional and inferior attitudinal questions, such as whether respondents "support" participation or are "willing" to participate in a hypothetical action. Again for ethical and practical reasons, the questions about violence could not be as concrete. Practically speaking, questions about prior violent action amount to requests for admissions of illegal behavior and are therefore subject to measurement error: violent respondents might lie and deny prior actions. Ethically speaking, the nonviolent aftermath of Beslan was still potentially fragile, and the survey could have roused negative thoughts and feelings as much as measured them. In asking questions about retaliatory ethnic violence, the goal was to minimize this possibility.

As a result, the measure of retaliatory violence is subject to the same criticisms leveled at prior studies of participation. The analysis includes the measure of support for an action, in this case retaliatory violence, rather than the actual action. The study is thus imbalanced: the findings about political participation are rigorous, whereas the findings about retaliatory violence are suggestive and require further study for corroboration. The strategy to deal with the imbalance is, whenever possible, to be explicit about measuring support for retaliatory violence rather than actual retaliatory violence and to discuss what the connection between the two might be.

A final limitation of this study is one that is common to cross-sectional survey research: the impossibility of providing conclusive evidence of the direction of causality between variables. The study aims to understand post-violence political participation and post-violence support for retaliatory violence. These were measured at a single point in time with questions about past political action and current attitudes and emotions. The survey questions were theory-driven, meaning they were constructed based on testable hypotheses about attitudes and emotions that might "cause" behavior. Still, the possibility of some endogeneity or reverse causality, whereby the behavior actually caused the attitudes and emotions, is real. For example, victims of violence could attend a protest and, through participation, better formulate grievances and articulate anger. The strategy to deal with this possibility is to describe the compatibility or incompatibility of the survey results with preexisting theories and evidence about political participation and retaliatory violence. Also, the survey results are supplemented with news reports, prior scholarly discussions of Beslan, and focus group discussions, and the possibility of reverse causality is thoughtfully and honestly considered and discussed.

Contributions and Implications

The aftermath of the Beslan school hostage taking offers important lessons about anger, prejudice, and other variables and their influence on behavioral responses to violence. Findings contribute to the literatures on ethnic violence and political participation, as well as contemporary Russian politics, emotions and politics, and other dimensions of political psychology, social movements, and contentious politics.

The study finds that anger was a productive force in fueling the extraordinary outpouring of peaceful political participation after the hostage taking and that anger had surprisingly little to do with support for retaliatory violence. This finding is consistent with a recent wave of literature in political science and psychology that extols the virtues of anger for political participation and, ultimately, interest representation. To the degree that individuals need to assert themselves in the political system to secure rights and redress grievances, anger seems to be a previously undervalued but significant, positive motivator.

However, the finding challenges the research (as well as conventional wisdom) on violence, which usually stresses the dangerous ramifications of anger and holds anger responsible for an individual's violent behavior. Despite long-standing hypotheses linking frustration and aggression (Dollard et al. 1939; Berkowitz 1993), the assumption that anger "causes" an individual to retaliate violently is weak theoretically and unfounded empirically. Rigorous testing on aggrieved individuals—actual victims of violence in Beslan—revealed no difference in support for retaliatory violence between the angriest victims and least angry victims. There was an abundance of anger and other emotions after the hostage taking, and there was an abundance of talk about "getting even," but those who supported retaliatory violence against the co-ethnics of the perpetrators cannot rationalize their support by blaming their emotions.

The single most important factor explaining support for retaliatory violence after the hostage taking was not anger but ethnic prejudice, regardless of whether or not that prejudice induced an emotional response. The perpetrators of the violence in Beslan in 2004 were mainly of Chechen and Ingush descent, about whom most Beslan victims and other North Ossetians felt negatively. On average, they would not want to dine with these "others," send their children to school with them, or have a relative marry one. Most victims and other North Ossetians often thought of the perpetrators not simply as individual terrorists but as representatives of their presumably violent and barbaric ethnic groups, and most blamed the Ingush and Chechen people for causing the tragedy in the school. Victims who expressed these sentiments with the greatest intensity were the most likely to approve of killing ethnic "others" in retaliation.

It may seem inappropriate to talk about the prejudice felt by victims of violence. Prejudice has a pejorative connotation, as if we are judging and blaming the victims for their sentiments rather than understanding and validating them. After all, if we were viciously attacked and watched our babies killed by members of another ethnic or religious group, surely we too would generalize from our negative feelings toward the perpetrators and feel hostility or loathing toward people who look, act, speak, or pray like them.

It is actually this very leap of logic that this study questions, but based on data rather than moral condemnation. The study is motivated by sympathy for victims of violence and aims to be respectful of Beslan victims and do justice to their cause by reporting their grievances and actions accurately. However, the data show that a value judgment against prejudice is warranted, even among victims, because prejudice, with or without anger, can fuel violent sentiment.

Importantly, not all Beslan victims felt negatively toward the Ingush and Chechen people, and among those who were not prejudiced, approval of retaliatory violence was extremely low. The grievances of the non-prejudiced victims were no less legitimate and their emotions no less real. They simply did not scorn all Ingush and Chechens nor hold the ethnic groups accountable for the actions of its criminal members, and these attitudes made them more likely to disapprove of retaliatory ethnic violence.

Other results of the Beslan study focus on alienation, efficacy, and optimism. The study finds that victims who were politically alienated from Russia, as evidenced by decreasing pride in their country since the hostage taking, were significantly more likely to pursue peaceful political activism. Politically alienated victims were also significantly *less* likely to support retaliatory violence. Victims who were not politically alienated and retained or even increased their pride in Russia since the hostage taking were more likely to support further violence over peaceful activism.

The lesson about political alienation is thus similar to the lesson about anger: although much maligned, political alienation may actually be a reasonable and productive response to ethnic violence. Victims who lose pride in their country may be the very victims to give a voice to their community that distracts the community from further violence, whereas victims who retain or increase their pride have no such distractions. The unalienated or politically proud victims have the greatest potential to perpetuate the cycle of violence.

Efficacy is an important factor in explaining individual responses to violence, but the type of efficacy matters a great deal. For Beslan victims, political efficacy was strongly correlated with peaceful participation, whereas self-efficacy was strongly correlated with support for retaliatory ethnic violence. The implication here is that feeling personally efficacious, but not efficacious in the political arena, may be a recipe for approving of extra-judicial or extra-governmental reactions to violence. While self-efficacy is found to have beneficial consequences in many life arenas, in a post-violence context, efficacious individuals may think it is acceptable to take matters into their own hands and meet violence with violence. Here, the study emphasizes the possibility of this negative outcome but does not condemn self-efficacy as it condemns prejudice, because self-efficacy has many valuable qualities and may even have played a small role in motivating political participation.

Additional insights from the study of the Beslan school hostage taking include findings about social alienation and social networks, optimism and pessimism, past political participation, past victimization by violence, perceived risk of political activism, and the extent of harm suffered during the hostage taking. Many of these findings, as well as those above, support prior research findings about ethnic violence or political participation, but many are novel and controversial.

These differences may be attributed in large part to the rigor of the research design and its individual-level evidence. The data derive from interviews and focus group discussions with indisputably aggrieved individuals who were all experiencing genuine emotions, holding genuine attitudes, participating in actual political actions, and contemplating the pros and cons of retaliatory violence, which truly could have materialized on a large and tragic scale.

Thankfully, it did not. Support for retaliatory ethnic violence was low in Beslan, and actual violence was even lower. Peaceful political participation was high. In this sense, the aftermath of the hostage taking may provide a positive example. This study of individual victims' responses to violence may prove useful for understanding how and why future victims of violence turn toward participation over retaliation.

Chapter Summary

In the pages that follow, a political history of the aftermath of Beslan is blended with a political science analysis of individual emotions, attitudes, and behavior. Part I provides details on the context of the Beslan school hostage taking. Chapters 1 and 2 are devoted to the numerous grievances of the victims. These include grievances against their historical ethnic rivals, the Ingush and Chechens, as well as political grievances against the governments of North Ossetia and Russia. Chapters 3 and 4 are devoted to victim action and inaction after the hostage taking. Support for retaliatory violence among victims is reported, along with their numerous political actions, using data from the victim survey and supplementing with anecdotal evidence from focus groups and newspapers. Appendix A chronicles these post-violence activities in even greater detail.

Part II analyzes variation in individual responses to the hostage taking. Why do some victims support retaliatory violence while others do not? Why do some victims take political action while others do not? Chapters 5 through 10 each explore a different explanatory variable in depth, including anger and other emotions, prejudice, political and social alienation, political efficacy and self-efficacy, and experiences with ethnic violence or political participation prior to the hostage taking. Chapter 11 tests the findings of Chapters 5 through 10 more rigorously with multivariate analysis, providing support for the bivariate findings in the preceding chapters.

Part III deals with the question of generalizability. Chapter 12 asks whether the above findings about Beslan victims apply to nonvictims—that is, individuals of varying degrees of personal and geographic proximity to the Beslan victims who were themselves not surviving adult hostages, parents or guardians of underage hostages, or next of kin of deceased hostages. The chapter relies heavily on data from the surveys of nonvictims in Beslan and Vladikavkaz and compares with data from the victim survey. Chapter 13 discusses whether and how the findings might apply to victims of violence in other geopolitical and cultural contexts. The book concludes with thoughts on the implications of the findings for stopping cycles of ethnic violence, increasing interest representation, and advancing research methods.

PART I

THE BESLAN SCHOOL
HOSTAGE TAKING

Before the horror, the day promised to be one of joy and celebration. It was September 1, traditionally the first day of school in Russia and known as the "Day of Knowledge." Whereas in other countries, the start time for school and its associated customs may vary by region or locality, in Russia there is a great deal of uniformity in the timing and rituals. The Day of Knowledge is a festive holiday when children dress in their best clothes, with girls in traditional white hair ribbons and bows. They are accompanied by one or more parent or other adult relatives, and they bring bouquets of flowers for their teachers. In nice weather, everyone may gather outside, clustered by class and grade level, as the school director and local dignitaries greet the children and the school year and especially welcome the first graders who are just beginning their journey for knowledge. The oldest students, the eleventh graders, lead the youngest, the first graders, into an assembly, where they listen to songs, poetry, and inspirational speeches by school administrators, teachers, war veterans, politicians, and other visitors. Parents and other adult guests stay for the assembly. At the end of the ceremony, a first grade girl sits on the shoulders of an eleventh grade boy and rings a bell, signifying the beginning of the school year. Typically, the Day of Knowledge is not a full school day, and parents and children return home together after the festivities.

These rituals have been part of Russian life since 1935, when legislation harmonized school calendars across the Soviet Union (Kelly 2007:511). In 1969, the *Komsomol*, or Communist Youth League, decreed that the event should be celebrated in every school in the country (Phillips 2007:32), and by 1984 the Supreme Soviet of the USSR officially designated September 1 as the Day of Knowledge. The holiday evokes warm feelings of nostalgia for many citizens and is eagerly anticipated by school-age children and their parents. As Beslan School No. 1's headmistress Lydia Tsaliyeva remarked, "The first of September was always the happiest day of my year. It was a genuine celebration. Children, teachers, and parents alike all loved it. *I* loved it" (Phillips 2007:10). Beslan victims likely began their day with hopeful thoughts for the coming school year. And there were many such hopeful people. Somewhere between 1,100 and 1,400 students, parents, teachers, and guests arrived at School No. 1 expecting to participate in Day of Knowledge celebrations.

Instead, their arrival marked the beginning of the worst three days of their lives. Most students were standing outside in a ceremonial line called a *lineika* when the first shots were fired (Chivers 2007). Many of them carried balloons that their teachers planned to have them release at the climax of the ceremony (Chivers 2007; Phillips 2007:11–12). Headmistress Tsaliyeva congratulated the students on beginning the new academic year. Then music began and, with it, gunfire (Milashina 2006d).

Hearing the shots, many high school students and adults, especially the most able-bodied and strategically positioned closer to the outskirts of the school grounds, ran away ("Khronika zakhvata" 2009). Approximately 150 people escaped hostage status in this way (Chivers 2005b). Those who could not run were herded into the school gymnasium, panicked, screaming, crying, shocked, confused, and pushed so tightly in the crowd being forced into the gym that they sometimes stepped or trampled on those who fell (Phillips 2007:27–29,44–49). Among these victims was thus an abundance of younger school-age children, as well as many preschool children who were accompanying parents and older siblings on the would-be joyous occasion. The number of preschoolers in attendance was even higher than past years, because a shortage of natural gas meant that local day care centers had not yet opened (Milashina 2004a; Uzzell 2004).

Sheer terror followed for over two grueling days inside the school and during the final explosions and shoot-outs that marked the event's tragic end (Dunlop 2006, 2009).[1] During the violent fifty-three-hour siege, hostages were herded into cramped and stiflingly hot quarters, often with hands over their heads. Talking or crying was met with frightening and credible threats. They "had seen friends executed, been threatened with shooting, denied food and water, forced to drink urine, and obliged to soil themselves where they sat" (Parfitt 2004).

By the afternoon of September 3, 2004, one in every hundred Beslan residents had been killed, meaning few Beslan residents were spared the loss of a relative or friend. Beyond the dead, hundreds of victims remained seriously injured, many maimed for life. Some victims were missing for weeks or months after the tragedy, and some bodies were destroyed beyond recognition and returned to their families in pieces or remnants, sometimes to the wrong families. Surviving victims and their families, friends, and neighbors, even those without enduring physical injuries, were psychologically traumatized. The fifty-three hours of violence scarred the small town and the entire North Ossetian republic (Images 1.1, 1.2, and 1.3).

---

[1] See also www.pravdabeslana.ru, which contains links to official commission reports, dissenting views, proceedings of the court case against the captured hostage taker Nur-Pasha Kulayev, and many other valuable documents.

Image 1.1. People searched for relatives among the dead hostages at the morgue in Vladikavkaz, North Ossetia, on September 4, 2004.
VLADIMIR SUVOROV/GAZETA/AFP via Getty Images.

Image 1.2. Family and friends buried their children and other loved ones in Beslan, here during a mass funeral in the rain on September 6, 2004.
Scott Peterson/Getty Images.

Image 1.3. Portraits of some of the 330+ victims hung on the wall of School No. 1.
YURI KADOBNOV/AFP via Getty Images.

Part I takes an in-depth look at the aftermath of Beslan, or the post-violence context. Victims were left with grievances against the hostage takers, co-ethnics of the hostage takers, and the political officials and institutions responsible for managing the rescue efforts. These grievances are described in Chapters 1 and 2, before moving to victims' responses to the grievances in Chapters 3 and 4. Political grievances are discussed at greater length than grievances against ethnic rivals, but the difference in text allotment does not mean that all Beslan victims placed a higher weight on political grievances. The difference reflects the complexity of the political grievances compared with the more straightforward grievance against the individual militants and members of their ethnic groups for taking the hostages in the first place and for the resulting deaths and devastation.

1

Grievances against Ethnic Rivals

The siege of School No. 1 was one of many incidents of ethnic violence in the North Caucasus and the larger Russian Federation. By most accounts, the militants were part of the insurgency in the ongoing Chechen war, and the school hostage taking took place in the context of Russian-Chechen historic military conflict (Schaefer 2011). Beslan residents were selected by militants because they were not Muslim. Although predominantly ethnic Ossetians rather than Russians, they were Orthodox Christians who lived within the Russian Federation more agreeably than residents of Chechnya, Dagestan, and Ingushetia. The favored status for Ossetians had a long history: Ossetians were the primary beneficiaries of Soviet Russian atrocities committed against Muslims during the Stalinist era when Muslims were forcibly evicted from their homes, and as recently as the first Chechen war (1994–1996), federal air raids had been launched at Chechnya from the airfield near Beslan (Grodnenskii 2007; Harding 2012:132). Ossetians therefore served as proxy targets for militants seeking to harm Russia. Ossetians were also relatively easy targets, given that Beslan and School No. 1 are located in close proximity to the border between North Ossetia and Ingushetia.

A less widely promoted version of events focuses on the militants' demand for the release of their Ingush comrades who were recently imprisoned for a June 2004 attack on an armory in Ingushetia. This account places the school hostage taking in the context of Ossetian-Ingush historic rivalries and violence. The school gymnasium where the vast majority of hostages were kept had been the site of a prior and similarly brutal hostage taking of Ingush civilians by Ossetians during the 1992 territorial conflict over the Prigorodny region, described below. The 1992 Ingush hostages, many of them women and children, were packed together, denied food and water, and threatened at gunpoint, with several male hostages executed (Rodriguez 2004b; Weir 2005b). While few if any analysts interpret the 2004 hostage taking as vengeance for 1992, the more common assessment is that militants in 2004 were cognizant of the potential to reignite violence between Ossetians and Ingush. The hostage taking would leave the Ossetians and their Russian patrons blaming and retaliating against Ingush who would then draw closer to their Chechen cousins and thus further destabilize the Caucasus to the advantage of regional insurgency (Schaefer 2011:230). This was the explanation for the hostage taking offered by the sole surviving hostage taker Nur-Pasha Kulayev at his trial.

After Violence. Debra Javeline, Oxford University Press. © Oxford University Press 2023.
DOI: 10.1093/oso/9780197683347.003.0002

The two interpretations are complementary. The hostage taking was either a direct tactical maneuver in the Russian-Chechen conflict or an indirect tactical maneuver to inflame Ingush and Ossetians to participate in the broader Russian-Chechen conflict, or it was both. In both interpretations, the perpetrators of the 2004 hostage taking were clearly ethnic "others" and were acknowledged as such by the victims and by Ossetians and non-Muslims more generally. Grievances surrounding the hostage taking were therefore easily couched in ethnic terms. This chapter documents those grievances.

History of Ingush-Ossetian Ethnic Violence

Ossetians are descendants of ethnic Iranian Alans and Sarmatians who moved to the Caucasus around the sixth century AD and settled in the low-altitude hills and plains, surrounded by indigenous Ingush and Chechens residing at higher elevations in the mountains (Cornell 1998:410). The Ossetian language too descends from Eastern Iranian or Alanic and bears little resemblance to the languages of other Caucasian populations. Ossetians are predominantly Orthodox Christians; the Ingush, Chechens, and many other neighbors are Sunni Muslims. North Ossetia has traditionally been less rural and more multinational and multireligious than these other Caucasian republics: According to the Russian census, the population of Ingushetia in 2002, two years before the hostage taking, was 77 percent Ingush and 20 percent Chechen, and the population of Chechnya was 94 percent Chechen. North Ossetia's population just before the hostage taking was approximately 63 percent Ossetian and 23 percent Russian, with minorities of Ingush, Armenians, Kumyks, Georgians, Ukrainians, and other ethnic groups.

North Caucasian societies, including Ossetians, are typically described as conservative, traditional, hierarchical, patriarchal, oriented toward extended families, and authoritarian (Savva and Tishkov 2012:62). They are mostly poor and suffer high unemployment, inequality, corruption, and criminality, and youth unemployment has been particularly extreme (Dzutsev 2011). Ethnonationalism has long played a role in education, political appointments, access to resources, and general social mobility (Savva and Tishkov 2012:62).

Historically, Ossetians and their Muslim neighbors were mutually suspicious but peaceful. Conflicts arose largely as a result of Russian involvement in the region (Cornell 1998:410). The Soviet regime played with borders and created territorial divisions within the new USSR to serve political ends that would set the stage for decades of interethnic hostility. The two most important conflicts for Ossetians involved Ingush in North Ossetia and Georgians in South Ossetia, and both conflicts factored in the 2004 Beslan school hostage taking.

In the 1920s, the Soviets dissolved the Gorskaya ("Mountain") Republic, populated by both Ossetians and Ingush, and gave the Ingush an autonomous oblast that included the Prigorodny District. Ossetians were separated into two geopolitical units, North Ossetia in the Russian Federation and South Ossetia in the Georgian Republic. Because the Ossetians were loyal to the Soviet regime while Georgians were not, the creation of South Ossetia was intended to weaken Georgia's drive for secession and independence. South Ossetians were dissatisfied with this arrangement and occasionally pursued reunification with other Ossetians (Birch 1995; Cornell 1998).

During World War II, Stalin accused Ingush and Chechens of collaboration with German forces, forcibly deported them from the North Caucasus, and divided and reorganized the region. The reorganization included a transfer of control of the previously Ingush-populated Prigorodny District, which accounted for almost half of Ingushetia's territory, to the North Ossetian Autonomous Republic. In 1956 and 1957, Khrushchev issued decrees that rehabilitated the Ingush, allowed them to return to their region, and reinstated the Chechen-Ingush Autonomous Republic. However, Prigorodny was still part of North Ossetia, and the decrees were never accompanied by plans to settle property disputes between original Ingush owners and current Ossetian residents who had often settled in the region at state encouragement and had built homes, farms, and businesses. If anything, both the Soviet and North Ossetian authorities acted in ways that obstructed peaceful resolution. The authorities passed decrees to prevent housing sales, limit the issuance of residency permits (*propiska*), discriminate in jobs and education, and introduce other rules that restricted the ability of Ingush to return to the Prigorodny region ("Russia: The Ingush-Ossetian Conflict" 1996).

In the 1970s, many Ingush protested these discriminatory practices, and in October 1981, after an Ingush killed an Ossetian taxi driver, Ossetians in Prigorodny participated in one of the worst civil disturbances in post–World War II Soviet history, with the goal of expelling all Ingush from Prigorodny. Meanwhile, many Ingush moved into Prigorodny, some legally and some illegally (Birch 1995; Cornell 1998).

By Gorbachev's perestroika era, when ethnic groups throughout the Soviet Union were asserting rights, Georgia's independence movement meant a permanent solidification of the North–South Ossetian divide. Rejecting this outcome, South Ossetians renewed their quest for reunification. Mass violence erupted in the early 1990s, as attempts by Russia and Georgia to resolve the crisis nearly brought the two countries to war. The conflict spilled into North Ossetia, along with refugees from South Ossetia, and led Russia to declare a state of emergency in Vladikavkaz, the North Ossetian capital, and other parts of the republic. Peace was eventually achieved with the help of European peacekeepers, but the more than 100,000 South Ossetian refugees now in North Ossetia required food, shelter, and employment and thus put a strain on the North Ossetian republic and increased its dependency on the Russian government. Some South Ossetians moved into the Prigorodny region recently vacated by Ingush. Some were militant and sought weapons to return to fighting in the South, and some engaged in criminal economic activity (Birch 1995; "Russia: The Ingush-Ossetian Conflict" 1996).

Around the same time, Ingush demands for the return of the Prigorodny region intensified, and both Ingush and Ossetians attended growing demonstrations to assert their opposing claims. Once more, the now-floundering Soviet government issued perhaps well-intentioned but half-baked decrees, such as the April 1991 Law on the Rehabilitation of Repressed Peoples, which raised Ingush expectations for returning Prigorodny to Ingushetia, raised Ossetian agitation and defensiveness of their right to Prigorodny, and provided few if any helpful details on how to execute the peaceful resolution of competing territorial claims ("Russia: The Ingush-Ossetian Conflict" 1996; Tishkov 1997:ch. 8). Russia's recognition of the "independence" of South Ossetia encouraged North Ossetians to resist Ingush claims in Prigorodny and even to promote the settlement of South Ossetians in Prigorodny (Nichol 2010:12; Cornell 1998).

The conflict in Prigorodny flared violently in 1992 and left nearly 500 individuals killed in the first six days alone, more than 1,000 hostages taken on both sides, approximately 260 individuals missing, thousands of homes wantonly destroyed, and most of the estimated 34,500–64,000 Ingush residents of Prigorodny forcibly displaced and living as refugees in tent camps in Ingushetia and Chechnya ("Russia: The Ingush-Ossetian Conflict" 1996). Tanks, armored vehicles, and automatic weapons were distributed to Ossetians by republican officials or the Russian military and were seized by Ingush from Russian army units or were given to Ingush by Chechens (Birch 1995). Atrocities were committed by both sides, and the conflict never quite resolved, despite a state of emergency in North Ossetia and Ingushetia declared by Russian President Boris Yeltsin on October 31, 1992, and lasting until late February 1995. Paramilitary groups remained or, if disbanded, were not disarmed. The proliferation of weapons among the general population in the North Caucasus was clear during the 2004 hostage taking when large numbers of armed bystanders appeared.

In terms of sheer numbers of deaths, injuries, lost homes, and forcible displacement, Ingush were the losers in the 1992 conflict, but Ossetians nevertheless retained grievances over the violence. Many Ossetians also have their own version of the events. In the focus group of female activist victims thirty-five years or younger, participants discussed what they perceived to be the distortion of Ingush-Ossetian relations by the mass media.

BELLA: I came across it many times in publications. For some reason, publications support the Ingush. I have never come across publications in favor of Ossetians. Perhaps I am mistaken?

BELA: Nothing of the kind has appeared for quite a long time.

BELLA: Right, such publications haven't appeared for quite a long time. In any case, I haven't come across any. As a rule, 90% of publications, if not all 100%, support the Ingush. That is, a person who doesn't know the situation, doesn't know either Ossetians or Ingush, will say: "Oh, what terrible people these Ossetians are!" They are the suffering party.

BELA: We attacked them.

BELLA: And I will tell you why. It was in 1992 when there was a conflict. But nobody asks the question, who expelled them. And who expelled them? Nobody did. I have an [Ingush] girlfriend. We studied together since first grade. We then were in tenth grade. During the week, I associated with her at school. It was Sunday morning; my neighbor came and said, "War!" I immediately called her at home, but nobody picked up. After this, we lost touch, but neighbors told me that they had left at night. They had all been informed. [To the moderator] Have you ever heard about this? Most probably not. [Outside Ossetia, people have] the opinion presented by the central mass media: "My God, how does your daughter live there in Ossetia? They are such monsters over there, they expelled poor women with breastfeeding babies. How does your daughter live there? Isn't she afraid?" And [it is difficult to argue] that Ossetians are normal people. No one was expelled. It was them who attacked Ossetia.

BELA: It is difficult to argue with the central television.

The perception of media bias in favor of the Ingush and to the disadvantage of Ossetians was repeated in the focus group of male activist victims over thirty-five years old.

TOTRAZ: What is being written [in the mass media]? Different things. Once a commissioned article was written saying that Ossetians do what, on the contrary, Ingush people are doing.

KAZBEK1: Yes, it created the impression that we were doing it.

TOTRAZ: That we are acting there in this way. For sure [the information is distorted].

BORIS: It is deliberately distorted.

TAMERLAN: [The media report] was an order. Someone ordered it.

VITALY: Someone pays for and orders programs against Ossetians. Take an average Muscovite. Will he double check these facts? Why would he need to? He accepts this on faith.

ALIK: For example, I am absolutely sure that when there was this conflict in 1992, since then these actions have been on the Ingush side . . . because we didn't attack. Ossetia didn't attack Ingushetia. They came here. Not one house was burned in the territory of Ingushetia. And no political appraisal has been given since then.

BORIS: That's right.

ALIK: If the guilty had been punished, I am sure nothing would have followed. And I don't know why they are indulged. I can't understand it at all.

BORIS: And the most important thing is, when the events evolved, do you know how they treated it? It should be Ingush-Ossetian, and it is treated as Ossetian-Ingush. You see? Such information is in the press. The other way around.

KAZBEK1: As if we had attacked them.

In the focus group of male nonactivist victims, participants were initially asked to discuss the current possibility of retaliatory ethnic violence. The moderator, despite repeated efforts, could not get the men to distinguish current hostilities from the violent interethnic history.

TAMERLAN: Ethnic discord [has existed], let's not say for centuries, but for decades.

MODERATOR: But still a war didn't break out [after this current tragedy], and on the contrary, people united somehow. Tell us about this.

RUSLAN: The war started in 1992 when they attacked us.

MODERATOR: Well, this is a different topic.

TAMERLAN: It started even earlier, in the last century.

RUSLAN: . . . when they attacked us the last time.

MODERATOR: That's different. If the point of reference is the tragedy . . .

RUSLAN: Ossetian television didn't say that Ingush missiles are aimed at Ossetia, but said that Ossetian missiles attacked Ingushetia, our tanks. And our people were sleeping when they came to us. Even here there is no justice.

Seen through the eyes of Beslan victims and other North Ossetians, the 2004 hostage taking is just further evidence of the continued barbarism of people who should not be allowed to live near them in the first place. After 1992, North Ossetians believed that "the conflict represents Ingush aggression against their republic. According to the Ossetian perception, the return of Ingush—especially in the absence of any judicial proceedings—would mean letting the guilty back into 'their home'" ("Russia: The Ingush-Ossetian Conflict" 1996:40). This sentiment, by now decades old, was reinforced by the school hostage taking. The discussion among Ossetians after 1992 was about (preventing) reconciliation and the return of displaced Ingush more than about retaliation, but the predominant Ossetian sentiment to prevent return of the displaced was the foundation for attitudes about retaliatory violence after the 2004 school hostage taking.

Even popular culture captures this century of mutual distrust and conflict. A nonactivist male victim explained.

BORIS: Ill feelings were stirred on that side and on this side. There is an old movie. It's called "*Druzya* [Friends]." I think it was shot in the 1930s. Cherkasov plays the part of an Ossetian, and somebody else plays the part of an Ingush. They were moving a stone. The one who got up earlier in the morning moved the stone to have more land. The stone was their border. If the Ossetian gets up, goes, and sees, "Oh, an Ingush moved the stone at night," he moves it again and hides. An Ingush gets out in the morning, "Oh, an Ossetian moved the stone again," and he moves it again. The movie was taken during the period of the revolution, but it has been this way since. These ill feelings are instigated. They are instigated against us, and we have it here. It has been the case, and it will be so [in the future]. If only people stopped talking about it, but they don't.

History of Chechen-Ossetian Ethnic Violence

The Prigorodny region was historically populated by Ingush more than Chechens, and the conflict was only peripherally connected to the Russian-Chechen wars.[1] Still, ethnic ties between Ingush and Chechens mean that historic animosity of Ossetians toward Ingush was also felt toward Chechens.

Ossetians also understood the insecurity of North Ossetia as the result of purposeful action by Chechen militants who strategically sought to destabilize the entire North Caucasus. When the USSR collapsed along republican lines in 1991, it seemed logical to some Chechen nationalists to declare independence too, despite their inconvenient status as a republic within, not adjacent to, the Russian Federation. Chechnya was always one of the poorest regions of the Soviet Union, having little industrial development or agriculture and depending on massive subsidies from the central government. Despite this dependence, the long history of Russian conquest and deportation of the Chechen people and their mutual hatred and distrust fueled conflict and obstructed the kind of successful

---

[1] Some saw the connection as more than peripheral. For example, Sokirianskaia (2007) argues that the 1992 violence in the Prigorodny district was an attempt by Russia to provoke Chechen intervention and thus justify Russian retaliation in Chechnya. She also notes that during the 1994–1996 Chechen war, many Chechens fled to Ingushetia, where they were welcomed by their ethnic kin. In this sense, most violence in the North Caucasus was probably related in some way to the Russian-Chechen conflict.

negotiations that were taking place in other potentially secessionist Russian regions. By December 1994, failures in leadership and governance on both the Chechen and Russian sides led to the first Chechen war, conducted under President Boris Yeltsin (Evangelista 2002).

In August 1996, the war formally ended with the signing of the Khasavyurt Accord by representatives of Russia and Chechnya, but in reality, both sides lied and reneged on promises. Russian authorities never sent the promised aid to repair the destruction, and Chechen authorities did little to stop lawlessness and violence in the region. In 1999, the second Chechen war resumed in full force under President Putin, at tremendous cost to human life and infrastructure, and while the Russians "won," the Chechen insurrection continued, along with rampant criminality. The Russian state violated human rights and committed unthinkable atrocities, including torture, disappearances, and summary execution, and the rebels increasingly relied on the use of terror and appeals to radical Islam (Evangelista 2002; Jack 2004; Schaefer 2011). Some analysts questioned the sincerity of the rebels' commitment to Islam and saw the rebels as entrepreneurs of violence—warlords and criminals who seemed interested in fighting for its own sake (Zurcher 2009:88).

The devastation in Chechnya meant that even ordinary citizens participated in the criminality. There were few if any legal ways to survive, and many families earned income by stealing oil, illegally refining oil, kidnapping for ransom, or profiting from Chechnya's de facto status as a free trade zone where illegal contraband or even perfectly respectable goods could be smuggled into Russia, without paying duty or tax or passing border checks, and resold at enormous profit. The distance between the Chechen capital of Grozny and the North Ossetian capital of Vladikavkaz was a mere fifty miles, and less between other towns, leaving the Ossetians with a mess in their backyard and the frequent victims of Chechen banditry and militancy.

There were direct, high-profile instances of Ossetians being targeted by Chechens. On December 16, 1996, a delegation consisting of North Ossetian presidential advisor Georgy Dzhikayev, Deputy Minister of Internal Affairs Soslan Sikoyev, Secretary General of Russia's Assembly of National Democratic and Patriotic Forces Schmidt Dzoblayev, and a police escort headed to Grozny in order to prepare for a conference on problems in the North Caucasus. Instead, they were seized and held hostage. The hostages were released ten days later, except Dzoblayev, whose ordeal lasted almost eight months due to his captors' assertion that he was disloyal to Chechnya. Other North Ossetians were still being held in Chechnya and Ingushetia at the time ("Ossetian Official" 1997; Grodnenskii 2007:689–690). Given the captors' demands for six million dollars in ransom, these events could be dismissed as basic criminality and not interethnic violence, but their occurrence amidst the Chechen conflict meant for many Ossetians that there was very little difference between criminals and Chechens.

Violence perpetrated by Chechen militants or their sympathizers continued in the North Caucasus both before and after the Beslan school hostage taking. Although official data on terrorist attacks in the region are unreliable, there were at least sixteen other "major occasions of violent conflicts/insurgency/terrorism" outside Chechnya between 1995 and 2006, with at least four of these directly in North Ossetia and the others in close proximity (Baev 2006). These included a March 1999 explosion in a Vladikavkaz market that killed 50–70 people; two separate suicide bombings a month apart in 2003 in Mozdok, one in a bus and another at a hospital, that killed 20 and 50 people, respectively; and multiple explosions targeting pipelines and power lines in North Ossetia in January of 2006 (Baev 2006; Phillips 2007:200–202). The Vladikavkaz market was attacked again in 2008 and 2010, with casualties, as was a Vladikavkaz bus stop, also in 2008 and also with casualties (Abbas 2008; Dzutsev 2011; Hammarberg 2011; Parfitt 2011). In 2008, Vitaly Karayev, the mayor of Vladikavkaz, was assassinated, presumably by an Islamist group with links to Chechen militants. A month later, his predecessor Kazbek Pagiyev, mayor from 2002 to 2007 and a former North Ossetian deputy prime minister, was also assassinated (Abbas 2008; "Former Vladikavkaz" 2008).

If we consider not just the major events but all security incidents, large and small, North Ossetia experienced fewer than Chechnya itself or the other neighboring republics of Ingushetia, Dagestan, and Kabardino-Balkaria, and many of the incidents were likely related to Prigorodny, Muslim-Christian conflicts, or organized crime, not the Chechen conflict per se (e.g., Abbas 2008; O'Loughlin and Witmer 2011). Nevertheless, in absolute terms, the incidents in North Ossetia were too many, and enough were linked to Chechnya to matter. They were seen as part of a pattern of Chechen terrorism that included the 1995 hostage taking at a hospital in Budennovsk in Stavropol Krai and the 2002 hostage taking at the Dubrovka theater in Moscow, which each left over 120 dead (Zurcher 2009:83; Javeline and Baird 2007). As then-President Dmitry Medvedev stated when addressing a meeting of the National Anti-Terrorism Committee held in Vladikavkaz on February 22, 2011, "[i]t is here that our citizens are faced with terror on a daily basis. Terror exists in other parts of our country too, but in the North Caucasus it is present almost everywhere, and terrorist attacks occur quite regularly, unfortunately. The root of contradictions that generate extremism and radicalism is here" (Hammarberg 2011:7). The not-so-subtle implication by Medvedev, and by many North Ossetians, was that the root—the problem—was Chechen.

The Ethnicities of the Hostage Takers

The Russian authorities initially claimed that many hostage takers in Beslan were Arab or were involved in international terrorism with links to al-Qaeda.

News reports from the final day of the hostage taking were inconsistent about the number and nationalities of the hostage takers, but one common thread was that the terrorists were not Russians, neither by ethnicity nor citizenship. North Ossetian Federal Security Service chief General Valery Andreyev initially claimed on Russian state television that ten of the twenty-seven "destroyed bandits" were from Arab countries, and one of the ten was black, but none were Russian citizens (Dunlop 2006:63; Tuathail 2009:9). Presidential advisor Aslambek Aslakhanov arrived in Beslan and declared that an "international gang" was responsible for the attack, with the gang comprised of eleven Arabs, two blacks, one Kazakh, one Tatar, and no Chechens (Tuathail 2009:9). Russian Defense Minister Sergei Ivanov claimed at an informal session of the Russia-NATO council in Romania that five of seventeen destroyed and identified terrorists were citizens of Arab states (Dunlop 2006:64fn). President Putin repeated the claim that nine hostage takers were from Arab states and one was from Muslim Africa and that these were terrorists with links to al-Qaeda and global jihad (McAllister and Quinn-Judge 2004).

The evidence quickly suggested otherwise, and by the day after the tragic end, even Andreyev conceded that some of the terrorists were Russian citizens (Tuathail 2009:9). Not all officials were forthcoming with similar concessions. Russian Deputy Prosecutor General Sergei Fridinsky was still telling journalists on September 6 that the hostage takers were an international group with representatives of ten nationalities (Tuathail 2009:9). Many other officials propagated the clearly false story of al-Qaeda and international terrorism well past the time when they probably knew better.

In fact, the majority of hostage takers were ethnic Ingush or Chechen. The undisputed leader of the terrorists was Ruslan Tagirovich Khuchbarov, also known as "the Colonel" (*Polkovnik*). Khuchbarov was born in Ingushetia in 1972 to an Ingush father and Chechen mother, and when his parents separated, he and a younger brother moved to Chechnya and became Chechen fighters, and his brother was killed during the first Chechen war (Tuathail 2009). Victim eyewitness accounts confirm the ethnicity of Khuchbarov and many of the other hostage takers. Nur-Pasha Kulayev, the accused and convicted hostage taker and allegedly sole survivor among the terrorists, also confirms the ethnicity of the hostage takers. Indeed, Kulayev himself and his older brother and fellow hostage taker Khan-Pasha were Chechens from Chechnya.

At his trial, Kulayev was asked about the Colonel:

What was the Colonel [ethnically]?

[Kulayev]: The Colonel was an Ingush ...

In the school when you were there in what language did they give commands?

In Ingush. The Colonel [he added] also spoke fluently in Chechen.

Did you understand him when he gave commands in Ingush?

No, I didn't. But he knew Chechen well . . .

Who in the school decided who should stand where?

The Colonel and one other Ingush. (Pravdabeslana.ru, III, 38, in Dunlop 2006:38)

According to Kulayev, the Colonel and former Ingushetia president Ruslan Aushev spoke in Ingush when Aushev visited the school (Pravdabeslana.ru, III, 10, in Dunlop 2006:38).

Prosecutors also asked Kulayev:

What nationality were the thirty-two persons in your group?

Ingush, one Arab and one Ossetian [presumably Khodov], and one slant-eyed person. The remainder were Ingush and Chechens. There were four or five Chechens. . . . (Pravdabeslana.ru, III, 38, in Dunlop 2006:43)

Kulayev's testimony did confirm that not all the hostage takers were Ingush and Chechen. One of the leaders was Vladimir Khodov, also known as "Abdul" or "Abdulla," an ethnic Ukrainian who was adopted by his ethnic Ossetian stepfather and raised in the Muslim enclave of Elkhotovo in North Ossetia and who later converted to Islam (Buse et al. 2004; Dunlop 2006:30). However, the diversity of ethnicities was narrow, and even those who were not tied to ethnic violence in the North Caucasus by birthplace and ethnicity were nevertheless connected to the Chechen cause. They were homegrown terrorists rather than international jihadists, and they claimed to represent or act on behalf of a local ethno-religious group.

As further evidence, demands of the hostage takers were consistent with causes espoused by ethnic Ingush and Chechens. They demanded full Russian troop withdrawal from Chechnya, recognition of formal independence for Chechnya, the presence at the school of particular political officials such as the presidents of North Ossetia and Ingushetia, and the release of approximately 30 suspected rebels detained in a June 2004 crackdown in Ingushetia. The crackdown was in response to the bloody raid on the Ministry of Internal Affairs (MVD) armory in Ingushetia on June 21–22 that left 80 people killed, 106 wounded, and 1,177

firearms and 70,922 bullets in the hands of the radical Chechen warlord Shamil
Basayev and his militants (Dunlop 2006:24–25).

Basayev claimed responsibility for the school hostage taking. He was probably
operating autonomously from the rest of the Chechen independence movement,
including Chechen separatist leader Aslan Maskhadov, who denied involvement and condemned the action, calling it a blasphemy. Nevertheless, the role of
Basayev as the mastermind behind the school hostage taking clarified to most remaining doubters that the siege was an act of terror by one ethno-religious group
against another.

Some observers have tried to distinguish the Ingush hostage takers from the
Chechen hostage takers, asserting that Ingush militants dominated and that
only after the school had been seized was the attack "Chechenized," with Shamil
Basayev adding the demand of Russian troop withdrawal from Chechnya to the
smaller demand for releasing the thirty mostly Ingush rebels from prison where
they were being held for their attack on the armory (Dunlop 2006:44). It is also
noteworthy that Chechens and Ingush have had their own historic disagreements
and antagonisms and, while related in many ways, still retain distinct identities
and interests (Tishkov 1997:ch. 8).

For the victims and their friends and neighbors, these distinctions were probably not so meaningful. The mere involvement of Besayev, let alone his leadership,
almost certainly "Chechenized" any attack, and the original cause of the raid on
the Ingushetia armory was itself related to the conflict in Chechnya. It was very
difficult to parse out Ingush-only issues from Chechen-only issues. As one of the
terrorists said as he herded hostages into the school gymnasium at the start of the
siege, "We are from Chechnya. This is a seizure. We are here to start the withdrawal
of troops and the liberation of Chechnya" (Chivers 2007). Similarly, Khodov, who
was neither Chechen nor Ingush, apparently told Dr. Larisa Mamitova, the Beslan
doctor who with her young son was among the hostages, "We have only one goal.
The Russian army must leave Chechnya" (Buse et al. 2004).

This empirical study provides some evidence that the distinction between
Ingush and Chechen people, let alone their causes, was largely irrelevant to
Beslan victims and other Ossetians, especially to those who perceived the school
siege in ethnic terms. For the victim surveys, pretest results revealed very similar attitudes toward Ingush and Chechen, so similar that interviewers risked
generating annoyance among respondents for asking duplicative questions,
and thus the final surveys asked about Chechens for some questions and
Ingush for others. This lack of differentiation may reflect racism, the perceived
interconnectedness of Chechen and Ingush issues, or the shared history, culture, religion, and linguistics between members of the two ethnic groups who are
jointly known as *Vaynakh*. Either way, most victims knew about the dominance
of Chechen and Ingush among the hostage takers, and those who tended to think

in ethnic terms had grievances not simply against Basayev, Khuchbarov, Kulayev, and the other deceased militants but against the ethnic groups they represented, Ingush and Chechen. The school hostage taking was perceived as a Chechen-Ingush attack.

Behavior of the Terrorists

The terrorists involved in the school siege were unbelievably cruel, and many victims generalized from the cruelty of these individuals to the cruelty of the Chechen and Ingush people. The terrorists refused to give the children food and water and strove to make the incident as traumatizing as possible. The Colonel allegedly told the children that he did not come there to joke around, and when asked if they could use the bathroom, he answered, "I am not your uncle, I'm a terrorist. I cannot let you do whatever you want. I also have children. I came here not simply to make jokes. I came here to kill" (Pravdabeslana.ru, VIII, 17, in Dunlop 2006:39).

The terrorists summarily executed twenty-one male hostages during the first two days of the incident, presumably to get rid of the physically strongest hostages who could cause difficulties and to intimidate the other hostages and convince the Russian authorities of the credibility of their threats (Dunlop 2006:54). The men's bodies were later dumped outside the building. In one such instance, Ruslan Betrozov, a forty-four-year-old father of two sons at the school, stood to translate the terrorists' rules, including no talking without permission, all speech in Russian rather than Ossetian, handing over cell phones, cameras, and video cameras, and the meeting of any resistance with mass executions, including the women and children. The terrorists let him speak, but when he stopped, one approached and asked, "Are you finished? Have you said everything you want to say?" When Betrozov nodded, the terrorist shot him in the head, leaving his dead body in front of the terrified children and remaining adults, mostly women (Chivers 2007).[2]

---

[2] Phillips (2007:67) tells Betrozov's story a bit differently: "One man, forty-six-year-old Ruslan Betrozov, was so worried about what the terrorists might do next that he resolved to try to defuse the situation.... he walked up to the terrorists and started trying to calm them down. He told them that if they stopped shooting and behaved less aggressively the hostages would quiet down by themselves. He said that their behavior was only making the situation worse. The terrorists carried on regardless and the chaos in the hall continued, but Betrozov did not retreat. He continued to plead with the gunmen to hold their fire.... [Larisa Tomayeva] was standing near Betrozov as he attempted to reason with the terrorists. She says, 'They forced him to the ground and shouted that if we weren't all as silent as the grave immediately, they would shoot him. But there was no way of getting everybody to be quiet. Betrozov was crouched down and he just kept calmly asking us all to quieten down. He was begging us to be silent. But, since nobody could get everybody quiet, the terrorists took him and dragged him a bit more into the centre of the gym and shot him through the back of the head.'" In all versions of the story, Betrozov was helpful to other hostages during the initial stages of the attack until his murder.

Other instances involved kicking and beating school boys. One former hostage, a forty-one-year-old biology teacher, reported, "I saw one of the rough guys shouting at this boy. He was saying, 'Why are you staring at me? You want to remember my face do you? Well, I'll give you something to remember me by.' He slammed the butt of his rifle into the boy's face. He fell over, moaning on the ground" (Franchetti and Campbell 2004).

There was certainly variation in behavior among the terrorists, and not all were as overtly cruel as the Colonel. There is evidence that many of the hostage takers had little knowledge about the plans and even objected to seizing a school (Phillips 2007:18). Russian Prosecutor General Vladimir Ustinov confirmed as early as September 9, 2004, that some militants quarreled with the Colonel over holding children hostage and that one was shot and killed by the Colonel in response (Abdullaev and Voitova 2004). The Colonel also intentionally detonated the explosives worn by two female suicide bombers and blew them up. While there is no conclusive evidence about his motivation, several hostages reported that the women objected to the choice of children as targets, especially when an alternative and less repulsive target, a police station, was practically next door (Chivers 2007; Tuathail 2009). Former hostage Alla Khanayeva heard one of the women say, "No. No. I won't do it. You said that we were going to attack a police station" (Phillips 2007:86).[3]

Other former hostages also reported variation in the militants' treatment of hostages. In a focus group of female activist victims thirty-five years and younger, participants recounted disagreements between the female suicide bombers and their boss and between those wearing camouflage and others who secretly helped some hostages when the camouflaged militants could not see.

VIKA: There was a conflict amongst themselves.
ANGELA: And people said that one of them gave the children water to drink.
BELA: More than one.
ANGELA: One of them did that, hostages saw it, and the "black" one noticed it. And people say, he was taken out, and we never saw him again. He never came back.

Indeed, not every Chechen and Ingush hostage taker was necessarily there of their own accord. Several times during his trial in the summer of 2005,

---

[3] Khanayeva told her story at the public meeting at the House of Culture on November 3, 2004, described in the Introduction, after Deputy Prosecutor General Shepel and other officials left but the more than one thousand residents remained to share thoughts on the hostage taking and updates on their well-being. Khanayeva quoted one of the female hostage takers as saying, "You promised that we would take the police department, the police, but this is a school!" (Shavlokhova et al. 2004:1).

Kulayev said that he, his older brother Khan-Pasha, and his friend Islam had been forced by the terrorists to join their band (Dunlop 2006:48; Tuathail 2009:7). All of them, he said, were accused by the terrorists of collaboration with the Russian authorities and were threatened with murder, and Nur-Pasha and Islam were even forced to dig holes for their own graves (Phillips 2007:21). In the younger Kulayev's case, he had applied to work with [pro-Moscow deputy Chechen premier] Ramzan Kadyrov, and he maintained that he "possessed a certification from an employee of the security services of the [pro-Moscow] president of Chechnya" (Dunlop 2006:48). If Kulayev is to be believed, he and perhaps other hostage takers were kidnapped and therefore hostages and victims themselves and had no plans to traumatize, let alone murder, children.

At least some hostages did believe this, or at least saw the Ingush and Chechen hostage takers as pawns rather than autonomous evil-doers. In a focus group of female activist victims over thirty-five, participants discussed whether the school siege was part of a Muslim movement with Ingush culprits.

LARISA: No. . . I am not saying that these were not Ingush. These were Ingush, but they were put there on purpose. They were told to go to Ossetia. It was known whom to bring: Ingush and Chechens. And they came, and they were hostages in this situation like we were. It was then visible with your own eyes. Their leaders left, and those who stayed until the end, until the explosion, were also hostages. They didn't even know what would happen next, what was happening. And they were dying with us.

TATIANA: Kulayev came out with us. We were in the cafeteria. She is correct in saying that he didn't even know. He himself said, "I swear to Allah, I didn't know that they brought us here to kill people. I have two children myself."

LARISA: Right. That's what they said. "Do you think I don't want to go home? I have five children myself." They were constantly talking on the phone, waiting for some information, which was never given to them.

TATIANA: Even when terrorists forbid us to drink water saying that it was poisoned, when we went to the toilet, one of them was secretly saying to everybody: "Drink water, they are telling lies. Drink water, and don't worry." It means that some of them really . . . either didn't know or simply had some humaneness in them.

Still, even if victims witnessed variation in the brutality of their captors, the most vicious of the captors left a lasting impression. Given that the vicious captors were mostly Ingush or Chechen, some victims associated the despicable behavior with those ethnicities.

Did Ordinary Ingush and Chechens Know of the Coming Terror?

Many Beslan residents believe that Ingush living in North Ossetia had advance notice of the impending siege, did not warn their Ossetian neighbors, and, anticipating retaliation, left the republic the evening before or even days and weeks before. Alan, a taxi driver from Beslan, reported, "They ran away, leaving their women, children, and elderly. They knew that we would not touch their children. I alone made four trips to [the predominantly Ingush North Ossetian village of] Khurikau" (Dyupin 2004). Former hostage Larisa Tomayeva reported, "During the last days of August, all of the Chechen and Ingush patients started to check out of the hospital and go home. We're always treating loads of them in our hospital because it's owned by the railway company and it's easy for them to get referrals for treatment. We noticed the same thing happening in the run-up to every terrorist attack there's been here, and just before the Ossetian-Ingush conflict in 1992. There's no denying that they all knew about it beforehand. They always know if something's going to happen in North Ossetia and then they make damn sure to get out" (Phillips 2007:248–249).

In a focus group of female activists thirty-five years or younger, participants had similar observations.

LARISA: Before the terrorist act, people from Ingushetia lay in our hospital. They studied at Medical Institutes. And after the terrorist act, they were off and away.

BELA: It means that they knew there would be a terrorist act.

MADINA: It really happened. Even now my mother-in-law says that they had a friend of the family, an Ingush. And within some short period of time—at that moment they didn't understand what he was talking about—he said good-bye to them. He warned them. That is, he knew beforehand what was going to happen, and he left for his motherland.

Participants in the focus group of female activist victims over thirty-five years old agreed.

TATIANA: Ingush attacked Ossetia. They all left at night. They left their apartments and went. Everybody knew that Ingush would attack us in the morning. We have Ingush neighbors, and when all this started we saw that they were not in their apartments. They left their furniture. They left everything that was there and went.

Participants in a focus group of male activists over thirty-five years old also agreed.

TAMERLAN: No one has ever given an unequivocal assessment of the latest, let's say, aggression. And it was aggression. Who came? Did Ossetians go to Ingushetia in bullet-proof KamAZ cars? They clad KamAZ cars with sheets of iron. It was all prepared. Then they informed [their Ingush people] two to three days before. It was planned very well there. And the day before all Ingush people who lived in North Ossetia hid and no one remained in North Ossetia, so that, God forbid, they wouldn't come to harm from their own people.

Immediately after the siege, even the bigger city of Vladikavkaz was devoid of Chechens and Ingush. Chechen and Ingush students withdrew from university, and Chechen and Ingush families picked up and left (Farniyev 2004).

The difficulty, of course, is in proving that Ingush people left North Ossetia before the siege and not afterward, when any cautious person in their place would have done the same (Dyupin 2004). By October 2004, reports said that thousands of Ingush had left, fearing revenge, and that remaining "Ingush students in North Ossetia were told to leave 'for their own protection'" (Weir 2004). Nevertheless, grievances are based on perception rather than reality, especially where the reality may never be known thanks to poor census data from the North Caucasus, purposeful concealing of residency and migration information, and the general chaos of the time and place. To the degree that the perception existed of prior knowledge of the school siege by the Ingush population, it added to the victims' grievances against not simply the terrorists but also their co-ethnics.

The perception that many if not most Ingush had prior knowledge of the hostage taking extends to former president of Ingushetia, Ruslan Aushev. Aushev is the only official to have saved any hostages, having been allowed to enter the school on the second day of the siege, receive a videocassette and note with written demands, and then leave with twenty-six people, mostly nursing babies and their mothers. While some celebrated this achievement, others viewed it skeptically and wondered if Aushev himself was a co-conspirator and "freed" some hostages just to keep up the smokescreen. Some hostages reported that Aushev told the terrorists that they had done great work and would go to heaven for their actions. However, the main evidence in support of the conspiracy theory was that Aushev remained alive and was Ingush and therefore, it was thought, would have had no incentive to help (Phillips 2007:247–248).

Conclusion: The Grievance Context of Ethnic Conflict

An Ossetian victim of Ingush and Chechen terrorists in the Beslan school would seem to have ample justification to seek out Ingush and Chechens for revenge.

Although Chapter 2 will now document the more numerous and nuanced grievances of victims against political officials, the weight given to the respective grievances was not clear, and the relatively simple-to-describe grievance against Ingush and Chechens was quite a powerful one. Most victims disliked, and many victims despised, members of these two rival ethnic groups, the Chechens and Ingush. All grievances against political officials involved in the counterterrorism operation would not have existed had the hostage taking not occurred in the first place. The decision to hold children hostage in a situation likely to result in mass death was attributed by many victims and other North Ossetians to the barbarism of the hostage takers and, by association, their ethnic groups.

In the minds of many victims, the association—the leap from person to individual of a particular ethnicity—made sense. The identities of the hostage takers as Ingush and Chechen—and not Arab or "international," as the authorities not-so-secretly hoped—played a prominent role in the story of the hostage taking. Many victims felt a powerful grievance against the particular terrorists and also against the ethnic groups they represented.

2

Political Grievances

The terrorist act in Russia involved children in an agonizingly prolonged, frightening, and traumatic event, but the event remains unexplained to this day. Since
the hostage taking, Beslan victims and their sympathizers lived in a stressful state
of frustration and disbelief that, years after the tragedy, basic facts remained in
dispute or were perhaps intentionally concealed. They had a long list of questions
that kept their community in limbo trying to establish exactly how it happened
that so many of their children, spouses, parents, siblings, and friends died.

Most grievances are informational. Beslan residents have their suspicions that,
although Ingush, Chechen, and other terrorists certainly took them and their
loved ones hostage, it may not have been the terrorists who ultimately killed and
maimed. Many questions surround the explosions that triggered the chaos, gunfire, and burning and collapse of the gymnasium roof that took the lives of a significant portion of the hostages, and the conventional wisdom in Beslan is that
the authorities, not the hostage takers, initiated the horror or at least exacerbated
it once the bloody finale began.

Table 2.1 shows the vast array of hotly contested questions that continue to
surround the hostage taking almost two decades later. These grievances are
discussed in greater detail below.

Most likely, we will never know the conclusive answers to many questions
in Table 2.1. North Ossetians and other Russian citizens anticipated this
non-outcome as early as 2004. Evidence was carted away prematurely, and
investigators who should have been questioning were instead proclaiming the
truth and even threatening witnesses whose accounts differed from the official
line. A nationwide poll conducted in July 2005 by the Moscow-based Public
Opinion Foundation found that only 15 percent of Russians expected the official parliamentary investigation headed by Federation Council Deputy Speaker
Aleksandr Torshin to discover the truth about what happened, and another
20 percent thought the commission would discover the truth but keep it secret
(Weir 2005a).

Most likely, the scale of the tragedy was the result of horrible mistakes. No one
really seemed to benefit from the early explosions, which took the terrorists by
surprise and thwarted their plans and which killed and wounded hundreds of
innocents, not to mention Russian security forces, leaving the authorities with
bloodshed on their watch. Blunders and negligence are the most reasonable

After Violence. Debra Javeline, Oxford University Press. © Oxford University Press 2023.
DOI: 10.1093/oso/9780197683347.003.0003

Table 2.1. Hotly Contested Questions about the September 2004 School Hostage Taking in Beslan

- The number of militants involved
- The ethnic identities of the militants
- Why some high-profile hostage takers had been released from FSB custody only shortly before the hostage taking
- How these same hostage takers then evaded the authorities
- How the militants arrived in Beslan
- How the militants got into the school
- How so many weapons got into the school and whether the weapons were hidden under the floor of the school library in advance
- Whether federal and/or local authorities received advance warnings of an impending terrorist attack
- Whether the militants issued demands
- The number of hostages
- Whether the government deliberately provided misinformation about the number of hostages and hostage takers
- Which precise authorities were guilty for misinformation
- Why no secure perimeter was established by troops to bar civilians from the scene
- Who made the real operational decisions during the crisis, such as the decision to use heavy weapons
- Why law enforcement bodies failed to coordinate operations
- Why President Putin and other top Russian and North Ossetian officials kept their distance from the scene
- Whether a terrorist or government sniper or armed civilian triggered the first explosion in the gymnasium and, if a government sniper, whether he was FSB Spetsnaz, army, internal affairs, police offer, or OMON or SOBR police commando
- Whether government troops fired incendiary weapons (flamethrowers known as *Shmel* rockets) into the school
- Whether they fired flamethrowers while some hostages were still alive inside
- How many flamethrowers were fired
- Whether commandos began to fire from machine guns, grenade throwers, tanks, and armored personnel carriers while hostages were still alive inside
- What options were available to Russian troops once the shooting started
- Why no fire trucks and firefighting equipment were at the scene

(continued)

Table 2.1. Continued

- Why two full hours went by after the fire started before firefighters were called
- Why the fire trucks were ill prepared with insufficient water and unable to connect to hydrants when they finally arrived
- Why so few ambulances were at the scene
- Why rubble and crucial evidence from the wreckage were so quickly removed from the scene before thorough forensic investigation
- Why body parts of victims were put in the local garbage dump
- How many victims died
- How many died in the gym versus the cafeteria and whether those in the cafeteria were killed by tanks
- Why some people were not told whether their children were alive or dead even months after the siege
- How many members of Russia's elite special forces died
- Whether some militants escaped and, if so, how many
- Why the scene continued to be open to the public after the standoff ended rather than sealed for investigation
- Overall how competently or incompetently the government managed the crisis and which government officials were responsible for competence or incompetence

explanations based on the currently available evidence. But whose blunders and whose negligence will likely remain a matter of debate and potential source of grievance indefinitely.

Blunders and negligence of any kind were galling to victims, because the Russian government by the time of the school hostage taking had a decade of fighting experience in the North Caucasus and Russia as a whole, including the two Chechen wars and several large-scale terrorist incidents. As described in Chapter 1, the Beslan school hostage taking was preceded by the 1995 Budennovsk hospital hostage taking and the 2002 Moscow theater hostage taking. Both cases ended badly, with Russian special forces storming the buildings and over 120 deaths, hundreds more severe injuries, and widespread trauma (Zurcher 2009:83; Javeline and Baird 2007). In the eyes of many Beslan victims, Russia should have learned from its years of failed conflict prevention and resolution. Beslan's horror should have ended better or never should have happened in the first place.

Who Killed Our Children?

If the terrorists had fired their weapons in the first few hours of the hostage taking and killed not just the men who posed a potential threat to their siege but the vast majority of hostages, a major issue would be removed from the victims' list of concerns: the question of who killed our children. Instead, the vast majority of deaths occurred during the supposed rescue operation, which included many acts of bravery and heroism but on the whole was bungled. Beslan victims suspect their loved ones were killed not only by terrorists, but by vigilantes and federal agents in the chaos that followed a perhaps unintentional explosion in the school ("Seeking Public Accountability" 2004).

Emma Tagayeva was a leader of Voice of Beslan and also the wife of Ruslan Betrozov, the hostage who attempted to calm the terrorists and fellow hostages and was executed for his efforts. Tagayeva explained, "My whole family was killed in school No. 1. My husband was shot right in front of my sons' eyes. I agree that my husband was killed by terrorists. But I do not agree that terrorists killed my sons. No one has proved that they did" (Allenova 2006).

According to Federation Council Deputy Speaker Alexander Torshin, who headed the parliamentary commission investigating Beslan, the tragedy resulted from a lack of leadership and the mistakes of the security services, especially in failing to organize a joint command of the counterterrorism operation in the first thirty-six hours and failing to collect and process intelligence information (Yasmann 2004). Even without the accidental explosion, official policies probably would have resulted in casualties. Russian authorities strictly refuse to negotiate with terrorists, which many Russians believe left Beslan hostages vulnerable, since storming and the loss of hostages' lives were the likely remaining response. The authorities concealed the number of hostages and casualties from residents of Beslan and the rest of Russia, and even now there is less than full disclosure of the number of victims.

Who Shot First?

Everyone agrees that the hostage taking ended with explosions, gunfire, and ultimately the collapse of the gymnasium roof and a raging fire. However, the source of the explosions—the "which came first?" question—is a matter of serious debate. Just before the first two big explosions at 1:03 and 1:04 p.m., the Russian Ministry for Emergency Situations had reached some agreement with the terrorists to remove the bodies of the twenty-one murdered male hostages that had been lying for two days in the courtyard. During the removal effort, the shooting and storm began.

The official line is that the hostage takers started the mayhem. When President Putin met with some members of the nongovernmental organization Mothers of Beslan on September 2, 2005, he informed the women that a hostage taker was reading the Koran and took his foot off the pedal that controlled a powerful bomb, leading to an explosion. Prosecutors repeated this line and insisted on the impossibility of alternative scenarios that might exonerate the hostage takers and point elsewhere for the initial explosions. The main alternative proposed by hostages and surviving hostage taker Kulayev had a Russian sniper killing the terrorist whose foot was on the pedal, but prosecutors said that scenario was impossible because the terrorist controlling the bomb was located behind non-transparent windows and therefore not visible to a sniper (Dunlop 2006:83).

The victims had many reasons to doubt the official line. It was inconsistent with eyewitness accounts, forensics, and terrorist motivations. The eyewitness accounts come from numerous former hostages whose stories corroborate each other. Yuri Savelyev, a dissenting member of Torshin's parliamentary commission who later issued his own report, explains, "The investigation asserts that the first explosions occurred in the western part of the gymnasium as a result of the detonation of explosive devices laid by terrorists. But the majority of hostages describe effects from explosions which originated in the opposite (eastern) part of the gymnasium. . . . This is the first incongruity" (Milashina 2006e) and suggests that the explosions were triggered from outside the school.

The surviving hostages further insist that the bombs placed by the terrorists on the basketball hoops, chairs, and center of the gym did not explode (Milashina 2006d). They tell a consistent story of hearing a first explosion, seeing a hole in the gym ceiling and the shattering of the roof, laying on the floor, watching a fire develop around the hole, and feeling burning fragments fall down upon them (Milashina 2006e). Svetlana Margiyeva, a former hostage who spoke at the Supreme Court during the victims' appeal of the Kulayev verdict, said, "I saw the terrorist who was at the pedal [controlling the explosive device] fall sideways. And then we were told that he had detonated the bomb. But it was not him! There was no fire, and a flame flew right down the hall. My body directly burned. The terrorists did not shoot; the shooting came from the street. But they accuse only Kulayev" (Allenova 2006:4).

At his initial trial, Kulayev told a similar story. Kulayev claimed that the hostage takers had removed the plastic from the windows so people could breathe, an action confirmed by former hostages and suggesting that the terrorist controlling the bomb with his foot could indeed have been visible to a Russian sniper. According to Kulayev, the Colonel shouted that a Russian sniper killed the terrorist at the pedal (Pravdabeslana.ru, III, 35, in Dunlop 2006:83).

Forensic investigation seems to support these eyewitness accounts. According to Yuri Savelyev, whose investigative credentials come from his expertise in explosions and firearms as much as his political position on the Torshin commission, "the first explosion was the result of the use of an RPO-A [a thermobaric 'flamethrower'] fired from the roof of an apartment building (Shkolnyi pereulok [School Lane], No. 37) at the roof of the gymnasium in its northeastern corner.... The second explosion was the result of a shot fired from the roof of an apartment building (Shkolnyi pereulok [School Lane], N. 41) by an RShG-1 [grenade-launcher] using a high-explosive fragmentation grenade" (Dunlop 2009:4). Savelyev supported his conclusions with explanations about weapons, those rigged by the terrorists and those used by the Russian counterterrorist operation, and their respective capacity for destruction, as compared with the actual destruction of the gymnasium and the rest of the school. Savelyev also concluded that "after the first explosions in the gymnasium, the explosive devices set by the terrorists did not explode. (They detonated later, as a result of a fire in the gymnasium.) . . . In the span of time separating the first [two] explosions in the gymnasium—approximately 22 seconds—not one homemade explosive device placed by the terrorists went off" (Milashina 2006e).

Still other forensic evidence was provided by two "sappers," Andrei Gagloyev, a lieutenant colonel and commander of the engineering troops of the Fifty-eighth Army, and Bakhtiyar Kara-Olgy Nabiyev, also a lieutenant colonel. Gagloyev and Nabiyev went into the school on their own initiative and against orders on September 3 to try to de-mine the gymnasium and save lives. According to Gagloyev, the homemade explosive devices that should have been connected were a mess and incapable of exploding. Therefore, the hole under the window could not have come from an explosion occurring inside the gymnasium. Nabiyev added that he and Gagloyev "dragged out the children, and not one of them had shrapnel. And around (on the walls) there was also none," and he confirmed that there were no explosions inside the room (Tskhurbayev 2007b; Milashina 2007c; Dunlop 2009:6).

Importantly, Gagloyev and Nabiyev's remarks were not clouded by the passage of time or the possibility of evidence contamination. The sappers' actions are captured on film at least twenty-five minutes before the gymnasium roof collapsed at 3:25 p.m., and they are questioned on tape very shortly thereafter, at 5:50 p.m. On tape, they unequivocally say that none of the terrorists' explosive devices had gone off (Milashina 2007c; Dunlop 2009:6). Also importantly, the videotape of Gagloyev and Nabiyev was supposedly lost by the North Ossetian Prosecutor General's Office for three years and became widely disseminated only after it was anonymously sent by mail to the Mothers of Beslan at the end of July 2007 (Tskhurbayev 2007b; Dunlop 2009:5). The convenient misplacing of the tape strengthened the conviction of many Beslan victims that the authorities indeed had shot first, were responsible for the start of the bloody end, and were attempting a cover-up.

The sappers' videotape may not be the only videotape suggesting that the authorities shot first. According to Savelyev and several journalists and former hostages, there were many other tapes documenting the entirety of events of September 1–3, including the ultimate storming of the school. These tapes were made by the Federal Security Services (FSB), the Ministry of Internal Affairs (MVD), the North Ossetian Procuracy, and an assistant to North Ossetian Minister for Emergency Situations Boris Dzgoyev. Most were classified by the FSB, Russia's successor to the KGB, and, despite repeated requests, were not made available to the hostages, General Procuracy, parliamentary commissions, the court, and even the president (Dunlop 2009:8).

Savelyev and others surmise that the authorities' first shot was motivated by the presence of a terrorist sniper sitting on the school roof and shooting at the courtyard, the site of two armored vehicles and a future counterterrorist storming of the school. They wanted to kill the sniper (Dunlop 2009:4). This potential motivation undoubtedly sounded plausible to many victims and other observers.

Conversely, the motivations for the terrorists to shoot first were unclear. At the time of the explosion, an agreement had supposedly been reached with former Chechen president and current rebel leader Aslan Maskhadov for him to travel to Beslan. North Ossetian president Dzasokhov confirmed in his testimony at the Kulayev trial that Maskhadov, widely recognized by Chechens and Ingush to be the lawful leader of Chechnya, was due to arrive. Moreover, Ingushetia president Ruslan Aushev and Aslambek Aslakhanov, retired MVD general and Putin's advisor on the Caucasus, were even closer to arriving at the school. If true, the terrorists had reason to believe that the hostage taking could end well for them with some negotiations and satisfied demands, making an explosion at that precise moment unproductive.[1]

Documented conversation between the terrorists and unofficial counterterrorist negotiators seem to support this conclusion. "At the moment when the first explosion and initial gunfire sounded, negotiator Mikhail Gutseriyev and the Colonel were engrossed in negotiations concerning the imminent arrival of Aslakhanov and Aushev at the school. Both were reportedly taken by complete surprise" (Dunlop 2006:87).

"What have you done?!" screamed Gutseriyev into the receiver.

"You deceived us. Now you will bear responsibility for everything," roared the Colonel in response.

---

[1] Aslakhanov arrived in Beslan at 5 p.m. on September 3, after the storming of the school (Milashina 2006d).

"There is no storm," Gutseriyev tried to calm him, unsuccessfully as the situation spun out of control. (Khinshtein as cited in Dunlop 2006:87; also Buse et al. 2004)

The phone call between the Colonel and Gutseriyev could suggest that neither the authorities nor the terrorists had motivation to shoot first, and the first shot was unintended. Perhaps a rogue terrorist or rogue Russian sniper was to blame. Here is where most victims and their supporters combined their assessment of motivations with their understanding of the forensics. While it was plausible that the terrorist at the pedal could have accidentally caused the explosion, the forensics strongly suggest that his bomb did not explode. Conversely, it was both plausible that a trigger-happy Russian sniper acted on impulse rather than command, and the forensics corroborate this possibility.

How Did the Gymnasium Roof Ignite and Collapse?

According to most former hostages, after the first two explosions, the gymnasium roof remained intact, and there was no fire. As former hostage Marina Karkuzashvili-Miskova explained, "The roof began to burn when they [Russian forces] began to fire some kind of missiles at it. These exploded, and a sizable fire started immediately. Plastic ceiling panels quickly got caught and fell on people with fiery flakes. People lit up like torches" (Milashina 2004c). Other former hostages also believed the military used weapons with projectiles that ignited the school roof, causing the burning roof to collapse on the wounded but still living hostages and set them on fire (Dunlop 2006:89–90). The weapons in question were the *Shmel*, "flamethrowers" that launch rocket-propelled projectiles with shells that, depending on the type, either explode, ignite, or create smoke (Medetsky and Voitova 2005; Dunlop 2006:90).

The authorities vehemently denied such charges. Nikoai Shepel, Russian Deputy Prosecutor General for the Southern Federal District, initially declared that the flamethrowers had been used by the hostage takers, not Russian forces (Bobrova and Milashina 2005). Shepel later admitted on July 12, 2005, that Russian forces did use the *Shmel*, but he denied that their actions led to the burning and collapsed roof. Shepel even claimed that the type of *Shmel* used, the RPO-A, was incapable of causing that damage because, unlike the RPO-Z which have napalm as their primary ingredient, the RPO-A "don't have an incendiary effect." Fire from the RPO-A, he said, lasts only a split second, but exposure would have had to last three to five seconds to burn a person or set a building on fire (Milashina 2005a; Medetsky and Voitova 2005). Shepel's reversal followed an earlier reversal in April 2005 by other officials investigating in Beslan. In response to repeated, direct probing by victims and journalists, head of the North Caucasus Procuracy's press service Sergei Prokopov admitted that flamethrowers were used, but like Shepel, he insisted that these particular flamethrowers had a thermobaric not incendiary effect, meaning that their shells burn instantly, leave a vacuum, and cannot set fire to a roof (Bobrova and Milashina 2005).

Most victims did not buy the official line. Again, their beliefs were buttressed by eyewitness accounts, forensics, and their understanding of the respective motivations of the authorities and the terrorists. At Kulayev's trial, Beslan police officer Chermen Khachirov testified that soldiers shot at the school with flamethrowers from an adjacent five story building thirty minutes after the first explosion occurred. "They carried more than twenty *Shmels* up there. I saw them myself." Another Beslan police officer, Alan Khodikov, testified that he personally was "a witness of how at a minimum ten shots were fired at the school from flamethrowers" (Dunlop 2006:93). Many local residents also claimed that the flamethrowers were fired from roofs where Russian special forces, not rebels, were located (Bobrova and Milashina 2005).

Victims collected and in some cases held on to the remnants of these shots. When President Putin told representatives of the Mothers of Beslan at their September 2, 2005, meeting that the flamethrower did not have an incendiary effect, the Mothers replied, "we discovered flamethrowers at the crime scene. With two strips (RPO-A) and with three (RPO-Z). And we have all the parts. That is, during the storming of the school both thermobaric and incendiary ones were used" (Kaboyev 2005). When the president then claimed that the flamethrowers were not fired at the gymnasium but at other parts of the school, Mothers of Beslan leader Susanna Dudiyeva replied, "Vladimir Vladimirovich! In the school not one classroom was burned, not one window opening has a trace from a flamethrower. Not one wall was burned through by a flamethrower. Only the gymnasium burned, which means that the flamethrower was fired only at the gymnasium" (Kaboyev 2005).

An explosives expert who examined the school wreckage confirmed that a flamethrower was the most likely reason for the fire on the gym roof. If someone outside the building fired from a flamethrower, "[t]he roofing would immediately have begun to burn and virtually any detonation would have been sufficient for its collapse." The expert also said that a few explosions inside the gym would not explain how the roof burned in its entirety. He judged the diameter of the holes in the walls of the gym and where they occurred and determined that they were localized and could not set a fire of that breadth (Dunlop 2006:92).

Others with relevant expertise seemed downright annoyed by the repeated "party line" that certain types of flamethrowers could not start fires and did not ignite the school roof. Anatoly Ermolin, a State Duma deputy and a former commander of the elite FSB special forces unit known as *Vympel*, declared, "To claim that the roof could not ignite from the use of a *Shmel* is nonsense. Any explosion can cause a fire" (Dunlop 2006:91). The head of the North Ossetian parliamentary commission to investigate the hostage taking Stanislav Kesayev agreed, stating that the roof burned only from above, and he cited the testimony of State Duma deputy and doctor Vorobyeva that the burns of each victim were from a substance similar to napalm (Dunlop 2006:89).

Many Beslan victims themselves well understood various weapons and their capabilities, thanks in part to living in a region replete with weapons and in part to their personal research after the tragedy. As Dudiyeva told Putin, "I know the effect of a flamethrower. I picked up literature on the flamethrower and read that it is used to destroy a sniper" (Kaboyev 2005). At various times, victims asserted that it was impossible to fire from flamethrowers within a building (Bobrova and Milashina 2005). Even more frequent was the basic observation by Beslan resident Zifa Tsirikhova that "the ceiling caught fire and fell down . . . and that would not have happened if the blast came from inside" (Walsh 2005).

In terms of motivations, victims were hard pressed to understand why the terrorists would use flamethrowers or start a roof fire in the gym at that particular point in the siege. Conversely, the Russian special forces, as Dudiyeva mentioned, were presumably trying to kill a sniper on the roof (Kaboyev 2005). This assumption was widespread and provoked disgust. Victims and journalists frequently pointed out that Russia had ratified the third protocol of the eighty-year-old Geneva Convention that prohibits the use of incendiary weapons "under any circumstances, against any object near a concentration of civilians" (Milashina 2004b). As Mothers of Beslan member Zalina Guburova said with fury, "How can you use such weapons if there are children in the school? I cannot trust this kind of government" (Stephen 2005a).

When Did Russian Tanks Start Firing?

According to the official version of events, Russian tanks opened fire on School No. 1 only after all the surviving hostages had been evacuated from the building and terrorists alone remained in the basement. The timing, then, was about 8:30 p.m. (Dunlop 2006:93). In a meeting with some members of the Mothers of Beslan, President Putin confirmed that he had information, including military officer eyewitness reports, that the tanks started firing at 9 p.m. (Kaboyev 2005).

However, several accounts have the tanks firing as early as 1:30 p.m. Yuri Savelyev maintained that more than twenty eyewitnesses saw tanks being used at about 1:30 p.m., when hundreds of live hostages would have still been in the school (Dunlop 2006:93). Chair of the North Ossetian parliamentary commission investigating the hostage taking, Stanislav Kesayev, claimed, "In my presence, three shots were fired from a tank located in the courtyard into the school. I asked, 'What are you doing?' They answered, 'There are rebels.' I responded, 'But there are people there too'" (Dunlop 2006:17). One witness, Teimuraz Konukov, watched a tank fire into the school at 2:30 p.m. Responding to the official accounts that the timing was six hours later, he incredulously pointed to the spot behind a tree across the street where he stood at the time and said, "I was right here" (Chivers 2005b:1). By approximately 3 p.m., according to most accounts, Russian special forces had begun a full-blown assault.

Eyewitness accounts of Russian tanks firing much earlier in the day also came from former hostages who were the unintended recipients of that fire. Those who did not escape or die under the collapsed and burning roof but could still move were herded by the militants out of the gymnasium and into the auditorium, first floor cafeteria, and workshops of the school's central building. The militants then forced women and children to stand on the windowsills and wave white "flags"— curtains or school blouses, according to different reports—so Russian forces would not shoot at the windows. According to Rima Kusrayeva, "Then armored personnel carriers drove up from which three soldiers jumped out and began to fire at the windows. I myself saw how a woman fell, after which there was a mountain of corpses on the windowsill" (Farniyev 2005a:3). Sergei Urmanov similarly recounted, "I personally saw two women who were mown down as they tried to do this. I don't know which side got them, but I saw them fall. Then a shell was fired into the room. It came in spinning and smoking and burst into flames. It fell on my daughter" and burnt her and filled her with shrapnel" (Phillips 2007:233). Marina Karkuzashvili-Misikov's story was the same. "My sister Lora and my daughter Diana stood on the windowsill, and they were shouting ["Don't shoot!"]. But who would hear them? Lora somehow pushed my Diana down to the floor. One woman fainted. The rest, including Lora, were shot" (Milashina 2004c). Zarina Daurova heard a girl scream that they were being shot at by tanks. Vera Salkazanova heard children shouting at the windows for the soldiers to stop shooting (Phillips 2007:233–234).

Medics confirmed to Marina Karkuzashvili-Misikov that the women standing on the windowsills were shot in the chest, not in the back; that is, Russian forces shot them (Milashina 2004c). Other forensics were equally convincing to victims. On one of the above-mentioned videotapes, this one recorded by an employee of the North Ossetian Procuracy, special forces began firing grenade-launchers and flamethrowers at 3:08 p.m., after which three mushroom clouds rose over the school, two white and one black. Thirteen explosions followed in the next half hour. The tape shows civilians shouting on the street and pointing to the roof of the five-story building No. 37 on School Lane where there were people wearing helmets and where members of the parliamentary investigative committee later found used flamethrowers and grenade-launchers (Milashina 2007c). Army tanks were also firing at the school at this time, stopping by about 4 p.m. when members of the special forces entered the cafeteria through the windows (Dunlop 2009:9).

There were 106–110 hostages who died in the cafeteria, auditorium, and other parts of the southern wing of the school, not in the gymnasium (Milashina 2006d). These people—approximately a third of the total dead—died during the storming of the building by Russian special forces, and victims wondered whether they potentially may have otherwise survived.

How Could This Have Happened?

Beslan victims also had their suspicions about how the terrorists and their impressive stock of weapons got into the school in the first place. Again, the authorities, not the hostage takers, were the focus, here for their corruption and negligence. Victims questioned how the advance planning for such an attack could have gone undetected, both in the months prior in Ingushetia and in the days and hours prior when the security situation seemed to be unusually weak and when at least some officials had prior warning.

How Could So Many Terrorists Gather, Plan, and Escape Detection?

The terrorists who ultimately entered Beslan School No. 1 on September 1, 2004, had gathered since August 20 at a camp in the woods near the village of Psedakh in the Malgobek District of Ingushetia (Buse et al. 2004). Very early in the morning of September 1, the militants got in their GAZ-66 army truck and crossed the border from Ingushetia into North Ossetia, an internal Russian border but a potentially insecure one, given interethnic violence in the North Caucasus. By 7:20 a.m., they had taken captive an ethnic Ingush police officer, Sultan Gurazhev, who had stopped their vehicle outside the North Ossetian but predominantly Ingush-populated village of Khurikau (Buse et al. 2004). They now had two vehicles, their truck and Gurazhev's white Lada.

Two roads went south from Khurikau to Beslan, the main and tightly controlled road and an old unpaved road through the small village of Razdzog. Residents reported that the unpaved road was more heavily trafficked than the paved road and was used by those trying to avoid police, mainly drivers of unauthorized gasoline trucks. Residents also reported that there were no fixed checkpoints on the unpaved road, but independent wild police brigades were usually there trying to get "customs duties" from smugglers (Dyupin 2004). Upon arrival at the school, the terrorists released Gurazhev, apparently on the Colonel's orders because Gurazhev was a cousin of one of the terrorists (Buse et al. 2004). Gurazhev testified at the Kulayev trial that the covered military truck carrying the militants had passed several checkpoints, but police had not tried to stop it (Voitova 2005).

Upon learning of these circumstances, most victims were outraged. First, they questioned why the Ingush police, supposedly on high terrorism alert, failed to detect such a large gathering of terrorists. The training camp was in full force for a week and a half. The terrorists had sleeping bags and tarps and used sticks and twigs to build shelter, and the Malgobek district had a reputation for danger and weapons proliferation (Buse et al. 2004). At some point the terrorists managed to acquire a military truck stacked with grenade launchers, flamethrowers, sniper rifles, machine guns, and other weapons (Buse et al. 2004). Someone should have noticed.

Apparently, someone did. A year later, a young North Ossetian police officer showed journalists on a map the road the terrorists took to Beslan. "They came this way, through Psedakh and Khurikau. . . . They were staying in the woods between Psedakh and Sagapshi [villages in Ingushetia]. Right under the high-tension electric line. The locals have barbeques there. We already knew that something was brewing on that side. We informed higher ups. But they were supposed to handle it on that [the Ingushetia] side. We can't work there" (Allenova 2005a).

Equally devastating for the victims, official corruption likely played a big role in enabling the hostage taking. Due to tensions in the region, North Ossetians have to pass through many checkpoints in their ordinary affairs, and most residents believed that the only way terrorists with weapons and explosives could have entered the republic and ultimately the town and the school was through corrupt officials who accepted bribes. In particular, driving from the woods of Psedakh, Ingushetia, to Beslan School No. 1 required passing four police posts, where apparently only a few rubles allowed a vehicle to pass (Dyupin 2004; Buse et al. 2004). Although residents could not prove a payoff, Beslan drivers say that it would have been impossible to drive through the Sunzhenskii forest, as the area between the terrorist camp and Beslan is known, for free, especially with wanted men like the Colonel on board and an enormous cargo of weapons (Dyupin 2004). As one Beslan resident complained, "How could [the attackers] bring these weapons here if they [police] check tomatoes 20 times?" Another agreed, "If [the authorities] fulfilled their duty, this wouldn't have been possible" (Herman 2004).

The connection between police corruption and the hostage taking was not contested by the authorities. Russian and North Ossetian officials confirmed the victims' charges. According to the North Ossetian parliamentary investigative commission, "the militants traveled by roads used for smuggling oil out of Chechnya that were under the protection of corrupt law enforcement officials" (Voitova 2005:1; see also Gurin 2004). Head of the commission, Kesayev, noted that "[t]hey traveled right under the noses of our security forces" to reach Beslan, and they bribed corrupt roadside guards to bypass local checkpoints (Mainville 2005b). Former North Ossetian Interior Ministry and Tax Police official Batraz Takazov commented that "coming into [North] Ossetia there are two lines—'legal' and 'special.' You could bring an atom bomb through the 'special' line" (Gurin 2004). President Putin himself acknowledged that corruption among police officers was a contributing factor to terrorism ("Seeking Public Accountability" 2004). Beyond the checkpoint bypassing, corruption also likely led to leaked information about facilities where explosives were manufactured and failing to secure—or intentionally leaving insecure—those facilities.

Given the admissions of police corruption, victims were particularly outraged over the lack of accountability. For example, Putin may have acknowledged the problem, but he did not offer details on the corruption or his plans to combat it ("Seeking Public Accountability" 2004). In October 2004, three Beslan police officers were charged with criminal negligence over the school siege in their failure to provide adequate patrols of the border area, and two Malgobek officers were later charged with negligence for failing to detect the presence of a rebel camp in Ingushetia ("Police Charged over Beslan Siege" 2004; Allenova 2005a), but by May 2007 the Beslan officers were granted amnesty, and by October of the same year the Malgobek officers were acquitted by a jury in Ingushetia. Many victims disagreed with the cavalier handling and ultimate dismissal of the negligence charges, especially because the more deliberate crime of corruption in the form of bribe-taking was not even engaged by either court. Perhaps more importantly, victims believed the outcome then begged the question: If not these officers, who then should have detected the terrorists, but failed?

Why Did Officials Fail to Act on Intelligence about the Impending Siege?

Victims also questioned whether the Russian and North Ossetian authorities had advance notice of the planned siege. Believing that they did in fact have such warning, victims questioned why the information was not conveyed nor acted upon.

The prelude to Beslan was the assault on the Ingushetia armory a few months earlier. On June 21 and 22, 2004, about 200 militants attacked the armory, killing, wounding, and looting (Buse et al. 2004). As a result, they were able to stockpile weapons and ammunition, including 1,177 firearms and 70,922 bullets (Dunlop 2006:24). Some of the perpetrators of this early summer attack, and the firearms and ammunition, would make a second appearance on September 1 at the Beslan school—or perhaps a third or fourth appearance, given that police and detectives fought other gunfights and searched for and sometimes found stolen weapons throughout the summer, all within ten kilometers of the terrorists' camp in the forest (Buse et al. 2004).

On August 18, 2004, two weeks before the hostage taking, the Russian Ministry of Internal Affairs apparently sent a telegram to regional police saying that Chechen rebels were planning an operation in North Ossetia that might resemble a prior raid in the summer of 1995 on the hospital in nearby Budennovsk, approximately 240 kilometers north of Beslan (Buse et al. 2004). On August 28, just days before the siege, Beslan resident Valiko Margiyev was stopped by traffic police who searched his vehicle and told him that a group of rebels had penetrated into Beslan (Meteleva 2005b; Dunlop 2006:22). Just four hours and five minutes before the siege at 5 a.m. on September 1, 2004, a person named Arsamikov was taken into custody in the city of Shali, Chechnya, and revealed during interrogation that a seizure was being planned that day at a school in Beslan. This information was sent in a report to the Russian Minister of Internal Affairs Rashid Nurgaliyev (Meteleva 2005b; Dunlop 2006:22).

The information taken from Arsamikov was apparently not conveyed to the special services in Beslan, or it was conveyed but ignored. There were no armed police in the school and no armed traffic police parked in vehicles near the school, as was the practice in recent years when tensions were high in general but authorities had no such specific threat alerts. Beslan School No. 1 was protected on September 1 by just one policewoman, Fatima Dudiyeva, who had neither a telephone nor a gun.

Beslan victims wanted explanations for the failed security. There were only four schools in Beslan, so logistically, the conveyance of information would have been relatively straightforward, and beefing up security should have seemed appropriate. Head of the investigations department of the Beslan police Elbrus Nogayev, who lost his entire family in the school, was asked during the Kulayev trial if law enforcement agencies had taken sufficient measures to protect the school before capture. He replied, "No, of course not. There was no one there except for one [unarmed] female officer" (Farniyev 2005a:3).

Beslan residents, who did not have privileged access to the advance warning, were themselves always on high alert, just as a matter of course. There are massive amounts of weapons in Beslan homes, and at least one Beslan parent brought a pistol with him that day to school and managed to kill one terrorist and wound two others (Buse et al. 2004; Dunlop 2006:51).[2] Rusik Gappoyev, a resident of

[2] Phillips (2007:56) suggests that it was an armed and trained police officer who fired at least one of the shots that harmed the terrorists.

a nearby apartment building and professional hunter, and Taimuraz Gasiyev, a twenty-nine-year-old former student of School No. 1, along with other local men, also had guns and tried to shoot at the militants (Phillips 2007:56). Surely, thought victims, the authorities could have been at least as prepared as ordinary citizens.

At one point, Gasiyev found himself amidst local police officers whose guns were loaded with blanks. He asked them, "What did you think you were coming to? A fairground shooting gallery? This is war!," to which the police replied that their armorer had gone to the city and taken the key to the arsenal with him (Phillips 2007:57–58).

The authorities did not contest the charge of failed security and made a meager attempt to assign responsibility. Director of the Pravoberezhny District Department of the North Ossetian Interior Ministry, Miroslav Aidarov, and two of his subordinates, Taimuraz Martazov and Georgy Dryayev, were dismissed from their posts after the terrorist act and were charged on September 21, 2004, with negligence (Allenova 2005a). Deputy Prosecutor General Nikolai Shepel claimed that they had received instructions from their superiors "to take relevant measures due to the threat of terrorist attacks on September 1" but had ignored orders and instructions. Instead, two officers who were supposed to be guarding the school were sent to the Caucasus Highway, presumably to guard Dzasokhov, the president of North Ossetia (Dunlop 2006:23).

The lone unarmed policewoman and hostage Fatima Dudiyeva attributed the lack of armed traffic police to lack of personnel. "They said that they never have enough people. They had to protect the highway because a high-ranking official was due to pass by. Until now, however, they haven't been able to figure out who he was supposed to be" (Dunlop 2006:24). Dzasokhov in fact had no travel plans that day, as he himself testified at the Kulayev trial. A piece of the story was missing, and Beslan victims again suspected that corruption—perhaps payoffs to keep armed guards away from the school—filled in the blanks. Terrorist leader Vladimir Khodov was said to have boasted during the hostage taking that "[y]our police sold you out for $20,000" (Dunlop 2006:24), and to many Beslan victims, the boast rang true.

How Did Terrorists Gain Access to the School?

Russian authorities maintained that the militants brought their weapons with them and entered the school for the first time when they attacked the school at around 9 a.m. on September 1.

Many victims asserted that some terrorists had been walking freely in Beslan for at least a week before the hostage taking, that the terrorists must have had access to the school before September 1, and that some had already taken the school on the night of August 31, before the main group attacked at 9 a.m. the next morning. These victims variously claimed that they witnessed terrorists already in the building, were forced to help terrorists get weapons hidden at an earlier date under floorboards, noticed construction material conveniently located near broken windows as evidence of a break-in, and noticed a floor plan of the school in the hands of the terrorists.

For example, as the building was raided from the outside, policewoman Fatima Dudiyeva was seized on the second floor where she had run to call headquarters from a school telephone. At Kulayev's trial, Dudiyeva said that the terrorists who seized her had been there all night and warmly embraced the hostage takers from the main group when they ascended the stairs to the second floor. Former hostage Kazbek Dzarasov told a German newspaper that he was one of the men who had been forced to pull up the floorboards to extract weapons and ammunition. Former hostage Sarmat Khudalov told the same story at the Kulayev trial, as did one other male hostage, a teacher who died in the school, to a female hostage (Dunlop 2006:26–29). Former hostage Larisa Tomayeva ran from the militants in the schoolyard and climbed into the school through a broken window by standing on piles of bricks and sand that were lying on the ground. She was in high heels and with two children, but nevertheless got into the school easily. Because the schoolyard is usually cleaned for Day of Knowledge celebrations and because the construction materials were laid so conveniently below the high and otherwise difficult-to-reach and now smashed windows, Tomayeva and other victims suspected that terrorists used that very opening in advance of September 1 (Phillips 2007:50).

Russian officials conceded only one of these points. The fact that the terrorists brought with them a detailed floor plan of the school seems relatively uncontested and was admitted even by the head of the Russian parliamentary commission, Alexander Torshin (Dunlop 2006:27). The advance stashing of weapons was more controversial. Head of North Ossetia's FSB Valery Andreyev said that "weapons and explosive materials were carried in and hidden on the territory of the school" before the terrorist act occurred, but Shepel and other officials denied that rebels had advance access to the school and insisted that they brought their weapons with them (Dunlop 2006:26).

Russian officials rarely engaged the question of whether terrorists were in the school the night before and, if so, how they got there. They even more rarely engaged the obvious question about how the attack could have been so well prepared. Importantly, the start of the Day of Knowledge celebrations had been moved to an earlier time at the very last minute, with some students and parents learning about the change only the night before. The terrorists, however, seemed fully aware of the change. The victims wondered how (Phillips 2007:26–27).

How Could These Particular Terrorists Be at Large, Given Their Atrocious Criminal Records?

Many, if not most, of the hostage takers were known criminals and terrorists well before September 1, 2004, and were even on Russia's wanted list. Among the victims' grievances was how officials could have let these individuals roam free for so long.

Second-in-command Khodov was on the Russian wanted list since 1998 on suspicion of rape, but he nevertheless appeared at his brother's funeral on July 22, 2003, talked to neighbors, and spent weeks following the funeral in Elkhotovo, his predominantly Muslim hometown within North Ossetia, at the home of local Muslim Hadji Ali. Hadji Ali himself was considered a shady character whose cellar had been searched for weapons only a few months before the school hostage taking. Two days after the funeral and during his stay at Hadji Ali's, Khodov was arrested by North Ossetian Interior Ministry police in connection with the rape, but he was immediately released and even given a ride home by police. Possible reasons for his release range from carelessness and laziness—a failure to investigate or a broken computer in Elkhotovo that did not allow police to see the prior arrest warrant—to the more sinister, such as bribery or Khodov's professed agreement to become a police agent (Buse et al. 2004; Franchetti and Campbell 2004).

After his release, Khodov became a deadly terrorist, killing two and wounding ten in a car bomb in Vladikavkaz, North Ossetia, on February 3, 2004. Police issued another warrant for his arrest and circulated his photograph widely. He exploded two similar bombs near the station of Elkhotovo on May 29, 2004, that sent a Moscow-Vladikavkaz train off the rails. Nevertheless, he visited Elkhotovo regularly, moved about freely, stayed at his mother's home, was a regular in the town mosque, and was not arrested by local police chief Lieutenant Colonel Valery Dzhibilov (Khinshtein 2004; Buse et al. 2004; Dunlop 2006:31–32).

Khuchbarov, the leader of the terrorists whom they called "Colonel," was also on Russia's wanted list. He joined Islamic terrorists and participated in several armed attacks. His targets included a column of Russian troops outside his hometown of Galashki, Ingushetia, in May 2000 that left eighteen dead; an FSB building in Ingushetia in September 2003 that left three dead; the armory in Nazran, Ingushetia, on June 21–22, 2004; and other Ingush towns. The Russian police attempted to arrest Khuchbarov many times and failed. Like Khodov, Khuchbarov made occasional public appearances during his time on the wanted list, including a visit to Galashki in 2004 to attend a memorial service for his deceased mother (Buse et al. 2004).

More generally, five of eighteen terrorists who had been identified by October 2004 had previously been in the custody of Russian special services, and five others were on the wanted list. Some hostage takers had at some point been tried and freed, often with the help of the Ingushetia criminal justice system (Khinshtein 2004; Dunlop 2006:45–48). For example, Musa Tsechoyev, owner of the GAZ-66 truck used to bring most of the militants to Beslan, was a convicted kidnapper who served only a brief prison term and as recently as July 23, 2004, was involved in a shootout with police outside his home (Buse et al. 2004).

Allegedly, many of these barbaric hardened criminals were released with the goal of turning them into secret collaborators with the FSB, which would explain their free movement prior to the hostage taking and also that many of them were identified from fingerprints (Meteleva 2005a; Dunlop 2006:49–50). Khan-Pasha Kulayev, brother of surviving hostage taker Nur-Pasha, was one of those who was previously arrested and released, which Nur-Pasha claimed made the terrorist leaders suspicious that the Kulayevs and their friends were working for the Russian security services (Tuathail 2009:7). Perversely, the release of the elder Kulayev made victims suspicious too, but for different reasons. His release, the other arrest-and-release cases, and the failed arrests again suggested police negligence, incompetence, and/or corruption.

Why Did Russian Authorities Refuse to Negotiate with the Terrorists?

Notwithstanding the unauthorized conversations between the Colonel and Ingush politician and businessman Mikhail Gutseriyev, there was little interaction between important Russian political officials and the hostage takers during the duration of the siege. Russian officials asserted the correctness of this strategy. Many, including Prosecutor General Vladimir Ustinov, Deputy Prosecutor General Nikolai Shepel, and President Vladimir Putin,[3] claimed that the terrorists made no demands, implying that there was no negotiation to be had (Uzzell 2004). Shepel and other Russian officials also claimed that most of the terrorists were drug addicts, again implying that negotiation would have been pointless (Osborn 2004b). The Torshin commission even pondered whether the first explosion could be blamed on narcotic use and the consequent carelessness of the terrorist controlling the explosive device (Buse et al. 2004; Milashina 2005b).

Perhaps most importantly, the Russian government had a firm policy of not negotiating with terrorists. As Putin said almost four years later, "Any country that makes concessions to terrorists will ultimately bear greater losses than those

---

[3] Putin asserted this position during his September 2, 2005, meeting with four members of Mothers of Beslan.

experienced in the course of special operations. In the final analysis, it destroys the state and increases the number of victims" (Dunlop 2009:10).

Beslan victims disputed the claims about unclear demands and drug addiction, and they vehemently disagreed with a policy position that essentially ensured hostage deaths on a massive scale.

Most victims were aware that the terrorists' demands were made in written notes, verbal communications, and video. Dr. Larisa Mamitova, a hostage and mother of a hostage, was treating Khodov for a gunshot wound to the arm and suggested to him that a message be sent outside. Mamitova was taken to the Colonel, given a sheet of paper and pen, and told to write a phone number for the Russian government to call him. The Colonel then dictated his demands to Mamitova for the following individuals to come to the school to negotiate: the presidents of North Ossetia and Ingushetia, Dzasokhov and Zyazikov; retired MVD general and Putin's advisor on the Caucasus, Aslambek Aslakhanov; and Moscow pediatrician Leonid Roshal. The Colonel also demanded water from Nazran, Ingushetia (Buse et al. 2004).

Just over two hours after the start of the siege—that is, at about 11:30 a.m. on September 1—Mamitova left the school. Waving a piece of yellow curtain as a substitute for a white flag, she delivered the message and returned to the school where her young son Tamerlan was being held as collateral. Mamitova would have no reason to fabricate these events, and her leaving the building and handing over a note with demands is chronicled in several places (Buse et al. 2004; Milashina 2006d; Dunlop 2006:52–53; Phillips 2007:99–105).

Only an hour later, the terrorists handed over a videocassette showing what happened inside the school and another note demanding the freedom of the rebels who attacked the Ingushetia armory in June. Although authorities at the time suggested that the cassette was empty, the Russian television channel NTV showed on September 7, 2004, a videotape filmed inside the school and most likely made on September 1, just hours after the seizure and likely from the "empty" cassette (Dunlop 2006:55). By the morning of September 2, the telephone number that the Colonel dictated to Mamitova no longer worked, prompting queries of whether the Russian crisis staff actually blocked the number, since it had been working earlier. The Colonel dictated a new number to Mamitova who again left the school, delivered the message, and returned (Buse et al. 2004; Phillips 2007:126–127).

More specific demands came in a subsequent note given to former Ingushetia President Aushev when he was allowed to enter the school at about 2 p.m. on September 2. Aushev remembers the demands as:

> stop the war; withdraw forces; Chechnya enters into the CIS but remains in the ruble zone; in addition, Chechnya, together with the federal forces, introduces

order in the North Caucasus and does not permit any third force there. The decree of the president of Russia concerning a withdrawal of forces must be read on television. (Dunlop 2006:75)

Aushev was also handed a videocassette that several former hostages saw being taped earlier when he was led into the gymnasium to observe the situation of the hostages. Upon exiting the school, Aushev handed the note with demands to FSB General Valery Andreyev who then sent it to Moscow. The videotape, again declared by officials to be empty, later ended up in the hands of CBS television (Dunlop 2006:74–76).

Many hostages witnessed these various attempts of the terrorists to convey their demands. While it may have been reasonable for authorities to claim that demands such as the immediate withdrawal of the over 50,000 troops stationed in Chechnya were unrealistic (Phillips 2007:124), it seemed unreasonable to deny the very existence of demands, especially the quite realistic ones of talking with specific named political leaders. It may also have been reasonable to doubt that the terrorists would negotiate in good faith. They were terrorists, after all, and swore, insulted, and threatened (Phillips 2007:124–128). Again, however, the authorities did not simply describe the terrorist demands as unclear or irrational or express doubt in their trustworthiness as negotiating partners. The authorities said that the terrorists made no demands, and that, to victims, seemed suspiciously self-serving.

Hostages distinctly did not witness drug taking, only high professionalism among the militants. Importantly, the North Ossetian parliamentary commission concluded, "No traces of strong narcotics were found in the bodies of the rebels" (Milashina 2005b). Skittish or erratic behavior of the terrorists, when reported by former hostages, was usually described as a reaction to some unplanned part of the attack, like the surprise explosions.

In response to Putin's remarks about the impossibility of negotiations, victims saw this as a choice, and a very bad one. For example, participants in a focus group of female victim activists thirty-five years old or younger discussed whether terrorists who take hostages should have their demands met.

VIKA: When the fate of so many children is at stake . . .
BELA: Thousands of lives.
BELLA: I think yes. No matter what demand they make, even withdrawing troops from Chechnya and so on, I think yes, because the underlying motto of the state is that everything is for children. Children are our future, and so on. That is, it sounds nice, but when it comes to real life . . .

Former hostage and then nineteen-year-old Zarina Daurova agreed. "They think it is better to piss in the shithouse than to try to hold negotiations in it," she said, referring to Putin's famous 1999 television interview when he vowed to pursue terrorists everywhere, even wasting them in the outhouse. "But this time they got it wrong. A school full of children isn't the shithouse" (Phillips 2007:246).

Some victims went so far as to claim that the president's unyielding stance violated their constitutional rights. According to Voice of Beslan leader Ella Kesayeva, "We believe that his [Putin's] own words indicated his participation in the blame for the Beslan tragedy and the deaths of the hostages. The repudiation of negotiations and the use of armed forces de facto also cost the hostages their right to life, which is guaranteed by the Constitution" (Dunlop 2009:11).[4] Victims were backed up by independent Duma deputy and Torshin Commission member Yuri Ivanov who argued, "For the sake of saving the children, Putin, in my view, should have entered into negotiations precisely with [former Chechen President Aslan] Maskhadov" (Dunlop 2009:11).

Maskhadov would never have been allowed to arrive in Beslan, critics charged, because the Kremlin could not tolerate the possibility of making a hero out of him. The Kremlin considered Maskhadov a terrorist himself and could not lose face. Even allowing Aushev, an informal leader, to become a hero, was presumably too unpalatable (Dunlop 2009:14–15). Some critics even charged that the storm of the school by Russian special forces was intentionally accelerated to remove any possibility of Maskhadov's involvement, since Maskhadov had already agreed on the morning of September 2 to come to Beslan to facilitate a peaceful resolution to the crisis (Dunlop 2009:11). Victims suspected that elite power struggles took higher priority than their lives.

Understanding that the authorities had not even the remotest intention to negotiate, victims were convinced that storming the school was the authorities' only plan all along. Additional evidence for their conviction came from the authorities' assertion that there were no demands when in fact there were. The assertion allowed the authorities to portray the hostage takers as irrational suicide bombers who were not explaining what they wanted and could not be satisfied. From the point of view of Beslan victims, the authorities provided themselves with an excuse to do what they always intended: storm the school.

There *was* an official designated negotiator at the school, Vitaly Zangionov, a relatively low-ranking officer of the North Ossetian FSB. Zangionov received orders from the head of the North Ossetian FSB Andreyev but not from the higher-ranking officers at the scene, Russian FSB deputy directors Vladimir

---

[4] See Voice of Beslan's "Declaration of criminal case against the official person of former President of the Russian Federation Vladimir Putin," available at http://www.golosbeslana.ru/zayav040 608.htm.

Pronichev and Vladimir Anisimov and head of the FSB Center for Special Operations Alexander Tikhonov. Zangionov was missing crucial facts that would have allowed him to be effective in his job. The facts he did not know included: the number of hostages in the school; the demands of the terrorists to withdraw Russian troops from Chechnya; decisions made by the counterterrorist headquarters; who besides himself (like Mikhail Gutseriyev and presidential advisor Aslakhanov) was telephoning and conducting negotiations with the terrorists; that Ruslan Aushev was to enter the school; that Gutseriyev negotiated to bring out the bodies of the executed hostages; that Dzasokhov advocated for the participation of Maskhadov; or that the terrorists sent a videocassette and note to Putin (Milashina 2006a). The seemingly deliberate effort to keep Zangionov in the dark, combined with his low rank, convinced many Beslan victims that his negotiating efforts and therefore their safety were sabotaged by the authorities.

Taken together, the authorities' actions convinced the hostage takers that there would be a storm, which caused conditions for the hostages to deteriorate and increased the likelihood that the terror would end badly. As discussed later in this chapter, the number of hostages held in the school was reported as far lower than the reality. According to former hostage Zalina Albegova, Khodov heard the small number of hostages and said, "They [the government] don't need you. You are expendable. They are lying so that when they storm the building they can cover up the casualties" (Franchetti and Campbell 2004). The Colonel too claimed to school principal Tsaliyeva that "such misinformation [about 354 hostages] proved that Moscow had written off the hostages" (Franchetti 2004). The misinformation led the militants toward greater and greater cruelty in their treatment of the hostages. Whereas the first day they permitted children to use the bathroom, after the announcement of only 354 hostages, they forbade bathroom visits. According to former hostage Marina Kantemirova, the terrorists said, "We can do anything we want with you, since there are not 1,200 of you but only 354, and the authorities don't need you" (Dunlop 2006:65–66). Former hostage Svetlana Dzheriyeva recalls another one saying, "If they want there to be only 354 hostages in here, then we can do that for them" (Phillips 2007:118).

Who Led the Counterterrorist Operation, How Were Various Forces Coordinated, and What Went Wrong?

Many different forces responded to the crisis in Beslan. On the North Ossetian side, there was President Dzasokhov, parliamentary speaker Taimuraz Mamsurov, other political officials, the North Ossetian FSB headed by Andreyev, and the North Ossetian MVD headed by Kazbek Dzantiyev. On the Russian Federation side, there were numerous FSB officials, including Pronichev (who oversaw the 2002 storming of the Moscow theater building), Anisimov, and Tikhonov; special forces (*spetsnaz*) from the two elite FSB counterterrorist units, Alfa and Vympel; and troops and officers of the MVD and the military. There were prominent former officeholders, including Mikhail Gutseriyev, the ethnic Ingush former deputy speaker of the Russian State Duma and current president of Rusneft oil company; his brother and former minister of Internal Affairs of Ingushetia, Khamzat Gutseriyev; and former president of Ingushetia, Ruslan Aushev. And of course there were armed civilians.

Many victims complained that this multitude of organizations and individuals was uncoordinated at best and unprofessional, chaotic, and dangerous at worst. According to Lieutenant Colonel Elbrus Nogayev, the police supervisor whose wife and daughter died in the school, confusion reigned. "I heard a command saying, 'Stop shooting! Stop shooting! While other soldiers' radios said, 'Attack!' " (Chivers 2005b:1). The North Ossetian parliamentary investigatory commission drew similar conclusions. Almost a year after the attack in August 2005, head of the commission Stanislav Kesayev declared that his local investigators were unable to establish who was in command of the security operation at Beslan: "We can't even say who was giving the orders" (Weir 2005a:6). Four different headquarters were working at once, and "[t]o this day we do not know who was in actual command" (Chivers 2005b:1; see also Buse et al. 2004; Mainville 2005b).

One source of dangerous confusion was the chain of command between federal and regional officials. Technically, Andreyev had authority over the FSB deputy directors Pronichev and Anisimov, because Andreyev was officially named leader of the counterterrorism headquarters either in the first hours of the crisis (Voitova 2005) or on the second day of the crisis (Milashina 2005b; Dunlop 2006:62)—even the timing was unclear. However, many Beslan victims believed that Andreyev lacked de facto authority and that Pronichev and Anisimov were the real decision-makers. The FSB deputy directors, along with Tikhonov and General Taimuraz Kaloyev, head of the FSB for the Southern Federal District, had flown in and left General Andreyev in the awkward position of directing his bosses, while these Moscow FSB leaders truly had their own parallel headquarters that did not involve Andreyev or Dzasokhov (Milashina 2005b; Dunlop 2006:62). Andreyev's testimony at the Kulayev trial seemed to confirm that senior FSB officers overruled him. He claimed that he had not ordered the use of flamethrowers and tanks and that "[t]his matter was not under my authority" but under the authority of head of the FSB Center for Special Operations Alexander Tikhonov (Voitova 2005:1).

Federal issues aside, poor communication or outright dysfunction between agencies at the same level of government contributed to the chaos and disaster. Discussing the late arrival of firemen to the burning school and their empty water tanks, Andreyev accused the North Ossetian minister of Emergency Situations, Boris Dzgoyev, of negligence. In turn, Dzgoyev accused Andreyev of issuing the order to fight the fire too late (Voitova 2005). At the federal level, the FSB and MVD went their own ways. According to one MVD officer, "there existed two headquarters acting in parallel. One, under the leadership of the FSB, concentrated on the operation to free the hostages. But what occurred there and what decisions were made—no one knew. The second, the operational headquarters of the MVD, worked on the territory: it set up cordons, evacuated residents, reacted to all announcements. There was no coordination between the two headquarters" (Meteleva 2005b). The director of the FSB, Nikolai Patrushev, whose role in the crisis management was itself unclear, confirmed later during a secret Federation Council session that there had been little coordination between the MVD, the FSB, and the army during the hostage taking (Buse et al. 2004).

The various headquarters also failed to coordinate with influential and potentially helpful individuals present at the school. Officials like Aushev and the Gutseriyev brothers were involved, but because they were disliked by Moscow or perhaps for some other reason, they largely acted on their own and were not allowed in the crisis staff building. Aushev instead worked from the yard outside, using his cell phone to call well-connected figures who might be able to act as intermediaries in the crisis (Buse et al. 2004).

Noticeably absent from the scene or even from the larger story of the crisis was the Russian president. Aside from a televised meeting in Moscow with Jordan's King Abduallah II, Putin remained out of public view until the morning of September 4, after the school building had been stormed and the hostage taking ended by bullets, fire, and death. Given the centralization of power in Russia, most victims and observers suspect the president played some decision-making role, but the details of that role are unknown as of this writing and may never be known (Phillips 2007:253–254).

Noticeably present at the scene were swarms of unauthorized people, including many men with weapons. Victims were dismayed that the situation outside the school got so out of hand, with the area not cordoned and many armed civilians and representatives of the South Ossetian MVD accumulating, some holding AK-47 assault rifles and sophisticated sniper rifles (Dunlop 2006:68–69).

Retired North Ossetian parliament deputy Kazbek Torchinov lived in the apartment building across from the school and called the military headquarters, " 'What are you doing? This may also provoke tragedy! I live across from the school, I can see everything. Why are armed civilians there? You say that [elite

FSB counterterrorist unit] Alfa is here, all special forces are here! Why are there still civilians? To provoke reprisals from the militants against hostages? So there will be extra victims?' They answered, 'It's okay, don't disturb our work.' That was the reaction" (Milashina 2004a).

The presence of armed civilians likely exacerbated the crisis, and there were rumors that the armed South Ossetians may have been among those to open fire first (Dunlop 2006:68–69). Had the authorities been better organized and coordinated, thought many victims, the vigilantes could not have done damage.

The presence of civilians may not have been all bad: in the end, civilians may have compensated for lack of coordination by the authorities and saved lives by rescuing hostages from the burning rubble of the gym during the two hours that the gym burned before firefighters were given the signal to put out the fire and by providing vehicles to transport wounded hostages to hospitals (Images 2.1, 2.2, and 2.3). The authorities, despite having well over two full days to prepare, had woefully insufficient numbers of emergency vehicles and personnel near the school, meaning that the privately owned vehicles had to substitute. Still, official coordination and the availability of expert medical staff would clearly have been preferable. Well-intentioned civilians loaded hostages into their vehicles "inexpertly, in a way that could have worsened their injuries and may even have caused death in some cases" (Phillips 2007:222–223, 234).

Image 2.1. Ossetian civilians mixed with soldiers during the school siege on September 3, 2004.
YURI TUTOV/AFP via Getty Images.

Image 2.2. Approaching the burning school with stretchers, Ossetian civilians hoped to find survivors among the hostages who died when the roof caved in.
YURI TUTOV/AFP via Getty Images.

Image 2.3. Ossetian civilians and soldiers attended to the wounded, here carrying an injured student.
YURI TUTOV/AFP via Getty Images.

Why Were There No Preparations to Put Out the Fire and Save Hostages?

At the time of the initial explosion at 1:05 p.m. on September 3, 2004, Boris Dzgoyev, North Ossetian minister for Emergency Situations, reported a fire in the building and claims he was told to await further orders and not extinguish the fire (Meteleva 2005b). Head of the FSB's Center for Special Operations General Alexander Tikhonov for several hours forbade firemen to go to the fire, even when it was small enough to be extinguished with a single fire extinguisher, and he gave the command to enter and extinguish the fire only at 3:10 p.m. after more than a hundred hostages burned (Milashina 2006d, 2007b). Only at 3:20 p.m. did Dzgoyev send seven fire engines, which then took some time to arrive (Meteleva 2005b). Minutes later—3:27 or 3:28 p.m.—firemen started putting out the fire at about the same time that the roof collapsed and killed any hostages who might have remained alive. Firemen first entered the gymnasium at 4:37 p.m., and the fire was finally extinguished at 5 p.m. (Milashina 2006d).

By then, the gym smelled of burned meat (Meteleva 2005b). Thermal shock with no other wounds from bullets or fragments was the singular cause of death for many hostages, meaning "almost 100% of their skin covering had been scorched" (Milashina 2007c).

Mothers of Beslan asked President Putin during their September 2, 2005, meeting, "Why did it take forty minutes for the command to extinguish the fire to come to the firemen and still another forty minutes for the firemen to get to the school? During those eighty minutes everyone burned up. . . . There should be accountability for the fact that there was not an immediate extinguishing of the fire and the fire departments were not prepared" (Kaboyev 2005).

Victims wanted officials higher than the firefighters to provide explanations and be held accountable. By the time the fire had been put out and hostages had fully burned, the evidence that grenade launchers had fired at the school had conveniently burned too (Milashina 2007c). That, to victims, seemed telling. It suggested that the authorities prioritized eliminating militants—and then covering their own tracks—over saving the lives of hostages (Milashina 2004b).

Why Can't We Get a Clear Answer?

Beslan victims were unsatisfied with the efforts of official investigators to answer these questions, and they disputed official interpretations which seem predetermined to absolve officials of blame while not clarifying what happened to their loved ones. Rumors and speculation would have been minimized had official information been released in a timely and accurate manner (Farniyev 2004). Instead, silence was followed by the release of perceived misinformation that just made matters worse for victims.

What Were the Basic Numbers of Hostages—Dead, Alive, and Missing?

The number of hostages was in dispute from the very beginning of the crisis when authorities provoked the hostage takers by repeatedly publicizing that there were a mere 354 hostages in the school, a number that almost all observers immediately knew to be impossibly low (Phillips 2007:117–121). According to Beslan's Department of Public Education, School No. 1 enrolled at least 800 children from first through eleventh grade (Meteleva 2005b), and North Ossetian Minister of Education Alina Levitskaya remembers asking one of her civil servants to pass along information to the crisis headquarters that there had been 986 students enrolled at the end of the previous academic year (Phillips 2007:199). Given that the first day of school is a traditional day of celebration, many parents and other family members would certainly have been present. With just this limited information, it would have been reasonable to estimate that the hostages numbered well over 1,000. The official number was eventually revised upward from 354 but not quickly, clearly, or consistently.

Getting a clear answer was a victim grievance from the moment the siege ended. At unsanctioned rallies in Beslan on September 4, 2004, participants were spurred by the failure of the North Ossetian Ministry of Internal Affairs to announce the names of the dead and wounded hostages by noon that day, as promised. Beslan residents wanted to know what became of their missing relatives and demanded the "immediate publication of the names of all victims and escaped terrorists (banditov)" (Popova 2004).

In the next few weeks, lists of names were gathered and publicized but always with discrepancies. For the number of hostages, Prosecutor General Vladimir Ustinov announced the official figure of 1,156, whereas School No. 1 teachers listed 1,380 names, and the humanitarian organization Caucasian Refugee Council listed 1,345 names (Vlasova 2004a). On the website www.beslan.ru, which was originally started by teachers and relatives but then converted to a local government site, there were 1,338 names listed as either killed, injured, or missing ("Hundreds Still Missing" 2004). Across the various lists, the number of hostages varied by nearly 200, and discrepancies existed even between federal agencies, with both the transportation and interior ministries reporting higher numbers than the prosecutor general's figure (1,347 and 1,189, respectively)

(Walsh 2004b). Newspapers seemed to pluck different numbers out of a hat and then repeat these differing numbers in later stories or settled on round numbers like "1,100 hostages" (Parfitt 2004) or approximate quantities like "roughly 1,200" or "some 1,200 hostages" (Sands 2004b; Chivers 2005c). By November 2005, the North Ossetian Parliamentary Investigative Commission headed by Stanislav Kesayev released its report, which had the number of individuals standing in the celebratory *lineika* as 1,269 and those taken hostage as 1,127 (Table 2.2), but those numbers, too, would continue to be contested.

Table 2.2. Number of Hostages, Deaths, and Injuries, according to the North Ossetian Parliamentary Investigative Commission

Individuals in the celebratory *lineika* at School No. 1 on September 1, 2004	1,269
Individuals taken hostage	1,127
Freed by Ruslan Aushev on September 2, 2004	26
Hostages who left the school unassisted after two explosions	349
Dead	331*
Children	186
Women	99
Men	33
TsSN FSB (Vympel) employees	10
Ministry of Emergency Situations employees	2
Non-hostage civilian	1
Injured	783
Hostages and civilians	728
TsSN FSB, Interior Ministry, Emergencies Ministry, military personnel	55
Hostages freed during the power phase of the operation	461
Hostages whose identities were established on examination	96
Total number of identified victims	1,343
Children	415

Source: North Ossetian Parliamentary Investigative Commission, released in November 2005, available at http://www.pravdabeslana.ru/trigoda/doklad.htm#_ftn3.

* By 2006, two additional hostages died of injuries, bringing the most commonly reported total of deceased hostages to 333. The number grew to 334 by 2008 and 335 by 2009. See note 5 for further details.

Initial discrepancies were especially glaring when it came to the dead. Lists sometimes omitted deceased hostages and sometimes included hostages who survived. One focus group member found her traumatized and ill but very much alive sister-in-law listed along with the dead. Raisa Daurova, a Beslan resident who lost her sister in the school, showed an official published list and explained, "Look here . . . it leaves out, for example, Albina Alikova, a young teacher who was killed. Yet a little lower on the exact same page, condolences are printed to her family and friends. And such inaccuracies abound. But it is unclear why there is such a mess. After all, we all know each other here" (Vlasova 2004a).

A reasonable best guess on the death toll is over 360. The number includes 320 hostages (186 children, 134 adults),[5] ten Federal Security Service special forces, two Emergency Ministry personnel, and one non-hostage civilian,[6] along with thirty-one hostage-takers. Nearly 800 more Beslan residents were hospitalized, injured, or missing.[7]

The unavailability of a reliable list of victims was partially blamed for the inability of authorities to distribute the over $30 million donated during the first few weeks after the tragedy (Vlasova 2004a). The errors also contributed to the widespread feeling of disregard by the authorities for the people of Beslan. Most importantly, as described on the Pravda Beslana website,[8] the errors led victims to distrust other information peddled to them by officials who could not get right something so basic as the number of hostages and who is dead or alive. As one man said, "Just look at the number of graves" (Walsh 2004b).

[5] The number of deceased hostages tragically evolved over time. One young female victim, Marina (Tagziyeva) Zhukayeva, was in a coma for almost a year after the tragedy and died in August 2005 (Chivers 2005c; Page 2005d; Borisov 2006a). Another victim, Taisia (Bziyeva) Dauyeva, who suffered multiple injuries and was thought to be improving, died suddenly on August 9, 2006 (Borisov 2006a), and 33-year-old school librarian Elena Avdonina also died after multiple operations and coma on December 4, 2006 ("In Northern Ossetia" 2006; Myers 2006b). New deaths, plus errors and controversies (see next note), mean that reports of victim deaths—that is, all deaths besides the militants—ranged from 331 to 335. For the September 2006 commemoration of those who died, schoolchildren released 333 balloons into the sky shortly after 1 p.m., the time when the first explosion went off in the school (Sageyeva 2006b). Most sources report 333 balloons released in 2007 as well, but by 2008 there were 334 balloons, with little reporting on who had perished in the past year (Savina et al. 2008; Arutunyan 2008). In 2009, RIA Novosti reported that 335 balloons were released ("Over 5,000" 2009).

[6] Disputes exist over the number of non-hostage civilians who were killed. Most reports list a single casualty, but they are usually referencing the same sources, and other reports list higher numbers. For example, Pravda Beslana lists the names, birth years, and injuries of non-hostage civilians involved in the fighting, and seven of these are men who were killed at the scene (one), died afterward (three), or went missing (three). See http://www.pravdabeslana.ru/trigoda/spisok_g.htm.

[7] See http://www.beslan.ru/index.php/remember_cat_sltd/category/o_sobytiyah/, http://www. pravdabeslana.ru/trigoda/spisok_z.htm, and the report of the North Ossetian parliamentary commission, also known as the Kesayev report, http://www.pravdabeslana.ru/trigoda/doklad.htm#_ftn3.

[8] http://www.pravdabeslana.ru/trigoda/spisok_z.htm.

What Were the Basic Numbers of Hostage Takers—Dead, Alive, and Missing?

Even more contentious was the number of hostage takers. The authorities insisted that thirty-two terrorists were in the school and that all but one, Nur-Pasha Kulayev, were destroyed in the counterinsurgency. The authorities claimed that Kulàyev himself first offered the number thirty-two, which he said was told to him by the Colonel.

Surviving hostages gave numerous accounts of where rebels stood during the attack, casting strong doubt on the official total of thirty-two terrorists and suggesting double that number or more. Beslan School No. 1 consisted of several buildings, auditoriums, classrooms, auxiliary rooms like a boiler, and an interior courtyard. The terrorists needed to keep control of some 1,200 hostages while patrolling the perimeter of the school and also taking turns getting some rest. Realistically, thirty-two terrorists could not control such a vast territory and number of people. Moreover, many hostages said they had attempted to count the number of terrorists while they were in captivity and arrived at numbers far higher than thirty-two (Dunlop 2006:42–43).

Witnesses just outside the school corroborated the higher numbers of militants. According to one, Kazbek Torchinov, the retired North Ossetian parliament deputy who lived in the apartment building across from the school:

> I spent all three days in my home opposite the school. I saw everything. . . .
> A masked man wearing military camouflage came running from the gates of the school. And then a covered GAZ-66 truck drove up. As soon as it stopped, the guy who was running raised the cover, and out of the truck came pouring still more people in camouflage and masks. All of them were armed. Together with the first man, I counted 27 people. . . . I'm quite convinced that there were more [than 32]. While they were jumping out of the vehicle, at the same time [other] militants were driving people from all sides of the school to the entrance. And they were shooting along the whole perimeter. On the other side of the school, in the courtyards, there were no fewer than ten men. (Milashina 2004a)

Some analysts of the Beslan tragedy argue that the attack likely involved at least five or six groups of terrorists, totaling sixty to seventy people, getting to Beslan via different routes, different vehicles, and at different times (Milashina 2006d). The official insistence on thirty-two terrorists did not even make sense when combined with another part of the official story, that the militants entered Beslan in the single GAZ-66 military truck. Based on its size, the GAZ-66 could not fit all the weapons found in the school plus the thirty-two militants or even the twenty-eight who would have remained after four militants rode in the kidnapped Gurazhev's Lada (Milashina 2006d). To stick with the claim that all terrorists came together in these two vehicles, the terrorists would have had to number *less* than thirty-two, but an official claim to such an effect would have been so incongruous with the evidence that authorities simply allowed the inconsistency to stand.

There was also debate over how many females were among the hostage takers, which would influence the total tally. In part five of his report, Savelyev concluded that people saw four so-called suicide bombers, two of whom were killed by the terrorists themselves who detonated the women's explosive devices, and that there was a fifth woman with a sniper rifle (Milashina 2006d). This conclusion does not square with official versions that only two of the hostage takers were female, the ones destroyed by their explosives.

The discrepancies mattered because they implied that children and loved ones were killed in the name of a counterterrorist operation that ultimately failed to catch all the terrorists. Victims widely believed that many hostage takers stripped off their camouflage under which they had track suits or other sports clothes and then disappeared into the crowd (Farniyev 2004). The victims' belief was buttressed by reporting in *Caucasian Knot* that "an unaccounted number of [terrorists] escaped into the crowds, into neighboring apartment blocks, into the town and even as far as Nalchik" (Harding 2012:181). The bad guys were still out there.

Indeed, the *main* bad guys may still have been out there. Khodov, for example, was pronounced dead by a coroner's report that claimed to use fingerprints and his mother's identification, yet he was also rumored to have been captured alive and simultaneously continued to appear on the federal wanted list (Franchetti and Campbell 2004; Dunlop 2006:34). Khuchbarov, the "Colonel," probably got away (Dunlop 2006:39–40).

Victims felt that the authorities were outright lying to cover themselves. In Kulayev's initial interrogation, he claimed not to know how many rebels were in the group (Pravdabeslana.ru, III, 22 and XI, 31, in Dunlop 2006:41). Then the number thirty-two appeared and stuck. As Susanna Dudiyeva explained, Deputy Prosecutor General Nikolai Shepel "saw thirty-one [dead] bodies and Kulayev, and he thinks that this is the evidence that gives him the right to say that there were only thirty-two terrorists. He should stop lying to the whole world and to us" (Mereu 2005:3).

Evidence of a cover-up was supported by police activity outside of Beslan just after the end of the attack on the school. Sometime on September 3, information was released that the militants who had escaped from the cordon in Beslan possibly drove off toward Nalchik, the capital of the Republic of Kabardino-Balkaria that borders North Ossetia to the west. At 5 p.m. that day, traffic police in Nalchik attempted to stop and inspect a Volga car, but the driver failed to obey and instead drove through town and reached the Volnoaulsky Bridge, where the three Chechen occupants of the vehicle, armed with automatic weapons and pistols, had a shootout with police and were killed. Potentially related police activity was reported to the east of North Ossetia as well. On September 4, the Chechen Ministry of Internal Affairs reported that security measures were increased in Chechnya, including the closure of administrative borders "in order to rule out the possibility of infiltration into Chechnya by the terrorists, *who managed to escape from the school in Beslan*" (Harding 2012:169).

Victims may not have known about these police activities, and they may not have known about reporting by *Caucasian Knot*. However, most of them did not need this additional evidence of surviving terrorists to confirm what they had seen with their own eyes.

Why Can't We Get an Honest, Objective, and Thorough Investigation?

Some political grievances might have been alleviated by the creation of a commission to investigate the tragedy. However, the Beslan commission was actively resisted by Putin at first and then formed reluctantly, mainly from members of the ruling party. On September 10, 2004, Putin asked the Federation Council, the upper house of the Russian Parliament, to hold an open inquiry and provide a "complete, objective picture" of the siege and its gruesome ending ("A Welcome Russian Inquiry" 2004). Less than a week later, Russian officials announced that the Duma, the lower house of Parliament, would join the upper house in investigating the tragedy ("Parliament to Investigate" 2004). The commission became known as the Torshin investigation after Federation Council Deputy Speaker Alexander Torshin who was selected to be its head by Federation Council Speaker Sergei Mironov. It was composed of twelve Federation Council members and ten Duma deputies, and its intended length of work was originally no longer than six months (Abdullaev 2004; "Hundreds Still Missing" 2004).

From the start, victims and independent and opposition politicians complained that the commission would not truly look into the root causes of terrorism and the failed rescue operation. According to Communist Duma Deputy Viktor Ilyukhin, the true goal of the Beslan commission was "to cover up what happened" ("Seeking Public Accountability" 2004). Their expectation seemed fulfilled in the months that followed, as prominent federal officials perpetuated misinformation or shined light on partial truths in order to distract from truths more damning to the authorities. As late as February 2005, Prosecutor General Nikolai Shepel, whose investigation ran parallel to Torshin's, was conceding the discovery of *Shmels* on the roofs of apartment buildings near the school, but he hinted that the weapons probably belonged to accomplices of the terrorists (Walsh 2005), and most victims suspected that by this time he knew full well that Russia's own special forces had used these weapons. Also as late as February 2005, Shepel was still telling reporters that one of the gunmen was a Saudi citizen and that Arab mercenaries trained the militants in the Sunzhenskii forest (Walsh 2005). The participation of an Arab or two in the hostage taking, while likely true (Buse et al. 2004), was a minor detail, and the retelling seemed designed to distract from the more central story of the Chechen conflict and the bungled storming of the school. On September 11, 2005, over a year after the siege, Shepel again said that the Beslan hostage takers were "international terrorists," leading Ella Kesayeva, then of the Mothers of Beslan, to call Shepel's words "one more link in a chain of lies" demonstrating that "the official investigation is desperately trying to cover up the crimes" committed by the Russian special forces, such as the use of flame throwers (Fuller 2005). Victims believed Shepel even lied about his lies. For example, after the court verdict on Kulayev, Shepel remarked, "The investigation has never asserted that there were thirty-two bandits" (Milashina 2006d).

When the Torshin commission got underway, victims complained that they gave countless hours of interviews and evidence, only to see conclusions that did not at all incorporate what the victims themselves saw and reported. At the January 2005 highway blockade, victims told Deputy Prosecutor General Vladimir Kolesnikov that the facts they told members of the Torshin commission were not reflected in the materials of the investigation (Tokhsyrov 2005). In the words of one female activist focus group member who complained about victims being "dragged to court for our evidence":

> Just think of all those places I was being summoned. . . . All those interviews they took from me, explanations they asked for each word I uttered. . . . And there he is, this man from the FSB, and he argues with me: "A huge work has been performed. How dare you say that nothing has been done?" But what has been done in fact?

Supposedly responding to complaints about Shepel, Putin agreed during his September 2, 2005, Moscow meeting with victims to send an overseer, Kolesnikov, to the investigative process. Kolesnikov's presence originally inspired hope that the investigation would be more objective and thorough, but by October 20, 2005, Kolesnikov held a press conference and indicated that he agreed with Shepel on all points, and he refuted most claims made by victims' families. For example, Kolesnikov agreed with Shepel that there were no weapons placed in the school in advance, that only one tank fired and only after hostages had been evacuated, that the use of flamethrowers had nothing to do with the fire, that the fire burned hostages who were already dead, and that North Ossetian FSB head Andreyev and the firefighters did not commit any crimes (Gatsoyeva 2005).

Voice of Beslan leader Ella Kesayeva responded to this news by saying, "Everything he says is not true" (Gatsoyeva 2005:3). Intensive care nurse and former hostage Larisa Tomayeva was in the staff room that adjoined the gym when the roof began to burn and offered further rebutting details. "I can say with absolute certainty that many, many people were burned alive: people with stomach injuries or whose legs had been severed; people who were stunned. They couldn't get to their feet and they started to burn. I saw it with my own eyes" (Phillips 2007:229).

The initial promise of wrapping up the investigation in only six months proved unrealistic, and the Torshin commission extended its investigation several times (Voronov 2006). The Prosecutor General's office too was nowhere near wrapping up its own investigation. At a meeting on November 3, 2004, Shepel informed victims that the investigation had been extended to January 1, 2005, because the first testimony from eyewitnesses was too emotional, and witnesses were going to be questioned again (Shavlokhova et al. 2004). After other extensions, Shepel resigned as the Deputy Prosecutor General for southern Russia in July 2006 and was replaced by Ivan Sydoruk in August 2006, who himself then extended the timetable of the Prosecutor General's investigation until January 1, 2007. At the time of the extension, the case already contained 130 volumes, over 1,700 people had been questioned, and over 1,200 expert examinations had been carried out ("Beslan Victims Met" 2006).

Victims were upset by the delays but even more upset by the inadequacies of the reports. The Torshin commission finally released its 240-page final report and 400+ pages of appendices on December 22, 2006,[9] and several lawmakers then declared the commission's work done and called for its abolition. This seemed outrageous to victims. Mothers of Beslan leader Susanna Dudiyeva pointed out, "In his report, Torshin did not answer the basic questions: how could the militants prepare for the terrorist act for such a long time, moving freely around Ingushetia and forming a camp there? Why was false information given about the number of hostages, and why were negotiations not conducted?" She concluded, as did many other victims, that the commission's conclusions were "unobjective" and "another attempt to shield the guilty from punishment for their irresponsibility and negligence" (Moshkin and Bondarenko 2006:3; see also Voronov 2006).

---

[9] See the website www.pravdabeslana.ru for links to the official commission report and related documents.

Two other reports had the potential to bring closure to victims with honest, thorough investigations.[10] The North Ossetian Parliament launched its own independent investigation that the federal prosecutor's office declared illegal but that at the beginning seemed to offer promise of objectivity. In late August 2005, the head of the North Ossetian parliamentary investigative commission, Stanislav Kesayev, was on record as finding fault with the counterterrorist operation and criticizing the lack of coordination between the different forces, the corruption and incompetence that allowed the militants to reach Beslan in the first place, and the lack of preparation for the storming and its aftermath (Mainville 2005b; Voronov 2006). However, the actual written report and subsequent statements by Kesayev were less critical, suggesting to victims that he was convinced to pull punches and participate in the whitewash. Released on November 29, 2005, the Kesayev report "was met with disappointment and surprise in North Ossetia." Ella Kesayeva (no relation) called the report "evasive" and said that it "differs significantly from statements made earlier by members of the parliamentary commission" (Migalin 2005; see also Voronov 2006).

The second major alternative to the official federal investigation was better received by victims ("Beslan Victims Back" 2006). Yuri Savelyev, who became a dissident member of Torshin's parliamentary commission, launched his own investigation into the siege based on the testimony of former hostages, witnesses, photo and video evidence, and various expert tests. He released his 700-page report, "Beslan: The Truth about the Hostages," on August 28, 2006, on the website www.pravdabeslana.ru. The report largely went against the official version of events. Savelyev, an explosions and firearms specialist, claimed among other things that (1) the two explosions that triggered the fire in the gymnasium were caused by RPO-A flamethrowers fired from outside, likely by Russian security forces positioned on the roofs of neighboring five-story apartment buildings across from the school; (2) commandos fired from machine guns, grenade throwers, and tanks while hostages were still being held, contrary to denials by prosecutors; (3) officials in command of the rescue operation waited more than two hours to send firefighters to the blazing school gym, leaving many hostages to be burned alive; (4) twice as many hostage takers were present as officials claim—60 to 68—meaning that half managed to escape; and (5) reliable information about a terrorist attack in Beslan was available at least three hours before the school was seized (Voitova 2006b).

Savelyev's thorough and professional report, although not without critics (Kiselyev 2006; Rechkalov 2006; Voronov 2006), confirmed victims' suspicions,

---

[10] See the website www.pravdabeslana.ru for links to the North Ossetian Parliamentary report, Savelyev's dissenting report, proceedings of the court case against the captured hostage taker Nur-Pasha Kulayev, and many other valuable documents.

and the fact that he needed to write such a dissent exacerbated their frustrations. Savelyev was a member of the Torshin commission but could not get a hearing for his findings. As he himself explained:

> I asked that my materials (and that included more than 800 pages of text and hundreds of testimonies by eyewitnesses) be taken into account in the report. . . . the majority of the members of the commission, who represented the ruling faction [Edinaya Rossiya] in the Duma, ignored my request. Moreover, several members of the commission told me directly that no one intended to read my report. They intended simply to sweep my investigation under the rug. . . . I was therefore required to bring to the people the results of my investigation. My duty as an [elected] deputy and my conscience as a scholar obliged me to do that. . . . Of all the members of the commission I was the only one who had a professional understanding of issues involving explosive technology. (Dunlop 2009:5)

A few days later, on September 2, 120–300 copies of Savelyev's report were confiscated at the Vladikavkaz airport, treated, in the words of one journalist, as "subversive literature." The reports were to be distributed free of charge to Beslan victims who did not have Internet access to read the report on the Pravda Beslana website where it was posted. The courier was detained. He and the reports were released three hours later after protests from victims, including Rita Sidakova, Aneta Gadiyeva, and Viktor Yesiyev, with Gadiyeva calling and successfully enlisting the help of new North Ossetian president Taimuraz Mamsurov (Mishtein 2006; Panyushkin 2006b; Tlisova 2006b; Tskhurbayev 2006).

Savelyev's findings were not the only evidence that authorities tried to ignore or conceal. As described earlier, for as long as possible, Shepel and other federal officials tried to deny that Russian forces used flamethrowers. North Ossetian parliamentary commission head Kesayev told reporters in late June 2005:

> The first batch of the flamethrowers that were used, which a member of the Federation Council Panteleyev found in my presence, was given to the investigation. But the investigation simply washed them away. . . . it was done very simply. The wrong [serial] number [for the flamethrower] was written down, as if it were a mistake. Then when an inquiry [zapros] was submitted, it turned out there was no such batch. . . . Later when they found other flamethrower parts, I advised the citizens to hand them over, but with that action being filmed by a television camera and with the numbers and everything written down according to protocol. (Dunlop 2006:89)

Aware of such actions, victims thought the federal authorities were not just innocently disagreeing and reaching different but honest conclusions. The authorities were intentionally concealing evidence.

After victims found tubes used by flamethrowers and shell cartridges shot by tanks, the prosecutor's office backpedaled, but it continued to lie, in the minds of victims, by changing the story to fit the now incontrovertible evidence and still protect the authorities. The new claim was that the weapons were used, but only when no living hostages remained at the school (Milashina 2006d). Worse, it seemed that the incontrovertible evidence could still be ignored and the original lie perpetuated. After Shepel reversed his earlier statement and admitted on July 12, 2005, that the Russian special forces had used flamethrowers in the counterterrorist attack, some of Russia's most authoritative news sources, including *Kommersant*, Mayak, and NTV, reported the precise opposite, saying that Shepel still claimed flamethrowers were not used (Milashina 2005a).

Victims and opposition political leaders felt compelled to search for evidence on their own because existing evidence was being withheld from them. This was the case, for example, with the videocassettes taken by various officials during the course of the supposed rescue effort. Victims requested to see the footage taken by the prosecutor's cameraman and were told for three years that it was lost (Milashina 2007c). They, along with Savelyev and various journalists, also insisted that there were many other tapes made by the various ministries and security services that would clarify the events of September 3, especially the storming of the school, and that they were being denied access. Deputy prosecutor Sydoruk admitted, "If you request data from the FSB, then in accordance with the law, it will be necessary to classify it" (Milashina 2007b).

Where Does the Buck Stop?

The victims sought not only to unravel the chain of events but to place blame. Victims wanted to know who said what and who did what during the course of the three days in September 2004 that ended in the deadly fire and deaths. Once those individuals were identified, victims wanted them to face criminal proceedings or at least some kind of meaningful punishment, such as dismissal from current and future political office.

In the words of Susanna Dudiyeva, victims demanded that "all of those whose actions or failure to act led to this tragedy be held responsible" (Mainville 2005c:A04). These included the individual(s) who disseminated misinformation that there were only 354 hostages; refused to negotiate with hostage takers; failed to prepare for a rescue operation and instead left residents to take the wounded to hospitals in private cars; failed to cordon off the area around the school for two days and left residents free to wander the area, contaminate the crime scene, and prevent proper forensic work; and approved the use of tanks, flamethrowers, and grenade launchers during the storming of the school (Mainville 2005b, 2005c; Milashina 2005b).

Male activist victims over thirty-five years old discussed their frustration with the obfuscation and lack of accountability.

TOTRAZ: Even regarding this car hired from there [Ingushetia]. Who gave the order? These are details. There are very many such details. Where is the scoundrel who allowed them to come from there unpunished . . .

KAZBEK: There are no little boys, no children here, and they [the authorities] tell us some kind of fairy tales. They assure us, "No, the minister of internal affairs has nothing to do with it." How come? And who has something to do with it? . . . Look, the traffic patrol stands here. Someone gave them the order to leave their place, right? Someone gave it. Who is your boss? Here he is. Who gave you the instruction? Let's say it's the police chief. And who gave the order to the police chief? If you go down this chain, you get to a concrete person and call him to account. The same with the firefighters, policemen. But this is not done.

Victims named names. They at various times demanded the resignation of North Ossetian president Dzasokhov and criminal prosecution against former head of North Ossetia's Federal Security Service Valery Andreyev and former North Ossetian minister of Internal Affairs Kazbek Dzantiyev (Tokhsyrov 2005). Immediately following the attack, Dzasokhov said that he could not in good conscience remain in his position and that he and his government would resign, yet shortly thereafter he was evasive about leaving and said he had urgent tasks to solve. He dismissed his government but remained himself and claimed that he could not fire local security chiefs because they reported to Moscow ("Seeking Public Accountability" 2004).

At the federal level, victims named various military and FSB leaders, including Nikolai Patrushev, the head of Russia's Federal Security Service. And finally, as Ella Kesayeva said in August of 2005, "The most important name—the one we are all afraid to say—is Putin, the head of state, who is guilty of everything that happened. He is finishing his presidential term and is being held accountable for nothing. He has still not deigned to meet with us and offer an apology" (Mainville 2005c:A04).

There were smaller fish called to accountability, although the call ultimately went unanswered. For not maintaining adequate supervision at checkpoints on the North Ossetian border with Ingushetia where the terrorists were able to pass, the Prosecutor General's Office charged three individuals with negligence: the head of the Pravoberezhny district division of internal affairs Miroslav Aidarov, chief of staff Georgy Dryayev, and deputy head of public security Taimuraz Martazov, all of whom were dismissed after the terrorist act (Allenova 2005a). The three pleaded not guilty and were granted amnesty on May 29, 2007 (Farniyev 2007c).[11] For not locating the terrorist camp within their territory, the Prosecutor General's Office initiated negligence cases against head of the Malgobek [Ingushetia] district division of internal affairs Mukhazhir Yevloyev, his deputies Bagaudin Yevloyev and Akhmed Kotiyev, and head of the district criminal investigation department Khamzat Mamilov (Allenova 2005a). The case was pursued against Mukhazhir Yevloyev and Kotiyev, but Ingushetia's Supreme Court acquitted them on October 5, 2007, using a jury that included the defendants' relatives, and Russia's Supreme Court upheld the verdict in June 2008 ("Russia Supreme Court" 2008).

Even if these individuals had been found guilty of the specific transgressions in question, victims felt there was plenty of blame left to assign for the tragedy as a whole. At the very least, victims wanted the higher-ranking officials to be questioned, as they themselves were, and ideally in a public setting where victims could hear the testimony. For example, high-ranking FSB personnel had their own operational headquarters and led the counterterrorism operations but to the victims' dismay were never questioned about the event. As Ella Kesayeva expressed during a meeting with Dmitry Kozak on September 1, 2005, "The fact is our children were burnt, our children were executed, and no one wants to get involved in this question" (Page 2005d:39; also Allenova 2005b).

To the degree that official investigators did engage the blame question, it was usually to absolve officials from blame and usually, from the victims' perspective, without foundation or honest inquiry. As Stanislav Kesayev commented, "Every agency wants to be first in line for the medals and last in line to take responsibility for the failures" (Chivers 2005b:1). According to a report posted on the Prosecutor General's Office website on December 27, 2005, "The expert commission does not see . . . any violations in the actions of the crisis headquarters and units . . . that could be responsible for the harmful consequences that resulted from the terrorist act in Beslan" (Saradzhyan 2005). Victims and other North Ossetians found such a conclusion impossible and frustrating.

BESLAN PUBLIC COUNCIL CHAIRMAN MAIRBEK TUAYEV: "There was a horrible tragedy, but it turns out that nobody is responsible for this." (Olisayeva 2004)

IRA GIBILOVA, WHOSE DAUGHTER-IN-LAW, THIRTEEN-YEAR-OLD GRAND-DAUGHTER, AND TEN-YEAR-OLD GRANDSON DIED IN THE SCHOOL: "We will never know the truth about who let the terrorists come here and how

---

[11] The full text of the verdict can be found here: http://www.pravdabeslana.ru/poamnistii.htm.

our children died. The people who let this happen will never be punished."
(Mainville 2005b)

SHOUTS FROM THE BLOCKADE OF THE ROSTOV-BAKU/CAUCASUS FEDERAL
HIGHWAY: "The truth still won't be told!" (Tokhsyrov 2005)

SUSANNA DUDIYEVA: "It is important in principle to know the truth so that something like this cannot happen again, and so that incompetent, irresponsible,
corrupt people—people without morals—will be punished. That is not what
is happening." (Chivers 2005b)

Victims were joined in their sentiments by the majority of Russian citizens.
According to a 2005 poll by Russia's Public Opinion Foundation, only 15 percent of Russians thought Torshin's parliamentary commission would reveal what
really happened at Beslan, 19 percent thought the commission would get to
the bottom of events but keep the results to itself, and most of the remaining
respondents thought the panel would not find answers (Cullison 2005). By 2007,
a poll conducted by the Levada center showed that only 8 percent of Russian
citizens believed that they were being told the whole truth about Beslan, 51 percent said they were being told only a part of the truth, 24 percent thought that
the authorities were concealing the truth, 6 percent said the authorities were deliberately misleading them, and 11 percent were not sure one way or the other
("Chuzhoye gorye" 2007).

How Does a Twenty-Four-Year Old Named Nur-Pasha Kulayev
Fit in the Story?

According to the Russian official interpretation of events as offered by the Russian
General Prosecutor's Office, Nur-Pasha Kulayev was the sole surviving terrorist
of the school hostage taking, with all the others killed. Many Beslan victims were
unconvinced and were certain that several terrorists succeeded in getting away
(Dunlop 2006:99). Victims largely viewed Kulayev as a bit player whose trial provided a potential opportunity for learning the truth about the hostage taking and
its aftermath, but they believed that opportunity was squandered by officials who
instead used the trial to bring closure to their investigation, even when crucial
questions remained unanswered.

During the first day of the Kulayev trial, one woman shouted, "Say something concrete. You always talk about Kulayev and his band, but what exactly
did Kulayev do?" ("Courtroom Chaos" 2005). As the head of the North Ossetian
parliamentary investigation Kesayev described, "There is a general feeling here
that Kulayev will be convicted, and that will be the end of it" (Weir 2005a:6).
According to Ala Khanayeva-Romanova, a former hostage who lost her

fifteen-year-old daughter, Marianna, "The Kulayev trial, the investigation, it's all a smoke screen, a farce. It's a cover-up. We are fed up with this show. We want the truth and won't stop fighting until we know it" (Franchetti 2005). A lawyer for the victims, Olga Mikhailova, similarly claimed that the purpose of the proceedings in the Supreme Court of North Ossetia was "a write-off of blame for the whole terrorist attack on one person" and bemoaned the fact that the victims were denied the right to pose questions to experts at the trial. "They could not even inquire about the distance from which their relatives were shot," meaning that the judicial investigation was incomplete, the circumstances of the hostages' death were not properly studied, and the case demanded a retrial (Allenova 2006:4).

In the focus group of female activist victims thirty-five years old or younger, participants shared this frustration, with some even expressing doubt that Kulayev was in fact one of the terrorists.

VIKA: How could it happen that the children were herded like a flock of sheep and underwent all kinds of insults and suffering, and the only person in the whole country to be held responsible was some pathetic Kulayev? Where did they pick him out? Maybe they brought him from some prison. . . . they started looking for the culprit, spent four years on this. The only one they could find was Kulayev. Nobody but Kulayev is to blame for everything!

BELLA: Just to ease up the tension, to show that everything is in order. Roughly speaking, they found a scapegoat. To tell the people, "Here is the guilty one." That is, the people demanded a guilty person—here he is. But in fact, we are all adults, and we all understood that he was simply a punching bag.

ANGELA: This trial of Kulayev is in fact a kind of show. . . . everybody knew that he was a pawn. . . . what can we do with him? How can we take him to task? What? He knew nothing, it seems to me, absolutely nothing. Even if he was indeed there. There are versions that he wasn't there at all, and there are versions that he was. Even if he was there, he was told to go there and do a certain job, which he did.

ANGELA: He was there with someone who was the boss of them, and this boss was given instructions. The boss who was there gave his instructions down the line.

In the focus group of male activist victims thirty-five years old or younger, this same doubt about Kulayev was expressed:

PAZIL: Maybe this is some person who was brought here to show demonstratively: Here he is. Someone has been caught. Who knows? Maybe he was already convicted once. Maybe he was already serving time in jail. Here is a person sitting in jail, and he can be brought under a different name. They show that he is intimidated. He can't say two words, this person.

The male nonactivist victims had the same conversation:

BORIS: It was just a show. It's still not known whether Kulayev was there or not. They tell us that he was there, but whether he was or not is still unknown.
TAMERLAN: Who didn't identify him? Everyone cannot identify him.
ARKADY: Most people didn't identify him.
TAMERLAN: I personally saw Kulayev, and yes, he was there. He gave me water.
ARKADY: All right, let's not argue whether he was there or not, but it's also impossible that this is all [of the story]. He is guilty, and that's all.

The evidence suggests that Kulayev *was* one of the hostage takers. He himself admitted as much during his testimony, although claiming that he was there against his will, never fired on the hostages, and therefore did not commit murder. Other victims claim they saw or even interacted with him during the three-day siege. He was found cowering under a truck and was "pulled from a would-be lynch mob of citizens by masked Russian commandos, who then paraded him on camera" ("Courtroom Chaos" 2005). Russia had a moratorium on capital punishment, and in 2006, Kulayev was instead sentenced to life in prison, but his sentence was unsatisfying to many victims who saw it as shutting down an investigation that had barely begun.

Why Are Insults Added to Our Injuries?

Many of the above grievances might be less passionately felt if Beslan victims believed they were given appropriate respect and were treated with compassion and dignity. Instead, victims witnessed rewards bestowed on the very officials they believe were accountable for the destruction of their families. They also witnessed or were themselves subject to official harassment, either because of their advocacy on behalf of victims' concerns or simply because they, as firsthand eyewitnesses, had information that sometimes contradicted the official line.

Why Were Potentially Culpable Officials Rewarded with Promotion?

The few officials who were presumably "punished" for the botched rescue operation ended up in other jobs, as good or better than the ones they had before.

On September 6, 2004, Kazbek Dzantiyev resigned from his position as head of North Ossetia's Ministry of Internal Affairs, and a week later, Putin removed Valery Andreyev from his position as head of North Ossetia's FSB ("Timeline" 2004; Gurin 2004). In early 2005, however, both men received prestigious new posts: Andreyev became deputy chief of the FSB Academy, and Dzantiyev became deputy commander of the internal troops of the Moscow Military District (although State Duma deputy and member of the Torshin commission Arkady Baskayev said that both Dzantiyev and Andreyev were later dismissed from service) ("Chuzhoye gorye" 2007; see also Voitova 2005). Former North Ossetian presidential press secretary Lev Dzugayev, who notoriously announced the inflammatory number of 354 hostages, got promoted less than two weeks after the attack to the region's minister of Culture and Mass Communications (Osborn 2004a).[12] The acquitted Malgobek police chief Mukhazhir Yevloyev got offered a new job in the Ingushetia police force that was equivalent to his old one, and his acquitted deputy Akhmed Kotiyev was promoted to head of the police department in Ingushetia's largest city, Nazran (Dadashova et al. 2008).

Former North Ossetian president Dzasokhov resigned from office on May 31, 2005, and a week later on June 7, 2005, he became a member of the Federation Council (Migalin and Samarina 2005). In U.S. terms, he was effectively bumped from governor to senator. In the words of one female victim activist, "After such events in the republic such a person is appointed for such a position!"

At the federal level, Vladimir Pronichev, FSB first deputy director and overseer of the storming operation of Beslan School No. 1, was in mid-2005 promoted to the rank of four-star general (Dunlop 2006:98). Russia's Minister of Internal Affairs Rashid Nurgaliyev retained his post until 2012 when he was made deputy secretary of Russia's Security Council. Russia's director of the FSB, Nikolai Patrushev, also retained his post until 2008 when he was made secretary of the Security Council (Buse et al. 2004). Dmitry Peskov, the then deputy press secretary charged by victims, as well as Savelyev and the North Ossetian parliamentary commission, with promoting the erroneous 354 hostage figure that provoked the militants to behave more aggressively toward the hostages, remained Putin's press secretary through the latter's permutations from president to prime minister to president again (Litvinovich 2005; Milashina 2005b,

---

[12] At the time of the attack, Dzugayev was head of the North Ossetian President's Information and Analysis Office and had the job of announcing official estimates. By most accounts, Dzugayev was the original source of reports that the hostages numbered 354. Dzugayev was questioned as a witness at the Kulayev trial, where he angrily explained that 354 was the number of hostages who were definitively identified in a preliminary list created amidst the chaos and that any number released at that time would have been incorrect (Phillips 2007:120–121). However, it was not established who authorized Dzugayev to release and repeat the number 354 during the course of the hostage taking (see http://www.pravdabeslana.ru/47-151205.htm). Dzugayev himself said he received the information from Andreyev (Tagayeva et al. 2012: 44).

2005c; Tagayeva et al. 2012:10). Peskov became deputy head of the presidential administration and presidential press secretary in May 2012.

Officials who were not promoted went about business as usual, or if they were fired, it was at a later date and for unrelated reasons. Boris Dzgoyev retained his position as North Ossetian minister for Emergency Situations. Pyotr Vasilyev, who was the member of the operational headquarters in charge of contacting journalists and who, according to Savelyev and the North Ossetian parliamentary commission, was responsible along with Peskov for the misinformation about the number of hostages, retained his position with Russian State Television (Litvinovich 2005; Milashina 2005b, 2005c; Tagayeva et al. 2012:10). Alexander Tikhonov, whom Andreyev claimed gave the order for the use of heavy weapons and who for two full hours did not give the order to extinguish the fire in the gym, retained his position as head of the FSB's Special Operations. Commander of the 58th Army, Lieutenant General Viktor Sobolev, who was in charge of military operations at the school and admitted to the use of tanks and flamethrowers, retained his position until 2006 and then became the chief military advisor to the Russian Embassy in India before retiring in 2010 (Osborn 2004c). FSB Deputy Director Vladimir Anisimov retained his position as well, until being fired in 2006 in connection with a high-level corruption scandal (Yasmann 2006).

Why Have Authorities Been Grotesquely Insensitive?

While officials went on with their lives, many victims could not get on with theirs. This was partly because loved ones were still missing, and relatives were busy identifying charred corpses and searching for body parts. Their search revealed new horror.

Russian authorities had cleared out School No. 1 in great haste right after September 3, and on September 4, they hosed down the ruins to clean off the blood and human tissue, although a year later, blood-soaked children's clothing could still be found in the school and bloody handprints and streaks on the walls (Page 2005c; Wexler 2005; Chivers 2005b). Unbeknownst to most victims, debris was taken to an abandoned quarry about a mile outside of Beslan. A half year after the attack, in February 2005, some Beslan residents were rummaging in the quarry and found clothes, old shoes, and clumps of hair and shreds of dried skin. Within an hour, relatives of deceased hostages "descended on the grim pile to search for traces of their loved ones" (Page 2005c). Rita Sidakova found a white blouse belonging to her nine-year-old daughter Alechka who must have disrobed with the other children to endure the stifling heat before being burned alive in the fire in the school gym (Wexler 2005).

The startling discovery at the dump conveyed a grotesque insensitivity on the part of the authorities. It also conveyed their extreme incompetence, if accidental—or malfeasance, if deliberate—since presumably the found body parts were evidence for the investigation (Voronov 2006:7). The motive for the malfeasance, according to Voice of Beslan's Ella Kesayeva and many other victims, was to conceal the authorities' use of flamethrowers and tanks (Allenova 2006). The malfeasance charge was substantiated by driver Murat Katsanov who claimed he found the dump two and a half months prior, in December 2004, and informed both local officials and Torshin's parliamentary commission investigating the siege. According to Katsanov, "There were body parts and clumps of hair. Dogs and foxes ate most of them" (Page 2005c). In the words of Susanna Dudiyeva who lost her thirteen-year-old son Zaurbek in the siege, "First they let those bandits kill our children, then they let the dogs eat their bodies. Why did they not tell us about it? It should have been examined, then buried or burnt" (Page 2005c).

The callous dumping of body parts was not the only evidence victims had of grotesquely insensitive treatment of their loved ones' remains. They also saw a crime-scene video taken on the morning of September 4 and leaked to the Mothers of Beslan that showed how casually investigators shoveled ashes among the dead and how, upon finding a dead girl, they "unceremoniously toss[ed] her blackened body into a bag" (Chivers 2005b:1).

By September 17, 2004, the families of School No. 1 still could not understand what had happened to 122 people, including 84 unrecognizable and unclaimed bodies in the morgue, and many surviving relatives spent their days examining the charred bodies and picking through pieces of bone, flesh, teeth, and hair set aside in trays. Searching this way for her twelve-year-old niece, Madina, Aza Pukhayeva offered this description, "It's hell in there. There's just charred fragments in there. You can't tell if it's a boy or a girl. Some have their hands up by their heads like a baby in a cradle. We've looked at every fragment, every finger, the hair, the teeth." Vova Tumayev identified his only daughter, also named Madina, by an earring, and his wife, Zinaida, by a mole on her pinky. Searching for his 70-year-old mother, Maria, Vladimir Kusov said, "We've been out checking hospitals. I've been to the morgue 8, 10, 12 times. We have no idea what else to do" (Mydans 2004a).

In this context, victims could reasonably have expected sensitivity to be heightened, if anything. Instead, it seemed to them that the government just wanted to put the whole business to rest, regardless of whether relatives were truly matched with their missing persons. A July 2005 shipment of unidentified body parts came from a government forensic lab so rancid that families had to bury the caskets immediately (Cullison 2005). Many families were uncertain if they buried their own children, partly because so many hostages were burned beyond recognition but also because the government's desire to finish the task left little room for scrutiny. Vladimir Kisiyev, a grandfather of eight, disagreed with the results of the genetic examination of the remains of his eight grandchildren, noting, for example, that the feet supposedly belonging to his grandson were the wrong size and shape for a little boy. Experts suggested that he bury them as his grandson's anyway. Eighty-year-old Georgy Agayev and his relatives were told something similar by prosecutors (Tokhsyrov 2005).

Participants in a focus group of male activist victims older than thirty-five described their comparably agonizing ordeals.

TAMERLAN: My wife and my elder son came out of the gym, although with injuries, and they were treated for a long time afterwards. And my younger son, his fate is unknown because I didn't find him among the dead. . . . There was a person there, a witness, who saw my younger son as they were taking him away. And later this witness was very strongly pressured, and I was forced to compromise. She was threatened to be sentenced to 20–25 years [of imprisonment] for aiding terrorists. And I agreed to bury the kid whom I hadn't found. That is, I buried someone else's child. I even know whose child it was. The poor devil was exhumed twice.

BORIS: I didn't find my granddaughter among the dead. They haven't given me the DNA results to this day, not to mention any kind of documents at all. Fragments were lost in the course of the investigation. Amazing what this examination was based on. This is one thing. Second, there were no representatives of the prosecutor's office, no medical personnel, nobody. "Is this your coffin?" "Judging from the inscription, it's mine. Can I look inside?" "No, it's a zinc coffin." They didn't let me open it. "Give me the documents from the medical examination." "There are none." "Who should I appeal to?" "I'm sorry, but I put my signature in the register. I accepted [this result]." What can she [the morgue employee] do? She is a medical nurse. She just gave me [what she was told to give]. December 6, it happened more than three months after the tragic events.

KAZBEK: Imagine, they did this very, very fast, just to get rid of people. You can't conduct a genetic examination in a week. And how fast they did it! As Boris says, many zinc coffins, all sealed off, went to Rostov. They have numbers on them. They arrive. I say, "Where is ours?" They say, "Here." "There is only a number there!" "Well, we took your blood sample, didn't we!" "So what? Open it. You have done everything. You have conducted all medical procedures. Open it!" No, they say, we won't. They put them [coffins] into KamAZ vehicles without asking anybody. We are standing behind the gates and see two echelons of KamAZ, "refrigerators," leaving. We got into our cars and followed them in a column. And we got them only here in the Beslan morgue, still not opened, nothing.

BORIS: Yes. The strangest thing is that, at that moment, there were no prosecutor's office representatives, no medical personnel. They didn't offer any explanations. "That's yours. Take it away." And that's it. Okay, so after this, they then accused us. "Who hurried you? Why did you take it away?" when we started demanding a genetic examination. And that's what we still have.

In an effort to compensate victims for their losses, the authorities authorized money. The federal and regional government each gave 100,000 rubles ($3,500) to the families of the deceased, along with 18,000 ($630) and 25,000 ($875), respectively, for funeral expenses (Tagayeva et al. 2012).[13] This meager amount was perceived by victims as insulting ("An Empire's Fraying" 2005).

It is also not even clear when the money arrived. As victim Rita Kudzyyeva explained, although 18,000 rubles were promised for funeral expenses of deceased victims, the authorities could not even determine the number who perished, and the funerals could not wait. "There were not enough coffins in Vladikavkaz, so we drove some here from Nalchik at our own expense. You tell me, who is so generous, appraising our lives at 100,000 rubles?" Another victim cried and shouted while trying to stretch her arms around the four coffins in her yard containing her son, daughter-in-law, and two grandchildren, "Putin gave me money! Putin gave me money! I will buy myself new children" (Milashina 2004a).

The government's callousness extended to some 120 survivors who were left permanently disabled, including 70 or more children ("Over 5,000" 2009; Schepp 2009).[14] Injuries included burns, disfigurement, and severe trauma, and there was a desperate need for operations, medicine, and long-term physical therapy and psychological therapy. The compensation from the federal government and regional governments for these victims was also perceived as meager and insulting, ranging from 15,000 ($525) rubles and 25,000 rubles ($875), respectively, for "unharmed" hostages (meaning lack of physical injury; there were

[13] Dollar amounts are based on the average exchange rate during November and December 2004 of 1 ruble to $.035.

[14] Just as reports differed on the numbers of hostages, hostage takers, and the deceased, so too did they differ on the number of disabled former hostages. The Russian Red Cross suggested in 2006 that there were 500 disabled people living in Beslan and that 200 of them were survivors of the hostage crisis (Plotnikova and Mitrophanova 2006). Lyudmila Dzytseva, head of Beslan's new school that replaced School No. 1, said in 2006 that there were 300 former hostages at the new school, 24 who lost their hearing, 40 who lost limbs, and all of whom suffered from post-traumatic stress disorder (Church 2006). Deputy head of the new school, Olga Shcherbinina, said in 2007 that over 400 of the 700-plus students at the school were disabled ("Beslan Kids Still Haunted" 2007). Most likely, the definition of "disabled" varied, and this accounted for the discrepancies. Numbers between 120 and 130 were most commonly reported and probably referred only to the severest physical injuries.

no unharmed people in the full sense of the word) to 50,000 rubles ($1,750) from each government for the seriously or gravely injured (Tagayeva et al. 2012). Many of the latter could not possibly attend to their ongoing medical expenses with these sums.

In the beginning, private donors came through with compassion and assistance, including compensation of 1,000,000 rubles ($35,000) to next of kin of deceased hostages and 700,000 rubles ($24,500) to those with serious injuries (Tagayeva et al. 2012; Schepp 2009). At this point, the government too had the injured hostages on its radar. In November 2014, the North Ossetian government paid between 350,000 ($12,250) and 1,000,000 ($35,000) rubles per victim based on injuries or deaths, and in the next few years the federal government provided funds for a multi-functional medical center and an institute of social support for children and families (Tagayeva et al. 2012). In 2007, the government built the new hospital on the outskirts of Beslan (Schepp 2009).

Over time, however, disabled victims began to feel forsaken. Dr. Alan Adyrkhayev complained, "The government does nothing. There are no regular examinations, and there is no central government office for those seeking help" (Schepp 2009). By 2009, the new hospital still lacked the funding and licenses to open, and hospital plans did not include a pediatric psychology department anyway. Also due to lack of funds, the existing hospital could not be renovated and stood empty, and the salaries of doctors and nurses were reduced by 20 percent by the city administration. As a result, desperately needed operations did not happen. Medicines initially acquired in Moscow or abroad when attention and compassion still ran high were not refilled. Fifteen-year-old Fatima Dzgoyeva, whose head was pierced by shrapnel during the storming of the school and who suffered a nineteen-day coma followed by three years lying in bed, went on to have five operations that allowed her to walk and say a few words. Her aunt and caretaker, Lana, wrote to the North Ossetian governor to request help raising the money for Fatima's operation and treatment in Berlin. Lana's sentiments captured the feeling of many in Beslan, "I am so thankful that the government helped us. But indifference set in soon afterwards. No one wanted to pay for the long-term consequences, and the ailing survivors were relegated to the status of supplicants" (Schepp 2009).

A male activist victim who lost grandchildren put his grievance in historical context. "Our fathers after the war had much greater protection than we do in today's day. The state provided them, the war veterans, with much better social protection. What status did we receive in today's day? None. It's as if we don't exist. We are empty."

Victims reported that they were even the targets of extortion. As one female activist victim described, "After the terrorist act, when somebody calls you at home and says we will take away your child's status as having medium gravity injuries or grave injuries if you don't pay this amount, what should our attitude to the authorities be?"

Why Were Innocent Victims Harassed by Authorities?

Victims also claimed that they were treated suspiciously by the authorities, as if their insider knowledge and grief needed to be controlled and manipulated so as not to challenge official interpretations of events. Victims felt pressured and even threatened into giving false testimony about what they saw and did during their captivity. The pressure turned to harassment for those victims who spoke up, or had the potential to do so, and especially for those who became activists.

As described in the Introduction, on November 3, 2004, over a thousand Beslan residents met at the House of Culture with Deputy Prosecutor General Shepel and other authorities. There, victims openly discussed being bullied. Former hostage Ruslan Boloyev, whose daughter was one of the schoolchildren killed, stepped up to the microphone and turned toward Shepel and senior investigator Konstantin Lyufi:

BOLOYEV: You shouldn't lie. You shouldn't lie and say that there weren't any weapons in the school. I myself was forced to carry plastic explosives and guns from the library to the gymnasium.

LYUFI (rising from his seat and approaching Boloyev): Wait a minute. Let's clear this up now, in front of everyone. I questioned you, didn't I? You told me that there weren't any weapons in the school. Didn't you?

BOLOYEV: I did. But what else could I do, when two men in uniform came to my home and threatened me. "If you say anything about weapons, we'll make sure you rot in jail."

UNIDENTIFIED MALE 1: They came to see me too!

UNIDENTIFIED MALE 2: And two soldiers told me the same thing!

LYUFI (to Boloyev, taking him by the elbow and leading him off to the side): Why don't you come with me and we'll get to the bottom of this.

PEOPLE IN THE CROWD: Leave him alone! Do you want him to rot in jail too?!

Later in the meeting, residents continued to discuss how witnesses were being pressured to keep certain information quiet and give false testimony (Shavlokhova, et al. 2004). In June 2005, Kazbek Dzarasov gave a story similar to Boloyev's. Dzarasov admitted publicly that three men dressed in camouflage uniforms forced him to give false testimony at the trial of Nur-Pasha Kulayev, specifically forbidding him from saying that the terrorists forced him to open up the floor of the building to extract weapons hidden there in advance (Dunlop

2006:27). Former hostage Madina Sasiyeva-Salbiyeva was on record in the pre-liminary investigation as having said that the hostage taker at the controls of the bomb was reading the Koran and then took his foot off the controls, but during the actual trial of Kulayev, she said that she did not notice if the hostage taker took his foot off the controls. Victims and other observers speculated that she was originally pressured by investigators into giving false testimony and then mustered the courage to talk honestly at the trial (Dunlop 2006:85).

Persuasion and coercion by officials were accompanied by interference with victims' rights to speech and assembly. On February 25, 2005, Mothers of Belsan gave notice of a "Mothers Against Terror" rally to be held at Freedom Square in the heart of Vladikavkaz, and their permit was denied. They persisted by ap-pealing to presidential representative to the Southern Federal District, Dmitry Kozak. When Kozak's assistant Alexander Smirnov arrived in Beslan, the rally was permitted, but the North Ossetian deputy prosecutor Alexander Popov warned residents to stay away from the square due to potential attacks, and Ossetian elders went on national radio and television warning that the rally was designed by those trying to "sow discord among people." On March 7, the day before the scheduled event, the radio station VGTR "Alania" announced that the rally had been canceled altogether, which it had not (Racheva 2005a).

Despite all these attempts to thwart the rally and silence the victims, on March 8 more than a thousand people gathered at Freedom Square. The official tactic was now harassment. On that morning, attempts were made to provoke conflict and prevent the Mothers of Beslan from coming to Vladikavkaz. At the rally it-self, participants were threatened with physical violence, and police warned them that they could lose their jobs. Despite the fact that Freedom Square was packed with people, officials held a press conference immediately afterward to announce that only 270 people had showed (Racheva 2005a). Other harassment included threats to journalists covering the rally, threats to a Beslan-Vladikavkaz bus driver that he would lose his license for making the trip, and slanderous leaflets denouncing Mothers of Beslan chair Susanna Dudiyeva and placed in Beslan mailboxes (Racheva 2005b).

On May 12, 2005, the North Ossetian Ministry of Internal affairs banned "rallies, meetings, and other events that attract large numbers of people," defending the decision by saying, "this is not a ban on holding rallies and large demonstrations, only a suspension of the acceptance of applications for permis-sion to hold them." The reason was the possibility of terrorist attacks and the inability to divert security forces from other obligatory duties to instead patrol rallies. They claimed to have new information about possible impending attacks (Farniyev and Kashin 2005).

Beslan victims expressed outrage at this decision, with Susanna Dudiyeva dismissing the terrorist threat as an excuse, "as if there really was some time in the past seven years when we lived without the threat of terrorist attacks? If someone wants to hold a rally, then let the police make it so that the rally is not penetrated by a single terrorist, not a single suicide bomber." In Dudiyeva's opinion, the real reason for the ban was that "they simply don't want to hear us or listen to us anymore." The ban was "political" because the government feared a "wave of popular anger" (Farniyev and Kashin 2005:8).

Eventually, there were conflicts between victims and police. On October 27, 2005, eight victims of either the Beslan school hostage taking or the 2002 Moscow theater hostage taking were arrested and taken to the Tverskoye police station for picketing the building of the Russian Prosecutor General's office. The women had been given permission to picket, just not at the Prosecutor General's main office but at its reception room, which is in a different location, and the police refused the women's request to continue for a half an hour where they were. The women were forced to stay in the police station for three hours ("Beslan Activists Arrested" 2005). A year later, also in Moscow, police and special riot forces detained at least 10 participants in unauthorized protests about Beslan, while about 80 protesters remained near Lubyanskaya Square, and a rally commemorating Beslan was also broken up in St. Petersburg ("Moscow Police Break Up Rally" 2006). In August 2009, victims tried to pass a letter to then President Dmitry Medvedev who was visiting Vladikavkaz for a military awards ceremony. They were greeted with "a tight cordon of bodyguards, threats, rudeness, and the use of force," including being grabbed by the arms and warned that they would be fired upon if they tried to run toward the president ("Beslan Victims' Mothers" 2009).

The authorities also used the judicial system to harass victims, especially the activists. In late August 2007, the Leninsky Court in Vladikavkaz ordered the termination of the Voice of Beslan in its present composition and the expulsion of its chair Emma Tagayeva and most outspoken member, Emma's sister Ella Kesayeva, allowing another more Kremlin-friendly organization to register itself under the same name (Milashina 2007d).[15] In November 2007, Voice of Beslan leader Ella Kesayeva was charged in court for "arbitrary behavior and improper use of roadside areas," specifically her putting up signs that pointed at the school wreckage with the message, "Putin's course [Kurs Putina]," sarcastically playing on the promotional language of Putin's party, United Russia, in its campaign for upcoming elections (Mereu 2007). On December 19, 2007, the North Ossetian Supreme Court upheld the lower court ruling and again ordered the Voice of

---

[15] Emma Tagayeva lost her husband, Ruslan Betrozov, to a summary execution by the terrorists described in Chapter 1, and she lost her two sons, Alan and Aslan Betrozov, during the storming of the school. In some news articles and possibly even legal documents, she is referred to as Emma Betrozova, but in the application to the European Court of Human Rights that bears her name and in most other documents, she appears as Emma Tagayeva.

Beslan to disband ("Court Orders" 2007). By 2008, Voice of Beslan members were being charged by prosecutors in Ingushetia with extremism, thanks to their "appeal to all those who care about the Beslan tragedy," which accused President Putin of abetting terrorism (Osadchuk 2008; Parfitt 2008). By 2009, Voice of Beslan's appeal was banned and included on the Federal List of Extremist Materials and remains there as of this writing ("Voice of Beslan Appeal" 2010; Tagayeva et al. 2012:69).

Legal harassment came in various other forms. In perhaps the most serious and intimidating instance, the victims' lawyer, Taimuraz Chedzhemov, received death threats after trying to help the victims bring charges against high-level officials. On September 1, 2007, Chedzhemov quit ("Lawyer of Russian School" 2007; Allenova and Farniyev 2007). On the more inexplicable and pathetic side, Beslan children who were attending a free boarding school in Moscow Oblast received notice that they would have to pay taxes, accrued fines, and penalties on their tuition (Kozenko and Farniyev 2009).

Victims were joined by journalists as targets of harassment, which indirectly added to victims' grievances, because the targeted journalists were the ones covering their story in the greatest depth and with the greatest compassion. The pattern began even during the hostage crisis. Anna Politkovskaya, a famous journalist for *Novaya gazeta* and book author, decided to fly to Rostov-on-Don and travel by car to Beslan but was poisoned on the flight (Haraszti 2004:9; Dunlop 2006:60). Andrei Babitskii of Radio Free Europe/Radio Liberty was held by police at the airport in Moscow, roughed up, and taken by police to court on a criminal charge, which was conveniently dropped after the terror ended (Haraszti 2004:9–10; Dunlop 2006:60). Just days afterward, Raf Shakirov, editor of *Izvestiya*, was forced to resign due to the newspaper's critical coverage of the siege (Haraszti 2004:8–9; Cozens 2004).

Journalists continued to be targeted in the years that followed. Svetlana Meteleva of the newspaper *Moskovskii komsomolets* wrote a three-part report, cited heavily in this chapter, that was based on classified documents that had been leaked to her. The official Russian investigative commission demanded that Meteleva reveal her sources of information, and, in the presence of her colleague Aleksandr Minkin, a federal investigator directly threatened her and warned that her sources would be punished no matter what (Dunlop 2006:20). Marina Litvinovich, founder and publisher of the fact-finding and fact-disseminating website Pravda Beslana ("The Truth of Beslan," http://www.pravdabeslana.ru/), also helped create the Mothers of Beslan and became a spokesperson for victims, not only through the website but also by organizing rallies and financial assistance. On March 20, 2006, Litvinovich was beaten on the head and left unconscious with two missing teeth but no missing valuables in an attack many suspected was related to her Beslan investigation (Schreck

2006a). Many victims felt a message was being sent that any attempt to learn the truth about their dead, wounded, and traumatized loved ones was a punishable offense.

Why Were Victims Ignored, Discredited, and Demeaned?

Condescending treatment by the authorities, especially of female victims, was a mainstay of the aftermath of the hostage taking. Authorities portrayed the women as incapable of their own thoughts and opinions, the emotional puppets of more clear-thinking actors with political agendas. The women were alternately ignored or charged with hysterics, or both.

The campaign to discredit the victims was not subtle. Beslan Mayor Oleg Gobuyev said, "There are some forces that direct these women to make their demands—it is not their own idea" (Page 2005c). A North Ossetian government official claimed that there were not more than a dozen mothers on the Mothers of Beslan committee, which was really dominated by former leaders of the republic, especially those in the United Ossetia movement who hoped to capitalize on the tragedy and force Dzasokhov to resign (Farniyev and Kashin 2005; Naidenov 2005b). Federation Council Deputy Speaker Alexander Torshin asserted that the Beslan mothers were acting from emotions and "not being logical" in their accusations against Russia's leadership (Weir 2005a:6).

Over the course of the Kulayev trial, some victims began to pity the captured hostage taker or at least to see Kulayev as a potential avenue in their search for the truth. They did not want him executed, since his death would mean closing the door to discovering any new information about the siege. Head of Mothers of Beslan Susanna Dudiyeva said, "It is obvious that Kulayev will be found guilty. What we want is to see the responsible government officials on trial" (Page 2005a). Dudiyeva told the court in June 2005 that she and others would apply for a pardon for Kulayev if he told the truth (Cullison 2005; Page 2005a). Prosecutor Maria Semisynova reacted by saying, "It's immoral to talk about forgiving someone who has killed children and taken over a school. In their pain and their grief, [the victims' families] are losing control of themselves" (Cullison 2005:A1).

After their twenty-eight-hour sit-in at the Vladikavkaz courthouse where Kulayev was being tried, the Beslan victims left dissatisfied, noting that the authorities refused to take their demands for accountability seriously. Protester Zalina Guburova said that the authorities were treating them "like a gang of hysterical women not worthy of meeting with" (Mainville 2005a:A10). Shepel pretty much confirmed Guburova's assessment. "We cannot simplify the case just because the mothers' committee insists on that. As a prosecutor, I cannot be governed by emotions. The investigation must be based upon facts which are proven" (Page 2005a).

From the victims' perspective, Shepel and other officials were creating a smokescreen by making the issue one of emotions versus fact, when fact is precisely what the victims were disputing. Whether or not they did so emotionally was beside the point. The basic premise of Semisynova's statement was something victims questioned: Did Kulayev actually kill any children? Many victims believed Kulayev's claim that he did not shoot anyone, and they still wanted to know who—or at least, who else—did. The families did not believe they were "losing control of themselves." They were trying to take control by making sure the authorities did not "disappear" a crucial piece of evidence, namely the person of Kulayev. Calling them illogical and emotional was adding insult to their injuries, a clear attempt to dismiss their deeply felt grievances.

Deputy Prosecutor General Shepel took the insult to the greatest height when he accused Beslan victims not just of emotionality and poor logic but of fabrication. Shepel charged that victims who testified at the Kulayev trial gave "evidence that is not based on their personal experiences but on reports in the national and regional media—on gossip. They are not saying what they saw but what they have read in the papers or seen on TV." In particular, their claims that there were more than thirty-two hostage takers were "lies" based on "gossip and fantasy." The newspapers that ultimately influenced the victim-witnesses based their articles on "gossip, unchecked information, and the fantasy of their authors" (Mereu 2005:3).

Susanna Dudiyeva responded, "Mr. Shepel is accusing everyone of lying. He is accusing more than 1,000 people of Beslan of lying. He is accusing the journalists of writing invented reports. How is it possible that he is the only one who is right when 1,000 people say he is not? Shepel was not at the school" (Mereu 2005:3).

The victims did not go quietly but fought against marginalization. The Mothers of Beslan repeatedly demanded that they meet with the president himself to discuss their grievances. As a result of one of the most notable victim protest events, the highway blockade discussed in Chapter 4, the victims did get a meeting with presidential envoy to the South Federal District, Dmitry Kozak, who promised to pass along an appeal to Putin. In response to their later frustration that the president did not respond, Kozak explained that the president probably did not have time. The victims replied, "But we understand that he [the president] has time for his dog, but for us he has no time" (Allenova 2005b).

When Putin finally agreed to meet with the women, he insulted them by choosing September 2, 2005, a date that was in the middle of the first Beslan memorial services (September 1 to September 3), a year after the attack, when most Beslan residents had planned to visit the remains of School No. 1 and the cemetery where the victims were buried. Kozak's response to the victims' outrage about the proposed timing was supposedly, "So what?" (Allenova 2005b). The Mothers of Beslan accepted the meeting but accused the Putin administration of being grossly insensitive or trying to deflect media attention from the cere-monies in Beslan, which some parents would have to miss in order to meet with President Putin (Page 2005b; Weir 2005a). Susanna Dudiyeva explained, "To in-vite us on September 2 is the height of cynicism. But we are putting our pain and sense of insult to one side for the sake of our cause" (Page 2005b). Victims were offended and resentful, and when confronted with the need to miss the com-memorative ceremonies, fewer accepted the invitation than otherwise would have (Page 2005b).

The campaign to harm the victims' reputations and cast doubt on their mental acuity continued after the meeting with Putin. When some prominent members of the Mothers of Beslan met with and began to follow a charlatan named Grigorii Grabovoi who promised to resurrect Beslan children for a fee, some observers suspected that this was a plot of the authorities to discredit the sen-sible, credible, and increasingly prominent organization. Their suspicions were confirmed when, a few days after the visit between Grabovoi and the victims, "a videotape of the meeting mysteriously made it into the media. . . . This is a tech-nique repeatedly used to discredit various political forces" (Semyenova 2005:1). They questioned how in Beslan—a place where the authorities watched all the actions of journalists and kept them under close scrutiny—the representatives of Grabovoi's sect operated in complete safety (Semyenova 2005).

The dismissive attitude of the authorities toward the victims partly explains why Yuri Savelyev, dissenting member of Torshin's parliamentary commission, was revered by victims, journalists, and other observers. They appreciated not only his expertise in explosives and weaponry but the respect he gave to the victims. In his own words, "I never shared the opinion that the former hostages and victims were inadequate people. On the contrary, I believe that they in particular remembered forever and brought to us everything that happened in the three days in the Beslan school. And if you really have a desire to un-derstand the causes and consequences of this terrorist act, if you try to take away some kind of lesson, then the evidence of these people must be treated very seriously. . . . if you study all the evidence of the hostages . . . you will see a serious difference with the investigation's official version" ("Seeking Public Accountability" 2004).

Why Are We Still Unprotected?

Of course, victims doubted that the authorities really had "a desire to understand the causes and consequences" or to "take away some kind of lesson." Indeed, victims believed that lessons were not learned and they were no safer after the fatal ending of the assault on School No. 1 than they were before.

The security situation in Beslan and the rest of North Ossetia still was not resolved. In the assessment of Stanislav Kesayev about the Russian ability to respond to terrorist threats a year after the school hostage taking, there had been "no radical changes as a result of the Beslan events. I wouldn't want to see our security forces put to the test in another such crisis" (Mainville 2005b). At the January 2005 highway blockade, Rita Naifonova explained what this meant for victims and other North Ossetians. "We live like we are on a powder keg. When children go to school, we are afraid that they won't return. And our government doesn't move a finger. And we were tired of waiting for these official truths" (Tokhsyrov 2005:3).

Participants in a focus group of female activists thirty-five years and younger expressed similar frustrations:

MADINA: Where is the guarantee that there won't be another Beslan?
BELA: No guarantee, nobody has one. I live with that thought every day.
VIKA: No, there is no guarantee. That's what frightens us, the thought that our government can't guarantee that there won't be another tragedy.

The concerns and fears were both general, related to all potential terrorists in the region, and specific to the precise terrorists who had already claimed so many lives in Beslan. Indeed, at least one terrorist, Ali Taziyev, was declared dead after the 2004 counterterrorism operation at the school, only to reemerge in 2006 as a suspect in the assassination of Ingushetia's Deputy Interior Minister Dzhabrail Kostoyev. One newspaper mocked, "It seems that in Russia the terrorists destroyed by the federal forces don't die but are transformed into zombies and continue executing their black affairs" (Parfitt 2006). By 2010, Taziyev was arrested in Ingushetia on multiple charges, including an attempt to assassinate Ingushetia's President Yunus-Bek Yevkurov, and in 2013, he was sentenced to life imprisonment ("Notorious North Caucasus" 2013). Confusingly, or perhaps conveniently, Taziyev was not found guilty of participating in the Beslan school siege or even charged with participation ("Delo obvinyayemogo" 2012; "Captured Ingush" 2013). Most likely, a terrorist was misidentified as Taziyev back in 2004 and Taziyev was never in the school, but acknowledgment of such a mistake would reinforce the victims' point that the insistence on thirty-two terrorists was arbitrary, the authorities were uninformed or deliberately misinforming, and threats remained.

Ella Kesayeva spoke at the Russian Supreme Court hearing of the victims' appeal of the Kulayev trial (which the Supreme Court denied), and she described the victims' feelings of insecurity due to inconsistent and at times wildly implausible information about the terrorists. "How do we prove that there were about thirty-two terrorists? Witnesses indicated that they saw two times more militants. And where is the guarantee that those eight so far unidentified bodies were terrorists from the school and not imported federal corpses? Where is the guarantee that all participants in the attack on Beslan were killed and tomorrow they will not come to another school?" (Allenova 2006:4).

And if terrorists did return, whether they were the same ones or different, where was the guarantee that the authorities would behave differently and save more lives next time? Looking at the evidence, victims believed that the authorities prioritized the military operation to eliminate militants over a special operation to free hostages (Milashina 2004b). They believed this was a matter of ongoing and terribly misguided federal policy (Politkovskaya 2006:7).

The general Russian public seemed to share this grievance with the Beslan victims. Government counterterrorist operations came to be viewed as a death sentence for hostages in Russia. The message from the Russian government to the Russian people was, "We can't protect you from terrorists. And when you do become the victim of a terrorist attack, you have a 20–30 percent chance or worse of being killed by one of our own forces during the rescue" ("Seeking Public Accountability" 2004). The message resonated with Zita Sidakova, mother of seven-year-old Georgy and five-year-old David and widow of Albert, one of the men identified by the terrorists as a potential threat and therefore shot and killed on the first day of the hostage taking. Sidakova was adamantly opposed to sending Georgy back to school. "Who will guarantee he will be safe?" (Finn 2005b).

Conclusion: The Political Grievance Context

Victims of the Beslan school hostage taking had many unanswered questions. They wanted to understand who precisely killed their children, what enabled such a hostage taking in the first place, what enabled the tragic ending, why investigations seemed to cover up more than reveal, and why they, innocent victims, were being so callously mistreated. Victims were repeatedly told "facts" about the hostage taking by officials who were not present at the scene. These facts frequently conflicted with their own eyewitness memories and with evidence that they themselves uncovered when they returned to the scene. Their version of the story was nevertheless deemed "wrong," they felt, simply because of the power differential.

The victims' pursuit of answers is ongoing as of writing this book, and many suspect they will never get the answers they seek. For that, their grievances were directed not at the terrorists and not at the Ingush or Chechen co-ethnics, but at political authorities ranging from regional officials in various emergency, military, and police capacities to the highest-ranking officials in the Russian Federation, including President Putin himself.

3

The Surprisingly Nonviolent Aftermath

Some research and conventional wisdom suggest that retaliatory violence would have been a regrettable but very understandable response by victims to the violence in Beslan. Aggression is widely perceived as justifiable, tolerable, and sometimes even necessary when it is in retaliation for a previous wrong or injury (Miller 2001:534). The motivation to punish perpetrators is powerful (Miller 2001:535, 541), as is the motivation to direct aggression toward members of a categoric unit, such as the ethnic group of the perpetrators (Horowitz 2001; Petersen 2002; Turner 2011).

However, research also shows that interethnic cooperation is more common than interethnic violence (Fearon and Laitin 1996; Lake and Rothchild 1996; Olzak 2006) and that interethnic violence is unlikely when the rival ethnic group has little power and is therefore not resented (Peterson 2002). The existence of a wrong or injury does not always inspire aggression or motivate victims to punish perpetrators or their co-ethnics. Individual support for violence may depend on many factors.

Consistent with findings about the infrequency of interethnic violence, large-scale post-Beslan retaliation and ethnic conflict did not occur. The anticipation of retaliatory violence far exceeded its practice. Still, consistent with other theories about the motivations for retaliatory violence—especially those emphasizing the role of prejudice, political pride, social alienation, self-efficacy, and pessimism—the predictions and fears of a retaliatory bloodbath in the North Caucasus had foundation. In a conducive context—where, for example, charismatic elders encouraged retaliation—some victims could have been convinced to kill. Studying such a "near miss" can provide useful insights into the sources and dynamics of retaliatory violence (Horowitz 2001:32, chapter 12).

This chapter describes retaliatory violence in the aftermath of the Beslan school hostage taking. It reviews evidence from news reports, focus group discussions, and survey data that retaliatory violence was widely anticipated by victims, other North Ossetians, and observers in the North Caucasus, Russia, and the world. It then examines the actual retaliatory violence that did occur and the variation in individual support for retaliatory violence among Beslan victims. Particular attention is paid to measurement issues and the use of survey questions to measure this support.

After Violence. Debra Javeline, Oxford University Press. © Oxford University Press 2023.
DOI: 10.1093/oso/9780197683347.003.0004

Anticipated Retaliatory Violence

In the North Caucasus, historical, anthropological, and cultural studies suggest longstanding practice and acceptance of blood feuds and related violence (Jersild 2002). Individual clans or families are considered blood communities, and members defend each other's rights, dignity, and property. Vendettas have been launched in response to offenses ranging from mild slights to mass deportations, and trauma is thought to reinforce these values and customs (Isaenko and Petschauer 1999:162–163). In many cases, retaliatory violence has been not only acceptable but obligatory for restoring the honor of a family or a clan.

After the hostage taking, observers of Russia and the North Caucasus thus predicted and feared outbreaks of violence by Ossetians against ethnic Ingush or Chechens, the presumed (and later confirmed) ethnicity of the majority of hostage takers. These observers cited the very recent past history when heavily armed civilian militias of Ossetians and Ingush mobilized against each other for the purpose of ethnic cleansing ("Russia: The Ingush-Ossetian Conflict" 1996). Their fear of retaliatory violence was also based on statements made right after the hostage taking by Beslan residents who condoned retaliation (Chivers 2004; Dyupin 2004; Weir 2004).

There were two time frames when observers closely watched Beslan in expectation of retaliatory violence: immediately after the hostage taking and immediately after the traditional forty-day mourning period. Technically, Ossetians are forbidden to touch a weapon while mourning, but rumors circulated that not everyone would wait. Directly after the hostage taking, police and Russian troops were on high alert to prevent retaliatory violence, mostly in the Prigorodny District, the disputed region of North Ossetia that was formerly part of Ingushetia and that continues to be populated by ethnic Ingush (Sands 2004a). Many Beslan residents expressed support for violence but in some hypothetical future. Young men in particular expressed a readiness to take up arms and fight (Rodriguez 2004a).

At the end of the forty-day mourning period—on or just after October 13, 2004—observers again anticipated revenge. Ingush families who still resided in North Ossetia fled across the border into Ingushetia. Police officers were again on high alert, internal border crossing points were reinforced, and the local agricultural institute gave Ingush students an indefinite leave (Mydans 2004b).

Participants in the focus group of female activist victims thirty-five years old or younger recalled the anticipation of retaliatory violence at this time.

MADINA: At the time when it all happened, so much was going on! We will bury our people, wait until forty days have passed, and here it will begin! We won't leave this alone! If a man is a Caucasian. . . .

BELA: Like Kaloyev, do you remember Kaloyev? [Bela was referring to Vitaly Kaloyev, the North Ossetian architect who went to Switzerland and tracked down and stabbed to death the air traffic controller whose negligence caused the death of his wife and two children in a 2002 plane crash. Kaloyev was greeted as a hero by most Ossetians, receiving accolades and even an appointment as a deputy minister in the North Ossetian government ("Ossetian Revenge" 2008).]

MADINA: He is a warrior. This stereotype has been developed for centuries.

BELA: Blood for blood.

A *Christian Science Monitor* report, entitled "In Beslan, a Tense Bid for Calm" and filed on October 14, 2004, captures the mood:

> As the 40-day mourning period observed by the mainly Orthodox Christian population of North Ossetia ended Tuesday, many here said they are struggling to master their feelings of rage and fear. The key hope now, some say, is that tough law enforcement coupled with community pressure will prevent a few angry neighbors from launching violent reprisals against Ossetia's hereditary enemies, the mainly Muslim Ingush, who are widely blamed for the school siege that ended with at least 331 dead, half of them children. . . . "There is an outward calm, but inside people are seething with feelings of aggression brought on by fear and anxiety," says Inna Abayeva, a psychologist at the Psychological Training Center in Vladikavkaz, where many of the survivors are being treated for post-traumatic stress. . . . Indeed, a vengeful point of view is not hard to find, especially among the small knots of young men hovering on Beslan's street corners. . . . "The further you get from the Ingush border, the quieter things are," says Marat Dzanayev, a young engineer in the North Ossetian capital, Vladikavkaz. "There has always been trouble with them, and our patience can't last for much longer." (Weir 2004:6)

The prevalence and even comfort in discussions about retaliatory violence were seen in parenting decisions after the hostage taking. One visitor to Beslan in October 2004 noticed that most children, even the littlest ones, played very violent video games for hours at a time, often with snipers, blood, and military ambushes. The visitor was told that the children would not play with other games that were offered to them. "They could not have control of anything when they were held by the terrorist, but they can fight back in these games," said a Beslan English teacher. Another English teacher added, "After what they have seen, computerized blood is not so bad" (Lansford 2006:50).

The anticipation of retaliatory violence was reinforced by mass action that was nonviolent but looked like it could turn otherwise. Anti-Ingush rallies were held on September 4 and 5, 2004, mostly in the long-disputed Prigorodny district. Police and Russian troops patrolled the area and prevented ethnic violence (Sands 2004a). In the very recent post-violence context, the near miss was nevertheless noteworthy to most observers.

The sentiment expressed by Madina Pedatova, a teacher at Beslan's School No. 8, was common, "Everyone here is always talking about getting ready for war with the Ingush, to get even with them. I'm terrified of it, but I'm sure it's coming" (Weir 2005a:6). As one participant in the focus group of female activist victims thirty-five years old or younger put it, "At the moment, everyone was sure that something would happen, that it wouldn't remain simply as it was."

The days and weeks after the hostage taking resembled a typical lull before a deadly ethnic riot. In such a lull, the precipitating event is unexpected and of grave significance but not clearly determinant of a violent response, and victims and their co-ethnics are interpreting the precipitating event in a wider context (Horowitz 2001:89–90). A lull is not a "calm before the inevitable storm," because the lull is not calm, and the storm is not inevitable (Horowitz 2001:91). In Beslan, the storm was dodged, but the rumors, expectations, and expressed support for violence suggest that the situation could have gone either way.

Incidents of Retaliatory Violence

Not all incidents were near misses, and some post-Beslan anti-Ingush and anti-Chechen harassment and violence did occur after the hostage taking. Hours after the siege ended on September 3, Ossetians reportedly took some Ingush residents hostage in the village of Chermen, twenty kilometers southeast of Beslan (McAllister and Quinn-Judge 2004). On the night of September 4, 2004, a group of 300 armed Ossetian men reportedly walked from the village of Sunzha to the largely Ingush neighboring village of Kartsa in Prigorodny. Apparently calmed by South Ossetian president Eduard Kokoity, the enraged men went home but promised to return after the last victim had been buried (Farniyev 2004). Only days later, some Beslan residents were rumored to have headed into Ingushetia where they abducted ten Ingush men (Walsh 2004a). Hostility toward Ingush and Chechen students and hospital patients was reported, as were nine cases of disappearances of Ingush civilians in the Prigorodny District between the summer of 2005 and April 2006, including one who was found dead with evidence of beatings and torture (Sokirianskaia 2007:48). Other reports document abductions of nineteen Chechens and Ingush in 2006–2007 (Fuller 2007), and in 2007, a Russian FSB officer, Lieutenant Colonel Alikhan Kalimatov, sent to investigate the kidnappings of ethnic Ingush in North Ossetia, was shot dead on the Caucasus highway in Ingushetia ("High-Ranking Security Officer" 2007).

Acts of hostility and violence continued to be reported sporadically in the coming years. For example, on September 11, 2010, two days after a Vladikavkaz market attack that left seventeen people dead and over 150 injured, some young Ossetians are reported to have gone to Kartsa with the goal of vengeance against Ingush (Dzutsev 2011). In February 2011, a wealthy Muslim businessman tried to build a prayer room and minaret in his garden in the southern part of North Ossetia and in the midst of building was met by some 300 protesters who broke into his home, slashed the tires on his car, and demanded he tear down the emerging minaret (Parfitt 2011).

The words "reported," "reportedly," "apparently," and even "rumored" or "rumors" are used frequently in discussions of post-Beslan retaliatory violence for two reasons. First, incidents of ethnic violence are difficult to document systematically and with any sort of confidence for the North Caucasus. Routine census data from the region are notoriously unreliable, given that there are political, economic, and security implications to verifying the precise number and location of people of different ethnicities. A more controversial statistic, such as deaths due to ethnic conflict, does not exist and, if it did, would be even less reliable than simple demographic information.[1]

Second, even if verifiable data existed on ethnically motivated deaths, injuries, and destruction in the North Caucasus after the school hostage taking, it might be difficult to label all such violence as retaliatory. Ethnic conflict in the North Caucasus and the Ingush-Ossetian conflict in particular predated the school hostage taking, and some violence probably would have occurred after September 2004, even without the tragedy. There are no meaningful data to serve as a baseline showing a "typical" year of Ossetian violence toward Ingush or Chechens and how the baseline compares to such violence after the school hostage taking, with any increase presumably attributable to the hostage taking and therefore deserving of the label "retaliatory." Most of the above-described incidents, while likely retaliatory, still represent random, isolated reports, rather than a systematic understanding of what Beslan victims thought about retaliation or how they acted after the 2004 incident.

Focus group discussions can help fill in some of the blanks. Although focus groups also do not provide systematic evidence, they provide convincing corroborating evidence that retaliatory violence was widely considered among victims and other North Ossetians but was widely rejected. Indeed, there was no variation across the six focus groups on this score. The theme of all discussions

---

[1] John O'Loughlin and Frank Witmer (2011) have compiled an impressive database of 14,177 violent events that occurred in the North Caucasus from August 1999 to August 2007, with events coded by precise day of occurrence and geographic location. However, to calculate Ossetian retaliatory violence for the Beslan hostage taking, we would need, at a bare minimum, the ethnicities of victims and perpetrators and ideally some evidence that the violence was ethnically motivated.

was, "Yes, we contemplated and even discussed retaliatory violence. No, we did not commit such violence and don't know people who did."

Some of these assertions may seem self-serving. Focus group participants were, after all, denying illegal and uncivilized behavior. Still, the consistency of their stories, their reasons for avoiding retaliatory violence, and the simple fact that, after 2004, an all-out war between Ossetians and Ingush or even major on-going violent skirmishes with casualties did not occur strongly suggests that the scale of retaliatory violence after the school hostage taking was small and certainly far smaller than anticipated.

In the focus group of male activist victims older than thirty-five, participants confirmed that retaliatory violence was very much on the table at the beginning.

TOTRAZ: There was mourning for a long time. And I am telling you that you get an impulse to grab weapons and rush headlong in the first month. But a month goes by, and already then [everything is different].

KAZBEK1: Yes, longer.

TOTRAZ: You want to know, you ask why there was no outburst. . . . An outburst could have happened!

But it did not, and in the focus group of male nonactivist victims, participants discussed instigators who were trying to get men to retaliate but failed.

BORIS: People had such thoughts. Common sense prevailed. Right after the terrorist act, everybody was about to rush in that direction, but gradually everybody realized that . . .

VALERY: These [people who wanted to shoot Ingush] are unbalanced people.

Other participants in this same focus group discussed how retaliatory violence was prevented by a particular elder.

RUSLAN: The teacher, Guteyev, head teacher, war veteran, spoke on television. He was spared in this tragedy.

ALAN: There is even a cassette.

RUSLAN: He was approached, "Let's go and attack," and he calmed them down. . . . "You calm down for now." His former students had children who died, relatives, acquaintances died, and he as an elder calmed them down. "You wait. What are you doing?" And the young people listened to the elders.

Guteyev and other anti-violence elders were notably not countered by a prominent, violence-provoking Ossetian leader, which is perhaps surprising, given the larger context of historical violence in the North Caucasus described in Chapter 1. However, after the hostage taking, almost anyone in a position of political power seemed to bear some responsibility for the lax security situation in North Ossetia and/or the bungled counterterrorism operation described in Chapter 2, and entrepreneurial political leaders who tried to exploit the situation by calling for violence may have risked drawing negative attention to themselves and their own shortcomings.

In the midst of discussing why no one battled against the Ingush, participants in the focus group of female activists thirty-five years old or younger discussed what some Ossetian men did do: They armed themselves and organized their own patrol of the border with Ingushetia. The women claimed that many men prioritized armed defense over retaliatory violence.

BELLA: Honestly, there were some calls.

VIKA: I'll say this, our men went out. We have a license to carry weapons, officially registered and all. Because my husband worked for fifteen years in such places that he and his circle, his friends, have weapons. . . . They carried out a lot of children, his friends, even though they had no relatives in the school. Then starting from October they used to take our car. The men split up along the border with Ingushetia and drove out there, and each car had a group of people who had their own section, their own day of the week. They took their lawful weapons and went by car. I concretely speak for my family. They took their own car and drove there, although it strained my nerves, and I always said that my two bullet and three missile wounds were more than enough and I was crawling on my side. Who will raise the children if something happens to you? But in our family it is customary for the women to keep silent, while the man does whatever he considers necessary. They went out until there emerged, what is it called, *kazachestvo* [Cossack units].

BELA: Yes.

VIKA: They started paying money. It was voluntary at first. Then they decided that some money could be raised from defense plants at least, so that the men would be warmly dressed. They had such purely everyday demands, and they stood there because they waited for dirty tricks from any side. The more so that when they were in the gym, they examined everything. They also were strongly aggressive, but none of them tried to knife somebody on the quiet. They decided to do something, and they did it. But then Cossack units were created, and people were paid wages officially. And when all the armed men were restored, our men left. I know that not one of them remained in the Cossack units.

BELA: This war wouldn't have led to something. Poor people would simply have killed each other, and that's all.

This observation about the futility of retaliatory violence was repeated frequently among victims.

BORIS [MALE NONACTIVIST]: What's the point in going? You go today, come back. You go tomorrow, you don't come back. And what? Well, you will kill three to four people, and what will be next? One day you will also be killed.
BELLA [FEMALE ACTIVIST THIRTY-FIVE YEARS OLD OR YOUNGER]: Had we actually risen up, it would have resulted perhaps in a second Chechnya.

Most Beslan victims agreed with the sentiment that retaliatory violence would have been impractical at best and dangerous and deadly at worst. Both news reports and victim testimony provide evidence of anti-violence attitudes compatible with the low violence outcome.

TEACHER EMMA MEDOYEVA: Everyone here is filled with sorrow, and for some it is unbearable. It is so hard to forgive and try to live for the future, but this is our only chance. Most people here want peace. (Weir 2004:6)
SERGEI KAZYENNOV, AN EXPERT WITH MOSCOW-BASED INSTITUTE OF NATIONAL SECURITY AND STRATEGIC RESEARCH: In the Caucasus, just one spark is all it takes to set off an explosion. But people are exhausted. . . . The majority just wants peace. (Weir 2004:6)
VOICE OF BESLAN LEADER ELLA KESAYEVA: The terrorists who seized the school in Beslan also said that their families had died, their loved ones killed and that is why they had come to kill. But this is a vicious circle that has to be broken. ("Ossetian Revenge" 2008)

In the focus group of male activist victims older than thirty-five, participants put the matter starkly.

TOTRAZ: No one would kill children. If someone comes to you armed, that's a different story, but to go and create troops—there is no such thing, and there won't be such a thing. And there is no desire for this either.
KAZBEK1: What are we, barbarians?

Male activist victims thirty-five years old or younger offered their reasoning for not taking revenge against the Ingush.

VLADIMIR: It would be more correct to avenge the guilty ones.
MARAT: They are also people. We can't know which [of them participated in the terrorist act]. What, we'll shoot everyone?

VLADIMIR: Ingush people also studied at school, and during the conflict they just took their things and left. I mean, I saw this person every day. I greeted him every day. We had lunch together. It doesn't mean that if there was a conflict here and someone said that this is an Ingush, I should go and kill him. They are the same people [as we are].

Individual Variation in Support for Retaliatory Violence

There was certainly ambivalence toward retaliatory violence across the Beslan community and even within individuals. The majority opposed violence, but there was a spectrum ranging from extreme support for nonviolence to extreme support for violence, with gradations in between.

Even at the early stage, when the wounds and graves of the hostage taking were still fresh, Beslan victims debated among themselves about the virtues and vices of retaliation. A teenage Beslan boy whose little sister died in the school declared, "I'm ready to kill them, to finish this threat forever," while his friend Oleg insisted, "No, that's not good. We don't want war" (Weir 2004:6).

Time passed, and the most extreme pro-violence assertions became rarer and more muted, but retaliatory violence was still debated. For example, differing levels of anti-violence conviction were evident across participants in the focus group of female activists thirty-five years old or younger when they were asked whether they would have supported their men if the men had attacked Ingush.

BELA: No.

BELLA: I would not.

IRINA: No.

MADINA: I can't say anything for sure, because, if, God forbid, there had been a situation where my child . . . I can't speak calmly about that. I don't know.

BELA: All the same, no. This war wouldn't have led anywhere.

BELLA: You know, maybe I wouldn't have supported, but I can't guarantee that I would have stopped them. You can express your opinion, but they will do what they consider to be necessary. That is, I wouldn't have supported them, but if you give it a good thought, you understand that there would have been new victims. Though Madina correctly said, I don't know how I would have reasoned if my child had perished.

IRINA: Then you would have reasoned in the same way, "I lost my child. I don't want to lose you too."

BELLA: Well, maybe so.

BELA: This isn't the way out of the situation.

VIKA: I have a smart acquaintance, a very interesting girl with two children, who has completely changed her attitude toward her husband since the terrorist act. He is a bit older, and she is now absolutely set against him aggressively because she was there with her two kids and suffered insults from these Chechens, Ingush, so how could he stand all this and forgive them for everything. Each has his own opinions.

BELLA: Well, yes.

VIKA: You can't speak for everyone, of course.

Measuring Support for Retaliatory Violence

Which Beslan victims unequivocally supported retaliatory violence, which victims were unequivocally opposed, and which had more middling attitudes? Measuring actual violent behavior is a challenging and highly error-prone task, because a violent respondent might worry about the ramifications of going on record with admissions of illegal acts. Perpetrators of violence usually do not confess, take credit, or brag, but instead conceal and obfuscate (Horowitz 2001:224–225). A direct survey question about violent behavior is a sensitive one that might elicit socially desirable responses—lying about violent behavior—and thus measurement error.

To minimize these problems, support for violence was substituted as a proxy for actual violence. The two are by no means equivalent, since support for violence is not the only factor influencing actual violence, and the impulse toward aggression is much more common than the realization of that impulse. For example, asked about episodes of intense or recent anger, individuals felt an impulse toward physical aggression or punishment in 40 percent of the episodes but actually responded with physical aggression in only 10 percent of episodes, or a quarter of the time when aggressive impulses were felt (Averill 1983:1148). Substituting an attitudinal question for a question about actual violent behavior is thus subject to the same limitations as attitudinal questions about political participation that are critiqued in the next chapter.

These very real limitations are difficult to avoid when studying violent behavior, given the ethical constraints described in this book's Introduction and the need to minimize response bias. Research should not inflame respondents with violent thoughts nor encourage the systematic misreporting (likely underreporting) of violent behavior that could jeopardize the validity of statistical results.[2]

---

[2] List experiments are often helpful in estimating aggregate levels of sensitive behavior that individuals might otherwise not disclose. However, list experiments cannot identify which precise individuals engaged in the behavior, as required for data analysis in a study that seeks to explain individual behavior.

Still, understanding violent impulses is an essential step toward understanding violence itself. Supporters of violence are more likely to report intentions to engage in violence (Muller 1972), and supporters of violence are presumably more likely perpetrators of violence than opponents of violence. For individuals to behave violently, they need to imagine violence and to talk themselves into it (Apter 1997:2; Schroder and Schmidt 2001:9; Demmers 2012:132). Also, supporters of violence are the very individuals responsible for perpetuating community norms in favor of violence and facilitating violence by government and vigilantes. They provide the social approval that allows the perpetrators of violence to act without fear of stigma or other social sanction (Horowitz 2001:258, 266). For example, public legitimation of violence has facilitated militancy in Africa (McDoom 2013; Linke et al. 2015).

In the context of Russia and the North Caucasus, survey questions asking about support for retaliatory violence are probably less subject to social desirability bias than in other contexts. Given the recent Chechen wars under Yeltsin and Putin, the various atrocities committed by either side, mostly in Chechnya but also in Moscow and other parts of Russia, and the extreme popularity of the second war under Putin, support for retaliatory violence has been socially acceptable discussion in Russia, and signals sent by the authorities could be seen as imparting "a sense of empowerment and license" to harm (Beissinger 1998:402). Putin himself has used violent language in reference to Chechens, including his famous remark on Russian television in 1999, defended on numerous occasions afterward, that, if he caught Chechen terrorists, he would "waste them in the outhouse." Professional Russian politicians have seriously discussed the use of thermonuclear weapons in Chechnya, and members of the Russian public, including the supposedly progressive middle class and intelligentsia, have advocated killing Chechens (Evangelista 2002:74–75). If anything, interviewer debriefings suggest a social norm in North Ossetia such that the socially desirable response might be negative attitudes and aggressiveness toward Ingush and Chechens.

Given the permissiveness of this violent discourse, and given that support for violence is already likely to be higher than the commission of violence, a measure of support for retaliatory violence that asked about only mildly violent behavior might not sufficiently discriminate between the sincerely violent respondent and the flippant respondent. Instead, the analysis in this book relies heavily on a survey question about support for outright murder, assuming that affirmative responses would come from only those victims with the most extremely violent impulses. Here Kalyvas offers relevant guidance:

> Intentional and direct physical violence takes several forms, including pillage, robbery, vandalism, arson, forcible displacement, kidnapping, hostage

taking, detention, beating, torture, mutilation, rape, and desecration of dead bodies. Although I refer to various forms of violence, my primary focus is on violent death or homicide. As just stated, homicide does not exhaust the range of violence, but is an unambiguous form that can be measured more reliably than other forms (Spierenburg 1996:63; Buoye 1990:255), which is why it is used as the primary indicator of violence in quantitative studies (e.g., Poole 1995; Greer 1935). In addition, there is a general consensus that homicide crosses a line: It "is an irreversible, direct, immediate, and unambiguous method of annihilation" (Straus 2000:7); in this sense, death is "the absolute violence" (Sofsky 1998:53). (Kalyvas 2006:20)

Here, too, the focus is on violent death or homicide in order to separate truly violence-prone victims from victims who might offer pro-violence responses off the top of their head but were not sincerely committed to violence. Asking about such an "irreversible, direct, immediate, and unambiguous" act of murder seemed to hold the highest promise of generating valid responses.

We measure support for retaliatory violence with a question about whether it would be acceptable to kill the same number of Chechens as were killed in Beslan. Table 3.1 shows that 6 percent of victims fully approved and 8 percent somewhat approved of such a retaliatory act, numbers consistent with the low level of reported violence after the hostage taking but high enough to merit concern and analysis: one in every seven victims supported retaliatory murder. The vast majority of victims somewhat disapproved (34%) or completely disapproved (41%).

Table 3.1. Support for Retaliatory Violence among Beslan Victims

"I will now read some specific strategies that some people recommend to resolve problems in North Ossetia. For each one, please tell me whether you fully approve, somewhat approve, somewhat disapprove, or completely disapprove."

	Fully Approve	Somewhat Approve	Somewhat Disapprove	Completely Disapprove	Refused	Unsure
Kill the same number of Chechens as were killed in Beslan	65 (5.9)	88 (8.0)	371 (33.8)	446 (40.6)	83 (7.6)	45 (4.1)

N = 1,098; number of victims (%).

Contribution to Violence Measurement

This measurement approach represents an advance over preexisting studies of individual support for violence, which are plagued by challenges to construct validity, or the ability to measure what they purport to measure—in this case, support for violence. Often, the nature of the violence has been undefined, and respondents were asked whether they understood certain reasons for the use of the violence, whether they had sympathy for those reasons, whether the violence was justified, or whether they supported the use of violence (Tausch et al. 2011:136, 139). Given that respondents may have had multiple interpretations of the word "violence," some may have been evaluating their understanding, sympathy, perceived justifiability, or support for murder, while others may have been evaluating their attitudes toward bodily injury, property destruction, or far tamer forms of violence.

Also, questions about ambiguous acts of violence have sometimes conflated support for the violence with perceived efficacy—for example, *Rate your agreement on a 7-point scale from "do not agree at all" to "fully agree." Sometimes violent protest is the only means to wake up the public*—so that it is not clear what was being measured, support for the violence or a neutral assessment of whether violence is an effective strategy (Simon and Ruhs 2008:1357). Even when a violent action was specified, like "expanding the war on terror," and respondents were asked to express support, the ramifications of that support were left to respondent interpretation, and some might have been endorsing retaliatory murder, whereas others might have held an idealistic hope that a war could be expanded without casualties (Skitka et al. 2006). A study that was most specific about the violent action in question, suicide operations and the 2005 London bombings, asked only about the respondents' understanding of the perpetrators' reasoning or whether the actions were justified (Tausch et al. 2011:139). Justification questions are probably the closest to support questions and may be a reasonable choice if there are ethical concerns with asking about support. Still, construct validity would have been maximized by measuring support with a question that used the word "support" or "approve" in conjunction with the specified violence.

The question about retaliatory murder for the atrocities in the Beslan school is phrased in such a way as to resonate with victims in the context of their culture and traditions in the North Caucasus. Over 330 members of the Beslan community, half of them children, were killed in the hostage taking. A question about killing a single Ingush or Chechen in retaliation probably would not have been a very valid measure of retaliatory attitudes, because the single murder may have seemed insufficiently retaliatory, even by opponents of violence who were simply analyzing the appropriateness of the question. Violence in many situations and regions of the world is often characterized as tit-for-tat—having some equivalency in retaliation—and the characterization is fitting for the North Caucasus where violence has increasingly taken on a dispersed tit-for-tat pattern (O'Loughlin and Wittmer 2012:2388–2389). At the individual level, perpetrators of violence often "work on the basis of a scorecard mentality; they wish to even the score, if it is uneven" (Horowitz 2001:402). Thoughts of an-eye-for-an-eye or blood-for-blood, as one victim described above, are common in the Caucasus, where vengeance is considered a justifiable, honorable, and even necessary response to an assault or other offense against a family member. Given the large number of murdered victims in the school, and given the likely resonance of a tit-for-tat or eye-for-eye approach, victims were asked whether they would approve of "killing the same number of Chechens as were killed in Beslan." The assumption was that victims who approved were unambiguously distinct from victims who did not approve.

Limitations to the Measure of Individual Support for Retaliatory Violence

Three challenges to this measurement approach are: (1) the use of a single question instead of a battery of questions that could be combined into an index or composite score representing support for retaliatory violence, (2) the reference to Chechens rather than Ingush as the ethnic group to be targeted for killings, and (3) the passage of time from the hostage taking until the measurement of support for violence with the survey instrument, during which attitudes and behavior may have changed.

In terms of the single question, although multiple-item measures combined in an index or composite score are often preferable to single-item measures, the goal was to strike an ethical balance between measuring support for retaliatory violence and not re-traumatizing the victim respondents or putting hateful, negative ideas in their heads, so the use of too many measures, even about support for violence, was ill-advised. Perhaps more importantly, evidence shows that validity can sometimes be increased by a particularly relevant single measure (Rossiter 2002; Heath, Martin, and Spreckelsen 2009). The direct question about killing Chechens arguably is such a measure. Indeed, as discussed above, it represents a major contribution to the literature on individual support for violence, which often infers the advocacy of murder without ever having asked the question so bluntly.

The decision to refer to Chechens rather than Ingush as the reference group in the survey was driven mainly by pretest results, consultation with local experts, and anecdotal evidence that either choice would have produced similar results, because Ossetians have similar attitudes toward Chechens and Ingush.

The pretest included questions about a relative marrying an Ingush, bringing an Ingush home for dinner, and sending children to school where half the children were Ingush. These same questions were asked about Chechens, and the responses were virtually identical. The non-differentiating attitude of Ossetians toward Ingush and Chechens may be driven partly by racism—Muslims from the North Caucasus are often lumped together as "blacks," with no attempt to see their ethnic individuality—and partly by genuine similarities between the groups, because both are Muslim and have related ancestry, language, culture, and histories of Russian and Soviet oppression and because Ingush and Chechens were joined together from 1936 to 1992 in a single political unit, the Chechen-Ingush Autonomous Soviet Socialist Republic.

In terms of questions about retaliatory violence, the lack of differentiation between Ingush and Chechens may also be driven by the continued lack of clarity on the hostage taking. The ethnic identities of the hostage takers are still a matter of dispute, as are their motivations. Most analysts see some connection between the Beslan hostage taking and the war in Chechnya (Sokirianskaia 2007:47), and indeed the hostage takers are said to have demanded Russian troop withdrawal from Chechnya and recognition of Chechen independence, but Ossetians and Ingush have tensions of their own, especially due to the bloody 1992 territorial dispute over the Prigorodny District of North Ossetia, and one of the hostage-taker demands involved releasing 28–30 suspects detained for earlier rebel raids in Ingushetia. Therefore, a question asking about either Chechens or Ingush would be a reasonable measure of support for retaliatory violence.

The time lag between the hostage taking and the research represents a limitation of this study. It is possible, for example, that more victims approved of killing Chechens in September 2004 during the heat of the moment than during the 2007 survey. Had the survey been conducted during the fall of 2004, responses might have reflected this greater approval.[3] It is also possible that some victims acted violently during the time lag between the tragedy and the survey, and it is unclear whether such violent victims remained proponents of violence or regretted their behavior and became opponents of violence (Petersen 2002:5). The latter issue is probably not too troubling for this study, because it would apply at most to a very small minority of respondents, given that, according to all available evidence, very few victims actually committed retaliatory violence after the hostage taking.

More generally, even if the estimate of 14 percent of Beslan victims who approved of retaliatory violence might have varied by a few percentage points

---

[3] Importantly, the response rate would likely have been much lower in 2004 due to burials, mourning, convalescence, trauma, other life issues, and general fatigue from talking constantly to reporters and officials with little reprieve. A low response rate would have introduced other potential biases to the study.

during different post-violence time frames, the variation was likely small, given the evidence of peace-promoting mediators as early as September 4, and should not affect statistical analyses of the correlates of support for retaliatory violence. All variables in this study, including support for retaliatory violence, were measured at the same point in time. An argument that the timing of the survey influenced conclusions would require hypotheses for why the passage of time should influence the *relationships* between variables. The reverse hypothesis seems stronger: variables such as prejudice and political pride were probably as correlated with support for retaliatory violence in September 2004 as they were during the 2007 survey.

Measuring Support for Less Extreme Retaliatory Violence

As a further check on the single measure of support for retaliatory violence, five other questions were asked about support for less "absolute" forms of violence, including forbidding Ingush from entering North Ossetia, forcibly evicting Chechens from the Caucasus, raiding (committing military operations) in the hometowns of terrorists even if this led to the deaths of Ingush who were not terrorists, and holding the relatives of Chechen soldiers hostage (Table 3.2). These actions, all short of deliberate murder, were widely discussed in North Ossetia and Russia more generally. For example, the idea of holding terrorists' relatives hostage was a familiar enough idea for head of the parliamentary faction Rodina, Dmitry Rogozin, to issue a warning in November 2004:

> I am sure that it is necessary to create a permanent parliamentary commission for controlling the activity of the special forces. Because in a country where the prosecutors general suggest taking terrorists' relatives hostage, the special forces can cross that thin line beyond which work to prevent terrorism turns into a restriction of citizens' rights and interference in their personal lives. (Farniyev and Gorodetskaya 2004)

Some of these alternative forms of violence were not even seen as violence by many victims. For example, the female activist victims thirty-five years old or younger discussed whether retaliatory violence could resolve the Ingush-Ossetian conflict, and some women seemed to have a definition of violence that excluded forcible deportation. That is, violence was not associated in their minds with moving Russian citizens against their will from one part of the Russian Federation to another.

VIKA: Why violence? They simply have to be moved from the territory of our republic. Why are they registered here? Why do they live here?

Table 3.2. Support for Less Extreme Retaliatory Violence among Beslan Victims

"I will now read some specific strategies that some people recommend to resolve problems in North Ossetia. For each one, please tell me whether you fully approve, somewhat approve, somewhat disapprove, or completely disapprove."

	Fully Approve	Somewhat Approve	Somewhat Disapprove	Completely Disapprove	Refused	Unsure
Forbid Ingush from entering North Ossetia	632 (57.6)	206 (18.8)	88 (8.0)	56 (5.1)	73 (6.6)	43 (3.9)
Forcibly evict Chechens from the Caucasus	243 (22.1)	153 (13.9)	316 (28.8)	245 (22.3)	84 (7.7)	57 (5.2)
Raid the hometowns of terrorists* even if this leads to the deaths of Ingush who were not terrorists	219 (19.9)	166 (15.1)	317 (28.9)	245 (22.3)	76 (6.9)	75 (6.8)
Hold the relatives of Chechen soldiers hostage	118 (10.7)	183 (16.7)	418 (38.1)	262 (23.9)	83 (7.6)	34 (3.1)

* Russian: "commit military operations in towns where the terrorists are located"

"Given what happened in Beslan, some people support violent measures against Ingush, even against those who are not terrorists. Other people think that, despite the tragedy in Beslan, violent measures against Ingush who are not terrorists are unacceptable. Which view is closer to your own? Do you feel this way strongly or only somewhat?"

Support Violent Measures, Strongly	Support Violent Measures, Somewhat	Violent Measures Unacceptable, Somewhat	Violent Measures Unacceptable, Strongly	Refused	Unsure
191 (17.4)	126 (11.5)	319 (29.1)	155 (14.1)	99 (9.0)	208 (18.9)

$N = 1,098$; number of victims (%).

With questions about such wide and varying types of retaliatory violence, victims might seem split or ambivalent in their support for violence. In the aggregate, victims expressed approval of some forms of retaliation but not others. Most likely, the differences reflect the level of violence proposed. Victim approval decreased substantially as the suggested means of retaliation become more and more threatening to human life. The vast majority would forbid Ingush from entering North Ossetia (76.4 percent), but that majority drops to only a minority favoring forcible eviction of Chechens from the Caucasus (36 percent) and military operations in towns where terrorists are located even if this leads to the deaths of non-terrorist Ingush (35 percent).[4] The minority shrinks even further when it comes to supporting violent measures against non-terrorist Ingush (28.9 percent) and holding relatives of Chechen soldiers hostage (27.4 percent).

Even these small pro-violence minorities are large compared to the much smaller percentage of victims who affirmatively answered the most direct and unambiguous question about retaliatory murder. Indeed, holding relatives of Chechen soldiers hostage and supporting violent measures against non-terrorist Ingush was supported by roughly twice as many victims as the 13.9 percent who approved of killing the same number of Chechens as were killed in Beslan. Given that actual retaliatory violence after the hostage taking was lower than anticipated and that most news reports and focus group discussions suggest a nonviolence social norm among Beslan victims, later chapters focus analysis on trying to explain the small percentage of victims who supported violence when defined in the unambiguous and irreversible sense of retaliatory murder. What makes these victims distinct?

Conclusion: The Nonviolent Majority and Potentially Violent Minority

Approximately 6 percent of Beslan victims fully approved of a tit-for-tat retaliatory killing in order to resolve problems in North Ossetia, and another 8 percent somewhat approved. These numbers are low in the context of the abundant warnings about retaliatory violence after the hostage taking in School No. 1 and its devastating ending, but the survey results are consistent with the aggregate picture of post-violence nonviolence in Beslan. From a Chechen or Ingush perspective, it may be cold comfort to know that "only" one in every seven or eight Ossetians wanted you killed, and from a global peace perspective, that percentage should ideally shrink to zero. However, in the reality of conflicts in the North Caucasus and the emotional aftermath of the Beslan hostage taking, it is important to note that most Beslan victims did not support retaliatory violence.

There *was* support for retaliatory violence among victims, if retaliatory violence was defined more broadly to include keeping unwelcome ethnic rivals out of North Ossetia or bringing other harm to Ingush and Chechens, short of deliberate killing. Between a quarter and a third of victims approved of forcibly evicting Chechens from the Caucasus, committing military operations that could lead to the deaths of innocent Ingush, and even holding the relatives of Chechen soldiers

---

[4] Note again that any differences are not due to the referent ethnic group. Our pretest results demonstrated that Ossetian attitudes toward Ingush and Chechen are virtually interchangeable, despite the differences in these two groups and their historical relations with Ossetians.

THE SURPRISINGLY NONVIOLENT AFTERMATH   131

hostage, not to mention the majority who approved of forbidding Ingush from entering North Ossetia. These attitudes are an important component of the post-hostage taking—and likely pre-hostage taking—landscape in Beslan.

However, most victims drew the line at approving of outright murder. A question about support for intentionally deadly retaliation thus meaningfully distinguishes the minority of pro-violence Beslan victims from the rest. This minority was the likely pool from which truly violent retaliators or their supporters would have been drawn, had the post-violence context in Beslan been more encouraging of retaliation. The focus on "absolute violence" improves upon previous individual-level studies, which often seem to measure "support for violence" with questions that are ambiguous about the precise nature and extent of the violence in question or that really tap into sympathy with violent people, their causes and motivations, and not necessarily approval of their violent actions.

4

The Surprisingly Political Aftermath

Just as some grievances after the hostage taking seemed to justify retaliatory violence, other grievances seemed to justify political action. Nevertheless, observers of Beslan rarely predicted that political action would become the frequent, widespread, and protracted reaction that it did.

In the context of post-Soviet politics, such a prediction might have even seemed far-fetched. Russia at this point had become an electoral patronal system with elements of both democracy and autocracy (Hale 2010; Robertson 2011), open to some peaceful political participation but relatively intolerant of challenges to authority perceived as irreverent or threatening. The Russian mass public endured numerous hardships after Soviet collapse, yet political action against the regime of then-President Boris Yeltsin was relatively low (Javeline 2003a, 2003b) and continued to be low throughout the first term of the highly popular President Putin. By the time of the Beslan school hostage taking in 2004, Putin had just been re-elected with 71 percent of the vote and was managing political action by working closely with apolitical and pro-state civil society organizations while discouraging adversarial action such as protest. Anti-state activists had come to expect harassment and detention, and challenges from below were limited (Robertson 2009). The idea that some provincial, poor, Caucasian, and mostly female Russian citizens would take on the authorities did not fit with this portrait of a largely compliant public.

The scope of post-tragedy activism was staggering and began almost immediately after the crisis ended on September 3, 2004. In this chapter, the post-tragedy activism is described and grouped by moderate political action, extreme political action, and moderate and extreme legal action. The amount of victim participation is then quantified using the victim survey data. Appendix A chronicles these many political acts, as well as the major events that spurred the activism.

Moderate actions are those that are normatively acceptable to the larger polity, even if the actions drew large numbers of participants and provoked repercussions, whereas extreme actions such as blockades and hunger strikes seem to violate community norms. In reality, however, moderate and extreme action, or normative and non-normative action, may be in the eye of the beholder, and the categories more fluid than rigid. In Beslan, moderate action like filing an appeal was often tied to extreme action like a courtroom sit-in. The moderate

After Violence. Debra Javeline, Oxford University Press. © Oxford University Press 2023.
DOI: 10.1093/oso/9780197683347.003.0005

rally often included protesters holding inflammatory signs and led to a disruptive highway blockade.

The groupings therefore serve descriptive, not analytical purposes: they help illuminate the breadth and depth of victim activism. All actions, whether moderate or extreme, drew from the same finite pool of victims and their relatives, friends, neighbors, and coworkers in the small town of 36,000 residents. The hundreds or thousands of participants overlapping in so many of these actions represented unprecedented sustained mobilization.

Moderate Political Action

Moderate political actions taken by victims included rallies; meetings with political officials; public announcements, statements, letters, and petitions; watchdog functions over official investigators; and victim-led investigations. Although described separately below, most actions were interconnected and also were linked to the two nonprofit organizations, Mothers of Beslan and Voice of Beslan, that emerged after the hostage taking.

Organizations

Only days after the siege, Beslan victims were already organizing, with some on their way to becoming full-fledged political and civic activists. Although not officially registered at the time, the Committee of Beslan Mothers (or Mothers of Beslan) and the Committee of Beslan Teachers formed and were leading civic activities, such as aid distribution and informal grief counseling, and soon after, political activities (Page 2005c). The Committee of Beslan Teachers operated partly as a charity that collected information on victims to help potential donors decide how best to distribute funds. Some of the teachers, including Vice Principal Elena Kasumova-Ganiyeva, physical education teacher Marina Bitsoyeva, math teacher Fatima Ramonova, and kindergarten teacher Zhanna Kanukova, were largely responsible for establishing the website www.beslan.ru, which solicited donations for relatives and victims, even allowing donors to designate specific victims by name (Lavelle 2004). The website also posted lists of victims, including whether they were injured, killed, or missing; the names of donor individuals and organizations; offers made by groups to victims for rehabilitation vacations and material goods; and a news archive on events related to the aftermath of the siege, including updates on victims' health.

The teachers' efforts were painstaking. They went door to door to all students' houses, asking about the children and their parents. They studied the school's registers and spent enormous time gathering details on the listed victims and updating the website (Lavelle 2004; "Russia: Beslan Teachers" 2004). Although the news archive was not maintained over time and the committee itself stopped functioning, the website eventually became the official local government site for the town of Beslan, with a small "we remember" section that included numbers from the attack and photos of victims (Official Kremlin International News Broadcast 2005).

The Mothers of Beslan, however, continued and thrived. By February 25, 2005, the Mothers of Beslan was an officially registered public organization with a sophisticated website (http://www.materibeslana.com/rus/index.php). Their mission was to "unite all mothers of the Earth against war and terror," and their specific goals were to (1) preserve the memory of those who died in terrorist acts, (2) assist in an objective investigation of the terrorist act in Beslan, (3) provide social protection to those injured in terrorist acts, (4) promote anti-terrorist activity, (5) engage in charitable activities, and (6) assist with the construction of a memorial on the site of School No. 1. Less than one year after the attack, Mothers of Beslan had 150 members, a long list of political initiatives to their credit, and a detailed website chronicling their many activities. At the time of this writing, the organization boasted 200 members.

The Mothers of Beslan actively engaged with President Putin, starting as early as November 3, 2004, when they decided to write an appeal to him outlining the discussion from the day's town meeting with Deputy Prosecutor General Nikolai Shepel, as described in detail in the Introduction to this book, and explaining what they expected the president to do (Shavlokhova et al. 2004). By November 18, 2004, the Mothers of Beslan, headed by Susanna Dudiyeva, began collecting signatures from members of injured families in Beslan for an accusatory open letter to Putin and the parliamentary investigative commission, stating that "corruption, permissiveness, and incorrect national policy" were to blame for the hostage taking, that the republic's leaders were "absolutely unready for action in this critical situation," and that Putin should punish the corrupt officials responsible. They achieved 300 signatures by November 19 and sent the letter to major news organizations (Tokhsyrov 2004; "Beslan Locals" 2004; Sands 2004b). In February 2005, after some victims found the decaying remains of victims' bodies dumped in a local quarry, it was Dudiyeva who called local prosecutors, security officials, and journalists, forcing the head of the North Ossetian administration, Vladimir Khodov, to appear on local television, deny his involvement, and promise to find the culprit (Page 2005c).

More generally, for almost two decades since the hostage taking, activists from the Mothers of Beslan tenaciously pressed their case, and Dudiyeva and other representatives appeared in countless news reports and interviews whenever the political aftermath of the hostage taking was documented. Such tenacity led Russia's most famous pollster, Yuri Levada, to note that the Beslan victims were a rarity among the otherwise politically passive Russian public. Mothers of Beslan, he claimed, was the only truly influential protest organization in the country. Levada also noted that "the attitude [of the authorities] toward them is both frightened and spiteful. They seek to scare them [the Mothers] and to split their ranks" (Dunlop 2006:102), which in fact happened, although not necessarily due to official pressure.

By October 2005, some leaders of the Mothers of Beslan, including Ella Kesayeva and Emma Tagayeva, disagreed over strategy and tactics and left to form a new organization. Voice of Beslan emerged and was officially registered as a public organization on November 25, 2005, and began to maintain a website with contact information, press releases about its activities, and appeals for monetary support (www.golosbeslana.ru). The organization went on to become highly visible and tenacious in its own right and increasingly bold in its statements and actions. Although Mothers of Beslan and Voice of Beslan frequently worked toward the same ends, collaborated, and sponsored some of the same actions, it was often Voice of Beslan that adopted some of the most radical positions, such as opposing the death penalty for Kulayev for fear of losing him as evidence, charging President Putin with responsibility for the botched rescue effort and resulting deaths, and calling Putin "an accomplice of terrorism." Voice of Beslan also took some of the most radical actions, such as hunger striking and appealing to foreign governments and international organizations with statements that officials would dub "extremist" (Bobrova 2011).

Rallies

The school was stormed on Friday, September 3, 2004, and rallies began the very next day, including an hour-long rally in Beslan's central square, a rally lasting over six hours and involving more than three hundred people at the House of Culture, and a rally lasting over two hours and involving one hundred people near the school wreckage. Protesters were spurred by the failure of the North Ossetian Ministry of Internal Affairs to release the promised lists of dead and wounded hostages and escaped terrorists. They demanded the immediate disclosure of the names and the resignation of President Alexander Dzasokhov and Minister of Internal Affairs Kazbek Dzantiyev (Popova 2004; Sands 2004a).

This was only the beginning of rallies with political demands. On September 7, 2004, a furious crowd of about 1,500 people gathered near government headquarters in Vladikavkaz, with men speaking emotionally into microphones before people decided to disperse in favor of first burying the dead. The next day, however, the crowds returned. On September 8, by 11 a.m., 3,000–3,500 North

Ossetians gathered and listened for two hours to emotional speeches before about a thousand of them tried to enter a government building known as the "Gray House." One woman held a sign saying, "Corruption is the Accomplice of Terror." After about three hours, some protesters began throwing tins and bottles at the building's windows. The crowd demanded Dzasokhov, whose represent-atives in turn asked if they would meet with him in the Hall "October." Instead, the crowd sent ten envoys to present their demands to Dzasokhov. Coming out of the Gray House, one of these negotiators announced that Dzasokhov agreed to dismiss all of the power ministers. The crowd was not appeased, and Dzasokhov then promised to fire all of his ministers, the entire government, while the crowd continued to shout, "Resign, Resign." The protesters threatened to return in three days and take further action if nothing changed (Abdullaev and Voitova 2004; Farniyev 2004) (Image 4.1).

The month of October saw relatively few rallies, but outdoor activism picked up again in November after the angry town meeting at the House of Culture. Protesters at rallies on November 10 in Beslan and Vladikavkaz demanded

Image 4.1. Protesters in Vladikavkaz shouted at North Ossetian interior minister Kazbek Dzantiyev in the week after the hostage taking, demanding a meeting with North Ossetian president Alexander Dzasokhov.
MAXIM MARMUR/AFP via Getty Images.

Image 4.2. More than a hundred people rallied at the school wreckage on December 17, 2004, holding portraits of their children and posters reading. "We are waiting for a meeting with President Putin"; "Our children had the right to life"; and "Who will answer for our children."
STRINGER/AFP via Getty Images.

truthful investigation and disclosure of results, and they threatened to block the regional highway if their demands were not met before the new year ("Russia: Prosecutor" 2004; Smirnov 2005). The one hundred or so participants in a rally on December 17 at the school wreckage similarly demanded an "objective and transparent investigation of the tragedy" and referenced the November rally in Beslan, noting that the promise made by authorities in November for an honest and open investigation was not fulfilled (Olisayeva 2004; "Russia: Prosecutor" 2004) (Image 4.2). After a reprieve on rallies during which time victims turned to other forms of activism, approximately 1,000 people gathered on March 8, 2005, in Vladikavkaz's central Square of Liberty (Image 4.3). The rally was called "Mothers against Terror" and was organized by Mothers of Beslan who were threatened and repeatedly hindered in their efforts and harassed by officials (Farniyev and Kashin 2005).

Over time, rallies played a lesser role in victims' political strategy, but there were occasional large turnouts, especially on the anniversary of the hostage

Image 4.3. Over 1,000 people gathered in Vladikavkaz's central Square of Liberty on March 8, 2005, for a "Mothers against Terror" rally, organized by Mothers of Beslan, despite threats and harassment. Signs included " 'Terrorists' in power are more frightening than al-Qaeda"; "Imagine! Terrorists kill us, and the authorities humiliate us!"; "Parliament should be for the people!"; "Nord-Ost, Beslan, never again"; and "Mamsurov, who are you with?"
AFP via Getty Images.

taking, such as the rally held in Moscow on September 1, 2007, attended by a few hundred protesters who demanded that criminal charges be brought against members of the headquarters in Beslan responsible for the hostage release operation, along with FSB director Nikolai Patrushev and former Security Council secretary Vladimir Rushailo (Taratuta 2007). The victims also held many memorial events. For example, on May 29, 2007, they staged "1,000 nights without the children" at the Beslan memorial cemetery and lit candles on every grave ("Russian Court Amnesties" 2007). The organizers also asked all residents of North Ossetia to place burning candles in their windows in memory of the dead children. A statement issued by Mothers of Beslan read, "We want to show that the children that died in a burning gymnasium or were shot dead by militants are not forgotten, and to remind everyone about a terrible tragedy that should not happen again" ("Russia: Beslan Marks" 2007). For another example, on November 13, 2010, sixty victims rallied in the center of Vladikavkaz to demand that all terrorist attacks committed in North Ossetia be investigated and that a law on the status of terror victims be adopted ("Russia: Beslan Terror" 2010).

Meetings with Political Officials

Victims met with North Ossetian President Dzasokhov as early as September 14, 2004, less than two weeks after the crisis ended, and they met with various Federation Council members and Duma deputies who visited Beslan as part of the Torshin commission from September 20 to 27 ("Dzasokhov vstretilis" 2004; Abdullaev 2004). On November 3, more than a thousand Beslan residents gathered at Beslan's House of Culture for the volatile public meeting with political officials, including Shepel, the ex-mayor, and the senior investigator (Shavlokhova et al. 2004). Otherwise, victims generally had to fight for meetings with high-ranking officials.

Thanks to their blockade of the Rostov-Baku/Caucasus Federal Highway, described below, victims were granted a meeting with presidential envoy to the Southern Federal District Dmitry Kozak on February 1, 2005, in Rostov-on-Don. Kozak promised that the decision about Dzasokhov's resignation would be made by the Ossetian Parliament, which never happened and led victims to appeal to Putin with petitions and public statements (Bondarenko 2005; Smirnov 2005). On September 1, 2005, victims again succeeded in meeting with Kozak, this time because they intentionally disinvited Putin to the commemorative events for the first anniversary of the siege. Kozak came unannounced in Putin's place. Accompanied by newly appointed North Ossetian president Taimuraz Mamsurov, he talked to victims for two hours (Allenova 2005b). The victims pushed Kozak aggressively on many of the disputed issues and were frustrated with his response (Allenova 2005b).

Up to the point of the second Kozak meeting—that is, the entire year after the hostage taking—victims had been requesting to meet with their country's top leader, President Vladimir Putin. On September 2, 2005, that meeting finally occurred in the Moscow suburb of Novo-Ogaryevo. The timing of the meeting irked many victims because it coincided with commemorative events back in Beslan for the one-year anniversary of the hostage taking, making victims choose between attending memorial services or attending the long-awaited meeting where they could express their grievances to their president.

Still, some victims did choose to attend what became a three-hour meeting with the president, and while describing the meeting as frank and difficult, some of the participants left feeling optimistic that their grievances were heard and would be addressed (Ratiani 2005). The victims presented Putin with voluminous information about the attack and the official investigations, including their complaints about the delays, poor coordination, and lack of objectivity. They expressed their opinion that the currently separate criminal proceedings against Kulayev, North Ossetian police officers, Ingush police officers, and Ministry of

Emergency Situations personnel should be merged into a single case in order to maximize the possibility that the full truth would be revealed. Mothers of Beslan leader Susanna Dudiyeva explained that the president had incomplete information that victims tried to correct.

Dudiyeva and some other attendees believed Putin's assurances that he would "work for the truth" and "look into everything and take a very responsible approach to resolving these issues" and that they would see changes in the coming days (Ratiani 2005:3). After the meeting, Putin sent Deputy Prosecutor General Vladimir Kolesnikov and other prosecutors to Beslan "to conduct a comprehensive additional review of the entire body of information available about the case" (Gritchin 2005:1). Unfortunately, Kolesnikov's visit did not persuade victims that the investigation was any more objective than before. If anything, antagonisms between the official investigatory committee and local officials and individuals increased, and any initial optimism from the Putin meeting faded quickly on the ground back in Beslan (Berseneva 2005). In an attempt to make amends, Kolesnikov appeared on the scene of the school ruins on October 3, 2005, and met unexpectedly with some Mothers of Beslan and promised them that there would soon be "high profile trials" of "bungling bureaucrats" (Shavlokhova 2005b:1).

On May 23, 2006, victims again met with presidential envoy Kozak who promised to organize a meeting between them and Russian Prosecutor General Vladimir Ustinov, boss of Shepel and Kolesnikov. That meeting materialized in Moscow on June 1, 2006, but Ustinov himself canceled at the last minute. Instead, Shepel and Kolesnikov met with five male Beslan residents who had lost relatives in the school: Elbrus Tedtov, Mairbek Tuayev, Ruslan Tebiyev, Azamat Sabanov, and Valery Karlov. Sabanov had been part of the delegation that met with Putin in September, and all of these men had testified at the Kulayev trial and had given evidence that did not coincide with the official version of events. For example, Tedtov claimed that at least four terrorists fled from the scene and that he could name three of them. Kolesnikov promised the men that he would provide answers within a month, and, if necessary, arrange a meeting with Ustinov (Farniyev and Allenova 2006; Farniyev 2006a; "Zhiteli Beslan vstretyatsya" 2006).

It is unclear whether the June 1 meeting had any effect or follow-up. On June 2, 2006, Ustinov resigned (Farniyev 2006a). By early July 2006, Deputy Prosecutors General Shepel and Kolesnikov, along with four other deputies, were fired in a shake-up ordered by Ustinov's replacement, the new prosecutor general, Yuri Chaika. The Beslan case was only one minor factor in a larger overhaul to rid the Prosecutor's Office of incompetence and corruption and give Chaika a free hand in appointing his own people (Abdullaev and Yablokova 2006). At the time of their firing, Shepel and Kolesnikov had not fulfilled their promises to the five male Beslan victims.

On Chaika's orders, Shepel's successor, Ivan Sydoruk, then met with victims on August 9, 2006, and promised that the investigation would continue until at least January and that he would work more closely with them (Sageyeva 2006a; Tlisova 2006a; Sergeyev 2006). The meeting was held in Vladikavkaz for two hours and also attended by North Ossetian president Taimuraz Mamsurov, North Ossetian prosecutor Alexander Bigulov, and the Prosecutor's Office investigative team leader, Alexander Solzhenitsyn (Farniyev 2006b; "Poterpevshiye Beslana" 2006). Almost a year later, on July 13, 2007, members of Mothers of Beslan met again with Sydoruk and Kozak in Nalchik, the capital city of the neighboring Kabardino-Balkar Republic, with the officials stipulating that the more radical Voice of Beslan members be excluded from the meeting. By this point, the victims' complaints and the prosecutors' official responses were familiar, including explanations to the victims that their requested information was classified and that they should not expect officials to be held criminally liable, especially for failing to prevent a crime. All that seemed different was the substitution of Chaika and Sydoruk for Ustinov, Kolesnikov, and Shepel (Milashina 2007b).

To mark the third anniversary of the tragedy on September 1, 2007, a delegation led by Duma Speaker Boris Gryzlov visited Beslan and included Kozak, Duma security committee head Vladimir Vasilyev, and other officials. The delegation ignored the children's graves and portraits, as well as the photo exhibition of dead children hung along the walls of School No. 1 and the slogans written below: "The FSB and the Interior Ministry are responsible for terrorism," "There is no forgiveness for the authorities who allowed Beslan," and "President Putin! We demand an objective investigation into Beslan and punishment for all the guilty." The Mothers of Beslan peppered the officials with questions about the investigation and the amnesty for the police officers responsible for allowing the militants to get to Beslan. The officials again asked the victims to wait while experiments were conducted and investigations could be completed, and Kozak told Dudiyeva that if victims were unhappy with a court decision, they could appeal, at which point Dudiyeva raised the possibility of going to Strasbourg and joining the Voice of Beslan members who had already filed a complaint with the European Court of Human Rights (ECHR) (Allenova and Farniyev 2007).

Not all attempted meetings by victims transpired. On August 9, 2009, Voice of Beslan members tried to meet with Russian president Dmitry Medvedev in Vladikavkaz where he was visiting to commemorate the anniversary of the 2008 war in South Ossetia. The women went around the tightly cordoned off 58th Army headquarters and tried to deliver a letter to Medvedev requesting the meeting. Instead, they were asked for passports, threatened with the use of firearms, blocked from walking, had their posters torn and arms grabbed, and were left in tears as they drove out of Vladikavkaz. Once on the road, they were stopped by road police inspectors and the section chief for countering extremism who wrote down the details of the driver ("Beslan Victims' Mothers" 2009). Unsuccessful in handing the letter in person, in the next months and years, Voice of Beslan wrote letters to Medvedev requesting a meeting.

While these requested meetings never materialized, two victims, Elvira Tuayeva and Mziya Kokoity, had an impromptu meeting with Medvedev on February 22, 2011, when he arrived at the Beslan City of Angels cemetery unannounced. Medvedev offered condolences and promises but claimed he had not received any of the prior requests for a meeting (Granik and Farniyev 2011). On March 24, 2011, Susanna Dudiyeva and other victims met with Alexander Khloponin, presidential envoy to the newly created North Caucasus Federal District that President Medvedev carved out of the Southern Federal District. Victims gave Khloponin documents and videos, and Khloponin promised to fulfill their demand for a meeting with Medvedev in the next few months (Farniyev 2011a; Marzoyeva 2011). On May 5, 2011, Tuayeva and Dudiyeva flew to Moscow in anticipation of finally meeting with Medvedev in an official capacity. On their arrival, the women learned that the meeting was canceled, possibly because Medvedev's team feared a public relations failure for selectively inviting only the less radical victims from Mothers of Beslan who wouldn't criticize Medvedev's patron, former President Putin (Bobrova 2011; Odynova 2011). By June 1, 2011, Tuayeva and Dudiyeva, accompanied by North Ossetian president Mamsurov, finally met with Medvedev for two hours in Moscow, presented him with their frustrations and requests, and received promises in return to reconsider the investigation materials (Farniyev 2011b).

Victims succeeded more quickly in meeting with the head judge of North Ossetia's Supreme Court, Tamerlan Aguzarov, on May 3, 2007, after pulling an all-night sit-in at the court the night before ("Beslan Mothers Given" 2007; "Russian Court Overrules" 2007). Representatives of Mothers of Beslan and Voice of Beslan refused to leave following a reversal of a Vladikavkaz district court ruling to open criminal cases against officials who oversaw the hostage rescue operation, possibly including former North Ossetian president Dzasokhov and former FSB head Andreyev ("Beslan Mothers Given" 2007; "Beslan Mothers Stay" 2007). While victims were pleased with the one-hour meeting and the judge's promise for a fair hearing into possible misconduct of the officials, Ella Kesayeva commented, "We think there will always be a way to stall our pleas. We think the prosecutor's office will not open a criminal case because it would require summoning high-ranking officials to court as witnesses, and the prosecutor's office is acting in the interests of the Kremlin, which is not interested in digging into the Beslan tragedy" ("Beslan Mothers Stay" 2007).

Meetings were also held with internationally known high-profile individuals, including the Council of Europe's Parliamentary Assembly member Anne

Brasseur, UN High Commissioner for Human Rights Louise Arbour, and Council of Europe's Human Rights Commissioner Thomas Hammarberg (Revazova and Teziyeva 2005; "Voice of Beslan Members" 2006"; "Russian Rights" 2006).[1] Ella Kesayeva became especially active in the international arena through conference participation and networking with other activists on behalf of terror victims and human rights.[2] On September 1, 2010, a delegation of European Parliament members headed by Heidi Hautala ate at the home of Kesayeva who had invited them to Beslan (Milashina 2010).

Meetings between victims and political officials, high and low ranking, continued for years after the hostage taking. Notable among them was the September 28, 2009, meeting between three victims, Ella Kesayeva, Emilia Bzarova, and Svetlana Margiyeva, and deputy presidential envoy for the southern district, Nikolai Fedoryak. The victims complained that the replacement for inspector Solzhenitsyn, Alexei Khalin, was no more objective than his predecessor and that Khalin even attempted to intimidate them by claiming that their effort to protract the investigation was a criminal offense. Their request to have Khalin replaced was denied, but victims had more positive discussions with Fedoryak on the law on the status of victims of terror acts (Marzoyeva 2009).[3]

Public Announcements, Statements, Letters, and Petitions

Between meetings and rallies, and sometimes during them, victims issued public announcements and statements and sent public and private letters to officials, including multi-signatory petitions. The letters began as early as September 20, 2004, when hundreds were sent to members of Torshin's parliamentary commission who had arrived in Beslan (Abdullaev 2004). Then, provoked by the tense November 3 meeting with Shepel, on November 18, 2004, over three hundred Beslan residents signed an open letter to President Putin and the Torshin commission blaming "corruption, permissiveness, and incorrect national policy" for the siege and demanding punishment of negligent local officials (Sands 2004b; Tokhsyrov 2004). The text of the letter was written by Susanna Dudiyeva who headed a nascent organization then called "the Association of Mothers and Children of Beslan" and reflected a similar letter sent by activist victim Mairbek Tuayev two weeks before (Tokhsyrov 2004). The letter was sent to Putin, the parliamentary commission, and major Russian newspapers ("Beslan Locals" 2004).

---

[1] http://golosbeslana.ru/2007/hammarberg.htm, http://www.golosbeslana.ru/2011/tomas1
605.htm.
[2] http://www.golosbeslana.ru/obce.htm, http://www.golosbeslana.ru/2009/gavel.htm, http://www.golosbeslana.ru/2010/spain.htm.
[3] http://golosbeslana.ru/2009/fedoryak.htm.

The demands quickly became more specific and bolder. A few months later, on February 17, 2005, members of Mothers of Beslan traveled to Moscow with a petition to President Putin asking him to dismiss North Ossetian president Dzasokhov, and the Mothers held a news conference calling for Dzasokhov's resignation (Eckel 2005; Smirnov 2005). On July 5, 2005, they issued a statement expressing lack of confidence in federal investigator Konstantin Krivorotov and Deputy Prosecutor General Nikolai Shepel and demanding a change in leadership (Gritchin 2005). In late August 2005, just before the first anniversary of the siege, the Mothers of Beslan brazenly asked President Putin not to attend memorial events (Chivers 2005b; Page 2005b). On August 31, 2005, Beslan teachers sent a letter to Putin expressing frustration that neither Dzasokhov nor Mamsurov would meet with them and that the names of the guilty had not been revealed ("Beslan Teachers Send" 2005) (Image 4.4). On that same day, hundreds of victims from more than thirty families signed a letter to the international community expressing lost hope in hearing the truth and asking for asylum or immigration status from foreign governments (Mainville 2005d; Stephen 2005b). The following day was September 1, the first anniversary of the siege and the start of mourning, and Ella Kesayeva read the political asylum statement aloud to journalists in front of the school, possibly against the wishes of Susanna Dudiyeva, Julieta Basiyeva, and other Mothers of Beslan members who had planned to announce it differently (Allenova 2005b).

Image 4.4. Mothers of Beslan leader Susanna Dudiyeva addressed the press in Beslan on August 31, 2005.
KAZBEK BASAYEV/AFP via Getty Images.

This commitment to bold announcements was especially pronounced after Kesayeva and other victims split from Mothers of Beslan and founded Voice of Beslan. In November 2005, shortly after the organization's official registration, it posted a statement on its website addressed to "everyone sympathetic to Beslan's tragedy." Voice of Beslan argued that "none of the acts of terrorism that occurred during Putin's presidency has been investigated properly" and that Putin had become "the guarantor for terrorists" by not punishing senior officials who botched the Beslan rescue operation (Osadchuk 2008:2). On January 18, 2007, Voice of Beslan posted on their website an open letter signed by 101 victims asking the North Ossetian Parliament to invite Savelyev to present his report in the presence of the victims.[4] On March 6, 2007, Voice of Beslan published a statement demanding that Putin, Chaika, and Sydoruk press criminal charges against heads of security forces and other government officials who oversaw the hostage release operation, including former North Ossetian FSB director Andreyev, head of the special operations center of the Russian Federal Security Service Alexander Tikhonov, and Dzasokhov (Farniyev 2007a).

Voice of Beslan's boldness was not limited to statements about Beslan itself. The organization followed political developments on related issues and took adversarial positions. For example, when a new anti-terror law was proposed at the federal level, Voice of Beslan expressed opposition in an appeal published on March 13, 2006.

> We, mothers of the children killed in School No. 1, state that this law is a convenient way only for the authorities to commit absolute, unlimited, and anti-constitutional arbitrariness. The law, under which a hijacked plane can be shot down and hijacked ships can be destroyed if "all measures conditioned by the circumstances are exhausted," is simply amoral. The new law proposed by our authorities is a dog-eat-dog law. . . . While in Beslan there was a semblance of legality, under the new law citizens of the Russian Federation will be deprived of even a theoretical possibility of justice. We call on the Russian people to think about the dangers of the new law: this monstrous invention of lawmakers can ruin thousands of lives on absolutely legal grounds. ("Beslan Victims Denounce" 2006)

By mid-April 2006, Voice of Beslan was publicly condemning the possibility of allowing President Putin to seek a third term and released a statement entitled "Why prolong Putin's regime?" (Schreck 2006a).[5]

---

[4] The Parliament answered on February 1 that they would consider hearing Savelyev's report after the criminal investigation was complete. http://golosbeslana.ru/2007/odoklade.htm, http://golosbeslana.ru/2007/otvetparlamenta.htm.

[5] http://golosbeslana.ru/2006/3srok.htm.

Anniversaries of the hostage taking were occasions for open letters to high-ranking officials, since media attention was focused on Beslan for a few days each September. On the three-year anniversary of the hostage taking in 2007, victims sent appeals to President Putin, Mrs. Putin, and the government of Moscow. They asked Moscow officials whether they remembered about Beslan and, if they did, why they were spending grandiose sums on festivities in honor of Moscow's birthday. They asked Mrs. Putin why she never came to Beslan nor expressed sympathy for the mothers when she herself was a mother. They reserved their strongest words for the president, including complaints about Kolesnikov, who simply accused local officials, and Torshin, who would not admit that any officials could be guilty.

> Two years have passed since our meeting with you. Two years of useless waiting and illusions. We were hoping that we would bring home to you the truth, which perhaps you did not know fully. But over time, we realized how naïve we were. . . . [The main truth] is that our children were sacrificed to bureaucratic interests. (Allenova and Farniyev 2007:4)

Approaching the four-year anniversary of the siege, on August 25, 2008, Voice of Beslan posted the text of a letter addressed to Medvedev and other high-ranking officials with signatures from seventy-five victims, who appealed again for a thorough, objective investigation and the adoption of a law for the social protection of victims of terrorism.[6] On the five-year anniversary, September 1, 2009, Mothers of Beslan sent a statement to Medvedev pointing out that the investigation had been extended thirty-one times, with political considerations taking precedence over accountability of members of the operational headquarters. They also denounced the lack of ongoing medical and psychiatric care for child victims and the humiliating requirements for disability status extension (Farniyev 2009). Noting Medvedev's silence on the anniversary, Voice of Beslan sent him yet another letter on November 14, 2009, with yet another request to meet to discuss the investigation.[7] On the sixth anniversary, September 1, 2010, Voice of Beslan sent Medvedev another statement, this time with 864 signatures, requesting to meet with him and requesting help in adopting the law for victims of terrorist acts. "We are again and again appealing to you for help" ("Beslan Victims Demand" 2010).[8] They received a reply on December 1, 2010, that seemed to address Kesayeva personally rather than any organized group of

[6] http://www.golosbeslana.ru/zayav250808.htm.
[7] http://www.golosbeslana.ru/2009/medvedevu1411.htm.
[8] http://www.golosbeslana.ru/2010/medvedevu0109.htm.

victims. The reply explained that requests to meet the president must be sent to a different address.[9]

At times, the victims' letters, petitions, and public statements had less to do with their intended activities and more to do with defending themselves and their organizations. By 2008, Voice of Beslan was being accused of extremism by the Nazran Prosecutor's Office due to the organization's 2005 appeals to the European Parliament and United States, which included a description of Putin as an "accomplice of terrorism" who bore responsibility for the botched rescue and deaths of hostages (Osadchuk 2008).[10] In response, on January 11, 2008, the organization sent an appeal to Putin requesting that the extremist label be dropped and the pressure on the organization be ended ("Voice of Beslan NGO" 2008).[11] Two days later, the victim activists sent a telegram to the Nazran court saying they would not attend the trial without an independent expert appraisal of the text, which they did not believe to be extremist ("Russia: NGO Leader" 2008). Putin replied to the Voice of Beslan letter on January 30, saying that it was not within his power to end the extremism proceedings. A letter from Deputy Prosecutor General Sydoruk said the same ("Russian NGO Disappointed" 2008).

In the midst of this distraction came another: in mid-February 2008, Ella Kesayeva found herself the defendant against the Federal Court Marshals Service branch in Vladikavkaz, which claimed that she and other Voice of Beslan members assaulted seven officers and one judge. Kesayeva submitted her written denial, posted a statement to the Voice of Beslan website, and submitted a complaint with 230 signatures to the ECHR about pressure from the Russian security agencies ("Criminal Cases" 2008; Nowak 2008).[12] In mid-2009, parents of Beslan children attending a boarding school in Korallovo in Moscow Oblast were ordered to pay taxes on the "income in kind," as well as fines and penalties of between 20,000 and 70,000 rubles per family, money they did not have, especially because most were unemployed. Kesayeva and Voice of Beslan again found themselves distracted from their main mission by the need to write letters, request details about the taxes, and prepare to take on the authorities and defend the rights of these children to attend the school without paying taxes to do so (Kozenko and Farniyev 2009).[13]

Letter writing became strategic and relentless. On November 20, 2009, Voice of Beslan posted an appeal to Russia's Human Rights Commissioner Vladimir Lukin, asking him to ask Medvedev, the Federation Council, and the Duma to

[9] http://www.golosbeslana.ru/2010/obrap.htm.
[10] The precise wording was "We have every right to accuse the present Russian regime of aiding domestic and global terrorism" (http://golosbeslana.ru/2005/301105.htm).
[11] http://www.golosbeslana.ru/putinu110108.htm.
[12] http://www.golosbeslana.ru/zayav150208.htm.
[13] http://www.golosbeslana.ru/2009/nalogi.htm, http://www.golosbeslana.ru/2009/nalogi1.htm.

pass a law to protect victims of terrorist acts.[14] On November 27, 2009, Voice of Beslan petitioned Ella Pamfilova, chair of the Presidential Council for Civil Society and Human Rights, and Alexei Golovan, Russia's Children's Rights commissioner. They demanded to be invited to participate in discussions of the human rights situation in the North Caucasus and to be given assistance in keeping their legal status as an NGO.[15] On February 4, 2010, Voice of Beslan sent a letter signed by seventy-five victims to Alexander Khloponin, the president's envoy to the North Caucasian Federal District, asking to meet to discuss the status of the investigation and the proposed law for victims of terrorist acts.[16] On March 30, 2010, after bombings in the Moscow metro, Voice of Beslan released a statement appealing to the president, prime ministers, and ministers to fight terrorism more effectively.[17] When letters to Khloponin were sent back to Voice of Beslan with no answer, Kesayeva and others from Voice of Beslan sent a letter on February 25, 2011, to Sergei Naryshkin, head of the president's administration, asking for Khloponin's address and noting Medvedev's failure to reply to the letter signed by 864 Beslan residents about the law on the status of victims.[18] On March 25, 2011, Voice of Beslan again appealed to Medvedev, this time with a statement signed by 117 victims requesting that he comply with the constitution, meet with victims as promised, and improve investigations into terrorist acts and the ability to fight terrorism.[19]

Victim letters, appeals, and public announcements to the media were often combined with other forms of activism to ensure that complaints and demands were in written form and more likely to be received and recorded accurately. For example, any time there was a requested, planned, or actual meeting with the Russian president, letters, appeals, and other written documents were always involved, often with hundreds of signatories and published on websites and newspapers. In sum, victims had quickly and consistently learned to integrate multiple forms of political action to maximize attention to their activities and their cause. Activities were preceded by announcements and were followed by letters and statements, usually emphasizing the sizable number of victims who shared the specific grievances and demands. Victim activists had become professionalized.

[14] http://www.golosbeslana.ru/2009/lukinu.htm
[15] http://www.golosbeslana.ru/2009/panfilovoy.htm, http://www.golosbeslana.ru/2009/pan.htm, http://www.golosbeslana.ru/2009/panfilovoy.htm, http://www.golosbeslana.ru/2009/pan.htm.
[16] http://www.golosbeslana.ru/2010/hlopo.htm.
[17] http://www.golosbeslana.ru/2010/terakt.htm.
[18] http://www.golosbeslana.ru/2011/nary.htm.
[19] http://www.golosbeslana.ru/2011/obr2503.htm.

Watchdogs over Official Investigators

Victim activities went beyond simple calls for action. Victims acted as watchdogs over the official investigators, pushing them vigilantly. Watchdog activity came about less immediately than other activities and was born of frustration with the pace and integrity of officials and their investigations.

Deputy Prosecutor General Vladimir Kolesnikov was sent to Beslan by Putin after the president's September 2005 Moscow meeting with victims. Intended as a peacemaker, Kolesnikov swiftly angered the victims by endorsing the conclusions of the Shepel investigation and criticizing the independent investigation being conducted by the North Ossetian Parliament under the leadership of Stanislav Kesayev. On October 3, 2005, Kolesnikov unexpectedly showed up at the school ruins where victims routinely gathered, and those present pressed him with criticisms of the federal investigation, leading Kolesnikov to his promise of "high-profile trials" of "bungling bureaucrats" (Shavlokhova 2005b:1).

Ella Kesayeva was particularly aggressive in her questioning of Kolesnikov at the school wreckage.

KESAYEVA: Well, now are you convinced that flamethrowers were used at the school?

KOLESNIKOV: I did not deny this.

KESAYEVA: What do you mean? And on Friday, when you gave a press conference?

KOLESNIKOV: I did not talk about this.

WOMEN: Will Ustinov get rid of Shepel?

KOLESNIKOV: No. This [removing Shepel as prosecutor at the Kulayev trial] isn't his issue. This is a question decided by the Supreme Court. Everything is in its hands.

WOMEN: Why have you criticized the testimony of victims and witnesses?

KOLESNIKOV: No one thought that they were being subjected to criticism. It's simply that those who gave testimony say something completely different to me. So I call the person and say to him, "You will be prosecuted for perjury." And he starts to give what is necessary. He begins to think sensibly. . . . I want to work with you. Ordinary people are much more important to me than those bureaucrats who are sitting with you here. You will soon hear about the high-profile trials which will be held in your republic. (Shavlokhova 2005b:1)

Of course, it was not Kolesnikov who ended up working closely with victims, but dissident parliamentary investigator Yuri Savelyev. Savelyev's independent report had the support of both Mothers of Beslan and Voice of Beslan, partly because of Savelyev's credentials, rigorous investigation, and conclusions that dovetailed with the victims', but also because Savelyev treated the victims as partners in investigation. According to Mothers of Beslan leader Susanna Dudiyeva,

> All information from the report which does not tally with the official probe was gathered by us together. Savelyev worked with us throughout the two years. He worked with every hostage and witness individually; we spent a lot of time in the gym of the school. We support the people's deputy and his report and we will work to make it public. ("Beslan Victims Back" 2006)

The cooperative relationship with Savelyev contrasted with the distrustful and confrontational relationship between victims and other officials. Victims participated with these officials largely by trying to obstruct potentially deceptive "research" that they thought was designed to exonerate officials rather than learn the truth. For example, on August 17, 2006, when authorities and firefighters under the orders of new Deputy Prosecutor General Sydoruk tried to go to the burned out wreckage of the school to recreate the rescue operation, twelve victims stood in their way, saying that the action was part of a larger cover-up of the botched rescue operation ("Beslan Victims' Relatives" 2006; Sergeyev 2006).

Later that same month, however, cooperation improved when Ruslan Tebiyev, Elbrus Tedtov, and other male victim activists joined the prosecutor's office in conducting an investigative experiment. Beslan residents had long doubted that all thirty-two terrorists—let alone the much greater number they suspected were in the school—plus the overwhelming number of explosives, grenade launchers, machine guns, and assault rifles had traveled the extremely poor roads from Ingushetia to Beslan in a single GAZ-66 truck, as accused hostage taker Kulayev testified at his trial. Using an identical truck traveling on the same roads, they were not able to recreate the official version of events. The truck took forty minutes to drive only ten kilometers from Psedakh, the village in Ingushetia, to the administrative border between Ingushetia and North Ossetia, constantly getting stuck and finally sinking into a rut. They concluded that such a truck could have transported only a few of the terrorists and only some of the weapons (Borisov 2006a).

In the focus group of male activist victims over thirty-five years old, participants described this experiment in greater detail.

KAZBEK: We went for an investigation to the city, to Tarskoye. . . . They brought soldiers as thin as rakes and put them, thirty-two armed people, into the car. We tell them [the authorities] that there were more weapons there [in the Beslan school]. Where did they disappear? You know, I should have brought a photograph. I have a photo left. They [the soldiers in the car] sat like sardines in a can.

TOTRAZ: Any person, especially of such an age—everyone served in the army—understands what a GAZ-66 is. Everyone drove in this car. Thirty-two people [in such a vehicle], and they were supposed to be taken there [from Ingushetia to Beslan via the Ossetia border]. I can believe they can transport them a short distance [in such a car]: 500, even 1,000 meters for some purpose. But as for going from somewhere [far] . . . I don't know, they should have at least invented something else.

Indeed, the results of the experiment should not have surprised anyone, because investigators already knew the official capacity and limitations of a GAZ-66. At some point, lead investigator Alexander Solzhenitsyn had sent a formal request to the factory that makes the GAZ vehicles, and the factory confirmed that the GAZ-66 could not carry more than two tons, about 4,400 pounds and less than the weight of thirty-two men alone without weapons. In early July 2006, in an effort to ensure widespread public dissemination of evidence, male activist victim Valery Karlov then shared the information from the GAZ factory with the newspaper *Kommersant*. Karlov also shared his inference that all the terrorists, armaments, and explosives together weighed more than a single GAZ-66 could withstand and could not possibly have been transported in the single GAZ-66 from Ingushetia to North Ossetia. His inference resonated with most victims because, as the focus group members noted, the vehicle was extremely familiar to them, so familiar that it had a nickname, *shishiga* (Borisov 2006a). The new evidence that contradicted the official version of events shined light, according to victims, on all the many other errors evident in the official version (Farniyev 2006a).

Most of the victim watchdog activities were far less dramatic and involved constant oversight of officials and publicly taking them to task when they made missteps. For example, in mid-September, 2005, victims received the news that a new prosecutor, Igor Tkachov, would now lead the official investigation, and Ella Kesayeva from Mothers of Beslan publicly responded.

We are very curious as to why Tkachov in particular was put in charge of the investigation. . . . He investigated the case back at the beginning and only created chaos by making a lot of mistakes. We plan to speak with him. We no longer intend to let things run their own course the way we did with Shepel, whom we trusted at first. (Revazova and Teziyeva 2005)

When Deputy Speaker Stanislav Kesayev delivered his commission's oral report to the North Ossetian Parliament on November 29, 2005, victims pointed out the commission's unfounded backtracking from its initial conclusions. Kesayeva described the report as "evasive" and said that it "differs significantly from statements made earlier by members of the parliamentary commission" (Migalin 2005).

The tenacity of the victims became a constant thorn in the side of officials. After Torshin decided to delay the release of his commission's report, originally scheduled to be published on September 22, 2006, the report was leaked and published on the website www.pravdabeslana.ru. Torshin's report supported most of the conclusions of the official prosecutors' investigations: there were, it said, 32 militants; the use of heavy weapons at the school was justified and could not have caused casualties among the hostages; and operational headquarters took necessary measures to minimize consequences of the terrorist attack. Besides the terrorists, the culprits in the tragedy were identified as employees of Ingushetia's Ministry of Internal Affairs who did not detect a camp of militants on its territory and employees of North Ossetia's Ministry of Internal Affairs who failed to protect the administrative border between Ingushetia and North Ossetia and thus did not prevent the terrorists from entering Beslan (Allenova and Maksimov 2006). By releasing the Torshin findings right on the heels of the release of Savelyev's dissenting report, victims put the discrepancies squarely in the public eye and made Torshin feel obliged to conduct further investigations and prolong his commission's work (Allenova and Maksimov 2006).

Victims were equally relentless in following the work of the various prosecutors' offices and courts. For example, on January 5, 2008, Voice of Beslan called for the removal of Alexander Solzhenitsyn from his role as lead investigator. Ella Kesayeva told Ekho Moskvy radio that Voice of Beslan intended to file an appeal to the Prosecutor General's Office against Solzhenitsyn, who they thought was impeding the investigation by claiming progress when nothing was being done ("Russian NGO Calls" 2008). For another example, after the capture of terrorist leader Ali Taziyev who was rumored to have played a role in organizing the attack on the school, on December 22, 2010, Voice of Beslan sent a statement to investigation departments and the adviser to Justice A. N. Khalina asking to question Taziyev (also known as Magomed Yevloyev or Emir Magas) about his involvement in Beslan and asking for Taziyev's photo to verify with victims whether he was in the school (Latynina 2010; Elder 2010; "Captured Ingush" 2013).[20]

Victim-Led Investigations

Victims did not wait around to be asked to join official investigations. Where possible, they became investigators themselves. In 2005, members of the

---

[20] http://www.golosbeslana.ru/2010/hodat2212.htm.

Mothers of Beslan found and submitted to the court during Kulayev's trial several launch tubes from *Shmel* flamethrowers, which they contended were used in the assault. Their evidence was supported by leader of the North Ossetian parliamentary investigation Stanislav Kesayev who said that traces of napalm were found during the medical investigations and would have had to come from incendiary napalm grenades launched by the flamethrowers. This evidence forced Deputy Prosecutor General Shepel to admit in court that flamethrowers had been used in the siege, something he previously denied. The Mothers also forced Russian authorities to admit that two T-72 tanks fired several cannon rounds into the school during the battle on September 3, although authorities insisted that they did not shoot at the gym where hostages were held (Weir 2005a).

Along the way, victim investigators had help from as yet undisclosed sources. In July 2007, the Mothers of Beslan received a video by mail from an anonymous source. The video showed army officers Gagloyev and Nabiyev concluding that the initial explosions were triggered by weapons fired from outside the school building, meaning the shooter was someone other than the terrorists. The video also showed children running from the building before two loud blasts were heard from outside the gymnasium, again implicating a non-terrorist as the source. The Mothers of Beslan, having been told for three years that this video was lost, promptly released it on their website (Tskhurbayev 2007b; Dunlop 2009:5).

Again, while such assistance was welcome, victims did not wait around for it. They actively solicited help, including from abroad. For example, on November 30, 2005, Voice of Beslan issued the statement, declared more than two years later to be extremist, asking leaders from the United States and the European Union to help investigate the attack.[21] The statement became known for labeling Putin "a guarantor of criminals" and an accomplice of terrorism, but it was mainly a call for help. The organization requested that U.S. leaders publish satellite photographs of the school made during the siege and that those photographs be presented to local citizens at Kulayev's trial. They also requested that journalists or anyone else with information about the attack or video footage come forward with it for the investigation. Addressing the European Union and European Parliament whose members had already signaled the possibility of holding an international investigation, the statement said, "We cannot demand, but we ask for support for our efforts to investigate the terrible crime that took the lives of our loved ones" ("Beslan Mothers Ask" 2005).

[21] http://golosbeslana.ru/2005/301105.htm.

Extreme Political Action

When moderate action failed to produce results, victims resorted to more extreme action. The label "extreme" probably reflects official perspectives and community norms prior to the hostage taking, for these actions garnered much support and, given the new circumstances of unresponsive government, seemed normatively acceptable to the Beslan community. Importantly, the high turnout makes any attempted distinction of criminal or disruptive activists from peaceful protesters somewhat artificial. Those most engaged in moderate action were also most engaged in extreme action.

Blockade

By January 2005, Dzasokhov and the North Ossetian republican leadership still had not delivered on their November promises for quicker and more transparent disclosure of information. Members of the Torshin commission had visited Beslan, but victims were dissatisfied with their official investigation, and some victims did not want Torshin to return to town. Deputy Prosecutors General Vladimir Kolesnikov and Nikolai Shepel held a brief press conference on January 19, 2005, to report on the progress of their official investigation, but the prosecutors refused to address the question of which political leaders were to blame for the tragedy. Instead, they said that the attack remained under investigation, and the results would be available to victims in a month (Tokhsyrov 2005). The inattention to victim grievances prompted some victims to move beyond rallying and to choose more creative forms of protest that would be difficult for officials to downplay or ignore.

At 11 a.m. on January 20, about fifty victims started to gather in what would become a blockade of the Rostov-Baku/Caucasus Federal Highway. The protesters demanded the resignation of North Ossetia's still-president Dzasokhov and criminal prosecution against North Ossetia's former Federal Security Service director Valery Andreyev and the former minister of Internal Affairs, Kazbek Dzantiyev. Protesters carried signs saying, "Why were our children killed?"; "We demand an international investigation"; and "Dzasokhov is a puppet of Moscow." They initially intended to march eighteen kilometers from Beslan to a rally at the house of the republican government in Vladikavkaz, but when the procession swelled in size to two hundred and reached the Caucasus Highway, a major thoroughfare for the region, the blockade was born (Tokhsyrov 2005; Shapovalov 2005).

Kolesknikov arrived at the highway with North Ossetia's prosecutor Alexander Bigulov and was greeted with a banner saying "Put Andreyev on trial!" The prosecutors asked the protesters to unblock the highway, and the victim protesters replied with complaints about the investigation, such as the underreported number of terrorists, misinformation about weapons at the school before the siege, and the misidentification of deceased hostages. People in the crowd shouted, "What's left to talk about with him?" and "The truth still won't be told!" (Tokhsyrov 2005:3).

By the evening of January 20, some four hundred people were blocking the highway, lighting bonfires to keep warm and eating sandwiches and drinking tea brought by supporters. They threatened to stay until Dzasokhov resigned the presidency and the borders with Ingushetia were secured (Tokhsyrov 2005). The blockaders built tents across the highway (Chivers 2005a), and on the morning of January 21, they managed to get Dsazokhov to address them in person, although without addressing their demands (Shapovalov 2005).

Only on day three of the blockade did it finally come to an end. Dmitry Kozak, presidential envoy to the Southern Federal District, called the blockade leaders by telephone and agreed to meet with them in person on February 1, if the protesters agreed to legal approaches to addressing their grievances, including allowing Russian law to determine the question of Dzasokhov's resignation, as Dzasokhov himself had said the day before (Shapovalov 2005; Bondarenko 2005).

Hunger Strikes, Pickets, and Sign Postings

Beslan victims occasionally ventured other dramatic acts of protest, such as hunger strikes and pickets at critical moments when victims felt that insults were being added to their injuries. One such moment was on June 7, 2005, when it became known that Dzasokhov's May 31 resignation was not a punishment and that he would go on to become a Federation Council member, while Taimuraz Mamsurov, former head of Parliament and Dzasokhov's "double," according to one victim, would replace Dzasokhov. Learning the news, approximately twenty members of the Mothers of Beslan began a picket in the center of Vladikavkaz to protest. A day later, nine of the women decided to stage a three-day hunger strike, saying they would sit in front of the Parliament building like their children sat, without water and food (Migalin and Samarina 2005; Tskhurbayev 2005).

The hunger strike was used again on February 9, 2006, when Judge Aguzarov signaled that oral closing arguments in the Kulayev trial would begin. Voice of Beslan demanded that the Court continue questioning witnesses, especially former Ingushetia president Aushev who had been in the school, helped release some hostages, and had agreed to come to court in a week. Their demand denied, Ella Kesayeva and six other members of Voice of Beslan —Alma Khamitseva, Emilia Bzarova, Svetlana Margiyeva, Marina Melikova, Zalina Dziova, and Emma Tagayeva-Betrozova—then launched a hunger strike (Karacheva 2006a).

The women repeated their demand for the "interrogation of all witnesses who may shed light on the circumstances of the terror attack" ("Beslan Women Continue" 2006). Kesayeva conveyed the victims' dismay that "the true culprits have not been named" (Myers 2006a).

> We never expected the presentation of arguments to begin as early as yesterday. We weren't warned about it. I barely had a chance to read my petitions requesting that Aushev be called as a witness. The court turned them down, because Shepel stood up and said that Aushev didn't have to be heard, that he had nothing to do with Kulayev's case. Shepel said there was enough evidence for sentence to be passed on Kulayev. It appears that he [Shepel] doesn't need any more witnesses. I filed a petition stating that we don't trust the prosecution or Prosecutor Shepel. We don't think he was objective in his investigation of the case. And we think that a new, independent investigation should be conducted with the participation of new, independent experts. (Karacheva 2006a:1; also "Zhenshchiny" 2006)

Although victim Zalina Dziova and her daughter got sick on the fourth day of the hunger strike, causing Dziova to withdraw, the other six Voice of Beslan members, led by Kesayeva, continued their hunger strike for eleven days, losing 5–8 kilograms each and ending in hospitalization for Bzarova and Margiyeva and very high blood pressure for Tagayeva. Tagayeva received emergency assistance only after twenty-five minutes had passed. The hospital was a mere five-minute walk from Voice of Beslan's headquarters (Milashina 2006b, 2006c).

The hunger strike was not widely covered in North Ossetia, with some newspaper editors directly telling their staff not to cover it. A representative of the presidential envoy Kozak, Balikoyev, met briefly with the hunger strikers, so briefly as not to attract attention to the protest. The telephone was turned off to the office building where the hunger strike was taking place and reconnected only on the seventh day. Eviction was threatened. The women met this intimidation by threatening to carry on the strike in front of President Mamsurov's house in Beslan. Mothers of Beslan did not support the Voice of Beslan hunger strikers, preferring instead to concentrate their efforts on restoring the death penalty, so they could see Kulayev put to death (Milashina 2006b). After eleven days, the hunger strikers were convinced by North Ossetian parliamentary deputies that further protest was pointless, and they decide "to halt the strike, regain strength, and continue fighting" ("Beslan Women End" 2006).

Voice of Beslan resorted to a hunger strike again on December 19, 2007, when North Ossetia's Supreme Court ordered the group to disband. Ella Kesayeva and three other victim activists began their hunger strike simultaneously with a picket outside of North Ossetia's Supreme Court ("Court Orders" 2007; Farniyev

2007f). They ended their strike and formally appealed the decision on December 21, 2007, to no avail. Voice of Beslan ceased to exist in its original form as of February 7, 2008, while its members soldiered on and took the new name, "All-Russian Public Organization of Victims of Terrorist Acts, Voice of Beslan," under which they continue to operate today (Litvinovich 2008). The organization's old name continued to exist in the official registry but was inactive and, by October 2009, abolished.

Hunger strikes were notable but rare during the political aftermath of Beslan. Pickets were more frequent. For example, on October 20, 2005, Deputy Prosecutor General Vladimir Kolesnikov told a news conference that the fire in Beslan School No. 1 did not result from the use of flamethrowers, so there were no grounds to prosecute those who used them. Angered over the comment and the implication that no one was responsible for the children's death in the fire, on October 27, 2005, eight women who lost children in Beslan or lost relatives in the Dubrovka theater picketed the Prosecutor General's office in Moscow. Their signs said, "Let international experts probe Beslan!"; "Citizens of Russia, any of you could find himself in our place, think of it!"; and "Bring Putin, Patrushev, Nurgaliyev to account for the lives of our children!" (referring to the president, FSB director, and Internal Affairs minister). The protesters were arrested and taken to the Tverskoye police station ("Beslan Activists Arrested" 2005).

Similar pickets with different but related signs were a regular feature of the Beslan activists' repertoire. Other examples include the aforementioned 2007 protest in front of the Vladikavkaz Prosecutor's Office against the amnesty decision for the Beslan police officers. The very aggressive messaging included "Terrorists' helpers are terrorists themselves" and "The FSB and Ministry of Internal Affairs are responsible for the act of terror." Messaging at an October 31, 2010, picket in Vladikavakaz included the aforementioned "Mr. Putin, we demand a law on terrorist victims and not your charitable handouts!" as well as "We demand an investigation of the terrorist attacks in Ossetia."[22] Signs at a March 31, 2011, picket in Vladikavkaz also read, "we demand the adoption of a law on the status of terror victims"; "we require an investigation into terrorist acts"; and "we demand security."[23] The latter picket was followed by police harassment, with officers telling victims who had already ended their picket that they had violated an unspecified law and would have to come to the police station. Nothing further came of the incident.

Much more came from the wooden road sign erected by members of Voice of Beslan and Mothers of Beslan together in late November 2007, in advance of Russian elections and with the words "*Kurs Putina* [Putin's course]" and an arrow

[22] http://www.golosbeslana.ru/2010/piket_zakon.htm.
[23] http://www.golosbeslana.ru/2011/3103.htm.

Image 4.5. Voice of Beslan members held a sign saying *Kurs Putina* [Putin' course] with an arrow pointing to the destroyed school. Court charges against leader Ella Kesayeva followed, one of several attempts by officials to harass and intimidate victims, their attorney, and journalists.
Voice of Beslan, http://golosbeslana.ru/2007/protivkursa.htm.

pointing to the destroyed school (Image 4.5).[24] Ella Kesayeva was then charged with arbitrary behavior and improper use of roadside areas, but Judge Besolov indefinitely deferred the hearing on the charges after more than fifty people arrived at the Beslan district court to support her ("Russia: NGO Leader" 2008). The sign was perhaps one of the most brazen and risky challenges by victims to authority.

Moderate and Extreme Legal Action

Legal actions by victims were largely intended and implemented as moderate measures. Victims worked within the institutionalized judicial process to try to achieve truthful investigations and government accountability. However, when that process seemed, by design, to deflect and stifle more than clarify and bring

---

[24] See http://golosbeslana.ru/2007/protivkursa.htm for photos.

justice, victims turned to extreme action to disrupt the process. In almost every case, the moderate and extreme actions were intertwined, and the participants much the same.

Kulayev Trial

The event drawing perhaps the highest participation from Beslan victims after the siege was the trial of the only hostage taker to be captured alive, twenty-four-year-old Chechen carpenter and father of two, Nur-Pasha Kulayev, who faced eight charges, including terrorism, murder, and hostage taking. Starting in May 2005, victims packed the courtroom, protested outside the courthouse, and in general let their thoughts about the trial, the hostage taking, and the aftermath be known. Inside the courtroom, they screamed at the chief justice of North Ossetia's Supreme Court, Judge Tamerlan Aguzarov, for officials to be held responsible and put on trial. Outside the courtroom, they held signs such as "Government corruption feeds terrorism" ("Courtroom Chaos" 2005; "Give us a Gun" 2005). Attending the Kulayev trial required effective organizing and financing. Two mornings a week when the trial was in session, a bus carried members of Mothers of Beslan to the courthouse in Vladikavkaz, twenty minutes away (Cullison 2005).

On August 23, 2005, fifteen mothers of children who died in the siege staged a sit-in for twenty-eight hours in the Vladikavkaz court during Kulayev's trial. They insisted on meeting with Shepel and demanded that Putin and other top officials be held responsible (Mainville 2005a). Supporters, many of whom were victims or victims' relatives, gathered outside the courthouse and passed food and water to the women. Victim Ella Petrozova spoke by phone from the courtroom to *AFP* news agency. "We believe that witness testimony before the court is being ignored and that the real guilty parties are not at the defense table. What about President Putin himself? Where was he during those three days when our children were held hostage?" ("Beslan Mothers Lash" 2005). Victim Marina Pak relayed the same message by phone to *Radio Free Europe/Radio Liberty*. "We have grievances against the investigation. We demand an objective investigation. This means no official should bear responsibility for another. Nobody should be able to hide behind anyone else's back" (Bigg 2005). Standing on the steps of the Vladikavkaz courthouse, Susanna Dudiyeva explained, "We are demanding that all of those whose actions or failure to act led to this tragedy be held responsible. Since legal measures have failed us, we have to take extreme measures" (Mainville 2005c:A04).

Victims wore their watchdog hats during the trial. They were aware that the trial was about much more than Kulayev; it was quite possibly their singular fact-finding opportunity, and they tried to maximize its usefulness in that capacity. On September 29, 2005, in a court session during Kulayev's trial, a group of victims and their attorney, Taimuraz Chedzhemov, demanded that the judge replace Shepel whom they accused of pre-planning the trial. Dudiyeva said, "He fills up an already made skeleton with the witnesses' evidence." Chedzhemov also charged that Shepel failed to investigate the siege and its consequences properly by refusing to question crucial senior officials. A few days later, on October 4, Aguzarov refused their requests, saying that any mistakes Shepel made were during the preliminary investigation ("Beslan Court Rejects" 2005).

When North Ossetian FSB head Valery Andreyev took the stand in mid-December 2005, victims were again unrelenting. Shouting "tell the truth!" or weeping, they accused Andreyev of lying when he refused to say why authorities had initially released a hostage count much lower than the actual number. When North Ossetian Emergency Situations Minister Boris Dzgoyev took the stand and claimed that the fire occurred more than one and a half hours after the first explosions and after all hostages were already dead, one man stood up, accused Dzgoyev of lying, and said, "These are false statements. We ran into the gym and carried children away from there. They were burning alive" (Voitova 2005).

On December 27, 2005, when the federal prosecutors led by Shepel made their findings known, victims again used the Kulayev trial to draw attention to their dissatisfaction. Thirty members of Mothers of Beslan and Voice of Beslan protested the prosecutors' report by refusing to leave the courtroom and demanding that the judge summon three deputy directors of the FSB to testify and hopefully contradict the official version of events (Saradzhyan 2005). Ella Kesayeva cautioned that, if the truth were not established during Kulayev's trial, the prosecutors would drag their feet and let the Beslan case fade without resolution. "This is a ploy. When the time comes, they will close the case and no one will bear any guilt" (Saradzhyan 2005).

North Ossetian president Dzasokhov's testimony finally came on Thursday, January 12, 2006. Victims began the session by trying to pull Dzasokhov's bodyguards from the front seats of the courtroom, yelling that their children had needed security. Dzasokhov's four-hour testimony then commenced, and when he insisted that, although there were warnings of possible attacks in North Ossetia, "There was no information that would indicate exactly that a school would be seized," victims shouted, "Shame on you!" Women in the courtroom blamed Dzasokhov for not exchanging himself for children at the school and pinned a handwritten poster to the courtroom wall saying, "Dzasokhov, you are a coward." One woman held a sign accusing Dzasokhov and other regional officials of having "sold our children," and another stood up from a bench and asked, "How am I supposed to live on if my eight-year-old son was killed?" Dzasokhov explained his position on several counts, including the fact that security officers said they would arrest him if he went to the school. His explanations were met with weeping and yelling victims (Voitova 2006a).

Less than two weeks later, on January 24, Judge Aguzarov announced that all information had been gathered and so the trial would end shortly. Victims disagreed, saying, as they had for months, that they wanted more witnesses to be brought before the court, especially high-ranking federal officials. The victims refused to leave the Supreme Court building in Vladikavkaz and would not let the prosecutors go ("Beslan Protesters" 2006). Voice of Beslan also submitted a petition to the Supreme Court of North Ossetia-Alania to disqualify Aguzarov in Kulayev's trial. They accused Aguzarov of "clear bad faith and lack of impartiality," especially in acting as a defender of Dzasokhov; taking a pro-government position more generally and trying to please the authorities and protect officials; and not giving victims the appropriate opportunity required by law to get acquainted with the reports from the court sessions.[25]

On February 9, 2006, after questioning the last witness, Dr. Leonid Roshal, who had attempted to negotiate with the terrorists, Judge Aguzarov signaled that oral closing arguments in the Kulayev trial should begin. Voice of Beslan's Ella Kesayeva demanded that the court continue the process of questioning witnesses, since not all witnesses had been called, and some, like former Ingushetia president Ruslan Aushev, agreed to come to court in a mere week, February 16. Aguzarov denied Kesayeva's request (Karacheva 2006a).

Kulayev was declared guilty on all counts on May 16, 2006, and thanks to a moratorium on the death penalty in Russia, he was sentenced to life in prison. In response, the Voice of Beslan kept their grievances and demands in the news, pointing out that the end of the trial should not obscure the ongoing need to hold officials accountable for their failures. According to Kesayeva, "We know the terrorists came to kill, and they should be punished, but those who were supposed to save the hostages are also guilty. They are criminally liable for the death of innocent people. It's not negligence on the part of the authorities, it's murder" (Finn 2006).

On May 24, 2006, in anticipation of the conclusion of the lengthy reading of Kulayev's verdict, twenty women held signs outside the courtroom in Vladikavkaz saying, "President Putin! We demand an objective investigation and the conviction of all the guilty!" and "No forgiveness for the officials who let Beslan happen" ("Beslan Mothers Protest" 2006). When the sentencing ended on May 26, victims, many dressed in black, carried banners reading "There is no forgiveness of the authorities who let Beslan happen" ("Beslan Kidnapper" 2006). By May 31, Voice of Beslan filed a preliminary appeal to the Russian Supreme Court through the Supreme Court in North Ossetia, claiming that the court approached

[25] www.golosbeslana.ru/2006/aguzarov.

the Kulayev case in a one-sided manner and ignored conflicting evidence about the attack and the government response, especially victims' testimonies about the actions of the authorities. The appeal was designed not to exonerate Kulayev but to force more information to be revealed and to encourage further investigation ("Russia: Beslan Victims" 2006; "Victims File Appeal" 2006).

The Voice of Beslan did not believe their appeal would be effective in the Russian Supreme Court; they were already prepared to take the matter further and apply to the Russian Constitutional Court and then to the ECHR in Strasbourg. According to Ella Kesayeva, "All our actions are now directed towards the European Court. We will go through all the procedures in Russia, and put up with all the refusals which we have received and will continue to receive in the future, and we are certain that these will be refusals, and then we will go to the European Court of Human Rights. We have all the proof we need of our leaders' guilt. I think that Strasbourg will give us the answer which will suit us" ("Russia: Beslan Victims" 2006).[26]

On September 1, 2006, Voice of Beslan filed an extended appeal with the Supreme Court, reiterating their claim that the case ignored necessary details about the siege and that their right to life, guaranteed under Article 2 of the European Convention on Human Rights, was broken during and after the attack.[27] The detail in the 200-page appeal was painstaking. It represented countless hours of time and intellectual effort in piecing together evidence and crafting argument. The main points concerned the court's refusal to establish the circumstances that enabled the capture of the school; who commanded the operational headquarters; the origin of the earliest explosions; the true causes of the deaths of hostages; and that heavy hardware was used, despite the exhaustive witness testimony to this effect ("Beslan Committee Ready" 2006). A press release about the appeal ends harshly. "If the President of the Russian Federation cannot guarantee us our rights, he must go. If he remains and the results of the Prosecutor General's Office satisfy him, it means he is covering for criminals."[28]

On December 26, 2006, Russia's Supreme Court upheld Kulayev's life sentence, denying the appeal of the Beslan victims who had asked for a retrial. Only four of the thirty victims who signed the complaint were in court because many of the victims, as well as their lawyer, Taimuraz Chedzhemov, did not think their presence would accomplish anything. Still, many other victims addressed the court and argued that the investigation had been one-sided and that the trial served to pin all the blame for the tragedy on one person, Kulayev, while not properly investigating the hostages' deaths (Allenova 2006).

---

[26] The text of Voice of Beslan's appeal can be found at http://golosbeslana.ru/2006/kass.htm.
[27] The text of the appeal can be found at http://golosbeslana.ru/2006/kassall.htm and the press release at http://golosbeslana.ru/2006/relis.010906.htm.
[28] http://golosbeslana.ru/2006/relis010906.htm

Nur-Pasha Kulayev did not attend his Supreme Court hearing on December 26 for the appeal against his sentence, arousing suspicion among victims that the authorities may have had him killed. While some victims would have welcomed such news, many victims, especially Voice of Beslan activists, saw Kulayev as evidence not to be destroyed, at least not before the full and thorough investigation they had been demanding. On January 4–5, 2007, Ella Kesayeva told Ekho Moskvy radio that the victims intended to submit an inquiry to relevant government agencies demanding proof that Kulayev was still alive and asking for a meeting with him ("Russian Campaign Group" 2007).

Trial of Beslan Police Officers

From their earliest experiences with the Kulayev trial, victims learned their way around a courthouse and became vigilant about overseeing related judicial proceedings. On January 13, 2006, a hearing began for the trial of three Beslan police officers who had been senior members of the Pravoberezhny District's Interior Ministry branch. Former head of the branch Miroslav Aydarov, his deputy Taimuraz Martazov, and chief of staff Guram Dryayev were accused of negligence in allowing terrorists to cross through a checkpoint, which presumably enabled the Beslan attack. The case had been open since October 27, 2004, when Russian Deputy Prosecutor General Shepel announced the charges. Victims demanded that journalists be allowed in the courtroom and that the officers' case be linked with the trial of Nur-Pasha Kulayev, since testimony at Kulayev's trial would clearly influence the trial of the police officers. Neither demand was met for the hearing, and the victims submitted more formal petitions, one from the Mothers of Beslan calling for the trial of the police officers to be linked to the wider investigation into the hostage taking and another from the Voice of Beslan asking for the trial to be suspended until the end of the main investigation ("Negligence Trial" 2006; "Russia: Trial of Police" 2006). These petitions too were not granted.

The trial began on March 16, 2006,[29] and victims consistently tried to transform the proceedings from a small case against three local police officers into a wider investigation of political officials responsible for public safety in Russia. The hearings became "a forum for a rare sustained public challenge to the Kremlin" (Chivers 2006). After testifying against the police officers, victim Sergei Oziyev remarked, "The guilt of our leadership is incomparably higher than the guilt of the local police." Former hostage Taisiya Nogayeva whose daughter did not survive concurred. "I consider these police officers guilty, but they are not

---

[29] Transcripts of the trial are available at http://www.pravdabeslana.ru/stenmentindex.htm.

the main people who are guilty." Retired police colonel Elbrus Nogayev lost a wife and daughter in the siege and also concurred. "Only negotiations could have stopped it, not these three men." Victims were hoping that the trial would reveal information about the incompetence, deceit, and callousness of government officials in their handling of the siege and its aftermath, officials whose failings were perceived to be greater than those of the local police (Chivers 2006).

A year later, victims' hopes were dashed. On May 10, 2007, about thirty representatives of Mothers of Beslan and Voice of Beslan attended the negligence hearing. The court announced that amnesty might be possible for the Beslan police officers and that litigation might be stopped. Ella Kesayeva responded, "We left the court in protest. This is a violation of our constitutional rights to justice. The authorities are afraid of court hearings; they are afraid to summon high-ranking witnesses. And this amnesty was declared deliberately to shut the mouths of law-enforcement officers who are accused now and who could be accused in the future" ("Beslan Mothers Report" 2007).

The defendants had submitted a petition to stop the trial based on a September 22, 2006, decision by the State Duma called "On the Announcement of Amnesty Concerning the Persons Who Committed Crimes in the Process of Counterterrorist Operation in the South Federal District." The police officers claimed that their actions in Beslan were considered a "counterterrorist operation" and therefore not subject to prosecution, a position supported by Vladimir Lozitsky from the Prosecutor General's Office (Farniyev 2007b). The defendants also argued that the terrorist attack was made possible due to the poor performance of the FSB, not them, because the FSB is responsible for preventing attacks.

Judge Valery Besolov of the Pravoberezhny court in Beslan invited comments from the different parties and then adjourned for a decision on May 25, despite the protest of victims and their families. Dudiyeva said that the policemen were essentially a bone thrown to the victims, and now the bone was being taken away ("Power Agents" 2007; Tokhsyrov 2007a).

Rita Sidakova of Mothers of Beslan told the judge, "If you no longer have the guilty parties, then judge me. I am to blame for sending my child to school on September 1." Sidakova then walked into the cage, closed it from the inside, and refused to leave the courtroom until the court made a decision. Three hours later, Dudiyeva persuaded Sidakova to leave the courthouse, and the women planned a picket outside the North Ossetian prosecutor's office (Tokhsyrov 2007a).

The Beslan women held signs saying, "The Beslan tragedy is beyond amnesty!"; "Terrorists' helpers are terrorists themselves"; and "The FSB and Ministry of Internal Affairs are responsible for the act of terror." They marched with these signs from Vladikavkaz's Friendship Square to the Office of the Public Prosecutor where they held a small rally and lodged a complaint with the Public

Prosecutor of North Ossetia, Herman Shtadler, about the termination of the case. The women argued that the policemen should first be declared guilty before amnesty could even be considered (Tokhsyrov 2007a).

On May 29, 2007, at 10 a.m., Judge Besolov read out the amnesty decision and endorsed the defendants' position that they fell under the State Duma's amnesty decision. About fifty victims were in the courtroom to hear the reading, but the defendants were not and had submitted written statements instead. Women began to cry out "Enough! Let them come, and then you will read!" As the judge continued to read the decision to terminate the case, the victims began to bang and clap, louder and louder, and some tried to break through the police officers to get to the judge. The judge stopped and declared that they would resume again at 4 p.m. (Farniyev 2007c:5).

When the defendants still did not appear and the judge again started to read the verdict, victim Elvira Tuayeva broke through to the judge and tried to take a file from his hands. The judge then left the room. Ella Kesayeva cried, "If the decision is read, then no one will be able to call them to account anymore!" Another victim added, "So then he will not read it. They decided a long time ago that there is not a single guilty person among them. We ourselves are guilty because we sent our children to school on that day" (Farniyev 2007c:5).

Elvira Tuayeva then cried out, "We must destroy everything here!" and rushed toward the window. Some other women started to wreck the blinds and shouted, "If they don't want to listen to us the good way, then we will do it the bad way." Responding to a police officer who warned that they would have to pay for the damage, victim Marina Pak said, "Let them try. If they do that, then we will burn down this court." Ella Kesayeva added, "And let it remain in history why this court was burned down." Some women seized chairs and beat the windows with them, and one broke a Russian flag. A woman said quietly in Ossetian, "The state does not need us. Why should we respect its symbols?" Some women broke tablets on the doors of the lobby (Farniyev 2007c:5).

The judge left the main courtroom and pronounced his amnesty verdict in an empty room with only the state prosecutor, a secretary, a bailiff, and two video cameras present. The victims remained in the usual courtroom and were unaware that the verdict had been reached and read. Learning that the judge had announced his decision, they refused to leave the courtroom, but by 9 p.m. they went to attend the memorial service commemorating 1,000 days since the tragedy (Farniyev 2007c).

The victims immediately planned to appeal, arguing that amnesty is appropriate only for someone who has been convicted of a crime, so the police officers would first have to plead guilty or be tried and found guilty (Farniyev 2007d). The appeal was filed on June 6, 2007, with the Supreme Court of North Ossetia. Victims argued that, if the defendants were not guilty, evidence should have been presented and the defendants should have been acquitted, but as it stood, the question of their guilt remained open ("Russia: Beslan Families" 2007). Their lawyer Taimuraz Chedzhemov also pointed out that the charges in the case were not about the officers' behavior during the terrorist attack itself, only the time period beforehand, so there was no relevant counterterrorism defense, and therefore amnesty was granted illegally—an argument that had been made by victim Valery Karlov during the trial and that went unanswered by Judge Besolov (Milashina 2007a).

Shortly afterward, it was the victims themselves who were found guilty. On July 20, 2007, Mothers of Beslan activists Rita Techiyeva, Zalina Guburova, and Mziya Kochishvili were charged with petty hooliganism and "failure to obey a lawful demand issued by a public official attempting to maintain public order" when they ransacked the courtroom on May 29. It is unclear why these three women were targeted for prosecution and not the many other participants in the ransacking. The women escaped the typical punishment for this crime of fifteen days in jail but were fined 1,000 rubles each. They refused to pay, announcing that they would admit their guilt when the real culprits of the siege—the operational staff in the hostage release—admit theirs. Mothers of Beslan activist Aneta Gadiyeva commented, "We always said that in the end we would be the ones held responsible for everything. Now our women are the first people since Nur-Pasha Kulayev to be officially found guilty in connection with the Beslan terrorist attack" (Farniyev 2007e:4).

Trial of Ingushetian Police Officers

Just before the Beslan police officers were amnestied, a similar case began against two police officers from the Malgobek Department of Internal Affairs in Ingushetia. Department Chief Mukhazhir Yevloyev and his deputy Akhmed Kotiyev were also accused of negligence resulting in the school siege but in their case for failing to prevent the formation of a gang of terrorists in their territory. In early May 2007, the Supreme Court of Kabardino-Balkaria decided that the verdict should be rendered by a jury in Ingushetia. Beslan victims objected, arguing that the location and method would guarantee the release of the officers from criminal liability, and they planned to boycott the process. Victims had originally petitioned for the proceedings to take place in North Ossetia because many of them were injured and would have trouble getting to the neighboring republic. The judge ultimately decided on a jury trial by the Supreme Court of Ingushetia but taking place in Nalchik, capital of Kabardino-Balkaria, because the alleged crime happened in Ingushetia and was technically a case for an Ingushetian court.

The victims accepted the more neutral location of Kabardino-Balkaria but not the Ingushetian jury, since they believed that Ingushetian juries often pronounced "not guilty" verdicts on insurgents (Tokhsyrov 2007b). Victims publicly pointed out the contrast between the Beslan police who were not judged by a jury and the Ingushetian police who would be. They also noted the likely negative influence of the amnesty verdict for the Beslan officers on the verdict for the Ingushetian officers and that Vladimir Lozitsky from the Prosecutor General's Office would probably support a new amnesty petition (Farniyev 2007b).

The Supreme Court of Ingushetia, presiding in Kabardino-Balkaria, officially charged the Malgobek police officers with negligence on June 27, 2007, and the officers pleaded innocent ("Russian Court Charges" 2007). To no one's surprise, in October 2007, the officers were acquitted because, according to the Supreme Court of Ingushetia, the prosecution "failed to prove the fact of the offense." The prosecution and injured parties appealed the decision, but in March 2008, the Russian Supreme Court upheld the acquittal. In May 2008, Russian Deputy Prosecutor General Sydoruk submitted a petition to the Supreme Court claiming that the injured parties' rights had been denied in the first trial and their arguments ignored in the appeal, and he asked that the acquittal be set aside. Ella Kesayeva repeated the victims' prior objections about the location, noting that many victims weren't physically able to endure the one-and-a-half hour drive from Beslan to the trial in Nalchik. She also noted that the judge failed to explain to the victims their rights at the beginning of the trial to challenge the entire jury and that the two state prosecutors gave no support when victims petitioned for additional witnesses to be called (Dadasheva et al. 2008).

When Mothers of Beslan filed their complaints with the ECHR, one of the complaints dealt with the Malgobek police officer trial and the Russian courts' failure to punish the officers ("Beslan mothers expect" 2009).

Seeking Accountability of Powerful Political Officials

Beslan victims were unsatisfied with the singling out of low-level officials such as police officers who were at most bit players in the tragic outcome in Beslan. They wanted higher officials to be questioned and held accountable. Rather than waiting for judicial cases that the authorities would never bring, they aggressively initiated and pushed for such cases. On March 3, 2006, the Mothers of Beslan petitioned the Russian General Prosecutor's Office for Dzasokhov to be tried for "criminal negligence and incompetence" during the hostage rescue operation and to face criminal liability. They also wanted to try other former local officials, including FSB director Andreyev, Minister of Emergency Situations Boris Dzgoyev, and Minister of Internal Affairs Kazbek Dzantiyev, for "concealment of information about circumstances that endanger the life and health of people" (Tskhurbayev and Migalin 2006).

Beslan victims often used public statements to publicize their demands for judicial action or to accompany the filing of court papers or appeals of judicial rulings. For example, on March 6, 2007, Voice of Beslan published a statement to demand that Putin, Prosecutor General Yuri Chaika, and Chaika's deputy in the Southern Federal District, Ivan Sydoruk, press criminal charges against government officials who oversaw the hostage release operation. Voice of Beslan claimed that they had evidence that should convince the Prosecutor General's Office and Russia's leadership that these officials are at fault ("Beslan Families" 2007).[30] Voice of Beslan then filed an appeal at the Leninsky Court of North Ossetia-Alania on March 19, 2007, demanding the same: prosecution of members of the crisis center and leaders of the Federal Security Service and Interior Ministry who participated in the hostage-release operation.[31]

The quantity of paperwork, the level of detail, and the legal knowledge required for this kind of activism within the Russian judicial system was massive. Judicial appeals and other courtroom activities occasionally became full-time operations for some activists. In the March 2007 appeal, victims argued that "the investigation never established the identities of the people who arranged, planned, and executed the terrorist act" or even accurately dealt with the number of involved gunmen and their accomplices, so the government's claims—for example, that the president of Ichkeria and Chechen guerrilla leader Aslan Maskhadov was one of the organizers—were unsubstantiated. Specific officials were named in the appeal, along with details of their allegedly criminal actions. Andreyev allegedly provoked the terrorists with his inability to organize negotiations or make arrangements for the terrorists to meet with Dzasokhov, Ingushetia president Murat Zyazikov, and presidential aide Aslambek Aslakhanov. Andreyev also failed to prepare the security forces for the September 3 operation and instead allegedly ordered the use of tanks, grenade launchers, and flamethrowers, which, combined with his other failings, caused the terrorists to execute twenty-one hostages on the first day and hundreds more to die on September 3, 2004. Voice of Beslan blamed FSB General Tikhonov for dereliction of duty and abuse of power by ordering the deployment of tanks and armored personnel carriers. They accused Dzasokhov of not admitting his command of the crisis center on the first day of the tragedy, lying to the court, and failing to take preventive measures while knowing that terrorists were active in the Caucasus (Farniyev 2007a). Victims went on to name other officials and their alleged crimes too.

[30] http://golosbeslana.ru/2007/zayav070306.htm.
[31] http://golosbeslana.ru/2007/jaloba125.htm.

In response to the March 2007 appeal, the Leninsky District Court in Vladikavkaz essentially agreed with the victims. The Court ruled on April 3 that the regional prosecutors acted illegally when they refused to initiate a criminal investigation into the conduct of officials in charge of the siege such as Dzasokhov, Andreyev, and Tikhonov. With this ruling, the Leninsky District Court effectively ordered the local Prosecutor General's Office to begin the appropriate investigation. The ruling was not initially well publicized but became known by the end of April ("Court Rules" 2007; "Beslan Mothers Stay" 2007).

Prosecutors appealed the Leninsky District Court decision to the North Ossetian Supreme Court. On May 2, 2007, the Supreme Court, headed by North Ossetia's top judge, Tamerlan Aguzarov, sent the case back to the lower court for a new hearing, citing procedural violations such as the absence of a secretary at the court hearing and the reference to the wrong articles in the transcribed text. This amounted to a reversal of the ruling of the Leninsky Court ("Beslan Mothers Stay" 2007; "Russian Court Overrules" 2007).

Victims opposed the ruling, and representatives of both Mothers of Beslan and Voice of Beslan camped out overnight in the Supreme Court. On May 3, as described above, Aguzarov met with them for an hour and offered assurances that the lower court would oversee a fair hearing. Voice of Beslan's Kesayeva, among those who camped out, expressed doubt that the investigation would ever be opened ("Court Rules" 2007; "Beslan Mothers Stay" 2007; "Beslan Mothers Given" 2007).

By August 2007, Voice of Beslan was back in the Leninsky Court, but not because of the investigation. This time, the organization was forced to defend its very existence and its current leadership. The Court stripped Kesayeva of her title and effectively handed the organization to individuals who had previously been minor and even troublesome members. On December 19, 2007, North Ossetia's Supreme Court ordered the old Voice of Beslan to disband and upheld the lower court ruling that Ella Kesayeva was not the group's leader. These judicial challenges prompted public replies from Kesayeva and others, as well as another appeal to the North Ossetian Supreme Court ("Court Orders" 2007).[32]

Perhaps the most daring judicial action of all came on June 4, 2008, when the still-functioning Voice of Beslan filed criminal charges against Vladimir Putin for violations of eleven articles of the Russian Criminal Code, including negligence and murder. Among Putin's stated offenses were the refusal to engage in negotiations, the use of non-selective weaponry, abuse of power, the disregard for life, and intended bodily harm. The victims argued that the command to use tanks and flamethrowers must have come from the president because the law "On Defense" states that the president alone wields the power

---

[32] http://golosbeslana.ru/2007/nadzorjaloba.htm.

to deploy the regular army in situations outside the army's normal functions. Victims quite publicly and explicitly claimed that the president carried the same level of responsibility as the terrorists for the deaths of hostages (Savina and Dzhodzhua 2008).

Some activist victims—Svetlana Margiyeva, Zhanna Tsirikhova, Emilia Bzarova, Annetta Misikova, Emma Tagayeva, Nona Tigiyeva, Ella Kesayeva, Valery Nazarov, and Vladimir Kisiyev—wrote a book chronicling their judicial actions. They called it *Doroga k pravdye. Beslan i Rossiskaya sudebnaya sistema* [The Road to Truth: Beslan and the Russian Judicial System] (Milashina 2012).

European Court of Human Rights

Unsatisfied with the Russian justice system, victims pressed forward with their appeal to the ECHR. By June 25, 2007, eighty-nine of them had filed a lawsuit claiming violations of their rights to life, objective investigation, fair trial, and efficient legal defense, as set forth in the European Convention on Human Rights (Shavlokhova and Balburov 2007; "Russia: Beslan Victims' Families" 2007; Tskhurbayev 2007a).[33] The case was labeled "Application no. 26562/07 Emma Lazarovna Tagayeva and Others against Russia and 6 other applications." From January 21, 2008, through April 2, 2009, materials were submitted from different applicants, for a total of 447 former hostages or next of kin who brought complaints (Tagayeva et al. 2012).

The female activist victims over thirty-five years old, especially those who were teachers, discussed how they joined the Strasbourg action.

TATIANA: When we appealed to the court asking to punish the people who allowed it to happen, teachers participated as well, collected signatures, all so that the documents could be sent to the Strasbourg Court.

TATIANA: They [teachers] informed us. They didn't offer for us to join. They just reported that they were appealing to the court. If you want, if someone wants to come, please sign the documents and support us. Those who wanted supported them. Those who didn't kept out of it.

BERTA: You know when such an action is conducted, it's based on the opinion of all people, all of us, not just the opinion of these ten people. They learn our wishes and requests in advance. Based on this, they make a questionnaire. And only then they call and tell us about it. And those who agree sign the papers.

---

[33] http://golosbeslana.ru/2007/izjaloby.htm.

In April 2012, the 447 victims who signed the papers began to get responses from the ECHR to their complaints. The Court had recently considered a similar complaint from victims of the Moscow theater hostage taking in 2002 and ordered sixty-four applicants from that case to be paid an unprecedented €1.3 million. Now the ECHR agreed to accept the complaint of Beslan victims and continue with proceedings, noting that the prior terrorist incidents in Russia, combined with local notifications of an impending terrorist attack, meant that North Ossetian officials should have been on high alert. The ECHR posed serious questions to the Russian government, with a request for answers within 2–3 months (Butorina and Lepina 2012).[34]

In November 2012, victims claimed that the Russian authorities, who still had not answered the ECHR's questions, were intentionally delaying and attempting to avoid participating in the ECHR process ("The European Court" 2012). Only on September 1, 2014, a decade after the Beslan tragedy, did the ECHR announce that a public hearing would be scheduled for October 14, 2014. It was anticipated that the Court would hear all the statements and then move to closed proceedings, taking at least a year before rendering a decision ("Slushaniye po delu" 2014).

The entire hearing of October 14 was open, webcast, and posted on the ECHR's website, simultaneously translated into Russian, all of which was rare for the Court and designed "so the citizens of Russia would hear and understand" (Milashina 2014) (Image 4.6).[35] Victims were represented by attorneys Kirill Koroteyev, Jessica Gavron, and Sergei Knyazkin, and the Russian Federation was represented by an entire legal team headed by Deputy Minister of Justice Georgy Matyushkin. Anticipations changed, and the final decision at the ECHR was then expected to come within two months of the hearing. If decided in favor of the applicants, compensation decisions would follow (Farniyev and Sergeyev 2014; Milashina 2014).

Only by April 13, 2017, did the ECHR render the verdict of *Tagayeva and others against Russia*, with the final judgment on September 18, 2017. A full thirteen years after the hostage taking, victims were validated in their claim that the Russian state had violated their human rights. While acknowledging that the Russian state, like other states, faced challenges in the fight against terrorism, the ECHR nevertheless held that states have a positive obligation to prevent threats to life before, during, and after a hostage taking. As victims had long claimed, the Russian state failed in its planning and control of the rescue operation, failed to minimize recourse to lethal force, and failed in its procedural obligation to

---

[34] See Tagayeva, et al. (2012:74–76) for the precise questions posed by the ECHR to the Russian government.
[35] http://www.echr.coe.int/Pages/home.aspx?p=hearings&w=2656207_14102014&language=en&c=&py=2014.

Image 4.6. Representatives of the victims, including Ella Kesayeva (second from left) and Emma Tagayeva (middle) attended the October 14, 2014, hearing of the European Court of Human Rights in Strasbourg, France, where they ultimately won a historic legal victory against the Russian state for its human rights violations.
FREDERICK FLORIN/AFP via Getty Images.

conduct an effective and independent investigation (Galani 2019). The ECHR ordered Russia to pay €2,955,000 in damages to victims and €88,000 in legal costs, for an unprecedented verdict against the Russian state of over €3 million. The Russian Justice Ministry appealed the ruling, but the appeal was rejected by the ECHR, and in September 2017, Russia agreed to comply with the ruling ("Beslan Siege" 2017). By September 2019, the Justice Ministry claimed that all but one victim had received the ECHR-awarded payout ("Only One" 2019).

Victim Welfare

Most of the judicial and legal action after the hostage taking involved quests for accountability and truth about the deadly event. However, some victim actions related to their individual problems and claims, or the actions downplayed the contentious issue of blame and focused on getting victims the help they needed.

Personal judicial action was rare but largely involved victims' frustrations over identifying the bodies of their loved ones. One male activist victim over thirty-five years old explained.

ALIK: I understood from the very beginning that it's impossible to find the truth, when they made me bury one burned leg of my sister. And for several months my wife went to courts, and we made them take [the remains] to Rostov, conduct an examination, and confirm that it is not my sister. We made them [conduct this examination] via the court again. It took a few months and, finally, in the morgue we found out that she had been buried under a different name.

Legislative action became an increasing focus of victim activity as the years wore on. Starting around the fifth anniversary of the attack in 2009, public statements by activists from Mothers of Beslan and Voice of Beslan frequently included references to the status of victims of terrorist acts, their difficult medical and social situation, and in the words of Mothers of Beslan activist Aneta Gadiyeva, "the humiliating process of getting their disability status extended" year after year (Farniyev 2009). Victims wanted a new federal law that specified the rights of victims and their relatives and determined measures for social protection and benefits. They were motivated by the ongoing need of disabled victims for expensive medical treatment, psychological services, and continuous rehabilitation years after the tragedy when victims were forgotten, especially because some illnesses developed or became apparent after the funding dried up ("Russia: Beslan Mothers" 2009).

On August 18, 2009, Voice of Beslan wrote a letter to the North Ossetian Parliament asking that the Parliament appeal to Medvedev to adopt a federal law on victims of terrorist acts.[36] On November 18, 2009, Voice of Beslan's Kesayeva announced the creation of a new public movement called "For the Status of Victims of Acts of Terrorism" to push for a law guaranteeing social support for victims of terrorism. Her announcement followed a November 17 meeting of the Federation Council where former North Ossetian president and now Council member Alexander Dzasokhov himself asked for a working group between the Federation Council and the Duma to draft legislation. Kesayeva noted that the concept of "victim of terrorism" did not exist in the current legislation ("Survivors of school" 2009). Similarly, journalist Olga Bobrova explained:

The legal status of "victim of terrorist attack" in the present Terrorism Law is not at all defined. Compensation to victims rests on the terrorists themselves. The state participates in the fate of these people no more than for any other "socially disadvantaged" citizen. A child mutilated in the Beslan school is formally listed as a disabled child, while adults are listed as having a work injury. (Bobrova 2011)

---

[36] http://golosbeslana.ru/2009/ozakone.htm.

Through the remainder of 2009 and 2010, victims repeatedly emphasized the injustice of a state of affairs that reduced them to beggars through no fault of their own. For example, at a "sanctioned picket" on October 31, 2010, one of the signs read, "Mr. Putin, we demand a law on terrorist victims and not your charitable handouts!"[37] Beslan victims continued these types of efforts in 2011 and also joined forces with other victim organizations. On January 25, 2011, Voice of Beslan, Nord-Ost (representing victims of the 2002 Moscow theater hostage taking), and Volga-Don (representing victims of a 1999 terrorist explosion in Volgodonsk) co-signed a statement calling for the speedy adoption of a law to protect the status of victims of terror. The statement noted that terrorists had attacked Russia for more than ten years while the government avoided responsibility for taking care of victims afterward.[38]

Victims understood the creeping pace of legislative action about terrorism in Russia and argued that programs for victims could and should be put in place while the law on the status of victims was in the process of being adopted. In anticipation of a May 2011 meeting with Medvedev, Voice of Beslan members convened the meeting with 258 victims, described above, during which they drafted an official appeal with a long list of required programs. The list was sent to Medvedev and posted on the Voice of Beslan website.[39]

Going beyond Victim Grievances toward Broader Activism

Beslan victims who became full-time political activists began very quickly to conceive of their role in expansive terms. They networked across social movements and bridged the specific complaints about the hostage taking with more general issues of counterterrorism policies and human rights protections.

Networking materialized mostly with victims of other terrorist attacks and botched rescue efforts. On October 25, 2005, survivors and relatives of Beslan victims teamed with survivors and relatives of the Moscow theater hostage crisis, sometimes known for the street, "Dubrovka," where the theater is located and sometimes known for the title of the musical that was playing in the theater, "Nord-Ost." The families created a new nongovernmental organization called Nord Ost and issued an appeal at a news conference for Putin to take another look at the "biased" official Beslan investigation. The appeal boldly demanded, "We also want you, the president of the country, to admit your own responsibility for the death of our children, relatives, and loved ones and to disclose the

---

[37] http://www.golosbeslana.ru/2010/piket_zakon.htm.
[38] http://www.golosbeslana.ru/2011/zakon.htm.
[39] http://www.golosbeslana.ru/2011/sobr0805.htm, http://www.golosbeslana.ru/2011/sobranie0805.htm, http://www.golosbeslana.ru/2011/sobranie0805.htm.

entire truth . . . about Nord Ost" (Buribayev 2005:6). The relationship of Beslan victims with Nord-Ost victims and Volga-Don victims continued over the years and led to occasional joint actions, such as the 2011 co-signing of a statement demanding a law to protect the status of victims of terror.

Victims also branched out from their initial grievances specific to Beslan and protested over general issues about violence, counterterrorism, and human rights. For example, as described earlier, Voice of Beslan appealed on March 13, 2006, against the new Russian anti-terror law, arguing that the law granted the authorities unlimited authority to commit grievous injustices ("Beslan Victims Denounce" 2006). On May 1, 2006, one thousand Beslan victims and other residents protested the armed raid on the home of Cossack leader Khariton Yedziyev, demanding an end to the arbitrary behavior of law enforcement agencies, illegal security sweeps, and the persecution of Cossacks for fulfilling their obligation to guard the administrative border ("1,000 Protest" 2006). On October 31, 2008, twenty-six members of Voice of Beslan sent a letter to President Medvedev calling for the release from prison of Svetlana Bakhmina, the Yukos lawyer who was jailed while eight months pregnant and who Voice of Beslan activists angrily pointed out was being punished more than the murderers of their children.[40] On September 13, 2010, Voice of Beslan members joined other public figures, including Dagestan's Mothers for Human Rights, and signed a statement expressing solidarity with Memorial Human Rights Center director Oleg Orlov who was being tried for allegedly slandering Chechen president Ramzan Kadyrov when he suggested a link between Kadyrov and the murder of one of his center's employees in Grozny ("Rights Activists" 2010).

In March, 2012, members of the Voice of Beslan attempted to become election observers "to monitor the purity of elections" in the upcoming presidential race. Initially accepted by the local Communist organization, they were asked to retract their request, and no other party would grant them observer status. Still, Voice of Beslan activists encouraged citizens to show up at the polls and vote for any candidate but Putin. "Not a single vote in Beslan should go for Putin," they argued (Kusov 2012).

Over time, the extension from initial Beslan-specific grievances grew to include international issues. On December 18, 2012, Beslan residents gathered in School No. 1's old gymnasium and lit candles in memory of the new victims of a shooting at the Sandy Hook Elementary School in Newtown, Connecticut. A letter written to the mothers of children lost in Newtown was read out loud and filmed and posted on YouTube (Valieva 2012). On September 4, 2013, Susanna Dudiyeva sent an open letter to President Obama, urging him not to strike Syria

---

[40] http://www.golosbeslana.ru/bahmina.htm.

with military force and thereby aggravate the situation and bring more grief to the Syrian people, especially their children (Sageyeva 2013).

Measuring Political Participation

The narrative of political activism after the hostage taking includes repeated reference to a handful of supremely active victims. In addition, many more victims played repeated roles as attendees at rallies, signatories to statements and petitions, and participants in various events. On the other end of the activism spectrum, many victims did not participate at all. Here the aggregate amount of participation is measured, along with the variability among victims. This measure is then used in Part II to understand the correlates of political activism in the aftermath of violence.

Political participation again refers to "action by ordinary citizens directed toward influencing some political outcomes" (Brady 1999:737). Among the many challenges to measuring political participation with survey questions are the need to (1) identify and ask about all forms of participation or else risk omitting important political activities and misrepresenting a respondent's level of activism; (2) minimize recall and social desirability bias and misreporting by respondents; and (3) aggregate participatory actions that vary in duration, intensity, and other factors and are thus difficult to collapse into a unidimensional scale (Verba and Nie 1972: chaps. 3–4; Brady 1999).

To address these challenges, Henry Brady (1999) recommends the following rules for improving survey items on participation:

- Aim for concreteness through detailed description of the act.
- Ask about a short and definite time interval (e.g., one year).
- Ask for details of the activity to help the respondent remember it.
- Ask for amounts of time or money, if possible.
- Design questions to discourage overreporting and social desirability bias, meaning the respondents' editing of responses to give favorable impressions of themselves.

The advice was followed here by combing news reports in the days, weeks, months, and years following the horrific hostage taking at the Beslan school and identifying over thirty very concrete public participatory activities that had occurred by the time of our 2007 survey. The search specified the word "Beslan" from September 1, 2004, until the present day and was conducted in LexisNexis Academic, which included access to international newspapers, Moscow newspapers, Russian regional newspapers, ITAR-TASS, RIA Novosti, Radio

Free Europe, news wires, and Current Digest of the Post-Soviet Press, and then supplemented with EastView, World News Connection, and EBSCOhost. Beslan was chosen as the search word because any story on the hostage taking and related events necessarily mentioned the town, whereas the town rarely made the news for any other reason. A broad search on just the town name—rather than a narrower search on "Beslan AND protest," for example—maximized coverage of relevant participatory activities. While the possibility cannot be excluded that some major rally, letter writing campaign, or meeting with a public official was missed, any omissions were probably minor and should not result in the accidental mischaracterization of an activist as a nonactivist, or vice versa.[41]

Most of the identified activities involved a specific political official, a specific public location, and/or a specific date. The detailed descriptions recommended by Brady could thus be provided, and recall problems could be minimized. The focus groups suggested that social desirability bias was not a big factor in influencing responses to survey questions about participation, mostly because the socially desirable response in Beslan is not especially clear. There is no high premium placed on political activism in Beslan nor any public scorn or ridicule for participation in any of the named events. Participation in the controversial Mothers of Beslan or Voice of Beslan is an exception, but organizational membership was not included as a political activity, only participation in specific actions sponsored by the organization, and for these, participation did not require membership.[42] To the extent that social desirability bias played a role, it may have led to item nonresponse (refusals to answer) for questions about unlawful behavior, such as sitting in and refusing to leave a courthouse, blockading a highway, or meeting with a federal official in the name of resolving the unlawful blockade, activities usually undertaken by the most active respondents who were likely to score high on the participation count variable nonetheless.

As an added precaution, interviewers were instructed to use language designed to minimize social desirability bias, as well as recall bias. The participation questions were preceded by the following introduction:

> In the two years since the tragedy in the school, some former hostages and their families have engaged in political action. Others have not participated in these activities—either consciously or because they have simply been physically or psychologically unable to do so. I will now describe some events. Please tell me whether or not you were one of the participants. If you did not participate in an event, please feel free to say so, even if that is your response to every question. Also,

---

[41] This painstaking work was accomplished principally by Elizabeth Brooks, research assistant extraordinaire.

[42] Members of these two organizations tended to participate in most of the organizations' activities. The participation questions therefore capture their membership.

some of these events occurred two years ago, and it may be difficult to recall, so
please feel free to say if you do not remember.

Respondents were thus told that many in Beslan did not participate for very
good reasons. Implicitly, the message is that nonparticipation was perfectly acceptable, as was participation. A poor memory too was acceptable.

Beslan victims were then asked about their participation in thirty-one
documented political activities that occurred after the hostage taking between
2004 and 2006, drawn from those described above. Questions included details
like place, date, and public official in attendance to minimize the possibility of recall bias. Table 4.1 shows the number of Beslan victims who participated in each
of these concrete activities in declining order of participation rate. An extraordinarily high number of activities (nineteen) had participation levels of 5 percent
or higher, and seven activities had participation levels of 10 percent or higher.
Among the most popular forms of participation were attending some part of the
trial against accused hostage taker Nur-Pasha Kulayev (roughly 1 in 3 Beslan
victims), meeting with then North Ossetian president Taimuraz Mamsurov
(1 in 5), writing to a newspaper, calling a news show, or speaking to a reporter
since the tragedy (also 1 in 5), and attending a meeting with Russian Deputy
Prosecutor General Nikolai Shepel (1 in 6). Even those activities with the least
amount of participation still often involved quite impressive numbers of people
when considering the effort involved, such as meeting with Putin in Moscow,
meeting with Putin's special envoy in Rostov-on-Don, and traveling to another
North Ossetian town to participate in a rally. Indeed, it is difficult to think of another community in recent years that has demonstrated such an impressive level
of political activism, especially a community so far from an urban power center
and with relatively low per capita income.

To measure cumulative peaceful participation in politics, the activities in Table
4.1 were aggregated in the most basic way in a count variable ranging from 0 to
31 possible activities. These activities represent many types of political participation, including signing letters, meeting with various political officials, attending
rallies, picketing, hunger striking, and refusing to leave a courtroom. No single
kind of participation dominates the count variable; the various types of activities
(attending rallies, writing letters, meeting with officials, and engaging in high-
intensity activities like lawbreaking and hunger-striking) are represented in relatively equal numbers (7, 6, 11, and 7, respectively) and vary in the amount of
effort and perceived risk involved. The greater number of activities in which a
person participated, the more they fit the description of a political activist.

Alternatively, a Guttman scale could be used to distinguish people who
participated in more difficult or high-intensity activities from those who
participated in less intense activities. However, given that participatory activities

Table 4.1. Political Participation of Beslan Victims in Specific Activities

	Participated (%)	Refused to Answer (%)	Don't Know (%)
Attended some part of the trial against accused hostage taker Nur-Pasha Kulayev (inside the courtroom during proceedings) starting in May 2005	357 (32.5)	17 (1.5)	0 (0.0)
Met with North Ossetian president Mamsurov since the tragedy	213 (19.4)	10 (0.9)	4 (0.4)
Wrote to a newspaper, called news show, or spoke to a reporter at any time since the tragedy	206 (18.8)	14 (1.3)	9 (0.8)
Attended meeting with Russian Deputy Prosecutor General Shepel at the House of Culture on November 3, 2004	176 (16.0)	15 (1.4)	4 (0.4)
Participated in rallies in Beslan right after the tragedy in early September 2004	122 (11.1)	8 (0.7)	10 (0.9)
Picketed the Rostov-Baku/Caucasus Federal Highway in January 2005	118 (10.7)	37 (3.4)	1 (0.1)
Signed the open letter to Putin and the parliamentary investigation committee in November of 2004	117 (10.7)	17 (1.5)	20 (1.8)
Traveled to Vladikavkaz to participate in a rally since September 2004	93 (8.5)	10 (0.9)	8 (0.7)
Supplied the picketers of the Rostov-Baku/Caucasus Federal Highway with food, bonfire wood, or other supplies in January 2005	93 (8.5)	40 (3.6)	32 (2.9)
Met with other political official since the tragedy (besides those specifically named)	91 (8.3)	13 (1.2)	11 (1.0)
Met with federal officials from the Federation Council and Duma who visited Beslan three weeks after the tragedy	88 (8.0)	10 (0.9)	14 (1.3)
Wrote or signed a letter to any other political official since the tragedy (besides those specifically named)	88 (8.0)	21 (1.9)	29 (2.6)
Attended meeting with new Deputy Prosecutor General Sydoruk at the House of Representatives on August 9, 2006	85 (7.7)	9 (0.8)	3 (0.3)
Protested outside the courtroom where accused hostage taker Kulayev was tried starting in May 2005	84 (7.7)	36 (3.3)	2 (0.2)

(continued)

Table 4.1. Continued

	Participated (%)	Refused to Answer (%)	Don't Know (%)
Helped write the open letter to Putin and the parliamentary investigation committee in November 2004	82 (7.5)	13 (1.2)	19 (1.7)
Met with Deputies Prosecutor General Shepel or Kolesnikov or General Public Prosecutor Ustinov any other time since the tragedy	79 (7.2)	21 (1.9)	3 (0.3)
Signed the letter to the international community fearing that authorities will not reveal truth and requesting asylum or immigration in August 2005	79 (7.2)	36 (3.3)	38 (3.5)
Participated in any other rallies or acts of protest in the two years since the tragedy (besides those specifically named)	74 (6.7)	17 (1.5)	24 (2.2)
Wrote a letter to federal officials such as Federation Council members or Duma deputies	72 (6.6)	10 (0.9)	20 (1.8)
Participated in a sit-in at the court where accused hostage taker Kulayev was tried in August 2005	63 (5.7)	35 (3.2)	11 (1.0)
Refused to leave the courtroom at any other time during accused hostage taker Kulayev's trial (besides the August 2005 sit-in)	59 (5.4)	54 (4.9)	25 (2.3)
Participated in rallies outside of Beslan such as Prigorodny or Vladikavkaz right after the tragedy in early September 2004	58 (5.3)	7 (0.6)	12 (1.1)
Supplied with food and water those sitting in the courtroom where accused hostage taker Kulayev was tried in August 2005	54 (4.9)	41 (3.7)	37 (3.4)
Participated in a hunger strike at the end of accused hostage taker Kulayev's trial	50 (4.6)	51 (4.6)	6 (0.5)
Met with Putin's special envoy to South Federal District Kozak any other time since the tragedy (besides February 2005)	41 (3.7)	64 (5.8)	9 (0.8)
Met with President Putin in Moscow in September 2005	38 (3.5)	10 (0.9)	3 (0.3)
Signed any other letters to Putin in the two years since the tragedy (besides the open letter in November 2004)	38 (3.5)	19 (1.7)	34 (3.1)
Met with Putin's special envoy to South Federal District Kozak in Rostov-on-Don in February 2005	31 (2.8)	61 (5.6)	13 (1.2)

(*continued*)

Table 4.1. Continued

	Participated (%)	Refused to Answer (%)	Don't Know (%)
Called the special hotline to speak with federal officials such as Federation Council members or Duma deputies	29 (2.6)	10 (0.9)	23 (2.1)
Traveled to another town in North Ossetia to participate in a rally since September 2004	17 (1.5)	10 (0.9)	10 (0.9)

$N = 1,098$.

do not fall readily on a unidimensional scale, it is not always clear whether one activity is more difficult than another. For example, it might be uncontroversial to claim that signing a letter to an official is relatively easy, while blocking roads, sit-ins, refusing to leave a building, hunger-striking, or other forms of civil disobedience are relatively difficult, but there may be less consensus on the rank ordering of activities in between. For example, is it more difficult to participate in a rally or to meet with an official? The answer is heavily context dependent, since the amount of time spent on either activity and the exposure to risk may vary.

It is also not always clear whether one activity is more radical than another. The term "radical" has no precise, agreed-upon meaning in the literature on political behavior or social movements. At times, "radical" seems to mean all non-institutional forms of political participation including peaceful demonstrations. At other times, "radical" suggests illegal or violent behavior. Some scholars argue that the distinction between conventional and unconventional forms of participation is obsolete and meaningless, with social movements now a common form of politics (Klandermans 2003). Once-radical protest has in many cases become politics by other means. Even letter-signing is not always easy to place on a conventional-to-radical scale. The letter may contain safe demands for financial assistance or risky demands for accountability from powerful officials, perhaps coupled with inflammatory remarks such as calling the president an accomplice of terrorism. With such different demands, the letter can represent very different political actions.

A count measure of political participation therefore seems a reasonable choice, but as a test of its robustness, two different Guttman scales were created and found highly correlated with the count scale.[43] A factor analysis of the 31

[43] For each Guttman scale, letter writing was rank ordered as the easiest political activity and illegal or other high-effort activities like hunger-striking as the most difficult political activity. For one scale, rallies were rank ordered as second most difficult and meeting with officials third. For the other scale, these middle rankings were reversed, and meetings were put second and rallies third. Within each

participation items found that all loaded heavily onto a single first factor with an Eigenvalue of 12.3 explaining 63.4 percent of the common variance and that this first factor score correlated highly with the count scale. Finally, as suggested by the literature that continues to differentiate activities based on their level of radicalness, moderate or normative political action was distinguished from extreme or non-normative political action (Becker, Tausch, and Wagner 2011; Tausch et al. 2011; Valentino et al. 2011), and the results of multivariate analysis in Chapter 11 were substantively the same on each of these alternatively aggregated variables. For clarity in analysis, the count scale is used throughout the rest of the book.

The results are shown in Table 4.2. Table 4.3 collapses the data in Table 4.2 into categories for easier viewing. Fully half of Beslan victims surveyed had participated in at least one activity. More than a third had participated in two or more activities, and 16 percent had participated in four or more activities. An astonishing 7 percent of victims had participated in more than ten activities and would by most definitions be labeled political activists.

To the extent that these results are biased, they likely represent an underestimate of political activism. The focus groups revealed that some victims shied away from the word "participate" and would instead say, "we could not stay away if all other people were there," "we were full of emotion and wanted to ask the authorities why it happened," and "we wanted the truth." Many victims conceived of their activities as private affairs rather than political activism, even if they participated in several political activities, and therefore may have at times underreported their actions. Nevertheless, the assumption of this research is that attendance at a public demonstration, even if just to listen, or signing a petition, attending a meeting with a political authority, or otherwise putting one's person, name, or voice in a public setting constitutes political activism, regardless of the participant's own definition of political activism.

The impressiveness of the post-violence activism in Beslan cannot be overstated. Political participation, even by aggrieved individuals, is usually very low, due to the high, concentrated, and certain costs of participation and the low, dispersed, and uncertain benefits (Olson 1965; Lichbach 1998; Javeline 2003a, 2003b). As aggrieved as Beslan victims were, many factors worked against their politicization. They largely lacked resources such as money and access to policymakers, especially

---

category, activities seem similarly difficult and were therefore counted rather than ranked. If a person participated in all seven of the very difficult activities, then they received the highest score of 31 on the Guttman scale. If a person participated in none of the very difficult activities but participated in the maximum number of activities at the next level of difficulty, then they received a 24 on the scale. If they participated in all but one activity at the next level of difficulty, they received a 23, and so on. The correlation between the two Guttman scales is .99. The correlations between the count scale and the two Guttman scales are .73 and .76. Therefore, empirically, the scales are quite close.

Table 4.2. Cumulative Political Participation of Beslan Victims

Number of Activities	Number Participating (%)
0	548 (49.9)
1	158 (14.4)
2	98 (8.9)
3	37 (3.4)
4	54 (4.9)
5	50 (4.6)
6	23 (2.1)
7	16 (1.5)
8	14 (1.3)
9	12 (1.1)
10	8 (.7)
11	11 (1.0)
12	3 (.3)
13	9 (.8)
14	18 (1.6)
15	7 (.6)
16	2 (.2)
17	6 (.5)
18	3 (.3)
19	2 (.2)
20	3 (.3)
21	1 (.1)
22	2 (.2)
23	0 (0)
24	2 (.2)
25	0 (0)
26	2 (.2)
27	0 (0)
28	2 (.2)
29	2 (.2)
30	4 (.4)
31	1 (.1)

$N = 1,098$.

Table 4.3. Categories of Political Participation of Beslan Victims

Number of Activities	Number of Victims Participating (%)
None	548 (49.9)
One	158 (14.4)
Two or three	135 (12.3)
Four to ten	177 (16.1)
Eleven to thirty-one	80 (7.3)

$N = 1,098.$

given their remote location and the inhospitable transportation options. They were debilitated by the most extreme form of grief imaginable, the loss of children and other loved ones, and many of them suffered life-changing injuries that would prevent activism, or they found themselves in new roles of full-time caregivers to injured children and other relatives, with little time for anything else. Many of the victims were women and therefore faced considerable challenges in asserting their interests in a paternalistic region and country. Perhaps most importantly, many of the grievances amounted to accusations against some of Russia's most powerful political leaders that they, in essence, killed Beslan's children. That one in two victims nevertheless engaged in some form of political activity and one in fourteen became full-fledged activists is astounding.

Contribution to Participation Measurement

This measurement approach represents a considerable advance over most participation studies which fail to heed Brady's now twenty-year-old advice and instead continue to rely on very general measures of participation that invite recall and other bias. For example, as recently as 2010, the following questions were used:

Now I'd like you to look at this card. I'm going to read out some different forms of political action that people can take, and I'd like you to tell me, for each one,

whether you have actually done any of these things, whether you might do it or
would never, under any circumstances, do it.

- *Signing a petition*
- *Joining in boycotts*
- *Attending lawful demonstrations*
- *Joining unofficial strikes*
- *Occupying buildings or factories.* (Dalton et al. 2010:61)

Similar measurement strategies appear in many thoughtful and acclaimed works (e.g., Inglehart 1990: chap. 9; Norris 2002: chap. 10; Inglehart and Welzel 2005: chap. 9). Unfortunately, however, it is not entirely clear what these measures capture. They do not specify time frame, frequency, intensity, or any other information for any of the activities. Someone who joined one boycott is lumped together with someone who joined many boycotts. A joiner of a relatively conflict-free activity is lumped together with a joiner of a more aggressive activity. A joiner twenty years ago who is currently inactive is lumped together with a current activist. The statistical analysis in these works is sophisticated, but the measurement of the most crucial variable is too vague and error-prone to be meaningful.

These other measurement strategies also fail to account for the nature of the grievance. Actions are disconnected from issues. A signer of a petition over cafeteria food is lumped together with a signer of a petition over human rights violations. From a normative perspective, the unstated value equivalency of issues is problematic. From a research perspective, the unstated assumption that action over these very different issues is similarly motivated is also problematic. For example, a signer of a petition over cafeteria food may be loath to get involved in politics, whereas a signer of a petition over human rights violations may be loath to get involved on behalf of such a trivial issue as cafeteria food. A single, soup-like variable composed of ill-assorted ingredients may simplify analysis but lead to results with questionable validity.

The above measurement strategy also conflates actual behavior with stated intentions to act or the possibility of action ("I might do it"). Prior research has shown that hypothetical participatory behavior and actual participatory behavior are different. For example, three-fifths of survey respondents who stated an intention to participate in a planned peace demonstration eventually did not go, largely because of the numerous barriers to participation (Klandermans and Oegema 1987). From a measurement perspective, this finding tells us that willingness to participate is important to the degree that it differentiates the willing from the unwilling, but willingness to participate cannot be equated with actual participation or included in a scale with actual participation. Individuals who state their willingness but fail in the end to participate have not actually done something more than other nonparticipants.

Such problems are especially prevalent in the psychological literature, which tends to focus on action tendencies over observable actions (Elster 1998:47). For example, one study asked how willing respondents were on a 9-point scale (1 = "not at all willing"; 9 = "very willing") to engage in actions to change British foreign policy toward Muslim countries, including petition signing, rallying, and lobbying, thus implicitly conflating intentions with actual participation (Tausch et al. 2011:139; see also Simon et al. 1998; van Zomeren et al. 2004; Jost et al. 2012; and in political science, Valentino et al. 2011). At times, the prior research compounds the problem by structuring the survey questions as attitude statements, such as "*I would participate in a demonstration*" (van Zomeren et al. 2004) or "*I intend to attend a meeting*" (Jost et al. 2012:204) and asking for simple answers of "yes" or "no" or "agree" or "disagree." Attitude statements often encourage a positivity or yay-saying bias (Schuman and Presser 1996:chap. 8; Javeline 1999), and studies using these statements as measures of participation could potentially grossly overestimate participation due not only to the statements' hypothetical nature but also to their bias toward acquiescence.

This effort to get precise measurements of actual political participation represents an advance over such research.

Conclusion: The Overwhelming but Variable Political Participation of Beslan Victims

Of the 1,098 victims of the Beslan school hostage taking who were surveyed in 2007, half had acted politically on one or more occasions, and at least 7 percent had become political activists. Much of this activism they conducted in Beslan, but their activities also took them to Vladikavkaz, Rostov-on-Don, Moscow, and Europe. They rallied, petitioned, met with officials, conducted independent investigations, picketed, and starved. They boldly worked the Russian judicial system. By August 31, 2012, Beslan victims had been involved in 127 judicial proceedings in a journey described as "the longest campaign for justice in Russia and the most sorrowful." Fifty Russian judges, including thirty-eight North Ossetian judges and judges of the Russian Supreme Court and Russian Constitutional Court, all ruled against the Beslan victims, who did not take the rulings as the final word. Instead, they sought justice outside of Russia. The petitions by Beslan victims to Strasbourg's ECHR weighed 43 kilograms (Milashina 2012).

Of course, not all Beslan victims became activists. Half of them did not participate in a single political activity in the aftermath of the tragedy. Indeed, the appropriateness of a political response to the hostage taking was debated by the Beslan victims, with some saying that "true grief is silent" (Wexler 2005). A major puzzle is what accounts for the variation in victim responses. Who were the adherents of silence, and who fought in the political arena? In Part II, we analyze which factors increase the probability of an activist response to victimization by violence.

PART II

WHY POLITICS AND
NONVIOLENCE?

What explains the surprisingly political but nonviolent aftermath of the Beslan school hostage taking and the differing individual responses? Victims themselves pondered this question. In a focus group of female activist victims thirty-five years or younger, one participant explained, "Well, it was impossible to remain passive in that situation. That's my opinion." Asked by a reporter, "Why are you so political?," another victim responded, "We entered politics to the extent that politics entered us" (Wexler 2005). Mothers of Beslan leader Susanna Dudiyeva explained, "There is a class of people here who are not indifferent, who will remind the authorities that without action, without someone taking responsibility, this type of [terrorist attack] could happen again" (Eckel 2005).

Although victims were thoughtfully analyzing their own actions, their explanations are nevertheless theoretically and empirically unsatisfying. Why was it impossible for some victims to remain passive, when it was quite possible for others? With the botched counterterrorism and rescue operation, politics arguably entered each and every Beslan victim, so why did only some respond by entering politics? If a class of people were not indifferent and reminded the authorities about accountability, why did this class of people emerge and not some other?

Part II probes the systematically gathered survey data from 1,098 victims, along with the extensive focus group discussions, to provide more satisfying explanations. Theories from political science, psychology, and sociology are explored to develop hypotheses about individual victim behavior. These hypotheses are then tested on the data from Beslan victims. Each chapter is devoted to a single explanatory variable or collection of related explanatory variables and how those variables correlate with support for retaliatory violence and political participation.

Space constraints preclude exploring all factors plausibly related to post-violence behavior. The goal is to explore those variables that played a key role in the Beslan aftermath and that are potentially influential in other post-violence contexts where retaliatory ethnic violence and political action are both plausible responses. The focus is also on variables that have been previously neglected or the subject of recent attention but poorly studied due to the prevailing use of out-of-context laboratory experiments compared to richly contextualized survey data.

Chapter 5 explores how the emotions of victims of violence might influence their behavioral reactions. It describes the novel and important contribution of measuring victims' genuine emotions in response to genuine, salient grievances, and it shows how emotional reactions to violence vary among victims. However, contrary to expectations, emotional variation has little to do with support for retaliatory violence. After violence, victims may be angry, hate-filled, resentful, anxious, fearful, worried, or even hopeful or proud, and those emotions played little if any role in their decisions to support retaliatory violence. Also contrary to popular expectations—but consistent with recent research on emotions— emotional variation is indeed meaningful for political participation. In particular, angrier victims were more likely than less angry victims to engage in peaceful political action to redress grievances.

Chapter 6 explores the role of ethnic prejudice or racial attitudes on the aftermath of violence. Using standard measures of ethnic prejudice, such as how victims feel about dining with, marrying, or attending school with ethnic Ingush, the analysis shows that such prejudice was rampant among Beslan victims and highly correlated with support for retaliatory ethnic violence but played no role in peaceful political participation. Importantly, the relationship between prejudice and support for retaliatory violence existed independent of the victims' emotions, including anger and hatred. Prejudice and its harmful ramifications cannot be blamed on the emotional provocation of the violent episode.

Chapters 7 and 8 explore how the alienation or integration of victims of violence might influence their behavioral reactions. In Chapter 7, political alienation is conceived in terms of pride and shame in Russia and especially the perceived change in such pride since the hostage taking. Pride in Russia varied among Beslan victims and strongly influenced their behavioral reactions, with politically unalienated or proud victims being more supportive of retaliatory violence and less likely to participate in politics. The finding is corroborated with analysis of related variables such as blame toward political officials, including President Vladimir Putin, and satisfaction with their punishment.

Where political alienation discouraged support for retaliatory violence, social alienation may have done the opposite and encouraged support for violence (Chapter 8). However, social alienation is a complicated concept that, even when simplified, can be difficult to apply to individuals whose relationships and networks are also complicated. In Beslan, victims experienced both social support and social isolation, and the correlation between social alienation and support for retaliatory violence was not especially strong. Social alienation played no role in peaceful political activism.

Chapter 9 explores the role of efficacy in victim reactions to violence, distinguishing political efficacy, the perceived effectiveness of political action, from self-efficacy, or a more generalized sense of empowerment outside the political arena. Not surprisingly, politically efficacious victims were much more participatory in political action than less politically efficacious victims, while politically efficacious victims were no different from the less politically efficacious in their support for retaliatory violence. More surprisingly perhaps, efficacy outside the political arena was influential in both political participation and support for retaliatory violence, with the latter relationship especially strong. The higher the self-efficacy of Beslan victims, the more likely they were to support retaliatory violence.

Chapter 10 considers the victims' biographies, including their demographic background and experiences prior to victimization. Victims who had family or friends harmed by Ingush or Chechens on a previous occasion were more likely to support retaliatory violence for the hostage taking and also more likely to participate in politics, suggesting that repeat victimization heightens the propensity to respond to the victimization, but the nature of that response could vary. Victims who participated in politics before September 2004, whether as voters or activists, were more likely to continue that activism after the hostage taking, a finding consistent with the extant research in political science. Perhaps less obvious, those who did not participate in politics before the hostage taking were more supportive of retaliatory violence. This is one of the only findings suggestive of a politics-violence trade-off in the data set—that perhaps those socialized to articulate claims in the political arena are less inclined to entertain a violent response to a new harm—even though participants in politics after the hostage taking showed no similar trade-off and were no more or less likely to support retaliatory violence than inactive victims.

Chapter 11 ties together Chapters 5 through 10 with multivariate statistical analyses designed to test the robustness of the relationships found to be important at the bivariate level. Responses to the survey question about approval of killing Chechens described in Chapter 3 are analyzed in an ordered logit model, and the count variable of thirty-one participatory acts described in Chapter 4 is analyzed in a negative binomial model. The results buttress the conclusions drawn from the bivariate correlates of political participation and support for retaliatory violence in the aftermath of violence.

5

Anger and Other Emotions

Does the response to violence depend on the victims' emotions? Victims of the very same violent incident might experience different emotional reactions, such as anger, anxiety, or sadness, singularly or bundled in different combinations, or victims might experience the same emotional reactions at different levels of intensity. Theories from psychology and sociology suggest that these emotions should influence victims' reactionary behavior, but how?

This chapter explores theories of emotion, especially anger, and the effects of emotional variability on behavior such as retaliatory violence and political participation. It then analyzes the data from Beslan victims to test whether their responses to violence support these theories. Because the data come from victims of a real-world incident that was highly provocative of emotion, they are much better suited to the study of emotions and behavior than data from artificially induced emotions over often trivial and sometimes fictitious incidents, such as those typically created in laboratory experiments.

Consistent with other recent research, the analysis shows that angry victims were more likely to pursue peaceful activism than less angry victims. Similarly, victims filled with hate were more likely activists than less hate-filled victims. However, unlike past research, the analysis shows that anger, hatred, and other emotions surprisingly had no bearing on support for retaliatory violence. The sources of support for retaliatory violence are probably less emotional and, as shown in Chapters 6 and 7, more political, social, and psychological.

Anger and Emotional Reactions to Violence

Anger is a negative and often disparaged emotion, one that we are taught from childhood to try to minimize or at least to control. It is a response to a perceived misdeed, an unpleasant emotional state resulting from the perception of unwanted, unfair, or undeserved consequences, especially when the inflicted harm is perceived as intentional (Averill 1983:1146; Smith and Ellsworth 1985; Tomkins 1991; Elster 1998:57; Miller 2001:536; Carver and Harmon-Jones 2009; Petersen and Zukerman 2009).

By this definition, anger seems a justifiable reaction to the Beslan hostage taking. Children were the primary targets and victims, and children are

After Violence. Debra Javeline, Oxford University Press. © Oxford University Press 2023.
DOI: 10.1093/oso/9780197683347.003.0006

invariably described as innocent, their victimization as undeserving and there-fore maddening. Moreover, the intentionality of the perpetrators to inflict harm was clear. The deaths, physical injuries, and emotional devastation of the hostage taking were all the result of deliberate acts of terrorism and thus highly provoc-ative of moralistic anger. The intentions of government actors before, during, and after the hostage taking were arguably less clear, but the still-unresolved discrepancies in information and the perceived callous indifference to victims mean that even government-inflicted harm was often perceived as intentional and anger-provoking.

Truth can "quench anger" by clarifying the causal chain of events, but without a true accounting, victims may ruminate and excessively attribute in-tentionality and feel anger (Petersen and Zukerman 2009). Punishment can also quench anger by restoring power and control, getting "even in suffering," honoring the memory of the dead, relieving survivor's guilt, externalizing grief, or bringing closure, and apology can quench anger by showing the hu-manity of the perpetrator, separating the perpetrator from the offense, or repairing relationships and equalizing the status and control of the victim and perpetrator. However, without punishment or apology, victims may perceive that the perpetrator remains unfairly advantaged. They may dehumanize and demonize the perpetrator and hang on to their anger (Petersen and Zukerman 2009:573–574).

In Beslan, where there was neither truth nor punishment nor apology, anger could easily perpetuate. Male activist victims over thirty-five years old offered some insight into how their anger built.

TOTRAZ: I waited the whole time. For example, our president. It seemed to me that during the first days they were all in bewilderment. No one knew what to do.

KAZBEK: On the one hand, they say that there were headquarters. And who was in the headquarters? It's incomprehensible.

TOTRAZ: The headquarters are created anyway. But we had no idea who was the leader of these headquarters.

KAZBEK: This is one question, and then comes the fifth, the twentieth, and people start getting angry. They don't believe anybody. How can you believe?

TOTRAZ: Everything was strange. I mean, I expected our then-president [of Ossetia] at the most basic [to say], "People, I am sorry. Forgive me." Certainly, I am not accusing him, but just go and say that! And his behavior—he was clinging to power. Such [an event] happened. In normal countries, [the leader] resigns and apologizes. What can anyone do about him? What claims can we make against him? And he behaved as if nothing had happened. "Well, it has just happened, hail has beaten your roofs. What does it have to do with me?" Why not come out and speak [with the people], addressing your question and everyone who was standing there?

KAZBEK: And it never happened during all these four years. Not once did a single representative of the authorities ever come out and explain something in earnest.

TOTRAZ: This is clear.

KAZBEK: State Duma representatives were here, but what good things did they do? We at least expected them to come out and objectively tell things in front of people. They could have held a meeting and explained what had happened and why it happened, but no one did that. They quickly-quickly read out [the results of the investigation]. That they conducted an investigation—this is also nonsense. I don't believe it.

KAZBEK: You know what people whom I personally know, whose relatives died or were wounded or were in the school building think? If the authorities had officially recognized us as hostages, if they had officially apologized to us as it is normally done, then people would have calmed down much more. But it never happened, and people are all angry.

Not everyone angers equally, however. People vary in their readiness to anger or vulnerability to anger (Carver and Harmon-Jones 2009:187). Despite how anger-provoking the Beslan hostage taking appeared, it is plausible that the violence evoked other emotions, or was even rationalized by victims and that anger was not necessarily aroused (Miller 2001:533–534). The variation in emotional reaction may then have implications for the behavioral response.

Other emotions potentially evoked by an experience with violence include hatred, resentment, anxiety, and sadness. Like anger, hatred is a negative and disparaged emotion. It is an intense or passionate dislike and hostility that usually involves attributing to others stable negative characteristics such as intrinsic evil (Elster 1998:71; Halperin et al. 2011:276). In the case of ancient hatred, the others are often members of an ethnic out-group who have evolved historically into the traditional enemy (Petersen 2002:82). Again, like anger, hatred seems if not a justifiable then at least an understandable reaction to the hostage taking. As described in Chapter 1, historical animosities between Ossetians and Chechens and Ingush made it easy for victims to demonize members of the ethnic groups of the hostage takers, extrapolating from the Chechen and Ingush ethnicity of many terrorists to the idea that "Chechens and Ingush are the types of people who would do this sort of thing."

Hatred of government is not an idea that receives primary attention in the literature on emotions, but passionate dislike and attributions of intrinsic evil may not be reserved only for rival ethnic groups. Government also can come to be seen as an enemy, with particular government individuals seen as possessing deeply negative and unchangeable characteristics warranting hostility. Similarly, resentment, or bitterness over unfair treatment, could emerge after an experience with violence such as the Beslan hostage taking, and the resentment could be directed toward rival ethnic groups or government.

Anxiety, sadness, and many other emotions are also justifiable reactions to the Beslan hostage taking. Like anger and hatred, they are categorized as negative and unwanted, but they are less subject to normative condemnation. Exposure to violence is expected to generate unpleasant emotional responses. Anxiety is triggered by uncertainty, loss of control, the anticipation or threat of harm, and the violation of norms, particularly for norms that are "strategically central" to people and for violations that are extreme (Marcus et al. 2000:138; Carver and Harmon-Jones 2009:184; Valentino et al. 2009:310; Jasper 2011:292). In Beslan and arguably everywhere in the world, one strategically central norm is that children in a school building are never acceptable targets of violence, even in situations of ethnic or other conflict. In Beslan, that norm was egregiously violated, and after such violence, high levels of anxiety and depression are common (Huddy et al. 2005:595, 600). Victims are understandably preoccupied with past and future threats.

Experience with violence also sometimes triggers positive emotions such as hope. For example, about three-quarters of Israeli youth who were exposed to terror incidents reported feelings of posttraumatic growth (Laufer and Solomon 2006). The feelings include seeing new possibilities, relating more positively to others, sensing personal strength, changing spiritually, and appreciating life (Tedeschi and Calhoun 1996). People may reconstruct schemas to accommodate their violent experience, understand the trauma in personal terms, and allow the world to be comprehensible and meaningful again (Tedeschi 1999:320). They may feel gratitude for their safety and the safety of their loved ones (Fredrickson et al. 2003:365).

Negative and positive emotions after violence can coexist. They are separate, independent emotional dimensions rather than opposite ends of a continuum (Linley and Joseph 2004; Laufer and Solomon 2006). Growth after experiencing a terrorist incident, for example, can be accompanied by anxiety and depression (Tedeschi 1999:322).

Like anger and hatred, negative emotions such as anxiety and sadness and positive emotions such as hope vary across victims. Those physically closest to the violence, either by direct harm or via the killing or injury of a close relative, are typically the most emotionally aroused (Huddy et al. 2005:595, 600; Laufer and Solomon 2006:439). Even within this class of emotionally aroused victims of violence, individuals vary in the intensity and combination of their emotions. The variation may be due to personality, cognitive style, pre-trauma mental health, subjective interpretation of the violent episode, and other factors

(Tedeschi 1999:326–327; Laufer and Solomon 2006:442). The differing emotional reactions may then explain the differing behavioral responses to violent incidents such as the school hostage taking.

Anger's Dubious Role in Retaliatory Violence

Anger and hatred are the emotions most frequently hypothesized to lead to aggression or retaliatory harm (Averill 1983:1146; Elster 1998:51, 71; Harmon-Jones and Sigelman 2001; Petersen 2002; Skitka et al. 2006; Halperin et al. 2011; Tausch et al. 2011; Turner 2011:51; Jackson et al. 2019:325–326). The urgent need of angry people to right a perceived wrong supposedly encourages confrontation and violence (Halperin et al. 2011:275). When anger is defined as rage, violence even becomes subsumed in the definition ("violent, uncontrolled, explosive anger" or "a fit of violent wrath"), making it nearly impossible to disentangle the concepts and conceive of an anger that does not involve aggression. When violent acts are labeled "hate crimes," the causal role of emotionality is assumed with no evidence of emotion beyond the violent act itself.

Such propositions have their roots in a decades-old literature that described how otherwise normal and rational individuals were supposedly transformed by angry mobs to become angry themselves and therefore irrational and violent (Goodwin and Jasper 2006:612). Anger has been linked empirically to support for violent responses to the September 11 terrorist attacks in the United States (Skitka et al. 2006:375), support for the Iraq war (Huddy et al. 2007), opposition to peace agreements in Northern Ireland and Basque country (Halperin et al. 2011:275), and attacks against Jews and Germans in Lithuania, Poland, and Czechoslovakia (Petersen 2002). Accordingly, victims of violence who are angry might be expected to respond with retaliatory violence, and victims who are not angry might be expected to have less violent impulses (Petersen and Zukerman 2009).

However, the relationship between anger and retaliatory violence is actually not so clear. The literature on ethnic violence certainly includes discussion of emotions such as hate, resentment, and fear (Olzak 1992; Petersen 2002), but it also focuses on violence as a means of attaining short-term instrumental goals, independent of emotions (Kalyvas 1998, 2006). Moreover, action tendencies are socially regulated, inhibited or promoted by social norms (Elster 1998:51), and retaliatory violence in many if not most circumstances is a socially unacceptable channel for anger (Miller 2001:540). The mere presence of individual-level anger, hatred, or another negative emotion reveals very little about contextual factors such as instrumental goals, prevailing social norms, or the existence of provocateurs, political entrepreneurs who exploit anger and increase the acceptability and necessity of a violent response (Lake and Rothchild 1996; Fearon and Laitin 2000:846; Brass 2003; Kalyvas 2003; Wilkinson 2004; Bhavnani 2006; Varshney 2010). Thus, anger may reveal little about the propensity for retaliatory violence.

The suggestion that anger and other supposedly aggression-producing emotions lead to retaliatory ethnic violence also glosses over the unclear causal mechanism linking the two. Anger most likely provokes action, but why must that action be violent, particularly if the violence targets members of the perpetrators' ethnic group rather than the perpetrators themselves? Evidence from sociology shows that anger is often swallowed rather than released, and when released, anger assumes the form of bluster and bluff more than physical aggression (Collins 2008:21). Evidence from neuroscience shows that anger and aggression are even activated in distinct parts of the brain (Klimecki et al. 2018). Although some scholars distinguish the component measures of anger— arguing, for example, that hatred is more instrumental than rage (Petersen 2002)—there remains a black box between the feeling of hatred and the readiness for aggression. The causal mechanism is slightly clearer for resentment, or the intense feeling that status relations are unjust (Petersen 2002:51), but resentment is rarely hypothesized to prompt retaliatory violence against a rival ethnic group that occupies a lower position in the status hierarchy. Microlevel motivations for retaliatory violence probably involve other factors that enable individuals to commit physical harm.

Anxiety is also sometimes hypothesized to lead to violence. Intense ethnic conflict is supposedly "caused by collective fears of the future" (Lake and Rothchild 1996:41). Citizens are supposedly "willing to support extreme ends when they fear for their livelihoods, lives, and families" (de Figueiredo and Weingast 1999:263). They supposedly respond to ethnic appeals for extreme violence when they fear that their group's existence is threatened (Kaufman 2006:53) and that they face a choice of becoming a victim or perpetrator (Horowitz 2001:548). However, these hypotheses are tested mainly in macrolevel analyses that include no direct evidence of the fundamentally individual-level variable, anxiety, or the relationship between individuals' anxiety and their support for violence. The analyses also ignore the vast literature on emotions, cognition, and behavior that does not treat anxiety as a mobilizing emotion.

In more recent studies in microsociology, psychology, and neuroscience, anxiety is hypothesized to have the opposite effect on violence. Fear is shown to hinder the initiation of violence, confining people to bluster and backing down. When violence does occur, fear makes the violent person incompetent, misfiring, for example (Collins 2008:10). When there are already antagonistic groups, as in ethnic conflict, the predetermined social organization helps some individuals overcome fear to engage in violence (Collins 2008:11), but anxious individuals are unlikely to do this. Anxious individuals are more preoccupied with threat, aware of risks, prone to overestimating risks, and risk-averse than less anxious individuals. Through anxious eyes, retaliatory action is seen as dangerous and risky and therefore not worth supporting (Huddy et al. 2005:595). Instead, anxious individuals avoid the danger and risk that characterize many forms of violence, including retaliatory ethnic violence (Huddy et al. 2005:603– 605). By implication, we might expect that the least anxious victims after the Beslan school hostage taking were the most supportive of retaliation.

This logic, although based on thoughtful consideration of emotional processes, still requires a leap. The causal mechanism is again unexplained. While it makes sense that anxious victims have more barriers to violent action than less anxious victims, it is unclear why less anxious victims are motivated to behave violently, simply because barriers are fewer. The underlying assumption is that retaliatory violence is the default, ready to be unleashed if only the risks were few or perceived as such. The question remains why any victim would respond to their victimization by victimizing others who did not directly cause their victimization. What are the motivations?

The literature has very little to say about the role of positive emotions such as hope, gratitude, pride, joy, contentment, or enthusiasm on support for retaliatory violence. Positive emotions have been shown to broaden people's receptivity to a variety of behavioral options and to facilitate coping during crises (Fredrickson et al. 2003:366). However, it is unclear whether retaliatory violence is among the behavioral options that victims with positive emotions could consider and whether support for retaliatory violence is consistent with coping. Perhaps retaliatory violence, because it is normatively undesirable to most people, is inconsistent with coping, and support for retaliatory violence is therefore not a logical effect of positive emotions. With such limited guidance from prior research, there should be no firm expectations for whether Beslan victims who reported high levels of hope, enthusiasm, and pride were more supportive of retaliatory violence than other victims.

Anger's Powerful Role in Political Action

Post-violence anger is here hypothesized to manifest in peaceful political activism, and the lack of anger in post-violence situations is hypothesized to be demobilizing. Anger is an empowering emotion, in the sense that anger demands expression and action (Averill 1983:1152; Miller 2001:533; Carver and Harmon-Jones 2009; Valentino et al. 2011). An angry victim often has a stronger "approach motivation" than a less angry victim (Mikulincer 1988), more optimistically appraises risk (Skitka et al. 2006:376), and thus may be more likely to

do *something* in response to violence. Constructive action such as political mobilization is a likely contender. The hypothesis about post-violence contexts is
supported by recent empirical work on the mobilizing potential of anger in nonviolent contexts (Simon and Ruhs 2008; Halperin et al. 2011; Tausch et al. 2011;
Valentino et al. 2011; Jost et al. 2012).

Where the logic connecting anger and retaliatory violence seems incomplete,
there is no black box separating anger from political activism. A huge wave of research in the past decade or two provides explanation for the causal mechanism.
The research shows that, contrary to conventional wisdom that pits emotions
against reason, many emotions are mobilizing and even constructive. Emotions
help motivate individuals to act quickly, avoid procrastination, and make good
decisions. Often, a "decision guided by emotions and reason is better than what
can be achieved by rational deliberation alone" (Elster 1998:58). For example,
brain-damaged patients who lack emotion lose their decision-making capacity
(Elster 1998:61). Emotions turn "a thinking being into an actor," as in the case
of a person concerned about the needy who is stirred to help only after an emotional impulse (Frijda et al. 2000:3–4).

Anger in particular has been shown to have this mobilizing capacity
(Goodwin and Jasper 2006:619). In interpersonal relationships, anger often
serves not to dominate the person who caused the anger but to bring attention
to previously ignored issues and, when resolved, leads to repaired relations and
the reinstatement of trust and joint social goals (Oatley 2000:98–99). During
elections, anger can motivate people to participate when they otherwise
might not (Valentino et al. 2011:168). Anger has politicized Turkish migrants
in Germany (Simon and Ruhs 2008:1360) and citizens in the United States,
Greece, and Britain (Jost et al. 2012), and it has increased support for reconciliation and risk-taking in peace negotiations between Israelis and Palestinians
(Halperin et al. 2011:275). Anger over the violent repression of peaceful protest can motivate people to join the protest, even if the prospect of finding
themselves on the receiving end of the repression should motivate otherwise
(Jasper 2011:292).

The often high correlations between anger and hatred suggest that hatred too
might be a politically mobilizing emotion (Becker et al. 2011:7). Similarly, resentment might be politically mobilizing, particularly resentment directed toward a
government once thought to be caring and then revealed as callously indifferent,
as in the case of the Russian government after the Beslan school hostage taking.

The relationship between other emotions and political participation are less
clear. Anxiety, for example, is sometimes thought to make a voter more receptive to new, often negative information and thus trigger involvement in politics
(Marcus et al. 2000; Robbins et al. 2013). However, anxiety can make people feel
incapacitated, paralyzed, and unable to act. In the 2008 American presidential

elections, anxiety was demobilizing (Valentino et al. 2011:162). Because anxiety may work in complex and sometimes contradictory ways, its effect on post-violence political participation in Beslan might be minimal.

Pride can encourage action (Goodwin and Jasper 2006:619), and again, positive emotions can broaden the range of acceptable behavioral options for victims, especially personal coping strategies (Fredrickson et al. 2003:266). To the degree that political action to redress grievances serves as a coping strategy, positive emotions might be mobilizing. However, political action to redress grievances is by definition a somewhat negatively motivated behavior. Victims are dissatisfied, and dissatisfaction is not logically coupled with pride, hope, and enthusiasm. The positive emotions might therefore be demobilizing. Because the influences are potentially contradictory, positive emotions might have minimal effects on post-violence political participation in Beslan.

Measuring Anger and Other Emotions

To measure anger, Marcus, MacKuen, Wolak, and Keele (2006:12–13) recommend markers including hatred, contempt, and resentment. They also recommend framing questions either in terms of the perceived frequency or intensity of emotion, noting that there appear to be few empirical differences.

Consistent with these recommendations, this analysis adapts the widely used question format for measuring depression—"how many days during the past week (0–7) have you felt . . . ?" (Weissman et al. 1977; Mirowsky and Ross 1989)—and replaces "sad," "lonely," and other depression emotions with relevant anger markers: "angry," "hatred," and "resentful." A mean index of 0–7 was then created, where 0 represents the least angry victim and 7 represents the most angry. The same logic was followed in measuring the emotions of enthusiasm, inserting "hopeful," "enthusiastic," and "proud," and of anxiety, inserting "anxious," "afraid," and "worried."

The component measures of the anger index are not identical or interchangeable. Research shows, for example, that anger and hatred have some distinct causes (Fisher and Roseman 2007). However, anger, hatred, and resentment are highly correlated, and indeed hatred sometimes develops from previous or prolonged anger, especially with individuals who are not intimates of the victims and not within their control (Fisher and Roseman 2007). Here results are reported for both the combined anger index and its three component measures. The results of multivariate analysis reported later in Chapter 11 are mainly based on the index. Anger, hatred, and resentment are tested separately in the multivariate models and, despite their theoretical distinctiveness, lead to very similar results.

Table 5.1 shows that, on average, Beslan victims felt angry two of the past seven days before they were surveyed, a reasonably high frequency of anger but not that different from the frequency during which they felt positive emotions like enthusiasm and pride (probably a testimony to human resilience) and less than the average of three days during which they felt anxiety. Most importantly, for all the emotions measured, standard deviations are very high—usually higher than

Table 5.1. Emotions of Beslan Victims

Number of days during past week (0–7) feeling . . .	Mean	Standard Deviation
Anger	2.28	1.96
Resentment	2.30	2.43
Hatred	1.64	2.20
Anger index (anger, resentment, hatred)	2.11	1.88
Hopeful	3.23	2.69
Enthusiastic	1.99	2.10
Proud	1.83	2.30
Enthusiasm index (hopeful, enthusiastic, proud)	2.29	1.90
Anxious	3.66	2.54
Afraid	2.90	2.62
Worried	3.41	2.56
Anxiety index (anxious, afraid, worried)	3.38	2.25
Couldn't get going	3.39	2.52
Getting or staying asleep	3.80	2.54
Sad	3.75	2.47
Everything was an effort	3.43	2.53
Lonely	2.74	2.71
Unable to stop melancholy	3.12	2.67
Trouble keeping focused	2.99	2.39
Depression index (above seven questions)	3.32	1.96
Played sports or exercised	1.58	2.47
Done something enjoyable like music, art, reading, or hobby	2.11	2.65

$N = 1,098$.

two points on a scale that is only eight points. This suggests great emotional variation among Beslan victims and confirms that not everyone angers equally—or frightens equally or rebounds with hope equally—and this variation might have meaningful implications for post-violence behavioral reactions.

This approach to measuring emotions has several limitations, including the measurement of emotion years after the hostage taking and the cross-sectional research design, which challenge the ability to make causal claims linking emotion to behavioral outcomes. These challenges are discussed at length below. Still, even with these challenges, this approach to measuring emotions represents an improvement on previous studies, mostly because the study victims are believable. In survey terms, the measures of emotions are probably high on face validity and construct validity. When a Beslan victim reported emotions, the full team of researchers, including interviewers, field managers, and study designers, can convey with 100 percent confidence that these emotions were genuine, many having witnessed crying and other emotional outbursts firsthand, and plenty of journalistic accounts and other observations attest to the fact that the hostage taking was a deeply emotion-provoking incident. Given the horrific details of the Beslan school hostage taking, no reasonable argument could be made to suggest that Beslan victims are inappropriate people for testing the effects of anger on behavior because their grievances are not believably anger-provoking.

Most previous studies of the behavioral effects of emotion are based on less valid measures of emotions. They select test subjects who may or may not have experienced a deeply emotional incident, and they attempt to manipulate emotion experimentally in a laboratory setting. For example, researchers inform subjects of a real or fictitious issue involving procedural unfairness or ask subjects to recall emotion-provoking events and to describe the resulting emotion (e.g., van Zomeren et al. 2004; Tausch et al. 2011; Jost et al. 2012). Compared to survey research, this approach has the virtue of supposedly allowing researchers to assign emotions randomly and thus be more certain of the causal direction from emotion to participation, rather than vice versa (e.g., Valentino et al. 2011). However, while these studies may indeed minimize such problems of survey research, they introduce other, bigger problems.

First, researchers using experimental manipulations of emotion cannot be certain that they have indeed succeeded in inducing a true emotion rather than one "recalled" simply for the experiment. Participants often try to be "good" at their assigned task, attempting to please the researcher by giving answers when asked (Schuman and Presser 1996: chap. 5; Javeline 1999), and if the task calls for remembering anger or fear, most participants will likely oblige, but that does not necessarily mean that they are or have been angry, anxious, enthusiastic, sad, or any other emotion to a noteworthy degree (Klimecki et al. 2018). Indeed, for many of these studies, it is plausible to imagine participants reporting deep anger, frustration, or irritation during one minute and leaving the laboratory and happily skipping off to lunch the next, in a way we have more difficulty imagining with victims of violence.

Second and related, to the extent that emotions are induced in laboratory experiments, they likely fall at the low end of the intensity scale, even when the participants themselves indicate high-intensity emotions. (And intensity in such manipulations is often not even assessed by the participants but by the researchers who are trying to adhere to a coding scheme, despite the great subjectivity of emotion.) Such artificially induced emotions are likely to be "transient" and not comparable to the emotions of victims of violence (Petersen and Zukerman 2009). Indeed, it is probably not feasible to induce in a laboratory the kind of powerful, important emotions that are relevant for many kinds of behavioral reactions (Elster 1999:404), especially if the goal is to generalize to victims of violence.

The root of the problem for experimental manipulations of emotions is issue salience, or the lack thereof. Many issues that are the focus of psychological studies are either minor, such as ethical-political aspects of cafeteria food (Klar and Kasser 2009), tuition fees (van Zomeren et al. 2004; Becker et al. 2011; Tausch et al. 2011), or additional course requirements (van Zomeren et al. 2004), or the issues are removed from the individual and therefore not directly experienced, such as environmental protection (Becker et al. 2011) or the government bank bailout (Jost et al. 2012). It is difficult to imagine that these less salient issues could truly provoke the same emotions and behavioral responses as something so deeply felt as victimization by violence. Compare any of the above issues, for example, to the inexplicable murder of a child—literally inexplicable for the tens if not hundreds of Beslan parents who are still not even sure of the causal chain of events that led to their children's deaths.

Moreover, although political position (for or against tuition fees, for example) is often gauged, laboratory experiments rarely include measures of the intensity of the grievance or the commitment to the position. Do participants even care about tuition fees, for example—a question so rhetorical about the Beslan hostage taking or violence in other communities that it would be shockingly insensitive to ask. Strength or centrality of concerns is the major determinant of emotional intensity (Frijda and Mesquita 2000:62). Yet, for laboratory studies focusing on questionably salient issues, salience is an essential but often omitted control variable in multivariate analysis, rendering the resulting study less useful. Issues at the focus of political science studies, such as job prospects and a viral outbreak, seem more salient (e.g., Brader et al. 2011) but often involve hypothetical scenarios (a fictional outbreak, for example) and still probably fall far short of the salience of victimization by violence. They can therefore make only limited contributions to the study of emotions and political behavior. In the words of Halperin et al. (2011:286):

> It seems that although experimentalists have made great strides in manipulating short-term anger responses, a fuller understanding of emotion—particularly as it applies to real-world situations such as long-term conflicts—requires that we put anger back in context.

Limitations to Emotion Measurements

Still, studying anger via survey research, even in context, is not without challenges. Potential limitations to this study's measurements of emotions are that emotions were measured (a) almost three years after the emotion-provoking violent incident, (b) simultaneously with measurements of participation and support for violence, (c) in a diffuse sense without reference to specific targets, and (d) with similarly structured questions, making them subject to "straight line response strategies," or respondents mechanically giving the same answer to all questions (Herzog and Bachman 1981), rather than validly differentiating based on their true emotions. Each of these challenges is addressed in turn.

Measuring Emotion Years after the Incident

The Beslan victim survey was conducted in the spring and summer of 2007, and the questions on emotions referenced "how many days in the past week (0–7)." It could be argued that, to be valid, the emotion measurements should have been taken much earlier in some narrow window after the hostage taking but directly preceding the hypothesized behavioral effect. Measurements of emotions taken so long after their hypothesized effect may not be accurate, and statistical analysis using these later flawed measurements as explanatory variables may thus be error-prone.

There is no simple answer to the timing problem of the survey, and to a large extent this limitation must simply be acknowledged. However, there is also no simple answer as to what timing would have been more appropriate. One of the dependent variables, political participation, is a count of a range of activities that occurred from 2004 to 2006, some occurring as early as days after the hostage-taking. Ethical concerns prohibited approaching victims and asking about their emotions at that most sensitive time, as did the very practical issue of needing to secure research funds, but assuming researchers were callous and flush, the question still remains: Which point in time would be most appropriate for emotion measurement?

First, it is entirely plausible that later measurements of anger and other emotions are as accurate as immediate measurements. Everyday anger seems to have a modal duration of about a half hour, but even everyday incidents like consumer dissatisfaction can last weeks (Petersen and Zukerman 2009), so it can reasonably be assumed that anger after a violent hostage taking would be slower to decay and could last months or even years (Petersen and Zukerman 2009). It can also reasonably be assumed that other emotions and mood states like anxiety and depression also endure. Anger, anxiety, depression, and other emotions have been shown to be more severe and longer lasting for victims of hate crimes than for victims of other types of crimes (Green et al. 2001:493).

Even if emotions lose strength or otherwise change over time, the change may not jeopardize analysis when the main goal is to differentiate victims based on emotions relative to one another. Measurement error of emotions is most devastating for analysis if the rank ordering of victims changes over time, but it is less problematic if emotional intensity for individuals changes but not their emotional intensity relative to other victims. In the latter case, the relationship between the emotion and the outcome of interest should not change. For example, anxiety decreased in the United States after the September 11, 2001, terrorist attacks, but the relationship between anxiety and support for national security policy remained the same (Huddy et al. 2005:599). Anger as a temperament or personality trait is highly correlated with anger as a reaction (Zimprich and Mascherek 2012), suggesting that the rank ordering of victims by their level of anger would probably be similar if the survey was conducted in 2004, 2005, or 2006.

Second, it is also plausible that the later measurements are more accurate. People may take a while before even noticing or acknowledging their anger (Elster 1998:58). When they do notice their anger, the emotion does not necessarily remain constant over time. It is just as likely, or more likely, that anger grows. Anger often feeds on itself and persists through rumination: a focus on the angering episode can exacerbate and prolong anger, independent of any action taken (Frijda and Mesquita 2000:54; Horowitz 2001:186; Petersen and Zukerman 2009). Even without rumination, the passage of time can bring new information to bear and intensify the grievances and emotions. For example, Beslan victim Felisa Batagova remarked, "The government tells us only lies, and people are just getting madder and madder" (Sands 2004b:A01). Anger is not the only emotion with snowball potential. Anxiety, for example, demonstrates the same tendency. Anxious individuals tend to perceive more danger and vulnerability as they ponder their anxiety (Eysenck 2000:182).

Beslan victims certainly ruminated and pondered, as evidenced not only by the reports of interviewers and focus group moderators but also by very public displays of emotion, such as the wearing of mourning clothes every day for years after the hostage taking ("Beslan Teachers Send" 2005). Therefore, measurement of emotions within the first few hours or days after the hostage taking might have been most predictive of participatory acts occurring hours or days after the emotion measurement, but those measures might not have retained their validity over time and thus not held any advantage for predicting later participatory acts.

In an ideal research design, it would be possible to measure victims' anger and other emotions minutes before each and every participatory act—to monitor the growth or subduing of anger over time, track the emotion trend with the behavior trend, and tease out the direction of causality. Of course, ethical, financial, and practical concerns make such a research design highly unlikely: it would be indecent to bother victims of violence with requests for interviews at the frequency necessary to test causality, given the rapid cascade of participatory acts during 2004–2006, and finding the research funds and time necessary for such an endeavor would be unlikely. More importantly, such a research design is ideal in theory only: asking victims of violence to report their emotions so frequently would surely lead to attrition (dropping out of the survey) and poor quality survey response (satisficing or otherwise answering quickly and superficially to be dutiful but minimize the hassle). Realistically then, any study of the behavioral effects of emotion will probably involve a single opportunity to interview victims, and that single opportunity, whenever it may be, will likely involve some error in the measurement of emotions.

The relevant research question is whether measures taken in 2007 were systematically biased so as to consistently over- or underestimate emotions in some way that is correlated with the dependent variables, political participation or support for retaliatory violence. For example, could anger have increased by 2007 only for those Beslan victims who were politically active? This leads to the question of "reverse causation."

Inferring Causality with a Cross-Sectional Survey Design

The use of a single cross-sectional survey to study the aftermath of violence means that questions about emotions and political participation were necessarily asked in the very same interview, with no conclusive way to determine causal order. Although the goal is to test the effects of emotion on behavior, behavior could plausibly be causally prior to emotions. Individuals could become angry by virtue of having participated politically, as in the case of students whose collective action against government inflamed their anger (Becker et al. 2011:1593) or more generally when attempts to address an injustice produce few results and come to be perceived as futile (Tausch et al. 2011:141). Individuals could also manufacture and report anger or other feelings to be consistent with actions taken. People are often uncomfortable with cognitive dissonance and try to reduce this discomfort, sometimes by changing beliefs or attitudes to be consistent with behavior (Harmon-Jones 2000). In terms of post-violence behavioral reactions, an individual could plausibly think, "I acted, therefore I must be angry."

As with the timing problem, there is no simple answer to the challenge of "reverse causation," and to a large extent this limitation must be acknowledged. However, there are very good reasons to suspect that the causal direction is largely from emotion to behavior, even if there is some feedback in the other direction.

First, the multi-method approach employed here allows for the triangulation of sources of information, including survey data, focus group discussions, and media reports. The sources are highly consistent in showing that the grievance context in Beslan was a major, if not the major, source of anger after the hostage taking. Real problems, real complaints, and at least some amount of anger and other emotions predated political action in Beslan, and these complaints and emotions varied across individuals. Participators may have gotten more emotionally charged from their participation, but the rich contextual evidence casts doubt on the possibility that participants began their activist journey emotionally similar to other victims and could attribute their emotional arousal exclusively or mainly to political participation.

Second, the post-violence Beslan story focuses not only on emotion, but on political alienation and political efficacy. Beslan victims who were angry, politically alienated, and politically efficacious were among the most likely political activists. If instead causation was reversed and political activism caused anger, presumably it would do so only because the activism was unsuccessful (Becker et al. 2011:1596). However, if the activism was unsuccessful, presumably it would lead not only to anger but also to a decline in political efficacy (Valentino et al. 2009), yet this combination—high political activism, high anger, and low political efficacy—is rarely found in the data. Beslan victims who were politically active and angry also tended to be high on political efficacy. Such a combination of characteristics makes most sense if anger and political efficacy precede political activism and its successful or unsuccessful outcome.

Further evidence suggesting that emotion is causally prior to action comes from analysis of the effects of emotion on retaliatory violence. As shown below, anger and other emotions have no bearing on support for retaliatory violence among Beslan victims. Presumably, if victims were altering their survey responses to resolve cognitive dissonance, they would be most likely to do so in the case of support for violence. "I reported that I support killing Chechens as a response to the hostage taking, therefore I must be angry." That there is little if any evidence of such attempts to resolve cognitive dissonance and that angry victims are just as likely to oppose retaliatory violence as support it suggests that respondents were independently assessing their emotions and their behavior.

This is not to discount the standard problem with any cross-sectional survey of establishing cause and effect when cause and effect were measured simultaneously. Rather, it is an acknowledgment of the complexity for all research that aims to measure emotion and behavior and establish causality between the two. The approach taken here—measuring the emotions and behavior of a genuinely aggrieved population whose emotions, attitudes, and behavior seemed equally genuine—represents an important advancement over previous studies.

Measuring Diffuse Rather than Targeted Emotions

Some psychological theory and evidence suggest that anger results partly from the attribution of blame to an individual, group, organization, or government entity (Brader et al. 2011), thereby suggesting that anger usually has a target and should be measured with reference to a specific target. Individuals tend to specify perpetrators and get angry at those perpetrators, not at situations (Keltner et al. 1993; Frijda and Mesquita 2000:62; Petersen and Zukerman 2009:566). "The object of anger is the person whom we believe to have hurt us" (Elster 1998:49).

However, in some cases, the object of anger may be indeterminate (Elster 1998). The existence of anger does not necessarily mean there is clarity about the target of anger (Gamson et al. 1982; Goodwin and Jasper 2006:617). For example, anger at ethnic violence could be directed at initiators of violence within one's own ethnic group or at retaliators among a rival ethnic group (Fearon and Laitin 1996). If "A causes B to hurt C"—arguably the case in Beslan, where A could be the Chechen and Ingush terrorists and B could be the government forced to launch a counterterrorist operation, or where A could be the government and B could be the Chechens and Ingush enabled by the government's laxity and corruption—then the Beslan victims, C, could plausibly be angry at A or B or both (Elster 1998:49–50).

Indeed, many studies dealing with anger are explicitly concerned with the effects of diffuse anger. Presumably, diffuse anger involves a somewhat arbitrary selection of targets, with targets often being substitutable and not coherently blameworthy (Petersen 2002:31; Goodwin and Jasper 2006:617), and presumably, diffuse anger has the greatest potential to lead to violence:

[B]reaking the connection with the source of the emotion generates a "heat-seeking emotional missile" without a guidance system. It is this kind of free-floating emotional arousal that can, of course, generate personal aggres-sion and violence against anyone or any thing (Turner 2011:47), including members of a categoric unit such as an ethnic group.

The argument is not that anger is appropriately targeted at the ethnic group because the ethnic group is sincerely and accurately held responsible for some harmful action. Rather, the argument is simply that diffuse anger gets vented and is sometimes even misattributed, displaced, or targeted erroneously (Clore and Gasper 2000; Goodwin and Jasper 2006:617). For example, despite Iraq's lack of involvement in the September 11 attacks, the United States invaded Iraq anyway, supposedly displacing anger toward al-Qaeda (Turner 2011). Post-9/11 anger at Muslims could also be described as displaced, with some 2,000 violent incidents of individuals reportedly seeking out Muslims for retaliation (Singh 2002). The cognitive distortions associated with displaced anger are said to lead to scape-goating, or creating "enemies" to be attacked (Petersen 2002), enemies who are sources of frustration, even if not the primary source (Horowitz 2001). In regard to rage,

> the emotion exists before targets are selected. . . . residual frustration might op-erate to find a target through substitution. The group that is the cause of the frustration is unavailable, but the emotion remains and drives the individual to find a new object, a substitute target. (Petersen 2002:80)

Arguably, "accurate" targeting of anger in Beslan would have been toward the terrorists, without whom the hostage taking and its bloody aftermath indisput-ably could not have happened, but the terrorists were all said to be dead, save for Kulayev whom some believed may be dead too rather than imprisoned for life. Even if many terrorists escaped, their unknown identities and whereabouts made them inconvenient targets for anger. In this sense, any and all anger about the hostage taking had been displaced to other sources, and the anger might well be "free-floating" or diffuse.

This study tests specifically for the effects of diffuse anger. Testing for the effects of targeted anger seems tautological and less worthy of investigation. Of course, victims who are most angry at Chechens and Ingush will be more likely to act against Chechens and Ingush, whereas those most angry at government will be more likely to act against government. However, what of victims who are just plain angry—angry at Chechens, Ingush, government, society, the global com-munity, and so on? What does this emotion of diffuse anger provoke them to do?

This study also tests for the effects of other emotions in their diffuse states, even those said to be less diffuse by definition. For example, hatred usually has a historical target with historical justification, based on previous antagonistic experiences (Petersen 2002). Still, it is important to test for the effects of diffuse hatred, the feeling itself independent of the source. In a post-violence situation like Beslan, it is quite plausible to "hate the world," to feel the emotion of hatred welling up inside and not necessarily have clarity on the source of the feelings. As an *Izvestia* correspondent noted in his award-winning coverage[1] of the psychological aftermath of the hostage taking:

> A year after the tragedy, Beslan still brims with hatred: hatred toward the Ingush, who are viewed as either terrorists or their accomplices; hatred toward the authorities, who did not do everything in their power to save the hostages; women's hatred toward men for not having taken revenge for the deaths of their children and reciprocal hatred from the men toward the women for their endless mourning. . . . Beslan residents stew in this hatred. (Naidenov 2005c)

Although objects of hatred are named in the *Izvestia* article, they seem incidental. The hatred is broadly felt; targeted individuals, groups, and institutions, a secondary part of the story.

Similarly, states such as depression are characterized by the lack of a salient object or the presence of a rather amorphous, broad object such as "things in general," and "the unassigned feelings are available to be displaced to stimuli that are irrelevant or only partially relevant" (Clore and Gasper 2000:17). Emotions such as happiness, sadness, and fear too can sometimes occur without objects (Oatley 2000).

To the extent that targets are important for behavioral reactions to violence— and of course they are—several questions on blame attribution are included in the survey. Questions ask victims to assess the accountability for the hostage taking of various government actors as well as Chechens and Ingush (see Chapters 6 and 7). In multivariate statistical analysis, controls are added for blame, including blame of Chechens, Putin, and other federal officials, so the targets are already part of the models. If measures of emotions had also included targets, they would likely have been highly collinear with the measures of blame and would have made it difficult to test for the independent effects of each on retaliatory violence and political participation.

---

[1] Igor Naidenov won the 2005 Andrei Sakharov Prize from the Glasnost Defense Foundation. See "Spetskor 'Izvestii' Igor Naidenov stal laureatom premii imeni Andreya Sakharova [The special correspondent of *Izvestia* Igor Naidenov became the winner of the Andrei Skaharov Prize]," December 12, 2005, available at https://iz.ru/news/309285.

212 WHY POLITICS AND NONVIOLENCE?

Are Respondents Answering in "Straight-Line Response Sets"?

When survey questions have identical response scales and are asked one after another, there is a risk that respondents will choose the identical response category for all questions or at least concentrate responses at the same end of the scale. This is especially true when fatigue sets in at the end of lengthy surveys and for attitudinal items more than personal demographic questions (Herzog and Bachman 1981). If Beslan victims chose a straight-line response strategy for the emotion questions, there would be little differentiation among the emotions, which would compromise the ability to make valid inferences from the data.

This challenge could and should be leveled at almost every study of emotion and behavior, including or especially laboratory experimental manipulations. Most other studies measure emotions using attitude statements with six-, seven-, or nine-point response scales ranging from strongly agree to strongly disagree ("I detest people who advocate tuition fees") or from not at all to very much ("When I think about the pension bill the government is trying to pass, I feel angry"). They too risk straight-line response sets, as well as the probably bigger problem of acquiescence bias, or the propensity of respondents to agree with a statement regardless of its content (Schuman and Presser 1996: chap. 8; Javeline 1999).

Moreover, several of these other studies measure other key variables with the same style of survey question (using response scales with the same number of points), biasing the studies toward positive findings. For example, "action tendencies" in other studies have been measured with questions about how likely respondents were to participate in future political activities, and the response scales were also seven-point scales ranging from very unlikely to very likely (Tausch et al. 2011). If respondents tend to stay on a single side of the scale when responding to questions on both emotions and political participation, findings would be statistically significant, potentially strong, and yet entirely spurious. It is up to the researchers to address this methodological issue and demonstrate that findings are genuine and not a methodological artifact.

The responses from Beslan victims can be examined to gauge whether respondents were differentiating their responses, answering sincerely rather than "checking the same box" for assessments of each of their emotions. Correlations matrices between the emotions suggest that few respondents employed straight-line response strategies. Emotions that are theoretically related to one another, such as anxiety, fear, and worry, were empirically related as well, with correlations higher than .6 ($p < .001$). Emotions that are theoretically unrelated—such as the negative emotions of anger, hate, and resentment with the positive emotions of hope, enthusiasm, and pride—were also empirically unrelated, with all nine correlations lower than .1 and not statistically significant. If Beslan victims were thoughtlessly responding to emotion questions by giving answers at the same end of the scale, it is unlikely that the empirical results would line up so sensibly.

As a separate test, factor analysis was conducted on all eighteen questions asked in the same list with the same response set of "0–7 days." These results also suggest meaningful responses rather than straightline responses strategies. If respondents were answering all questions similarly, factor analysis would reveal only a single or very few factors with Eigenvalues over 1.0, because the dimension common to all emotions would not be the substance (whether it is a positive or negative emotion, for example) but just the structure of the question (eight-point scales). Instead, factor analysis revealed much greater differentiation among respondents. The analysis generated seven separate factors with Eigenvalues over 1.0, suggesting that some dimensions are common to one group of questions (hope, enthusiasm, and pride all load heavily on the same factor, for example), while other dimensions are common to other groups.

As a final test, in the same list as the emotions questions, victims were asked how many days in the last seven they played sports or exercised and how many days they did something they enjoyed like music, art, reading, or some other hobby. Exercise was positively correlated with measures of enthusiasm and negatively or not at all correlated with measures of anxiety and anger. Enjoyable activities were related to emotions with much the same patterns, only the negative correlations with measures of anxiety were even stronger. These quite reasonable results again suggest that respondents made meaningful differentiations when reporting the frequency of their emotions.

Beslan Victim Data on Emotions and Behavior

The data from Beslan victims show that anger has a very strong positive correlation with political participation. Victims were asked how many days in the last seven had they felt anger, and they were then asked the same questions about hatred and resentment. These responses were then averaged into a single anger index, ranging from zero to seven. As Table 5.2 shows, the angriest victims—those who felt these strong negative emotions over five days a week—were extraordinarily unlikely to sit on the sidelines. More than half of the angriest victims (53.1 percent) participated in four or more activities, and more than a quarter (28.6 percent) participated in eleven or more activities. Thus the angriest victims were roughly six to nine times more active than the less angry victims. Only a quarter (26.5 percent) participated in no political activities, as compared to the majority of those who were never angry (59.3 percent) or angry only one day a week or less (57.6 percent).

Table 5.2. Anger and Political Participation

Anger Index (0–7 mean scale of responses to "How many days in the past week (0–7) have you felt angry? hatred? resentful?")

	No Activities	One Activity	Two or Three Activities	Four to Ten Activities	Eleven to Thirty-one Activities	Missing	N
0 days	73 (56.2)	19 (14.6)	17 (13.1)	5 (3.8)	4 (3.1)	12 (9.2)	130 (100.0)
> 0 to 1 day	94 (56.3)	28 (16.8)	18 (10.8)	13 (7.8)	3 (1.8)	11 (6.6)	167 (100.0)
> 1 to 3 days	135 (44.7)	33 (10.9)	46 (15.2)	38 (12.6)	14 (4.6)	36 (11.9)	302 (100.0)
> 3 to 5 days	38 (41.3)	8 (8.7)	8 (8.7)	7 (7.6)	10 (10.9)	21 (22.8)	92 (100.0)
> 5 to 7 days	16 (25.8)	4 (6.5)	8 (12.9)	11 (17.7)	15 (24.2)	8 (12.9)	62 (100.0)

$N = 1,098$; number of victims (%); Pearson's $r = .26$, $p < .00$.

Hatred ("How many days in the past week (0–7) have you felt hatred?")

	No Activities	One Activity	Two or Three Activities	Four to Ten Activities	Eleven to Thirty-one Activities	Missing	N
0 days	167 (52.5)	50 (15.7)	39 (12.3)	19 (6.0)	8 (2.5)	35 (11.0)	318 (100.0)
1 day	49 (47.1)	13 (12.5)	26 (25.0)	8 (7.7)	2 (1.9)	6 (5.8)	104 (100.0)
2 or 3 days	70 (50.7)	14 (10.1)	13 (9.4)	21 (15.2)	9 (6.5)	11 (8.0)	138 (100.0)
4 or 5 days	21 (38.9)	4 (7.4)	8 (14.8)	6 (11.1)	5 (9.3)	10 (18.5)	54 (100.0)
6 or 7 days	11 (17.7)	3 (4.8)	8 (12.9)	11 (17.7)	19 (30.6)	10 (16.1)	62 (100.0)

$N = 1,098$; number of victims (%); Pearson's $r = .33$, $p < .00$.

Of all the component measures of the anger index, hatred is the most significant. A victim who felt hatred six or seven days a week was roughly ten times as likely to be a political activist, with 37.1 percent participating in eleven or more activities, compared to only 3.8 percent of those who never felt hatred or felt it only one day a week. Fewer than one in five (17.7 percent) of the most hate-filled victims refrained from activism altogether, compared to roughly half of the least hate-filled victims. The relationship between anger, hatred, and peaceful political participation is among the most statistically robust in the data. No matter which other demographic and attitudinal measures are added to the multivariate analysis in Chapter 11, anger and especially hatred have consistently significant positive effects on political participation. Although the conventional wisdom denounces hatred and other aversive sentiments, the data suggest that hatred, anger, and resentment can be peaceful, productive emotions.

Does anger also heighten the tendency to "lash out" (Petersen 2002)? Does it encourage aggression? Emotional theories of displaced anger might seem to explain why Beslan victims would support attacking individuals of Chechen or Ingush nationality who were not militants. The potential retaliators would presumably not need to tell themselves a coherent story that links their victimization to their lashing out, and to the extent that they did try to tell such a story, they could engage in cognitive distortions, greatly inflating the connection of ordinary Chechen or Ingush civilians to the militants (see Petersen 2002:115).

However, what of anger that does not lead to such cognitive distortions (or leads to cognitive distortions of a different kind with a different, non-ethnic target)? As shown in Chapter 6, theory and empirical evidence convincingly and directly connect ethnic prejudice and scapegoating with retaliatory violence, suggesting that an aversion to Ingush people and a readiness to blame Chechens as a whole for the actions of a few should be highly correlated with support for retaliatory violence. The theory and evidence are weaker in drawing causal links between diffuse anger and support for violence. As described above, even the angriest and most hate-filled of victims might refrain from retaliatory violence in the presence of community norms discouraging violence (Averill 1983:1147–1148; Lake and Rothchild 1996; Elster 1998:51; Fearon and Laitin 2000:846; Miller 2001:540; Kalyvas 2003; Bhavnani 2006) and self-censorship of long-reviled behavior, even when norms start to change. Contemporary humans in most places at most times, no matter how emotional, do not support violence.

As Table 5.3 shows, there is no statistically significant correlation between anger and support for retaliatory violence. The angriest and least angry victims in Beslan expressed relatively similar (low) approval of killing Chechens as a response to the hostage taking. This finding holds true in the multivariate analysis in Chapter 11, again suggesting that anger is not necessarily channeled violently, and the target of anger is not necessarily rival ethnic groups. The benefits of anger are thus reinforced: evidence from Beslan victims indicates not only a constructive role for anger in mobilizing political participation but also a negligible role for anger in support for retaliatory violence.

Table 5.3. Anger and Support for Retaliatory Violence (Killing the Same Number of Chechens as Were Killed in Beslan)

Anger (0–7 mean scale of responses to "How many days in the past week (0–7) have you felt angry? hatred? resentful?")

	Completely Disapprove	Somewhat Disapprove	Somewhat Approve	Fully Approve	Missing	N
0 days	54	52	7	10	7	130
	(41.5)	(40.0)	(5.4)	(7.7)	(5.4)	(100.0)
> 0 to 1 day	72	59	18	3	15	167
	(43.1)	(35.3)	(10.8)	(1.8)	(9.0)	(100.0)
> 1 to 3 days	132	110	29	18	13	302
	(43.7)	(36.4)	(9.6)	(6.0)	(4.3)	(100.0)
> 3 to 5 days	36	30	8	9	9	92
	(39.1)	(32.6)	(8.7)	(9.8)	(9.8)	(100.0)
> 5 to 7 days	25	20	3	6	8	62
	(40.3)	(32.3)	(4.8)	(9.7)	(12.9)	(100.0)

$N = 1,098$; number of victims (%); Pearson's $r = .05$, $p < .21$.

Table 5.4 shows even more clearly the relationship of anger, resentment, and hatred with peaceful political participation but not with support for retaliatory violence. The correlations between these emotions, singularly or bundled in an index, and participation are statistically significant and substantively meaningful, with a particularly noteworthy correlation of .33 ($p < .001$) between the number of days victims felt hatred and the number of activities in which they participated. The correlations between these emotions and support for retaliatory violence are not statistically significant, a finding reinforced in multivariate analysis in Chapter 11.

Other emotions prove less important for motivating political participation. Consistent with other research (Brader et al. 2011; Valentino et al. 2011), anger is found to mobilize more than anxiety or enthusiasm. Table 5.4 shows that the anxiety index and the individual measures of anxiety, fear, and worry that form the index are significantly correlated with political participation at the bivariate level, but these findings do not hold when controlling for a variety of other variables in multivariate analysis: in Chapter 11's full models of political participation of Beslan victims, measures of anxiety are not statistically significant. The enthusiasm index and its component measures of hope, enthusiasm, and pride are not significantly related to political participation in either bivariate or multivariate analysis.

Table 5.4. Emotions, Political Participation, and Support for Retaliatory Violence

Emotion	Political Participation	Support for Retaliatory Violence
Anger	.19*	.005
Resentment	.17*	.06
Hatred	.33*	.07
Anger index (anger, resentment, hatred)	.26*	.05
Hopeful	−.02	−.08
Enthusiastic	−.09	.03
Proud	−.07	.11
Enthusiasm index (hopeful, enthusiastic, proud)	−.07	.02
Anxious	.21*	.07
Afraid	.21*	.12
Worried	.20*	.03
Anxiety index (anxious, afraid, worried)	.23*	.08

Correlations (Pearson's r), $N = 1,098$; * $p < 0.001$.

Table 5.4 also shows that anxiety and enthusiasm, whether measured by indices or individual survey items, are unrelated to support for retaliatory violence. Anxious victims and enthusiastic victims, just like angry victims, do not differ significantly from other victims in their approval of killing Chechens. Support for retaliatory violence in Beslan does not appear to be emotion-driven.

The Supposed Conditionality of Anger?

In response to the finding that anger and hate do not influence support for violence, a plausible objection is that only the direct effects of anger have so far been analyzed. Perhaps anger matters for violence in some circumstances but not others, and analysis of its direct effects fails to capture this conditionality (Halperin et al. 2011:276). In statistical terms, anger is hypothesized to affect support for violence in interaction with other variables. Specifically, prior research suggests that anger may matter in its interaction with social alienation, blame attribution, political efficacy, self-efficacy, prejudice, and even other emotions like hatred. However, although the logic of each of these hypothesized interactions in many cases is quite plausible, they are unsupported by the data from Beslan victims.

Anger is sometimes hypothesized to mobilize individuals in interaction with (the lack of) social alienation. Anger presumably leads to violence only in the case of those who believe their anger is shared, understood by others, and supported by others. This social support presumably affirms their emotional responses like anger (van Zomeren et al. 2004:650). Anger without perceived social support for the emotion loses its validation and might not mobilize individuals for peaceful action or feed anger's aggressive action tendency.

Although plausible, such logic neglects alternative and directly contrasting hypotheses for the role of social alienation in support for retaliatory violence. In particular, the presence of social alienation, not its absence, could be meaningful for retaliatory violence, making predictions about the interaction of social alienation and anger less clear. As discussed in Chapter 8, believing that one is isolated in opinion and emotion—that others do not share or validate one's anger and have little concern for the angering experience—may be somewhat meaningful for retaliatory violence. Socially alienated individuals may be the very individuals less bound by anti-violence community norms.

The question thus remains whether anger influences support for retaliatory violence, but only for socially integrated victims or perhaps only for socially alienated victims. Table 5.5 shows the results of a short version of the ordered logit model discussed more fully in Chapter 11. The short version includes only three variables: the anger index, a measure of social alienation ("How interested do you think Russian society is in listening to the victims' side of the story?"), and a variable representing the interaction of the two. There are four possible values for social alienation, ranging from 1 (low alienation, meaning "I think

Table 5.5. Interactive Effects of Anger and Social Alienation on Support for Retaliatory Violence

	Support for Retaliatory Violence Ordered Logit Estimates Coef. (SE)
Anger	−.11 (.09)
Social alienation	.02 (.13)
Interaction: anger × social alienation	.07 (.04)

Russian society is very interested in the victims' story") to 4 (high alienation, meaning "I think Russian society is very uninterested"). To interpret the results, each of these different values is used to calculate the coefficient for anger, ranging from −.04 (when social alienation is lowest) to .17 (when social alienation is highest). Given that the standard error for anger in this reduced model is .09, these calculations show that anger is not statistically significant for any level of social alienation. The hypothesis that anger leads to support for violence in cases where victims feel social support is not backed by the data. Anger's lack of statistical significance is reinforced in the full multivariate model on support for violence in Chapter 11.

The interaction term can also be used to interpret the effects of social alienation at different levels of anger, which has a maximum value of 7. When anger is low (1, 2, or 3), the coefficient for social alienation is .09, .16, and .23 and the standard error is .13, which might suggest that social alienation has no significant effect on support for retaliatory violence. However, when anger is high (4 or greater), the effect of social alienation on support for retaliatory violence is indeed statistically significant. The effect of social alienation on support for retaliatory violence may thus be conditional on anger, and that is about the only case to be made for the importance of anger in motivating violence among Beslan victims.[2]

Besides the hypotheses about the interaction of anger and social support or alienation, many disparate hypotheses are proposed in the literature about the power of anger in interaction with other variables. Anger is hypothesized to drive action, both peaceful and violent, only against those held responsible (Gurr 1970:34; van Zomeren et al. 2004:650), meaning that anger should lead to support for violence only for victims who can attribute blame for their victimization. Anger hypothetically interacts with prejudice, meaning that anger should lead to support for violence among those who hold negative opinions of Ingush and Chechens. Anger hypothetically interacts with political alienation, because anger accompanied by pride in one's country leaves the angry person with only

[2] Perhaps anger is accelerated in some cases by social support and in other cases by social alienation, which would explain its lack of statistical significance in a two-way interaction with social alienation, but evidence of such conjecture would require a three-way statistical interaction with an additional, unknown variable. Based on existing theories, community norms might be such a variable, with anger mattering for retaliatory violence in the joint context of social support and pro-violence community norms and in the joint context of social alienation and anti-violence community norms. Such a test is beyond the scope of this study, given the focus on a single context of largely anti-violence community norms and the incredible difficulty of implementing a real-world research design involving multiple communities, but it is still an open possibility that anger may be relevant in a pro-violence community context. Because anti-violence community contexts are prevalent in the world (Fearon and Laitin 1996), the finding that anger is largely irrelevant for retaliatory violence applies widely.

non-political targets for aggression. Anger hypothetically interacts with political efficacy and self-efficacy, because anger accompanied by the perception that action is ineffective should not lead to action, whereas anger accompanied by efficacy is mobilizing (van Zomeren et al. 2004:649; Skitka et al. 2006:376; Carver and Harmon-Jones 2009:187).

In more nuanced hypotheses, anger is said to have effects on support for violence through its interaction with hatred. Anger should be destructively mobilizing among individuals with high levels of hatred because hate-filled individuals believe their anger results from stable, negative characteristics of the rival group, and aggression is therefore justified (Halperin et al. 2011:277). Anger should be constructively mobilizing among individuals with low levels of hatred because they are more likely to believe in the possibility of a changed rival group or at least in negotiation, education, and compromise (Halperin et al. 2011:277).

Men are supposedly more prone to both anger and aggression, so anger is hypothesized to interact with sex (Carver and Harmon-Jones 2009:191; Dorius and McCarthy 2011). There may be social payoffs to men who are perceived as aggressive (Daly and Wilson 1985, 1989), whereas conventions often discourage displays of anger by women who, in turn, are more likely to suppress anger (Hochschild 1975; Holmes 2004:209; Jasper 2011:296). It is therefore possible that anger provokes violence among men but not women.

Table 5.6 shows that none of these interaction hypotheses is supported by the data from Beslan victims. When interactions of anger and blaming President Putin or anger and blaming Chechens are added to models of support for retaliatory violence—either to the full model in Chapter 11 or to reduced models such as the one in Table 5.5—the interactions are not statistically significant. The same is true for interactions of anger with the many other significant variables in the analysis throughout this book: prejudice, political alienation, political efficacy, self-efficacy, hatred, and sex. Interaction terms are also not significant in any models of political participation (analyses not shown), meaning that anger has direct effects on participation and is not conditional on other factors.

Given the abundance of hypotheses that all assume an important role for anger in causing violence, every effort was made to look for significant effects. The strongest effect found involved social alienation: anger has no statistically significant effect on support for violence at any level of social alienation, but the effects of social alienation on support for violence are stronger for the angriest victims. Otherwise, the data again support the conclusion that anger has an independent, positive, statistically significant effect on political participation and no effect on support for violence, either independently or in interaction with other variables.

Table 5.6. Hypothesized Interactive Effects of Anger on Support for Retaliatory Violence

Anger Might Be Conditional on . . .	Hypothesis: Anger Leads to Support for Retaliatory Ethnic Violence When Victims . . .	Measurement*	Finding
Social alienation	. . . believe their anger is shared, understood by others, and supported by others	Perceived interest of Russian society in listening to the victims' side of the story	No support, although the reverse has some support (effects of social alienation are stronger at higher levels of anger)
Blame	. . . can attribute blame for their victimization	Perceived guilt of President Vladimir Putin for causing this tragedy	No support
		Satisfaction with punishment of federal officials who are guilty for what happened	No support
		Perceived guilt of Chechens for causing this tragedy	No support
Prejudice	. . . have negative opinions based on ethnicity	Feelings about dining with Ingush, marrying, going to same schools	No support
Political alienation	. . . are proud of their country	Change in political pride since hostage taking	No support
Political efficacy	. . . perceive that political action is effective	Self-assessment of how politically informed	No support
		Perceived effectiveness of demonstrating or protesting	No support
Self-efficacy	. . . perceive that personal action is effective	Perceived ability to help solve problems that led to tragedy	No support
Hatred	. . . feel hatred	Number of days feeling hatred in last seven	No support
Sex	. . . are male	Binary variable	No support

* See Table 11.4 for precise survey questions and descriptive statistics.

Is Anger Mediated by Other Factors?

Some research suggests that anger still may play a role in retaliatory violence, not in interaction with other causal variables, but as the emotional predecessor of other variables. In a two-step process, anger is hypothesized to be the primary variable that influences intermediate variables, which themselves influence support for violence. Anger supposedly causes individuals to remember selectively; attribute blame; feel efficacious or optimistic about the chances of successful retaliation; heighten prejudice and the propensity to stereotype; reduce estimates of risk; and engage more willingly in risky behavior (Petersen and Zukerman 2009:566–567; see also Gamson et al. 1982; Skitka et al. 2006:376; Huddy et al. 2007). For example, anger triggered causal attributions in the United States after September 11 (Small et al. 2006), and in turn, causal attributions presumably motivated support for retaliatory violence. Anger also triggered higher presidential approval ratings during international conflict (Lambert et al. 2010; Robbins, Hunter, and Murray 2013:498), and if presidential action involved violence, the anger-induced higher presidential approval presumably motivated support for that violence.

Still other research suggests the very opposite: anger is not causally prior to other variables, but other variables are causally prior to anger. Such hypotheses are discussed in both the political participation and violence literatures, often with opposing logic and expectations. For example, political efficacy may facilitate anger, which in turn may facilitate political participation, meaning that anger serves as the intermediary variable between efficacy and political participation (Valentino et al. 2009). Or the lack of political efficacy may facilitate anger because the inability to influence policy decisions is itself angering, in which case anger still may serve as the intermediary variable between efficacy and action, but only non-political and violent action (Tausch et al. 2011:139–141). Blame attribution also may be causally prior to anger, which then supposedly encourages aggression (Keltner et al. 1993; Turner and Stets 2006:35), and when efficacy is combined with blame attribution, anger is especially likely, and so is political participation (Frijda and Mesquita 2000:62; Brader et al. 2011; Valentino et al. 2011). Political alienation might be causally prior to anger and might encourage political protest through the mechanism of anger, whereas lack of political alienation—the presence of political pride—might reduce anger and therefore reduce protest (Jost et al. 2012:199).

Of course, feedback loops are entirely possible. Just as political efficacy causes and is caused by (successful) political participation (Valentino et al. 2009), some variables may cause and be caused by anger. For example, anger may increase blame, which, in turn, increases anger (Petersen and Zukerman 2009:566; see also Keltner et al. 1993).

However, none of these hypotheses about a mediating role for anger or for other variables finds support in the survey data from Beslan victims. First, the statistical relationship between anger, either as an individual measure or an index, and support for violence is so low as to approach zero, meaning that there cannot be a causal pathway to support for violence that involves anger in either a primary or intermediary role. Other variables cannot "work through" anger if anger has no significant independent effects on violence.

Also, as future chapters show, some variables hypothesized as intermediary variables are themselves unrelated to support for retaliatory violence, meaning that anger could have neither a direct nor indirect impact through the nonsignificant variables. For example, reduced risk estimates had surprisingly little effect on post-violence behavior in Beslan. Even if anger had the hypothesized effect of reducing risk estimates for Beslan victims, the relationship would not help explain individual variation in political participation or support for retaliatory violence after the hostage taking. Blaming President Putin for the hostage taking and trust in government also had no statistically significant effects on support for retaliatory violence, so any relationship between anger and blaming Putin or anger and trust would not help explain variation in support for violence.

Table 5.7 offers other reasons to doubt these many claims about the mediating effects of anger or other variables on support for retaliatory violence. Many variables said to be primary or intermediary are not highly correlated with anger. Anger is not significantly correlated with ethnic prejudice, blaming Chechens, political efficacy, self-efficacy, optimism about the future, or dissatisfaction with the punishment of political officials. Anger is correlated in statistically significant but substantively small ways with other variables that are not hypothesized to have mediating relationships with support for violence, including voting prior to the hostage taking, prior nonvoting behavior, and household income. The only variable that is correlated with anger to a meaningful degree is anxiety, but there is no meaningful hypothesis about anger mediating the relationship between anxiety and support for violence, or vice versa. Also, anxiety, like anger, has no significant relationship to support for retaliatory violence, so could not serve as a primary or intermediary variable.

Only two variables are significantly correlated with both anger and support for retaliatory violence: political alienation and one measure of optimism, believing it is possible to solve the problems that led to the Beslan tragedy. Even for these two variables, anger could not play the hypothesized mediating or mediated role in support for retaliatory violence.

First, although the correlations between anger and political alienation and anger and optimism are statistically significant, they are substantively small. Second, there are debates in the theoretical literature about whether anger always

Table 5.7. Anger and Other Explanatory Variables

	Anger
Anxiety	.43*
Enthusiasm	.06
Political alienation (decreased pride)	.15*
Putin's guilt	.13*
Dissatisfaction with punishment of officials	.07
Social alienation	−.01
Blame toward Chechens	.002
Prejudice toward Ingush	.11
Politically informed	.08
Perceived effectiveness of protest	.00
Self-efficacy	.01
Optimistic about future	−.10
Possible to solve Beslan's problems	.14*
Prior voting	.19*
Prior nonvoting behavior	.14*
Prior harm to relatives	.11
Hostage	.05
Child/children died	.09
Spouse died	.07
Number of relatives affected	−.01
Perceived risk of political activism	.09
Trust in government	−.15*
Female	.11
Age	.02
Household income	−.16*
Education	.03

Correlations (Pearson's r), $N = 1,098$; * $p < 0.001$.

influences political alienation in a positive direction. Some theorists of emotion conceive of anger as a component of alienation (Turner 2011:8–9), suggesting that angry Beslan victims should also be alienated. However, some empirical researchers suggest that anger decreases alienation, noting, for example, the above U.S. example where anger led Americans to support the president in a rally-around-the-flag effect during international conflict (Lambert et al. 2010). Of course, the relationship between anger and political alienation probably depends on the target of anger, and anger at political officials should increase political alienation while anger at Ingush and Chechens should decrease political alienation or perhaps have no effect. However, once the target of anger is added to the definition of anger, the causal path becomes murky, because the variables are no longer conceptually distinct. If anger directed at political officials is part of political alienation, then it is tautological and meaningless to say that anger causes political alienation. The independent role of anger in motivating support for retaliatory violence would be unclear.

Third and most important, as shown in later chapters, political alienation and optimism are negatively, not positively, related to support for retaliatory violence. If anger led to increased political alienation and political alienation led to decreased support for violence, then to the extent that anger played a role in support for violence, it would have paradoxically decreased the support. Similarly, if anger led to increased optimism and optimism led to decreased support for violence, then anger mediated by optimism would have decreased support for violence. These causal pathways are not hypothesized in the literature and make sense only with post hoc explanations.

In short, the vast majority of claims about the conditional, prior, or mediating effects of anger on support for retaliatory violence are unsupported by the empirical evidence gathered in Beslan. The sheer multitude of hypotheses lead to a messy, nearly unintelligible portrayal of anger's supposed role in retaliatory violence, especially because some of the hypotheses are contradictory. There may well be interactive or indirect effects of anger, ways in which anger serves as a causal mechanism, primary variable, or intermediary variable, but the many potential hypotheses sometimes seem designed to salvage the pet notion that violence must be about anger. Data from Beslan victims fail to support this notion. Political participation is about anger. Support for retaliatory ethnic violence is not.

Extreme versus Moderate Political Action

Some prior research suggests that moderate and radical collective actions are stimulated by different emotions (Becker et al. 2011; Tausch et al. 2011). For example, anger is said to predict normative action (conforming to the norms of the wider social system), such as letter writing, meeting with political officials, and demonstrating, but anger is supposedly unrelated to non-normative action (violating these norms), such as terrorism. Contempt is said to do the opposite and predict non-normative but not normative action (Tausch et al. 2011). Anxiety is said to stimulate low-cost action but have little effect on high-cost action (Valentino et al. 2011). Perhaps, then, the Beslan victim survey results are misleading, and the findings linking anger and hatred to peaceful political participation are erroneously driven by the aggregation of both moderate and extreme action into a single count variable. Disaggregating the variable into moderate versus extreme actions and analyzing each separately could plausibly reveal a stronger role for emotions like anger and anxiety in only moderate political action but not more extreme actions, while hatred might matter only in the more extreme actions.

Although this logic is plausible, there are equally plausible reasons to doubt that the related emotions of anger and hatred would affect behavior in unrelated ways or that anger would mobilize individuals for low-cost activities who would then check their anger for high-cost activities. First, participants in moderate and extreme action, or normative and non-normative action, are often the same people. For example, many American civil rights activists were recruited by their ministers to participate in multiple types of activities, including voter registration drives, sit-ins, interstate bus rides, bus boycotts, and other dangerous or even illegal acts, which varied in terms of their costs to the participant's pocketbook, time, energy, and personal security. "The four students who sat in at Greensboro and sparked the widespread sit-in movements had been members of the NAACP Youth Council" and didn't simply choose radical action after spurning conventional activism (Morris 1984:198). Prior evidence supports the importance of perceived costs in individual decisions to participate in collective action (Klandermans and Oegema 1987), making it reasonable to expect higher participation in normative over non-normative actions, but the costs themselves have an independent impact on participation, not necessarily one conditional on anger or hatred.

To the extent that emotions are related to cost acceptance, prior evidence suggests that anger increases risk taking (Skitka et al. 2006:376). If anger also reflects a desire for reconciliation and therefore reduces the desire to act contrary to norms (Becker et al. 2011; Tausch et al. 2011), it is unclear which "action tendency" of anger is stronger. Similarly, for hatred, it is unclear why hatred is mobilizing only for norm-breaking activities. An intense or passionate dislike, along with its accompanying attribution of intrinsic evil to the hated individuals or groups, supposedly triggers a desire for harm (Elster 1998; Halperin et al. 2011), but harm could potentially be pursued through moderate as well as extreme action. Harm is the end product of successful action, not necessarily the action itself. Hate-filled victims might therefore mobilize for moderate action and extreme action, whenever either opportunity presented itself.

Second, during times of heightened activism prompted by victimization by violence, norms may be in flux, and it may be difficult to put each activity into a neat box of normative versus non-normative. For example, were the Beslan victims who blockaded the highway acting non-normatively, given the illegality of the action and the inconvenience to commercial interests and drivers, or normatively, given the support they had from their local community? What about the victims who supplied the blockaders with food, drink, and bonfire wood—was their behavior normative or non-normative? To the extent that "normative" is defined as "actions conforming to the norms of the existing social system," it will be difficult to apply the definition to many post-violence situations in the world that have several, potentially competing social systems, some disapproving of extreme action and some approving or simply not considering the very same action to be extreme.

Nevertheless, the activities of Beslan victims can be roughly distinguished into categories reflecting moderate and extreme political action. Of the activities Beslan victims have pursued, the most extreme and perhaps non-normative include blockading the Rostov-Baku/Caucasus Federal Highway, participating in the courthouse sit-in, refusing to leave the courtroom at other times, and participating in a hunger strike at the end of the Kulayev trial. Less extreme and probably normative activities involved participation in rallies, meetings with political officials, and petitions or letters to political officials.

Table 5.8 shows that these distinctions are not especially meaningful. Political participation is differentiated into moderate and extreme political action, with the three forms of moderate political action in separate indices representing letter writing or petition signing, meetings with political officials, and rallies. Each cell shows the correlations of these indices, and the index for extreme political action, with different emotions, represented by single-item measures and multi-item indices. (The results are the same when the three separate indices are combined into a single "moderate political action" index.)

The correlations indicate that the type of political action does not matter: anger and hatred are statistically significant for both moderate political action and extreme political action. Hatred is consistently the most powerful emotion driving each type of political action. Although hatred is more highly correlated with extreme action than with moderate action, the small difference in degree does not support a conclusion that hatred matters only for extreme action. There is also no support for a conclusion that anger and resentment matter only for moderate action. Finally, two emotions, anxiety and enthusiasm, that appear nonsignificant in multivariate analyses of political participation in Chapter 11 and are therefore

Table 5.8. The Similar Role of Emotions in Moderate versus Extreme Political Action

Emotion	Moderate Political Action			Extreme Political Action
	Wrote or Signed Letters (Count of 0–6 Activities)	Met with Official (Count of 0–11 Activities)	Participated in Rally (Count of 0–8 Activities)	Blockaded Highway, Hunger Strike, Courtroom Sit-in (Count of 0–5 Activities)
Anger	.18*	.11	.20*	.19*
Resentment	.15*	.15*	.14*	.14*
Hatred	.28*	.27*	.29*	.36*
Anger index (anger, resentment, hatred)	.23*	.21*	.24*	.28*
Anxiety index (anxiety, fear, worry)	.20*	.20*	.17*	.19*
Enthusiasm index (hope, enthusiasm, pride)	−.04	−.07	−.01	−.04

Correlations (Pearson's r), $N = 1,098$; * $p < 0.001$.

not emphasized much in this current chapter, also seem to correlate similarly with the different forms of political action, with no distinction between moderate and extreme action. In the bivariate correlations, anxiety has a statistically significant relationship with participation, whether moderate or extreme, and enthusiasm has no significant relationship with participation, whether moderate or extreme.

These results make sense because, as suggested by the literature, moderate and extreme political actions are highly correlated. Beslan victims who participated in extreme actions very often participated in moderate actions, and vice versa. Participation in extreme actions in Beslan was correlated at .7 with meeting political officials, .77 with letter writing and signing, and .78 with participation in rallies. Activists seem to commit to activism and embrace many forms of action.

Perhaps the more important distinction than whether an action is normative or non-normative, within-system or out-of-system, moderate or radical, or constitutional or extraconstitutional (Tausch et al. 2011:131) is whether the action is violent or nonviolent. Evidence suggests that if non-normative behavior is further distinguished by violent versus nonviolent action, anger is unrelated only to the violent action (Tausch et al. 2011:135). The argument here is that the decision to be violent is on a different dimension than the decision to participate in normative or non-normative action. Violence is not simply the most extreme end of the non-normative spectrum. Rather, it reflects a different calculation and is influenced by a different set of variables.

Beslan victims did not act violently toward government, and ethical and safety concerns precluded asking survey questions along these lines, so the effects of anger and hatred on anti-government violence cannot be tested here. However, questions did indeed ask about support for retaliatory violence against Chechens, and there too, anger and hate have similar effects: both are nonsignificant. Presumably, if hatred has the greatest impact on violence when there are no reconciliatory intentions, then it would most certainly have its greatest impact on those victims of Beslan who are hate-filled and have little desire to preserve social relations with Chechens. Hatred should be a positive, statistically significant predictor of violent tendencies toward Chechens. That hatred is not significant in this context suggests that it would also not be a significant predictor of violent tendencies toward government. However, the possibility is left open that hatred might play a more significant role in anti-government violence in the context of post-violence situations where the goal is to sever relations with the current government or challenge its legitimacy and overturn the existing social order.

Depression as a Reaction to Violence

As a mood state or mental illness, depression is worthy of special consideration for its role in the aftermath of violence. Depression is conceived as "psychological distress," or "the unpleasant subjective states of depression and anxiety, which have both emotional and physiological manifestations" (Mirowsky and Ross 2002:1286). Depression is measured by the victims' self-assessments of the frequency of depression ("How often do you feel depressed?") and also a seven-item index of psychological distress that is a short version of the Center for Epidemiological Studies' Depression Scale, widely used and tested by psychologists for validity and reliability (Radloff 1977; Mirowsky and Ross 1989). The seven-component survey questions of the depression index ask, "How many days during the past week (0–7) have you (1) felt you just couldn't get going? (2) felt sad? (3) had trouble getting to sleep or staying asleep? (4) felt that everything was an effort? (5) felt lonely? (6) felt you couldn't shake the blues? (7) had trouble keeping your mind on what you were doing?" The resulting scale is a mean index from 0 to 7.

Although higher scores on the Depression Scale increase the odds of a clinical diagnosis of depression, the index is intended not to diagnose mental illness, as is the case with depression scores used by psychiatrists. The index is intended to identify gradations in distress (Weissman et al. 1977; Mirowsky and Ross 1989:7, 2002). Levels of psychological distress that would not meet the psychiatric criteria for "diagnostic depression" often still constitute very real problems for the individuals suffering at these distress levels and for the medical system. It is therefore more useful to conceive of psychological distress or other mental health issues on a continuum rather than as a dichotomy of "depressed" or "not depressed" (Mirowsky and Ross 1989).

Is there a relationship between levels of psychological distress and retaliatory violence and peaceful political action? On the one hand, depression is usually conceived as a demobilizing mood state (Goodwin and Jasper 2006:619). Component measures of depression even include the inability to "get going" and "feeling like everything is an effort." Therefore, it is reasonable to hypothesize that more depressed victims are less likely than other victims to take action, either peaceful or violent.

On the other hand, more depressed victims may have a vested interest in the outcome of any post-violence action and might be more likely to seek coping mechanisms to mitigate the depression, such as action to redress the grievance. Political action in particular could provide a meaningful distraction. Indeed, many Beslan victims testified to the therapeutic nature of political action, although few if any attributed the same therapeutic benefit to retaliatory ethnic violence.

IRINA, FEMALE ACTIVIST VICTIM THIRTY-FIVE YEARS OR YOUNGER: The ones who get involved in social activities communicate with people and they get distracted so that's easier for them to cope.

RITA SIDAKOVA, WHO LOST HER DAUGHTER: Without this, I don't know how we could go on. This is the best therapy. (Eckel 2005)

ZALINA TYBLOYEVA, WHO LOST THREE RELATIVES: Ours is the politics of grief. The politicians have done nothing for us. From this grief comes our politics. (Eckel 2005)

These competing hypotheses, especially if both operate and potentially counteract one another, suggest that there should be no strong effects of depression on behavioral reactions to violence. The lack of effects is also suggested by the multivariate analysis in Chapter 11 in which anxiety, an emotional component of depression and found to predict depression in other post-terrorism conditions (Huddy et al. 2005:599), had no significant effect on either political participation or support for retaliatory violence after the violence in Beslan.

Indeed, empirical evidence on the correlation between depression and activism seems mixed. There are examples like victim Marina Pak, who, while undoubtedly grieving over her daughter killed in the hostage taking, was probably not depressed in terms of the seven-item index and became a prominent member of Mothers of Beslan and engaged regularly in their activities (Panyushkin 2006a). However, data from the victim survey show that, on average, the most psychologically distressed Beslan victims engaged in peaceful political activism more than less distressed victims. The two variables for measuring psychological distress, frequency of feeling depressed and the psychological distress index, are positively correlated with the number of political activities ($r = .25$ and $.26$, respectively, $p < .00$). The same psychological variables are correlated much less with support for retaliatory violence ($r = .1$ and $.09$, respectively, $p < .00$ and $.01$). While the evidence is mixed, it can be reasonably concluded that, at the very least, depression in Beslan did not prevent political activism in response to the violent hostage taking.

The fact that depression does not preclude peaceful political activism lends support to the testimony of Beslan activists that politics may be therapeutic, whereas support for violence appears much less so. Nevertheless, it is a huge leap from acknowledging the frequent coincidence of depression and political activism to inferring that depression is a source of activism, especially when there is no theoretical justification for the inference, no logical reason why the inability to "force yourself to do anything" or the feeling that "everything is an effort" should possibly mobilize victims of violence. The contrary hypothesis that depression is demobilizing also provides no logical reason why the *lack* of depression should mobilize victims, only that it should be permissive of mobilization should victims be so inclined. The latter hypothesis is at once more logical yet unsupported by the empirical evidence.

Therefore, depression is not treated as an independent causal variable in the models in Chapter 11. The decision to omit depression as an individual-level variable is reinforced by the fact that one concrete measure of harm, the loss of a child, is correlated with depression ($r = .18$ and $.24$, $p < .00$, for the self-assessment of depression and the index, respectively) and already included in multivariate models of participation and support for retaliatory violence. Some variation in depression is likely tapped by this more directly relevant factor.

Depression as Part of the Post-Violence Context

Depression is inextricably linked with the grievance of victimization and therefore still part of the post-violence story. Depression is so pervasive among victims of extreme violence that it forms the context for the research question: Given the depressing circumstances of victimization, why do only some victims mobilize?

This section therefore takes a brief moment to document the depression context in Beslan, which likely mirrors the context in other communities victimized by terrorism or other acts of extreme violence. After the school hostage taking, Beslan victims were plagued by posttraumatic stress and other psychological reactions such as survivor's guilt and the torment of hearing about relatives who acted heroically and then did not survive. Many were unable or afraid to return to work, and many rarely left their homes.

According to Alma Khamitseva, who lost her sister Lema in the siege, "It can never be normal here for me. I don't even leave my house because I don't know what to do or where to go. We have all lost sense of our lives" (Sands 2004b:A01). Male activist victims described the mood in the town.

BORIS: Our life has turned upside down after these events. Life has taken a completely different course, in a different key. Our life had been different before these events. After this we don't live. There is no joy inside. We can smile, but it's not from the soul, not from the heart. That's what they have done to us. Not only we, the victims. The whole Ossetia is ill after these events.

TOTRAZ: There were some people among the victims, they didn't leave the cemetery for a long time. They spent nights and days there. They spent long time there in a direct sense. They stayed near the tomb, just came and lived there. Brought food there, and that's all, and they didn't leave.

Stress-related illnesses like heart attacks made the mortality and morbidity toll continue rising well after the siege (Sands 2004b). For example, Elbrus Dudiyev, husband of Mothers of Beslan leader Susanna Dudiyeva and father to their killed thirteen-year-old son Zaur, suffered a stroke in 2008 (Franchetti 2009). Tsara Shotaev, a sixty-two-year-old retired banker, lost his daughter and seven-year-old granddaughter and himself suffered a heart attack in October 2004. He explained, "People still feel very depressed. A lot of my friends never leave their houses. You used to hear music in the streets, and you never hear that anymore. We had eight kids killed right on this little street. Can you imagine that? Eight kids. We plan to move as soon as we can sell the house. I cannot remain here. It is too hard on my heart" (Sands 2004b:A01).

Surviving child victims became afraid of the dark, loud noises, and men with beards (Sands 2004b). For years afterward, some had nightmares and woke up screaming; some slept with their parents, afraid to sleep alone (Franchetti 2009). Many tried to go back to school but became hysterical at the sight of men with automatic weapons standing guard at their school, now standard in Beslan, or even in response to a thunderstorm, construction noise, or the raised voice of a teacher. Many associated going to school with death, especially the youngest victims who had no other memory of school. Said seven-year-old Georgy Sidakov, "I don't want to go to school. I don't want to be dead." Fatima Bagayeva, a psychologist at Beslan's hospital who worked with these youngest survivors, explained, "They are living with terrible trauma and grief, but when they turn to parents or other relatives, they see that they [adults] can't cope either" (Finn 2005b).

Not all victims of violence are unable to cope. Depression varies among victims, even in response to the same circumstances, and in Beslan, some victims managed to soldier on with life. Two years after the tragedy, thirteen former hostages became new mothers, a new maternity hospital was built, and some new marriages had emerged from among the victims, such as the one between Mothers of Beslan member Marina Pak, whose daughter was killed, and Kazbek Adyrkhayev, whose wife was killed as she shielded her small children with her own body (Samoipova 2006; Panyushkin 2006a). Female activist victims thirty-five years or younger described this happier outcome:

BELLA: There was also another way out. People accepted the situation as it was and continued to live.

VIKA: My sister-in-law, for example, had a girl, eleven years old, who died. She adopted a newborn girl, without a husband. Her husband died even earlier before the birth of her son. She was pregnant when he died. She brought them up alone for eight years. And though she is single and not so young, she adopted a newborn girl.

BELA: And my sister who was in the terrorist attack, had a boy a year ago. Her boy (*another son*) died in the terrorist act.

Male nonactivist victims discussed why some people sank into depression and others soldiered on:

BORIS: It was easier for me because there were so many people there. If I had been alone, if it had happened in my family only, I would probably have gone crazy. It was the fact that there were so many people involved. People supported each other, sympathized, helped. I speak about myself. I don't know about the rest, but it helped me that I wasn't alone in this grief. It can be bad, of course. I am not saying that it's good. If it hadn't happened, it would have been much better, of course, but as so many people were injured, we [helped] each other in some way, even those who didn't take part sympathized with those who had something happen to them. It all helped to cope. And a person thought, "Well, what can you do now? It already happened. They are no longer living. Now you can do whatever: kill yourself, hang yourself. You can do whatever. Who will benefit from it?" Someone felt ill, someone's heart failed, some people died from it. Someone was wounded and died later. But, mostly, people kept going, because we had to go on living. Someone lost everyone, someone lost two, someone lost three, but someone remained. . . .

And someone thought that he had to go on living, feed his family, raise children who were left without a mother or a father. And someone didn't think. It seemed to him that it would be easier for him to drink, forget about what had happened, but there are few such people, you can count them on fingers.

How widespread was depression in Beslan, and how did it vary across victims? The survey results strongly suggest that there was an alarming mental health crisis in Beslan. As Table 5.9 shows, over a third of Beslan victims reported feeling depressed always or most of the time (14.7 and 24.4 percent, respectively). Sixty-one percent of victims reported experiencing psychological distress more than one day a week; 37 percent of victims reported experiencing psychological distress more than three days a week; and 16 percent of victims— or one in every six victims—reported distress more than five days a week. These percentages of depressed Beslan victims do not even include the large number of

Table 5.9. Depression among Beslan Victims

"How often do you feel depressed?"

Never	Rarely	Some of the Time	Most of the Time	Always	Refused	Unsure
22	188	444	268	161	6	9
(2.0)	(17.1)	(40.4)	(24.4)	(14.7)	(0.5)	(0.8)

Psychological Distress Index, mean score of the following seven questions. How many days during the past week (0–7):

1. could you not force yourself to do anything? [English: "felt you just couldn't get going"]
2. felt sad?
3. slept uneasily or could not fall asleep? [English: "had trouble getting to sleep or staying asleep"]
4. felt that everything was an effort?
5. felt lonely?
6. been unable to stop feelings of melancholy [English: "felt you couldn't shake the blues"]
7. had trouble keeping your mind on what you were doing?

0 days	> 0 to 1 Day	> 1 to 3 Days	> 3 to 5 Days	> 5 to 7 Days	Missing
29	87	263	232	176	311
(2.6)	(7.9)	(24.0)	(21.1)	(16.0)	(28.3)

In the two years since the tragedy in the school, how many times have you received professional psychological assistance of any kind?

None	1–2 Times	3–10 Times	> 10 Times	Refused	Unsure
524	307	125	72	25	45
(47.7)	(28.0)	(11.4)	(6.6)	(2.3)	(4.1)

$N = 1,098$; number of victims (%).

victims (28 percent) who were uncomfortable answering questions about their mental health, many of whom probably experienced at least some psychological distress and whose responses would have likely made the mental health picture portrayed above even grimmer. Negative mental health effects of trauma tend to diminish over time (Knudsen et al. 2005:261), so the rampant depression in Beslan two years after the hostage taking was alarming in itself and also for what it revealed about the potentially greater levels of depression in years prior.

Many Beslan victims sought treatment at the newly installed psychosomatic department of Beslan's hospital, using the twenty-four-hour hotline, or from the on-site psychologists available for consultation. Some traveled to the Psychological Training Center or the North Ossetian State Children's Rehabilitation Center in Vladikavkaz. Some even traveled to the Serbskiy State Center of Social and Forensic Psychiatry in Moscow for additional help (Parfitt 2004; Weir 2004; "Psychologists Provide Help" 2005). Treatments included art and play therapy for children and rehabilitation programs and vacations. In May 2005, the Russian Red Cross and the International Federation of Red Cross and Red Crescent Societies opened a psychological aid center. By that August, more than 1,200 people, including 300 former hostages, had applied to the center ("Psychological Aid Center" 2005; "Russian Red Cross" 2005). In March 2006, a Beslan branch of the joint UNICEF–North Ossetian government rehabilitation center finally opened in Beslan for families affected by the tragedy (Tsugaeva 2006).

These efforts encountered serious obstacles. Some groups attempted to take advantage of the vulnerable Beslan victims, especially those who had received compensation payments from the Fund for Aid to Victims of a Terrorist Act or from the Russian government. Religious sects flocked to Beslan and set up shop in children's clinics and other rehabilitation centers, some claiming to be volunteer psychologists and some promising to resurrect children from the dead for a fee. Local authorities responded by passing the "Law on Missionary Activity" and compelling Scientologists and other groups to leave Beslan (Sokolov-Mitrich 2004).

There were also cultural, social, and other obstacles to psychological treatment. Men had a particularly difficult time coming forward "because local tradition dictates that a man cannot openly show his feelings and emotions—his 'weakness'" (Parfitt 2004:2009). Children who were placed in therapy had often lost confidence in the ability of adults to protect them and needed to build trust first. More generally, according to a psychologist at the Children's Rehabilitation Center, "Ossetians are a proud people, and most personal problems are solved within their extended and tight-knit families," making it difficult to convince parents to send their children to therapy or seek therapy themselves ("Russian Federation: Beslan" 2005).

Still, as Table 5.9 shows, more than half of the Beslan victims reported receiving professional psychological assistance at least once in the two years between September 2004 and the survey, with sizable minorities receiving such assistance three to ten times (11.4 percent) or more than ten times (6.6 percent). The post-violence context in Beslan included rampant depression but also significant attempts to heal.

Conclusion

Negative emotions such as anger, hatred, and anxiety are often hypothesized to lead to violence. However, the survey of Beslan victims reveals no statistically significant correlation between these negative emotions and support for retaliatory violence against Chechens. Angry and hate-filled victims indeed mobilized more than less angry and hate-filled victims, but their mobilization was peaceful and political. Anxious victims were no different from less anxious victims in their support for retaliatory violence or their political participation, and the positive correlation between anxiety and political participation at the bivariate level fails to hold in multivariate analysis.

The significance of anger and hatred for peaceful political participation is not conditional on other variables or dependent on the moderate or extreme nature of the specific political act. The lack of significant correlation between these emotions and support for violence and the presence of a significant positive correlation between these emotions and political participation suggest that anger and hatred are constructive rather than destructive emotions. While anger and hatred have been demonized and worry-provoking, it seems they may be worthy of acceptance and even welcome, to the extent that they mobilize aggrieved individuals to attempt to redress their grievances through the political system and are not the prime culprits in instigating retaliatory violence.

The puzzle, though, is by no means solved. Anger and hatred are not the only variables influencing post-violence political participation, so what else matters? If anger and hatred play little role in encouraging support for violence, what does play a role? These questions are addressed in Chapters 6 through 11 with discussions of the influence on post-violence behavior of ethnic prejudice, political versus social alienation, political versus self-efficacy, and experiences prior to victimization, including prior harm and prior political participation.

6

Ethnic Prejudice

The hostage takers in Beslan School No. 1 were criminals. They were murderers, rapists, and thieves who later turned to the cause of Chechen independence. Some or most were even latecomers to devout Islam. For example, terrorist leader Khodov formally became a Muslim only in 2003 (Buse et al. 2004). Many of the hostage takers were on Russia's wanted list, including Khodov for rape and Khuchbarov for murder, both since 1998 (Buse et al. 2004; Milashina 2006d; Dunlop 2006:36–38). By their outlaw distinction alone, these were not "typical" Ingush and Chechens.

Nevertheless, many if not most Beslan victims thought it was reasonable to generalize from these criminals to their entire ethnic groups and to regard the co-ethnics as criminals too. At the very least, the hostage taking provided confirmatory evidence that Ingush and Chechens were undesirables. Mingling with such people was not palatable. Only a small minority of victims did not harbor such prejudice.

What is the role of ethnic prejudice in motivating responses to violence? This chapter explores prejudice, defined as negative preconceived opinions of ethnic others and measured as the seemingly innocuous opposition to mixed schooling, marriage, and dining, and the effects of prejudice on support for retaliatory violence. The relationship between ethnic prejudice and political participation is explored more briefly, given the dearth of hypotheses about such a relationship in the extant literature and the absence of a meaningful empirical relationship in Beslan.

The analysis shows that negative attitudes toward members of a rival ethnic group are not innocuous. Beslan victims who frowned upon interethnic mingling were more likely to support retaliatory violence after the hostage taking than victims who were willing to share meals, schools, and marriage with their Ingush neighbors. The latter, tolerant victims, were a small minority, and their commitment to nonviolence was probably the most robust in this entire study. The far larger majority of victims were prejudiced against Ingush and more likely to approve of killing Chechens. It will later be shown that the relationship between everyday prejudice and support for retaliatory violence is independent of anger, anxiety, and other emotions. Harmful outcomes emerge from the tendency to paint all members of an ethnic group with one brush, not from the emotion surrounding such generalizations. The potential for retaliatory violence

After Violence. Debra Javeline, Oxford University Press. © Oxford University Press 2023.
DOI: 10.1093/oso/9780197683347.003.0007

after the Beslan school hostage taking was thus very real, should a political elite or other entrepreneur within the community have tried to capitalize on the widespread prejudice and instigate mass revenge attacks.

Prejudice after Violence

For prejudice to exist, there must first be a sense of ethnic identity, a sense of in-group and out-group, we and they (Horowitz 1985:70). Members of an ethnic group share "a group name, a believed common descent, common historical memories, elements of shared culture such as language or religion, and attachment (even if only historical or sentimental) to a specific territory" (Kaufman 2001:16). This sense of identity serves some positive functions, including the fulfillment of emotional and physical needs by a community larger than the family (Horowitz 1985:81). Humans seem hard-wired for group membership (Lake and Rothchild 1996:55–56).

The downside of ethnic identity is that it is often sustained only in comparison with individuals and groups who do not share the ethnicity, and the comparison usually casts these others in a negative light. Pairs of rival ethnic groups often identify modal personality attributes of both groups in a contrasting and opposing way, with one characterized as backward and the other as advanced. These attributes are supposedly in the nature of group members who vary little across individuals or over time. Such stereotypes often serve as cognitive shorthands in peaceful social situations and situations of conflict (Green et al. 2001:485). Groups compete for self-worth (Horowitz 1985:142, 143), and individuals gain self-worth from successful group competition (Horowitz 2001:46–47). Feeling good about membership in one's own group may require vilifying the other group (Lake and Rothchild 1996:55–56).

Stereotypes and Prejudice in North Ossetia

Accordingly, in North Ossetia, Ossetians commonly contrasted the negative traits of the backward Ingush and Chechen ethnicities with the positive traits typical of their own more advanced group. For example, writing over a decade before the hostage taking, Tishkov (1997:176) reported, "During my numerous conversations with Ossets, both with representatives of local authorities and with many residents, strongly negative stereotypes concerning the Ingush were heard: lazy, insidious, dishonest, trespassers and so forth." Phillips (2007:198) concurred: "I was told that the backward, grasping Ingush required special handling by Ossetians, who by nature were welcoming of other nationalities.

A professor at Vladikavkaz Institute of the Humanities told me, 'We are on the threshold of modernizing our society. Our neighbours in Ingushetia are not quite there yet. Whatever else you say, Ossetia is still a multi-ethnic society, whereas Ingushetia is a mono-ethnic society. That has an impact on how people live.' "

The contrast between Ossetians and their rival ethnic groups was drawn especially starkly in the descriptions of the danger posed by Ingush and Chechens. According to Sveta Dzhioyeva, a reporter at the newspaper *Osetia Segodnya* [Ossetia Today], "It is only our tolerance that has stopped something worse happening with the Ingush. Even now, after all the explosions, they come to our bazaar to shop, and nobody bothers them. But I don't know an Ossetian who would go to Nazran [capital of Ingushetia]. It's far too dangerous. Do you see you any Christian suicide bombers? The Muslims need to ask themselves that question before they demand sympathy. We have a right to be afraid of them" (Parfitt 2011).

The negative ethnic stereotyping and bundling of Chechens and Ingush together were palpable during the focus groups. Many discussions had participants nodding in agreement as one described the civilized nature of Ossetians compared to their barbaric Ingush and Chechen neighbors. An exchange between female activist victims over thirty-five years old is illustrative.

LARISA: If we take the North Caucasus, Ossetians are the calmest, most peaceful people. The majority of nationalities in the North Caucasus live in Ossetia. Everybody lives peacefully here and loves each other. Each takes care of his family, works, raises children. And how many refugees there are in our Ossetia! From everywhere. The territory is small, all live peacefully, and everyone finds a place and work for himself. If we take the Republic of Ingushetia, no one lives there besides Ingush. Even birds of a different nationality don't fly there. Only Ingush people live there.

TATIANA: They have already killed the last Russian family.

LARISA: You know, no one can live with them. They can't even live with each other. And let's take Ossetia. We have plenty of nationalities living here, Germans, Jews, Poles, well, literally all.

BERTA: And speaking of the Georgian conflict, has a single Georgian stood and left here? Of course, not. And nobody oppresses them.

DINA: You know there is a village Chermen in the Prigorodny region [of North Ossetia]. There you can say, "Here is the house of an Ingush and here is that of an Ossetian." And they live like that. Fine. . . . you can also go to Ingushetia. Even children will tell you that they hate Ossetians. That's how they are brought up.

DIANA: And you go there and look for somebody's house, tell them the last name, first name, and patronymic, and they will tell you something different. If they live on the right side, they will tell you that it's to the left. They will never help you.

DINA: And they come here freely. In the maternity clinic, an Ingush woman will receive a better place than we. And they walk about the town.

TATIANA: The Ingush got what they wanted. They now live alone. Only Chechens and Ingush live in Chechnya and in Ingushetia. Nobody else.

DINA: And here everybody lives.

TATIANA: They got this through war. They did everything they could.

DINA: We receive refugees, but nobody goes there.

TATIANA: Since the time of Lermontov, "the evil Chechen is sharpening his dagger on the bank of the Terek [River]."

BERTA: Because they, other peoples, will be slaves there. They won't live, they will be slaves.

RAISA: And they can't exist by themselves.

LARISA: The conclusion is that we are the most civilized people.

The contrast between the primitive and even barbaric Ingush and Chechens, on the one hand, and the peace-loving, civilized Ossetians, on the other, was also noted in the focus group of female activists aged thirty-five years and younger.

MADINA: No Ossetian family brings up a child in such conditions. What am I saying? As a child is born in an Ingush family, he is told that an Ossetian is the enemy. Those are the conditions in which they bring up their children. Now, you for example, do you educate your child in such a manner? Do you?

BELA: No, God forbid.

MADINA: Who has children? I also don't do this. And how many Ingush people walk and drive across our republic!

LARISA: If we only tried to go there!

BELLA: No, they feel here absolutely at ease here. That is, they can come here calmly. I, for one, whatever emergency arose. . . . They say never say never. I am saying it at the given moment. I would never go there with my children, whatever the emergency. I would be scared not so much for myself as for my children, for the family. But they can calmly come here and feel at ease and unpunished. Let's say an Ingush woman sits next to me with her children, I wouldn't harm her.

In the focus group of female nonactivist victims, participants agreed that Ingush are socialized to hate:

VERA: They were expelled from here. . . . Their houses were taken, and it started from this. They hate us. There was an Ingush website, which was closed down.

I often opened it and read. It's terrible what the Ingush write about us. They take it in with their mother's milk.

INDIRA: Hatred.

VERA: This hatred toward Ossetians.

The men similarly described the contrasts between Ossetians and their Ingush and Chechen neighbors. Male activist victims over thirty-five years old repeated the theme of peaceful living within North Ossetia compared to the crude, parochial, and brutish life in Ingushetia.

TAMERLAN: You know, national hostility has become part of state policy in the republic of Ingushetia. I can say it for certain. And if we analyze it, clashes occur every 15–20 years. The young generation is brought up in hatred. Suppose, they reach mature age, full age, and again they come with their questions to resolve the territorial problem. It happens each 15–20 years and it will continue.

TOTRAZ: Have you ever heard that someone from Ossetia came to Ingushetia and did something? Not something like this, but did something in general. Apart from the rumors that some people disappear. And that is unknown. Maybe they kidnap them themselves.

KAZBEK: Provocations, rumors.

TAMERLAN: This [Ingushetia] is a mono-national republic. Russians ran away from there, and now they are dragged there by a noose.

ISRAEL: We don't [slaughter Ingush]. We just don't trust them. Nobody believes the Ingush. We just don't trust them with anything.

TOTRAZ: I, for example, would not want an Ingush to live near me, by the way. I don't want to go to him. Let him live by himself, but I don't want to see him near me.

KAZBEK: Near?! Not even in the immediate neighborhood.

One of the most common discussions about ethnic differences—initiated by focus group participants themselves rather than the moderator—was the hypothetical situation of role reversal. What might have happened had the perpetrators been Ossetian and the victims Ingush or Chechen? All comments ran in the same direction: retaliatory violence in that case was virtually assured. For example, a male activist victim thirty-five years old or younger explained, "I think that Ingush are more aggressive, and if this had happened there, they would have attacked us."

The female nonactivist victims concurred:

INDIRA: If it had happened in Ingushetia, we definitely wouldn't be in this world any longer.

ZINAIDA: No, they wouldn't have listened.

VALENTINA: They would have wiped us off the face of the earth.

ZARINA: You know I studied in Chechnya and lived for fifteen years all in all there. I know them. If it had happened in the reverse in their school, for example, even if the militants had been mixed, not mostly Ossetians, I am 100 percent [sure] that they would have gone and destroyed all of Ossetia.

VERA: Well, now they are destroying us one by one.

ZARINA: I am 100 percent sure. They would never have forgiven it.

VERA: Literally recently, an Ossetian student was killed in Moscow. He was killed by an Ingush. The Ingush is hiding in Nazran. Everyone knows it. The Ingush authorities don't extradite him.

ZARINA: If they needed such an act to start a war between Ossetia [and Ingushetia], they should have done it the other way around [using Ossetians to seize an Ingush school]. If they wanted that.

INDIRA: Probably they wanted that, yes. They failed.

ZARINA: They didn't take into account that Ossetians are noble. They [Ingush] considered things according to their own mentality: what would be their calculations for this. Had it been reversed, there would certainly have been war.

VALYA: They needed a war in the Caucasus for them [Ingush]. Yes, this [would have worked].

LIZA: There would be war. That's 100 percent.

In the focus group of nonactivist male victims, participants agreed about the likelihood of retaliatory violence had the militancy taken place in Ingushetia. They also speculated that the Ingush would have gotten away with retaliation, echoing the oft-stated theme that Ossetians are treated unfairly in politics and public opinion. Ossetians were perceived as burdened by their civility relative to Ingush and Chechens, who—like younger siblings benefiting from a parent's low expectations—are given a pass for bad behavior.

BORIS: That's different mentality, different laws, and different people. They live differently. You never know what would have happened there. Perhaps if it had taken place in Ingushetia, they would have attacked us. No one would have stopped them, also perhaps so. They are such a people. This people has such a mentality. And we still need to see how the authorities relate to this people, because some people are allowed to do many things, but Ossetians in particular are not allowed to do anything. Ossetians should be restrained like this! . . . For some reason, everything is possible in Ingushetia. What is permitted to them is not permitted to us. If we had just moved to that side, we would have been wiped off the face of the earth. They can't be touched for some reason. Nobody touches them, not their policemen who brought bandits here. Nobody touches them. They are considered deportees. They got up at night and each and every one left, and they are all considered deportees. Georgia attacked South Ossetia for some reason, and again South Ossetia is to blame for that.

Terrorist demands are often related to the grievances of their ethnic groups. Indeed, in Beslan, the problems confronting Chechens and Ingush were the backdrop for the school siege, and the terrorists called for resolution of the problems. Prejudice against Ingush and Chechens manifested not in the attribution of the terrorists' grievances to their ethnic groups but in the attribution of the terrorists' *actions* to their ethnic groups.

The Origins, Perpetuation, and Exacerbation of Prejudice

In Beslan, a sense of Ossetian ethnic identity—likeness and difference with Ingush and Chechens—predated the hostage taking. Ethnic prejudice—stereotypes and negative appraisals of Ingush and Chechens—also predated the violent episode. In the words of one female nonactivist focus group member, "We have always had the same attitude toward the Ingush."

The prejudice may be rooted in childhood socialization (Kinder and Sears 1981) and personality characteristics such as dogmatism and xenophobia (Gibson and Howard 2007). The prejudice likely had a historical basis in the many real episodes of interethnic conflict, which then evolved into legends, sometimes accurate and sometimes distorted, that bolstered the positive image of Ossetians (Lake and Rothchild 1996:55; Kaufman 2001:16). And the legends and prejudice were likely reinforced when Ossetians noted their contributions to their country relative to Ingush contributions. As a nonactivist male victim explained, "During the Great Patriotic War, the most heroes of the Soviet Union were Ossetian in relation to their number in the population. The Ingush did not have a single one. They didn't even fight." The Soviet and Russian governments contributed to the sense of ethnic difference and opposition with provocative discourse and actions.

The prejudice provided a pre-made ethnic narrative for the hostage taking that cast the militants as representatives of their ethnic groups. Where ethnic identity is salient, "group membership is the lens through which ingroup members explain the behavior of outgroup members" (Horowitz 2001:541). In the North Caucasus, hostage takers were remembered less by their names and criminal records and more by their Ingush and Chechen ethnicities. For many Ossetians, Ingush and Chechen were already synonymous with terrorists.

In turn, the school hostage taking may have inflamed the preexisting prejudice by providing confirmatory evidence of the despicable nature of Ingush and Chechens. The attack may have even generated new prejudice. Terrorism-generated and terrorism-enhanced prejudice is common in many geopolitical settings (Skitka, Bauman, and Mullen 2004). Attacks heighten in-group solidarity and the propensity to vilify out-groups, the perceived source of harm and future threat (Huddy et al. 2005:594). For example, after the September 11 attacks on the World Trade Center, Americans downgraded their ratings of Middle Eastern ethnic groups (Traugott et al. 2002:514). Equally plausible, the attack in Beslan may have had no effect at all on existing prejudice and simply gave license (and opportunity) to prejudiced individuals to express their prejudice to journalists, academics, politicians, other victims, and the larger Ossetian and Russian communities. Without data gathered prior to the hostage taking for comparison, inferences about the role of the attack on prejudice are speculative. However, it can confidently be asserted that prejudice in North Ossetia has a long history and endures as of this writing.

Variation in Prejudice

Writing about stereotypes and prejudice runs the ironic risk of lumping together all individuals in a community and falsely assigning them a uniform set of attitudes, when of course individuals differ. Not all Beslan victims were equally prejudiced against people of Ingush and Chechen descent. In focus groups, variation in attitudes was revealed, even if the prevailing sentiment was anti-Ingush and anti-Chechen.

For example, the group of male activist victims thirty-five years old or younger directly engaged the question of prejudice and whether it was appropriate to make sweeping generalizations about all members of an ethnic group.

AKHSAR: It seems to me that our people are more rational than these Ingush. They have altogether different notions.

VLADIMIR: In fact, none of us has any right to discuss their notions and what people they are. . . . Have any of you lived with them?

AKHSAR: We were acquainted with Ingush people. We have acquaintances among them, and I can say that we normally communicate with them. But still somewhere in the subconscious, they are somehow strange, even in conversation. They have different views. It seems to us that they are unpredictable.

MARAT: As they say, there is a black sheep in every family. In each nation, there are normal and abnormal people.

VLADIMIR: It is simply senseless [to wage a war with a different nation]. Fish begins to stink at the head. We should find the reasons here and not look for them in a different nation. It is easier to blame some other nation than influence it.

Some female nonactivist victims also questioned the appropriateness of ethnic generalizations.

ZARINA: These are people, a nation. They have all kinds. Do you think we don't? We have the same among Ossetians as well.
ZARINA: [Describing the terrorist Khodov] he lived here in Ossetia.
SIMA: He was raised here.
ZARINA: Yes, in an Ossetian family.
VALYA: And he spoke Ossetian.
ZINAIDA: At some point he studied at School No. 1. He studied there.

Female nonactivist victims frankly described their ethnic biases and openly wrestled with the idea that there are good and bad individuals in every ethnic group.

INDIRA: We were in the hospital in Moscow, and an Ingush operated on us. I think he performed an operation for you as well. He removed shrapnel. I had such fear! There was a boy there who ran from the operation the first time. He wouldn't let the doctor give him a shot when he learned that the doctor was an Ingush. He didn't want to. But there were no other options. We agreed again the second time that he would do it, and he didn't want to again, but with great difficulty—five people lay on him, an eight-year-old boy— they gave him a shot, and only then he had an operation. I was scared. I don't know, suddenly for some reason it seemed to me that he might not wake up. I don't know, I had this fear.
INDIRA: Maybe there are good people among them as well.
ANGELA: Of course, each nation has good and bad people.

Some victims were even able to discriminate among "good" and "bad" terrorists. According to Marina Khubayeva, a thrity-one-year-old housewife who escaped with shrapnel wounds but searched unsuccessfully for her twelve-year-old daughter, "I want to be fair. There were good ones and bad ones. This terrorist had been quite decent under the circumstances. He explained that they didn't want to hurt us but that his family had been wiped out and that they wanted Russian soldiers out of their country. He offered me a bottle filled with water. Then this other one came along shouting at him, 'Do you want a bullet in your head?'" (Franchetti and Campbell 2004).

Some male nonactivist victims made similar differentiations:

TAMERLAN: Executors came here.
BORIS: They are not guilty. They were hired. They were given a job. They fulfilled their task, and that's all.

Individuals may have varied not just in the degree of prejudice but in the type of prejudice. Some victims, while trying to avoid generalizing from the criminals to their ethnic groups, nevertheless revealed other kinds of stereotyping, prejudice, and occasionally, xenophobia. Some victims pejoratively discussed groups beyond Ingush and Chechen. For example, in the focus group of female nonactivist victims, even the more tolerant victims talked in ethnic terms.

INDIRA: Why hasn't anyone from the Ingush side or the Chechen side, though their nationalities were there, apologized to these children who were held hostage?
ZARINA: No, they said that it was not the nation [that did it].
VALYA: Bandits have no nation, no God. . . .there were not only people from Chechnya and Ingushetia. My God, it was the most multinational criminal bandit group. There has never been such a multinational bandit group in the world. . . . There were not only Chechens and Ingush, but also Ossetians, whoever you may think of.
ZINAIDA: There was a Kyrgyz there.
VALYA: Whoever you may think of. It was conceived at the level of not just Chechnya and Ingushetia. This was done at the level of America.
ZINAIDA: And a Kyrgyz, a militant, was with us in the gym all the night. He shouted all night, so that his voice became hoarse. No one even talked. Children cried, "Water-water!" and he shouted, "Shut up!" all night, and by the morning his voice became hoarse. And then he said, "Today we will make you go through the mincing machine. We'll make a mincing machine for you." You were not there, right?
SIMA: No.
ZINAIDA: I was. The whole night. And he was a Kyrgyz, with eyes like this.

Some Ossetians recognized that stereotypes ran both ways. According to Alan Tskhurbayev, a popular Ossetian blogger, "Many people in Ossetia are ready to put the words Islam, Ingush, and terrorist in a single chain. Equally, I'm sure that in Ingushetia just as many think of Ossetians only as 'the fighters who murdered us'" (Parfitt 2011).

A single nonactivist male victim went so far as to defend the average Ingush, while conceding the powerful influence of the more violence-oriented Ingush: "Before the terrorist act but after the Ingush events, I went to Ingushetia for a holiday a couple of times. They greeted me as a guest, no excessive words, and the common people are like us. They don't need war. They work, support their families. They don't need to be feuding with Ossetians or feuding with Dagestanis. They need to work, to support their families. There are some people who are itching to do it. Therefore, we are not going to attack them yet, but if they compel us, then there will be no way out. . . . Although they are already compelling us to that."

The Powerful Role of Prejudice in Retaliatory Violence

Ethnic prejudice can play a role in retaliatory ethnic violence for two reasons. First, as described above, individuals with strong ethnic identities and strong negative assessments of other ethnicities tend to view events through an ethnic lens. Prejudiced individuals are more likely than unprejudiced individuals to label criminal perpetrators by their ethnicities and to comprehend crimes in ethnic terms. They attribute behavior, including violence, to the innate characteristics of members of rival ethnic groups. Prejudiced individuals are thus more willing to punish not just the perpetrators of atrocities but those sharing the perpetrators' ethnicity. They may even be willing to punish members of ethnic groups only vaguely connected to the perpetrators by religion, place of residence, appearance, or some other characteristic. Such was the case, for example, after the September 11 terrorist attacks when at least 2,000 hate crimes were committed against Arabs, Muslims, and those perceived to be Arab or Muslim due to dress, skin color, or other physical attributes (Singh 2002). Some Americans endorsed deporting Arab Americans, Muslims, and first-generation immigrants and supported war against Iraq, even though it was by then acknowledged that Iraq played no role in the attacks (Skitka et al. 2006:382).

Second, prejudice is often accompanied by dehumanization (Bruneau and Kteily 2017). "[T]he lives of strangers against whom there is animus are believed to be of lesser value than those of ethnic kin, perhaps even of trivial value" (Horowitz 2001:542). Retaliatory violence is a less weighty action—less subject to deliberation, second thoughts, and remorse—if the lives of the targets of retaliation do not matter. Indeed, degradation is often a goal of violence. Perpetrators of violence often choose to kill their victims in ways that demonstrate that they do not count (Horowitz 2001:432).

What is commonly referred to in the United States as a "hate crime" is really a crime of prejudice. The "perpetrator is motivated by prejudice toward the victim's putative social group" (Green et al. 2001:480). Negative thoughts about ethnic others, not the emotion surrounding the negativity, is the decisive factor allowing victims or their sympathizers to leap from supporting vengeance against the criminals to holding the criminals' ethnic group responsible and supporting violence against them, no matter their connection to the actual crime.

Prejudice and Retaliation after Violence in Beslan

In Beslan, the idea that "a criminal has a nationality" was rampant among politicians, journalists, and the public. Local newspapers published the ethnicities of the mostly Chechen and Ingush terrorists next to their names (Mite 2004), and this tendency spilled over into international reporting. Even the Wikipedia entry for the "Beslan school siege" lists the nationality of each dead militant, which implies that this information is relevant and broadly conceived as relevant.[1]

At the very least, the identification of hostage takers by their ethnicity facilitated the blaming of ethnic Ingush and Chechens for the gruesome violence. Participants in a focus group of female activists thirty-five years old and younger were asked whether many people accused the Ingush people after the tragedy.

BELLA: Yes, I think so.
IRINA: Everybody did.

The male activist victims over thirty-five years old concurred:

KAZBEK: [On whether the Ingush people are guilty] Right.
TOTRAZ: Of course, for certain.
KAZBEK: All are guilty, all.
TOTRAZ: It is just easy there to find executors who would come to us.
KAZBEK: They have no brains.

Again, however, prejudice varies across individuals, leading some victims not to blame the co-ethnics of perpetrators. Victims may even be ambivalent in both their prejudice and their blame, at times trying to be—or appear to be—tolerant of rival ethnic groups and at times persuaded that tolerance is unfounded. Consider the discussion between nonactivist male victims about whether Ingush

---

[1] See https://en.wikipedia.org/wiki/Beslan_school_siege.

people are guilty for the tragedy, as one participant openly ponders and considers both sides:

BORIS: They are not guilty.

VALERY: No, why are they not guilty? The preparation went on there? Everyone saw this happening there [in Ingushetia], a kilometer from the administrative borders.

BORIS: The Ingush are such a nation. If it happened here, I am not sure that someone wouldn't have come and said something.

In the focus group of female nonactivist victims, participants also discussed the culpability of the Ingush people, and at least one participant gave contrary answers as the discussion ensued. First, she asserted, "Most people say that the majority of militants were Ingush people. Twenty-six people. Of course, they are guilty. There was a majority of them there." But later in the conversation, she asserted quite the opposite: "Common Ingush people are also not guilty." Another participant agreed, "There were not only Ingush there."

Quotations in news reports from North Ossetia suggest how the dominant sentiment of prejudice linked to support for retaliatory violence.

ALAN KURSRAYEV, A TWENTY-SIX-YEAR-OLD OSSETIAN FROM BESLAN: Don't blame us at all if we rise up. The Ingush were among the terrorists at the school, and as far as I'm concerned, all Ingush are terrorists. (Rodriguez 2004b)

BOYS TWELVE YEARS OLD AND UNDER PLAYING A VIOLENT GROUP COM-PUTER GAME IN VLADIKAVKAZ: Look, an Ingush, a terrorist—waste him! (Parfitt 2011)

EMILIA ADYRKHAYEVA, ELEVEN-YEAR-OLD IN A LETTER TO HER FATHER ABOUT HER DEAD MOTHER: This is dedicated to our mother Ira. The years have passed, but we will never forget your smile, your eyes and your tenderness. The Russians should kill the Ingushetians, just as they killed our Beslan. (Schepp 2009)

Focus group participants offered similar commentary:

VIKA [female activist thirty-five years or younger]: As for me, I can't bear to see them [Ingush] even in kerchiefs. I am against their staying in our republic at all because one terrorist act follows another. They annihilate absolutely inno-cent people time after time. Why aren't they expelled? You know, for centuries we have had a saying: if you boil an Ingush and an Ossetian in one pot, they wouldn't mix in a soup.

Ingush themselves well understood the connection between prejudice and retaliatory violence. According to Zarema Tochiyeva, a forty-year-old French teacher from the mostly Ingush town of Kartsa in North Ossetia, "The people of Kartsa knew this would happen and began to feel the danger even before the hostage-taking ended Sept. 3. The word is that the Ossetians are preparing to attack us here. To them, Ingush is not a nationality but an enemy. Monsters. That's it. Once they've decided on that, they don't need to think any further" (Mydans 2004b).

It is possible that prejudice or at least stereotyping may dissuade retaliatory violence, to the extent that violent behavior is contrary to the self-image of an ethnic group. Ossetians, for example, pride themselves on being more civilized than their barbaric ethnic rivals. As one male activist victim thirty-five years old or younger explained, "If a person commits a crime, it doesn't entitle another person to commit the same crime. If we went, 30–40 people, they would just have had more people. . . . Why should we turn into animals?"

Indeed, many victims denied that their prejudice, fully admitted, would cause them to commit an act of violence. A female nonactivist victim explained:

VERA: I don't know, I for example determined for myself: I won't go kill Ingush. I am not able to kill a person. But I won't shake hands with an Ingush. I won't talk with him, won't have any kind of contact with him. My child studies in a Moscow university, and she says, "Mama, an Ingush girl comes up to me, sees that I am not Russian, says, 'Who are you?' 'I am Ossetian.' 'And I am Ingush.' I turned away," she says. "'I have nothing to talk with you about, that's all.'" That is, she won't take revenge either, but she determined for herself that this is the nation with whom it's impossible to communicate. I won't try to find out whether an Ingush is good or not. Probably this will pass, but now they are all enemies for me.

The nonactivist male victims also denied retaliatory intentions while talking in ethnic terms:

BORIS: We have brains in our heads. We think about things and have to think with our heads. If we go [attack them], nobody will benefit from this. As opposed to [how they think].
ARKADY: A person nevertheless thinks about his descendants, and now, for example, if we start a war, tomorrow they will go after our children. We should think about this. That's what I think.
BORIS: . . . I am saying that unlike others, Ossetians have brains which they use. They think, and they do, perhaps not always correctly, but mostly they do things the right way.

TAMERLAN: We are peace-loving by nature. As for our relations with people, we usually treat people as guests, as acquaintances, as friends. Here in Ossetia is one of the most multi-national populations. I think 120 nationalities live together.

BORIS: Here nobody says that you are Russian, Armenian, or Georgian. When there was a conflict with Georgia, nobody touched Georgians here.

TAMERLAN: Such facts are really rare.

BORIS: This is very rare. Perhaps there are a few people who think and want to do something, but not everything turns out, but mostly, the whole multitude of Ossetians are sensible people who know what to do and how to do it. Do you think that no one provoked us to do something to Ingush people after the terrorist act? They tried to do this.

Factors Mitigating or Exacerbating the Prejudice-Violence Link

Prejudice alone does not cause retaliatory ethnic violence or even support for such violence. Other factors are of course at play, either fanning the flames or alleviating tensions, calming those most agitated, and otherwise making a situation less volatile. Consider, for example, the grievance context, in this case the school siege. Prejudice against Ingush and Chechens, absent the recent act of terror, may have had few attitudinal or behavioral ramifications, because there would have been nothing to retaliate against, no violent episode to be seen through an ethnic lens. If and when violence such as a hostage taking does occur to victims who harbor prejudice, a political entrepreneur may still be required to direct that prejudice toward retaliatory violence (Kaufman 2001:12).

Conversely, after violence befalls victims who harbor prejudice and could act upon the prejudice, in-group policing can be a powerful tool to halt the spiral of retaliatory violence (Fearon and Laitin 1996; Brubaker and Laitin 1998:439). Sinister political entrepreneurs may not exist or may flounder in their efforts, and peace-minded political entrepreneurs may prevail. Indeed, that is likely what happened in Beslan. Potential instigators of retaliatory violence were reined in by respected elders and prevented from organizing revenge attacks or swaying impressionable followers. As the female nonactivist victims explained:

ZINAIDA: People listen to elders here.

INDIRA: Elders and the authorities.

ZINAIDA: Probably the elders brought them to their senses and said that they shouldn't do that. Blood is not washed out in blood—we have this Ossetian proverb. The elders probably had a talk with them, and they listened. Ossetians are such people. They are the only one of all Caucasian peoples—I am saying this not because I am Ossetian. They always listen to others when people prompt or tell them something like that. And they listened. But Ingush people wouldn't do that.

The state too can play a role in provoking prejudiced individuals to commit retaliatory ethnic violence or in thwarting retaliation. Often the state supports violence or is perceived to do so and thereby serves as provocateur (Horowitz 2001:8), but sometimes ethnic violence does not serve state interests and is discouraged. In Beslan, mass retaliation would have made it difficult for the authorities to continue their propaganda that Beslan was yet another incident of international terror, a thing entirely separate from the Chechen conflict and other domestic problems in the North Caucasus, which were said to be under control. For days, weeks, and even months after the hostage taking, the Russian authorities inaccurately portrayed the ethnicities of the hostage takers as non-Caucasians (Harding 2012). Although the authorities had their own self-serving reasons for doing so, the lie may have had the positive ramification of staving off further violence. The participants in the focus group of female activists thirty-five years and younger discussed this explanation for why retaliatory fighting did not happen:

BELA: It seems to me our authorities did a lot to prevent that.
BELA: Well, there were conversations that no, they were not Ingush; they were completely different people.
BELLA: It is not just that there were conversations. They were categorically denying.
BELA: But I'm even happy about that.
BELLA: [Confirming that the authorities denied that the hostage takers were Ingush] Yes. Yes, they even started to say that mercenaries were there.
BELA: And there were Negroes and Arabs.

One factor that does not seem required for prejudice to play a meaningful role in support for retaliatory violence is emotion. Some scholars argue that ethnic appeals produce violence only when accompanied by fear and existential threat (Kaufman 2006:52–53; also Skitka, Bauman, and Mullen 2004:744) or when in-group love becomes out-group hate (Brewer 2001). However, Chapter 5 showed that prejudice was not conditional on fear, anger, or other emotions in its effects on support for retaliatory violence. Nor did fear, anger, or other emotions seem to be a preliminary or intermediary step in support for violence in Beslan whereby emotions heightened prejudice or vice versa. Anger or other emotions could not account, theoretically or empirically, for the leap from logical revenge (kill the killer) to generalized revenge (kill the killer's co-ethnics), whereas prejudice directly connects the two. The prejudiced individual thinks in ethnic terms and is likely to see a killer as representative of his or her ethnic group.

Emotions may be an excuse or rationalization that allows prejudiced individuals to vocalize ethnic attitudes that would otherwise be unacceptable, but a terrorist act itself also may have this effect. In Beslan, the hostage taking probably justified the expression of prejudice that was already there or was created or magnified by the event. Prejudice alone, with or without emotion, increased support for retaliatory violence.

Threat perception has been shown to influence support for retaliatory violence more strongly than emotions. For example, after the September 11 terrorist attacks, Americans who perceived a high threat of future terrorism were more supportive of aggressive military action against terrorists and less supportive of American isolationism (Huddy et al. 2005). The link between perceived threat and support for retaliatory violence is probably conditional on or mediated by prejudice. Threats, or terrorist attacks themselves (that is, proven threats), may cause or heighten prejudice (Struch and Schwartz 1989; Marcus et al. 1995; and Herrmann et al. 1999; Huddy et al. 2005:594) or allow preexisting prejudice to reveal itself. Either way, the perceived threats or actual attacks probably require the important intermediary of prejudice in order to motivate support for retaliatory ethnic violence—retaliation directed not toward proven terrorists but their co-ethnics.

The Irrelevance of Prejudice for Political Action

In situations of ethnic conflict, stereotypes and prejudice can hinder interethnic compromise (Horowitz 1985:54). Even in the absence of overt ethnic conflict, prejudice can influence electoral preferences and opinions on public policy issues. For example, prejudiced attitudes have led white Americans to oppose school desegregation (Giles et al. 1976), welfare spending on education, healthcare, and the elderly (Gilens 1995, 1996), and the candidacy of an African American for president (Piston 2010). Prejudiced individuals may act on their prejudice in the political arena, as they did, for example, by participating in antibusing movements in the United States (Schuman et al. 1997:6).

However, in a general sense, there is no reason to believe that prejudiced individuals participate in politics at a greater or lesser rate than those without prejudice. Research on racial prejudice in the United States focuses mainly on the implications of prejudice for public attitudes, policy preferences, and policy outcomes rather than on behavioral implications, such as voter turnout or the frequency of attendance at demonstrations. There is evidence that racial *identification* in the United States is linked with higher rates of participation in political campaigns, petitions, protests, and boycotts (Chong and Rogers 2005), but there is no evidence that racial *prejudice* is responsible for similar variations in mobilization.

In ethnically divided societies, research on ethnic prejudice focuses mainly on its implications for conflict resolution. When it comes to participation rates in institutionalized political processes or politics outside institutions, especially for issues that do not bear directly on ethnic relations, there is little theory or evidence to suggest that prejudice should matter. For issues that do bear directly on ethnic relations, participation might be motivated by prejudice if a specific ethnicity-related action was on the policy agenda. Otherwise, prejudice probably neither precludes nor encourages variation in political activism.

In Beslan, the policy agenda did not include legislation or debates about interethnic issues, such as formally resolving the dispute over the Prigorodny region (described in Chapter 1) in favor of ethnic Ossetians or encouraging the remaining Ingush and Chechen residents of North Ossetia to leave the republic. Such legislation was largely unnecessary, given that many Ingush residents had already left North Ossetia of their own volition after the hostage taking or were at least rumored to have done so (Dzutsev 2004). Also, as focus group discussions suggest, demands for blatantly racist legislation would probably have violated Ossetians' sense of themselves as a civilized people who welcome all ethnic groups. Over time, demands for political anti-Ingush or anti-Chechen solutions were rendered even less necessary, because the Prigorodny situation resolved in favor of Ossetians. In 2009, Ingush president Yunus-Bek Yevkurov announced that Ingushetia officially recognized the disputed region as part of North Ossetia, diminishing a primary source of interethnic conflict (at least for Ossetians) and prompting many Ingush to return to their homes in Prigorodny without threatening Ossetians' territorial claim to the region (Dzutsev 2009).[2] Most likely, even prejudiced Beslan victims did not see value in ethnic-based legislation, although there are spotty news reports just after the hostage taking of the occasional crowd demanding that North Ossetian president Alexander Dzasohkov expel all Ingush from the region (Dzutsev 2004). For the more pressing and prevalent issues that were on the policy agenda, both prejudiced victims and less prejudiced victims participated in politics at similar rates. While prejudice is a significant part of the story of post-violence support for retaliation, it did not play a meaningful role in post-violence political participation.

---

[2] Census data from the North Caucasus are notoriously unreliable, but it is worth noting that the data record 6,894 more Ingush in North Ossetia in 2010 compared to 2002. Of the 710,275 residents of North Ossetia in 2002, 21,442 were Ingush (3%), and 3,383 were Chechens (0.5%) (http://www.perepis2002.ru/index.html?id=17). Of the 712,980 residents of North Ossetia in 2010, 28,336 were Ingush (4%), and 2,264 were Chechen (0.3%) (Vserossiskaya Perepis Naseleniya 2010, http://www.gks.ru/free_doc/new_site/perepis2010/croc/perepis_itogi1612.htm).

Measuring Prejudice

Measures of prejudice borrowed from widely used and validated questions about approval of interethnic mingling in schools and marriage and at the dinner table (Biernat and Crandall 1999; Schuman et al. 1997; Shaw et al. 2015:240–241). These questions are among the nine most frequently asked questions in the American General Social Survey and many other surveys used for decades to measure racial or ethnic attitudes (Biernat and Crandall 1999: 305–307). Here, Ossetians and Ingush are substituted for whites and blacks.

Table 6.1 shows that Beslan victims generally disliked their Ingush and Chechen neighbors, hoped to be physically separate from them, and did indeed live physically or at least socially separate from them. Most (59.7 percent) would have objected strongly if a family member wanted to bring an Ingush home for dinner, and in the few years prior the overwhelming majority (86.6 percent) did not have an Ingush in their home for dinner. The victims did not want their relatives marrying into Ingush families (57.9 percent said they would be very uneasy about this proposition), and they did not want their children to attend the same schools as Ingush children, with 71.5 percent endorsing separate schools and 75.6 percent objecting to sending their children to a school where half the children were Ingush.

Three of these questions were combined into a mean index of 0–1, where 0 represents the least prejudiced victims—open to intermarriage, mixed schooling, and dining with Ingush—and 1 represents the most prejudiced victims, opposed to all three. The index includes only one of the two questions on schooling (preferring schools separate or the same), because the two schooling questions were highly correlated ($r = .76, p < .00$). The index omits the factual question about having an Ingush over for dinner in the past few years, because the question is not directly attitudinal, even if indicative of attitudes.

Table 6.2 shows that the majority of Beslan victims (53.2 percent) are prejudiced and get the highest score on the prejudice index, with another 21.9 percent being more prejudiced than not. However, there is a small minority that is unequivocally not prejudiced (4.2 percent), and another 8.7 percent who waver in their prejudice or lean toward nonprejudiced views.

The component survey questions of the prejudice index could be criticized for their simplicity at a time when questions from the literature on American racial attitudes have become more sophisticated and varied to reflect changes in the social and political context of race relations in the United States (Schuman et al. 1997:61). In Beslan, the basic questions about interethnic mingling are appropriate for the social and political context of the North Caucasus where such mingling is still widely frowned upon and where affirmative action, busing, and other Western public policies are less relevant. For example, as in many regions

Table 6.1. Attitudes of Beslan Victims toward Ingush

How strongly would you object if a member of your family wanted to bring an Ingush home to dinner?

Object Strongly	Object Mildly	Not at All Object	Refused	Unsure
656	196	62	107	77
(59.7)	(17.9)	(5.6)	(9.7)	(7.0)

During the last few years, has anyone in your family brought an Ingush home for dinner?

No	Yes	Refused
951	34	113
(86.6)	(3.1)	(10.3)

How would it make you feel if a close relative of yours were planning to marry an Ingush?

Very Uneasy	Somewhat Uneasy	Not at All Uneasy	Refused	Unsure
636	211	54	108	89
(57.9)	(19.2)	(4.9)	(9.8)	(8.1)

Do you think Ossetian and Ingush students should go to the same schools or to separate schools?

Same Schools	Separate Schools	Refused	Unsure
52	785	104	157
(4.7)	(71.5)	(9.5)	(14.3)

Would you have any objection to sending your children to a school where half of the children are Ingush?

No	Yes	Refused	Unsure
63	830	109	96
(5.7)	(75.6)	(9.9)	(8.7)

$N = 1,098$; number of victims (%).

Table 6.2. Prejudice of Beslan Victims: Index of Opposition to Interethnic Dining, Marriage, and Schooling

0 (least prejudiced)	46 (4.2)
< 0 and > .5 (leaning nonprejudiced)	23 (2.1)
.5 (mixed attitudes)	72 (6.6)
< .5 and < 1 (leaning prejudiced)	240 (21.9)
1 (most prejudiced)	584 (53.2)

$N = 1,098$; number of victims (%); 133 missing.

of ethnic conflict, endogamy in the North Caucasus is seen by many, especially the prejudiced, as a key to preserving ethnic identity (Horowitz 2001:49). Even in the United States, intermarriage is perceived as more threatening than job competition and other more complicated interracial issues (Glaser et al. 2002:177). There are of course nationalities policies in Russia, as there were historically in the Soviet Union, but for simplicity, questions here measure ethnic prejudice and not attitudes toward ethnicity-related policy issues (Carmines et al. 2011).

Simple measures of ethnic prejudice have the advantage of being clearly distinct from measures of emotion. They allow us to conceptualize negative assessments of a rival ethnic group separate from the emotions surrounding those assessments or from offending actions such as terrorism. This conceptual clarity and measurement clarity represent an important contribution. Other studies of ethnic violence attribute the violence to hate, contempt, or antipathy, but these terms are conceptualized as a bundle of prejudice-plus-emotion, making it unclear whether prejudice or emotion is the more powerful factor.

Consider, for example, the following argument: "Without feelings of antipathy, there can be no ethnic conflict" (Horowitz 1985:182). Antipathy, in this statement, includes both the concept of prejudice (negative attitudes toward an out-group) and the concept of emotion (the feeling of intense dislike, synonymous with hatred or perhaps a milder form). If antipathy were tested rigorously and found to be correlated with ethnic conflict, thus validating the statement, we would not be much closer to knowing the relative power of prejudice and emotion in provoking retaliatory violence.

Or consider a similar argument: "Antipathy or hatred toward the class or category means precisely a disposition toward generalization and away from individuation of targets within the group" (Horowitz 2001:542). Notice the qualification of antipathy or hatred as extending *toward the class or category*. The feeling of antipathy or hatred requires prejudice in order for the proposition to work. If the word "prejudice" were substituted for the first clause, the reference to class or category could be eliminated, because it is already embedded in the concept of prejudice. The argument would read simply, "Prejudice means precisely a disposition toward generalization and away from individuation of targets within the group," and it would make sense. "I don't want my children going to school with people of that ethnicity" may or may not be accompanied by emotion, but the argument here is that such ethnic prejudice is distinct from emotion and should be measured distinctly in order to test for independent causal effects.

It may seem obvious and overly simple to talk about the link between negative opinions of others and the willingness to kill them, but the simplicity of the relationship is the important and often missed point. In many places in the world, ethnic prejudice is ordinary. This ordinary sentiment can have grave consequences. Crimes of prejudice may sound less dramatic than "hate crimes," but it may be the more apt label, precisely because drama is an unnecessary part of the equation—a smokescreen for the simple but more powerful and sinister explanatory variable. To test this possibility, the attitude needs to be separated from the emotion.

Simple measures of ethnic prejudice may be worrisome in some countries where such questions elicit a social desirability bias. Expressed ethnic or racial attitudes in a survey or focus group may inaccurately reflect true attitudes, as respondents give answers that they think are in line with the attitudes of the interviewer or society at large. Answers to questions about racial or ethnic intermingling end up revealing social norms but are biased as measures of attitudes (Schuman et al. 1997:3). This is the case in the United States where some respondents are reluctant to reveal their prejudiced attitudes because the attitudes defy social norms and could be labeled "politically incorrect." Desiring to please the interviewer or an imagined community audience, respondents may hesitate to admit their prejudice and may misrepresent their opinions, systematically underreporting prejudice (Shaw et al. 2015:242).

For this study of Beslan victims, the potential underreporting of prejudiced attitudes is less of a concern. Negative assessments of ethnic groups may be uncomfortable in some cultures, but in Beslan, North Ossetia, and the Caucasus more generally, prejudiced thoughts are comfortably expressed. If anything, the socially desirable responses in Beslan are the ethnic exclusionary ones. Statements like those above ("I can't bear to see them" and "They have no brains") were offered nonchalantly to a nodding, accepting audience. In the focus group of female activist victims over thirty-five years old, participants offered similar insulting commentary about Ingush with the comfortable and correct assumption that prejudiced statements would be well received by most others.

TATIANA: Revengeful.
RAISA: Yes, such a repugnant people.
LARISA: They are a very peculiar nation. Very much so. And nobody knows them better than we do.

Limitations to Prejudice Measurements

Potential *over*reporting of prejudiced attitudes is the more relevant concern about data from Beslan. When there is a dominant group norm or sentiment, it may be difficult for an individual with minority views to express those views publicly or even in a private group setting, and the difficulty exists not just for prejudiced individuals in an unprejudiced group. Expressing unprejudiced views among prejudiced individuals can also be uncomfortable and possibly hazardous. Just as compromisers in interethnic conflict risk contempt by their co-ethnics for their presumed betrayal (Horowitz 1985:54), those who express sympathetic or defensive thoughts about members of a rival ethnic group may risk ostracism or hostility. In the study of Beslan victims, participants who were not prejudiced may have been the most circumspect in their comments. This concern was relayed by the focus group moderator and survey interviewers in the study. They questioned whether it would be possible in North Ossetia to express positive attitudes toward Ingush, given the social norm of negative attitudes and even aggressiveness toward Ingush.

These concerns have merit. In the focus groups, participants holding an anti-norm, nonprejudiced mindset may have stayed quiet, so nonprejudiced views may be somewhat underrepresented. However, even with some social desirability bias, questions about ethnic attitudes were still highly useful. The few individuals who dared speak positively about Ingush, in the sense of "there are good and bad people of all ethnicities," were defying norms and so were likely sincere in their statements.

Similarly, for the systematic surveys, there may be some noise in the responses of the majority of respondents who said they felt negatively about interethnic mingling: some nonprejudiced individuals may have intentionally selected prejudiced responses. The most that can be done in analysis is admit this possibility and note the very clear direction of the bias toward prejudice. However, it is also important to note that there should be little to no noise among the minority of respondents who expressed nonprejudiced—that is, anti-norm—sentiment. Their survey responses are likely valid, and as shown in this chapter and in multivariate analysis in Chapter 11, these unabashedly nonprejudiced victims were the least likely to support retaliatory violence.

A bigger concern is that social desirability bias may also affect expressed support for retaliatory violence. As described above, Ossetians have positive stereotypes of themselves as civilized and peaceful, and victims who supported violence may have concealed their support in their survey responses or focus group participation in order to conform to the peace-loving norm. However, in terms of the conclusion linking prejudice to support for retaliatory violence, social desirability bias may actually work against finding such a link. Some respondents presumably overreported their prejudice, and some underreported their support for violence. If these were the same people—the same people swayed by social norms to misrepresent their true attitudes in a socially acceptable way—they should have served to dilute the relationship between prejudice and support for violence. There should have been more victim respondents displaying prejudice while claiming an aversion to killing Chechens. A strong relationship between prejudice and support for violence is nevertheless found and suggests that the relationship might be even stronger had social desirability bias not played a role.

Beslan Victim Data on Prejudice and Behavior

Although research on racial and ethnic prejudice is abundant, research systematically connecting prejudice to behavior is not. This is especially true for violent behavior. According to a thorough review of the hate crime literature:

> Those seeking to understand the nature and origins of bigoted violence are likely to be disappointed by extant scholarship on prejudice, racism, and discrimination. . . . the laboratory experiments that dominate this literature are often contrived and rely almost entirely on undergraduate subjects. . . . scarcely any of this research [on prejudice] examines directly and systematically the question of why prejudice erupts into violence. . . . little rigorous empirical work on the causes of hate crime in North America and Western Europe has been published. . . . not much conclusive evidence has emerged, in part due to the persistent absence of reliable, consistent, and disaggregated statistical data. Most published work consists of speculative historical narratives that adduce evidence for a particular explanation of hate crime on the basis of journalistic accounts and aggregated statistics provided by government agencies or victims' advocacy groups. (Green et al. 2001:479–480, 491)

Data from victims of the Beslan school hostage taking fill this gap in the literature and systematically reveal the link between prejudice and support for violence. Victims who were prejudiced were more likely to support retaliation for the school hostage taking than victims who were not. This is the case whether prejudice is measured by individual survey questions or as an index of multiple questions.

Table 6.3 shows the correlations between the individual survey questions about interethnic mingling and approval of the retaliatory killing of Chechens. Approval of killing was most highly correlated with attitudes toward a member of the family bringing an Ingush home for dinner ($r = .20, p < .00$). Of those who objected strongly to dining with an Ingush, 8.5 percent fully approved of killing Chechens, and 11.1 percent somewhat approved, compared to only 3.2 and 0 percent, respectively, for those who did not object at all. The number of victims in the latter nonprejudiced category was very low—only 62—and only 3.2 percent (two individuals of the 62) supported retaliatory violence. All remaining victims who were not prejudiced according to this marker did not support retaliatory violence.

The relationship is the same between attitudes toward mixed schooling and approval of killing Chechens in retaliation for the hostage taking ($r = .15, p < .00$). Only 52 victims thought that Ossetian and Ingush children should go to the same schools, and only 1.9 percent of those victims (one of the 52) supported retaliatory violence. All remaining victims who favored mixed schooling were not supportive of retaliatory violence. These victims contrasted with those who favored separate schools for Ossetians and Ingush, with 7.6 percent of pro-separation victims fully approving of killing Chechens and another 10.7 percent somewhat approving.

Table 6.3. Attitudes toward Ingush and Support for Retaliatory Violence (Killing the Same Number of Chechens as Were Killed in Beslan)

How strongly would you object if a member of your family wanted to bring an Ingush home to dinner?

	Completely Disapprove	Somewhat Disapprove	Somewhat Approve	Fully Approve	Missing	N
Object strongly	222 (33.8)	259 (39.5)	73 (11.1)	56 (8.5)	46 (7.0)	656 (100.0)
Object mildly	93 (47.4)	76 (38.8)	12 (6.1)	4 (2.0)	11 (5.6)	196 (100.0)
Not at all object	36 (58.1)	16 (25.8)	0 (0.0)	2 (3.2)	8 (12.9)	62 (100.0)

Pearson's r = .20, p < .00.

During the last few years, has anyone in your family brought an Ingush home for dinner?

	Completely Disapprove	Somewhat Disapprove	Somewhat Approve	Fully Approve	Missing	N
No	372 (39.1)	358 (37.6)	81 (8.5)	61 (6.4)	79 (8.3)	951 (100.0)
Yes	18 (52.9)	7 (20.6)	6 (17.6)	1 (2.9)	2 (5.9)	34 (100.0)

Pearson's r = -.03, p < .45.

How would it make you feel if a close relative of yours were planning to marry an Ingush?

	Completely Disapprove	Somewhat Disapprove	Somewhat Approve	Fully Approve	Missing	N
Very uneasy	233 (36.6)	242 (38.1)	65 (10.2)	54 (8.5)	42 (6.6)	636 (100.0)
Somewhat uneasy	81 (38.4)	91 (43.1)	18 (8.5)	2 (0.9)	19 (9.0)	211 (100.0)
Not at all uneasy	26 (48.1)	20 (37.0)	0 (0.0)	5 (9.3)	3 (5.6)	54 (100.0)

Pearson's r = .10, p < .00.

(continued)

Table 6.3. Continued

Do you think Ossetian and Ingush students should go to the same schools or to separate schools?

	Completely Disapprove	Somewhat Disapprove	Somewhat Approve	Fully Approve	Missing	N
Separate schools	265 (33.8)	321 (40.9)	84 (10.7)	60 (7.6)	55 (7.0)	785 (100.0)
Same schools	34 (65.4)	15 (28.8)	0 (0.0)	1 (1.9)	2 (3.8)	52 (100.0)

Pearson's $r = .15, p < .00$.

Would you have any objection to sending your children to a school where half of the children are Ingush?

	Completely Disapprove	Somewhat Disapprove	Somewhat Approve	Fully Approve	Missing	N
Yes	300 (36.1)	327 (39.4)	81 (9.8)	60 (7.2)	62 (7.5)	830 (100.0)
No	34 (54.0)	16 (25.4)	5 (7.9)	3 (4.8)	5 (7.9)	63 (100.0)

Pearson's $r = .08, p < .03$.
$N = 1,098$; number of victims (%).

Similar patterns are revealed for the relationship between comfort with intermarriage and attitudes toward retaliatory violence ($r = .1, p < .00$). Fifty-four victims said that they would not be uneasy if a close relative was planning to marry an Ingush, and of those, 9.3 percent (5 of the 54) supported retaliatory violence. In contrast, about one in five of the numerous victims who were very uneasy about a relative intermarrying fully approved (8.5 percent) or somewhat approved (10.2 percent) of the retaliatory killing of Chechens.

The question about whether a family member brought an Ingush home for dinner in the past few years was the only one that did not reveal the same variation in support for retaliatory violence among victims. Victims who said yes and victims who said no were statistically similar in their approval of killing Chechens. This suggests that the mere fact of interethnic dining may not reveal prejudice or tolerance as much as attitudes toward that dining. A family member could have brought home an Ingush guest over the objections of other family members, and it is plausible that the objectors could have absented themselves from the table or home, meaning the Ingush was present while the victim was not—a potential flaw in the survey question that was not anticipated. More importantly, having an Ingush in the home for dinner was an extremely rare event. Only 34 of the 1,098 victim respondents were in this category of having such a recent ("last few years") experience. Conclusions from these experiences should be tentative at most.

Table 6.4 shows the relationship between the prejudice index described above and support for retaliatory violence ($r = .20$, $p < .00$). Of the 141 victims who fell in the three least prejudiced categories, only 2 percent (three individuals) approved of killing Chechens, either fully or somewhat. For those in the category leaning toward prejudice, 2.9 percent fully approved and 9.6 percent somewhat approved of killing Chechens. For those in the most prejudiced category of the index, meaning they gave the most prejudiced response to all three component survey questions, 9.2 percent fully approved of killing Chechens, and 10.8 percent somewhat approved. These last two categories, leaning toward prejudice and most prejudiced, represent more victims than any other categories in the index (three-quarters of the victims), so the connection between attitudes toward Ingush and support for retaliatory violence is quite meaningful. The small minority of victims who were not prejudiced stand out as uniquely and consistently nonviolent.

Table 6.4. Prejudice Index and Support for Retaliatory Violence (Killing the Same Number of Chechens as Were Killed in Beslan)

Prejudice Index (0–1 mean scale of responses to "How strongly would you object if a member of your family wanted to bring an Ingush home to dinner—strongly, mildly, or not at all?"; "How would it make you feel if a close relative of yours were planning to marry an Ingush—very uneasy, somewhat uneasy, or not uneasy at all?"; and "Do you think Ossetian and Ingush students should go to the same schools or to separate schools?")

	Completely Disapprove	Somewhat Disapprove	Somewhat Approve	Fully Approve	Missing	N
0 (least prejudiced)	25 (54.3)	13 (28.3)	0 (0.0)	2 (4.3)	6 (13.0)	46 (100.0)
< 0 and > .5 (leaning nonprejudiced)	16 (69.6)	5 (21.7)	0 (0.0)	0 (0.0)	2 (8.7)	23 (100.0)
.5 (mixed attitudes)	49 (68.1)	20 (27.8)	0 (0.0)	1 (1.4)	2 (2.8)	72 (100.0)
< .5 and < 1 (leaning prejudiced)	80 (33.3)	110 (45.8)	23 (9.6)	7 (2.9)	20 (8.3)	240 (100.0)
1 (most prejudiced)	206 (35.3)	216 (37.0)	63 (10.8)	54 (9.2)	45 (7.7)	584 (100.0)

$N = 1,098$; number of victims (%); Pearson's $r = .21$, p < .00.

Stated differently, 71.6 percent of victims who supported retaliatory ethnic violence fell in the category of "most prejudiced," and another 26.1 percent leaned toward prejudice. Not a single pro-violence victim had nonprejudiced or even mixed attitudes. In contrast, only 46.2 of victims who opposed retaliatory violence fell in the most prejudiced category, and another 17.9 percent leaned prejudiced, while 11 percent had mixed attitudes, and 3.6 percent and 5.6 percent leaned nonprejudiced or were among the least prejudiced, respectively.

The differences between pro- and anti-violence victims are even clearer in the component questions of the prejudice index. Of those who fully approved of killing Chechens, more than eight in ten strongly objected to having an Ingush over for dinner (86.2 percent) and were very uneasy about intermarriage (83.1 percent), and more than nine in ten wanted Ossetian and Ingush children to go to separate schools (92.3 percent). These numbers stand in stark contrast to the responses from victims opposed to retaliatory violence. Of those who completely disapproved of killing Chechens, only about half strongly objected to having an Ingush over for dinner (49.8 percent), were very uneasy about intermarriage (52.2 percent), and wanted separate schools for Ossetians and Ingush (59.4 percent). The latter are still uncomfortably high percentages of victims holding negative attitudes toward members of another ethnic group, but they are dramatically lower than the percentages for pro-violence victims.

This strong relationship between prejudice and support for retaliatory violence is robust. In Chapter 11, a variety of demographic and attitudinal variables are controlled in the multivariate analysis, and prejudice continues to have a positive, statistically significant effect on approval of killing Chechens.

As mentioned earlier, the correlations between attitudes toward Ingush and attitudes toward Chechens were so high in the survey pretest that it made no sense to ask the same questions about both ethnic groups. The above relationship between attitudes toward Ingush and support for retaliatory killing against Chechens would very likely hold if Ingush were substituted for Chechen and Chechen for Ingush in each question. A look at the related issue of blaming Chechens as a people for the attack on the school is suggestive of this non-differentiating approach. Table 6.5 shows that victims who believed Chechens were very guilty for causing the tragedy were more likely than other victims to support retaliatory violence. Of those labeling Chechens as very guilty, 8.8 percent fully approved of killing Chechens, and 10.1 percent somewhat approved. Of those labeling Chechens somewhat guilty, 5 percent fully approved, and 8.9 percent somewhat approved. In contrast, of the very small group of victims who thought Chechens were not at all guilty, only 6.3 percent (or one individual) fully approved of killing Chechens, and another 6.3 percent (another single individual) somewhat approved. Similarly, only 2.4 percent (two individuals) of those who thought Chechens were not very guilty fully approved of killing Chechens, and only 3.6 percent (three individuals) somewhat approved.

Table 6.5. Blaming Chechens and Support for Retaliatory Violence (Killing the Same Number of Chechens as Were Killed in Beslan)

"As I read the names of some people and organizations, please tell me whether you think they are very guilty, somewhat guilty, not very guilty, or not at all guilty for causing this tragedy? *Chechens*"

	Completely Disapprove	Somewhat Disapprove	Somewhat Approve	Fully Approve	Missing	N
Very guilty	167 (35.8)	177 (37.9)	47 (10.1)	41 (8.8)	35 (7.5)	467 (100.0)
Somewhat guilty	121 (31.7)	145 (38.0)	34 (8.9)	19 (5.0)	63 (16.5)	382 (100.0)
Not very guilty	48 (57.1)	30 (35.7)	3 (3.6)	2 (2.4)	1 (1.2)	84 (100.0)
Not at all guilty	13 (81.3)	1 (6.3)	1 (6.3)	1 (6.3)	0 (0.0)	16 (100.0)

$N = 1,098$; number of victims (%); Pearson's $r = .14$, $p < .00$.

The relationship between blaming Chechens and support for retaliatory violence is as robust as the relationship between prejudice and support for retaliatory violence. Prejudice and blame are related theoretically and empirically ($r = .25$, $p < .00$), but they each have independent effects on victims' approval of killing, even in multivariate analyses in Chapter 11.

Importantly, the effect of each variable is not conditional on anger. If interaction terms are added to the multivariate models in Chapter 11, prejudice and blaming Chechens consistently have significant and strong effects on support for retaliatory violence, anger does not, and the interaction terms do not. Table 6.6 shows these same effects for simple models of just anger, prejudice, and blaming Chechens. Prejudice and blame are consistently significant; anger, independently and conditionally, is not.

In contrast, there is little if any connection between prejudice and participation in politics as a response to the Beslan school hostage taking. Table 6.7 shows no statistically significant correlation between participation, measured as a 31-count variable or in five categories of participation, and most measures of ethnic prejudice. The single exception is the measure of attitudes toward intermarriage. The more uneasy victims were with a relative marrying an Ingush, the more likely they were to participate in politics. However, this correlation (.1 and .13, $p < .00$, for the count and categories, respectively) is not supported by findings from any other measures in the data set and does not hold up in multivariate analysis.

Table 6.6. Interactive Effects of Anger with Prejudice and Blaming Chechens on Support for Retaliatory Violence

	Support for Retaliatory Violence Ordered Logit Estimates Coef. (SE)
Anger	.12 (.19)
Prejudice	1.92 (.52)***
Interaction: anger × prejudice	−.14 (.22)

	Support for Retaliatory Violence Ordered Logit Estimates Coef. (SE)
Anger	.08 (.17)
Blaming Chechens	.39 (.14)***
Interaction: anger × blaming Chechens	−.02 (.05)

	Support for Retaliatory Violence Ordered Logit Estimates Coef. (SE)
Anger	.12 (.19)
Prejudice	1.76 (.51)***
Blaming Chechens	.24 (.10)*
Interaction: anger × prejudice	−.14 (.23)

$*p < .05; **p < .01; ***p < .005.$

When the measures of prejudice are bundled in an index, there again is only a small and not very significant correlation between prejudice and participation ($r = .07$, $p < .04$) (Table 6.8). There was certainly an abundance of prejudiced individuals among the activist Beslan victims (46 out of 57 victims who participated in eleven or more activities fell in the category of "most prejudiced"), and some highly visible activist leaders unabashedly expressed prejudiced views. For example, according to Mothers of Beslan chair Susanna Dudiyeva, "The Ingush say that not all Ingush are terrorists, but we can't help noticing that all the terrorists are Ingush" (Parfitt 2011). However, those "leaning prejudiced" had the highest percentage of politically inactive victims (62.5 percent), and inactivity was the modal participation category for victims of all levels of prejudice. The small potential relationship between the prejudice index and participation does not hold when controlling for other variables in multivariate analysis: In Chapter 11's full models of the political participation of Beslan victims, prejudice toward Ingush is not statistically significant.

Table 6.7. Attitudes toward Ingush and Political Participation

	Political Participation (Count 0–31)	Participation Categories
How strongly would you object if a member of your family wanted to bring an Ingush home to dinner?	.08	.08
During the last few years, has anyone in your family brought an Ingush home for dinner?	−.04	−.02
How would it make you feel if a close relative of yours were planning to marry an Ingush	.12*	.13*
Do you think Ossetian and Ingush students should go to the same schools or to separate schools?	−.002	−.01
Would you have any objection to sending your children to a school where half of the children are Ingush?	.02	−.01

Correlations (Pearson's *r*); * *p* < 0.001.

Table 6.8. Prejudice Index and Political Participation

Prejudice Index (0–1 mean scale of responses to "How strongly would you object if a member of your family wanted to bring an Ingush home to dinner—strongly, mildly, or not at all?"; "How would it make you feel if a close relative of yours were planning to marry an Ingush— very uneasy, somewhat uneasy, or not uneasy at all?"; and "Do you think Ossetian and Ingush students should go to the same schools or to separate schools?")

	No Activities	One Activity	Two or Three Activities	Four to Ten Activities	Eleven to Thirty-one Activities	Missing	N
0 (least prejudiced)	19 (41.3)	14 (30.4)	3 (6.5)	1 (2.2)	2 (4.3)	7 (15.2)	46 (100.0)
< 0 and > .5 (leaning non-prejudiced)	10 (43.5)	3 (13.0)	0 (0.0)	3 (13.0)	1 (4.3)	6 (26.1)	23 (100.0)
.5 (mixed attitudes)	31 (43.1)	10 (13.9)	11 (15.3)	5 (6.9)	4 (5.6)	11 (15.3)	72 (100.0)
< .5 and < 1 (leaning prejudiced)	150 (62.5)	19 (7.9)	19 (7.9)	22 (9.2)	4 (1.7)	26 (10.8)	240 (100.0)
1 (most prejudiced)	271 (46.4)	71 (12.2)	71 (12.2)	53 (9.1)	46 (7.9)	72 (12.3)	584 (100.0)

N = 1,098; number of victims (%); Pearson's r = .08, p < .02.

Conclusion

Retaliatory ethnic violence involves taking revenge on a perpetrator's co-ethnics. Victims who commit or support retaliatory ethnic violence are generalizing from the perpetrator's actions to the actions of others in the perpetrator's presumed community. They are making the perpetrator's ethnicity a relevant factor—sometimes the most relevant factor—and attributing the crime to characteristics supposedly typical of all members of that ethnic group. Making this leap from perpetrator to ethnic group, from targeting the killer to targeting his co-ethnics, is facilitated by prejudice. Prejudice motivates individuals to think in ethnic terms and to see a killer as a representative of his ethnic group.

In the Beslan school hostage taking, the most vicious captors were thugs—known serious criminals well before the hostage taking. Many were on wanted lists for murder, rape, robbery, and other crimes (Milashina 2006d). It is possible that they turned to terrorism simply as an outlet for their criminal tendencies, since many displayed the tendencies first and conversion to the cause of Chechen independence later (Dunlop 2006; Phillips 2007:18–19). These thugs and their willing or unwilling recruits were purported to be dead and therefore unavailable as targets of revenge.

The survey of Beslan victims shows that the most prejudiced victims of the carnage were the most willing to view the thugs' co-ethnics as legitimate substitute targets. As will be shown in Chapter 11, prejudice has significant effects on support for retaliatory violence even when controlling for a variety of other factors in multivariate analysis. Negative opinions of others based on ethnicity are common, and many if not most Beslan victims felt such negative opinions about Chechens and Ingush. The possible conversion of ethnic prejudice to retaliatory ethnic violence in the North Caucasus was substantial.

On the more optimistic side, research has shown that prejudice can lessen over time. After World War II, for example, prejudice in Europe became associated with anti-democratic ethnocentrism and was delegitimized, and with the delegitimization came a decrease in ethnic violence (Horowitz 2001:563–564). In Beslan, the few victims who consistently offered nonprejudiced responses to survey questions were consistently the least supportive of retaliatory violence. By revealing the link between prejudice and retaliatory ethnic violence, we at least identify a pathway for reducing future harm. In order to stop the cycle of violence, we must first tackle prejudice.

We must do other things, too, of course. Factors besides prejudice have effects on attitudes and behavior after an experience with violence. In the next chapters, discussion turns to the roles of political and social alienation, political and self-efficacy, prior political participation, and prior harm. Where prejudice was largely unrelated to political participation in Beslan, many of these other factors play a greater role.

7

Political Alienation and Blame

Victims of violence may have different attitudes toward their country and its leaders and institutions. Some victims are proud to be citizens of their country and perhaps even prouder after the episode of violence than before. Many are unchanged in their pride, perhaps not viewing the incident as relevant to their political attitudes. For still other victims, the violent episode, and presumably the state's inability or unwillingness to guarantee safety, makes them feel less proud of their citizenship.

What is the role of political alienation in the response to violence? This chapter explores victims' attitudes toward Russia and Russian citizenship after the Beslan school hostage taking and the relationship of these attitudes toward support for retaliatory violence and political participation. It also explores concepts related to political alienation, such as blaming President Putin for the hostage taking or its bloody ending, (dis)satisfaction with the punishment of political officials for their role in the hostage taking and its aftermath, and trust in government.

Political alienation turns out to be the main variable connecting the two potential outcomes, support for retaliatory violence and political participation, because political alienation has negative effects on the former and positive effects on the latter. Victims who are politically alienated from their country are significantly less likely to support retaliatory violence along ethnic lines, and they are significantly more likely to respond to violence with peaceful political activism. Victims who are not politically alienated—who are as proud or prouder of their country after the hostage taking as they were before—are more likely to support further violence over peaceful activism.

Political Alienation after Violence

The meaning of political alienation has long been discussed and debated in the social science literature (e.g., Seeman 1959). It has been confounded conceptually and analytically with other concepts, including (the absence of) political trust, loyalty, patriotism, perceived legitimacy, perceived representation or responsiveness, efficacy, support for incumbents, and approval of incumbents, and it has been associated with negative sentiments toward specific institutions such as legislatures or judiciaries, specific officeholders, different levels of government,

After Violence. Debra Javeline, Oxford University Press. © Oxford University Press 2023.
DOI: 10.1093/oso/9780197683347.003.0008

the type of political regime, the political party in power, specific policies, and the political system as an undifferentiated whole. The term has thus been criticized for its "function as a synonym for virtually all the maladies, real or imagined, that afflict modern man" (Citrin 1977:381).

Here, political alienation is intentionally defined narrowly as a subjective sense of disenchantment, estrangement, or detachment from one's country because the country is deemed unworthy of praise or pride (Citrin et al. 1975; Schwartz 1976; Reef and Knoke 1999:413). "At the far end of the continuum, the politically alienated feel themselves outsiders, gripped in an alien political order; they would welcome fundamental changes in the ongoing regime. By contrast, the politically allegiant feel themselves an integral part of the political system; they belong to it psychologically as well as legally" (Citrin et al. 1975:3). For simplicity and clarity, the latter can be described as proud; the former as disenchanted, lacking pride, and often ashamed.

Political alienation may be related to other concepts such as political efficacy, political trust, and patriotism, but the narrow definition allows these concepts to be distinguished clearly from one another. Theoretically, an individual may feel patriotism, defined as a love of country and concern for its welfare and improvement, but may simultaneously feel politically alienated if the country's behavior is perceived as shameful. Loss of pride and love of country may coexist. Theoretically, the opposite is also possible: disenchantment or loss of pride may correlate with or even cause loss of love. Either way, understanding individual motivations for retaliatory violence and political participation requires studying the independent effects of variables such as political alienation, which in turn requires keeping political alienation conceptually clear and distinct from a seemingly similar variable such as patriotism that actually taps into a different attitudinal relationship with one's country.

Political alienation should also be kept conceptually distinct from political trust and political efficacy. Political trust is another vague and long-disputed concept that may signify confidence in all government institutions, some subset of institutions, or particular officeholders (Citrin 1974; Miller 1974; Muller et al. 1982). Declines in trust may signify a negative trait such as cynicism, a positive trait such as political sophistication and realism, both, or neither. In studies of U.S. politics, "questions about pride in existing institutional arrangements . . . appear to be on their face more valid indicators of a basic attachment to the political regime than most" questions that ostensibly measure trust in government (Citrin 1974:975). Given its vagueness, political trust in the Beslan case is not discussed in depth, although given its prominence in the literature, it is frequently included in analysis. Political efficacy, or feelings of empowerment or disempowerment in the political process, is a clear and distinct concept, and Chapter 9 is devoted to its analysis.

Marginality is another important concept potentially related to post-violence contexts in general and the Beslan aftermath in particular, but the concept is murky due to its association with both political and social alienation. Marginality refers to a group's proximity to "the mainstream of the dominant socio-economic and political systems" of a country (Jackson 1973:876). It is often conceived in terms of affluence and political power and also as a perceptual variable that captures a group's perceived centrality to others in the polity—that is, whether members of the group think others care about them.

Such a sense of marginalization was voiced by veteran schoolteacher Tatiana Svetlova, who sustained numerous injuries during the hostage taking and witnessed the deaths of students and their parents: "The only thing that is known in our world is that everyone is in it for himself. No one will come to help you in the hardest moments of your life. Not even your government" (Lansford 2006:77). Observers of post-violence Beslan residents noted "the isolation these people feel from Moscow. Until the Beslan horror, North Ossetia had been an island of calm in a war that, having started in Chechnya, now rages across the Caucuses." Now, the feeling is that "such disasters can happen again" (Stephen 2005a).

The difficulty, however, with the concept of marginalization is that it reflects perceptions about both ordinary people and political officials. Given that it is reasonable to believe that ordinary people care about you while politicians do not, or vice versa, the concept is muddled and difficult to measure or analyze. More narrowly defined and precise concepts, such as the above-defined political alienation and the next chapter's social alienation, minimize conceptual confusion and should enable greater clarity and understanding of whether the victims' attitudes toward the public, the government, or both drive responses to violence.

After a violent episode, it is reasonable for victims to experience a change in political alienation, especially a change for the worse: decreased pride in one's country, or increased political alienation. It is this decrease, more than the absolute level of political alienation, that is hypothesized to be meaningful for responses to violence. Victims who perceive a loss of pride in their country, like other individuals with violated expectations, should be mobilizable, because they sense their own change in attitude and the salience of that change (Lind and Tyler 1988; Mikula et al. 1998; Tyler et al. 1997).

Political Alienation in Beslan

In the particular case of Beslan, expectations were tremendously violated, and for many victims, pride in Russia deteriorated. Ossetians have traditionally viewed

Moscow as "a protector and guarantor of political survival" (Sands 2004a). This view stemmed from the Ossetians' religious kinship with Russians, their longstanding loyalty to Russia, perceived favoritism from Russia that they consider earned and deserved, and their need for protection, given their ethnic and religious minority status in the volatile North Caucasus. Russia's inability to protect Beslan families from the terrorists, not to mention Russia's callous treatment of the hostages during and after the three-day siege, dealt victims a crushing psychological blow. Many victims questioned their traditional views and whether Russia was worthy of their pride (Stephen 2005a).

In focus groups, participants directly and emphatically discussed their changed attitudes toward Russia. For example, the male activist victims thirty-five years and older weighed in on questions of pride and shame:

TAMERLAN: Probably I was proud before 2004, before September 3. Now my opinion has changed a lot. I have no illusions. I won't get anything I expect from them. Until the people who, let us say, were inactive, didn't do anything, hopefully just didn't harm me and my family—as long as they are in power, I won't even get answers to the questions that I have posed, unfortunately.

BORIS: I apologize, but let's take the United States for comparison. They are far away from us. To defend their citizens, they are ready to annihilate anybody anywhere. To defend their citizens. What about our country? Just pretty words, they just present this Constitution to us. The most just, humane, and democratic? This is only on paper with golden letters. It doesn't work. It is idle! I will be glad if it works 15–20 percent.

KAZBEK: After 2004, the majority thought like this—that Russia had dumped us, abandoned us, nobody needed us, the authorities didn't solve anything, no actions were taken.

Other victims echoed this theme of disenchantment that the problems of the victims were an inconvenience to the Russian government. For example, a nonactivist female victim described reactions to the maddeningly prolonged waiting by the Palace of Culture for the authorities to release the names of the deceased children:

VERA: And the first night, when we were sitting and waiting in the palace, somebody came to speak to us every hour or hour and a half. On the second night, there was no one. One woman was in hysterics. The headquarters were in the administration building. There was absolutely no information, and we shuddered at each shot: Suddenly this was your child who was now killed.

It's the second night, and you understand that no one needs you with your problem.

Another example comes from a female activist victim under thirty-five years old who was in the school:

VIKA: It was a frightful sight. When you are in the gym laying with a bullet in your ass, I beg your pardon, from the very first day, and with a swollen leg, lying on your six-year-old child, ready to tuck him wherever possible to protect him from the exploding bombs and missiles. When you see the two-, three-year-olds straggling about absolutely neglected, crawling around half naked, shell-shocked, and rocking, what kind of respect can you feel toward our country, our authorities, and our special forces? I, for one, have no respect.

The female activist victims thirty-five years and older also reflected on how the tragedy influenced their attitudes toward Russia:

LARISA: I am ashamed.
FATIMA: Rather ashamed.
LARISA: We realized that nobody needs us in this country.

The women continued with a sarcasm that characterized their disenchantment:

TATIANA: We are unprotected.
LARISA: Totally unprotected. How could you give birth to another citizen for this country after having gone through all this? Sorry for the frankness.
RAISA: They raised the allowance [child benefit paid by the state]. Have as many kids as you please.

The male activist victims under thirty-five years old responded similarly to questions about how the tragedy influenced their attitudes toward Russia:

PAZIL: Of course, it has . . . for the worse. How can it be for the better? How could they allow such things to happen in Russia, I wonder?
ZAUR: If we study history, Russia is probably the strongest state. Probably, yes, I am proud. [But in terms of whether the Beslan tragedy influenced his attitude to Russia] Of course, it has. First of all, how did they [the authorities] allow it to happen? This is probably the most important.
PAZIL: [On whether he ever feels ashamed for Russia] I do, to be honest.
ZAUR: Probably I felt ashamed for Russia during these September events.

These young men went on to discuss what actions they expected from the Russian authorities during the tragedy and, implicitly, how those expectations were dashed:

PAZIL: [I expected] that there will be no victims.
MARAT: They should have looked for some other option.
VLADIMIR: Or they should have looked for some compromises so that there would be no victims.

Speaking at Strasbourg, Susanna Dudiyeva summed up much of her community's sentiment of political alienation: "Although the trial has the name, 'Victims of Beslan against Russia,' none of us is against Russia. We just want our country to begin to value human life" (Farniyev and Sergeyev 2014:3).

The male nonactivist victims used similar words:

TAMERLAN: I would like to feel proud that Russia is learning to value human life and dignity.
BORIS: For now it is not valued.

Variation in Political Alienation

Despite all this evidence of post-violence political alienation in Beslan, many victims did not share these views. Political alienation varied among victims after the hostage taking. In the focus groups, there were several strong declarations of pride in Russia and pride in Ossetia. Asked if they often feel proud of Russia, the female activist victims thirty-five years old and younger replied in a chorus, "Yes. Of course, yes." A male activist victim under thirty-five answered, "Right now, I am pleased to live in Russia. Yes, very much so." To the more direct question, "Do you feel proud that you are a citizen of Russia?" a male nonactivist victim offered an unequivocal "yes," and another "of course," and others gave similar unambiguous answers.

Some victims had mixed feelings about their pride and shame in Russia. In response to whether she sometimes felt ashamed for Russia's actions, one female activist victim aged thirty-five years or younger answered, "It happens." Pressed on whether pride or shame happens more frequently, she replied, "Probably more often I feel proud," to which another participant said, "I more often feel ashamed."

When victims thought of Russia and the pride or shame they felt about being a Russian citizen, the hostage taking was often not the foremost event or characteristic to come to mind. In focus groups, they expressed pride or disappointment in their country based on other characteristics and accomplishments. This was evident especially for the less alienated victims whose instinct was to think first about athletic victories and popular culture competitions. Olympic medals and the success of Russian singer-songwriter Dima Bilan on the annual international television song competition, Eurovision, were sources of pride. For the politically alienated victims, the conversations turned to low salaries, high prices for consumer goods, high taxes, income inequality, corruption, the decline of Russian education, the hard lives of pensioners, the state of the country's orphanages, the mortality rate, and the general decline in social welfare provisions in the country. These, they claimed, made them ashamed of Russia.

The two topics besides the hostage taking itself that were given the most attention in conversations about pride and shame were, first, Russia's 2008 military actions in South Ossetia, and second, the status of Ossetians in the Russian Republic. In South Ossetia, Russia acted on behalf of Ossetians against Georgians, which tremendously gratified victims and other North Ossetians. According to the male activist victims over thirty-five years old:

ALIK: After the August events, I became proud of being a Russian citizen.
BORIS: Yes, at least then they behaved in the right way.
ALIK: For the first time I wasn't ashamed for our state, for the first time. But they [the authorities] also realized that it was the last chance.
BORIS: This time it was pleasant.
KAZBEK: We are proud that Russia defended Abkhazia and Ossetia.

Male nonactivist victims connected their renewed pride in Russia to the prior vulnerability exposed by the hostage taking.

VALERY: When the events in Tskhinvali [capital of South Ossetia] took place in August, and when our troops repulsed the Georgian troops, I felt that someone can protect me, you understand?
TAMERLAN: That's when the pride appeared.
VASILY: Of course. How could it be no? How can we not feel it?

Female activist victims thirty-five years old and younger discussed their pride in hearing Vitaly Churkin, Russia's representative to the United Nations, give a statement in August 2008 at the U.N. Security Council where he described Georgia's actions against Ossetians as ethnic cleansing and genocide. Churkin demanded that Georgia withdraw from the territory of South Ossetia and agree to the non-use of force, and he formally expressed Russia's support for an independent South Ossetia.

VIKA: It was very pleasant for me when Churkin spoke.
BELLA: Then it's true, there was such pride! Really, we felt proud.

BELA: A dignified person, indeed.

BELLA: Yes, in this respect Eurovision wasn't so special. Well, yes, it was pleasant, but I can't say that I felt proud. And when Churkin spoke, there was really a feeling of some kind of pride that there are some figures in our government who can do something, that they can represent our interests on a decent level when they want to, when they feel like it.

BELA: When it's to their advantage.

BELLA: Yes-yes-yes. By the way, right. Because when it wasn't to Russia's advantage, then . . .

The relationship of Ossetian ethnicity, North Ossetian residency, and Russian citizenship provoked more complicated and conflicting feelings among victims. On the one hand, victims proudly wore all three identities and spoke highly of the historical bonds between Ossetians and Russians. The female victim activists aged thirty-five years and younger explained:

IRINA: [I feel proud] of Russia, of North Ossetia. They are united so that North Ossetia is part of the Russian Federation. And the Russian Federation is a unitary power, invincible only when its people rally together. [But in terms of the motherland] The motherland for me is my city. And that's all. [Responding to whether that means Ossetia is closer for her] Well, yes, of course.

MADINA: Well, you see, here in Ossetia we say, Ossetia, of course. Then comes Russia, that we are part of Russia, and abroad we say that we are from Russia. We don't say abroad that we are from Ossetia.

The male nonactivist victims offered a similar commentary on their connectedness with Russia:

VALERY: I live in Ossetia, but I live in Russia at the same time. You see, I can't imagine myself without Russia.

ARKADY: Russia, yes, I can't imagine Ossetia without Russia.

BORIS: Ossetia just won't survive without Russia.

On the other hand, many victims feel that they as Ossetians are unappreciated and mistreated by Russia. The male activist victims over thirty-five years old described the perceived lack of appreciation. In doing so, they make clear their violated expectations and disenchantment.

ALIK: Attitude to Russia? The point is that our great-grandfathers decided it long ago, appealed to Russia of their own accord and joined it. And since that time Russia has not had a single moment to doubt the loyal citizenship of Ossetians. Not one! That is why Russia's attitude to this particular conflict outrages me.

KAZBEK: You see how it turns out. Ossetia has been with Russia for many years. Has Ossetia ever betrayed Russia? Never! Has it ever spoken about separation? Has it ever been the case? It has never been the case and never will. And other republics. We love Russia, and it seems to push us away. It treats other republics better than us.

ISRAEL: More loyal, yes.

BORIS: They respect Chechnya. They love the Ingush. And what have Ossetians done bad?

TOTRAZ: This is my state. It's my country, how can I . . . no matter what it is like.

BORIS: It is ours, in any case.

TOTRAZ: With rare exceptions, this people wants to be with Russia.

The complaints of female victim activists aged thirty-five years and younger went beyond the perceived lack of appreciation and focused on the mistreatment of Ossetians by Russia. They themselves acknowledge the conflicted feelings and implicit struggle between pride and shame.

BELA: I was in Moscow once and I felt like I was in a different state, judging by the attitude to me, when they stopped me every now and then and checked my passport. I had to show them my train ticket. But the feelings are strange. Then you feel that your motherland is Ossetia, of course.

VIKA: It is absolutely all the same to them whether you are Ingush or Ossetian. We all are "black" for them. They also don't get especially absorbed in our conflicts.

BELA: No, judging by how they responded during the terrorist act . . .

Male activist victims over thirty-five years old had similar complaints:

BORIS: Why do we need to register when we leave Ossetia if we live in Russia?

KAZBEK: If I come to visit you in Moscow, policemen grab and drag me. "Why don't you have a registration? What are you doing here?" I say, "My cousin lives here." "Is he permanently registered here?" I say, "Yes." "And why aren't you permanently registered?" I say, "I came to visit him. Why do I need permanent registration?" What am I, in Germany?

BORIS: Registration for what? It's absurd! Idiocy. In Moscow the reaction is such: "Persons of Caucasian nationality." They have this reaction. Their adrenalin immediately begins. They are boiling.

Female nonactivist victims noted the same mistreatment:

VERA: You know yourself what bad names you can be called when you come to Moscow. I apologize, of course, but even "black ass." That's rude, of course. Darkeys, etc.

ZINAIDA: Caucasian or a person of Caucasian nationality.

VERA: Yes, here is this formulation. There are so many nationalities in the Caucasus. How can they put us under one abbreviation? I don't know.

Blame after Violence

After an experience with violence, victims may try to attribute blame for their victimization. Aggrieved individuals typically seek to identify culprits or failed problem-solvers and to assign causal responsibility or treatment responsibility accordingly (Iyengar 1989, 1991). Blame attribution is often a difficult task due to the complexity of problems and the blame avoidance strategies of political actors who intentionally confuse lines of accountability, among other factors (Javeline 2003a, 2003b). As a result, aggrieved individuals, including victims of violence, may be unable to specify blame. Still, blame is a subjective phenomenon, and despite difficulties in attribution, many victims nevertheless succeed in identifying blameworthy culprits and failed problem-solvers. Their attributions may be accurate or inaccurate in the sense of the objective facts that caused the violent episode or the resulting harm (Javeline 2003a, 2003b). Either way, the blame attributions can be critical factors in their post-violence response, especially to the extent that they attribute intentionality to wrongdoers (Brader et al. 2011).

Blame is often directed toward political officials. Although political alienation and blame toward officials are conceptually distinct, they merit joint discussion, because there are linkages between pride in one's country and blaming the officials in that country for their role in allowing or even enabling horrific violence or in exacerbating the pain of the aftermath. Victims may lump all political officials together as blameworthy, or they might single out specific individuals and institutions at the national or local level as particularly worthy of blame, absolution, or credit.

In the larger sense, blame is often linked to the frame that individuals or organizations use to interpret a grievance, potentially in the name of mobilizing collective action. The purpose of many collective action frames is to emphasize the seriousness and injustice of a social condition and to redefine as unjust and immoral what was previously seen as unfortunate but perhaps tolerable (Tarrow 1998). Civic activists face challenges in the process of frame alignment, or linking their interpretations with those of other aggrieved individuals (Snow et al. 1986;

Tarrow 1998:chap. 7). Activists compete with others in the political arena, including the media, government, other activists, and even the very individuals they are trying to recruit but who may interpret events differently.

Given the difficulties of constructing a mobilizing frame, it is truly remarkable that many victims in Beslan were relatively successful in dominating the discourse after the hostage taking or at least providing a very powerful counterbalance to the framing efforts of the government. The government worked hard to avoid blame and to link the hostage taking to the global war on terror (Harding 2012). The terrorists were characterized by Russian officials as "evil, cruel, and brutal. They shoot, and threaten to shoot at random, creating an almost unimaginably dangerous and horrific situation for the hostages" (Harding 2012:94). The framing goal of the authorities was to establish firmly "that all blame for the deaths of hostages is to be placed solely on the terrorists. Only after the official narrative of a 'successful operation to release the hostages' undertaken by heroic members of the special forces is elaborated in the aftermath of the siege are . . . graphic narratives included in the narrative text [of the official news source, RIA-Novosti], where they serve to endorse, rather than undermine, the overall narrative of an effective, benevolent state working diligently to protect its brave and heroic citizens from the inhuman evil of international terrorism" (Harding 2012:95). The authorities, "through the intensification of security measures, the mobilization of personnel, troops and medical equipment, are cast as a capable, resourceful, benevolent government working effectively and efficiently to protect its innocent citizens from this barbaric attack. The fates of a number of young, critically injured children, flown from the Beslan 'outpost' to Moscow, are attentively narrated [in RIA-Novosti] as they and their parents are welcomed and cared for by medical experts in the capital" (Harding 2012:102).

Despite these efforts by the state, its "international terrorism" frame was quickly rejected by most Belsan victims and other North Ossetians, and the "effective, benevolent state" frame was mostly rejected soon after. Instead, the dominant frame among North Ossetians was one of government incompetence and callousness. The government, in short, was seen by many as blameworthy.

The official frame and the social movement frame were not the only narratives surrounding the hostage taking. There was also the frame promoted by the Chechen armed resistance and conveyed largely through the Kavkazcenter News Agency. This alternative frame portrayed the Russian government in black-and-white terms as a force of evil, brutal and inhuman and planning the deliberate destruction of innocent children (Harding 2012:chap. 3). Beslan victims who heard these messages may have resisted them, and they may even have resisted pondering the parallels drawn by the Kavkazcenter between the child deaths in Beslan and the far more numerous child deaths in Chechnya. Still, it is possible that these additional narratives served to weaken receptivity to the official pro-government frame and strengthen receptivity to the anti-government mobilizing frame. The narrative of the Chechen resistance includes themes of Russian officials' lying, disregard for innocent lives, incompetence, rigidity, and interfering with and poisoning journalists who intended to report on the hostage taking, all of which are compatible with the mobilizing frame of blaming government.

Blaming Putin

President Vladimir Putin was singled out for much of the blame (Rodriguez 2004a). Ludmilla Jimiyev, whose fifteen-year-old son, Oleg, died in the siege, explained:

> I used to have great respect for Putin. Even Oleg used to look up to him because, like the President, he loved judo. I hate the terrorists for destroying my life, but with his policies Putin has failed us. His Government only worried about killing the terrorists, not saving our children. That is why he doesn't want to meet us. Because then he would have to look into our eyes and would not know what to say. (Franchetti 2005)

Some focus group participants were equally comfortable blaming Putin directly. In two different groups, victims used the Russian proverb, "Fish begins to stink at the head," implying that the president bears responsibility for the inaction, mistakes, and corruption of the vast body of officials who answer to him.

ARKADY [male nonactivist victim]: Will we name names? Let's start with Putin. And why not? The head of the state. Everything is under you. The Ministry of Internal Affairs is under you. The Federal Security Service is under you.

ISRAEL [male activist victim over thirty-five]: I think, about the heads, about Putin. They could have come to an agreement with the militants to avoid this terrible bloodshed. It's on their conscience, I think. I have such claims against them.

Complaints about Putin seemed to fall in two categories. The first, above, involved his role in the botched counterterrorism operation and hostage rescue. The second involved his less than humane treatment of the victims. The female victims under thirty-five years old discussed rumors of Putin's self-indulgence and callous behavior.

VIKA: As our President was allegedly sitting here afterward, everybody talks about it, he sat here drinking coffee. And as he was treated to a coffee with foam, just the kind he enjoyed most, there [in the school] the kids sat. And he had to get his exact espresso coffee, or whatever it is called.

BELA: Espresso.

VIKA: With foam, to be precise. Not simply coffee, but only with whipped foam.

The callous indifference was also noted by the female nonactivists: Putin ignored the suffering of ordinary people. For example, when Putin visited Beslan on Saturday, September 4, he met with very few survivors and did not visit the morgue to view the scope of the tragedy.

VERA: You know, I didn't understand it. Putin came after the terrorist act.

INDIRA: At night.

VERA: We were lying in hospital, and in the morning the doctor comes to the ward, laughing, and says, "Putin came at night, at three at night."

INDIRA: Why not during the day?

VERA: He dropped by the doctors' staffroom, dropped by [head of school] Lydia Alexandrovna's ward, that's all. He didn't enter a single other ward. At night. Why at night? And why didn't he at least go and see the children? Those wards where the children were laying? It is somehow incomprehensible.

INDIRA: Why didn't he meet with all the residents of Ossetia during the day?

VERA: Why wasn't [Federal Security Service Director] Patrushev here?

INDIRA: And many people say that both Putin and Patrushev were here all three days.

VALYA: But it's not so. We all know it. We all know that they were not here.

INDIRA: So many years have passed. He could have come and met people at least one time.

Blame toward the president was often bundled with blame directed at law enforcement agencies. The president earned his experience and reputation through the ranks of such organizations, and these authorities were so often put on a pedestal by Russians and by the president himself. That they failed miserably had reputational costs, as the male activist victims over thirty-five explained:

KAZBEK: Do you know to whom our attitude has changed? Not to the authorities on the whole, but to some authorities, to law enforcement bodies.

BORIS: To security agencies.

KAZBEK: And the president. The authorities. The Ministry of Internal Affairs.

BORIS: Law enforcement agencies. And who else?

VITALY: Why did they allow it to happen?

KAZBEK: If the FSB sends a telegram to the Ministry of Internal Affairs that such a terrorist act is possible—and we were shown this paper, by the way—why didn't the Ministry of Internal Affairs take any measures, moreover on September 1? The FSB of Russia sends a dispatch to Russia's Ministry of Internal Affairs, Nurgaliyev, or whoever they have there, and they also didn't do anything. The Ministry of Internal Affairs didn't do anything.

The female activist victims over thirty-five echoed the same themes as they each identified who is guilty.

DINA: Law enforcement agencies.
FATIMA: The authorities.
TATIANA: Most likely, the FSB because this is the intelligence service.
DINA: Yes. Law enforcement agencies.
TATIANA: It works very badly, especially, if they were in the forest. This base was formed not far from there. They prepared for half a year, and they didn't find out about them or recognize them. Of course the FSB is first of all.
DIANA: The FSB as well.

The failure to detect the terrorist plot was not the only reason to blame law enforcement agencies. The agencies also mishandled the hostage crisis once underway and then conspired to cover their tracks and avoid blame, as the male nonactivist victims explained:

TAMERLAN: There were many facts that are not disclosed. It is clear why, the main reason. The same people who examined these facts are responsible for all this. You wouldn't throw mud at yourself.
ARKADY: Actions were not coordinated. The Ministry of Internal Affairs acted on its own, the FSB on its own, the 58th army on its own. There was no connection.
TAMERLAN: The organization was quite wretched.

Criticism of the security agencies was categorically distinct from the praise lavished on the brave elite soldiers who were on the ground in Beslan and rushed into the school. Where Putin and law enforcement agencies were blamed for disregarding victims and costing lives, the soldiers were credited with saving them. Female victim activists over thirty-five years old captured a prevailing sentiment.

LARISA: [Regarding Alfa and Vympel] They are real heroes. These are heroes. These were the only people who saved children at the expense of their lives.
DINA: We can say about them that they are the pride of Russia. Not the president or anybody else.

LARISA: They just lay over children. That's not mere words. I saw it myself. At the expense of their lives.

TATIANA: Larisa said it correctly.

Putin and the Russian leadership more generally were also considered blameworthy for their actions in Chechnya that provoked the hostage taking. Many male nonactivist victims were convinced that someone was benefiting from conflict in the Caucasus.

BORIS: You know, someone needs to have a constant spark in the Caucasus, with one nation or another, at one place or another. There should constantly be tension in the Caucasus.

BORIS: Probably someone needs it.

VALERY: Resources. Oil, gas across the Caucasus to Iran, Iraq.

TAMERLAN: That's why there are always wars here.

RUSLAN: Let's take Chechnya—a small islet, so beautiful. How many years has Russia spent trying to stop them? Can't Putin bring all the troops there to annihilate them all? He can. And what for? It's a commercial war.

TAMERLAN: What are the troops there for? They have calmed down already. By themselves.

RUSLAN: Right! And was it impossible to calm down everybody immediately? Possible. It was possible. It's a commercial war. Someone makes money on it. And who? The leadership. The higher authorities in Moscow.

Female activist victims aged thirty-five years or younger were also convinced that someone benefited from tensions in the Caucasus and possibly from the Beslan school massacre itself.

VIKA: The state has been to blame since Yeltsin's time when they stirred up Chechnya. It all comes from there. The total lawlessness started then and there. It was there that our Russian government laundered all their money. This has been a well-known fact for a long time. Everything comes from there, all this contagion. It was Chechnya at that time. Had Russia wanted, it would have smeared all the militants with one spit by dawn. They simply benefited from it. They supported all that. And the sprouts grew in that soil.

BELLA: [In response to whether everything originated in Chechnya] Everything is interconnected, of course.

BELA: They were definitely Chechens, the militants.

BELLA: At some point I also had such thoughts that perhaps it was ordered [i.e., by a contract].

VIKA: Way back in September I was told that it's entirely possible that this had been planned by our government and brought from Chechnya in a roundabout way. I was foaming at the mouth. I was shocked. "How you can say such things! What are we! To be like this!" Then some time passed, two years, and I will not be surprised if one fine day after a hundred years, as the girl said, it turns out that . . . [it was indeed this way].

Variation in Blaming Putin

Not all victims found fault with Putin. Many continued to revere him, especially for his general leadership on issues unrelated to the hostage taking. One female activist victim thirty-five years or younger explained:

BELA: After Yeltsin my attitude toward him is good. I like him. I remember how we lived before Putin and how we lived during Putin's presidency. I remember my mother's salary was constantly delayed and all this. Life has become more stable.

For some victims, it was less a matter of liking or revering Putin and more about understanding his predicament. Some male activist victims thirty-five years old or younger were relatively forgiving.

ZAUR: I think, as the president he did everything possible to avoid it. He probably did everything he could.
PAZIL: And I think he didn't do anything. Nobody, not a single person [could do anything]. It is a terrorist act. All of them just killed each other. It's within their power. It's all the doings of their hands, these terrorist acts. That's obvious.

Victims openly debated about the blameworthiness of President Putin. When the victim advocacy organization, Voice of Beslan, issued a statement against a third term of office for Putin, Voice of Beslan leader Ella Kesayeva explained that "it's a shame of Ossetia to fawn upon a president who did nothing for saving Ossetian children." Some (predominantly male) members of Voice of Beslan disagreed with the statement and other criticisms of the Russian government and special forces made by Voice of Beslan leaders. The varying attitudes toward Putin led to a split in the organization, to the official harassment of Kesayeva and Emma Betrozova, and to judicial action that had the two women expelled from the organization and a new organization with new leaders put in their places (Milashina 2007d).

Splits were evident in the focus groups as well, including the group of male victim activists aged thirty-five years or younger.

ZAUR: And the heart of any state is—who?—the president. He is responsible for the state, so he should be responsible for the people who live here.
VLADIMIR: He can't be responsible for everybody.

A similar debate among female activist victims thirty-five years or younger contained a bit more sarcasm:

IRINA: He was here once. Visited the hospital. He behaved like an ordinary guy.
VIKA: Oh, sure, an ordinary guy. They sealed off the airport, and at night first one plane landed, all his bodyguards swarmed forth, sealed off the exits, then the second plane and he himself, and half of Beslan was sealed off. And where was this cordon when our children were sitting there or walked in underpants, poor things, over a pile of people, a pile of corpses trying to find where their mother or an acquaintance was. Concussed poor children. Where were they? . . . He could have done something for three days. He has such a huge army of officials to decide what to do. They know all these se-cret technologies, which we don't even suspect. I still think that something could have been done. [Referring to a prior notorious statement by Putin] All terrorists should be blasted in toilets. Everything was clear there from the very beginning. It was voiced long before these events.
BELA: So, here their goal was to kill terrorists, right? They just didn't expect so many people to die.

Male nonactivists also debated the culpability of Putin:

ARKADY: Putin was vacationing in Sochi and immediately flew to Moscow when it was reported to him. I think it was the radio station, Echo Moskvy. I dislike it a lot. We were listening to this channel as a car stood nearby, and Putin probably got wrong information where the seizure of the school was happening or he didn't understand. He flew not to Beslan but to Moscow.
BORIS: He came to Beslan at night, after all this already.
ARKADY: After the terrorist act, when people were already . . .
BORIS: He came at night, shook hands with an honored teacher, and flew away.
VASILY: Even if he had flown here, what could he have done? When it started on the first day, people watched. All the people were right there. Women, men were eager to enter. No one let them.

BORIS: No one says that Putin should have entered there. There was no need to do that. Putin could have arrived during the day, not at night. There was no need for him to enter the school but just to watch.

Blaming Local Authorities

Some victims combined their excuses for Putin with their blame toward local authorities, particularly the North Ossetian republican leadership. The female activist victims over thirty-five years old discussed the exercise of power in their region.

TATIANA: Of course, we can't say that the president is to blame for everything. He lives far away and doesn't see what is happening here in Ossetia, and, of course, in the first place, our Ossetian government should take care of its people.
DINA: Putin can issue a decree and it won't apply to the region. Our head may take it and simply not allow it anywhere. And it won't extend into the regions.
TATIANA: And all the same, if our [Ossetian] government had a better control over things, was concerned, this terrorist act wouldn't have happened.
LARISA: Well, that's for sure.

Some victims who focused on the North Ossetian republican leadership also doubted whether more localized officials had any authority or relevance whatsoever. The male activist victims over thirty-five years old discussed the administration of the city of Beslan.

TOTRAZ: And where was the administration at all?
EVERYBODY: Nowhere!
KAZBEK: And where was it? Where is it now?
TOTRAZ: What is that, the mayor of Beslan city, I don't know at all. Somewhere he may control someone or something, but as for his authority, that question of course is interesting.

Male nonactivist victims agreed that the Beslan authorities were not very involved and described the situation similarly:

BORIS: Beslan was almost immediately brushed aside. Beslan didn't loom anywhere. Mostly the president was there. There were headquarters. It's not clear at all. What headquarters were those, who was there, what were the leaders doing. They gave out disinformation to people all the time. And the Beslan administration was hardly visible at all.

ARKADY: They were immediately brushed aside. They stood on the sidelines.

The male activist victims over thirty-five years old continued their discussion by returning to the accountability of the more powerful republican politicians. Some wanted these individuals to accept accountability in a public way and seek forgiveness. They wanted their leaders to feel and display guilt.

TOTRAZ: As for Dzasokhov, the only thing I personally wanted and expected from him was to say, "I apologize to you, my people, that this happened under my leadership. Perhaps I am guilty somewhere." It's my personal opinion. I understand that in real life he would never say so because he is a politician. The same is true for Putin and Mamsurov.

KAZBEK: He [Dzasokhov] sits in Moscow and chatters there.

TOTRAZ: He explained it very well. I wanted to say just this.

BORIS: Such an attitude.

VITALY: They had information that there would be a terrorist act, and they could have prevented it.

KAZBEK: My attitude to them [authorities] is negative. It wasn't [negative before the tragedy]. After this terrorist act, you see, a person is dismissed. There was a revolution in Thailand, and the prime minister and a number of ministers resigned. And what do we have here? He [Dzasokhov] resigns, and they appoint him to a position in Moscow. He should have left politics altogether.

The male nonactivist victims also believed that the proper response of their republican leaders would have been to forfeit their positions.

ARKADY: Let's just assume, Dzasokhov is the leader of the republic. When such thing happened in the republic—it's not even correct to call it emergency, such a tragedy, there had been nothing like that in the world—did he just go to the people to say what was happening during these three days? Okay, then he should at a minimum have retired, at a minimum. He didn't retire. Now he holds a high position in Moscow, for God's sake. And the head of the Ministry of Internal Affairs, Dzantiyev. The commercial structure of the Ministry of Internal Affairs. Where is Dzantiyev now? In Moscow. Is it normal? How should we feel?

The absence of apology and resignation from official posts were relatively minor complaints of the victims, compared to the bigger violated expectation that their leaders should have sacrificed themselves in exchange for children's lives. In a region accustomed to death, revenge, and honor, the complaint of many focus group participants seemed to be that their local officials did not act honorably. Victims recalled that the terrorists demanded the presence in the school of Dzasokhov, Ingushetia president Zyazikov, Putin advisor Aslakhanov, and pediatrician Roshal.

VIKA [female activist victim thirty-five years old or younger]: Had the four of them come, something might have been different. And so, even if they were killed, they and their ancestors and successors would have become heroes for eternity, and they at least could have held their heads high. At least their names would have been revered throughout Ossetia, unlike now.

VERA [female nonactivist]: And Dzasokhov, it is my subjective opinion, even though they wouldn't let him in, I think he should have gone there anyway. They would have killed him, yes, but he would have died like a hero. I am talking as a mother now. I don't know. It was my opinion. He should have gone there.

The male nonactivists agreed.

VALERY: Dzasokhov—he was offered to enter the school building, but he didn't. If he had entered it, maybe 20–30 people would have been released.

ARKADY: If, suppose, Dzasokhov had entered [the school building], I don't know whether they would have killed him or not. That he didn't enter—I don't consider it cowardice. Fine. The only thing is, he would have been closer to people here.

VALERY: He would be a hero now.

Variation in Blaming Local Authorities

Just as some victims defended President Putin and absolved him from blame, some victims offered relatively forgiving words for the local authorities and tried to absolve them or at least understand their position. For example, male activist victims aged thirty-five years or younger described the powerlessness of the regional officials:

VLADIMIR: The federal authorities moved the authorities of North Ossetia aside. They didn't decide anything here anymore. They just approached people and spoke with them. Only the people who were trained for this could act the way we would like. For example, Vympel-Alfa—they were prepared for these actions. And the rest just behaved themselves simply. No one knew how he would behave in the next second.

ZAUR: [In regard to whether anything depending on the authorities] Probably not on ours.

The female nonactivists similarly described the powerlessness of the regional officials and also their perverse dual status as victims:

VERA: I think that our district administrators were puppets and had no voice whatsoever. It didn't matter whether they were there at the time or not.

INDIRA: Nobody considered their opinion, and nobody asked them for one. Mamsurov at the time was chairman of Parliament. He became the head only later. As Larisa said, his children were there, and when [former Ingushetian president] Aushev suggested, "Let's set your children free," he refused. I think his rating went up then. They would have been led out, and no one would have known that they were led out.

LARISA: And he requested to go to the gym. I heard it myself, not through someone. And his wife—we are neighbors with them—we stood together. And Larisa was on the same level as all the other parents. She cried the same. She stood the same.

Indeed, many North Ossetian authorities were caught in the devastating position of fending off blame for a tragedy that was out of their control and ended the lives of their own loved ones. The former chief administrator of the Pravoberezhny District Boris Urtayev explained his predicament. He "didn't try to make excuses. He said that four of his own relatives had been killed in the school. 'I had neither the men nor the means to protect them. I'm not a soldier. But if the district internal affairs department had been under my supervision, this tragedy would never have happened. But a chief administrator doesn't have that kind of authority'" (Shavlokhova et al. 2004).

Power and powerlessness were sources of disagreement when it came to the police officers who presumably should have thwarted the terrorist operation. The male nonactivist victims argued over what could have been done and how much blame to assign.

VALERY: Later on the first of September, they removed [police posts] from there.

BORIS: That's right. I say in general, who is guilty for all this? Why was there not a single traffic police inspector on the roads? There was not a single one. At least, near the school there was none.

TAMERLAN: Even if we take whatever volume of schools [we have], there aren't enough officers. Where can we find so many officers to cover everything?

There is information: "something, somewhere" [will happen]. Nothing more specific.

RUSLAN: You can drive up to the school from the one side and from the other. There are only two driveways. Put two people here. If the car is driving in, stop it.

TAMERLAN: Stop people armed with pistols?

RUSLAN: All right. Let them kill me, but they didn't save the children.

TAMERLAN: I want to say one thing. Even if there had been not 3–4 police officers, but, suppose, 10 people, they could have wounded as they did.

RUSLAN: I agree, but how many children died!

Perhaps the biggest disagreements about blame concerned local-level corruption and incompetence. For some victims, the bribery and lazy disregard that allowed the terrorists to pull off their carnage meant that the inept workers and takers of the bribes, no matter how small, were culpable. Other victims understood the hardships that gave rise to bribe-taking and laziness, or they focused on the lines of accountability for the larger issue, the culture and institutionalization of bribe-taking and laziness. As local journalist Murat Kabaev explained, "A soldier is a soldier, he follows the orders. The guilty guy is the one who gives the order" (Stephen 2005a). The latter victims were more tolerant of the low-level individuals who committed such transgressions. Both sides were argued by the male nonactivists.

ARKADY: Even if there had been ten people, they would not have stopped it, I agree, but the car passed two posts.

TAMERLAN: The post officer had a good reason. Who stands there? The youngest. And how much do they get? He is on duty there for twenty-four hours every other day. Is it realistic? Why? I was on duty for twenty-four hours every other day for four years.

TAIMURAZ: He should carry out his duties.

TAMERLAN: We are not paid anything. Four to five thousand rubles.

ARKADY: What are we coming to? That the state has this attitude to the Ministry of Internal Affairs.

TAMERLAN: The state should think over this issue. The state should really give some thought to things.

BORIS: I am sorry, but if you work for four thousand, go ahead and work. If you don't want to, if you are not happy with it, leave. Could they have a look into the car to see what a person is transporting?

TAMERLAN: How does he know who is driving? They give him 500 rubles, and he lets anybody go past. He just wants to feed his children.

The Elusiveness of Blame

Some aggrieved individuals, including victims of violence, fight a losing battle in their struggle to assign blame. They face obstacles from blame-avoiding institutions that cloud responsibility by diffusing authority between many agencies, branches, and levels of government (Javeline 2003a:86–94). They also face obstacles from blame-avoiding politicians who employ strategies such as pointing fingers at others, claiming powerlessness in decision-making, empathizing publicly with victims, taking ambiguous policy positions, rotating leaders in relevant political offices, and accommodating some of the aggrieved group with partial concessions (Weaver 1986; Javeline 2003a:76–85, 2003b). In Beslan, the task of blame attribution was thwarted at every turn by the complexity of events and abundance of actors who used blame-avoiding techniques. Many Beslan victims were thus left uncertain about who to blame.

In terms of finger pointing, for example, the Torshin Commission played the blame game and pointed fingers at regional and local authorities for the hostage crisis. It noted that the Russian minister of Internal Affairs, Rashid Nurgaliyev, sent telegrams to regional authorities warning about the need for tightened security at all educational establishments, only to have those warnings ignored, as evidenced by the fact that only a single unarmed policewoman was stationed outside School No. 1 right before the siege, and she too was taken hostage. Specifically, the Torshin Commission pointed fingers at North Ossetia's FSB director Valery Andreyev for poor coordination among the many security services and military units at the scene and at former president of Chechnya Aslan Maskhadov and even Abu-Dzeyt, an Arab who Torshin claimed played an important role in the siege, among others (Finn 2005a).

Rival officials joined the blame game and pointed fingers right back. They accused the Torshin Commission of whitewashing mistakes by high-level members of the federal government. According to Vladimir Ryzhkov, an independent member of Parliament, the report was "an attempt to put the blame on regional and local law enforcers and not on the leaders of federal ministries, who in my view bear responsibility for what happened. They didn't take preventive measures. They didn't check how their orders were being carried out" (Finn 2005a). North Ossetian president Dzasokhov also contradicted Torshin when testifying at the Kulayev trial in January 2006. Dzasokhov said that he never received warning of a possible school attack, only unspecific warnings of possible attacks in North Ossetia. "There was no information that would indicate that a school would be seized" (Voitova 2006a).

The sheer number of inquiries and reports, official and unofficial, also served to facilitate finger pointing and confound blame, because the reports arrived at different conclusions. For example, while the federal prosecutors absolved law enforcement, the North Ossetian regional parliament blamed law enforcement. The latter's report questioned whether North Ossetian FSB head Valery Andreyev had authority over two FSB deputy directors, Vladimir Pronichev and Vladimir Anisimov, who were in Beslan during the hostage taking. During the Kulayev trial, Andreyev's testimony suggested that the senior FSB officers overruled him and that he himself had not ordered the use of flamethrowers and tanks in storming the school. "Responsibility for the deployment of tanks and flamethrowers is borne by the head of the FSB Center for Special Operations Alexander Tikhonov. This matter was not under my authority" (Voitova 2005:1).

The many complicated dimensions of the bungled counterterrorism operation meant that a single political official was often involved in a multilevel blame game with different players over different mistakes. For example, Andreyev also pointed fingers at North Ossetia's Emergency Situations Minister Boris Dzgoyev, whom he accused of negligence. Andreyev argued that firemen arrived to the burning school too late and that some of their water tanks were empty. Dzgoyev pointed fingers right back. He denied any responsibility and testified at the Kulayev trial that Andreyev's order to begin fighting the fire came too late. "The firemen could not move in earlier because there was no order to do so" (Voitova 2005:1).

Finger pointing continued when it came to the official investigations or, as many victims came to see them, official cover-ups. For example, former Parliament leader and North Ossetian president since 2005, Taimuraz Mamsurov, explained the difficulty in clarifying the number of terrorists involved. "Back at the start of the investigation—on November 6, 2004—the deputy prosecutor general at the time said in a television interview that the number of terrorists had been determined conclusively to be 32, and that he would hold accountable anyone who doubted that. Imagine the situation the investigators found themselves in after that statement. After that, would you, as a uniformed officer, risk contradicting your superior, even if you later gathered sufficient evidence to the contrary?" (Borisov 2006b:1).

Some defense mechanisms employed by politicians required no adversary and instead involved the political strategy of pleading no way out, or claiming loss of control and therefore the inappropriateness of accountability. Dzasokhov employed such a strategy when he blamed the chaos and difficulty of circumstances for the incorrect estimates of hostages in the school. "Naturally, nobody could give exact information in that turmoil. But the figures were not low through any malicious intent" (Voitova 2006a).

Given the many conflicting stories, finger pointing, and other blame-avoiding mechanisms used by dozens of potentially accountable officials, it is not surprising that attributing blame for the hostage taking proved difficult for some victims. One response was to attribute blame abstractly, as did the female activist victim over thirty-five with her answer to the question about who is mostly to blame for the hostage taking: "Corruption. That is all." In other cases, victims were sure that some concrete authorities were to blame, but they could not say which one.

BORIS [male nonactivist victim]: We want only one thing: that those who are guilty are punished. We don't need anything else. They should be in jail, at least. And for a long term, because over 300 people died. Someone is guilty, right? Somebody should bear responsibility, shouldn't he? People get 15–17 years for killing one person, and here 334 people died and no one is guilty. No one. And those who were wounded and died later. And no one is guilty! We are not told who is guilty, we are not told who should be punished, and we are not told what in fact happened. We are not told anything.

Conspiracy Theories and Baseless Scapegoating

When blame is elusive, theories are often offered to fill the void. In Beslan, many victims resorted to conspiracy theories that had no basis in any investigation or evidence. Conspiracies, especially by the United States, were mentioned in almost every focus group, suggesting that they were widely discussed, if not endorsed. The female activists age thirty-five and younger debated such a theory.

BELA: But it seems to me that these are the intrigues of America. Why are you laughing? Really, I watch TV. I browse the Internet. I read. It seems to me that this is their plan that they developed a long time ago, and they are slowly implementing it. All the uniforms of the militants, I also read in the newspapers, and the drugs they took, I also read about this in a newspaper.
IRINA: My advice for you: don't believe everything you read in newspapers.
BELA: It seems to me that they needed such an act to instigate international strife here again with the Ingush. They probably thought that we would rise up and go, because there were conversations that the militants were Ingush, although nobody knew for sure. It seems to me that this is the same method of inflaming international strife, so that a new war would start, and the poor people who don't understand all the details would go out and kill each other. That's all.

A similar theory about U.S. culpability was put forth in the focus group of female activist victims over thirty-five and met with a much more receptive audience:

LARISA: I would say that this terrorist act wasn't even inside the country. It was international because it is a chain of terrorist acts. It is Islam. I don't even know how to put it. But it originated somewhere far away, not here. Probably it even comes from America.

RAISA: No, girls, America is guilty for everything. That's all. It is behind all such events. And now with Georgia and other countries it . . .

TATIANA: It has ruined other countries, and now it is ruining us, only gradually.

The men too occasionally named the United States as a likely culprit behind the hostage taking.

AKHSAR [male activist victim thirty-five years or younger]: I think that it is America. In my opinion, they even had this goal, as I understood, to start a war between the peoples, so that turmoil would begin again in Russia in the Caucasus. It was probably beneficial for someone. Such things are not done for no special reason.

TOTRAZ [male activist victim over thirty-five years old]: I got an impression that the international terrorism ordered this, the Americans. Yes, they [Ingush] were executors. And who conceived this idea and organized it so competently? There were many fortuitous circumstances there, very many.

The other widespread conspiracy theory in Beslan concerned the seventy-two-year-old principal of School No. 1, Lydia Tsaliyeva, who had worked at the school for fifty-two years. Tsaliyeva was a hostage herself along with her sister, nephew, and two grandchildren. She suffered severe wounds, underwent three operations, and mourned the loss of hundreds of her students. Nevertheless, she was accused of all manner of wrongdoing. Some Beslan residents claimed that she helped plan the terrorist attack (Shavlokhova et al. 2004). According to various rumors, Tsaliyeva hired workers over the summer who hid weapons and ammunition in the school for the terrorists and familiarized themselves with the layout of the building, and she arranged for the Day of Knowledge celebrations to begin an hour earlier to accommodate the terrorist act (Walsh 2005; Phillips 2007:251–252). Tsaliyeva allegedly knew that bearded men were in the building and told students that they were merely vagabonds, and she allegedly pointed out the children of government officials to the terrorists and tipped them off that one hostage was a former police officer (Chivers 2004). She allegedly drank tea with the terrorists after the other hostages were denied water (Franchetti 2004). While children were drinking urine to quench their thirst, she allegedly ate an apple and would not share (Franchetti 2004). Perhaps Tsaliyeva's biggest crime was surviving. According to Felisa Batagova, whose sister, niece, and grand-daughter died in the school, "She made damned sure she saved her own skin" (Phillips 2007:250). "A ship should sink with its captain" (Chivers 2004:3). Another woman added, "She left the gym on the third day with exactly the same hairdo that she had when she entered it on the first" (Phillips 2007:251). Others claimed that Tsaliyeva faked her injuries or lied about their severity to cover up her role in the tragedy (Phillips 2007:252).

Curses and threats to Tsaliyeva were written on the charred and bullet-ridden walls of School No. 1. Journalists declined to print some of the most vulgar (Chivers 2004). The tamer graffiti included: "Lidiya, you will burn in hell for the perished children"; "Lidiya, we will get you"; "Lida, you sold other people's children"; "Lida, you will not live"; "You should have died instead of the children"; and "Lida, School No. 6 hates you. Die!" (Chivers 2004; Franchetti 2004). When she returned home from her surgeries in Moscow, some Beslan residents shouted at her "Why didn't you save them?" "You don't belong here, you shouldn't be living here!" (Shavlokhova et al. 2004). Trying to enter the school building, angry mourners screamed "Murderer!" (Page 2005d). Accusers included Aneta Gadiyeva of Mothers of Beslan who argued, "They hid arms there. Lidiya was negligent and should have known" (Walsh 2005).

None of these accusations was proven. According to Sergei Ignatchenko, the senior spokesman for the Federal Security Service, and Aslanbek Aslakhanov, adviser on the North Caucasus to President Vladimir Putin, investigators ruled out the labor crew's role in preparing the attack, and others noted that it was a crew that had been working at the school for over a decade on annual repairs and maintenance (Chivers 2004; Franchetti 2004). The unshared apple was really a piece of chocolate given to Tsaliyeva because she suffered from diabetes (Franchetti 2004). According to fellow hostages, Tsaliyeva acted courageously during the ordeal (Page 2005d). Oleg Albegov, a neighbor of Tsaliyeva, surmised, "They need someone to blame. As long as the truth is not spoken, it will be like this" (Page 2005d:39). Tsaliyeva herself tearfully concurred. "It's very painful. I can't believe I have any enemies. How can people think I helped the gunmen? I can't bear to think of all the people I knew so well who died in the school. My only explanation for what some people are saying about me is they are so torn by grief they don't know who to blame" (Franchetti 2004).

Political Alienation, Blame, and Retaliatory Violence

Political alienation, or the absence of political pride, can be a strong inhibitor of support for retaliatory ethnic violence, because victims of the original violence are distracted by their grievances toward the state. This does not mean that politically alienated individuals will refrain from all destructive behavior. To the extent that behavior is directed toward the state or its actors, it may take an aggressive and even violent form. For example, alienated West Germans were more likely than other Germans to seize buildings, fight with police, or participate in violent acts intended to overthrow the government (Muller et al. 1982:246). However, such behavior is more appropriately categorized as extreme, radical, or illegal political action, not retaliatory ethnic violence, and such political action is expected to have a positive relationship with political alienation, as described below.

For retaliatory ethnic violence, political pride, or the absence of political alienation, can be a strong facilitator. Victims of ethnic violence often seek retributive justice, yet those who feel proud of their country are unlikely to interpret their grievance as government failure and unaccountability, and they may disqualify political institutions and actors as targets for retribution. For these unalienated victims, their grievance still requires some kind of response, and members of their perpetrator's ethnic or religious group may be the most "logical" remaining targets for indiscriminate retaliation. Pride in country leaves victims searching outside the political system for action.

Indiscriminate retaliatory violence is especially likely in places where the authorities themselves support or are perceived to support such violence. For example, ethnic rioters are often motivated by the perception that they have "a green light for violence against the target group" and that they are in some sense acting on behalf of the government (Horowitz 2001:344–345). With presumably tolerant or sympathetic authorities, retaliators may believe that law enforcement will not stand in the way of their actions and that their actions are even permitted and legitimate (Olzak 1992; Horowitz 2001:352). Their belief is often buttressed by the fact that retaliatory violence against the target group is rarely punished and by the fact that police and armed forces likely share the rioters' ethnicity, religion, or language and, importantly, their sentiments toward the target group (Horowitz 2001:355, 366). "Given the common human propensity to abdicate conscience functions to authority," retaliatory ethnic violence can thus be looked upon "as a form of thuggery that has been sanctioned and sometimes even glorified as a contribution to the welfare of the group, so that those who might otherwise see themselves as criminals are able to see themselves as warriors" (Horowitz 2001:359). Of course, in places where authorities clearly and consistently disapprove of retaliatory ethnic violence, there is less reason to believe that political pride (the lack of political alienation) would motivate support for retaliatory violence (Horowitz 2001:362). However, in the many instances where authoritative "green lighting" of violence exists, the politically proud are most receptive to the signal.

These arguments about political alienation (conceived as decreased political pride) are distinct from arguments about trust in government. Theoretically, a victim who trusts government, like a victim who absolves government from blame and supports political officials, may be more supportive of retaliatory ethnic violence. However, prior empirical evidence suggests that trust in government has a more complex relationship with violence, sometimes hindering and sometimes facilitating (Muller et al. 1982; Craig and Wald 1985). One reason might be the relative vagueness of the concept, which may signify confidence in all government institutions, some subset, or particular officeholders. Expectations for the relationship between political trust and retaliatory violence in Beslan are therefore unclear.

In North Ossetia and indeed all of Russia, it was widely thought that the authorities approved of violence against Caucasian Muslims, having conducted such violence themselves on numerous occasions and publicly advocated killing Chechens (Evangelista 2002:74–75). Had Beslan residents taken revenge on their Ingush and Chechen neighbors, there is good reason to suspect that law enforcement would not have done much to stop them or to identify and prosecute them after the fact. The Russian government rarely investigates disappearances of Ingush or Chechens, potentially signaling to Ossetians that their violent actions would go unpunished ("As If They Fell" 2008).

The victims most likely to receive and follow these signals were those who were proud of Russia, especially those whose pride in Russia increased after the hostage taking. For these victims, the Russian and North Ossetian leaders were off limits as targets of culpability and in some cases even retained their admiration and respect. Some proud victims might have also thought that their government shared their pro-violence sentiments. For victims who were politically alienated, it made less sense to take cues from the shameful government.

A similar dynamic was at play for blame attribution. For victims who were unable to attribute blame or who thought the authorities bore little responsibility and therefore did not deserve punishment, the response to their grievance could not be directed at those authorities. To the extent that their suffering required a response, retaliatory ethnic violence may have seemed more acceptable. Conversely, victims who did attribute blame to the authorities had less need to search for other culprits and were less receptive to authoritative signals about the acceptability of harming Chechens and Ingush.

Political Alienation, Blame, and Political Action

The presumed impact of political alienation on political participation has long been debated, with scholars hypothesizing that it could have both positive and negative effects. Some evidence suggests that political alienation increases political participation, although alienation is defined in ways that sometimes resemble political trust and efficacy (Jackson 1973). Much more evidence suggests that political alienation "may substantially diminish the willingness of citizens to participate in politics," although the definitions of political alienation also vary widely (Miller 1974; see also Vose 1959; Cortner 1968; Keniston 1968; Moore 1975; Leahy and Mazur 1978; Klandermans 1979; Morris 1981; Bobo and Gilliam 1990; Scheppele and Walker 1991; Gilliam and Kaufman 1998; Tate 2003; Adams et al. 2006). Still other evidence suggests that these effects of political alienation are conditional on factors such as social skills, ideology, organizational affiliations, interpersonal trust, and age (Citrin 1977; Herring 1989).

Overall, lessons about alienation drawn from the literature are confusing. On the one hand, disenchantment with government could lead to withdrawal from politics, but on the other hand, disenchantment is a grievance in itself that could mobilize political action, if participants seek to have their government address their disenchantment (Jackson 1973). To the extent that research has mentioned the roles of pride and shame, it has been mostly in regard to pride and shame in one's self, with personal shame crippling action and personal pride encouraging action (Goodwin and Jasper 2006:619), which again resembles a finding about efficacy more than one about political alienation. The effects on participation of pride in one's country or disenchantment and shame are rarely overtly discussed.

Still, there are hints in past research that a decrease in political pride should be mobilizing. Studies that include pride in their conception of political alienation find evidence that alienation is a significant factor in collective action (Muller and Opp 1986; Muller et al. 1991). Studies also show that a sense of betrayal by one's government or "moral shock" at government behavior can inspire political action. For example, because it so grotesquely violates expectations, state repression often ignites the very protests it was meant to suppress (Brockett 2005; Jasper 2011:292). Even in the absence of repression, disadvantage often promotes collective action when the disadvantage is perceived as unfair or illegitimate (Lind and Tyler 1988; Tyler et al. 1997; Mikula et al. 1998; van Zomeren et al. 2004:650), again suggesting that a negative change in perception of government can mobilize aggrieved individuals.

The Beslan victim study firmly supports the idea that political alienation, defined as decreased political pride, should be mobilizing. Focus group discussions reinforced the importance of moral shock and violated expectations for political participation. For example, male activist victims over thirty-five years old explained their sense of betrayal and how it motivated their action:

TOTRAZ: They published the results of the investigations, and I began to see that it was all wrong. Suppose they publish it for you. You, an outsider, will believe it, but I saw it with my own eyes. I can analyze a little bit. I am not saying that I am smart, but I can analyze and compare events. I see that it is all wrong, and this [political activism] is my reaction.

KAZBEK: In the school building, some representative of the authorities is speaking to you. He says one thing, and something completely different is shown on TV. Absolutely different! How can you not be surprised by this?

For some victims, the entire aftermath of Beslan represented their violated expectations of government, and along the way, each component violation generated very specific feelings of disenchantment that in turn manifested in political action. For example, Rita Naifonova explained in Chapter 2 her participation in the January 2005 blockade: "We live like we are on a powder keg. When children go to school, we are afraid that they will not return. And our government doesn't move a finger. And we are tired of waiting for the truth from these authorities" (Tokhsyrov 2005:3). For another example, Ella Kesayeva explained the picket organized to protest what victims saw as an attempt by officials to conceal the truth about the botched rescue operation. "Today the firemen arrived at the site in full gear and with their tanks full of water. But on September 3, 2004, when hundreds of children were dying in flames, firemen came without their protective suits, their equipment didn't work and their water tanks were empty" ("Beslan Victims' Relatives" 2006).

Not all Beslan victims felt betrayed by their country. Some continued to feel pride, and a rare few even felt their pride increase. Such "system justification" has been found in a variety of contexts to reduce an individual's willingness to take political action (Jost et al. 2012). The mechanism resembles the effects of perceived fair treatment (Miller 2001:544–545) and support for the political party in power (Oegema and Klandermans 1994:718), where attachment to the potentially offending party causes individuals to ignore, downplay, or excuse the offense. In Beslan, victims who continued to be proud of Russia or increased their pride after the hostage taking could hardly then participate in actions that called that pride into question.

Political trust should hypothetically operate the same as political alienation, meaning that individuals who trust the established political system should be less likely to challenge that system with political protest, and distrustful individuals should be the most likely participants, especially in unconventional action (Gamson 1968). Empirically, however, this hypothesis has found only limited support (e.g., Citrin 1974; Nilson and Nilson 1980), with some studies suggesting that the effects of political trust on participation may be conditional on other factors (Roefs et al. 1998). Political trust may encourage participation, to the extent that aggrieved individuals believed the trusted government would be responsive to their participation, but political trust could also discourage participation, to the extent that aggrieved individuals are less inclined to attribute their grievances to the trusted government in the first place. These two effects likely cancel each other out. In the case of Beslan, there are no significant effects of trust in government on political participation.

Blame should also hypothetically operate the same as political alienation, meaning that individuals who attribute blame for their victimization to specific political officials or institutions should be more likely to take political action (Javeline 2003a, 2003b). Beslan victims could have potentially attributed blame to a dozen or so high-powered officials in the security services, internal affairs, emergency situations, or executive branch of the regional or federal government, and many seemed very willing to draw lines of accountability all the way to the fish's head. Those who confidently assigned blame to President Putin or who expressed dissatisfaction with the virtually nonexistent punishment doled out to other political officials were more likely to participate in politics.

Those who defended Putin pulled their punches, and some even felt compelled to obstruct the participation of others. As described in Chapter 8, activists in Voice of Beslan split over the appropriateness of criticizing the president, with five pro-Putin members expelled. The expelled members then tried to stifle the criticisms of Kesayeva and other Voice of Beslan activists by taking over the formal organization and entangling Kesayeva and others in distracting lawsuits.

The inability to attribute blame also serves to discourage political action (Javeline 2003a, 2003b). Accordingly, focus group discussions among Beslan victims suggest that it was mainly the nonactivists who had difficulty attributing blame. Nonactivist victims pondered questions of accountability; they understood that there was a huge puzzle, but they had no answer. Indeed, in both the female and male nonactivist focus groups, participants went on at length about not knowing who is guilty. The vagueness of their blame attributions likely contributed to their low mobilization potential.

Asked who, in their opinion, was most guilty for what happened in the Beslan school, female nonactivists replied:

ZALINA: Who knows.
ZINAIDA: I have none [no suppositions], because I wonder: Suppose you come to my apartment. Do you know where I keep what? You don't know me at all. And how did they arrive to this very School No. 1 without obstacles?
VALYA: Why specifically School No. 1?

INDIRA: And how can we know who is guilty?

SIMA: If we knew who is guilty! The problem is that we don't know who is guilty.

INDIRA: But how did they get into School No. 1 without obstacles?

ZINAIDA: Exactly. They stood and waited.

INDIRA: Why not a different school?

ZINAIDA: And what were Ingush doing here? How could they?

INDIRA: This is interesting to us. If, let's say, we find ourselves in Hazrani, is there a School No. 1 there? I don't know. How will we find this School No. 1?

ZINAIDA: Exactly. How did they find the way?

VALYA: It means, apparently, that somebody tipped them off.

VERA: You know, when we lay in the hospital, we lay in hospital in Moscow, and women who were injured at Nord-Ost came to visit us. They said, "you were 'ordered,' and we were 'ordered.'" That's what the women said.

Male nonactivist victims also pondered the lines of accountability for the tragedy and their own inability to attribute blame.

BORIS: You see, it is difficult to say [who is guilty]. Practically everybody in Beslan knows that it was done on purpose, but proving it is not our business. That is, we won't prove it. And the one who should prove it won't. Officially nobody knows who is guilty, but judging by how it was all conducted, they certainly didn't just arrive.

RUSLAN: Somebody must have known. Now any information will somehow leak. Such a terrorist act, and no one in the Vladikazkaz Department of the Ministry of Internal Affairs could find evidence. No one. There were no informers that such a thing was being prepared. It is just impossible. Information leaks everywhere all the same.

ARKADY: And if we want to reason further, let's go further. After this Maskhadov was killed, [Chechen rebel leader] Basayev was found, and everybody was immediately found. Earlier they were not found. They were such uncatchable Joes. And why uncatchable? Because they were needed. And now—bang!— everything is all right.

The supposed success of capturing or killing all the hostage takers was just one of many strategies that helped political authorities avoid blame and discourage political action. Concessions to victims were another such strategy, as a male activist victim over thirty-five years old explained:

TOTRAZ: No one will fight the authorities. Each had children left here, and later on everyone depended on these authorities. They did take some steps after all. Compensation, treatment—we got all this. No one can deny it. It calmed people down, but questions remained. Let's say a girl remained wounded. She needs treatment. Suppose I will go [to fight the authorities], but now I think about her.

Measuring Political Alienation and Blame

Political alienation is defined as the estrangement from one's country as reflected in decreased political pride. This emotional detachment and disappointment are conceptually distinct from political efficacy (empowerment), political trust (confidence in institutions, political officials, or the system as a whole), patriotism (love of country and concern for its welfare), and a variety of other terms. The operationalization of political alienation reflects these definitional distinctions and avoids conceptual confusion. In everyday terms, pride and shame are "moral emotions of self-approval or self-disapproval, which entail a feeling of connection or disconnection from those around one" (Jasper 2011:289). In political terms, pride and shame are similar, only the referent is not one's self but one's country. Politically proud individuals approve of and feel a connection with their country. Politically alienated individuals do not.

The operationalization of political alienation as decreased pride also helps avoid the basic question-writing mistakes that plague the efficacy/alienation literature. For example, preexisting survey questions are often posed as negative attitude statements beginning with "I don't think public officials care" and "People like me don't have any say," for which disagreeing poses the cognitive challenge of double negatives (Reef and Knoke 1999). The resulting data may measure political alienation, but the data also may measure political efficacy or, given the measurement problems, nothing at all.

To measure political alienation, Beslan victims were instead asked direct questions about feelings of pride and shame in Russia. Table 7.1 shows that, at the time of the survey, a majority of Beslan victims felt very proud (27 percent) or rather proud (42 percent), but a minority felt not very proud (18 percent) or not at all proud (6 percent). Victims were much more divided on the question of shame, with roughly half feeling ashamed of Russia very often (11 percent) or rather often (33 percent) and roughly half not very often (35 percent) or hardly ever (9 percent).

Political alienation is likely a dynamic rather than static sentiment, and an increase in alienation, or weakened attachment to country, is likely the most relevant mobilizing factor. For clarity in operationalization and discussion, this change in alienation is measured as decreased pride in Russia. Victim respondents were asked to think back before the 2004 hostage-taking about how proud they were of Russia at that time. Although such a survey question is

Table 7.1. Political Alienation, Shame, and Blame among Beslan Victims

Current political alienation: "How proud are you to be a Russian citizen?"

Very Proud	Rather Proud	Not Very Proud	Not at All Proud
295	462	199	69
(26.9)	(42.1)	(18.1)	(6.3)

Shame in Russia: "How often do you feel ashamed of Russia?"

Hardly Ever	Not Very Often	Rather Often	Very Often
100	389	367	124
(9.1)	(35.4)	(33.4)	(11.3)

Past political alienation: "Thinking back to before the tragedy—that is, before September 2004—how proud were you to be a Russian citizen?"

Very Proud	Rather Proud	Not Very Proud	Not at All Proud
508	450	78	15
(46.3)	(41.0)	(7.1)	(1.4)

Changed political alienation: decreased pride in Russia since the 2004 tragedy (difference between responses to "How proud are you to be a Russian citizen?" and "Thinking back to before the tragedy—that is, before September 2004—how proud were you to be a Russian citizen?")

Pride Increased	Pride Stayed Same	Pride Decreased One to Two Steps	Pride Decreased Three to Four Steps
32	659	272	94
(2.9)	(60.0)	(24.8)	(8.6)

Blame toward President Putin: "Speaking just about the central authorities, please tell me whether you think the following authorities are very guilty, somewhat guilty, not very guilty, or not at all guilty for causing this tragedy? *President Vladimir Putin*"

Not at All Guilty	Not Very Guilty	Somewhat Guilty	Very Guilty
100	291	368	260
(9.1)	(26.5)	(33.5)	(23.7)

Dissatisfaction with punishment of guilty federal officials: "Now I will state some demands that have been made by several Beslan victims. Can you tell me whether in your opinion these demands have been completely satisfied, mostly satisfied, mostly not satisfied, not satisfied at all? *Punishment of federal officials who are guilty for what happened*"

Completely Satisfied	Mostly Satisfied	Mostly Not Satisfied	Not Satisfied at All
38	58	486	452
(3.5)	(5.3)	(44.3)	(41.2)

$N = 1,098$; number of victims (%).

obviously subject to recall bias, as some victims overestimate or underestimate their prior sentiments, recall bias is not problematic here, where the goal is to measure victims' perceptions of their attitudinal stability or change, their subjective assessments of their changed attachment to their country. In this case, recall or objectivity is less crucial than the perception of having become more or less proud of Russia. The difference is calculated between the respondents' current pride and former pride. Table 7.1 shows that the majority of victims perceived no change in pride (60 percent), whereas a third felt one step (16 percent), two steps (9 percent), three steps (8 percent), or four steps (1 percent) less proud of Russia after the hostage-taking, and a small minority felt one step (2 percent) or two to three steps (1 percent) prouder.

The virtue of using survey questions to measure political alienation should be obvious: pride is a psychological or perceptual variable and can be validly measured only by speaking to the holders of the perceptions (Citrin 1977). Indeed, a major criticism of the now discredited literature that cast protesters as deviants and protesting crowds as "lonely" is that researchers often inferred the presence of a psychological state, such as alienation, dissonance, or anxiety, from objective data rather than subjective data on perceptions (McAdam 1982).

The virtue of the particular survey questions answered by Beslan victims is their simplicity and clarity. Many alternative measures of political alienation have long histories, but those histories are accompanied by decades of criticism and validity challenges (Citrin 1977; Herring 1989). Time-"tested" questions supposedly tapping political alienation could easily be taken instead for measures of efficacy, trust, policy satisfaction, or incumbent support (Citrin 1977; Herring 1989). Very simple questions about pride in citizenship suffer no such confusion or measurement bias.

To corroborate analyses of political alienation, victims were asked questions about blame toward political officials and satisfaction with their punishment. While not measures of political alienation, presumably these variables should operate in the same direction as political alienation as they influence support for retaliatory violence and political participation.[1] Feeling politically alienated, blaming President Putin, and being dissatisfied with the punishment of officials for their role in the massacre should have similar behavioral effects. As Table 7.1 shows, most Beslan victims are ready to assign a fair amount of blame to President Putin, with over half saying he is very (24 percent) or somewhat (34 percent) guilty, and only a third saying he is not very (27 percent) or not at all (9 percent) guilty. They are even less willing to let other federal officials off the

---

[1] Political alienation and blame are conceptually distinct and also empirically distinct, although somewhat correlated at .24 ($p < 0.001$) for political alienation (decreased pride) and Putin's guilt and .13 ($p < 0.001$) for political alienation and the dissatisfaction with punishment of officials.

hook, and are not at all satisfied (41 percent) or mostly not satisfied (44 percent) with the punishments doled out.

Limitations to Political Alienation and Blame Measurements

The measure of decreased pride intentionally narrows the concept of political alienation to a single dimension. This runs contrary to the standard practice of treating political alienation as a multidimensional concept requiring measurement with a multi-item index. Without several survey questions to tap into political alienation, the measure used to determine the alienation of Beslan victims could potentially be biased.

The question, however, is what kind of bias, how much bias, and whether this bias is greater or less than the bias of alternative measures. The multi-item indices or scales used in prior studies of alienation are only as valid as their component survey questions. Some of the most rigorous scales used in equally rigorous analyses include measures of pride, but they also include assessments about whether courts guarantee the right to a fair trial, whether leading politicians have good intentions, and other aspects of the political system that should reasonably be correlated with decreased political pride but arguably represent specific appraisals rather than an emotion, feeling, or subjective sense that is the defining characteristic of political alienation (Muller and Opp 1986:486; Muller, Dietz, and Finkel 1991:1268). Appraisals of the performance of political institutions and personalities might turn out to be key determinants of an individual's pride in country, but they also might not; inclusion in the measure of political alienation precludes testing this relationship.

Scholars using such measures rightly point to high inter-item correlations and scale reliability that legitimize use of the scales, but the resulting analysis is still subject to multiple interpretations, depending on how researchers and readers understand the bundle of survey questions and the concept they supposedly represent. Also, many if not most items in these multi-item indices are similarly worded survey questions with similar if not identical response categories. The similarities mean that respondents have a higher propensity for straight-line response strategies, or mechanically offering the same response to all questions or concentrating responses on the same end of a scale (Herzog and Bachman 1981). Those high inter-item correlations may reflect, as researchers maintain, a common underlying dimension such as political alienation, or they may reflect the straight-line response strategies and therefore be a methodological artifact.

An additional challenge may come from the use of attitude statements with agree-disagree response sets, such as "The courts in the Federal Republic guarantee everyone a fair trial regardless of whether they are rich or poor, educated or uneducated" or "Looking back, the leading politicians in the Federal Republic have always had good intentions" (Muller and Opp 1986:486). In such cases, the component questions in the multi-item indices are also subject to acquiescence bias, or the tendency to agree with statements regardless of their content (Schuman and Presser 1996: chap. 8; Javeline 1999). If so, the high inter-item correlations may reflect correlated, but potentially erroneous, agreement more than an underlying sentiment.

This then is the point of comparison for the measure used here to represent political alienation. While there are valid challenges to the decision to define political alienation as decreased pride in one's country (or here specifically as decreased pride in being a Russian citizen), the measure is biased only to the extent that respondents may have inaccurately reported their own sense of pride, either current or past or both. Otherwise, it is a pure measure of a feeling or subjective sense, not confounded with appraisals, and it is not subject to straight-line response strategies or acquiescence bias.

Similarly, survey questions that ask directly about the guilt of President Putin or a respondent's satisfaction with the punishment of political officials for the Beslan tragedy are simple, clear, and valid on their face, but they also might be subject to challenges of bias as single-item measures. Previous research suggests that specificity in blame can be usefully measured with multi-step survey questions that allow respondents to be vague or specific in their blame attributions and that also test for the consistency of those attributions (Javeline 2003a, 2003b). Such a procedure demands space in a survey that was unfortunately not available in the Beslan victim survey, but as shown above, focus group discussions strongly support the finding that more specific attributions of blame encourage greater participation in politics.

Although the Beslan victim study cannot test systematically for the effects of blame specificity, it can test for the effects of a related but different concept, blaming a country's most prominent leaders. In the 1990s, 54 percent of Russians who were "specific attributors" of blame for Russia's wage delays and nonpayments crisis singled out then-President Boris Yeltsin as the main culprit (Javeline 2003b:112). In Beslan, there is no way to test the correlation between blame specificity and blaming Putin or between blame specificity and dissatisfaction with post-violence punishments, but the prior finding about Yeltsin provides strong rationale for asking about Putin and other officials. The question about Putin's guilt may be more valid and reliable than the question about satisfaction with the punishment of federal officials, because the punishment, or lack thereof, was fully apparent to some victims only over time, and in those cases, responses may have changed as disillusionment set in.

Also, respondents who questioned the anonymity of the survey and feared reprisals may have understated their criticism of officials, in which case the mission again is to ponder the direction and magnitude of potential bias. Presumably, fearful respondents would also be reluctant to participate in politics, leaving only the fearless to criticize officials and also participate in politics. The underreporting of blame could thus magnify any finding of a strong relationship between blame and political participation. This bias is plausible and should be kept in mind when interpreting statistical results. It would essentially mean that the measures of blame should be interpreted as the interaction of blaming powerful political officials and comfort in expressing that blame.

However, there is also strong reason to suspect that Beslan victims did not pull punches when responding to the survey, even the blame questions. Victims who participated in focus groups, a much more public venue for expressing opinions than a one-on-one survey, did not seem to self-censor during discussions of Putin or any other official. To the extent that they self-censored or chose not to participate altogether, they seemed motivated less by political fear and more by emotional exhaustion and a desire to avoid reliving the tragedy.

Beslan Victim Data on Political Alienation and Behavior

Political alienation is correlated with support for retaliatory violence in a negative direction: in Beslan, politically alienated victims were less likely to support retaliatory violence, and politically proud victims were more likely to support retaliatory violence. As Table 7.2 shows, victims who perceived an increase in their pride in Russia were the most likely to approve somewhat or fully of killing the same number of Chechens as were killed in Beslan (34.4 percent), and those who perceived no change in their pride were the next most likely group to approve (14.9 percent). However, victims who perceived that their pride in Russia decreased since the tragedy were the least likely to approve: only 12.1 percent of those whose pride decreased one to two steps and 8.5 percent of those whose pride decreased three to four steps somewhat or fully approved of killing Chechens. Victims whose pride decreased three to four steps were especially adamant disapprovers of retaliatory violence (almost 60 percent completely disapproving). The term "only" is used in a relative sense, given that 8.5 percent of any population supporting retaliatory murder is not trivial.

The above finding is corroborated by some but not all measures of political alienation (Table 7.3). There is no statistically significant relationship between feeling ashamed of Russia or blaming President Putin and supporting retaliatory violence. However, victims who were dissatisfied with the punishment of guilty federal officials were less likely to support retaliatory violence than victims who were more satisfied. While approximately a third of those who were mostly (34.4 percent) or completely (29 percent) satisfied with the punishment of officials

Table 7.2. Political Alienation and Support for Retaliatory Violence (Killing the Same Number of Chechens as Were Killed in Beslan)

Current political alienation: "How proud are you to be a Russian citizen?"

	Completely Disapprove	Somewhat Disapprove	Somewhat Approve	Fully Approve	Missing	N
Very proud	118 (40.0)	86 (29.2)	42 (14.2)	14 (4.7)	35 (11.9)	295 (100.0)
Rather proud	162 (35.1)	178 (38.5)	32 (6.9)	26 (5.6)	64 (13.9)	462 (100.0)
Not very proud	89 (44.7)	72 (36.2)	7 (3.5)	15 (7.5)	16 (8.0)	199 (100.0)
Not at all proud	36 (52.2)	18 (26.1)	5 (7.2)	6 (8.7)	4 (5.8)	69 (100.0)

Pearson's $r = .04$, $p < .19$.

Past political alienation: "Thinking back to before the tragedy—that is, before September 2004—how proud were you to be a Russian citizen?"

	Completely Disapprove	Somewhat Disapprove	Somewhat Approve	Fully Approve	Missing	N
Very proud	216 (42.5)	168 (33.1)	44 (8.7)	28 (5.5)	52 (10.2)	508 (100.0)
Rather proud	179 (39.8)	150 (33.3)	34 (7.6)	26 (5.8)	61 (13.6)	450 (100.0)
Not very proud	23 (29.5)	37 (47.4)	7 (9.0)	6 (7.7)	5 (6.4)	78 (100.0)
Not at all proud	3 (20.0)	7 (46.7)	2 (13.3)	2 (13.3)	1 (6.7%)	15 (100.0)

Pearson's $r = -.07$, $p < .04$.

Changed political alienation: decreased pride in Russia since the 2004 tragedy (difference between responses to "How proud are you to be a Russian citizen?" and "Thinking back to before the tragedy—that is, before September 2004—how proud were you to be a Russian citizen?")

	Completely Disapprove	Somewhat Disapprove	Somewhat Approve	Fully Approve	Missing	N
Pride increased	4 (12.5)	15 (46.9)	9 (28.1)	2 (6.3)	2 (6.3)	32 (100.0)
Pride stayed same	243 (36.9)	221 (33.5)	63 (9.6)	35 (5.3)	97 (14.7)	659 (100.0)
Pride decreased one to two steps	119 (43.8)	105 (38.6)	14 (5.1)	19 (7.0)	15 (5.5)	272 (100.0)
Pride decreased three to four steps	55 (58.5)	22 (23.4)	2 (2.1)	6 (6.4)	9 (9.6)	94 (100.0)

Pearson's $r = -.12$, $p < .00$.

$N = 1,098$; number of victims (%).

Table 7.3. Shame and Blame and Support for Retaliatory Violence (Killing the Same Number of Chechens as Were Killed in Beslan)

Shame in Russia: "How often do you feel ashamed of Russia?"

	Completely Disapprove	Somewhat Disapprove	Somewhat Approve	Fully Approve	Missing	N
Hardly ever	48 (48.0)	26 (26.0)	10 (10.0)	4 (4.0)	12 (12.0)	100 (100.0)
Not very often	110 (28.3)	159 (40.9)	49 (12.6)	13 (3.3)	58 (14.9)	389 (100.0)
Rather often	178 (48.5)	124 (33.8)	20 (5.4)	23 (6.3)	22 (6.0)	367 (100.0)
Very often	58 (46.8)	33 (26.6)	5 (4.0)	16 (12.9)	12 (9.7)	124 (100.0)

Pearson's $r = -.02$, $p < .48$.

Blame toward President Putin: "Speaking just about the central authorities, please tell me whether you think the following authorities are very guilty, somewhat guilty, not very guilty, or not at all guilty for causing this tragedy? *President Vladimir Putin*"

	Completely Disapprove	Somewhat Disapprove	Somewhat Approve	Fully Approve	Missing	N
Not at all guilty	42 (42.0)	32 (32.0)	7 (7.0)	5 (5.0)	14 (14.0)	100 (100.0)
Not very guilty	97 (33.3)	114 (39.2)	24 (8.2)	15 (5.2)	41 (14.1)	291 (100.0)
Somewhat guilty	152 (41.3)	121 (32.9)	36 (9.8)	19 (5.2)	40 (10.9)	368 (100.0)
Very guilty	120 (46.2)	86 (33.1)	12 (4.6)	22 (8.5)	20 (7.7)	260 (100.0)

Pearson's $r = -.02$, $p < .59$.

Dissatisfaction with punishment of guilty federal officials: "Now I will state some demands that have been made by several Beslan victims. Can you tell me whether in your opinion these demands have been completely satisfied, mostly satisfied, mostly not satisfied, not satisfied at all? *Punishment of federal officials who are guilty for what happened*"

	Completely Disapprove	Somewhat Disapprove	Somewhat Approve	Fully Approve	Missing	N
Completely satisfied	4 (10.5)	7 (18.4)	3 (7.9)	8 (21.1)	16 (42.1)	38 (100.0)
Mostly satisfied	7 (12.1)	15 (25.9)	14 (24.1)	6 (10.3)	16 (27.6)	58 (100.0)
Mostly not satisfied	192 (39.5)	192 (39.5)	39 (8.0)	18 (3.7)	45 (9.3)	486 (100.0)
Not satisfied at all	211 (46.7)	142 (31.4)	29 (6.4)	28 (6.2)	42 (9.3)	452 (100.0)

Pearson's $r = -.19$, $p < .00$.

$N = 1,098$; number of victims (%).

approved of killing Chechens, only small minorities of victims who were mostly not satisfied or not at all satisfied approved of killing (11.7 and 12.6 percent, respectively), again with the caveat about the use of the word "only" in relative terms.

Political alienation is correlated with political participation in a positive direction: the majority of victims who felt no change in their pride in being a Russian citizen, along with the very rare victims who actually perceived an increase in their pride, were among the least politically active. Conversely, victims who perceived the greatest decrease in their pride in Russia were far more active. As Table 7.4 shows, only 9.4 percent of proud victims participated in more than one political activity, and no proud victim participated in more than ten activities. Among victims who felt no change in pride, 21.6 percent participated in more than one activity and only a very few (2.3 percent) in over ten activities. Among the modestly politically alienated, participation in more than one activity and more than ten activities jumped to 29.1 percent and 5.9 percent, respectively. The most staggering levels of participation were among the most politically alienated: Over half (51.1 percent) participated in more than one activity, and over a quarter (27.7 percent) participated in an astounding eleven or more activities.

The above finding is corroborated by related measures of political alienation, such as feeling shame in Russia and blaming President Putin for causing the tragedy. As Table 7.5 shows, victims who felt ashamed of Russia "hardly ever" or "not very often" were far less active politically than victims who felt ashamed "rather often" or "very often." Indeed, a quarter (26.4 percent) of those who felt ashamed rather often participated in more than one activity, and half (49.2 percent) of those who felt ashamed very often participated in more than one activity, with a quarter (25.8 percent) participating in more than ten activities. Similarly, victims who thought Vladimir Putin was "not at all guilty" or "not very guilty" for causing the tragedy were less active than victims who thought Putin was "somewhat" or "very guilty": More than one-third (36.1 percent) of those who thought Putin was very guilty participated in more than one activity.

The only measure related to political alienation that does not correlate with political participation is dissatisfaction with punishment of the federal officials guilty for the tragedy, and here, the above-described measurement problem may be relevant. Victims were testifying about their level of satisfaction at the time of the survey, and it is plausible that victims became less satisfied over time, as the absence of punishments became more apparent. If even the nonactivists became disillusioned, the correlation with prior participatory acts is likely smaller than it would have been had the snapshot of victim attitudes and behavior been taken at an earlier point in time when the nonactivists may have been more satisfied. The bias is thus against a finding that (dis)satisfaction with the punishment of officials influences participation in politics and may explain the low correlation in Table 7.5.

Table 7.4. Political Alienation and Political Participation

Current political alienation: "How proud are you to be a Russian citizen?"

	No Activities	One Activity	Two or Three Activities	Four to Ten Activities	Eleven to Thirty-one Activities	Missing	N
Very proud	149 (50.5)	51 (17.3)	24 (8.1)	27 (9.2)	9 (3.1)	35 (11.9)	295 (100.0)
Rather proud	239 (51.7)	65 (14.1)	69 (14.9)	41 (8.9)	7 (1.5)	41 (8.9)	462 (100.0)
Not very proud	81 (40.7)	15 (7.5)	10 (5.0)	25 (12.6)	28 (14.1)	40 (20.1)	199 (100.0)
Not at all proud	23 (33.3)	5 (7.2)	7 (10.1)	8 (11.6)	12 (17.4)	14 (20.3)	69 (100.0)

Pearson's $r = -.23$, $p < .00$.

Past political alienation: "Thinking back to before the tragedy—that is, before September 2004—how proud were you to be a Russian citizen?"

	No Activities	One Activity	Two or Three activities	Four to Ten Activities	Eleven to Thirty-one Activities	Missing	N
Very proud	230 (45.3)	61 (12.0)	65 (12.8)	50 (9.8)	32 (6.3)	70 (13.8)	508 (100.0)
Rather proud	225 (50.0)	64 (14.2)	36 (8.0)	42 (9.3)	23 (5.1)	60 (13.3)	450 (100.0)
Not very proud	42 (53.8)	10 (12.8)	7 (9.0)	6 (7.7)	2 (2.6)	11 (14.1)	78 (100.0)
Not at all proud	8 (53.3)	1 (6.7)	2 (13.3)	2 (13.3)	0 (0.0)	2 (13.3)	15 (100.0)

Pearson's $r = .04$, $p < .21$.

Changed political alienation: decreased pride in Russia since the 2004 tragedy (difference between responses to "How proud are you to be a Russian citizen?" and "Thinking back to before the tragedy—that is, before September 2004—how proud were you to be a Russian citizen?")

	No Activities	One Activity	Two or Three Activities	Four to Ten Activities	Eleven to Thirty-one Activities	Missing	N
Pride increased	15 (46.9)	12 (37.5)	1 (3.1)	2 (6.3)	0 (0.0)	2 (6.3)	32 (100.0)
Pride stayed same	351 (53.3)	97 (14.7)	61 (9.3)	66 (10.0)	15 (2.3)	69 (10.5)	659 (100.0)
Pride decreased one to two steps	116 (42.6)	24 (8.8)	43 (15.8)	20 (7.4)	16 (5.9)	53 (19.5)	272 (100.0)
Pride decreased three to four steps	24 (25.5)	6 (6.4)	6 (6.4)	16 (17.0)	26 (27.7)	16 (17.0)	94 (100.0)

Pearson's $r = .34$, $p < .00$.
$N = 1,098$; number of victims (%).

Table 7.5. Shame and Blame and Political Participation

Shame in Russia: "How often do you feel ashamed of Russia?"

	No Activities	One Activity	Two or Three Activities	Four to Ten Activities	Eleven to Thirty-one Activities	Missing	N
Hardly ever	53 (53.0)	12 (12.0)	11 (11.0)	6 (6.0)	2 (2.0)	16 (16.0)	100 (100.0)
Not very often	216 (55.5)	63 (16.2)	49 (12.6)	18 (4.6)	5 (1.3)	38 (9.8)	389 (100.0)
Rather often	168 (45.8)	31 (8.4)	28 (7.6)	58 (15.8)	11 (3.0)	71 (19.3)	367 (100.0)
Very often	34 (27.4)	13 (10.5)	11 (8.9)	18 (14.5)	32 (25.8)	16 (12.9)	124 (100.0)

Pearson's $r = .32$, $p < .00$.

Blame toward President Putin: "Speaking just about the central authorities, please tell me whether you think the following authorities are very guilty, somewhat guilty, not very guilty, or not at all guilty for causing this tragedy? *President Vladimir Putin*"

	No Activities	One Activity	Two or Three Activities	Four to Ten Activities	Eleven to Thirty-one Activities	Missing	N
Not at all guilty	46 (46.0)	17 (17.0)	16 (16.0)	10 (10.0)	2 (2.0)	9 (9.0)	100 (100.0)
Not very guilty	163 (56.0)	31 (10.7)	42 (14.4)	24 (8.2)	3 (1.0)	28 (9.6)	291 (100.0)
Somewhat guilty	185 (50.3)	55 (14.9)	27 (7.3)	32 (8.7)	13 (3.5)	56 (15.2)	368 (100.0)
Very guilty	97 (37.3)	26 (10.0)	23 (8.8)	33 (12.7)	38 (14.6)	43 (16.5)	260 (100.0)

Pearson's $r = .23$, $p < .00$.

Dissatisfaction with punishment of guilty federal officials: "Now I will state some demands that have been made by several Beslan victims. Can you tell me whether in your opinion these demands have been completely satisfied, mostly satisfied, mostly not satisfied, not satisfied at all? *Punishment of federal officials who are guilty for what happened*"

	No Activities	One Activity	Two or Three Activities	Four to Ten Activities	Eleven to Thirty-one Activities	Missing	N
Completely satisfied	17 (44.7)	8 (21.1)	3 (7.9)	6 (15.8)	0 (0.0)	4 (10.5)	38 (100.0)
Mostly satisfied	22 (37.9)	6 (10.3)	9 (15.5)	1 (1.7)	1 (1.7)	19 (32.8)	58 (100.0)
Mostly not satisfied	242 (49.8)	66 (13.6)	49 (10.1)	58 (11.9)	20 (4.1)	51 (10.5)	486 (100.0)
Not satisfied at all	212 (46.9)	54 (11.9)	45 (10.0)	36 (8.0)	37 (8.2)	68 (15.0)	452 (100.0)

Pearson's $r = .07$, $p < .03$.

$N = 1,098$; number of victims (%).

The Supposed Conditionality of Political Alienation?

Some studies have proposed that political alienation has significant effects on either retaliatory violence or political participation, but the effects depend on other variables. For example, political pride (sometimes conceived as "system justification" or "procedural fairness") is hypothesized to reduce anger, which in turn decreases political action (van Zomeren et al. 2004; Jost et al. 2012). As already shown in Chapter 5's discussion of anger, such hypotheses find no support in the Beslan data. Anger and political alienation have independent effects on political participation, and anger has no statistically significant effect on support for retaliatory violence, whereas political alienation has an independent negative effect. The variables are not significant in interaction with one another, and one does not mediate the effects of the other.

Blame too has been hypothesized to influence retaliatory violence or political participation through its effects on other variables. For example, the attribution of blame supposedly triggers anger, which then motivates political participation (Valentino et al. 2011:159). Again, as described in Chapter 5, despite multiple— sometimes competing and sometimes complementary hypotheses—about blame heightening anger or anger heightening blame, the Beslan data offer no support for these hypotheses. Anger is correlated with blaming Putin and dissatisfaction with the punishment of political officials at low or nonsignificant levels ($r = .13$ and $.07$, $p < .001$ and $.08$, respectively), and to the extent that each variable has effects on support for retaliatory violence or political participation, the effects are independent.

Political alienation and blame are also hypothesized to be conditional on efficacy, either political efficacy or self-efficacy or both. The lack of political pride supposedly motivates political action only for someone who feels empowered, and the presence of political pride supposedly motivates support for retaliatory violence only for someone who feels empowered. Or perhaps the feeling of political pride is itself empowering, and politically proud individuals feel more in control, so there should be a significant negative relationship between political alienation and efficacy.

These quite plausible propositions also find no support in the Beslan data. As Table 7.6 shows, when interactions between political alienation and political efficacy or between political alienation and self-efficacy are added to models of support for retaliatory violence—either the full model in Chapter 11 or reduced models of just alienation, efficacy, and the interaction term—the interactions are not statistically significant. Neither are interactions of blame with political efficacy or blame with self-efficacy (not shown). When the same interactions are added to models of political participation, they are also not statistically significant. Political alienation and political blame do have effects on support for

Table 7.6. Hypothesized Interactive Effects of Political Alienation/Blame and Efficacy

Political alienation might be conditional on . . .	Hypothesis: Political alienation leads to support for retaliatory ethnic violence when victims . . .	Hypothesis: Political alienation leads to political participation when victims . . .	Measurement	Finding
Political efficacy	. . . perceive that political action is effective.		Self-assessment of how politically informed	No support for either hypothesis
			Perceived effectiveness of demonstrating or protesting	No support for either hypothesis
Self-efficacy	. . . perceive that personal action is effective.		Perceived ability to help solve problems that led to tragedy	No support for either hypothesis

* See Table 11.4 for precise survey questions and descriptive statistics.

retaliatory violence (negatively) and political participation (positively), but these effects are direct and not conditional on other factors.

Nor does political alienation mediate the effects of efficacy or require efficacy as an intermediary variable. For political alienation to be causally prior to efficacy, or vice versa, the two variables would need to be significantly correlated. As Table 7.7 shows, political alienation is not significantly correlated with either measure of political efficacy or with self-efficacy. It is not the case that feelings of pride in Russian citizenship make individuals feel efficacious. Blame too is largely uncorrelated with efficacy, although there is a low correlation between blaming Putin and believing that demonstrating or protesting is an effective way to address dissatisfaction. Interestingly, the correlation is positive, meaning that those who blame Putin are more likely to find protest effective, which makes sense if the target of protest is the perceived culprit. The low correlation suggests that one mechanism for blame to motivate political participation is through its impact on perceived protest effectiveness, although blame also has direct effects on participation, as shown in Chapter 11.

The effects of political alienation are also not mediated by prejudice. Politically proud victims are no more or less prejudiced than politically alienated victims ($r = .06$, $p < .09$). They are more inclined than politically alienated victims to

Table 7.7. Political Alienation/Blame and Efficacy

	Politically Informed	Perceived Effectiveness of Protest	Self-Efficacy
Political alienation (decreased pride)	.05	.08	.06
Putin's guilt	.01	.14*	.01
Dissatisfaction with punishment of officials	−.10	.09	−.04

Correlations (Pearson's r); $N = 1,098$; * $p < 0.001$.

support retaliatory ethnic violence, but the mechanism connecting their alienation to their propensity for ethnic violence likely depends on government signals about the acceptability of violence, not government signals about the desirability of interethnic mingling. The effects of political alienation and prejudice on support for retaliation are also not conditional on one another; they are strong and independent.

Conclusion

Beslan victims varied in their attitudes toward their country and its leaders. A majority reported no change in their pride in being a Russian citizen since the hostage taking, but a strong minority reported decreased pride, and a very small minority reported increased pride. A majority thought President Putin was guilty for causing the tragedy, and a much larger majority was dissatisfied with the punishment of political officials who were guilty for their roles in the tragedy, but here too, minorities dissented. This variation had meaningful consequences for the aftermath of violence.

Politically alienated individuals are less likely to support retaliatory violence and more likely to participate in politics. In Beslan, victims whose pride in Russia stayed the same or increased after the violent hostage taking were, on average, the most likely to approve of killing Chechens in response. Victims whose pride in Russia decreased after the hostage taking were, on average, the most likely to become political activists. The findings about blaming Putin and dissatisfaction with the punishment of officials are not as robust as the findings about political alienation, but where their effects are significant, they are always in lockstep with the effects of political alienation, suggesting that they tap similar causal mechanisms.

Political alienation is thus one of the few links between the post-violence responses of retaliatory violence and political participation. The statistical

316 WHY POLITICS AND NONVIOLENCE?

analysis in Chapter 11 will show that support for retaliatory violence and political participation are independent outcomes: victims might support retaliatory violence, participate in political action, both, or neither. However, it is possible that a variable might help understand both outcomes due to its significant effects on both, and political alienation may be one such variable. From a normative perspective, political alienation is especially important because it has the desired "politics not violence" effects. A politically alienated victim has a higher probability than other victims of becoming a nonviolent activist.

In the literature on violent and political behavior, political alienation has fallen somewhat out of fashion, possibly due to the methodological challenges of measuring and testing its influence. Instead, the non-political social world has recently generated much more interest, especially the subjects of social alienation, social support, and social networks. These are the subjects of the next chapter. However, findings from the Beslan victims provide a powerful argument to return attention to the disenchantment of aggrieved individuals with their country.

8

Social Alienation versus Social Support

A different kind of alienation, social alienation, is often presumed to influence support for retaliatory violence and political participation. The term "social alienation" is no longer extensively used in social science research, but the concept drives many investigations of its opposite, social integration and support. Social alienation is an implicit consideration in research on social capital and the component concepts of interpersonal trust, informal social networks, and formal associational activity, where the sometimes unstated and sometimes explicit mission is to prevent or counter widespread social alienation. Victims of violence are particularly susceptible to social alienation, especially after the violent death of a child (Murphy, Johnson, and Lohan 2002). However, victims also may vary in their real and perceived social integration or estrangement and especially in the most basic sense of whether or not they feel the concern and support of their fellow citizens who were not victimized.

This chapter explores how the victims of the Beslan school hostage taking related to each other and to Russian society in the aftermath of violence. The bulk of the analysis is qualitative, based on extensive focus group discussions that often dominated the allotted time. The social dimensions of life after the hostage taking were among the topics that focus group participants found most engaging. The chapter thus offers an in-depth exploration of victim networks and divisions and of the victim organizations Mothers of Beslan and Voice of Beslan, from the perspectives of victims who were active in these organizations and victims who were not. On the quantitative side, the chapter reports the victims' perspectives on Russian society and its interest in their plight.

Social alienation turns out not to be a very powerful factor in explaining responses to violence. In Beslan, social alienation is both limited and rampant, depending on how the term is conceived, and the contradictory forces of strong social networks and hard feelings seemed to push victims both toward and away from action. While there is some evidence that socially alienated victims are more supportive of retaliatory violence than other victims, the relationship is statistically and substantively weaker than expected, and social alienation plays no role in peaceful political participation after the hostage taking. These nonsignificant findings represent an important contribution in the context of prevailing assumptions to the contrary and in counteracting publication bias against null results (Franco et al. 2014).

After Violence. Debra Javeline, Oxford University Press. © Oxford University Press 2023.
DOI: 10.1093/oso/9780197683347.003.0009

Social Alienation after Violence

The term "social alienation" dates back to its Hegelian and Marxian roots and has been the subject of longstanding debates about its meaning. The term has referred at times to social structure and the objective reality of alienation and at times to the perception of that reality. Scholars have also debated about the nature and number of dimensions to the alienation concept. That the concept is multidimensional has been generally accepted, and dimensions of social alienation have been said to include powerlessness, meaninglessness, normlessness, cultural estrangement, self-estrangement, and social isolation (e.g., Seeman 1975). Within each dimension supposedly lay even more dimensions, such as unhappiness, negativism, loneliness, and despair.

The multidimensionality of social alienation makes it difficult to analyze. Scholars have sometimes referred to the "disunities rather than the unity of alienation" or "versions of alienation" (Seeman 1975:95). Therefore, to understand a phenomenon such as the aftermath of violence, it may be most productive to isolate for investigation one or two dimensions of social alienation that are potentially most relevant and analytically precise. For the aftermath of the Beslan school hostage taking in particular, those dimensions are powerlessness, discussed in Chapter 9 under its mirror-image concept, efficacy, and social isolation, or "the sense of exclusion or rejection vs social acceptance," discussed here (Seeman 1975:94).

Social alienation will thus be defined in the narrow and conceptually clear sense of estrangement and the perceived lack of social support and connectedness. Socially alienated individuals believe that others in society do not care about them. They believe that their thoughts and feelings are misunderstood or uninteresting to others in society and their well-being is a low priority for others. After a violent episode, these beliefs are common, particularly as the news cycle moves on and distant nonvictim citizens or, more devastating, community members grow "fatigued." The perception that one's personal tragedy has exhausted its time in the public attention space may be accurate or inaccurate; in either case, it is the perception that constitutes social alienation.

The state of social alienation is widely thought to be undesirable. Effects may include poor academic performance, deviant behavior, anxiety, loneliness, suicidal ideation, and other mental and physical health outcomes (Ernst and Cacioppo 1999; Lane and Daugherty 1999; Joiner 2005; Heinrich and Gullone 2006; O'Donnell et al. 2006; Van Orden et al. 2008; Justice 2018). After experiencing violence and profound loss, the objective absence of social support is problematic for logistical and emotional reasons, and the perceived absence of social support is frequently associated with psychological distress (Ifeagwazi et al. 2015). Fortunately, not all victims share perceptions of exclusion, rejection, isolation, and the callous indifference of the nonvictim world. Victims may vary in their degree of social alienation, and some may feel support from the nonvictim community and believe that others do care about their horrible situation.

Social Alienation and Support in Beslan

In many ways, Beslan might be described as a place with little social alienation. The small town represents one big social network where families have lived and mingled for generations. Social support, real and perceived, seemed pervasive, and the interconnectedness of the town's residents probably served to homogenize attitudes, particularly assessments of non-Ossetian Russian society.

During the hostage taking, the Beslan community coalesced even further, forming crowds outside the school. Many news reports described a dark side to these bonds: heavily armed vigilantes were said to have surrounded the school, some who potentially opened fire and inadvertently killed the very people they were trying to save (Voronov 2006). However, North Ossetia's Kesayev commission concluded the opposite, that community members were not perpetrators but saviors.

> It was only thanks to civilians from among the residents of Beslan and other cities and regions of Ossetia that the evacuation of the wounded became possible. . . . The role of ordinary residents of Ossetia in the release of hostages is invaluable. (Voronov 2006:8).

After the hostage taking, people in Beslan added to their bonds of kinship and residency the new bond of victimization. In the words of a male nonactivist victim, "This tragedy affected each family, because all relatives know each other here." While some victims moved away from Beslan as a means of coping, the interconnectedness and deep local patriotism kept most victims in place, carving out a future for themselves and their town together. Female nonactivist victims explained:

VALYA: I have the desire to pick up and leave, only not to save myself but for the children. The children, only this. And then I think, I will leave, she will leave, everybody will leave, we all will leave. And what will happen to our Beslan, to our Ossetia? That's what I think. Ossetians will simply disappear. And this is somehow frightful. Why? For what? We don't deserve such a shameful disappearance, extermination. We should do the opposite. I sometimes condemn those who left. They shouldn't have left. Everyone should have stayed. We should have demonstrated our strength. We should be here, should work here, should make it famous here.

VERA: Yes, we should raise our Ossetian Republic, our nation.

Discussions were peppered with "we" and "us" and sometimes blended feelings of social support and community embeddedness with ethnic and regional pride, as exemplified by male nonactivist victims discussing the possibility of moving:

BORIS: Those who wanted [to leave] have left, but I don't think there were very many of them.

RUSLAN: Where are they waiting for us? All people live in their own places [where they were born]. People live where they live. Maybe a few people, as Borya says, have left. For example, Russians lived here, were taken [hostages] here, and went to their parents.

ARKADY: And they want to return.

RUSLAN: And they probably also want to return.

ARKADY: No, we don't want to leave. That's for sure.

TAMERLAN: Not only we. Everyone. Koreans, Russians. So many acquaintances live all over Russia, and they say, "I will go crazy here. I want home."

RUSLAN: Everybody wants to return to Ossetia, because Ossetians are a peace-loving people.

One male activist victim over thirty-five years old summed up the sentiment emphatically:

KAZBEK: I personally am not going to leave. Even if an atomic bomb explodes here, I won't leave. . . . Everyone lives here. And the majority of people in the city know each other. They are relatives or friends.

Equally emphatic were some of the female activist victims over thirty-five years old.

LARISA: Generally speaking, we are very attached to our motherland.

DINA: I wouldn't go anywhere, even if I were offered a mansion abroad or something else. I love my town to that extent.

However, the hostage taking itself introduced divisiveness and animosity to Beslan and may have weakened bonds and perceived social support. A major division emerged between parents of dead children and parents of surviving but psychologically damaged and often gravely injured or ill children. The latter parents, as well as parents who were former hostages themselves and managed to stay alive, often felt survivors' guilt and claimed they were made to feel this way. Teachers and school administrators who lived through the ordeal suffered perhaps the worst survivors' guilt and public condemnation. Many residents in this once close-knit community felt their neighbors' insensitivity and disregard. In the aftermath of the hostage taking, feelings of social support gave way to feelings of mistreatment and resentment. "Everyone blames everyone, and no one has pity for anyone" (Naidenov 2005a).

In a focus group of female activist victims over thirty-five, participants straightforwardly discussed survivors' guilt and divisions within the Beslan community:

DINA: You know, Beslan was always a quiet peaceful town. Everyone knew everyone else. We were glad to see each other. But after this . . .

LARISA: It is very complicated to live here. You can't even imagine how complicated it is to live. Because when I see the woman who has lost her child, I even feel somehow guilty before her that this child sat near me in that gym, and he didn't survive. Honestly, I feel guilty. What should I tell her? And there are so many such people around! Can you imagine how complicated it is to look into each other's eyes.

TATIANA: You know that it wasn't your fault, and still you have a heavy heart. In Beslan, there are people who suffered and those who did not. The people who did not suffer for the most part sympathize with us. And there are some people, and there are quite a lot of them, among the victims as well, whose attitude to the victims is very negative. That's why it's difficult to live in Beslan, because you go along the street and you can hear an insult. During the first days after the terrorist act I heard, "You are alive, and my family is not. Why? You all should have died." It is very complicated when you live and know that there are people around you who hate you for that.

Beslan victims hurled many hurtful words at each other. Female nonactivist victims shared some of these encounters:

VERA: Some kind of hatred appeared. Why are your children alive? We were told this to our faces. . . . Why have your children survived?

INDIRA: At the expense of our dead children, your children survived. . . . You hid behind their backs, and therefore your children survived.

VALYA: I was just outraged when parents were saying behind my mother's back, "You survived because you didn't save the children. If you had saved the children, you wouldn't have survived." My mother says, "I was there with my only grandson when everything exploded. We flew apart." . . . And how many people accused teachers!

ZINAIDA: [Recalling an encounter with the grandmother of one of her students] She says, "You survived. Why did you survive, and my grandson died?" Are we people? How can someone say that?

Indeed, Beslan teachers felt so verbally harassed in their hometown that they sent a letter to Vladimir Putin a year after the crisis:

> We—the teachers—have been the object of constant criticism all year. We were accused of surviving. We were accused of non-fulfillment of our professional duties (while only special forces troops are professionals in those situations). They (local people) tried to split up our group. All this affected both us and our students and undermined our authority in their opinion ("Beslan Teachers Send" 2005).

> We were all in that [gym] hall, death threatened us, and many of our colleagues died. Many of those who survived lost their children and relatives. And we also have the right, unfortunately, to be called victims. ("Beslan Teachers Write to Putin" 2005)[1]

Male former hostages were unlikely to survive the hostage taking and were subject to particular resentment if they did, especially if they were teachers. In the patriarchal, macho culture of North Ossetia, a man who survives was considered by many to have been a coward or collaborator (Phillips 2007:87). Alik Tsagolov, the school's fifty-four-year-old physical education teacher, was one of those few survivors, and during the Kulayev trial, a female victim challenged, "I remember that you weren't made to leave the gym like the rest. But you're a man too, aren't you? And you were sitting right beside the path through the middle of the gym, weren't you?" After some back-and-forth, Tsagolov replied, "You'd need to ask the terrorists about why that was, wouldn't you? According to you, I should have filled out a form requesting them to shoot me?" (Phillips 2007:87–88).

Divisions also arose, often along the same fault lines, over the distribution of humanitarian aid and other financial issues. By mid-September 2004, various public and private foundations and organizations, Russian and foreign, had donated more than $30 million to Beslan victims. However, that money failed to reach most of the victims quickly and easily, and only twenty people had received an average of one million rubles (Vlasova 2004a). One year later, about one billion rubles had reportedly been transferred into the accounts of Beslan residents

---

[1] Original text of the teachers' letter to Putin can be found at http://www.echo.msk.ru/doc/102.html.

(Naidenov 2005a). As described in Chapter 2, the low compensation from the Russian government added insult to injury and contributed to political alienation. The *varying* compensation from all sources, with next of kin of deceased hostages receiving more than survivors and with some victims navigating the bureaucracy and receiving their money more quickly than others, contributed to social tensions and divisions.

Recipients of the compensation among female activist victims over thirty-five described these tensions and divisions:

TATIANA: At first, everyone was sympathetic. And then, probably after this humanitarian aid, all this started, people split up. And even my close neighbors looked at me differently, even envied me. And what did they envy? That we were given money?

FATIMA: Yes, yes, exactly. Even I was envied, although I lost my only child.

Female nonactivist victims who were not recipients of much compensation described the same tensions and divisions but through a different lens:

LARISA: There were families where parents couldn't afford to buy caramel for their child. And then families of the dead, they received such amounts of money, and then they certainly didn't realize themselves what they were doing. Forty days didn't pass after family members died, and these cars! These houses they built! It was just disgusting.

The increased purchasing power of some Beslan residents affected the housing market, nearly doubling the price of a three-room apartment (Naidenov 2005a). Rumor had it that a thousand new cars were in Beslan, and nine were involved in crashes, which some considered divine punishment for those who get rich off the blood of their relatives (Naidenov 2005a). Some recipients of humanitarian aid apparently flaunted their newfound wealth. One female under-thirty-five activist described a neighbor with two sons, one a firefighter who died in the school and another engaged to be married:

BELA: In our village, Ossetian village, many people are invited for the wedding, and neighbors and relatives always help. During thirty years of my life I have never seen anybody hiring waiters. Her son died in the terrorist act. He was killed. My neighbors. And it is clear for everybody where this money came from. In the street where I live everybody has about the same living standard.

And then came the apartments. In December 2004, Prime Minister Alexander Zhukov announced a new $49 million reconstruction project to finance Beslan's schools, an art institute, a nursery school, a hospital, and new apartment blocks for victims (Sands 2004b). In the focus group of female activist victims over thirty-five, participants discussed how the latter led victims to turn on each other:

LARISA: 1,200 hostages. They give fifty apartments to these 1,200 hostages. So, how should people [divide them]? From the very beginning, it was my personal opinion, I said that we all should have refused. We should have said, "Either give to everybody or to nobody." Because it was an apple of discord. It was the factor that distracted us from reality and turned people on one another. Why should you get it, not me?
BERTA: Let the children receive one apartment each, if they are entitled to it. And if not, they should have taken this amount and divided it equally among everyone. And no one would have said anything. Here they started dividing people into some kind of degrees, some kind of categories. When a child comes out and is immediately given a grave diagnosis, it starts: "No, he needs a different degree because this degree should be given to somebody else." Why did they start dividing people in this way?

The female nonactivist victims echoed these resentments about the distribution of apartments:

VALYA: To whom did they give them? Not the children, not the disabled children. Whom? It is not understood to whom these apartments were given. And I came, I said, "Tell me please, don't the rest need anything? Don't they need money? Don't they need apartments, some assistance, some attention, some treatment? Don't they need anything? We, the others, don't need anything?"
INDIRA: Be happy that you remain alive.

Female victims were far more inclined to discuss these divisions within the victim community, producing pages and pages of transcripts with great detail on specific incidents and the victims' impressions and feelings about the divisions. For the most part, the male victims refrained from discussing these issues, although given the same moderator prompts and opportunities. The male nonactivist victims seemed to know of the divisions created by controversies over distribution of material goods, as evidenced by the sentence or two in the transcripts, but the men were brief and thought it not worth elaboration:

BORIS: Do you know how much dirt there was there? I don't want to go into all this, with distribution of humanitarian aid, things, to say nothing of money. You won't believe what was going on! I don't want to get into all this.

Perhaps the more important aspect of social alienation involves the relationship of Beslan victims to the larger Russian society. For reasons noted below, the felt support or indifference of citizens outside the aggrieved community has been hypothesized to motivate reactions to violence. However, this topic generated less discussion in focus groups. As most victims saw it, Russian citizens reacted with interest and concern. Some victims experienced this concern directly during trips for medical treatment outside North Ossetia, where they were kindly received. Female nonactivist victims recounted the kindness:

LARISA: We were the first to go [for psychological rehabilitation], the very first group on September 18 to Sochi. . . . But for this trip, probably the children would have perceived all this differently, but there was so much attention and care there.

ZARINA: Yes, it helped our children a lot.

LARISA: Even waiters in the cafeteria, in the restaurant—they took care of these children as if they had been their own. I myself, for example, had no strength for that.

ZARINA: They distracted them.

LARISA: And they understood us much better. We got esteem, respect, sympathy, everything.

Social Alienation, Social Support, and Retaliatory Violence

Social alienation has long been linked to aggression and violence (Blalock 1967:43, 50; Horowitz 2001:351–352). Over half of lone-actor terrorists are socially isolated, whether they are mentally ill or healthy (Corner and Gill 2015). Low levels of social trust and low membership in voluntary associations—components of social capital that are related to social alienation—are linked to higher levels of violence, with causality likely running in both directions and with social (dis)trust and violence having the more robust relationship (Galea et al. 2002; Hansen-Nord et al. 2014). Social alienation presumably plays a role in anti-state violence (della Porta 1995), school violence (Baker 1998), rural youth violence (Osgood and Chambers 2000), soccer hooliganism and skinhead activity (Piotrowski 2004), and other aggressive behavior. The virtues of social integration and attachment and the dangers of social alienation seem widely accepted.

However, there is also evidence that most perpetrators of xenophobic collective violence are not marginalized within their local communities and are often employed, from stable families, and otherwise socially integrated (Green et al. 2001:494; McDoom 2013:454). Most participants in deadly ethnic riots are not socially marginal but are quite ordinary (Horowitz 2001:264–266). Even terrorists often have high levels of social support (Lee 2011). Prejudice— demonstrated in Beslan to be a forerunner of retaliatory ethnic violence—is no more likely among the alienated than the integrated (Gibson and Howard 2007:215).

A potential resolution to these contradictory findings may be found in the group or population in which an individual is alienated: social isolation from the wider community, accompanied by identification and cohesion within the aggrieved community, increases the acceptability of violence (Bhui et al. 2014). For example, it is plausible that the hostage taking itself was perpetrated by socially alienated Ingush, Chechens, and other militants (at least, those who were not coerced into the effort and not psychopathic). Believing that few people outside their networks understood, agreed and sympathized with, or even knew about their plight, they committed the heinous act to draw attention to their cause. Taking children hostage at a school might make the otherwise uncaring world care or at least take notice. The entire Chechen community is sometimes described as alienated and therefore prone to a higher percentage of violent actors than other communities.

> Leaving Chechnya in ruins after the first war, Russia alienated Chechnya, strangling it financially and cutting it off from the outside world. Some in Chechnya naturally turned to Islamic extremism, which was the only thing available that could provide them with moral and material support. The same thing has happened with some suicide recruiters and recruits. They have been alienated and abandoned. They have nowhere to turn, but to that which gives them moral and material salvation—Islamic extremism. (Reuter 2004:27)

Chechen terrorist organizations offer a support community, and fellow terrorists become "brothers" (Speckhard and Ahkmedova 2006:484).

The causal mechanism linking social alienation to retaliatory ethnic violence often hinges on a third contextual variable: community support for the violence itself. Indifference to aggrieved individuals, real or perceived, is rarely theorized directly to incite socially alienated individuals to act violently. Absent other factors, the perception that others don't care could plausibly contribute to anxiety or other emotions, described in Chapter 5, that do not prompt violence. Rather, the perceived indifference seems to matter when like-minded others legitimize both the perception *and* the appropriateness, justifiability, and even necessity of a violent response (Horowitz 2001:360–370). Solidarity among the alienated, particularly when they share a race, neighborhood, ethnic identification, religion, history, or acquaintances, provides a basis for would-be retaliators to predict comfortably how others will react, behaviorally and attitudinally, to retaliation (Rule 1988:266–267).

Thus, retaliatory ethnic violence is often a product of an unusual mixture of estrangement and integration. The socially alienated victims feel a lack of social support for their grievances outside the community, but if they feel strong social support for their violent reaction—community approval of retaliation—that reaction is more likely. Notably, the social norms surrounding retaliatory violence are also relevant for non-alienated victims. The independent role for social alienation in the story of retaliation may be modest.

Social Alienation, Social Support, and Political Action

The relationship between social alienation and political participation is less clear (Seeman 1975:99). On the one hand, social alienation, like political alienation, might provide a context of dissatisfaction and thus motivate post-violence participation. Evidence of socially alienated individuals participating in peaceful institutional politics includes supporters of Belgium's extreme right-wing party, the Vlaams Blok, who tended to feel socially isolated (Billiet and de Witte 1995) and who live in municipalities with weak associational networks (Coffé et al. 2007). Homicide survivors and other crime victims often seek out or create political organizations as a form of social support in attempts to overcome their isolation and powerlessness (Bateson 2012:572). Indeed, getting to know interesting people and making new friends may be an "affiliation incentive" or "social network selective incentive" that motivates otherwise unnetworked individuals to participate in politics (Muller, Dietz, and Finkel 1991). If individuals are already locally networked, their joint feeling of social alienation from the outside world may facilitate participation.

On the other hand, the perception of having problems that are of little concern to others might be demobilizing. Joining an activist group or participating in its activities depends to some degree on feeling the group's interest and support, which may give a sense of empowerment or affirm anger (van Zomeren et al. 2004). Successful redress of grievances in the political arena depends on public interest and support. If aggrieved individuals believe the interest and support is minimal or absent, joining activities may seem unrewarding and unpleasant, success may seem unlikely, and participation not worth the bother.

These two contrary forces might coexist within communities and even individuals and thus counteract each other: "Others don't care, which makes me aggrieved and want to act politically, but the fact that others don't care makes me feel unwelcome in activist circles and pessimistic about success and not want to act politically." In such cases, social alienation fails to explain political participation or the lack thereof.

When aggrieved individuals are not alienated—when they perceive that their concerns are shared by members of their own and the larger community—they might get just the boost they need for initial and ongoing political mobilization. Socially integrated individuals are more likely to vote, protest, and engage in other political action (McAdam 1982; Verba et al. 1995; Rüdig and Karyotis 2014:9), and they are more likely to be targets of mobilization in their preexisting networks (Klandermans and Oegema 1987). Group mobilization often depends on solidarity, or the shared sense of identity, fate, and commitment to the group (Fireman and Gamson 1988).

As with retaliatory violence, social alienation may have less powerful effects on political participation than the contextual factor of social norms about participation. When activism is held in high community regard, individuals sometimes go beyond avoidance of free-riding and seek out participation and take pride in activism (Chong 1991; Wood 2003). When activism is not held in high regard, or when there is community ambivalence, individuals are less likely to participate. In either case, the independent role of social alienation is complicated and unclear.

Social Alienation, Social Support, and Political Action in Beslan

Post-tragedy Beslan illustrates these complexities. Given the strong longstanding social networks and tragedy-prompted divisions within those networks, individuals in Beslan were at once integrated and alienated, pushed simultaneously to participate and to resist and resent participation. The push to participate at the aggregate level may have been aided by the relative lack of social alienation even from the wider Russian society: most victims sensed the concern of fellow Russian citizens outside the Beslan community. However, the relative homogeneity in perceived support again suggests a nonsignificant relationship between social alienation and political participation.

Certainly, local integration promoted participation. The small close-knit nature of the Beslan community prior to the hostage taking may be an objective contextual factor that varied little across individuals and therefore contributed to the unprecedented political mobilization in the aftermath. Although expectations of high turnout have been theorized to increase "free riding" and depress mobilization, significant evidence suggests the opposite: that group solidarity is an important determinant of participation. Aggrieved individuals are more likely to mobilize for events when they expect crowds of others to do the same (Klandermans 1984; Muller and Opp 1986; Klandermans and Oegema 1987;

Chong 1991). Small communities with informal networks allow individuals to support and even verify their expectations about turnout. They provide easy visibility of the actual protest actions, the absence of neighbors from their homes on days of action, and the communication of planned attendance at those actions. For example, the female activist victims thirty-five years old and younger explained how victims and other residents learned about rallies and other events:

BELLA: We were informed. People were somehow informed. There were no official sources of information. The people I knew, my relatives, called me and let me know. Because it was a personal matter for everyone.

BELA: I think these rallies were all spontaneous. For example, neighbors dropped in and said, "Let's go." For example, even when the road was blocked . . .

MADINA: Bella was correct in saying that there were no sources of information. Compared to Moscow or some other big city, ours is a very small town, and everyone knows each other. Everything is out in the open. One person said something, and it's heard on the other end of town. So, this wasn't a problem.

VIKA: Each funeral was a kind of rally.

VERA: There were funerals for a whole month. Naturally, all of Beslan went to the home that buried somebody.

VIKA: Not a month, two months.

VERA: Two months indeed. It was quite natural that the people gathered together.

Even nonactivist female victims confirmed that information about political action was accessible and that most victims were networked. There were few social obstacles to participation. Nonactivists were not especially alienated or especially integrated.

VERA: [Asked if information reached her.] Yes.

LARISA: A person learned about everything by telephone. No information was ever published in the newspaper or anywhere else. It was by hearsay.

Very quickly, the spontaneous and unorganized gave way to the organized: Members of Mothers of Beslan and Voice of Beslan devoted considerable thought and time into well-planned events. Still, social networks were crucial to attendance at these events and may have even led some victims to devalue the organizations' contributions. For example, in a discussion about the blockade of the federal highway, male activist victims over thirty-five years old tried to recall the level of organization:

KAZBEK: It came about spontaneously.

TOTRAZ: I wouldn't say that it was spontaneous. People were there.

KAZBEK: Mostly women initiated that.

TOTRAZ: Let's say I heard about it and went there immediately, but I didn't go just to look at what people were doing there. I went to listen and to support. It was purposeful. . . . There were mostly women. This committee, Mothers of Beslan. Generally speaking, it was their initiative.

KAZBEK: And then others heard about it, by phone or orally, and everyone started gathering there.

BORIS: As they say, word of mouth. People heard about it and went there, and that's all.

As time passed and rallies were organized, knowledge of their existence and the call to action continued to be spread by word of mouth through social networks. Activism was enhanced not just by the proximity of victims to one another but by their sense of community and collective fate. In a focus group of male activist victims thirty-five years old or younger, participants discussed whether they would do what the Mothers of Beslan asked them to do, whether it be signing a petition, participating in a protest, or joining in some event:

VLADIMIR: Yes. We'll support them. This is also our bond in misfortune.

ALAN: We'll do all we can.

However, political action itself can be divisive. Activist victims may seek and find social support among similarly engaged victims, and an unintentional by-product of these newly created bonds may be to enhance the perceived isolation of the nonactivist bystanders, who in turn make the activists feel misunderstood and isolated. Distrust, suspicion, scorn, and hostility can result. In Beslan, nonactivists frequently expressed these sentiments about the activists.

BORIS: Why did they create these organizations, Mothers of Beslan and Voice of Beslan? Voice of Beslan—who created this organization in general? Why was it created? All right, Mothers of Beslan was created spontaneously, and if you didn't like this [organization], you went and created a different one for yourself. And what are they engaged in? What do they do?

VALERY: Maybe they look for some advantage?

BORIS: Of course, they look for some advantage, both organizations. And they know themselves what advantage they look for, what they want and what they do. . . . Nobody even voted for them. They just formed it.

The divisiveness and resentment manifested in judgmental descriptions of the activists as self-serving and attention-seeking. Even those who themselves participated heavily in political action judged the top-level activists as performing the role of mourner and questioned the sincerity of the activism. The female activist victims under thirty-five explained:

VERA: They [the activists] display their grief everywhere. The child was killed. I understand, the child was killed. But somehow you get the impression that this is all for show. Okay, you don't take off your mourning scarf. It's your right. Wear your mourning scarf.

IRINA: But there ought to be some actions . . .

VERA: There ought to be some actions. You know how it is? The TV shows how they are going to Italy, they are going to some other place, they are going on holiday.

BELLA: Let me explain what is obvious to all of us. We have a certain national trait, a certain mentality. If you wear mourning clothes and go into mourning, you have to observe certain principles, canons, and it is unacceptable to break them. . . . Vera wants to say that they keep solely to the external appearance but . . . their behavior is at variance with the concepts.

These nonactivist/activist/super-activist divisions often overlapped with the divisions between parents of children killed versus injured. The two major issues of dispute were financial (for example, divvying up humanitarian aid) and the different nature of the heartbreaks of losing a child and caring for a sick or injured child. Many victims who lost children gravitated toward the organizations Mothers of Beslan and Voice of Beslan and their mission and goals of truth and punishment. Many victims whose children survived were often kept busy tending to injuries and trauma and other intensive parental caregiving and often had less time for activism but wanted the victim organizations to have a different focus: securing services for injured children. The female nonactivist victims explained:

VERA: In the beginning, the Committee immediately consisted of women who lost their children. That is to say, a kind of split occurred, and those who lost their children at some point started to relate to us completely differently.

LARISA: [After describing her daughter's still untreated shrapnel wounds.] They started [saying], "Your children have survived. What else do you need?" I don't need anything. I only wish that my child was well. And if you come to this Committee, such glances! What are you doing here? As though I wasn't involved in the terrorist act but was sitting on the third floor. I don't know. I personally think that's why I don't participate.

VALYA: I came to the Committee not long ago. If you can, please give advice. I don't ask for money. Just give some advice. In general, one answer was given to all my questions: "We don't need any of this because our children don't need it. You need this—you go." Each time they direct us to that thought: "Create your own committee for wounded children or some other children, your own Mothers' Committee. If you need our help, we will help, give advice how to organize everything, how to do everything."

INDIRA: They succeeded in getting benefits for the dead ones. When the survivors turned to them asking what they should do, they said, "You also will succeed. We have succeeded. You also will succeed in getting benefits." They did for themselves. We don't discuss anything.

Parents of surviving children wanted help with paperwork, finances, and logistics for international travel to seek medical treatment. They even wanted advocacy for basic services: a maternity hospital, school meals, and school heating. Many female focus group discussions turned to the minutiae of expenses in Beslan, such as the price of potatoes or butter for children's school lunch, and the corruption that leads to overcharges for such ordinary items. If they did not receive satisfactory assistance, they were upset: "This does not concern the Mother's Committee. Living children are not their business," as one under-thirty-five activist remarked. Also upset were the activists on the receiving end of what might have seemed impossible and insensitive demands.

The positions of the different types of victims are understandable. On the one hand, the parents of wounded kids desperately needed help and thought that help should be forthcoming from organizations claiming to represent all victims. On the other hand, the Mothers of Beslan and Voice of Beslan were NGOs, volunteer organizations. The leaders were parents who suffered and invested a tremendous number of hours trying to redress their grievances. They did not share one specific grievance with the parents of surviving kids: getting those kids medical and other kinds of attention. To ask them to take on this additional burden on a volunteer basis when that work would also contribute to their grief—helping other people's children when their own were dead—may have simply been too much for them. Seeing each side was tremendously difficult in Beslan, and focus group discussions suggest that empathy was in short supply. Parents of surviving children were often sure that material benefits motivated the poor parents who lost kids, whereas the activists resented that the parents of surviving kids failed to appreciate their better situation and that the mission of the activism was the quest for the truth.

Some nonactivist victims challenged the motives behind the activists:

VERA: [Responding to whether the purpose of the Mothers of Beslan and Voice of Beslan was to get material benefits] Such a conclusion is suggested.

ANGELA: So it turns out.

LARISA: Material benefits.

VALYA: They also received a pile of money for the [Teachers'] Committee and divided it between themselves.

VERA: Now, when you see what houses some teachers built within a year, then I think you make some conclusions. I am from a family of teachers. I know what a teacher's salary is. And in a year such a house was built.

VALYA: . . . why didn't people like [my mother or other long-term, respected teachers] head this Committee and instead some imposters gathered there? They handled huge piles of money, and it's not clear what has become of this Committee.

ZINAIDA: But it quickly fell apart. About a half a year, not more.

VALYA: Right, they were dissolved. There was an inspection. They inspected them once, and that's all.

VERA: Cash receipts stopped. That was the end. I work in the government. Due to this, I know a bit more than others. I know where they [Committee members] went, what they wanted to get. It all came to receiving some money, a monetary sum.

VALYA: Leaving children in the middle of the school year and going on a three-week trip!

ZINAIDA: They were in Spain and in Italy and who knows where.

VALENTINA: They traveled the whole world. A certain group of teachers.

Some victims were sympathetic to the activist parents of dead children and indicated that these activists did indeed work on behalf of surviving children. Female activists over thirty-five recounted some of these achievements:

TATIANA: They sent many children to Germany to get treatment. Sent many of them to the sanatorium and helped to send them via the ministry. As it was, they have done a lot.

DIANA: At one time boys who were in the terrorist attack were taken to the army. When it was said that these children shouldn't be drafted, they helped. Women got together whose sons were taken to the army and went to this Committee. Mothers of Beslan helped them. They were not drafted into the army and, I think, they even said that boys who were in a terrorist attack wouldn't be drafted.

Activists were also seen as praiseworthy by victims who hoped to keep the world interested in Beslan. Such victims in a sense hoped not to be socially alienated—in Beslan, Russia, and the globe—and acknowledged that activists within the victim community were central to this goal. As one female activist over thirty-five explained:

LARISA: They maintain contacts with the whole world. . . . I personally don't condemn them because no matter how they work and what they do, I would like to think that, at least, thanks to them, it hasn't been forgotten. And the world somehow remembers us. I bow to them. These are people who have left their jobs, left their families, and they exist. . . . They are doing a good job. They demand things from the state.

However, the dominant sentiments expressed in the focus groups reflected social alienation. The alienation resulted not only from the different fates of their children and different preferred goals for victim organizations but also from differences of opinions, such as those concerning President Putin, appropriate advocacy methods, and the death penalty. As one female activist over thirty-five pointed out, the Mothers of Beslan "allegedly expresses the opinion of all victims, all hostages, although this is not the case."

Notably, many if not most victims expressed similar feelings of alienation from others in Beslan. Discussion in activist and nonactivist focus groups was similar, as participants felt misunderstood and uncared for. These feelings in some cases drew victims toward a specific victim organization, in some cases away from the organization itself but toward its activities, and in still other cases away from activism altogether. These different responses suggest that social alienation has few predictable political responses.

Consider, for example, that the following discussion took place among female under-thirty-five activists, who were dismayed at the financial aftermath of the hostage taking, critical of organizational leaders, but nevertheless quite active themselves:

BELA: Here we are talking about how they improperly distributed humanitarian aid. As far as I understand, as far as I remember, they didn't send as many refrigerators as there were victims. This was why the disagreements started. They couldn't divide something.

IRINA2: Humanitarian assistance arrived. They didn't call anybody. They distributed everything among themselves. If they needed people for rallies or signing some documents, they immediately called, gathered people. But on other occasions—nothing.

BELA: They seem to have been organized in the first place for taking care of themselves.

IRINA: Indeed, some aspects of their behavior made people think that they created this organization not to try to investigate the crime but to get as much money as they could for themselves.

Consider too the response to social alienation by Beslan's teachers, who were both victims and targets of blame. The response was not uniform, as female activist victims over thirty-five discussed:

TATIANA: I wouldn't participate anywhere myself, but my work demands it. I am a teacher. And, in principle, we all, teachers, should be ahead of others. After the terrorist act, we fell from grace. I am saying it in front of the girls [i.e., the others in the focus group]. First, people seemed to understand us, and then for some reason it turned out that we were guilty. . . . That is too much for us. . . . We didn't participate in anything for more than a year. They wrote different dirty things about us. We had to bear a lot. But then, anyway, even the teachers split up. When the Mothers' Committee invited us for the first time to participate in the action on June 1, not all teachers went. Only some teachers participated. That is, some still felt insulted, and some understood that it was necessary to go.

Because both activists and nonactivists also had their share of preexisting community in Beslan, the divisive impact of activism was probably not strong enough to distinguish either group as more alienated than the other. Social alienation in relation to the local community therefore probably played little role in the political aftermath.

Social Alienation and Social Movement Organizations

The ambivalent role of social alienation manifested among the upper echelons of Beslan's victim leaders. These leaders worked closely with one another as megaphones to attract and retain support for Beslan, yet they themselves often seemed to embody isolation and disconnectedness. They publicly and loudly withdrew support from each other at critical junctures and thus realistically perceived a lack of social support within their own inner circles, while retaining more intense support and care within new, smaller circles. Rivalries and cooperation between social movement organizations are common (Morris 1984), and the disagreements and divisions among Beslan's most vocal activists is worth special mention in any retelling of the aftermath of school massacre.

About a year after the hostage taking, a self-proclaimed faith healer and "new Christ" named Grigorii Grabovoi promised victims to resurrect their children by October 15, 2005, and asked for 1,000 euros ($1,195) per resurrected victim. Some of the members of the Mothers of Beslan, including its leader Susanna Dudiyeva, supported Grabovoi, despite news stories directly calling him a charlatan or cult leader. As a result, the Mothers of Beslan Committee split, with some members changing the organization by-laws and electing a new chair, Anna Totrova. Totrova explained that "[e]ven the strongest of us start listening to miraculous stories" (JAC 2005). On September 17, Dudiyeva and at least ten other Beslan mothers attended a meeting with Grabovoi at the Kosmos Hotel in Moscow (Schreck 2006b). According to Ella Kesayeva, who eventually left the group to found Voice of Beslan:

> We don't know what to think, but one thing is clear—these women who went to this new-fledged messiah are in trouble. The story of our mothers' path to Grabovoi is very slippery. There are many questions, which we cannot answer. For example, it is surprising that the women who went to Grabovoi were the very same women who met with Putin—Susanna Dudiyeva, Aneta Gadiyeva, and Rita Sidakova. They returned not quite themselves—so joyful and saying only what a good guy Grabovoi is and how he will help them. How they changed and became zombies. The most sensible women of our movement somehow went mad. At present they look mad. They have forgotten that the goal of creating our committee was to find the truth. . . . Therefore we announced in an open appeal that this visit was a planned provocation aimed at eliminating our movement. The authorities and special forces planned for the liquidation of our organization through psychological influence. I think the government began to fear the Mothers of Beslan and now want to discredit and split the organization. We don't want a split, we just want to draw attention to our problems and help those women who are in trouble. (Semyenova 2005:1)

The women themselves who traveled to Moscow to meet Grabovoi did not see their actions as unusual and believed that a visit to a "great teacher" was their own business. As Aneta Gadiyeva explained, "We thought after meeting with President Putin that things would get easier. We were wrong, it got even harder. . . . Now we rely only in G-d, and if Grigorii Grabovoi has some opportunities, we cannot reject them" (Semyenova 2005:1). Another supporter of Grabovoi, Alla Batagova who lost her boy Timur, agreed, "I went to Grabovoi because I do not know what to do. A year has passed, but it became even harder for me. You know, I even think about how to hang myself. My husband already once had to pull me from the ropes" (Semyenova 2005:1; see also Shavlokhova 2005a).

By October 2, 2005, the rift over Grabovoi led some members to leave Mothers of Beslan and form Voice of Beslan, with Voice of Beslan declaring Grabovoi a con artist and expressing concern that the authorities were using him to discredit the cause of Beslan victims by making them appear gullible and even crazy (Farniyev 2005b; Shavlokhova 2005a; Shavlokhova and Sokolov-Mitrich 2005; Allenova 2005c). Voice of Beslan was officially registered as a public organization on November 25, 2005, and its members were among those who complained about Grabovoi to prosecutors, leading eventually to his April 2006 arrest during a séance at the Kosmos Hotel on suspicion of fraudulently obtaining money from parents of victims (Sageyeva and Khubezhova 2005; Schreck 2006b). Other disagreements involved different interpretations of the September 2005 meeting with Putin, with Mothers of Beslan tending to trust Putin, and those dissenting and forming Voice of Beslan remaining dissatisfied and becoming the more outspoken group.

Later, in mid-April 2006, Voice of Beslan itself had some internal divisions when five members were kicked out of the organization after objecting to the organization's denunciation of a pro-Kremlin referendum that would have allowed Putin to seek a third term. The former members objected to criticism of Putin, while many other members held Putin responsible for the attack. The five expelled members showed up with their relatives at the Voice of Beslan office and forced the one woman present to hand over the keys and vacate the premises. Head of Voice of Beslan Kesayeva obtained a duplicate key and retrieved possessions left in the office, and the building owner decided not to continue renting to them (Schreck 2006b).

Voice of Beslan also became a target of criticism by Mothers of Beslan. On February 7–8, 2006, Dr. Leonid Roshal, a prominent pediatrician who negotiated with the terrorists during the school siege, testified at the Kulayev trial at the personal request of Voice of Beslan leader Ella Kesayeva. During his testimony, Kesayeva asked Roshal why he had lied during the siege, saying that children could last eight or nine days without food or water, when he knew that the children were in critical condition and could have died much sooner. Roshal defended his decision based on the need to calm the crowd waiting outside the school and threatened to sue Kesayeva, who in turn threatened to sue Roshal. Susanna Dudiyeva commented on the incident by saying she felt ashamed. "Kesayeva's behavior shocked us all. She screamed at Roshal, calling him a liar. Two other women from the organization, Alma Khamitseva and Zalina Dziova, screamed in unison. It's beyond my comprehension, because Kesayeva herself invited Roshal to Vladikavkaz" (Karacheva 2006b:2).

When Voice of Beslan members went on a hunger strike in February 2006 in response to the judge's decision to end the court investigation and questioning of witnesses and to begin closing arguments before the victims believed all relevant witnesses had given testimony, many victims were critical. "The head of the administration of Vladimir Moves, whose grandson died in the school, did not respond to requests from Novaya Gazeta to connect Voice of Beslan's phone. Editor in chief of 'Life of the Right Bank' Elbrus Tedtov (whose high school son Timur was killed) gave an oral statement to his employees not to report on the hunger strike. However, the newspaper published the opinions of well-known Ossetians that the Voice of Beslan is engaged in politicking and 'a disgrace to the republic' by exposing their grief in public. Susanna Dudiyeva, head of the committee, Mothers of Beslan, said that she does not support the strike" (Milashina 2006b:6).

Mothers of Beslan supported the death penalty for Kulayev and the prosecutor's attempt to suspend the death penalty moratorium. After the May 16, 2006, conviction of Kulayev and his sentence of life imprisonment, Mothers of Beslan member Aneta Gadiyeva said, "Most of us are for the death penalty. If he is rotting in prison until his last minute, maybe it's adequate punishment. But he will still have some deliveries of food and little joys. Our children will never have those" ("Beslan Kidnapper" 2006).

In contrast, the Voice of Beslan spoke out against suspending the death penalty moratorium for Kulayev's sentencing: "the public organization The Voice of Beslan believes that the moratorium on the death penalty is a civilized measure. We do not want to become barbarians in response to barbarity. We do not support Deputy Prosecutor General Nikolai Shepel, who represents the state in the trial of Nurpashi Kulayev, in his call for the highest penalty for [the defendant]—the death penalty" ("Voice of Beslan Against" 2006).[2] Ella Kesayeva also argued for the practical value of keeping Kulayev alive as a witness: "Preserving Kulayev's life gives us hope that all circumstances of the terrorist act in Beslan sooner or later will be investigated. Alive, Kulayev can give evidence on the main part of the case. We hope to learn the truth about Beslan" ("Beslan Kidnapper" 2006).

These organizational disagreements and divisions reflected thoughtful convictions about how to redress the grievances of Beslan victims, and it might be reasonable to offer such a dispassionate interpretation. However, the divisiveness also reflected underlying feelings of support and lack of support, with victim leaders glomming on to some fellow leaders and passing judgment on and distancing themselves from others. The concept of social alienation, even when stripped down to a relatively simple dimension of perceived social support and connectedness, still fails to offer a clear portrait of victims, let alone an interpretation of the aftermath of violence. The impressive activists leading the Beslan victims felt simultaneously alienated and integrated, supported and abandoned, cared for and disregarded—just like the activists playing lesser roles and just like the nonactivists.

[2] The Voice of Beslan statement of March 7, 2006, is available on their website at http://golosbesl ana.ru/2006/obra0703.htm.

Measuring Social Alienation

The multidimensionality of the concept of social alienation has made it difficult to define and measure (Seeman 1975:95). Existing scales attempt to capture social alienation but suffer various issues related to validity and reliability and are therefore inadequate for many analytical purposes (Justice 2018). For example, many scales are context-specific and lack external validity, or the ability to be applied to other contexts and populations (Justice 2018). There is no widely accepted gold standard for measurement of social alienation.

Specifying a dimension of social alienation that might matter for post-violence behavior can clarify hypothesized relationships and simplify measurement. Therefore, social alienation is defined here as the perceived lack of social support and concern. Where focus group discussions followed the participants' interest in discussing social dynamics within Beslan, the survey measured the perceived lack of social support and concern from Russians outside Beslan. The question asked was, "How interested do you think the following groups are in listening to the victims' side of the story?" where "Russian society" was one of those groups. The more victims thought their fellow Russians were uninterested in their story, the more they were considered socially alienated.

The measure has weaknesses. It is a single survey question, rather than an index designed to tap into multiple dimensions of social alienation, and the survey does not offer other options to test for validity and reliability and thereby ensure that the question does indeed capture the essence of social alienation. The measure also does not offer insights into social alienation relative to the local Beslan community, as the focus group discussions did. The omission of Beslan-specific questions errs on the side of "do no harm." Heartbreaking tensions and divisions between community members in Beslan could have been exacerbated by extensive survey questions that drew attention to disparities in grief, hard feelings over material compensation, and blame toward fellow victims. Focus group discussions suggested that feelings of social alienation within the Beslan community were nearly universal but complicated and would have required numerous nuanced questions to tap. While such questions may have revealed interesting variation among victims, more likely the questions would have confirmed the complicated local dynamics of social alienation and an inability to paint individuals as clearly alienated or integrated or to place them on a linear scale from low to high perceived local support. As strongly suggested by the abundant qualitative evidence, the more thorough but potentially harmful line of questioning would also likely have confirmed the lack of correlation between social alienation and behavioral responses to ethnic violence.

Beslan Victim Data on Social Alienation and Behavior

Based on the measure of perceived support outside Beslan, most Beslan victims did not feel particularly alienated from Russian society. Four out of five victims said that they thought their fellow Russians were very or somewhat interested in listening to the victims' side of the story (39.7 and 39 percent, respectively). Only 13.8 percent thought their fellow Russians were not very interested, and only 2 percent thought they were not at all interested. Very few had difficulty answering the question (3.9 percent were unsure, and 1.5 percent refused to answer), despite the potential difficulty of evaluating the level of concern of over 140 million people.

As Table 8.1 shows, social alienation from the greater Russian community is not strongly correlated with support for retaliatory violence. Those who felt Russian society did not care about them were more likely to approve of killing Chechens than those who felt Russian society cared (27.3 percent versus 14.6 percent who somewhat or fully approved of killing), but the relationship is not statistically significant at the bivariate or multivariate levels (see Chapter 11).

Nor did social alienation play a role in political participation (Table 8.2). The more a victim believed Russian society was uninterested in the victims' story, the less likely that victim was to participate in politics, but again, this relationship is not statistically significant in bivariate or multivariate analysis (see Chapter 11). Most likely, social alienation is not a powerful force for post-violence political participation.

Table 8.1. Social Alienation and Support for Retaliatory Violence (Killing the Same Number of Chechens as Were Killed in Beslan)

Social alienation: "How interested do you think the following groups are in listening to the victims' side of the story? *Russian society*"

	Completely Disapprove	Somewhat Disapprove	Somewhat Approve	Fully Approve	Missing	N
Very interested	197 (45.2)	122 (28.0)	39 (8.9)	25 (5.7)	53 (12.2)	436 (100.0)
Somewhat interested	153 (35.8)	177 (41.4)	26 (6.1)	19 (4.4)	53 (12.4)	428 (100.0)
Not very interested	59 (38.8)	53 (34.9)	16 (10.5)	15 (9.9)	9 (5.9)	152 (100.0)
Not at all interested	10 (45.5)	5 (22.7)	4 (18.2)	2 (9.1)	1 (4.6)	22 (100.0)

$N = 1,098$; number of victims (%); Pearson's $r = .07$, $p < .03$.

Table 8.2. Social Alienation and Political Participation

Social alienation: "How interested do you think the following groups are in listening to the victims' side of the story? *Russian society*"

	No Activities	One Activity	Two or Three Activities	Four to Ten Activities	Eleven to Thirty-one Activities	Missing	N
Very interested	196 (45.0)	55 (12.6)	29 (6.7)	62 (14.2)	18 (7.3)	76 (17.4)	436 (100.0)
Somewhat interested	223 (52.1)	52 (12.1)	52 (12.1)	25 (5.8)	31 (7.2)	45 (10.5)	428 (100.0)
Not very interested	66 (43.4)	25 (16.4)	23 (15.1)	13 (8.6)	7 (4.6)	18 (11.8)	152 (100.0)
Not at all interested	6 (27.3)	3 (13.6)	4 (18.2)	5 (22.7)	1 (4.5)	3 (13.6)	22 (100.0)

N = 1,098; number of victims (%); Pearson's r = −.03, p < .45.

Social alienation may still play a small role in post-violence behavior in interaction with another variable, anger. As shown in Chapter 5, anger has a strong, independent, positive effect on political participation, whereas anger has no statistically significant independent effect on support for retaliatory violence. However, at the highest levels of anger, the effects of social alienation are statistically significant (see Table 5.5 in Chapter 5). Among victims who felt anger four days per week or more, those who were also socially alienated were more likely to support violence. Such daily anger is rare: only 13.6 percent of victims reported that they felt anger four days per week or more. Daily anger combined with social alienation in Beslan is rarer still: only 2.3 percent of victims (26 of 1,098 people) felt anger four days per week or more and also thought that Russian society was not very interested or not at all interested in the victims' side of the story. To the extent that social alienation increases the probability of supporting retaliatory ethnic violence, these few exceptionally angry victims may be most susceptible.

Conclusion

A defining feature of most conceptualizations of social alienation is a lack of support and concern, real and perceived, from others. Such emotional isolation has at times coincided positively with violent behavior and at times coincided negatively. Theories suggest that socially alienated individuals may be more, less, or equally predisposed to violence as the socially supported. Empirical evidence connecting social alienation to violence is mixed, and hypothesized causal mechanisms usually depend on other variables, suggesting at most a minor independent role for social alienation in retaliatory ethnic violence.

Similarly, the independent role of social alienation for political participation in the aftermath of violence seems negligible. Theoretically, social alienation could justify both action and inaction: the perception that one's well-being is a low priority for others is both a mobilizing grievance and a demobilizing assessment of the pointlessness of action. Again, other variables likely have more powerful effects on participatory behavior.

After the hostage taking in Beslan, the story of social alienation could be told in many ways. The tight social networks, born of a shared history living in the same town with large, extended families, offered Beslan victims an objective and subjective support system. Locally, concern was conveyed in the series of well-attended funerals, lengthy mourning period, and constant communication between relatives and neighbors. Nationally, concern seemed to be conveyed as well, with most victims expressing positive sentiments about the receptiveness of fellow Russian citizens to their plight.

Yet, what preoccupied most if not all Beslan victims was a sense of emotional abandonment. Loss and grief were so widespread that there often seemed little room for attention to someone's specific problems. Each individual victim seemed to cry, "Hear my pain! Hear my suffering!," and to be dismayed to receive the same cry in return, because few if any victims had the emotional bandwidth to listen.

Thus, Beslan victims embodied a complicated sense of social support and social alienation. If the role of social alienation in post-violence behavior is ambivalent theoretically, it is even more so for victims whose social alienation is ambivalent empirically.

The survey of Beslan victims did reveal variation in perceived alienation from Russian society at large. Most Beslan victims believed that Russians outside of Beslan were interested in listening to the victims' side of the story, and a minority believed otherwise. Still, the variation in social alienation mattered little for post-violence behavior. Victims who felt alienated from Russian society were slightly more likely to approve of retaliatory ethnic violence but were no more or less active politically than other victims. Social alienation seemed to matter most for the angriest victims, but even in this interaction, social alienation did not seem to be the primary motivator of retaliatory ethnic violence. Normatively, social alienation is a negative phenomenon and certainly makes life more difficult for survivors of violence, in Beslan and elsewhere, but it is the alienation itself and its implications for well-being, rather than its behavioral effects, that are problematic.

9

Self-Efficacy and Political Efficacy

A presumably essential factor for mobilization is the belief that a situation is changeable and that individuals or groups are capable agents of that change (McCarthy and Zald 1977; Gamson 1975/90; Klandermans 1997; Tausch et al. 2011). Perceptions of efficacy vary among individuals in daily life. Experience with violence may diminish efficacy, but variation among victims nevertheless persists, reflecting their pre-violence self-assessments, post-violence revelations, or both.

Whether the response to violence is retaliatory violence or peaceful political action, theories from sociology, psychology, and political science suggest that efficacy perceptions matter: those who act presumably believe that they and their actions make a difference. Efficacy can take different forms, and among the most relevant are self-efficacy and political efficacy. An important question is whether these different forms of efficacy manifest similarly or differently in post-violence behavior.

This chapter explores theories about efficacy perceptions and their effects on support for retaliatory violence and political participation. Primary sources and news reports provide background information on the relatively objective successes and failures of victims' actions. Focus group discussions reveal the victims' subjective assessments of the very same activities. The Beslan victim data are then used to analyze the effects of subjective assessments of self-efficacy and political efficacy on support for retaliatory violence and political participation.

The data suggest that self-efficacy and political efficacy are both mobilizing perceptions. Consistent with voluminous research, high political efficacy is related to political participation. Victims who considered themselves politically informed and who consider demonstrating or protesting to be effective mechanisms to address dissatisfaction were more likely to engage in political action. High self-efficacy has more normatively complicated effects that have received less attention in discussions of behavioral responses to violence. While feeling in control and able to solve problems after the tragedy may promote greater physical and mental health and even political activism, self-efficacy after tragedy may also encourage victims to exercise control in illegal or socially undesirable ways, such as supporting retaliatory violence.

After Violence. Debra Javeline, Oxford University Press. © Oxford University Press 2023.
DOI: 10.1093/oso/9780197683347.003.0010

Efficacy after Violence

An efficacious individual believes problems are solvable and that he or she can play a role in the solving. In apolitical contexts, such a feeling or perception is known as self-efficacy, which refers to individuals' assessments of their effectiveness, competence, and causal agency (Gecas 1989:292; Bandura 1995). In political contexts, if an individual thinks he or she can influence outcomes through political action, then the feeling or perception is known as political efficacy (Campbell et al. 1954; Balch 1974). Political efficacy can reflect an assessment of one's personal competence influencing political outcomes, and it can also or instead reflect an assessment of the political system itself and whether specific types of individual or group political action can be effective. Terms associated with efficacy include perceived agency, empowerment, competence, mastery, and control over life.

Some evidence suggests that self-efficacy develops as early as infancy in the interaction between an individual and the environment (Gecas 1989:300). Individuals then go on to develop their sense of efficacy in response to information from their life experiences, such as performance accomplishments that reflect personal mastery (Bandura 1977). Their self-assessments become fairly stable over time. Daily family interactions, work conditions, social relationships, and routine events, such as school graduation, marriage, parenthood, and retirement, have only minimal effects on self-efficacy (Gecas 1989:306–307). However, atypical events, such as victimization by violence or life-changing physical impairment, and off-time events, such as the death of a child or premature death of a spouse, can have more profound effects on self-efficacy. The sense of efficacy can be particularly diminished if individuals focus on their personal inadequacies during the atypical event rather than on situational factors (Bandura 1977).

After victimization in a violent hostage taking, individuals quite reasonably should feel inefficacious. Objectively speaking, they have lost control. The loss involved restricted freedom during the course of the hostage taking and irreversible life changes from physical and mental disabilities and murdered or disabled loved ones after the tragic ending.

Cognitive responses to this type of extreme adversity can depend on the initial sense of self-efficacy. Those who felt unempowered either personally, politically, or both before the hostage taking may find those perceptions reinforced by the extreme disempowering situation. They may go on to suffer from learned helplessness, or "a chronic sense of inefficacy resulting from learning that one's actions have no effect on one's environment" (Seligman 1975). Conversely, those who perceived greater control over their environment before the hostage taking may be better positioned to recover their sense of efficacy after the traumatic event (Luszczynska et al. 2009).

Perceptions of political efficacy after violence may also vary, depending on pre-trauma perceptions and post-trauma experiences. There are subjectively resourceful individuals who have a strong sense of political expertise and believe their own contributions make a difference to the likelihood of successful collective action (Finkel et al. 1989). Their efficacy perception is often grounded in reality, as some individuals do indeed have greater political influence and resources based on education, wealth, cognitive sophistication, or self-confidence (Lichbach 1998). Variations in post-trauma self-efficacy and political efficacy may in turn help explain differences in behavior, such as retaliatory violence and political participation.

Self-Efficacy and Retaliatory Violence

Victims contemplating retaliatory violence may first consider whether the violence is likely to be effective. For example, before confrontation, they might evaluate the strength of their group relative to the strength of the target group (Skitka et al. 2006:376). They might evaluate whether they have had previous success in using violence to achieve some end or have witnessed another group's successful use of violence (Gurr 1970:chap. 7). Will retaliation actually work?

The efficacy calculation presumably occurs whether the motivation for retaliatory violence is instrumental, intended to secure tangible goods, or expressive, intended to "blow off steam" and demonstrate anger or feel pleasure from administering punishment (Jackson et al. 2019:326–327). Victims might assess whether their actions promise to achieve a goal, such as a specific policy change or coerced compliance (Kalyvas 2006). Violence during civil wars, for example, is often used strategically (Kalyvas 2006:27). Victims might also assess whether their actions, the attack and resulting harm to the source of their frustration, would provide "an inherently satisfying response to the tension built up through frustration," even if the frustration itself is not reduced (Gurr 1970:22–23, 34; della Porta and Tarrow 1986:627). For example, insurgents in El Salvador believed that their participation would lead, not to the desired outcome of land acquisition, but to an assertion of their dignity, interests, and identity in the face of repression (Wood 2003). Chechen suicide bombings have also been characterized as expressive (Reuter 2004:21). Violence may be both instrumental and expressive (Hamlin and Jennings 2004:433). However, if retaliatory violence promises neither a desired tangible outcome nor the satisfaction of expression, victims presumably would judge the violence ineffective and would be less like to support it.

When assessing the potential effectiveness of retaliatory violence, victims may consciously or subconsciously conduct a cost-benefit analysis and weigh risks and rewards (McCullough et al. 2010). Retaliatory violence usually entails very real physical and legal risks, given that retaliation could incite further violence or judicial action if the victim-retaliator gets detained and indicted as a perpetrator. Victims of violence may thus anticipate death, injury, or punishment as the risks of their own violent response. Rewards could include the potential instrumental and expressive benefits of retaliatory violence but also material selective incentives provided only to the perpetrators of the violence, although there is little evidence that such incentives have played a large role in other forms of violence, such as mass insurgency in El Salvador (Wood 2003). Presumably, retaliation would be deemed effective if risks were low and rewards were high.

The Beslan victim survey does not include questions about the perceived instrumentality of retaliatory violence, perceived opportunity for expression, or the perceived risks and rewards, again to preclude any possibility of accidentally provoking violent thoughts and actions. However, focus group participants, as described in Chapter 3, conveyed the community narrative that nothing would be gained from retaliating against Ingush and Chechens. Although many victims felt an initial impulse to retaliate, they came to see such action as impractical, dangerous, and futile. The lack of perceived effectiveness of retaliatory violence in Beslan probably helps explain its infrequency at the aggregate level.

Among victims, however, the question remains whether efficacy, political or self, can help account for variation in individual support for retaliatory violence. Violence is sometimes hypothesized as a reaction to *inefficacy*, especially in the political arena. Having no other recourse, and frustrated by their inability to achieve goals or express themselves, aggrieved individuals may then resort to violence. For example, a feeling of powerlessness against the state has been said to drive terrorism (e.g., Moghaddam 2005), the Watts riots (Ransford 1968), and other violent action (Tausch et al. 2011). Conversely, if individuals feel empowered to act politically and think such action could effectively address their grievances, they would have no need to take a violent route.

The difficulty with this hypothesis is the unclear causal mechanism from political powerlessness to violent action. The logic suggesting that politically efficacious victims would feel little need for retaliatory violence is reasonably clear, but the corollary is unpersuasive: Why would victims become violent, simply because politics seem ineffective? Implied in the assertion that politically inefficacious victims would turn to violence is that anger or another emotional reaction provides the missing causal link. Victims presumably perceive their political powerlessness, become angry, and therefore act violently. However, as seen in Chapter 5, this logic too is unpersuasive, because anger does not cause retaliatory violence. Another implied causal mechanism suggests that, where politics is perceived as ineffective, violence then gets the benefit of the doubt as the default option and is assumed to be effective. However, such reasoning is purely speculative. There does not seem to be much evidence that victims reason this way. A feeling of political powerlessness is probably demoralizing and demobilizing for inspiring retaliatory violence, not mobilizing, or at least it is neutral and has little effect either way. Indeed, if victims did assume that violence is more effective than nonviolence in achieving goals, evidence suggests that they would be wrong (Chenoweth and Stephan 2011). Most likely, political efficacy plays no role in victims' support for retaliatory violence.

Self-efficacy, however, may indeed play a role. After extreme violence, a situation that understandably calls one's self-efficacy into question, victims emerge with varying perceptions of their control over life. In some respects, high self-efficacy might seem the more useful or productive perception. High self-efficacy is often beneficial and therapeutic for individuals as well as society, because it leads to better physical and psychological health, creativity, cognitive flexibility, problem-solving and coping, self-esteem, and greater community involvement. whereas low self-efficacy can be negative, maladaptive, and unhealthy (Gecas 1989:298, 311; Luszczynska et al. 2009). Those with the highest self-efficacy after victimization have a greater probability of post-traumatic recovery (Luszczynska et al. 2009).

However, perceived competence and control in such a tense and arguably uncontrollable situation may also manifest in normatively undesirable ways. Specifically, the highly efficacious may be more likely to take matters into their own hands. Studies of the effects of self-efficacy on violence are limited, but some evidence suggests that the feeling of empowerment describes victims and vigilantes who retaliate against offenders (Miller 2001:541). The feeling of empowerment also may describe teenagers who believe in their ability to behave aggressively and thus exhibit that aggression toward their peers (Barchia and Bussey 2011). Self-efficacy may both prompt the retaliatory violence and be restored or bolstered by the violence (Frijda and Mesquita 2000:65), and it may be difficult to tease out the direction of causality.

Evidence to this effect is more abundant on the related concept of self-esteem and its connection to violence, especially when the high self-esteem is unwarranted. Those who are egotistic, narcissistic, or simply believe in their own superiority and capability and who refuse to lower their high opinion of themselves tend to be more violent. The violent tendency is magnified when egos are threatened and those with high self-esteem feel that their superiority has been undermined, jeopardized, or contradicted (Baumeister et al. 1996). Individuals with low self-esteem are likely to avoid situations that hold the possibility of losing even more esteem. Individuals with high self-esteem often seek out situations where they can prove themselves and their worth. They do not anticipate failure so have fewer worries about lost esteem, and they are particularly motivated by threats that seem to provide opportunity for validation (Baumeister et al. 1996).

The relationship between self-efficacy and violence likely resembles the relationship between self-esteem and violence. In the context of the Beslan hostage taking, it is plausible that victims with high self-efficacy had a stronger reaction than other victims to the threat to self-efficacy posed by the victim experience. It is also plausible that victims with higher self-efficacy had a greater desire to assert that efficacy through retaliation.

Political Efficacy and Political Participation

Political efficacy, by definition, should be positively related to political participation. A subjective sense of competence in a particular domain, here politics, should inspire greater activity in that domain. However, politics is actually a multifaceted domain, comprising routinized institutional channels for participation, as well as possibilities to go around those channels and push for influence. Research in political science and sociology has at times questioned whether the effects of efficacy are similar for all types of participation or whether the effects depend on the type of activity.

Political efficacy was originally hypothesized to have positive effects on participation in electoral politics and other conventional institutional activities but negative effects on participation in extra-institutional political activities such as political protest (Campbell et al. 1954; Kornhauser 1959; Balch 1974). If goals could be achieved through conventional channels, why would anyone protest? A feeling of effectiveness in the political system presumably bred loyalty to the system and obviated the need to act in other ways, particularly in non-institutional contentious politics. For example, among young African Americans in the late 1960s, those with higher political efficacy participated more in traditional politics, but efficacy was said to be unrelated to protest activity (Jackson 1973:870–871).

Since the 1970s, however, research suggests that the effects of political efficacy on participation are positive, even for contentious politics. After all, if individuals do not think protest will work—if they feel inefficacious about protest—why would they do it? A sense of agency seems required or at least useful for most forms of political action. While perceptions of powerlessness keep people docile, a subjective transformation of consciousness can be mobilizing. The change in consciousness, sometimes known as "cognitive liberation," involves redefining a situation as unjust and subject to change through group action. Individuals' new belief in their capacity to alter their lot makes insurgency possible (Piven and Cloward 1977; McAdam 1982). Consciousness raising was a critical factor for the insurgency of unemployed people and industrial workers during the Great Depression and of African Americans during the civil rights movement (Piven and Cloward 1977; McAdam 1982). Perceptions of efficacy also influence the chosen venue for protest. University students stage anti-war protests on college campuses, rather than the nation's capital, because they can more effectively disrupt campus life. Similarly, factory workers strike and other aggrieved individuals disrupt those institutions where they have access and the potential for influence, even when the institutions themselves are not the direct targets of their grievance (Piven and Cloward 1977).

Within protest movements, evidence suggests that political efficacy helps explain individual variation in participation. High expectations of group success and of personal influence on outcomes have positively affected the participation of Dutch industrial workers (Klandermans 1984), German and American anti-nuclear protesters (Muller and Opp 1986), Dutch peace activists (Klandermans and Oegema 1987), and Greek anti-austerity protesters (Rüdig and Karyotis 2014:22–23). Political efficacy influences not only the decision to participate but the form of behavior, with individuals choosing the form that promises the greatest success (Opp 1988:861; Finkel et al. 1989:901).

Research is scarce on the connection between self-efficacy and political participation. Presumably, perceptions of self-efficacy and political efficacy are correlated, so that a self-efficacious individual may be more likely than an inefficacious person to perceive competence in politics as well. However, there is less reason to hypothesize a direct link from self-efficacy to political action without the intervening sense of political efficacy. To the extent that a direct link exists, the relationship is likely positive. A highly efficacious individual could plausibly feel generalized competence in addition to domain-specific competence, and an inefficacious individual could also generalize that negative perception. For example, Ugandan rebel abductees who experienced "posttraumatic growth" became increasingly involved in politics (Blattman 2009).

As with violence, efficacy may play a role in political participation whether the motivations are instrumental or expressive. For example, participants in electoral politics may vote to influence outcomes or to express identity, duty, and morality (Schuessler 2000; Hamlin and Jennings 2011). Participants in legal and illegal protests may be driven to achieve tangible goods or policy outcomes (Opp 1988) or to assert dignity, pride, agency, and defiance (Wood 2003; Goodwin and Jasper 2006:622). They may seek self-respect and the satisfaction of having aired disapproval or emotion (Chong 1991; Klandermans 2003). When the goal of protest is expression, not material gain, the role of efficacy may be less apparent but no less present: compared to nonparticipants, participants probably have a stronger belief in their own competence to express themselves. Instrumental and expressive goals in political participation, like violence, often coexist, and indeed, in post-violence contexts where the instrumental goal is a full accounting of the violence and all the emotions that accounting would provoke, it may be difficult to disentangle instrumental and expressive motivations. The subjective sense that goals of either type are achievable and that individuals have agency and empowerment probably influences participation.

Potential risks and rewards likely play a role in the cost-benefit calculation for political action, as they do for retaliatory violence. Victims of violence may expect or fear punishment for responding to the violence, even when the response is peaceful political participation. Especially in post-communist, authoritarian, or quasi-democratic countries, the peaceful demand for accountability often represents a challenge to local executives, security forces, or other political officials and is therefore risky. Anticipated punishment may color impressions of the potential effectiveness of political action and therefore be demobilizing, although some evidence suggests that such expectations can also add to grievances and make the aggrieved commit even stronger to the struggle and fighting the good fight (Muller and Opp 1986; Chong 1991; Javeline and Baird 2007).

Victims may also ponder the potential rewards of political participation, namely grievance satisfaction, and the odds of those rewards materializing. The promise of a selective incentive, or some excludable benefit to the participant regardless of its impact on the stated political goal, seems relatively unimportant (Klandermans 1984; Klandermans and Oegema 1987; Fireman and Gamson 1988:14; Muller et al. 1991). In the Beslan case, despite some victims' impression of the motivations of activist victims, it strains credulity to imagine that parents searching for information about their dead children, taking care of physically and emotionally scarred children, or nursing grave wounds of their own would be motivated to participate in politics by the promise of money or other material good, especially when such goods were being offered to victims as charitable donations. The main potential reward or benefit of political participation in the context of Beslan was the success of the participation itself—success in clarifying how the tragedy unfolded, who is responsible, and what happened to loved ones and in ensuring that new measures were in place to prevent a recurrence of such horror. Victims may assess the costs and benefits of collective political action to determine if activism would be effective and if they in particular could be effective contributors.

Activist leaders or political entrepreneurs well understand the role of efficacy in recruiting others to their cause. Part of their mission is to convince potential recruits of the possibility of change, the opportunities for action, and the crucial contribution of each individual (Gamson and Meyer 1996:283). For example, community organizers have emphasized the importance of efficacy in building support for social movements (Ennis and Schreuer 1987:395). Leaders see such value in the perception of efficacy that they often overestimate opportunities and odds of success.

In Beslan, the victims' political activities and their outcomes were highly visible and the effectiveness subject to direct scrutiny of both participants and nonparticipants, usually without the interpretive filter of activist leaders. Political participation after the hostage taking produced successes and failures. Victims tended to perceive the failures outweighing the successes but nevertheless varied in assessments of their own political competence and the effectiveness of political action.

The Objective (In)effectiveness of Political Action in Beslan

To some extent, assessments of the effectiveness of demonstrating or protesting are grounded in reality, and in Beslan, there are indeed some outcomes that represent objective wins for Beslan victims. Victims succeeded at forcing investigations that the authorities originally resisted. They succeeded at forcing North Ossetian president Dzasokhov first to dissolve his cabinet of ministers (Abdullaev and Voitova 2004; Sukhov 2004) and then to resign himself on May 31, 2005. Similarly, the firing of Russian deputy prosecutor general Nikolai Shepel in the summer of 2006 could be partly attributed to the victims' constant and aggressive complaints. On December 27, 2006, the Russian Supreme Court, while denying the victims' appeal for a retrial of Kulayev, determined that Shepel committed violations during his investigation of the Beslan incident, thus officially legitimizing the victims' complaints.

Victims succeeded at getting authorities to admit to previously denied actions during the siege, such as the use of flamethrowers. Thanks to their January 2005 highway blockade, they succeeded in getting an audience with a powerful Putin appointee, Presidential Envoy Dmitry Kozak, who had been encouraging them to refrain from unsanctioned protests (Bondarenko 2005). The meeting with Kozak materialized on September 1, 2005, and victims in attendance pulled no punches in presenting their case, both directly to politicians and indirectly via the media (Allenova 2005b). A day later, other victims succeeded in getting an audience with an even more powerful official, Vladimir Putin himself, who responded to their concerns about the lack of thoroughness of Shepel's investigation by sending Deputy Prosecutor General Kolesnikov and five other federal prosecutors to Beslan to review the evidence in a parallel investigation (Berseneva 2005; Mereu 2005).

During the courtroom sit-in in December 2005, one of the victims' demands was for Dzasokhov and North Ossetian FSB director Andreyev to testify at Kulayev's trial, and they succeeded in getting this testimony (Voitova 2005).

352 WHY POLITICS AND NONVIOLENCE?

When the main topic of discussion at the Kulayev trial on November 27, 2005, was the shelling of the school by tanks and the use of flamethrowers and which officials gave the orders, it was reasonably reported that, "[t]he efforts of the people of Beslan, who spent a whole year conducting their own investigation into the terrorist attack, were not in vain" (Milashina 2005c). That the topic of responsibility was even raised at the trial and that military use of inappropriate weaponry in the context of a hostage situation was admitted could be credited to the victim activists. Without their actions, the Kulayev trial and the official investigations would have been shorter, simpler, and even less forthcoming about the facts. More generally, information that has been accumulated over the years about the hostage taking—Russia's most atrocious terrorist act in the country's history—"is due in large part to the relentless digging carried out by North Ossetian and Russian women" (Dunlop 2009:1).

At the same time, many victim demands and objectives remain unmet to this day. The authorities admitted to some actions during the siege but continue to deny others, such as firing from tanks while hostages were still alive in the school. Some brave, long-lasting, and newsworthy actions produced few results, including the twenty-eight-hour sit-in at the Vladikavkaz courthouse, with Zalina Guburova, who lost a child, reporting, "We decided to leave [the courthouse after 28 hours] because of our extreme disappointment at the attitude of the authorities. . . . They are treating us like a gang of hysterical women not worthy of meeting with" (Mainville 2005a:A10).

Some initial successes backfired, such as getting Dzasokhov to resign, only to see him a week later on June 7 become North Ossetia's representative to the Federation Council, effectively moving from governor to senator, and to see him replaced by former parliamentary chairman Taimuraz Mamsurov, who was for some victims a no more trustworthy head of the republic. Ten years later, the post of North Ossetian president was handed to an official even less palatable to victims, former (by then) Supreme Court Chief Justice Tamerlan Aguzarov (Fuller 2015). Similarly, after Shepel's removal as Russian deputy prosecutor general, many victims understood that his replacement, Ivan Sydoruk, would likely be no better (Tlisova 2006a). The Supreme Court rebuke of Shepel was also a hollow victory, because Shepel had been sent into retirement by then and suffered no real consequences.

Kozak met with victims but provided less-than-satisfactory answers to their complaints and left them frustrated (Allenova 2005b; Bondarenko 2005). Putin gave victims assurances that he would seek the truth, but his dispatching of Deputy Prosecutor General Kolesnikov to Beslan hardly delivered on this promise, as Kolesnikov's additional review of the evidence amounted to aggressive attempts to re-interview and interrogate victims and witnesses rather than investigate objectively (Berseneva 2005). Dzasokhov and Andreyev testified at Kulayev's trial, but much of the testimony was deemed untruthful by the survivors and victims' relatives, and no authorities were subsequently held accountable. The long list of hotly contested issues described in Chapter 2, the lack of resolution to these questions years later, and the continued weak security of Beslan homes and schools are objective losses for victim activists.

Judicial action by victims was characterized by many losses but an important win. Chapter 4 chronicled the victims' rollercoaster ride through Russia's judicial system, with gains in one court overturned by a higher court. As noted above, victims failed in their appeal to the Russian Supreme Court for a retrial of Kulayev on the grounds that the investigation was conducted poorly, but the victims by that point anticipated the failure in Russia and were already looking to the European Court of Human Rights (ECHR). On April 13, 2017, the ECHR delivered the victims' most important success in affirming that Russia had violated the right to life. The ECHR judged that the Russian authorities had not taken preventive security measures, nor justified their use of force based on thorough and effective investigations as required procedurally. The Court also judged that the counterterrorist operation was not appropriately planned and controlled and that the Russian security forces had used disproportionately powerful and indiscriminate weapons. Russia appealed the ruling but, when the appeal was turned down, agreed to pay the awarded €2,955,000 plus legal fees.

Many victims considered the sum offensively small. It amounted to only €3,000–10,000 for most litigants, with the highest amount paid to those who lost a close relative. (The award was graded for each deceased, gravely injured, medium injured, or lightly injured former hostage. A half dozen litigants with two to five deceased relatives received between €20,000 and €50,000.) Nevertheless, the verdict represented a historic judgment against the Russian state, an important precedent for states responding to future acts of terrorism, and validation for the victims. *Tagayeva and Others v. Russia* has been called a landmark case for prioritizing the human rights obligations of states toward victims even in the context of national security interests when responding to terrorist hostage taking (Galani 2019).

The Perceived (In)effectiveness of Political Action in Beslan

To judge the potential for effective political action, Beslan victims were all presumably assessing the same circumstances, opportunities, and constraints and the same results of the same activism. However, in many ways, the success or failure of activism and the potential for success or failure are in the eye of the beholder. Efficacious victims may focus on the above successes. Less efficacious individuals may focus on the qualifications, caveats, and failures. Efficacy is essentially a perceptual variable, defined less by reality and more by an individual's interpretation of reality.

Focus group discussions revealed an enormous dearth of efficacy among Beslan victims. Inactive female victims were fairly unanimous and resolute when asked about whether the actions taken by others had any effect:

INDIRA: No.

VERA: No, absolutely not.

LARISA: If they haven't had any effect so far, this seems to be the end of it.

ZINAIDA: Yes, [I agree that there was no effect].

VALYA: Today, seeing the results, what do we see? Nothing. In fact, nothing. That Kulayev was displayed like a puppet, and everybody pounced upon him, but he is actually of no importance whatsoever. In this situation I can say that he was just thrown up, so that there was somebody to attack, like dogs at a bone. Nothing has been discovered, people don't know why they were ruined, why they suffered, why—nothing at all, absolute nil.

SIMA: God, what was the use of it?

VALENTINA: It made no sense at all. I went out. I was in solidarity. I was for all those principles that were put forward, that the people demanded. I just couldn't stay at home. This was the only [event], so to speak, where I took part. And what? Nothing. The people were dispersed, just dispersed. That simple. Promising, of course, promising to disclose the culprits, to let everybody know. That was all.

VALYA: Yes, there were sixty people among the victims [who attended the trial of police officers]. That is not a small quantity of people. And the representatives of the authorities, those power structures, in every way they protected and said that the policemen weren't guilty. They weren't guilty. No one is guilty. The proceedings went on from ten to five, and all—sixty people—explained, each of them differently, each with his own version, quite convincing, they say. They are not guilty. But then tell us, who is?

The futility of action was discussed by the male nonactivists as well, with the same unanimity and resoluteness:

RUSLAN: The federal road was blocked. And so what? [The cars] were allowed on a detour. And what's the use? Fadzayev came and explained, "We'll sort it out." Until now, they are sorting it out.

BORIS: Right, no one will gain understanding, and nothing will be known.

RUSLAN: People stood there, sat there at night, and what did they do?

BORIS: Even the trial was turned into a dog and pony show. They made some kind of pamphlet. Who needs that? Nobody does. Nobody will [do] anything, and I think it makes no sense to talk about it.

RUSLAN: They will reveal the truth in seventy years.

BORIS: Even in 100 years.

RUSLAN: Even if we ask someone from the authorities, where is Kulayev now? No one will say where he is. Maybe he is at home already. Who knows.

ALAN: Yes, most likely.

BORIS: And still we didn't achieve any objectives, and we will not achieve them. If we starve, if we die, if we do whatever, we still will achieve nothing. Some demands were advanced at each action, right? And were any of these requirements met? Nothing was met. And there were constantly these actions with the same demand: to punish those guilty. And who punished them? No demand was ever met. It means they were ineffective. Nobody will learn anything about this terrorist act, at least in the next fifty years.

RUSLAN: Nothing has been achieved during four years.

VALERY: Everything will be kept a secret for seventy years if it was planned at the top. It will be kept in the archives, and if some of us are alive in seventy years, we will know.

BORIS: If only you had been to this trial, you would have seen what farce it was. It wasn't a trial, it was a farce. No one cared about the things you added. Nobody listened. That is, they did it the way they wanted to.

TAMERLAN: I was interested, but I didn't see the sense in participating. Even this rally [the blockade]. What does it have to do with absolute strangers who are driving? What did they block the road for? What sense does it make?

BORIS: We just understood that it was useless. Useless. Trying to make them say who is guilty—they will never say it. Punishing somebody—they will never punish. They all were promoted. Those who should have been dismissed, put into jail—they were all promoted.

VALERY: It is still not known how many people were there, who came.

BORIS: There was nothing [that was solved]. Nothing was solved through these actions.

VALERY: The Mothers of Beslan went to Strasburg, but they didn't achieve anything either.

BORIS: And now time passes. You won't achieve anything at all. We keep silent and live. And if we don't keep silent, then we won't live either.

ARKADY: Nobody listens to us.

ALAN: Nobody listens to us. Can't we see that?

BORIS: We see by our town.

Participants in focus groups of activist victims also overwhelmingly expressed sentiments about their inefficacy, with one young female explaining, "To my mind, those rallies didn't result in anything." Asked in a bigger sense about whether it is possible to achieve anything in Russia, she answered, "In Russia, I think not." Her fellow young activist agreed and qualified, "In some minor specific cases, you may achieve something, but on such a scale, no. No, by no means."

The attitudes expressed by activists in the focus group match the written record of perceived inefficacy in media accounts. Beslan activists were frustrated at every turn and often spoke about a particular activity being ineffective, un-successful, or pointless. When former hostage Kazbek Misikov was asked about the results of the September 1, 2005, meeting with Kozak, he answered, "There were no results. . . . There is nothing to say" (Allenova 2005b). When Mothers of Beslan members met with the official delegation of Gryzlov, Kozak, and Vasilyev on September 1, 2007, and asked the officials a barrage of questions, most were answered with requests to wait for the results of the official investigation. On Gryzlov's departure, Beslan resident Vladimir Kisiyev, whose grandson was killed in the school, said, "In a half hour he will forget us." A woman corrected Kisiyev, "No, he has already forgotten us" (Allenova and Farniyev 2007:4).

However, the occasional activist in the focus groups held out the possibility for efficacy. One young female activist defended the victims' activism, saying, "I believe that it wasn't stupid. The only way out is for the parents, the family, to speak up, to tell the bosses, the top authorities, how was it possible to hurt chil-dren!" The female activist victims over thirty-five even recounted the role that efficacy perceptions played in their recruitment and the need for prior successes to stimulate bandwagoning. One older activist recalled, "Sometimes, when we asked people and collected signatures, some people refused. They said, 'Do it yourself. If you succeed, I will participate as well.' "

This predominantly inefficacious response of activists peppered with a few efficacious sentiments or people also matches media descriptions of activist perceptions. After the Supreme Court rebuked Shepel for lying to the victims, Voice of Belsan leader Ella Kesayeva explained to reporters that victims felt both satisfaction in the Court's acknowledgment of Shepel's wrongdoing and deep dis-satisfaction at the lack of consequences. Similarly, the activist victims expressed mixed perceptions of efficacy during their experience with the ECHR. On the one hand, the ECHR may be the one institution and activity that made victims feel effective. Journalist Elena Milashina, who covered the victims for over ten years, wrote, "I photograph them all together on the steps of the Strasbourg Court. And suddenly I realize that these women have NEVER been so happy AFTER the Russian courts. Not once in all these 10 years" (Milashina 2014). On the other hand, the ECHR verdict, while satisfying in some respects, still offered no answers to outstanding questions about the terrorist attack and counterter-rorism operation. Speaking for the victims, attorney Sergei Knyazkin explained, "We are not quite satisfied with the ECHR's ruling. So, for example, the ECHR considered that Article 13 of the European Convention on Human Rights ('Right to an effective remedy') was not violated. Besides, in our view, the court awarded rather small compensation—between 5,000 and 20,000 euros to each person. People have lost their children and are awarded such small sums" ("Lawyers for Beslan" 2017).

Measuring Efficacy

Self-efficacy is a general state of psychological empowerment, an individual's feeling of being in control. However, despite the seemingly comprehensive nature of the term, self-efficacy "is not a global construct but is linked to specific domains of functioning in the context of situationally specific demands" (Barchia and Bussey 2011:108, citing Bandura 1997). A systematic review of research on self-efficacy after collective trauma found that "studies targeting self-efficacy appraisals tied directly to the situational context generated more consistent results, compared to studies that measured self-efficacy unrelated to coping with event-specific demand" (Luszczynska et al. 2009:60).

Self-efficacy here is therefore measured specifically in the context of the aftermath of the Beslan hostage taking and its event-specific demands. Victims were asked, "Can you yourself do anything to help solve the problems that two years ago led to the tragedy in Beslan, or are the problems completely out of your control? Do you feel this way strongly or only somewhat?" Such a measure unambiguously captures a victim's sense of self-efficacy as it might relate to post-violence behavior.

Table 9.1 confirms the anecdotal evidence from focus groups and media reports that Beslan victims felt highly inefficacious. Fewer than one in ten victims felt they could do anything to help solve the problems that led to the tragedy, and only 2.6 percent felt strongly about their self-efficacy. Fully two-thirds of Beslan victims felt the problems were out of their control, with 32.0 percent feeling this way somewhat and 35.2 percent feeling this way strongly.

Political efficacy is also context-specific, by definition, and is here conceived in terms of individuals' perceptions of their own competence to participate in politics. In addition, because assessments of the potential for effectiveness in the political arena may reflect perceptions of group, rather than individual, potential to solve problems through collective political action (Bandura 1986:449–452), political efficacy is here also conceived in terms of the perceived effectiveness of political action. Self-assessed political competence is measured by responses to the question, "How informed do you consider yourself to participate in politics?" The perceived effectiveness of political activity is measured by responses to the question, "Suppose you were dissatisfied with your political or economic situation, to what extent is each of the following an effective way to address your dissatisfaction? *Demonstrating or protesting.*"

Table 9.1. Self-Efficacy and Political Efficacy among Beslan Victims

Self-efficacy: "Can you yourself do anything to help solve the problems that two years ago led to the tragedy in Beslan, or are the problems completely out of your control? Do you feel this way strongly or only somewhat?"

Out of My Control Strongly	Out of My Control Somewhat	Can Solve Somewhat	Can Solve Strongly
386	351	78	29
(35.2)	(32.0)	(7.1)	(2.6)

Perceived effectiveness of protest: "Suppose you were dissatisfied with your political or economic situation, to what extent is each of the following an effective way to address your dissatisfaction? *Demonstrating or protesting*"

Very Effective	Rather Effective	Not Very Effective	Not at All Effective
35	140	384	235
(3.2)	(12.8)	(35.0)	(21.4)

Self-assessed political competence: "How informed do you consider yourself to participate in politics?"

Very Informed	Rather Informed	Not Very Informed	Not at All Informed
20	215	590	183
(1.8)	(19.6)	(53.7)	(16.7)

$N = 1,098$; number of victims (%)

These measures offer distinct advantages over the conventionally used alternatives. Since the 1950s, political efficacy has been measured with attitudes statements, such as "I don't think public officials care much what people like me think"; "Voting is the only way that people like me can have any say about how the government runs things"; "People like me don't have any say about what the government does"; and "Sometimes politics and government seem so complicated that a person like me can't really understand what's going on" (Campbell et al. 1954). Respondents are asked to agree or disagree, usually on a five- or seven-point scale. Despite their persistence, the measures have obvious flaws, including ambiguity (who are "people like me"?), the cognitive challenge of double negatives when disagreeing, and the erroneous assumption that the questions covary over time and could be combined in a unidimensional scale (Reef and Knoke 1999:416–417). The measures also often conflate what is known as internal and external efficacy, with the former referring to perceived personal competence in the political system and the latter referring to the perceived responsiveness of the government and therefore potentially reflecting political alienation and blame as much as political efficacy (Balch 1974). Direct self-assessments of political competence and assessments of the effectiveness of political protest leave far less room for ambiguity, response bias, or conceptual confusion.

The low self-efficacy described in Table 9.1 is matched by low political efficacy, in terms of both self-assessed competence and assessed effectiveness of protest. Only two in ten Beslan victims considered themselves sufficiently informed to participate in politics, with only 1.8 percent describing themselves as very informed. Fewer than two in ten considered demonstrating or protesting an effective way to address dissatisfaction, with only 3.2 percent describing protest as very effective.

Importantly for both self-efficacy and political efficacy, variation among victims does exist. The efficacious are in the minority, but so too are the political activists and supporters of retaliatory violence. The question is whether these variations are correlated.

Beslan Victim Data on Efficacy and Behavior

Data from the Beslan victims suggest that efficacy indeed plays a role in post-violence behavior, although the different forms of efficacy manifest differently. As Tables 9.2 and 9.3 show, self-efficacy is significantly correlated with support for retaliatory violence ($r = .11$, $p = .00$), a relationship that proves robust and

Table 9.2. Self-Efficacy and Support for Retaliatory Violence (Killing the Same Number of Chechens as Were Killed in Beslan)

"Can you yourself do anything to help solve the problems that two years ago led to the tragedy in Beslan, or are the problems completely out of your control? Do you feel this way strongly or only somewhat?"

	Completely Disapprove	Somewhat Disapprove	Somewhat Approve	Fully Approve	Missing	N
Out of my control strongly	180 (46.6)	123 (31.9)	29 (7.5)	18 (4.7)	36 (9.3)	386 (100.0)
Out of my control somewhat	124 (35.5)	169 (48.1)	27 (7.7)	12 (3.4)	19 (5.4)	351 (100.0)
Can solve somewhat	35 (44.9)	24 (30.8)	7 (9.0)	9 (11.5)	3 (3.8)	78 (100.0)
Can solve strongly	11 (37.9)	9 (31.0)	4 (13.8)	5 (17.2)	0 (0.0)	29 (100.0)

$N = 1,098$; number of victims (%); Pearson's $r = .11$, $p < .00$.

Table 9.3. Self-Efficacy and Political Participation

"Can you yourself do anything to help solve the problems that two years ago led to the tragedy in Beslan, or are the problems completely out of your control? Do you feel this way strongly or only somewhat?"

	No Activities	One Activity	Two or Three Activities	Four to Ten Activities	Eleven to Thirty-one Activities	Missing	N
Out of my control strongly	192 (49.7)	58 (15.0)	37 (9.6)	35 (9.1)	6 (1.6)	58 (15.0)	386 (100.0)
Out of my control somewhat	197 (56.1)	31 (8.8)	36 (10.3)	28 (8.0)	33 (9.4)	26 (7.4)	351 (100.0)
Can solve somewhat	30 (38.5)	7 (9.0)	13 (16.7)	6 (7.7)	12 (15.4)	10 (12.8)	78 (100.0)
Can solve strongly	11 (37.9)	1 (3.4)	2 (6.9)	3 (10.3)	5 (17.2)	7 (24.1)	29 (100.0)

$N = 1,098$; number of victims (%); Pearson's $r = .21$, $p < .00$.

powerful in multivariate analysis in Chapter 11. The more a victim believed he or she could do something to help solve the problems that two years ago led to the tragedy in Beslan, the more likely the victim was to support killing Chechens as a response. Self-efficacy was also a significant correlate of peaceful political participation in bivariate analysis ($r = .21$, $p = .00$), but the relationship proves somewhat less significant in multivariate analysis.

Taken together, these findings corroborate the many conclusions in prior research that self-efficacy motivates action. The findings also suggest that self-efficacy has motivating effects regardless of the normative desirability of the specific action it motivates. The relationship between self-efficacy and the normatively *un*desirable action of retaliatory violence is particularly strong. Feeling power and control in a situation that most others would describe as beyond control may actually be delusional, and this unrealistic mindset may then facilitate unhealthy thoughts such as supporting retaliatory violence. The latter interpretation is speculative, because self-efficacy alone seems unlikely to turn an otherwise peace-loving victim into a supporter of murder. Nevertheless, the data justify caution in treating self-efficacy as an unambiguously positive perception.

Political efficacy, however, seems to be an unambiguously positive perception (Table 9.4). Although uncorrelated with support for retaliatory violence, political

Table 9.4. Political Efficacy and Political Participation

Perceived effectiveness of protest: "Suppose you were dissatisfied with your political or economic situation, to what extent is each of the following an effective way to address your dissatisfaction? *Demonstrating or protesting*"

	No Activities	One Activity	Two or Three Activities	Four to Ten Activities	Eleven to Thirty-one Activities	Missing	N
Very effective	2 (5.7)	5 (14.3)	5 (14.3)	7 (20.0)	5 (14.3)	11 (31.4)	35 (100.0)
Rather effective	73 (52.1)	10 (7.1)	15 (10.7)	9 (6.4)	13 (9.3)	20 (14.3)	140 (100.0)
Not very effective	176 (45.8)	48 (12.5)	49 (12.8)	37 (9.6)	32 (8.3)	42 (10.9)	384 (100.0)
Not at all effective	137 (58.3)	33 (14.0)	26 (11.1)	14 (6.0)	3 (1.3)	22 (9.4)	235 (100.0)

Pearson's $r = .17, p < .00$.

Self-assessed political competence: "How informed do you consider yourself to participate in politics?"

	No Activities	One Activity	Two or Three Activities	Four to Ten Activities	Eleven to Thirty-one Activities	Missing	N
Very informed	1 (5.0)	1 (5.0)	1 (5.0)	2 (10.0)	7 (35.0)	8 (40.0)	20 (100.0)
Rather informed	72 (33.5)	13 (6.0)	19 (8.8)	51 (23.7)	12 (5.6)	48 (22.3)	215 (100.0)
Not very informed	294 (49.8)	87 (14.7)	69 (11.7)	44 (7.5)	31 (5.3)	65 (11.0)	590 (100.0)
Not at all informed	123 (67.2)	22 (12.0)	16 (8.7)	5 (2.7)	5 (2.7)	12 (6.6)	183 (100.0)

Pearson's $r = .31, p < .00$.

$N = 1,098$; number of victims (%).

efficacy has a strong and robust relationship with political participation: the minority of victims who felt informed to participate in politics and who evaluated demonstrating or protesting as effective engaged in many more political activities than other victims ($r = .31$ and $.17$, respectively, $p = .00$). When tested in multivariate analysis in Chapter 11, both measures of political efficacy have consistently significant and powerful effects on political participation.

The Conditional or Mediated Role of Efficacy?

Self-efficacy and political efficacy are sometimes hypothesized to have not only direct effects on action but also effects that are conditional on other factors or mediated by other factors, especially anger, alienation, and blame. For reasons discussed in detail in Chapters 5 and 7, the evidence from Beslan victims suggests that the effects of efficacy are mainly or even exclusively direct, not conditional or mediated.

In terms of support for retaliatory violence, anger may hypothetically encourage efficacy by lowering estimates of risk and raising optimism about successful outcomes (Petersen and Zukerman 2009), and if angrier victims are more convinced that retaliation will work, they should take such action. Empirically, however, anger in Beslan was uncorrelated with both efficacy assessments (self and political) and retaliatory violence (Tables 5.6 and 5.7 in Chapter 5). A sense of empowerment, in an objectively disempowering situation, motivated retaliatory violence, whether victims were angry or not.

For political participation, the causal chain is supposedly reversed: efficacy hypothetically triggers or facilitates anger, which then should motivate participation (Valentino et al. 2009; Brader et al. 2011; Valentino et al. 2011:159). Simultaneity is also presumed important: anger accompanied by the perception that political action is effective should also motivate participation (van Zomeren et al. 2004:649; Skitka et al. 2006:376; Carver and Harmon-Jones 2009:187). However, empirically in Beslan, anger and political efficacy, and to a lesser extent self-efficacy, played important but independent roles in motivating action.

The absence of a conditional role makes sense in light of equally compelling hypothesizing about a negative relationship between political efficacy and anger (Tausch et al. 2011:139–140). Individuals who perceive a lack of control or ability to influence political outcomes may find their predicament angering. The mechanisms whereby the inefficacious and the efficacious become angry may differ, but it is unclear that one group stakes a greater claim to the emotion. Regardless of anger, efficacy motivates political action more than inefficacy.

Neither is efficacy conditional on political alienation or blame, despite the plausibility of these hypothesized relationships. For example, high self-efficacy or political efficacy supposedly matters little if blame for problems is unclear (Bandura 1982:143–144). Instead, blame toward political officials and alienation from the political system should motivate political action only when accompanied by a feeling of empowerment; a perceived absence of blame and political alienation should motivate support for retaliatory violence only when accompanied by a feeling of empowerment. Also, the perceived absence of blame and political alienation—that is, the converse perception, a sense of political pride and connectedness—should itself be empowering. The data from

Beslan victims show, however, that interactions between efficacy, self or political, and political alienation and blame are not statistically significant (Table 8.6 in Chapter 8), and indeed, efficacy and alienation are largely uncorrelated, meaning the effects of one are not mediated by the other (Table 8.7). Self-efficacy and political efficacy have strong independent effects on post-violence behavior, whether or not victims were politically alienated; political alienation and blame have strong independent effects, whether or not victims felt efficacious.

The one possible exception to the observed lack of conditionality of factors involves blaming Putin and believing that demonstrating or protesting is an effective way to address dissatisfaction. As Table 7.7 in Chapter 7 showed, these two factors are positively, although moderately, correlated, suggesting that blaming Putin may encourage greater belief in the efficacy of protest, especially if Putin is the target of that protest. However, the effects of the interaction of blame and protest efficacy are additional and complementary to the more significant, robust, and meaningful independent effects of each.

The Reverse Effects of Action on Efficacy?

Inferring causality with a cross-sectional survey design is difficult, and it is reasonable to consider the possibility of reciprocal or reverse causation. Perhaps efficacy does not cause behavior, but rather the support for retaliatory violence or participation in political action made victims feel efficacious. Existing research shows a high degree of reciprocity between self-efficacy and atypical life events, because perceptions of efficacy often become self-fulfilling prophecies. The highly efficacious take challenges and experience successes that increase their efficacy, while the less efficacious have difficulty coping and experience less success, which reinforces the initial low self-perception (Gecas 1989:308). For political efficacy in particular, the perception of empowerment may sometimes follow, rather than precede, political participation (Balch 1974; Wood 2003; Jasper 2011:292). Participation can provide skills and familiarity with the political system that in turn encourage further participation (Dahl 1961:288; Finkel 1985; Pierce and Carey 1971; Lichbach 1998). Crime victims, for example, are often driven by a quest for efficacy and use political participation as a tool for empowerment, a means to overcome feelings of helplessness (Bateson 2012:572). However, research also shows that only some forms of participation increase efficacy and that unconventional behavior such as political protest has little effect (Finkel 1985, 1987).

In the context of responses to victimization by violence, the more powerful causal direction is likely from efficacy to action. When efficacy is hypothesized to influence action, the objective outcome of the action and its subjective success or failure are not yet known and therefore not part of the hypothesized causal linkage. Efficacious individuals simply anticipate successful outcomes more than inefficacious individuals and therefore participate more frequently. However, when action is hypothesized to be causally prior to efficacy, the relationship is conditional on the perceived success or failure of action (Muller and Opp 1986:484). A positive experience where political engagement led to intended outcomes can increase efficacy, but a negative experience can decrease efficacy (Bandura 1977). Given that so many victim activist experiences are negative and disempowering, while the relationship between efficacy and activism remains strong, it seems likely that the efficacy-activism linkage is driven by the efficacy that predated the activism or persisted despite the negative outcomes.

In the case of Beslan, political activists often seemed jaded and cynical about the effects of their activism, and activism may have even decreased their efficacy. In each focus group of activists, male and female, older and younger, participants spoke so consistently and emphatically about the uselessness of their actions that they could easily have been mistaken for nonactivists. For example, female activist victims under thirty-five years old described how their participation reduced their political efficacy:

VIKA: When we once went to a rally, I understood that we were being used, just like this school had been probably used. Never again have I or my friends or relatives put ourselves out, because I think it was simply useless.
IRINA: Some people were initially smart ones, and the rest got smart later. Only later did they understand that all those rallies wouldn't lead anywhere. They simply came back home and quietly mourned for their children in silence. That's all.
BELLA: In principle, I agree, because I, let's say, have never considered myself very socially active. Before the tragedy, I never participated in any rallies. I never participated anywhere. After it, I participated. But now I will never put myself out anywhere, because it doesn't produce anything.

The female activists over thirty-five also volunteered that their participation reduced their political efficacy.

FATIMA: Well, we were at the rally. When the highway was blocked, we were there. But nothing was achieved. We were also at the rallies in Vladikavkaz, the meeting with Dzasokhov, and so what? We didn't achieve anything.
LARISA: Little was achieved. And until now nothing has been achieved.
BERTA: Well, I went to the highway with them. Of course, we went to that rally, blocked the road, stood there together with mothers who had lost their children. It is impossible to do otherwise. But it also didn't result in anything. Many questions remained.

FATIMA: What questions did they answer? No one has ever answered any questions.

TATIANA: And nobody will ever reveal the truth to us. If we know the truth, it may only be 2% and that's all. Nobody is likely to speak about it.

LARISA: Of course, it [the highway blockade] was ineffective. Moreover, it proved humiliating.

FATIMA: All other things, even the trip to Putin. How did we benefit from meeting with him?

TATIANA: In Vladikavkaz, the Mothers' Committee organized actions around International Children's Day. It was also futile. The government came to the square, and they mocked and insulted. At one time, we went to Moscow in groups, but there was absolutely no result.

LARISA: We can't imagine [any actions that could have helped]. I personally even spoke with lawyers. They told me that there is the Criminal Code, and there is the Civil Code. In these two books—and this is our law—there is nothing said about terrorist acts. As far as terrorist acts are concerned, we have no rights. That's all. Like a wall. You beat your head against it, and all they say to you is: Here is the book. There is nothing in here.

DIANA: I think it's hopeless.

FATIMA: It was a hopeless situation.

In the focus group of male activist victims thirty-five years old or younger, participants agreed that the activism had not achieved anything.

VLADIMIR: The truth is still not known.

ZAUR: If only Kulayev went on trial, it means there is no truth. I don't think that he was the only guilty one. He is guilty, but he is not the only one. If nobody else goes on trial, it means there is no truth. [As far as the highway blockade goes.] There is nothing to tell. We sat there, put a tent in the middle of the highway. Relatives, parents, young people were sitting there, even those who were not in the terrorist act. And so what? Nothing. Representatives of the city administration, the government came and asked us to clear the road. And so what? And nothing.

The young activist men then discussed whether it was worthwhile to take any sort of action.

PAZIL: It is worth it, but it will all be senseless, probably.

AKHSAR: First, we all believed that they would tell us the truth sooner or later, but it drags on for so long already.

ZAUR: In fifty years they will do a program [about Beslan] and will show the whole truth. But nobody will need it in fifty years.

MARAT: You won't know this truth no matter how hard you try. We have the Mothers of Beslan. They have been trying for so many years, and what have they learned? Nothing.

PAZIL: They put charlatan Grabovoi in jail, and that's all. All this is without results. The same meetings—it's just a clownery, in large part. What is it all for?

Similarly, when the male activist victims over thirty-five years old were asked if they got any results from their activities, they all answered "no."

BORIS: Because everyone was left with a negative mark. They treated us not like people but like a mob. That's all.

ISRAEL: They [the authorities] are not ready to tell the truth.

KAZBEK: They promised us that the investigation would start. We, they said, will tell you everything objectively, only we are asking you: Unblock the road, because this road is of federal significance. This will lead to catastrophe. All right. People again dispersed. They believed the government. Again the same [lack of result].

BORIS: All these Supreme Courts are just a farce, clownery. They laugh at us once again. This was derision of us.

KAZBEK: Do you know at how many court proceedings I have been? You won't believe! I've appealed to 14 courts. And everywhere, in each court they say the following: Let's suppose, the court proceedings are ongoing. All judges agree with our arguments. According to the documents, they agree. But the decision is made in favor of the state again! That is, we almost end up being the guilty party, not them.

TOTRAZ: Here only Kulayev was imprisoned, and that's all. But people want to find the culprits.

KAZBEK: And the prosecutor's office and the investigative committee for some reason don't institute any proceedings against these people, and it is all postponed.

Despite these relatively uniform claims, a small percentage of victims still felt politically efficacious and assessed themselves as politically informed and believed that demonstrating or protesting was an effective way to address dissatisfaction. As shown in Tables 9.1 and 9.3, although such politically efficacious victims were in the minority, there were more of them among the activists. Political efficacy on average was higher for activist victims than nonactivists. The efficacy differential between activists and nonactivists is what mattered and suggests that political efficacy has strong and likely prior effects on activism. In the words of one young male activist, who himself pointed to the lack of results from activism: "Well, to know the truth, it's necessary to turn everything upside down. We should pester them so much that they say, 'Leave us alone.' Then something will probably work."

Further evidence that political efficacy in Beslan had significant positive effects on political participation with little to no reverse effect comes from incorporating the role of anger. If political participation heightened the sense of efficacy, presumably it would do so because the participation was perceived as successful in achieving a desired outcome. However, the perceived success of participation should also diminish anger, and as described in Chapter 5, this combination of high political participation, high political efficacy, and low anger is rare among Beslan victims and makes for a relatively implausible post-violence story. Similarly, if participation was perceived as unsuccessful, which by most accounts it was, it should diminish political efficacy but heighten anger, and that combination too—high political participation, high anger, and low political efficacy—is rare among Beslan victims. Far more plausible is that angry and politically efficacious victims were motivated by their anger and efficacy to participate more frequently in political activities than other victims.

Pessimism and Retaliatory Violence

Optimism is conceptually distinct from efficacy, but both concepts involve expectations of positive outcomes. Self-efficacy refers to people's perception of their constructive role in achieving a desired outcome. Optimism refers to the general anticipation of a desired outcome, individual role aside. It is an inclination to expect the best. While pessimists explain bad events as permanent and pervasive, optimists see positivity and hope and explain bad events as temporary setbacks that will likely be overcome (Seligman 1998).

After violence, optimism would seem difficult to maintain. Nevertheless, in Beslan victims were not universally pessimistic. In response to the question, "In general, how optimistic do you feel about your future?," half the victims were not very or not at all optimistic (40.7% and 9.0%, respectively), but a sizable minority were rather or very optimistic (32.1% and 7.7%, respectively). In response to the question, "How possible is it to solve the problems that two years ago led to the tragedy in Beslan?," the majority gave the optimistic responses of rather possible or very possible (28.5% and 22.5%, respectively), with only 26.1 percent and 10.6 percent answering not very possible or not at all possible, respectively.

Because optimism and pessimism seem relevant to efficacy, their potential role in post-violence behavior warrants discussion here. Victims who feel optimistic about the future and the possibility for solving current problems may differ in their behavioral responses to violence from those who see the future as negative and hopeless.

In terms of retaliatory violence, pessimists are more likely supporters. Optimists consider problems solvable and look to a brighter future and therefore have less need for retaliatory violence, for either instrumental or expressive purposes. Pessimists, conversely, may be more mired in the hopelessness of a do-nothing strategy and feel they have little to lose by retaliating (Tausch et al. 2011:132). The causal mechanism that might trigger a pessimist to retaliate violently is relatively undertheorized but empirically supported: Prior research links pessimism to suicide ideation (Hirsch et al. 2009:48), suicide bombing (Politkovskaya 2001, 2003; Reuter 2004:2; Speckard and Akhmedova 2006:466–467), and extremist or non-normative political activities (Tausch et al. 2011:132).

In terms of peaceful political activism, the effects of optimism and pessimism are less clear. Pessimists probably feel their grievances more acutely than optimists, suggesting a greater propensity to participate in politics to address the grievances. For example, pessimists were more likely protesters in South Africa in the 1990s (Roefs, Klandermans, and Olivier 1998). However, pessimists may apply their pessimism to evaluations of the political process and believe that little good could come of participation. These sentiments may work at cross-purposes. Optimists, hoping and believing that problems will get solved, may feel that political action is unnecessary or at least not urgent, but they also may have greater hopefulness about the positive role of the public in the political process and therefore may be more inclined to participate. Participation of optimists could also be motivated by their initially high expectations that are then disappointed by the reality of negative outcomes and the need to revive their optimism (Lau 1985; Niven 2000). Optimists may even have high expectations for the success of bold, risky actions and therefore may be willing to participate in extreme political action (Satterfield and Seligman 1994). Again, the complex and sometimes contradictory effects of optimism suggest that it does not play a significant role in participation.

Evidence from media reports and focus group discussions support the idea that optimism and pessimism are not significant parts of the participation story. Activist victims in Beslan expressed both optimism and pessimism, and these sentiments often reflected realistic assessments of the stubborn resistance of the Russian government to address the victims' demands. For example, upon submitting a complaint to Russia's Supreme Court, Voice of Beslan leader Ella Kesayeva, offered a realistic and prescient appraisal:

> I cherish hope for our judicial system to have reason. Yet we should face the truth: our complaint will most probably be turned down. Then we will have a supervisory authority to go to and then Strasbourg. I am not pessimistic on this matter. All our actions today are just oriented towards Strasbourg. We stand to win our case against Russia in Strasbourg on the terrorist act in Beslan. I have no doubt. They will hand down a positive verdict to us. ("Beslan Committee Ready" 2006).

Low expectations of outcomes within Russia were commonly expressed by victims, but the low expectations were better characterized as warranted than pessimistic. For example, when Deputy Prosecutor General Shepel was removed from office and was replaced by Ivan Sydoruk, Kesayeva expressed doubt that anything would change. "I have no hope. Shepel concealed the facts but he knew everything. Sydoruk was aloof from the case, the tragedy. He will not go deep into the case and the falsehoods will go on" (Tlisova 2006a). Both at the time and in retrospect, most victims, activist and nonactivist, would label these assessments as not pessimistic but accurate.

For another example, on August 31, 2005, more than thirty families and hundreds of individuals signed a letter to the international community expressing lost hope in hearing the truth and asking for asylum or immigration status from foreign governments. The victims wrote:

> We—mothers, fathers, close relatives of the hostages, people treated like animals by terrorists, betrayed by our government, officials, security forces and "our" president—driven to despair, have lost any hope of hearing the truth about who is responsible for killing our families. We are asking you to accept us in your country, where we will be law-abiding citizens. . . . We ask you to treat our request with understanding. We are ready to exhume our children and relatives and leave Russia. We are not people driven insane by sadness, but people who have lost faith in truth and justice. . . . We . . . have been waiting patiently for almost a year to be told the truth about the bestial murder of our relatives and for the guilty to take responsibility. Time and the authorities' actions have shown us that the truth will never be revealed. (Mainville 2005d:A03).

> Putin sacrificed our children and our loved ones for a dirty policy. We . . . have lost all hope for a just investigation of the reasons and the guilty parties in our tragedy, and we do not wish to live any more in this country, where a human life means nothing. (Page 2005d:39; Stephen 2005b)

Victims occasionally expressed hope as well but usually in a larger context of pessimism, with neither optimism nor pessimism seeming a particular powerful motivator of behavior. For example, male activist victims over thirty-five discussed whether they still hoped to get some answer or truth and why they persisted in their activities, given their professed feelings of futility:

TOTRAZ: Of course, everyone hopes. No doubt about that.
KAZBEK: If not our government, then at least the world community will pay attention to us.
KAZBEK: For example, if I know that Mothers of Beslan Mothers is having some activity, I will go. I nevertheless want to find the truth. I don't believe [it's

possible], but all the same. How can I explain? You understand, to tell you the truth, I am 90% sure that nothing will come of it, but all the same my inner voice tells me that we need to fight anyway. There is some small hope.

KAZBEK2: Hope springs eternal.

Among Beslan victims surveyed, optimists were no more or less likely to participate in politics than pessimists. There was no statistically significant relationship between the two measures of optimism and the count variable of peaceful political action, at the bivariate or multivariate levels.

By contrast, supporters of retaliatory violence were highly likely to be pessimists (Table 9.5). The bivariate correlations of approval of killing Chechens

Table 9.5. Optimism and Support for Retaliatory Violence (Killing the Same Number of Chechens as Were Killed in Beslan)

"In general, how optimistic do you feel about your future?"

	Completely Disapprove	Somewhat Disapprove	Somewhat Approve	Fully Approve	Missing	N
Very optimistic	52 (61.2)	22 (25.9)	5 (5.9)	0 (0.0)	6 (7.1)	85 (100.0)
Rather optimistic	134 (38.0)	106 (30.0)	30 (8.5)	22 (6.2)	61 (17.3)	353 (100.0)
Not very optimistic	184 (41.2)	185 (41.4)	29 (6.5)	30 (6.7)	19 (4.3)	447 (100.0)
Not at all optimistic	32 (32.3)	35 (35.4)	10 (10.1)	7 (7.1)	15 (15.2)	99 (100.0)

Pearson's $r = -.10$, $p < .00$.

"In your opinion, how possible is it to solve/eliminate the problems that two years ago led to the tragedy in Beslan?"

	Completely Disapprove	Somewhat Disapprove	Somewhat Approve	Fully Approve	Missing	N
Very possible	142 (57.5)	66 (26.7)	14 (5.7)	16 (6.5)	9 (3.6)	247 (100.0)
Rather possible	129 (41.2)	139 (44.4)	16 (5.1)	14 (4.5)	15 (4.8)	313 (100.0)
Not very possible	115 (40.1)	94 (32.8)	26 (9.1)	21 (7.3)	31 (10.8)	287 (100.0)
Not at all possible	30 (25.9)	46 (39.7)	21 (18.1)	7 (6.0)	12 (10.3)	116 (100.0)

Pearson's $r = -.15$, $p < .00$.

$N = 1,098$; number of victims (%).

with generalized optimism and with optimism about solving the problems that led to the Beslan tragedy may appear small ($r = -.10$ and $-.15$, respectively, $p = .00$), but they are consistently negative, and when controls are added in the multivariate analysis, the correlations are much stronger. Supporters of retaliatory violence feel less hopeful about the future than other victims, both in general and specific terms.

The combined empirical results for self-efficacy and pessimism offer a nuanced insight into support for retaliatory violence. Victims who believe it is possible to solve the problems that led to the Beslan tragedy were *less* likely to support retaliatory violence. Victims who believe they themselves can do something to help solve the problems that led to the Beslan tragedy were *more* likely to support retaliatory violence. Expectations of positive outcomes in the abstract, without reference to personal agency, and expectations of positive outcomes as a result of personal agency thus have opposite effects on support for violence.

Conclusion

An individual's sense of effectiveness, competence, agency, empowerment, and control is usually described in positive terms. Forms of efficacy, such as self-efficacy and political efficacy, are considered helpful attributes in ordinary circumstances and, after violence, might seem particularly useful for motivating constructive behavioral responses to the violence.

Data from Beslan victims largely substantiate these assumptions. Political efficacy in particular has a positive significant effect on peaceful political participation. Victims who believed that demonstrating or protesting is an effective way to address their dissatisfaction and who believed in their own capacity to participate in politics engaged in a higher number of political activities than less efficacious victims. Although political efficacy is sometimes hypothesized to be the result of participation rather than its cause, the focus group discussions and other evidence from Beslan suggest that the causal direction is largely from political efficacy to participation and not the reverse. Activism in Beslan was widely perceived by both activist and nonactivist victims as ineffective, despite the historic nature of some accomplishments, such as the 2017 ruling of the ECHR against the Russian government and in favor of the victims. After repeated blows to political efficacy from the perceived failures of political action, some victims managed to continue to give high evaluations of their political competence and the effectiveness of protest, and these victims were among the most likely activists.

Self-efficacy also has a positive significant effect on political participation, although less powerful and robust than the effect of political efficacy. Self-efficacy, however, is a double-edged sword, because feelings of agency, power, and control may be channeled toward normatively undesirable behavior, such as retaliatory violence. Among Beslan victims, those who thought they could do something to help solve the problems that led to the tragedy in Beslan were more likely to support retaliatory violence. Those who thought the problems were completely out of their control were less likely to want to take matters into their own hands. Self-efficacy may therefore be somewhat culpable in perpetuating the spiral of violence, and an acknowledgment of lost control may sometimes better service peace.

Like self-efficacy, pessimism plays a significant role in encouraging support for retaliatory violence. While pessimism involves low expectations for positive outcomes, and efficacy involves high expectations, pessimism does not factor individual agency into those expectations. Lacking optimism about one's future and the possibility to solve the problems that led to the tragedy may create a dark, nothing-to-lose mood that could potentially be exploited by a call for revenge.

10

Biography

Demographics, Prior Harm, and Prior Activism

Behavior is often driven by biography, or all that came before today during the course of life. Demographic characteristics and personal history are thus usually the first descriptors of victims of violence and are assumed to be relevant in the aftermath. Demographic characteristics may include age, gender, education, and income. Personal history may include prior experiences of being harmed during incidents of ethnic violence and prior experiences with voting or extra-institutional political behavior.

Expectations of retaliatory violence in Beslan were largely driven by an awareness of the importance of biography. A vast amount of scholarly research and routine observations show that, probabilistically, violence begets more violence. When the hostage-taking incident became embedded in the personal history of every victim and in some sense part of the unvarying grievance context, it was reasonably predicted to motivate behavioral responses.

However, aspects of the victims' biographies that predated the hostage taking may also be important. Beslan victims whose families experienced violence prior to the current victimization might have especially deep unhealed wounds (Staub and Bar-Tal 2003:722) and might be more readily mobilized for retaliatory violence than individuals experiencing their first victimization. Repeat victims also might be more readily mobilized for peaceful political participation because their grievances are that much more severe.

Research also shows that political activism begets more political activism. Victims of violence who participated in peaceful politics prior to their victimization should already know the political ropes and have habits of participation to channel toward addressing the newly experienced grievance over violence. These same habits of participation should make prior political activists less likely to support retaliatory violence, because it is an unfamiliar course of action and because their longtime activism is often a manifestation of their nonviolent inclinations.

This chapter explores the significance of prior harm, prior activism, and demographic characteristics for behavioral responses to violence. The analysis shows that victims' biography mattered tremendously in terms of their personal history

After Violence. Debra Javeline, Oxford University Press. © Oxford University Press 2023.
DOI: 10.1093/oso/9780197683347.003.0011

but mattered very little in terms of demographics. Those whose family or friends suffered harm by someone of Ingush or Chechen descent prior to the hostage taking were more likely to support retaliatory violence and also more likely to participate in politics. Those who participated in politics prior to the hostage taking were more likely to participate in politics afterward and, notably, were less likely to support retaliatory violence. Longtime political activists are thus some of the most reliably committed to ending the spiral of violence while still demanding grievance satisfaction.

Victims' age, education, and income were not significantly related to support for retaliatory violence or participation. Gender, while anecdotally observed to be meaningful for political participation in Beslan, was less significant than anticipated. For retaliatory violence, to the extent that gender mattered, women were more supportive than men. Another component of biography, biographical availability, or victims' time constraints due to caretaking, work, medical problems, and other demands, was a critical factor in the aftermath of the hostage taking, because the life-altering terrorist act had time-constraining consequences for most victims. However, biographical (un)availability was less of a factor in accounting for variation among victims in how they responded to the violence.

Prior Harm

For many victims of violence, especially those in ethnically divided and violence prone communities, victimization has been experienced or witnessed before. Such victims often see the latest offense in the context of this violent history, part of a pattern or series, "rather than a single, discrete incident" (Horowitz 2001:531). Current violent conduct of the perpetrators seems consistent with prior violent conduct and therefore weighted more heavily than for first-time victims who may know the history but feel it less personally.

The decades-long conflicts between Ossetians and Ingush described in Chapter 1 mean that the school hostage taking was not the first time many victims were violated. Hostage takings, shootings, beatings, property destruction, and other human rights violations have been common in North Ossetia and the larger Caucasus and have been experienced by residents of all nationalities ("Russia: The Ingush-Ossetian Conflict" 1996). Many Beslan victims had therefore seen atrocities before. Indeed, instances of prior harm were so commonplace that they could be mentioned casually in the midst of discussion of other topics. For example, participants in the focus group of female activists thirty-five and younger dropped information about their prior experiences being harmed by Ingush:

VIKA: Our men also went by KAMAZ truck alone, until they were kidnapped and kept in a cellar.
MADINA: Our family has the same situation. My mother-in-law's brother was kidnapped.

Two women, in a room of only nine, had personal experiences with kidnapping, and it did not strike any of the participants as noteworthy enough to pause the conversation.

In the survey, victims were asked whether, prior to the hostage taking, any of their family or friends had ever been physically harmed by someone of Ingush or Chechen descent. Nearly one in five victims (17.7 percent, or 194 of 1,098 surveyed) answered yes.

The cumulative effects of victimization may increase the likelihood of a violent response. Evidence suggests that exposure to frequent violence breeds acceptance of violence as a useful or justifiable tool. Violence can be learned (Gurr 1970; Ross 1993; Paris 2004:169–170; Chapman 2008:522). In experimental research, people with histories of violence are more likely to be judged as currently intending violence and therefore met with preemptive violence. In empirical research on the renewal of violence in ethnically based civil wars, an opponent's prior violence often motivates an antagonist to resort to the same (Horowitz 2001:159). Among victims of Russian atrocities in the wars in Chechnya, the greater the trauma, the more likely the endorsement of generalized revenge, targeting Russians as an ethnic group rather than seeking to find a specific guilty party (Speckhard and Ahkmedova 2006:466–467). For those who turned to suicide terrorism, witnessing beatings and deaths of loved ones or personally experiencing torture was a common characteristic (Speckhard and Ahkmedova 2006:444; Tuathail 2009:7).

Thus, in Beslan, among victims who suffered from violence committed by Chechens or Ingush against them, their family, or their friends prior to the hostage taking, it is reasonable to expect greater support for retaliatory violence after the hostage taking. In Russian they might say, "A clever man won't step on the same rake twice." Or in English, "Fool me once, shame on you, but fool me twice—and with the atrocity of a school hostage taking, no less—and shame on me, a shame that will be avenged." For repeat victims, the hostage taking may have been the last straw.

Prior harm may play a similar role in political activism. For repeat victims, the longer or more intense history of victimization might exacerbate the political grievances associated with the most recent incident and thereby motivate action. For example, individuals who were most exposed to violence during Nepal's ten-year civil war had higher levels of civic participation (Gilligan et al. 2011). Those experiencing violence during African civil wars were also more likely voters, civic activists, and community leaders (Bellows and Miguel 2009; Blattman 2009). In Beslan, it is reasonable to expect a similar pattern. Victims of the hostage taking who suffered harm from violence committed by Chechens or Ingush before the hostage taking should have been more likely than first-time victims to participate in peaceful political action.

Analysis of the victim survey data supports these propositions. As seen in Tables 10.1 and 10.2, Beslan victims whose family or friends were physically

Table 10.1. Prior Harm and Support for Retaliatory Violence (Killing the Same Number of Chechens as Were Killed in Beslan)

"Prior to the hostage taking in the school, had any of your family or friends ever been physically harmed by someone of Ingush or Chechen descent?"

	Completely Disapprove	Somewhat Disapprove	Somewhat Approve	Fully Approve	Missing	N
No	353 (42.2)	322 (38.5)	59 (7.1)	33 (3.9)	69 (8.3)	836 (100.0)
Yes	78 (40.2)	46 (23.7)	28 (14.4)	31 (16.0)	11 (5.7)	194 (100.0)

$N = 1,098$; number of victims (%); Pearson's $r = .16, p < .00$.

Table 10.2. Prior Harm and Political Participation

"Prior to the hostage taking in the school, had any of your family or friends ever been physically harmed by someone of Ingush or Chechen descent?"

	No Activities	One Activity	Two or Three Activities	Four to Ten Activities	Eleven to Thirty-one Activities	Missing	N
No	441 (52.8)	100 (12.0)	75 (9.0)	87 (10.4)	30 (3.6)	103 (12.3)	836 (100.0)
Yes	51 (26.3)	25 (12.9)	33 (17.0)	15 (7.7)	28 (14.4)	42 (21.6)	194 (100.0)

$N = 1,098$; number of victims (%); Pearson's $r = .17, p < .00$.

harmed by someone of Ingush or Chechen descent prior to the hostage taking were more likely to support retaliatory violence ($r = .16, p < .00$) and also to engage in political activism ($r = .17, p < .00$). A personal history that includes some ethnic violence was thus an important motivator of responses to the hostage taking.

Prior Political Activism

Political participation may also be part of a victim's history prior to victimization. In Beslan, however, many victims asserted that political activism was low to nonexistent before the hostage taking and the accompanying political grievances. Indeed, in the focus group of male activist victims over thirty-five years old, participants were a bit confused by questions about prior participation in rallies, strikes, or other political activities.

TOTRAZ: What kind of rallies? Everything was quiet, normal.
KAZBEK: A small quiet town. What rallies would there be here?

Male nonactivist victims responded with similar confusion to questions about participation prior to the hostage taking:

BORIS: And what events or actions could there be before the events in Beslan? As always, a parade, some demonstrations.
VALERY: No [there were no meetings]. It was calm. Everyone knows each other.
BORIS: Nothing like that ever happened in Beslan. We didn't starve or rally, nothing.
RUSLAN: Here everyone knows each other from one end [of town] to the other end. What rallies and strikes?

But of course there was some political activism in Beslan before the hostage taking, just as there is some political activism in most towns in Russia and the world. In the survey, victims were asked about their participation in seven different activities related to voting, including whether they voted in the last presidential election, last Duma election, and last regional or local election, and whether they engaged in informal political persuasion or formal campaigning before national or local elections. Of these seven voting-related activities, victims on average participated in two of them, with a mode of three activities (reported by 40 percent of victims). Victims were also asked about their participation in nine different activities that went beyond voting, including whether they attended a mass meeting or speech by an elected official, demonstrated or protested, worked with others in the town to solve problems, formed a new group to solve a community problem, wrote a letter to a local official, went in person to see a local official, wrote a letter to a non-local official, wrote a letter to the media, or participated in a strike. Here the victims' impression of a largely quiet, apolitical Beslan is confirmed. Of these nine nonvoting political activities, victims on average participated in 0.4 of them prior to the hostage taking. The modal number of activities was zero, with 76 percent of victims having not participated in a single activity.

However, the remaining victims, though a minority, did possess relevant political experience. As described below, individuals who previously addressed grievances through conventional or even unconventional political channels should be more likely to return to those familiar channels when confronted with a new grievance. They therefore should be less likely to respond with the unfamiliar behavior of aggression (Muller 1982). Research supporting this claim has explored the role of prior activism on violent behavior toward the state, whereas the Beslan question is about support for retaliatory violence against members of the perpetrators' ethnic group. Still, the logic holds: in the case of Beslan, past political participation should have a dampening effect on support for retaliatory violence, because prior activists are alert to alternative venues for grievance expression. The relationship may not be causal and instead reflect the attraction of nonviolent individuals to civic institutions and activities (Chapman 2008).

Data from the survey of Beslan victims indeed suggest that longtime political activists were less likely to support killing Chechens as retaliation for the hostage taking. Although the correlation between prior voting behavior and support for retaliatory violence is not statistically significant, the correlation between prior nonvoting behavior and support for retaliatory violence is significant and negative ($r = -.11, p = .00$), and multivariate analysis in Chapter 11 shows the relationship is powerful and robust.

Past political participation is also probably one of the surest predictors of future political participation (Becker et al. 2011). Past behavior often contributes to a person's self-perception as an activist, which then creates cognitive pressures to be consistent and match future behavior to the self-perception (Moskalenko and McCauley 2009:252). Past behavior, when effective or perceived as such, also affords skills and confidence to be used in future action. Thus, participants in the 1964 Mississippi Freedom Summer project were more politically active throughout their lives than individuals who applied and were accepted but did not participate (McAdam 1989). Women activists of the 1960s were similarly more participatory later in life when compared to nonactivists (Cole et al. 1998). Individuals with past protest experience in Greece were more likely than others to participate in the 2010 strikes and demonstrations over austerity measures (Rüdig and Karyotis 2014). Past participation is one of the most salient pieces of information for political parties, candidates, and interest groups who seek to recruit individuals to undertake new political acts (Brady et al. 1999). Recruiters strategically investigate individuals' registration status, voting in past elections, and contributions to candidates and parties (Abramson and Claggett 2001).

These robust patterns should apply in Beslan. Victims who were politically active prior to the hostage taking should be more likely to engage in politics in response to the hostage taking. The victim survey data presented in Table 10.3 unambiguously support these expectations. Correlations of the number of post-violence political activities with prior participation in voting-related activities and nonvoting-related activities such as protesting, striking, attending a rally, or

Table 10.3. Prior Political Activism and Political Participation

Prior Voting Behavior

(Voting behavior prior to tragedy as calculated by a count of seven voting-related activities: voted in last presidential election, voted in last Duma election, voted in last regional or local election, persuaded to vote in last national election, persuaded to vote in last regional election, engaged in national campaign, engaged in regional or local campaign)

	No Activities	One Activity	Two or Three Activities	Four to Ten Activities	Eleven to Thirty-one Activities	Missing	N
0	133 (60.7)	32 (14.6)	10 (4.6)	10 (4.6)	3 (1.4)	31 (14.2)	219 (100.0)
1	45 (51.1)	17 (19.3)	11 (12.5)	4 (4.5)	5 (5.7)	6 (6.8)	88 (100.0)
2	53 (52.0)	8 (7.8)	14 (13.7)	7 (6.9)	4 (3.9)	16 (15.7)	102 (100.0)
3	202 (46.0)	52 (11.8)	47 (10.7)	62 (14.1)	24 (5.5)	52 (11.8)	439 (100.0)
4	4 (17.4)	1 (4.3)	2 (8.7)	3 (13.0)	11 (47.8)	2 (8.7)	23 (100.0)
5	2 (16.7)	2 (16.7)	2 (16.7)	3 (25.0)	3 (25.0)	0 (0.0)	12 (100.0)
6	0 (0.0)	0 (0.0)	1 (33.3)	0 (0.0)	0 (0.0)	2 (66.7)	3 (100.0)

Pearson's $r = .21$, $p < .00$.

(continued)

Table 10.3. Continued

Prior Nonvoting Behavior

(Nonvoting behavior prior to tragedy as calculated by a count of nine nonvoting-related activities: attended mass meeting or speech by elected official, demonstrated or protested, worked with others in town to solve problems, formed new group to solve community problem, wrote letter to local official, went to see local official, wrote to nonlocal official, wrote letter to media, participated in strike)

	No Activities	One Activity	Two or Three Activities	Four to Ten Activities	Eleven to Thirty-one Activities	Missing	N
0	471 (56.4)	119 (14.3)	89 (10.7)	48 (5.7)	22 (2.6)	86 (10.3)	835 (100.0)
1	11 (22.4)	11 (22.4)	8 (16.3)	10 (20.4)	3 (6.1)	6 (12.2)	49 (100.0)
2	10 (12.5)	1 (1.3)	10 (12.5)	30 (37.5)	6 (7.5)	23 (28.7)	80 (100.0)
3	4 (14.8)	1 (3.7)	2 (7.4)	4 (14.8)	15 (55.6)	1 (3.7)	27 (100.0)
4	1 (25.0)	1 (25.0)	0 (0.0)	1 (25.0)	0 (0.0)	1 (25.0)	4 (100.0)
5	1 (14.3)	1 (14.3)	0 (0.0)	0 (0.0)	5 (71.4)	1 (14.3)	7 (100.0)
6	0 (0.0)	0 (0.0)	0 (0.0)	1 (100.0)	0 (0.0)	0 (0.0)	1 (100.0)
7	0 (0.0)	0 (0.0)	0 (0.0)	0 (0.0)	0 (0.0)	2 (100.0)	2 (100.0)
9	0 (0.0)	0 (0.0)	0 (0.0)	0 (0.0)	1 (100.0)	0 (0.0)	1 (100.0)

Pearson's $r = .51, p < .00$.

$N = 1,098$; number of victims (%).

going to meet with a political official are statistically significant and high ($r = .21$ and .51, respectively, $p = .00$), and the relationship is among the strongest in multivariate analysis in Chapter 11.

Demographics

Individual demographic characteristics such as age, gender, education, and income are often hypothesized to influence support for retaliatory violence and peaceful political participation. For participation in particular, most studies include demographic variables as controls, if not central variables of interest. Empirically, age, gender, education, and income are consistently found to have significant effects on conventional and unconventional forms of political action (Leighley 1995).

However, there may be less reason to anticipate the same causal impact of demographic variables on post-violence behavior in Beslan or other post-violence contexts. For one thing, demographics were not highly correlated with the grievance of victimization; people of all backgrounds were affected. In terms of socioeconomic status, Beslan citizens were relatively homogeneous, and given the small size of the town, children of policymakers such as North Ossetian parliament-leader-turned-president Taimuraz Mamsurov studied with the children of ordinary citizens. Neither were people of one gender or age group spared. The violence affected entire families, no matter which member was among the dead or injured. Women, for example, were twice as likely as men to be among the hostages (35 percent of female victim respondents compared to 16 percent of male victim respondents), but men were more likely to have higher numbers of relatives, including their wives, among the hostages. Over 90 percent of the eighteen- and nineteen-year old victim respondents were hostages, compared to smaller percentages of victim respondents in their thirties and forties who, hostages or not, were usually parents of hostages.

More importantly, theories about the effects of demographic characteristics on post-violence behavior are often weak, contradictory, unclear, or unsupported by the empirical evidence. Still, given the prominence of demographics in discussions of retaliatory violence and political participation, age, gender, education, and income are discussed here and are included in analysis as control variables.

Age

Young people are often more likely to commit violence than older people (della Porta and Tarrow 1986:620–621), perhaps due to their higher economic insecurity (Goldstone 2001; Urdal 2006), the lower opportunity costs that accompany fewer family and career responsibilities (Goldstone 2001; Urdal 2006), attraction to new ideas and challenges to authority (Goldstone 2001), "hotheadedness" or youthful impulsiveness, and the youthful strength required for what is often a physical act. For example, participants in ethnic riots typically range in age from teens to thirties, and the more deadly rioters are typically closer to twenty than thirty (Horowitz 2001:259–260). Chechen suicide terrorists ranged in age from fifteen to forty-five and were commonly in their teens and twenties (Speckhard and Ahkmedova 2006).

In the focus group of male activist victims thirty-five years old or younger, participants discussed the effects of age on responses to the hostage taking in Beslan:

VLADIMIR: Yes [there were people who suggested striking back at the Ingush]. Other people were more rational and explained to them that they should first clarify who is to blame. [These more rational people were] the older generation.

AKHSAR: Yes, there are so many of our lads already on the borders! Yes, they were already ready to go.

VLADIMIR: Everyone needs to get together, and when they do, they discuss these issues—to go or not to go [to fight the Ingush]. They discuss at all levels, younger and older people.

ALAN: There are senior people whose opinion is respected.

To the extent that retaliatory violence was on the table in Beslan, young people were perceived as supporters, at least initially, whereas older people were perceived as more restrained. As a male activist victim over thirty-five years old reflected on his desire for revenge but subsequent reconsideration, young people "should be raised to listen to seniors."

Perhaps it is surprising, then, that evidence from the Beslan victim survey suggests that age had no meaningful effect on support for retaliatory violence. There is no reason to doubt the anecdotal accounts of young males publicly endorsing retaliation. These accounts were consistent across focus groups and in media reports and suggest that age may affect the willingness to express support for retaliatory violence out loud. However, at least some older victims shared these violent sentiments, even if unexpressed publicly, while many young victims quietly rejected retaliation. Systematic responses to the survey question about killing Chechens reveal that the low level of support for retaliatory violence was similar across all age groups. The correlation shown in Table 10.4 is close to zero ($r = .02, p = .55$).

Age has been thought to matter for political action as well, with older people often more likely to participate in institutional politics. As individuals age, they accumulate information, life experiences, resources, and community ties that increase their propensity to vote (Verba and Nie 1972; Wolfinger and Rosenstone 1980), and over the course of their lives, voting becomes habitual (Plutzer 2002). The effects of age may be even greater on other more information-demanding and status-dependent forms of participation, such as contacting political officials.

Table 10.4. Demographics, Political Participation, and Support for Retaliatory Violence

Demographic	Political Participation	Support for Retaliatory Violence
Age	−.01	.02
Female	.02	.04
Education	.12*	−.01
Income	−.02	−.01

Correlations (Pearson's r); $N = 1,098$; * $p < 0.001$.

The effects of age on extra-institutional forms of political action such as protest are less clear. Youthful idealism, rebellion, and energy often make these more physically demanding and risky actions the purview of the young (Lipset 1971), especially with the increasing use of social media as a communication tool for mobilization (Tufekci and Wilson 2012; Valenzuela et al. 2012). However, the frequently high organizational requirements for large-scale protest mean that seemingly youth-dominated actions may be coordinated by adults behind the scenes (e.g., Morris 1984). Older adults, and especially retirees or pensioners, have been especially active in the face of age-specific policy threats, such as proposed decreases in Social Security or Medicare spending in the United States (Campbell 2003) and decreases in state benefits and nonpayment of pensions in post-communist Russia (Javeline 2003a; Hemment 2009:41–42). There is also some evidence that age may not always matter. For example, Greek protesters against austerity measures in 2010 were of all ages, with a heavy presence of middle-aged people (Rüdig and Karyotis 2014:20).

Among Beslan victims, age had no meaningful effect on peaceful political participation. Systematic responses to the thirty-one survey questions about peaceful political participation reveal similarities across age groups: the level of participation for all was relatively high. Correlations between age and responses to violence, as shown in Table 10.4, are close to zero.

Gender

Men are often said to be more violent than women, partly based on their physical strength and testosterone levels (Carver and Harmon-Jones 2009:191) and mostly based on the empirical record. Participants in deadly riots and other forms of violence are "overwhelmingly male" (Horowitz 2001:158). Men are between 5 and 50 times more likely to be arrested than women worldwide, and they commit 9 out of 10 violent crimes in the United States (Baumeister et al. 1996:13). Young males are susceptible to group dynamics that urge them to commit collective, unplanned xenophobic crimes (Green et al. 2001:494). Men are also more prone to vengeful behavior (Jackson et al. 2019:322). Men have a greater sense of self-efficacy than women (Gecas 1989:305–306) and therefore a greater tendency to take matters into their own hands.

Women, conversely, are said to have heightened awareness and concern about the risks associated with war and terrorism (Huddy et al. 2005:595). Many women's organizations promote peace and nonviolence in conflict zones around the world (Schirmer 1989; Cockburn 2007), and those efforts are often portrayed as motivated by a violence-aversion associated with traditional female roles such as motherhood (Lemish 2000). When female legislators comprise a greater percentage of members of parliament, the state commits fewer human rights abuses such as political imprisonments, torture, killings, and disappearances (Melander 2005). Women who participate in ethnic violence typically incite rather than execute the violence (Horowitz 2001:259).

However, evidence is contradictory about whether women are, by nature or social construction, generally more peaceful than men (e.g., Smith 1984; Tessler and Warriner 1997). Gender differences in support for violence narrow when the violence is in retaliation for a gendered crime such as rape (Smith 1984:385). While not a single suicide bomber during the first Palestinian intifada was female and only 5 percent were female in the second intifada, women play greater roles in other violent rebellions. They comprised one-third of LTTE terrorists in Sri Lanka, have been the prime suicide terrorists in Hamas, have been involved in nearly 70 percent of Chechen suicide attacks, and have occupied leadership roles in the Tamil Tigers and Japanese Red Army (Reuter 2004:25–26). While women are usually not direct perpetrators of violence, they may play important roles in shaming men into violence (Brubaker and Laitin 1998:444).

It is thus not clear that women are less likely than men to support retaliatory ethnic violence, especially after experiencing an inhumane episode that included the torture and death of their own children. In Beslan, the anecdotal evidence is mixed. Many men clearly felt conflicted by the affront of the hostage taking to their masculinity. According to Murat Bolotaev, a Beslan man who saved many children from the school, although his own children were not among the hostages, "we have not avenged ourselves. I feel ashamed to visit our people in Russia. If I tell them that I am from Beslan, they will ask, 'Isn't that where your people had their asses whipped and just swallowed it?'" Yet, said Bolotaev, "Let's say we put some men together and go there. Whom do we kill there? Women and children again? How would we be any better than the terrorists?" (Naidenov 2005c).

Reports from Beslan commonly portrayed men with violent intentions restrained only by their more peaceful, sensible wives:

"The men in our family are talking about revenge. They are full of thoughts of fighting in Chechnya, to avenge the deaths of our children. We cannot let them! We are Ossetian people! Gentle, loving people. What will more blood do for this?," an older woman said pointing to the sea of dead people at the Beslan cemetery. "Nothing! They will still be dead, and then our men will be dead! No more! It is an Ossetian custom that when two men fight, if the woman throws a white cloth between them, then they must stop. The women of Beslan must gather all of our black clothes and change them into white clothes and lay them on the ground in front of our men and tell them to stop. Stop the flow of blood!" (Lansford 2006:51–52)

However, there are also stories in which the gender roles are flipped. Recall, for example, the story of Vitaly Kaloyev, the Ossetian man described in Chapter 3 who murdered a Swiss Air traffic controller for causing the air collision that took the life of Kaloyev's wife and two children. "The image of Vitaly Kaloyev haunts every Beslan man. . . . Only a rare Ossetian woman would fail to mention him as an example to follow" (Naidenov 2005c). Recall also from Chapter 3 the focus group discussion about a female victim who was held hostage with her two children and found herself at odds with her husband for his failure to retaliate. Although the majority of females in that focus group and in Beslan overall disapproved of retaliatory violence, established gender roles in North Ossetia and elsewhere seem to leave important room for women to serve as instigators. Women, apparently, were often reproaching "their husbands and brothers for not avenging the deaths of their children" (Naidenov 2005b). Head of Mothers of Beslan Susanna Dudiyeva is even reported to have said, calmly, "If a child had been killed, first suffering for three days and then returned to his father in pieces [and the father does nothing], then the father has no rights to produce any more children, ever" (Naidenov 2005b). As one Beslan mother who lost her child asserted, "I have to disappoint you; the story about the Caucasian woman throwing a white kerchief on the ground to stop the fighting between Caucasian men is a fairy tale, for tourists and journalists" (Naidenov 2005c).

These complicated dynamics suggest that gender plays no systematic role in support for retaliatory violence in Beslan. Accordingly, the bivariate correlation between female gender and approval of killing Chechens is near zero and not statistically significant (Table 10.4). Interestingly, gender is statistically significant when included in the multivariate model in Chapter 11, and the coefficient is positive, suggesting that, to the extent that gender mattered in Beslan, women may have supported retaliatory violence more than men. However, the finding is not robust enough to question the interpretation of a limited role for gender in post-violence retaliation.

It is also not clear that there should be gender differences in peaceful political responses to violence. Women are generally less participatory in politics than men, largely due to factors such as their lower income and education and greater family obligations (Schlozman et al. 1994; Verba et al. 1997; Dorius and McCarthy 2011:459). Differences between women and men vary somewhat across countries, but the relative dominance of men in political action is common (Paxton et al. 2007) and extends to Russia. However, the rise of protest movements by exclusively women's groups is also common, especially for issues surrounding reproductive rights, workplace fairness, domestic violence, war, education, and child health and welfare (Johnson and Saarinen 2011; Sasson-Levy et al. 2011), and female activists tend to commit more hours to their organizations (Dorius and McCarthy 2011). Despite challenges, women's movements have burgeoned in Russia since the collapse of the Soviet Union (Sperling 1999).

Indeed, the two most prominent nongovernmental organizations created in the aftermath of the hostage taking, Mothers of Beslan and Voice of Beslan, have been run and populated mostly by women. This creates challenges for male participation in a patriarchal society like North Ossetia. According to moderator debriefings after the focus groups, some men expressed reluctance to participate in activities organized and led by women. Leadership issues aside, some men considered the issue at the heart of these activities, protecting children, to be feminine, as compared to more masculine issues, such as providing financial support for the family. Some also perceived the activities themselves to be feminine, because they involved talking and expressing emotion, rather than real action taken by real men.

Male victims in Beslan reported being sent mixed messages about their political role relative to women and feeling conflicted about participation. Some of the men, such as the male activist victims over thirty-five years old, were comfortable with female leadership:

ISRAEL: Here in Ossetia, women are more socially active than men.
TOTRAZ: Men are more reserved.
BORIS: Women have it even on a genetic level.
KAZBEK: They say, "Come with us," and we go.

Others, such as the male nonactivists, suggested a bit more tension between women and men:

ARKADY: Let's take the committee of Mothers of Beslan, right? Its name tells everything already, that these are Beslan Mothers. Where a woman is fighting, what can a man do?

VASILY: There are only women there.

BORIS: [Regarding Voice of Beslan]: And who will go? No sensible man will join them.

ARKADY: I was present in the Palace of Culture. Someone came to us, "They say that parents of former hostages are gathering in the Palace." I arrived. I suppose it was organized there, but for some reason one of the members—I think she is still there—said, "We don't need men in the hall." I got up and left.

BORIS: And today they don't need them. Only when something should be signed, only then they call, "Come, sign."

The inclusion of men in the public organizations created in the aftermath of the hostage taking was a matter of dispute among the women, and when they split and Voice of Beslan became a separate official public organization on November 25, 2005, it explicitly included fathers who lost children in the siege. Leader Ella Kesayeva said that she believed the inclusion of men strengthened their position.[1] Female-only activism had both advantages and disadvantages. On the one hand, the authorities had to tread carefully when dealing with mothers who lost their children. Confronted by such sympathetic victims, the authorities at least had to go through the motions of meeting with them and pretending to listen. On the other hand, the women had to push hard to be taken seriously. As described in Chapter 2, female victims were routinely ignored, discredited, and dismissed. They were portrayed as emotional, hysterical, irrational, vacuous, or manipulated. For example, despite their own research and knowledge of weapons, Putin condescendingly explained to them how flamethrowers work. Despite the clarity and consistency of their demands, such as truthful investigation, presidential envoy Dmitry Kozak dismissed the women's hunger strike by saying, "Women do not know what they want" (Milashina 2012).

Table 10.4 shows that, despite the prominence of women in leadership positions in post-violence political action, there was little difference in male and female participation. Correlations between gender and the count variable of thirty-one political activities were approximately zero and not statistically significant.

Education and Income

The effects of education on support for violence are potentially contradictory. On the one hand, people who resort to violence are routinely and even

---

[1] "Комитет "Голос Беслана," ПравдаБеслана.ру; available at http://www.pravdabeslana.ru/golosbeslana.htm.

stereotypically portrayed as uneducated. Denied access to education, they are potentially more aggrieved, more stressed by threatening events, less sophisticated in reasoning about how to handle those threatening events, and therefore more violence-prone (Huddy et al. 2005:595; Humphreys and Weinstein 2008:447). Highly educated individuals are presumably more capable of reason, exercise better judgment, and behave less rashly. They are usually employed and financially secure and therefore have stakes in the current system and are less supportive of violent behavior that could threaten the system (Chapman 2008:521). On the other hand, in places where high levels of education are accompanied by a shrinking economy and limited job prospects, the highly educated individuals may be more aggrieved and violence-prone (Urdal 2006). Terrorists, for example, are often as educated or better educated than average. Most Chechen suicide terrorists studied by Speckhard and Ahkmedova (2006:454) graduated high school, and a quarter had finished college or university, with several more in college or university at the time they committed the acts.

The effects of income on support for violence, or the effects of resources more broadly conceived, are also potentially contradictory. Higher income individuals, like those with higher education, should have a greater stake in the stability of the current political system (Chapman 2008:521), whereas impoverished individuals may be more aggrieved and therefore violence-prone (Humphreys and Weinstein 2008:447). However, suicide bombers in places like Palestine and Chechnya have had no particular financial disadvantage and have sometimes even fared better than others (Reuter 2004:4; Speckhard and Ahkmedova 2006:453–454). Class differences sometimes fail to explain participation in violence, as was the case for the insurgency in El Salvador (Wood 2003). Issues besides poverty may be more central to the initial violence or the behavioral responses, in which case individual support for retaliatory violence may be unrelated to income.

The relative unimportance of education and income in support for retaliatory violence after the school hostage taking is shown in Table 10.4. Correlations approximate zero and are not statistically significant. Multivariate analysis in Chapter 11 reinforces these findings.

Perhaps surprisingly, the negligible role for these demographic variables extends to post-violence political participation as well. In other contexts, income and education matter for conventional participation such as voting, campaigning, and contacting political officials (Verba and Nie 1972; Wolfinger and Rosenstone 1980; Rosenstone and Hansen 1993; Verba et al. 1995) and for unconventional participation such as protest (Gamson 1975/1990; McCarthy and Zald 1977; Dalton et al. 2010:67–69). Opportunities for the poor and uneducated to influence politics are rare (Piven and Cloward 1977). In Beslan, some victims asserted that payoffs for murdered children introduced income inequality into the region where it had previously not existed and perversely made the newly wealthy victims less likely to participate in political actions that might jeopardize their payoffs.

Still, these anecdotes are not supported by the victim data, which suggest no significant role for household income in facilitating or obstructing political participation (Table 10.4). Income is not significantly related to participation at either the bivariate or multivariate levels. Education has a modest positive bivariate correlation with participation, but this relationship is not robust. When included with other variables in multivariate analysis in Chapter 11, education is not statistically significant. The latter finding is consistent with evidence that education may have only indirect effects on political mobilization, effects that operate mainly through prior political participation and disappear when prior participation is controlled in analysis (Rüdig and Karyotis 2014:20).

Biographical Availability

Demographics might still play a role in post-violence behavior to the extent that they determine an individual's "biographical availability," or the "absence of personal constraints that may increase the costs and risks" of participation (McAdam 1986:70; see also Beyerlein and Hipp 2006). These time- and energy-demanding constraints are also sometimes called "barriers to participation" and include full-time employment, childcare, elder care, and other family responsibilities (Klandermans and Oegema 1987).

As with the discussion of traditional demographic variables, a discussion of biographical availability leads to mixed expectations for political participation. On the one hand, people free from work or childcare obligations have few barriers to participation and have participated more frequently as a result (Rüdig and Karyotis 2014:20). Child-rearing can be particularly demobilizing due to not only the time pressures but the risk aversion associated with parenting. On the other hand, full-time employed individuals and others with less biographical availability typically have more income and other resources that enable them to participate more frequently (Corrigall-Brown et al. 2009; Rüdig and Karyotis 2014:9, 20). The presence of children in the home has not significantly affected the time allotted by activists to their causes, especially when those causes are child-related (Dorius and McCarthy 2011:467).

These conflicting pressures are less widely discussed in regard to retaliatory violence, but presumably a similar logic holds: a victim can be less biographically available for retaliatory violence than others, but the very lack of biographical availability may exacerbate the grievance motivating the violence. The conflicting pressures may counteract each other and suggest that factors beyond biography are more significant.

Data from the Beslan victim survey do not allow for a rigorous test of hypotheses about biographical availability. Objective circumstances, such as single-parenting due to spousal death or tending to injuries from the hostage taking, are plausible measures of unavailability because they limit time and energy in the aftermath of violence. However, deaths and injuries are also direct measures of grievances and more indisputably treated as grievances in analysis. Treating deaths and injuries instead as proxies for biographical availability would require subjective and possibly erroneous inferences, given the potentially greater relevance of other unmeasured factors such as assistance from family and friends and time management skills. Questions about how much time victims believe they have for activism were not asked in the survey, because the responses would be subjective and potentially reflect post hoc rationalizations: "I did not participate, therefore I must have been too busy."

However, focus group discussions credibly suggest that biographical unavailability, while an important part of the grievance context in Beslan, is not a meaningful variable for explaining behavioral responses to violence. After the hostage taking, few if any victims were biographically available. The morbid tasks assigned to the surviving next of kin, including searching for bodies and body parts and identifying and burying the dead, took up physical time and mental space. According to one focus group participant, "We hardly had time to go to funerals. Nine to ten people a day were buried." As the weeks and months wore on, some victims were home tending to loved ones who were injured either physically or psychologically or both, or they themselves were injured and convalescing. The demands of these duties varied across victims, but the variation was in a narrow range. After all, almost all adult victims in Beslan were parents or grandparents. Parenthood was the defining demographic characteristic of the entire victim community. Few if any Beslan victims emerged from the tragedy unburdened and fully available for whatever political or violent opportunities appeared.

Female nonactivist Beslan victims were nevertheless quite ready to see the connection between their biographical unavailability and political inactivity:

INDIRA: We were for two months in the hospital in Moscow, and there seemed to be some talk of rallies.
GALINA: We were not here either.
VERA: We were in the hospital. We know about it only by hearsay.
SIMA: [We know] only what we watched on television. We didn't go out ourselves.
VERA: I was told by telephone. Rallies went on both here and in town. First we were treated in the local hospital. Then we had to go to Moscow.

ZARINA: We were being rehabilitated.

INDIRA: Some were sent to Sochi, others were scattered among hospitals. All of us were undergoing medical treatment, dealing with funerals, had other concerns. But our relatives apparently took part.

The male nonactivist Beslan victims told a similar story about the effects of their biographical unavailability:

VASILY: For example, I didn't take part in anything because then all my children— some were in a Moscow hospital, some in whatever hospitals, and I visited them. So there was no time for rallies. We knew that people would do something, of course, but we actually didn't take part.

These professed explanations for inactivism, while reasonable, assume that activist victims had fewer constraints and therefore time on their hands for activism. Focus group discussions suggest otherwise. For example, female activists over thirty-five also explained how injuries limited their political involvement, yet they managed to participate in ten or more political acts since the hostage taking:

LARISA: I was in the hospital for half a year in Moscow, my children and I. And, generally speaking, I was far from all this. I had other concerns rather than participating in some actions.

RAISA: Same with me.

BERTA: Yes, in the beginning many people just had other concerns.

FATIMA: I looked for my child for a whole month.

BERTA: I personally was in hospitals with my children. Both of my children were in bad condition. One had burns, practically half the body was burned. The other was wounded by shards. I ran from one hospital to another. There was no time for rallies.

FATIMA: I first found my child on October 11.

BERTA: The people went in groups [to meet with government officials], because not everyone can go due to work or family or small children. Many people still have to go to have operations. For example, during the course of three years I have periodically gone to Moscow and to Germany.

DINA: We had other concerns.

FATIMA: I had other concerns. I went to morgues, to car coaches. I couldn't find her anywhere. Then they brought her to me from Rostov.

Again, these were women who were invited to this particular focus group because they reported their participation in at least ten political activities since the hostage taking. By their own accounts, they were unavailable for activism. They were active nonetheless.

Similarly, male nonactivist victims attributed the limited retaliatory violence after the hostage taking to the lack of biographical availability, when it is doubtful that even the most pro-retaliation Beslan victims had a great deal of availability to pursue the retaliation.

ARKADY: Right after that we had quite a different objective—to save our injured children who were in hospitals. Our children were treated in Moscow, in Rostov, and abroad. And I can personally say about myself: those, I don't know what to call them, instigators or what? Some waited armed, and some waited unarmed. And the injured had other concerns.

BORIS: My daughter and my wife died. I found my daughter three days later in a morgue. I buried her on the 8th. I didn't even find my wife, and in October they sent me her head and everything from Rostov. Before October, before they sent me this from Rostov, I went to the morgue every day. Then they were in the freight yard, in the freight car, in the refrigerator where I went every other day. I didn't have the strength to go every day. I went every other day. In my presence, seventy-five corpses were closed [identified]. They were closed and sent to Rostov. I couldn't find my wife. I looked them over, looked into their mouths, and turned these corpses. Could I think about attacking Ingush?

BORIS CONTINUES: I first buried my wife in October, and they sent her fragments after. Only after seventy-five corpses were identified did they send my wife. Dzhibilov received remains. He had his wife's leg there. And Ruslan Gapoyev also, they sent his wife, Dzhibilov's and mine. These three coffins were the last to come from Rostov, in October only. We had to bury them. We had to do forty days. We had to do a year. Could I think about going there? I had to protect my other daughter from that. And many people went through this. Some buried strangers. Some re-buried corpses. There were a lot of such people. People had other concerns. Some tried to stir up trouble, of course, but people were in such a state that they had other concerns. There were first impulses, but when people had to bury relatives, had to observe these rituals, everything. Therefore those who were injured hardly thought about it at that moment.

TAMERLAN: Many children died, but many of them stayed alive, and we had to take care of them.

ARKADY: The most important thing I can say for myself, children are at such an age now, I need to put them concretely on their feet. I have other concerns besides the Ingush.

The male activist victims concurred that biographical unavailability played as big a role in limiting retaliatory violence as in limiting political activism, while also not considering why violence-prone victims should have been any more available.

TOTRAZ: It was said already that it was necessary to bury people. When you go to this morgue and in front of your eyes they pour out of a sack parts of the body, fragments—legs, hands. It was necessary to understand all this. And this took a lot of time and strength. Was I supposed to run somewhere? I had to find and bury him. And I could run there with weapons later.

The role of biographical availability should not be discounted entirely. Parents with no surviving children were tragically deprived of the daily tasks and burdens of child-rearing and perhaps objectively had more time than parents of surviving children, whether injured or not. The most prominent leaders of Mothers of Beslan and Voice of Beslan lost their children. However, it is difficult to disentangle the grievance of a murdered child from the unwanted newfound time availability. It is also difficult to disentangle the grievance of being held hostage from the time demands of tending to injuries. Among Beslan victims, hostage status and injury are almost perfectly correlated ($r = .98, p < .00$).

More importantly, as shown in Chapter 11, the death of children and one's status as a hostage—along with other measures of grievance severity, including the death of a spouse and the number of relatives affected—had no statistically significant effect on peaceful political participation. Nor do other biographical variables such as marriage or employment have statistically significant effects. Whether variables more validly measured the extent of the grievance, biographical availability, or both, they were not primary motivators of activism.

Conclusion

Personal history influences responses to violence more than demographic characteristics. Victims whose family or friends experienced physical harm by someone of Ingush or Chechen descent prior to the hostage taking were more likely both to participate in politics and to support retaliatory violence after the hostage taking. Victims who were politically active prior to the hostage taking were more likely to continue that participation and less likely to support retaliatory violence. While age, gender, education, and income have had significant effects on political and violent behavior in other contexts, these characteristics played little role in the aftermath of violence in Beslan. Biographical availability, or lack thereof, features prominently in the aftermath, because almost all victims were overwhelmed with grieving, convalescing, and caregiving. However, these constraints are better understood as parts of the grievance context than as determining factors in how victims managed their unavailability.

The findings about prior harm and prior political participation are robust and powerful. A history of victimization by ethnic rivals makes a response to current victimization more likely, but whether the victim channels the response peacefully or violently may depend on other factors. A history of political activism, however, is a force for continued activism and against retaliatory violence. Only political alienation shares this dual positive effect on activism and negative effect on violence. Longtime activists are among the victims best primed for the normatively preferable peaceful approach to redressing their grievances.

11

A Portrait of Political Activists and Violent Retaliators

The previous chapters have focused on single factors or a few related factors that might influence political participation or support for retaliation in the aftermath of violence. In this chapter, factors are analyzed jointly in multivariate analysis to test the robustness of the conclusions drawn so far.[1] The bundled factors together paint a portrait of victims most likely to become political activists and those most likely to become violent retaliators.

Because there is no significant relationship in Beslan between political participation and support for retaliatory violence, the two outcomes are modeled separately. Findings from the earlier chapters about anger, prejudice, political and social alienation, self-efficacy and political efficacy, and other variables are corroborated. In addition, the statistically significant findings are described in terms of their substantive impact. How much greater is the probability of participating in politics if a victim is angrier, more politically alienated, or more politically efficacious? How much greater is the probability of supporting retaliatory violence if a victim is more prejudiced toward Ingush or less politically alienated?

The analysis shows that victims who were at the high end of the scales for anger, political alienation, political efficacy, or political activism before the hostage taking had much higher probabilities of becoming political activists after the hostage taking than victims at the low end of these scales—sometimes four or five times higher. Victims who were at the high end of the scales for prejudice or blaming Chechens had much higher probabilities of supporting retaliatory violence, as did victims at the low end of the scales for political alienation or satisfaction with the punishment of federal officials—sometimes as much as six times higher.

Uncorrelated in Beslan: Political Participation and Support for Retaliatory Violence

The relationship between civic activism and violence is often perceived to be negative and significant. When normal political channels are open, violence

[1] Vanessa Baird contributed greatly to the statistical analysis in this chapter.

After Violence. Debra Javeline, Oxford University Press. © Oxford University Press 2023.
DOI: 10.1093/oso/9780197683347.003.0012

presumably becomes superfluous. For example, access to political participation significantly decreases the likelihood of civil war recurrence (Walter 2004). Countries seeking transitional justice to address past human rights violations hope that the political process will serve as an alternative to retaliatory violence. International organizations and other donors to conflict-ridden countries assume that funding civil society development can prevent a resurgence of violence, ethnic or otherwise (Chapman 2008:515–516).

When normal political channels are blocked, or when governments are incompetent or unwilling to redress grievances, aggrieved individuals presumably seek other channels (Cunningham 2013:294). In the context of interethnic violence, "The ostensible fact that mass aggression has already occurred or is about to occur has the effect of closing alternative channels of peaceful activity. Of what use are the ordinary processes of politics when the other side has already taken up arms?" (Horowitz 2001:84). The vigilantes outside Beslan School No. 1 seemed to exemplify "the kind of desperation that people reach when a government cannot protect them. They take matters into their own hands, with deadly consequences" ("Seeking Public Accountability" 2004).

In the aftermath of the violence in Beslan, many observers assumed that the choice was dichotomous, either political participation or retaliatory violence. For example, a male activist victim older than thirty-five maintained that politics displaced his violent urges. "I swear I would have done so [committed retaliatory violence]. In the beginning, in the first two to three days, I could have done it. Then already a person starts thinking, 'and what will follow?' Nothing will come out of this war, shooting. It's necessary to somehow think politically."

Similarly, Voice of Belsan's Ella Kesayeva contemplated the behavior of Vitaly Kaloyev, the North Ossetian architect mentioned in Chapter 3 who committed retaliatory murder against a Swiss air traffic controller responsible for the death of his wife and two children in a 2002 plane crash. Kesayeva too understood the relationship between politics and violence to be negative:

> We feel sorry for Vitaly Kaloyev and his grief, and we understand him as no one
> else does. But the victims of Beslan should not go down that road, no matter
> what they have suffered. He was provoked by the Swiss authorities, and we are
> being provoked, but you can't commit illegal acts. ("Ossetian Revenge" 2008)

The presumed negative relationship between retaliatory violence and political participation was reflected in public discussions of blame for the hostage taking. A Levada Center poll conducted on September 7–8, 2004, asked Russians whether they blamed the terrorists, the security services for not protecting civilians, or the Russian leadership for perpetuating the war in Chechnya, and the poll allowed respondents to choose one or the other but not two or all ("Seeking

Public Accountability" 2004). Dr. Leonid Roshal, noted pediatrician and negotiator during the hostage taking, complained that Ossetians were blaming political officials and not the true culprit, the terrorist Basayev, as if it made no sense to consider the roles of both (Official Kremlin International News Broadcast 2005). Post-violence behavior presumably should have reflected this dichotomous blame attribution, with political participation justified by the exclusive or primary culpability of political leaders and retaliatory violence justified by the exclusive or primary culpability of terrorists.

However, some evidence casts doubt on these assumptions about the negative relationship between political and violent behavior. Civic institutions may or may not prevent communal violence, depending on whether ethnic rivals are networked through the institutions and whether the institutional missions involve interethnic dialogue or conflict resolution (Fearon and Laitin 1996; Varshney 2002). Participation in civic associations in Weimar Germany even facilitated violence (Berman 1997). Cross-national studies show that membership in civic associations has little to no effect on individual attitudes toward political violence (Chapman 2008), and the strength of civil society organizations has little to no effect on the onset of civil wars (O'Regan 2018). Longtime membership in civic institutions and acquaintance with avenues for political participation may be correlated with nonviolent inclinations (Chapman 2008), but the relationship between new political activism and support for violence in response to a fresh grievance is unclear.

In some cases, aggrieved individuals may engage in or endorse a wide range of activities, violent and nonviolent, in the hopes that one or several will work. Violent and nonviolent strategies were jointly pursued in apartheid South Africa, the El Salvadoran civil war, and Northern Ireland in the 1970s and 1980s (Seidman 2000; Dudouet 2013:403), and the characteristics of violent and nonviolent action are often similar (Tarrow 1998; Tilly and Tarrow 2007). In Beslan, even among the most politically active, there was some overt support for retaliatory violence. Mothers of Beslan leader Susanna Dudiyeva, for example, endorsed Kaloyev's retaliatory act while she devoted her own life to political action: "he behaved as a man should. . . . the machinery of state and justice does not work. That forces people to commit acts of summary justice" ("Ossetian Revenge" 2008). Dudiyeva also offered this rather extreme statement about retaliatory violence after the hostage taking: "I'm in favor of punitive methods. If a terrorist can kill innocent people, can kill children, why shouldn't the whole family that brought up that terrorist be executed?" (Parfitt 2011).

Fighting and voting are sometimes seen as reinforcing, such as when ethnic riots are used strategically to win votes (Wilkinson 2004; Dunning 2011:332–333). Some individuals may participate in numerous actions, peaceful and violent, and view them as strategic complements, whereas other individuals may choose between peaceful and violent action and view them as strategic substitutes (Dunning 2011:327, 330). Some change course over time, as when radicals turn into "within-system" participators (Muller and Godwin 1984:130, 137; Moskalenko and McCauley 2009).

In short, hypotheses about correlations between violence and participation are mixed and contradictory, as is the evidence. It is therefore reasonable to expect that these may be independent outcomes. Evidence from Beslan supports this expectation: According to data from the victim survey, there was little relationship between political participation and support for retaliatory violence ($r = -0.03$, $p < .32$). Victims spanned the spectrum from anti-retaliation activists to pro-retaliation activists to anti- and pro-retaliation nonactivists.

Table 11.1 shows the mean number of participatory acts out of a total of thirty-one that were taken by Beslan victims for four different categories of support for retaliatory violence. In three of the four categories—victims who completely disapproved of killing Chechens, somewhat approved, and fully approved—victims engaged on average in three political activities. In the remaining category—victims who somewhat disapproved of killing Chechens— they engaged on average in two political activities. The small differences in means are probably random and inconsequential: standard deviations are approximately five activities for each category of support for retaliatory violence, meaning there was a great deal of variation in political activism among supporters of retaliatory violence and among opponents of violence.

Figure 11.1 suggests some potential qualifications to the above statements. The figure shows support for retaliatory violence among victims who did not participate in any political activity since the hostage taking compared to those who participated in one activity, two or three activities, four to ten activities, or more than ten activities. While the linear correlation between the count variable of participation and support for retaliatory violence is not statistically significant,

Table 11.1. Participatory Acts of Beslan Victims by Level of Support for Retaliatory Violence: Comparison of Means

Kill the Same Number of Chechens as Were Killed in Beslan	Mean	N	Standard Deviation
Fully approve	3.31	65	5.38
Somewhat approve	2.74	88	4.47
Somewhat disapprove	1.93	371	4.69
Completely disapprove	3.17	446	5.10
Total	2.67	970	4.94

Minimum = 0, maximum = 31.

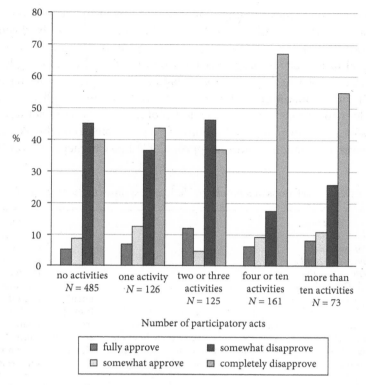

Figure 11.1. Support for retaliatory violence by level of political participation.

"I will now read some specific strategies that some people recommend to resolve problems in North Ossetia. For each one, please tell me whether you fully approve, somewhat approve, somewhat disapprove, or completely disapprove: *Kill the same number of Chechens as were killed in Beslan.*"

when victims are clustered into categories of political participation, we see that the most politically active Beslan victims are also the most forcefully opposed to killing Chechens: 67 percent of those who participated in four to ten activities and 55 percent of those who participated in more than ten activities completely disapproved of such retaliatory violence, compared to 37 percent of those who participated in two or three activities, 44 percent who participated in one activity, and 40 percent who participated in no activities.

Still, the difference between activist victims and nonactivist victims mostly reflects how emphatically victims at each participatory level stated their disapproval of violence. The greater proportion of activists who declared complete disapproval of violence is accompanied by a smaller proportion of activists who reported that they were somewhat disapproving, meaning that overall disapproval of retaliatory violence is similar in each participation category (between 81 and 85 percent disapproved).

400 WHY POLITICS AND NONVIOLENCE?

To corroborate these findings, the victim survey included questions about responses to the hostage taking that were harsh and potentially violent but stopped short of advocating outright killing. Victims were asked about their approval of forcibly evicting Chechens from the Caucasus, holding hostage the relatives of Chechen soldiers, forbidding Ingush from entering North Ossetia, and committing military operations in the towns where terrorists were located, even if this led to the deaths of Ingush who were not terrorists. As Table 11.2 shows, approval ratings of these actions are highly correlated. The lowest correlation is between approval of killing Chechens and forbidding

Table 11.2. Correlations of Support for Violent Responses to the Hostage Taking

I will now read some specific strategies that some people recommend to resolve problems in North Ossetia. For each one, please tell me whether you fully approve, somewhat approve, somewhat disapprove, or completely disapprove:	Kill the same number of Chechens as were killed in Beslan	Forcibly evict Chechens from the Caucasus	Hold the relatives of Chechen soldiers hostage	Forbid Ingush from entering North Ossetia	Commit military operations in towns where the terrorists are located, even if this leads to the deaths of Ingush who were not terrorists
Kill the same number of Chechens as were killed in Beslan	1 970				
Forcibly evict Chechens from the Caucasus	.47** .00 919	1 957			
Hold the relatives of Chechen soldiers hostage	.63** .00 944	.49** .00 935	1 981		
Forbid Ingush from entering North Ossetia	.22** .00 934	.32** .00 922	.31** .00 940	1 982	
Commit military operations in towns where the terrorists are located, even if this leads to the deaths of Ingush who were not terrorists	.33** .00 913	.04 .22 893	**.31 .00 920	**.28 .00 920	1 947

Pearson correlation, significance (2-tailed), N.
$*p < .05$; $**p < .01$.

Ingush from entering North Ossetia ($r = .22$, $p = .00$), and the highest correlation is between killing Chechens and holding hostage the relatives of Chechen soldiers ($r = .63$, $p = .00$).

Table 11.3 shows the mean number of participatory acts out of a total of thirty-one that were taken by Beslan victims in four different categories of support for these other potentially violent responses to the hostage taking. The standard deviations are again large, suggesting quite a bit of random variation and casting doubt on most conclusions that strong supporters and strong opponents of retaliatory violence differ in their political behavior one way or another. To the degree that there are any patterns in the data, the patterns are inconsistent. For the question about holding relatives of Chechen soldiers hostage, there is a small linear decline in participatory acts from approvers to disapprovers of such retaliatory violence that might suggest a complementary relationship between political participation and support for violence, but for the questions about forcibly evicting Chechens from the Caucasus and committing military operations even

Table 11.3. Participatory Acts of Beslan Victims by Approval of Responses to the Hostage Taking: Comparison of Means

"I will now read some specific strategies that some people recommend to resolve problems in North Ossetia. For each one, please tell me whether you fully approve, somewhat approve, somewhat disapprove, or completely disapprove."

	Forcibly evict Chechens from the Caucasus		Hold the relatives of Chechen soldiers hostage		Forbid Ingush from entering North Ossetia		Commit military operations in towns where the terrorists are located, even if this leads to the deaths of Ingush who were not terrorists	
	Mean (SD)	N	Mean (SD)	N	Mean (SD)	N	Mean (SD)	N
Fully approve	3.17 (6.45)	243	3.74 (6.45)	118	2.84 (5.11)	632	2.68 (3.86)	219
Somewhat approve	1.45 (3.75)	153	2.72 (4.76)	183	3.05 (5.29)	206	2.29 (4.52)	166
Somewhat disapprove	2.01 (3.71)	316	2.71 (4.88)	418	1.07 (2.86)	88	1.69 (3.39)	317
Completely disapprove	3.84 (5.19)	245	2.13 (4.39)	262	2.88 (4.72)	56	4.18 (7.08)	245
Total	2.69	957	2.68	981	2.73	982	2.67	947

Minimum = 0, maximum = 31.

if nonterrorists might die, the results might suggest a substitute rather than complementary relationship, with the highest mean participation scores for those who completely disapproved of harsh retaliation.

Figure 11.2 shows the relationship between categories of political participation and approval of these other harsh retaliatory measures that stop short of murder

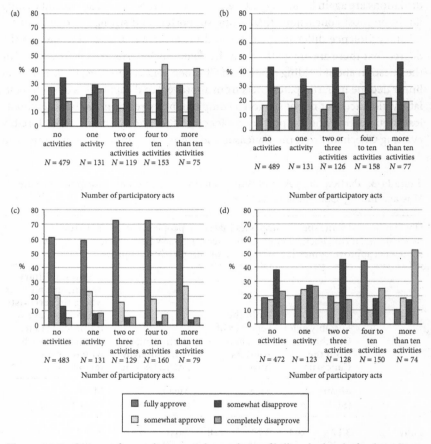

Figure 11.2. Support for retaliatory violence short of killing by level of political participation.

"I will now read some specific strategies that some people recommend to resolve problems in North Ossetia. For each one, please tell me whether you fully approve, somewhat approve, somewhat disapprove, or completely disapprove:"

a. Forcibly evict Chechens from the Caucasus

b. Hold the relatives of Chechen soldiers hostage

c. Forbid Ingush from entering North Ossetia

d. Commit military operations in towns where the terrorists are located, even if this leads to the deaths of Ingush who were not terrorists.

advocacy. Only one of these relationships—between participation and approval of the forcible evictions of Chechens—is statistically significant ($r = -.15, p < .00$), suggesting that victims in the highest participation categories are most likely to disapprove of forcible eviction, just as they were most likely to disapprove of retaliatory killing. However, the correlation is small, and none of the other relationships corroborates the conclusion of a substitute participation-violence relationship. Indeed, some relationships between participation and measures of support for violence, such as approval of retaliatory hostage taking or forbidding Ingush from entering North Ossetia, are actually positive ($r = .08, p < .01$, for both) or not statistically significant, as between participation and approval of military operations that could cause casualties of nonterrorists ($r = .02, p < .59$).

In sum, it would be quite difficult to predict a Beslan victim's support for retaliatory violence from his or her participatory behavior or to predict participation from support for violence. There is no consistent or strong relationship between political participation and support for retaliatory violence. The lack of correlation suggests that motivations for these two responses to violence may differ, although some overlap is certainly possible.

Modeling Political Participation and Support for Retaliatory Violence

Motivations for responses to violence have been discussed individually in Chapters 5–10. Multivariate analyses can test the robustness of the bivariate findings in those chapters. The analyses below corroborate the findings.

Variables and Measures

Table 11.4 shows the survey questions used to measure the outcomes of interest, political participation and support for retaliatory violence, as well as important explanatory variables and relevant controls. To review briefly: Violence in the Caucasus has been so widespread that support for outright murder—along the lines of an-eye-for-an-eye code of justice—can be a decisive factor distinguishing victims who support retaliatory violence from victims who do not. Support for retaliatory violence is thus measured as a four-category variable ranging from complete disapproval to complete approval of killing the same number of Chechens as were killed in Beslan. Political participation was measured by a count scale ranging from 0 to 31 activities, a scale that correlates highly with other potential measures such as Guttman scales but is easier to interpret.

Measurement of key explanatory variables described in Chapters 5–10 is also reviewed in Table 11.4. Variables include the emotions of anger, anxiety,

Table 11.4. Measures

Variable	Survey Questions	Percent, $N = 1,098$
Support for retaliatory violence	I will now read some specific strategies that some people recommend to resolve problems in North Ossetia. For each one, please tell me whether you fully approve, somewhat approve, somewhat disapprove, or completely disapprove: *kill the same number of Chechens as were killed in Beslan*	Fully approve 5.9%, somewhat approve 8%, somewhat disapprove 33.8%, completely disapprove 40.6%, refused to answer 7.6%, difficult to answer 4.1%
Political participation	In the two years since the tragedy in the school, some former hostages and their families have engaged in political action. Others have not participated in these activities—either consciously or because they have simply been physically or psychologically unable to do so. I will now describe some events. Please tell me whether or not you were one of the participants. If you did not participate in an event, please feel free to say so, even if that is your response to every question. Also, some of these events occurred two years ago, and it may be difficult to recall, so please feel free to say if you do not remember.	0–31 scale (no activities 49.9%, one 14.4%, two or three 12.3%, four to ten 16.1%, eleven to thirty-one 7.3%)
Anger	How many days in the past week (0–7) have you felt angry? hatred? resentful?	0–7 scale (mean 2.0, std. dev. 1.8)
Anxiety	How many days in the past week (0–7) have you felt anxious? afraid? Worried?	0–7 scale (mean 3.4, std. dev. 2.3)
Enthusiasm	How many days in the past week (0–7) have you felt hopeful? enthusiastic? proud?	0–7 scale (mean 2.2, std. dev. 1.8)
Prejudice toward Ingush	How strongly would you object if a member of your family wanted to bring an Ingush home to dinner—strongly, mildly, or not at all? How would it make you feel if a close relative of yours were planning to marry an Ingush—very uneasy, somewhat uneasy, or not uneasy at all? Do you think Ossetian and Ingush students should go to the same schools or to separate schools?	0–1 scale (mean .84, std. dev. .26)
Blame toward Chechens	As I read the names of some people and organizations, please tell me whether you think they are very guilty, somewhat guilty, not very guilty, or not at all guilty for causing this tragedy? *Chechens*	Not at all guilty 2%, not very guilty 8%, somewhat guilty 35%, very guilty 43%, refused to answer 8%, difficult to answer 6%

(continued)

Table 11.4. Continued

Variable	Survey Questions	Percent, $N = 1,098$
Changed political alienation (decreased pride)	[How proud is respondent now compared to before, as calculated by the difference between responses to current and past alienation questions on pride (How proud are you to be a Russian citizen? and Thinking back to before the tragedy—that is, before September 2004—how proud were you to be a Russian citizen?)]	Three steps more proud < 1%, two steps more 1%, one step more 2%, same 60%, one step less 16%, two steps less 9%, three steps less 8%, four steps less 1%, missing 4%
Blame toward and punishment of federal officials	Speaking just about the central authorities, please tell me whether you think the following authorities are very guilty, somewhat guilty, not very guilty, or not at all guilty for causing this tragedy? *President Vladimir Putin*	Not at all guilty 9%, not very guilty 27%, somewhat guilty 34%, very guilty 24%, refused to answer 3%, difficult to answer 4%
	Now I will state some demands that have been made by several Beslan victims. Can you tell me whether in your opinion these demands have been completely satisfied, mostly satisfied, mostly not satisfied, not satisfied at all? *Punishment of federal officials who are guilty for what happened*	Completely satisfied 4%, mostly satisfied 5%, mostly not satisfied 44%, not satisfied at all 41%, refused to answer 3%, difficult to answer 3%
Social alienation	How interested do you think the following groups are in listening to the victims' side of the story? Russian society (*Rossiiskoye obshchestvo*)	Very interested 40%, somewhat interested 39%, not very interested 14%, not at all interested 2%, refused to answer 2%, difficult to answer 4%
Political efficacy	How informed do you consider yourself to participate in politics?	Not at all informed 17%, not very informed 54%, rather informed 20%, very informed 2%, refused to answer 4%, difficult to answer 4%
	Suppose you were dissatisfied with your political or economic situation, to what extent is each of the following an effective way to address your dissatisfaction? *Demonstrating or protesting*	Not at all effective 21%, not very effective 35%, rather effective 13%, very effective 3%, refused to answer 16%, difficult to answer 12%
Self-efficacy	Can you yourself do anything to help solve the problems that two years ago led to the tragedy in Beslan, or are the problems completely out of your control? Do you feel this way strongly or only somewhat?	Out of my control strongly 35%, out of my control somewhat 32%, can solve somewhat 7%, can solve strongly 3%, refused to answer 3%, difficult to answer 20%

(continued)

Table 11.4. Continued

Variable	Survey Questions	Percent, $N = 1,098$
Optimism	In general, how optimistic do you feel about your future?	Not at all optimistic 9%, not very optimistic 41%, rather optimistic 32%, very optimistic 8%, refused to answer 2%, difficult to answer 8%
	In your opinion, how possible is it to solve/eliminate the problems that two years ago led to the tragedy in Beslan?	Very possible 23%, rather possible 29%, not very possible 26%, not at all possible 11%, refused to answer 4%, difficult to answer 8%
Prior harm to relatives	Prior to the hostage taking in the school, had any of your family or friends ever been physically harmed by someone of Ingush or Chechen descent?	Yes 18%, no 76%, refused to answer 5%, difficult to answer 2%
Prior political activism	Voting behavior prior to tragedy as calculated by a count of seven voting-related activities (voted in last presidential election, voted in last Duma election, voted in last regional or local election, persuaded to vote in last national election, persuaded to vote in last regional election, engaged in national campaign, engaged in regional or local campaign)	0–7 scale (mean 2.0, std. dev. 1.4), mode = 3 (40%)
	Nonvoting behavior prior to tragedy as calculated by a count of nine nonvoting-related activities (attended mass meeting or speech by elected official, demonstrated or protested, worked with others in town to solve problems, formed new group to solve community problem, wrote letter to local official, went to see local official, wrote to nonlocal official, wrote letter to media, participated in strike)	0–9 scale (mean 0.4, std. dev. 1.0), mode = 0 (76%)
Severity of grievance	Were you yourself a hostage?	Yes 29%, no 71%
	One or more children died	Yes, 20% no 80%
	Spouse died	Yes 6%, no 94%
	Number of relatives affected by hostage taking—count of relatives reported by respondent	0–7 scale (mean 2.3, std. dev. 1.3), mode = 2 (37%)

(continued)

Table 11.4. Continued

Variable	Survey Questions	Percent, $N = 1{,}098$
Perceived risk of political activism	In the future, how likely is it that Beslan residents who participate actively in making these demands will be punished or otherwise suffer for this?	Not at all likely 13%, not very likely 44%, somewhat likely 10%, very likely 4%, refused to answer 5%, difficult to answer 25%
Trust in government	How much of the time do you think you can trust the government in Moscow to do what is right?	Hardly ever 13%, only some of the time 54%, most of the time 16%, just about always 1%, refused to answer 3%, difficult to answer 13%
Demographics	Female	Female 66%, male 34%
	Age	Mean 45 years, std. dev. 14.5 years
	Household income	Mean 6,001–8,000 rubles/ month, mode = 4,001– 6,000 rubles/month (18%)
	Education	7 grades or less 4%, incomplete secondary 4%, complete secondary 15%, specialized secondary 39%, incomplete higher 7%, higher 30%, advanced degree < 1%

and enthusiasm; prejudice toward Ingush and blame toward Chechens; political alienation and blame toward and punishment of federal officials; social alienation; self-efficacy, political efficacy, and optimism; personal history of prior harm and prior activism; and demographics such as age, gender, education, and income.

Other factors that may influence responses to violence include the severity of the grievance, perceived risk of political activism, and trust in government. Although all Beslan victims were severely aggrieved, observers of violence often assume that the nature or extent of the grievance may matter. To test whether specific grievances might differentiate some Beslan victims from others and influence their responses, measures are included for being held hostage, death a child, death of a spouse, and having a large number of relatives affected by the violence. Observers also often assume that fear of punishment in an authoritarian or hybrid regime is a barrier to action. A measure is thus included for the perceived risk of political activism. Finally, some evidence suggests that general trust in government—as distinct from political alienation and blame specifically about the hostage taking—might be a factor for both support for retaliatory violence and political participation (Gamson 1968; Detges 2017). Beslan victims were therefore asked about their trust in the government in Moscow. Each of these measures is also described in Table 11.4.

Statistical results are unlikely to be biased by multicollinearity. Correlations between all explanatory variables in our models are mostly 0 or .1 and never higher than .3, except for the .43 correlation between anger and anxiety (see Table 5.7 in Chapter 5) and the .38 correlation between enthusiasm and optimism.

Omitted variable bias is also unlikely, because the results are robust in a variety of different models. However, there were undoubtedly numerous other unmeasured factors that affected victim responses to violence. Perhaps the most important is ethnic group identity, which has influenced peaceful and violent mobilization in other contexts (Moskalenko and McCauley 2009:247). While the perceived risk of political activism was queried, the perceived risk of retaliatory violence was not, and of course violence is objectively risky (Lake and Rothchild 1996:45). Also, closure, or lack thereof, on what happened to loved ones is an important type of grievance not captured by the other measures. Some focus group participants, such as a male activist victim over thirty-five years old, suggested that this particular grievance might be influential:

TOTRAZ: I told you we found our nephew. We are sure that it is he. In some way, it is easier for me because we have found him compared to those [who haven't found their relatives]. I am answering your question why I react this way, and he reacts that way, and someone else reacts differently.

Personality traits may be important for understanding individual behavior but were also unmeasured. For political participation, victims themselves offered explanations involving stubbornness, perseverance, and a desire to be "in the know." In the focus group of male activist victims over thirty-five years old, participants pondered these types of individuals:

BORIS: Some just can't stand it. Many people don't want to.
KAZBEK: But there are hard-headed people! They will even attack a tank with a spade. Some of us here are like that.
BORIS: You are quite right. There are obsessed people, obsessed.

The portrait drawn in this book of political activists and violent retaliators is valid but likely incomplete.

Dealing with Missing Data

Like all survey data, the Beslan victim survey has its share of missing data due to uncertainty and refusals to answer, with missing data for any given survey question varying from 3 to 30 percent. The correlation of the missing data with other variables in the data set is low (usually $r < .15$), but some data are not missing at random, which could bias estimates. To minimize the bias, strategies include listwise deletion of cases and modeling techniques to represent the missing responses with dummy variables, but these too introduce potential biases (Jones 1996; Allison 2002).

Instead, missing data in the Beslan victim survey is addressed using the method of multiple imputation and the ICE (Multiple Imputation by Chained Equations) program in Stata (Royston 2005). With multiple imputation, missing values are computed using other related variables in the data with random draws that include uncertainty, a method that has been found less biased than others. The ICE program created five data sets with imputed missing values of the variables described in Table 11.4, and analysis was then conducted on six data sets, including the initial incomplete (unimputed) data set. Results approximate a combination of results from all data sets and reflect a sample of 1,025 observations rather than the 1,098 in the actual survey. Standard errors were computed according to recommendations by Rubin (1987) to reflect the error of the nonmissing variables.

Results

The count variable representing participation in thirty-one political activities is analyzed using a negative binomial model. The four-category variable representing support for retaliatory violence is analyzed using an ordered logit model. Results are presented in Table 11.5. The analysis shows that anger, a perceived decrease in pride in Russia, and blame toward President Putin have positive, statistically significant effects on political participation.[2] While political alienation matters for peaceful participation, social alienation does not: victims who think that Russian society is uninterested in listening to the victims' side of the story are no more or less likely to participate than victims who think Russian society cares. The analysis also shows that, while a general sense of self-efficacy is somewhat significantly related to political participation, the more specific

---

[2] Dissatisfaction with punishment of the federal officials guilty for the tragedy plays no role in participation, probably because the punishment, or lack thereof, was apparent only long after the tragedy and most of the associated participatory events and therefore could not be causally prior to participation.

Table 11.5. Explaining Peaceful Political Participation and Retaliatory Violence

		Political Participation Negative Binomial Estimates Coef. (SE)	Support for Retaliatory Violence Ordered Logit Estimates Coef. (SE)
Anger		.16 (.03)***	.04 (.05)
Anxiety		.05 (.03)	.01 (.04)
Enthusiasm		−.03 (.05)	.12 (.04)**
Prejudice toward Ingush		−.03 (.22)	1.53 (.31)***
Blame toward Chechens		−.04 (.08)	.42 (.11)***
Political alienation (decreased pride)		.23 (.06)***	−.24 (.07)***
Blame toward and punishment of federal officials	Putin's guilt	.13 (.06)*	−.09 (.09)
	Dissatisfaction with punishment of officials	.001 (.07)	−.73 (.10)***
Social alienation		−.01 (.07)	.21 (.10)*
Political efficacy	Politically informed	.53 (.08)***	.01 (.11)
	Perceived effectiveness of protest	.28 (.07)***	.08 (.09)
Self-efficacy		.15 (.07)*	.32 (.11)***
Optimism	Optimistic about future	−.04 (.09)	−.49 (.13)***
	Possible to solve Beslan's problems	.07 (.07)	−.40 (.08)***
Prior harm to relatives		.48 (.14)**	.71 (.21)***
Prior political activism	Prior voting	.11 (.04)*	.05 (.07)
	Prior nonvoting behavior	.31 (.06)***	−.31 (.09)***
Severity of grievance	Hostage	.03 (.12)	.08 (.16)
	Child/children died	.20 (.13)	−.07 (.17)
	Spouse died	.35 (.21)	.38 (.28)
	Number of relatives affected	−.03 (.05)	−.01 (.05)
Perceived risk of political activism		.09 (.07)	.07 (.13)
Trust in government		.08 (.10)	.06 (.11)

(continued)

Table 11.5. Continued

		Political Participation Negative Binomial Estimates Coef. (SE)	Support for Retaliatory Violence Ordered Logit Estimates Coef. (SE)
Demographics	Female	.19 (.13)	.32 (.15)*
	Age	−.01 (.004)	−.0004 (.01)
	Household income	−.01 (.03)	.01 (.05)
	Education	.001 (.04)	−.02 (.05)
Constant		−3.29 (.67)	
Cutpoints	τ_1		−3.03 (.87)
	τ_2		1.92 (.88)
	τ_3		3.05 (.88)

Standard errors are in parentheses. See Table 11.4 for variable description and coding.
*$p < .05$; **$p < .01$; ***$p < .005$.

sense of political efficacy, as measured by self-assessed political competence and the perceived effectiveness of a particular political activity like protest, is more powerfully related to participation. *Anger, a decrease in pride in Russia, perceived political competence, and perceived effectiveness of political action can motivate victims of violence to participate in politics.*

Importantly, these relationships hold when controlling for past voting and past nonvoting political behavior, suggesting that anger, political alienation, and political efficacy have positive effects on post-violence political participation over and above the factors that influenced participation prior to the violence. The relationships also hold when controlling for past physical harm experienced by friends or family at the hands of Ingush or Chechens, as well as the severity of the grievance brought to the victim by the hostage taking. Anger, political alienation, and political efficacy have effects that are independent of the victim's status as a hostage or non-hostage, the victim's loss of spouse or child, and the number of family members who were held hostage.

As for support for retaliatory violence, generalized anger seems to play no role. Those who supported killing Chechens were no angrier than those who found killing Chechens repulsive.[3] Instead, prejudice toward Ingush and blame toward

---

[3] Enthusiasm appears statistically significant in the multivariate model of support for retaliatory violence, but enthusiasm is not significant in bivariate analysis (Table 5.4) or in other models tested.

Chechens play powerful roles in the advocacy of retaliatory murder. Political al-ienation is related to support for retaliatory violence but inversely to its relation-ship with peaceful political participation. A perceived decrease in pride in Russia has *negative*, statistically significant effects on support for violence, as does the related dissatisfaction with the punishment of guilty federal officials. Victims who emerged from the tragedy with equal if not greater pride in Russia and sat-isfaction with the treatment of guilty federal officials were more likely to support killing Chechens in retaliation.

Social alienation is not significant for peaceful political participation and only mildly significant for supporting violent retaliation: victims who think that Russian society is uninterested in listening to the victims' side of the story are somewhat more likely to support retaliatory ethnic violence, but the rela-tionship is one of the least robust. Self-efficacy and pessimism, however, matter quite a bit. Victims who are less optimistic about the future and less likely to believe it is possible to solve the problems that led to the school tragedy are more likely to support retaliatory violence, as are victims who believe they can do something to solve those problems. The measures of political efficacy that were so significant for influencing peaceful political participation are not sig-nificant for influencing support for violence. *Prejudice, pride in one's country, a perceived impossible interethnic situation, general pessimism, and confidence in the ability to take matters into one's own hands—but not anger or feeling po-litically informed or politically efficacious—can motivate support for retaliatory ethnic violence.*

Like with the model of peaceful political participation, the results of the model of support for retaliatory violence hold when controlling for past voting and past nonvoting political behavior, the degree of grievance brought to the victim by the hostage taking, and prior physical harm by Ingush or Chechens experienced by friends or family.

For both peaceful political participation and support for retaliatory violence, physical harm to family or friends by Ingush or Chechens prior to the school hostage taking is positive and statistically significant. Harm to loved ones is long remembered and, after a new and larger scale episode of violence, motivates people to do something. However, this deeply felt past experience does not tell us which type of reaction—peaceful or violent—will be chosen. A history of voting and nonvoting political behavior prior to the school hostage-taking is a strong predictor of post-violence political activism, whereas prior voting has no rela-tionship to support for retaliatory violence, and prior peaceful political behavior has negative effects on support for retaliatory violence. *Victims with histories of political activism are more likely to respond to violence with the desirable "politics and not violence" approach.*

The severity of grievance experienced by the hostage taking for the most part has no bearing on political or violent behavior, presumably because every single victim's experience could be labeled devastating, and the degrees of devastation are at the margins. The perceived risk of political activism, often discussed in the collective action literature, also has no bearing on political or violent behavior. Nor does general trust in government matter for either response to violence, probably because the more relevant political attitudes concern the government's role in the hostage taking and the change in pride in one's country in the aftermath of violence.

Direction of Causality Revisited

Like all survey-based research, the findings above are subject to challenges of endogeneity. It could be argued that the causal arrow is reversed and that Beslan victims first participated in politics and then became angry, politically alienated, and politically efficacious, or inferred that they must feel this way. As described in Chapter 9, victims widely believed their participation went nowhere, and perhaps this perceived inefficacy caused anger.

Although some reverse causation is plausible, a number of factors suggest strong relationships in the directions hypothesized. First, as described in Chapter 5, if victims act and then feel anger, the same logic should apply to either peaceful or violent action. Victims who supported retaliatory killing of Chechens should have also declared themselves angry, to express their true feelings or to project cognitive consistency, especially since questions about peaceful participation and retaliatory violence preceded questions on emotions. That anger is related to political participation and *not* to support for violence suggests that the emotion preceded and motivated participation.

Second, given the definitional distinctiveness of the concepts of political alienation and political efficacy, the hypothesized causal direction makes sense: decreased pride in Russia, because it provides a context of dissatisfaction and violated expectations, leads to participation, as does a sense of political competence. If instead participation was hypothesized as causally prior, it is unclear why participation would make a victim feel simultaneously less proud but more politically efficacious. Successful participation could presumably increase one's sense of political efficacy but would probably not decrease one's pride; unsuccessful participation could presumably decrease one's pride but probably not increase political efficacy. Therefore, the logic behind the endogeneity challenge is less coherent than the more straightforward portrait of angry victims feeling little pride in their country but nevertheless politically capable and therefore deciding to take action to redress their grievances.

The Probability of Supporting Violence or Participating in Politics

So far, the analysis tells us which relationships are statistically significant and the positive or negative direction of relationships but not the strength of these relationships. How much more would a victim support violence if he or she was more prejudiced or less politically alienated? How much more active in politics would the victim be if he or she were angrier or more politically efficacious?

Interpreting the substantive meaningfulness of the relationships shown in Part II requires understanding the magnitude of the effects of each explanatory variable. This is not easily done using the imputed models in Table 11.5. The underlying assumptions of these models allow for great rigor in determining statistical significance of relationships between variables but not for predicting the probabilities of participation and support for violence, given changes in anger, political alienation, and other variables.[4]

To predict such probabilities, models could, instead of imputing missing data, control for missing data in analysis. Dummy variables were thus created for whether respondents gave substantive responses or not to each explanatory variable, and then these dichotomous dummy variables were added to the models as controls. For the three emotion variables, missing data were correlated, so a single dichotomous dummy variable represented whether data were missing for any emotion. Inclusion of the dummy control variables does not alter substantive results. This older technique produced virtually identical coefficients and standard errors to the imputed models.

Support for retaliatory violence was measured with the survey question about approval of killing Chechens, but with one modification: the four-category variable was reduced to a trichotomous variable where those who approve of killing Chechens, whether strongly or somewhat, were treated as a single category. The models could then predict the probability that a victim would approve of killing Chechens.

Political participation was measured with the count variable of thirty-one possible political activities, as it was in the models with multiple imputation, and respondents who did not answer even a single question about the thirty-one events were counted as missing. Alternatively, only positive responses to participation questions could have been counted, and refusals or missing responses would have been treated as nonparticipation. However, such an approach risks inaccuracy if respondents were trying to conceal activism. Prioritizing accuracy

---

[4] In statistical terms, the assumptions required to generate predicted probabilities when using multiple imputation are not compatible with Rubin's rules, which assume normality when combining standard errors across the imputed data sets (1987). See White, Royston and Wood (2011) for a list of parameters and estimation techniques that should not be combined using Rubin's rules.

leads to the elimination of 155 respondents from our sample due to one or more missing responses to the thirty-one participation questions. Fortunately, the approach again does not alter results, and the models are very similar to the imputed models, with the advantage that they can be used to understand the magnitude of the effects of the significant explanatory variables.

To do so, all variables are held constant at their means, while the values are varied for each significant variable, one at a time. Given the modeling decisions described above, and given that the means of some variables have no real-world meaning (such as "mean gender"), the resulting predicted probabilities should not be treated as precise estimates. Rather, they are important and helpful in illustrating the probable difference in participatory or violent behavior, given differences in the explanatory factors.

Figure 11.3 shows the predicted number of political acts taken by a victim of the Beslan school hostage taking, depending on variation in one of the significant explanatory factors. Many of the variables have a similar substantive effect: they double, triple, or quadruple the likelihood of participation. At low ends of the scales (for anger, alienation, political efficacy, etc.), a victim participated on average in one activity. At high ends of the scales, a victim participated in two or more. For example, the least angry victims (never feeling anger, hatred, or resentment in the past week) participated on average in .82 activities, whereas the angriest victims (feeling anger, hatred, and resentment all seven days during the past week) participated in 2.23 activities, rounding to one and two activities, respectively. For political alienation, those at the lowest end of the scale participated in .55 activities, whereas those at the high end of the alienation scale participated in 2.18, again rounded to one and two activities, respectively, but really with a differential in participation of four times.

The variable with the greatest substantive effect on political participation is, unsurprisingly, prior political participation in nonvoting activities such as protests. A victim with no prior history of activism participated on average in .98 activities after the hostage taking, whereas a victim with a prior history of three activities participated in 2.67 activities after the hostage taking, and a victim with an extremely politically active past of six activities participated in 7.23 activities afterward. Given that less than one percent of victims exhibited such a commitment to political activism (Table 11.3), the predicted 7.23 activities is more hypothetical than real but nevertheless suggests the power of longtime activism in encouraging peaceful political responses to new grievances. The variable with the lowest substantive effect on political participation is prior harm to relatives. A victim with no relatives who suffered harm by Ingush prior to the hostage taking participated on average in one political activity after the hostage taking, whereas a victim with a family history of prior harm participated in 1.73.

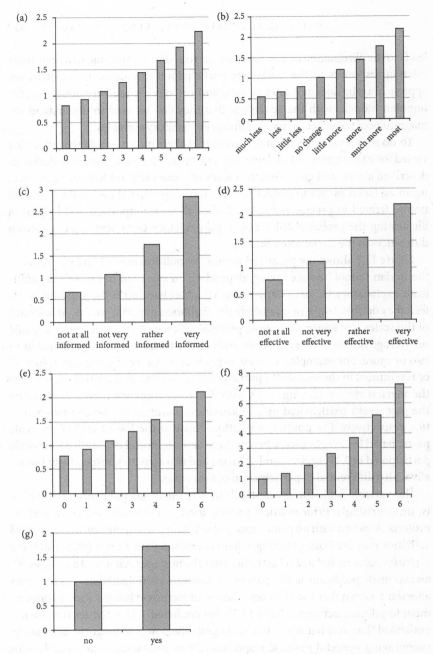

Figure 11.3. Predicted number of political activities with other variables held constant at means.

a. Effects of anger

b. Effects of political alienation

c. Effects of political efficacy (being informed)

d. Effects of political efficacy (protest)

e. Effects of prior political activism (voting)

f. Effects of prior political activism (nonvoting)

g. Effects of prior harm to relatives.

For most other variables, the effect on participation seems to be a jump from zero or one activity to two or three activities, on average. That difference for each variable amounts to roughly one to three thousand more participants across political activities, out of this pool of 1,098 victims, an outcome that could be highly meaningful for the successful redress of grievances.

Another way to estimate the magnitude of the effects is to predict the probability of specific levels of participation for different values of each explanatory variable. Figure 11.4 shows the predicted probabilities that victims at various levels of anger would participate in no political activities, one activity, two or three activities, four to ten activities, and eleven to thirty-one activities. It also shows the probabilities at various levels of political alienation, political efficacy, prior political activism, and prior harm.

There are powerful differences in the predicted probability of activism for the least angry and angriest Beslan victims. Victims who were at the low end of the anger scale were very likely to participate in no activities at all (probability .64) and very unlikely to participate in the high categories of four to ten activities or eleven or more activities (probability of .06 and .01, respectively). Conversely, victims who were at the high end of the anger scale had only a .27 probability of participating in no activities and a nearly equal probability of participating in four or more activities (.22 for four to ten activities and .06 for eleven or more activities). In other words, *the angriest victims had more than a one in four chance of being a political activist.*

The effects of the other variables are also powerful. The least politically alienated, least politically efficacious, and least politically active before the hostage taking had the highest probabilities of participating in no activities at all after the hostage taking, ranging from .58 for victims with no prior nonvoting activism to .77 for victims who felt much less politically alienated after the hostage taking. The least alienated, efficacious, and historically active also had the lowest probabilities of participating in four or more activities (ranging from .04 to .08 for four to ten activities and .01 to .02 for eleven or more activities). On the high ends of these scales, the probabilities of participating in four to ten activities ranged from .18 to .22 and eleven or more activities ranged from .05 to .06. *The most politically alienated, most politically efficacious, and most politically active in voting-related behavior before the hostage taking, like the angriest victims, had approximately a one in four chance of being a political activist after the hostage taking.*

Longtime activists who participated in six or more nonvoting-related political activities prior to the hostage taking had an astounding .86 probability of participating in four or more activities after the hostage taking, although again, so few victims had such extensive histories as longtime activists (Table 11.3) that this result is best interpreted as hypothetical. A history of participating in two

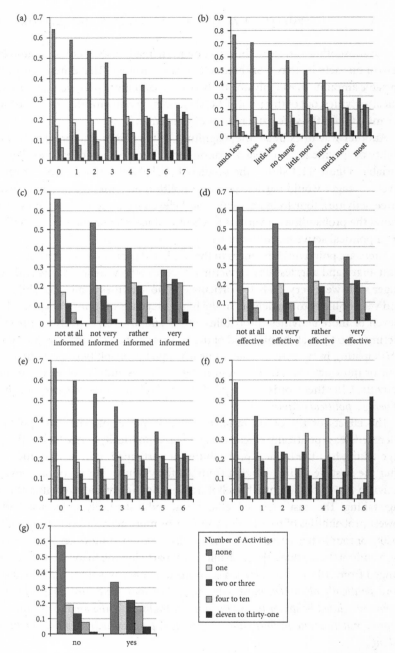

Figure 11.4. Magnitude of effects on political participation, predicted probabilities.

a. Effects of anger

b. Effects of political alienation

c. Effects of political efficacy (being informed)

d. Effects of political efficacy (protest)

e. Effects of prior political activism (voting)

f. Effects of prior political activism (nonvoting)

g. Effects of prior harm to relatives.

or three nonvoting political activities, however, was reasonably common, and even this limited prior activism had powerful results (.14 and .29 probability of participating in four or more post-violence activities, respectively), compared to victims with no prior activism whatsoever (.09).

Harm brought to relatives by Ingush or Chechen prior to the hostage taking, while significant for political participation in the aftermath, had less powerful effects than some of the other variables. Those whose relatives experienced no prior harm had a .57 probability of participating in no political activities after the hostage taking and only a .08 and .02 probability of participating in four to ten and eleven or more activities, respectively. Those whose relatives did experience prior harm were more politically active after the hostage taking, with a .18 and .05 probability of these higher categories of activism, more than double their fellow victims with no history of violence. This difference may seem unimpressive only in comparison to the more substantial effects of some of the other variables but is nevertheless quite meaningful.

Figure 11.5 shows the predicted probabilities of support for retaliatory violence, measured as the probability that a victim somewhat or fully approved of killing Chechens. The most prejudiced victims are over four times as likely to support retaliatory murder as the least prejudiced victims. A victim who would not object to having dinner with an Ingush, having a relative marry an Ingush, or having Ossetians and Ingush attend the same schools had a .03 probability of approving of killing Chechens in retaliation for the Beslan school hostage taking. A victim who would object to having an Ingush at the dinner table and would be uncomfortable with intermarriage and mixed schooling had a .13 probability of approving of killing Chechens in retaliation. The difference again is quite meaningful. *An unprejudiced victim had practically no chance of supporting retaliatory murder, let alone committing it, whereas a prejudiced victim had roughly a one in eight chance of thinking that murder is an acceptable response.*

The effects of blaming Chechens for the tragedy are similar to the effects of prejudice against Ingush. Victims who considered the Chechens not at all guilty had a .05 probability of approving retaliatory murder, while victims who considered Chechens very guilty had a .13 probability of approval.

The negative effects of political alienation and blame toward political officials on support for retaliatory violence are particularly striking. The least politically alienated victims had the highest probability of supporting retaliatory violence (.25), while the most politically alienated were roughly six times less likely to support violence (probability .04). Victims who were satisfied with the punishment of federal officials after the hostage taking were also highly likely to support retaliatory violence. A victim who was mostly satisfied had a .21 probability of approving of killing Chechens, or a one in five chance, and a victim who was completely satisfied had a .32 probability of approving of killing Chechens, or a

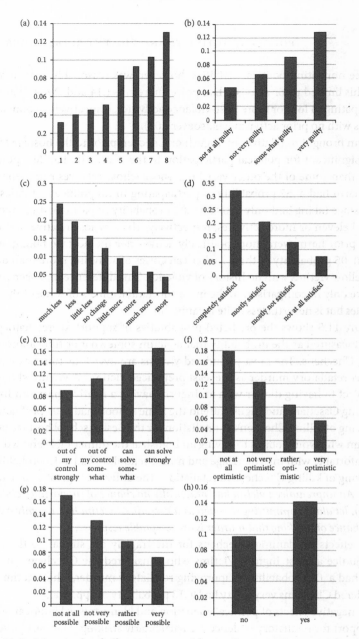

Figure 11.5. Magnitude of effects on support for retaliatory violence, predicted probability that a victim would somewhat or fully approve of killing Chechens.

a. Effects of prejudice

b. Effects of blaming Chechens

c. Effects of political alienation

d. Effects of dissatisfaction with punishment of federal officials

e. Effects of self-efficacy

f. Effects of optimism (about future)

g. Effects of optimism (solving Beslan problems)

h. Effects of prior harm to relatives.

one in three chance. The probabilities compare to the much lower .07 probability for victims who were not at all satisfied with the punishment of officials, only a one in fourteen chance. *Besides prejudice and blaming ethnic adversaries, political alienation has the biggest substantive impact on support for retaliatory violence, with the unalienated—the politically proud and satisfied with officials—being among the victims most likely to approve of murder.*

Self-efficacy and prior harm by Ingush or Chechens, although statistically significant, have less substantively powerful effects than the other variables. Victims lacking self-efficacy and having no relatives suffering prior harm had probabilities of supporting retaliatory violence that were lower than victims having high self-efficacy and previously harmed relatives but only by about 40 percent (.09 and .10 compared to .16 and .14, respectively). The effects of optimism were more substantial. Pessimistic victims were more than twice as likely to support retaliatory violence when optimism and pessimism were measured in terms of solving the problems that led to the Beslan tragedy (probability of .07 for the most optimistic victims and .17 for the most pessimistic victims) and more than three times as likely when measured generally in terms of the victims' futures (probability of .06 for the most optimistic and .18 for the most pessimistic).

Conclusion

In Beslan, there was no significant relationship between support for retaliatory violence and political participation. The two outcomes were independent. A supporter of retaliatory violence and an opponent of violence were equally (un)likely to participate in peaceful activism. An activist and a nonactivist were equally (un)likely to support violence. This is not an especially encouraging finding for peace-loving democrats who hope that participation in the political process can "cure" the desire for ethnically motivated revenge attacks. Nevertheless, the "cure" likely lies elsewhere in, for example, the eradication or at least minimization of ethnic prejudice.

Motivations for the two post-violence outcomes were mostly not the same. As shown in Chapters 5–10 and corroborated in this chapter with multivariate analysis, victims who had the greatest anger, political alienation, political efficacy, and prior experience with political participation were the most likely to respond to the hostage taking with peaceful activism. Victims who had the greatest prejudice toward Ingush, greatest blame toward Chechens, greatest pessimism, and least political alienation—meaning the greatest increase in pride in Russia—were the most likely to respond by supporting retaliatory violence. Other variables, such as self-efficacy and prior harm to relatives committed by Ingush or Chechens, also played roles in both outcomes. Little to no role was played in either outcome by the perceived risk of political activism, general trust in government, and importantly, the severity of the grievance as measured by the death of a child or spouse, the experience of being held hostage, or the number of relatives affected by the hostage taking. Rather, those grievances were the defining characteristics of almost all Beslan victims and thus important as the context that united them rather than as a variable that sorted them into a particular rank order.

For variables that have statistically significant effects, it is important to estimate their substantive importance, or the magnitude of the effects. To do so, the analysis predicted the probability of political participation and support for retaliatory violence at various levels of the significant explanatory variables. Victims who were at the high end of the scales for anger, political alienation, political efficacy, or political activism before the hostage taking had a roughly one in four chance of being a political activist after the hostage taking. Victims at the low end of these scales had less than a one in ten chance of becoming a political activist, sometimes—as for the least politically alienated—a less than one in twenty-five chance. Victims who were at the high end of the scales for prejudice or blaming Chechens had a roughly one in eight chance of supporting retaliatory violence, while victims at the low end of the scales for political alienation or satisfaction with the punishment of federal officials had between a one in five and one in three chance of supporting retaliatory violence.

These conclusions are in some sense conservative. Probabilities were predicted by varying each explanatory variable separately. The substantive impact of several variables jointly could of course be much higher. For example, an angry, politically alienated, and politically efficacious victim had a very high probability of participating in politics. A prejudiced and politically proud victim had a higher-than-average probability of supporting retaliatory violence.

The more rigorous analysis thus reaffirms some of the stark conclusions in the rest of Part II: increased pride in country, after a botched anti-terrorist operation, is a powerful driver of support for murdering members of a rival ethnic group. Prejudice toward that ethnic group and blaming an ethnic group for the atrocities committed by some of its members are also powerful drivers of retaliatory killing. Anger in the same situation is not the driving force but rather helps explain a more peaceful political response.

PART III
GENERALIZING FINDINGS FROM BESLAN VICTIMS

This study has examined the post-violence behavior of a group of similarly aggrieved individuals, Beslan residents who were directly victimized in the 2004 school hostage taking. These victims suffered varying but comparable and related harm. The logical next questions involve whether the findings about Beslan victims are generalizable to other people.

In social science terms, this is a question of external validity (Lucas 2003). The internal validity of the Beslan study has been bolstered by the comprehensive nature of both the survey questions and the victim sample: By interviewing such a large percentage of surviving adult hostages, parents or guardians of underage hostages, and next of kin of deceased hostages, it is highly likely that the survey results reflect the true experiences, attitudes, and behavior of the population of Beslan victims. If the results also have external validity, they might apply to nearby residents who did not suffer comparable harm and/or to victims of violence in other places and times.

Part III then examines external validity. Chapter 12 deals with the question of generalizability from victims to nonvictims. For political participation, the evidence does not support such generalizability. Variables explaining victim political behavior are rarely significant for nonvictims whose primary motivation is their geographic or social proximity to victims. For support for retaliatory violence, the evidence suggests some generalizability: Support for retaliation among nonvictims, like victims, is strongly connected to excusing government while blaming ethnic rivals for the actions of terrorists. Still, even for retaliation, the findings suggest caution in treating the nonvictim population as if it is or should be motivated by the same factors that motivate victims.

Chapter 13 deals with the question of generalizability from victims of violence in the small town of Beslan to victims of violence elsewhere around the world. Here the evidence is largely affirmative: Beslan victims are distinctive in terms of their culture, political environment, and the details of the ethnic conflict that exploded into the terrifying hostage taking and resulting massacre. However, these distinctions are generally not relevant for understanding individual-level motivations to respond to the violence with further violence or political activism. In important ways, Beslan victims are typical of victims of violence throughout the world. Many lessons can be learned from Beslan victims and validly applied to other victims of ethnic violence who are contemplating political and/or violent responses.

12

Should Results Apply to Nonvictims?

Should findings about victims of violence apply to nonvictims as well? In most situations involving an aggrieved population, there are individuals who are not directly aggrieved but who feel connected to the aggrieved population and share their pain and outrage. Some of these indirectly aggrieved individuals or sympathizers may act on that pain and outrage. As with the directly aggrieved population, the question is why some respond with retaliatory violence and some with political participation. Are the factors that explain the peaceful or violent mobilization of non-aggrieved populations the same as for the aggrieved?

This question is relevant for a wide range of subpopulations and problems in routine politics. For example, are men mobilized on behalf of women's issues for the same reasons that women are mobilized? Are native-born citizens mobilized to defend the rights of immigrant populations for the same reasons as the immigrants themselves? Or is greater theorizing required to understand the behavior of men, native-born citizens, and other individuals who sympathize with causes and harm not directly experienced?

In the context of Beslan, the question is what motivated nonvictim responses to the school hostage taking. This chapter explores whether the variables that are so important for motivating victim behavior—including anger, political alienation, and political efficacy for political participation and prejudice and political pride for retaliatory violence—are also important for motivating nonvictim behavior. Findings are based on original survey data from 1,023 nonvictim residents of Beslan and 1,020 nonvictim residents of the nearby North Ossetian capital of Vladikavkaz.[1]

The results show that models of victim behavior do not transfer well to nonvictims. While some explanations of victim and nonvictim behavior are shared, some are not. When added to study populations, nonvictims dilute findings, confuse analysis, and weaken our understanding of political behavior. The findings suggest the need for caution when generalizing from victim behavior to nonvictim behavior.

Perhaps more importantly, the findings suggest the inappropriateness of drawing inferences about post-violence reactionary behavior from population

---

[1] Vanessa Baird contributed greatly to the statistical analysis in this chapter, which builds on Javeline and Baird (2012).

After Violence. Debra Javeline, Oxford University Press. © Oxford University Press 2023.
DOI: 10.1093/oso/9780197683347.003.0013

samples, even if randomly and rigorously selected. The undifferentiated study of directly and indirectly aggrieved individuals may obscure the motivations of each.

Nonvictims by definition have less reason than victims to respond to violence, and their behavior to date is less studied and understood. Perhaps the single most important finding about such individuals concerns the role of grievances, which vary meaningfully among nonvictims more than among the universally ag-grieved victims. Proximity to victims—personal, geographic, and emotional—is a proxy for shared grievances and a strong motivator of political participation, but is unrelated to support for retaliatory violence. For retaliation, findings common to victims and nonvictims include the unimportance of anger and the importance of prejudice, blaming ethnic rivals for the crimes of their co-ethnics, and satisfaction with the punishment of officials.

Why Victims and Nonvictims May Differ

Direct experience with violence matters (Horowitz 2001:407). Direct victims of terrorism have heightened perceptions of personal vulnerability and greater anxiety, depression, posttraumatic stress disorder (PTSD), and other symptoms of emotional distress than nonvictims (Galea et al. 2002:985–986; DeLisi et al. 2003; Huddy et al. 2005).

Nevertheless, violence can have pervasive impacts in the population beyond the victims. Nonvictims are often psychologically affected by knowledge of a violent incident that they have not directly experienced, even if they are un-acquainted with the dead or injured (Schuster et al. 2001; Silver et al. 2002; Knudsen et al. 2005; Laufer and Solomon 2006). Their distress may emerge from sympathy with victims, personalizing and imagining themselves as victims, disappointed expectations about the state's ability to keep people safe, and concern about future attacks (Schuster et al. 2001; Knudsen et al. 2005:261).

Victims more than nonvictims should be expected to respond to the vio-lence. Personal victimization is more politically motivating than sympathy with victims, because "felt injustice is at the root of any protest" (Klandermans 1997:205). When individuals experience both personal deprivation and group deprivation, the personal is more likely to become political and motivate par-ticipation (Foster and Matheson 1999). When individuals sympathize but do not feel the injustice personally and deeply, they are more difficult to mobilize (Oegema and Klandermans 1994). At the leadership level, those who have been victims devote more time to their social movement leadership activities than nonvictim leaders (Dorius and McCarthy 2011).

Nonvictims may identify with the aggrieved collectivity, share feelings of injustice, believe in the possibility of social change, and therefore belong to the mobilization potential of a given social movement (Simon et al. 1998:648), but identity, feelings, and beliefs are more tenuous than the objective, unambiguous grievance of victimization by violence. Nonvictim sympathizers may even at times lose their sympathy and support for victims (Oegema and Klandermans 1994), a luxury not fully available to victims. In Beslan, for example, some nonvictims came to feel like second-class citizens, excluded from the material benefits received by victims, jealous, and increasingly desensitized to the victims' tragedy (Phillips 2007:256). While victims may lose sympathy for other victims or harden to their own situations, their connection to their grievance is a historical, unalterable fact and a more potent factor in converting potential mobilization to actual mobilization.

In terms of retaliatory violence or support for retaliatory violence, the differences between victims and nonvictims are less clear. Victims may at times be more forgiving than nonvictims and at times more supportive of revenge (Brewer and Hayes 2013, 2014). In Chechnya, for example, suicide bombers were typically victims traumatized by witnessing the beatings and murder of close family members at the hands of Russians or by being tortured themselves, and these victims were seeking vengeance (Speckhard and Akhmedova 2006:454–455). But after the Beslan school hostage taking, nonvictim South Ossetian refugees residing in North Ossetia were among those most vocal in calling for a violent response (Naidenov 2005c; Tuathail 2009:11fn), and retaliatory violence was pursued by nonvictims as far north as Moscow, where up to fifty young Russians attacked and severely injured four people from the Caucasus on a Moscow subway while shouting, "This is what you get for terrorist attacks" (Walsh 2004b). Either way, the views of victims, more than any other group in the population, may determine the outcome of post-violence peace processes (Brewer and Hayes 2013, 2014).

In addition to the variation between victims and nonvictims, there may be important variation among nonvictims. Proximity to the victims and the violence matters (Horowitz 2001:407). Among nonvictims, those who are or feel most similar to victims and identify with the victims based on these shared characteristics suffer more negative mental health outcomes (Knudsen et al. 2005:261). Geographic proximity to terrorist attacks or other acts of violence, as well as emotional proximity in the sense of knowing someone killed or hurt, also heightens psychological reactions such as anxiety, depression, PTSD, and threat perception (Galea et al. 2002:982; Schlenger et al. 2002; Silver et al. 2002; Veenema and Schroeder-Bruce 2002; Huddy et al. 2005; Knudsen et al. 2005:263). For example, after the terrorist attacks of September 11, proximity to the World Trade Center increased estimates of the probability of future terror-related events (Fischhoff et al. 2003). Beyond mental health reactions, other behaviors are also influenced by proximity. Riots generally occur closest to the initial acts of violence and decline in intensity with distance (Horowitz 2001:406–407).

Proximity is of course not the only factor differentiating nonvictims. Responses to terrorism and other acts of violence have a highly subjective dimension and vary greatly, as do coping strategies (Silver et al. 2002). However, efforts to identify these other factors and understand variation in nonvictim responses to a terrorist act like the Beslan school hostage taking have so far been limited.

Prior Research on Victim versus Nonvictim Mobilization

Few studies of retaliatory ethnic violence or political participation explicitly compare victim and nonvictim motivations. One challenge is in defining the nonvictim population, which incorporates a diversity of people. Some may sympathize with the victims and provide support, some may sympathize without providing support, some may be part of the bystander public and have yet to form an opinion on the circumstances or appropriate response, and some may even be opponents with competing opinions (McCarthy and Zald 1973, 1977; Ennis and Schreuer 1987; Cress and Snow 1996). Theories of post-violence behavior are difficult to develop and apply to such potentially dissimilar nonvictims, let alone to nonvictims and victims jointly.

Including or excluding nonvictims from studies of retaliatory violence or peaceful political behavior has typically depended on the role assigned to grievances for motivating such behavior. At one extreme, grievances have been treated as the primary motivation for activism (e.g., Gurr 1970), and discussing the behavior of non-aggrieved individuals has seemed nonsensical or at least a far less worthy topic of investigation. For people not victimized by violence, there is no expectation that they would respond to the violence. At the other extreme, grievances have been treated as ubiquitous and incidental to activism, suggesting that variables that mobilize or fail to mobilize directly aggrieved individuals should be the same as those affecting less directly aggrieved individuals (McCarthy and Zald 1977). A victim of violence and a nonvictim are subject to similar constraints and opportunities that could reasonably be modeled jointly.

In the middle of these extremes are studies that focus on deprived groups such as farmworkers (Jenkins and Perrow 1977), women (Freeman 1979), and African Americans (Oberschall 1973) or groups that are not traditionally deprived but find themselves confronted with a suddenly imposed grievance such as a major oil spill (Molotch 1970), court-ordered busing (Useem 1980), illness due to chemical waste (Levine 1982), or evacuation and water contamination due to nuclear accident (Walsh 1981). However, beyond simply saying "grievances do or do not matter" and insisting on the inclusion of grievances in theories and empirical analyses, few have analyzed the behavioral motivations of deprived or suddenly aggrieved groups in comparison to those who are less proximate to the grievance.

A notable exception finds that members of subordinate and dominant groups may both be mobilized by a critical mindset, also known as cognitive liberation, insurgent consciousness, or oppositional consciousness (Piven and Cloward 1977; McAdam 1982; Smith 1991; Mansbridge and Morris 2001), but, importantly, the process of fostering oppositional consciousness differs for members of each population (Nepstad 2007). To the question of whether victims and nonvictims are similarly mobilizable, the social movement literature seems equivocal but leans toward no.

Other bodies of literature also hint that nonvictims, a subset of people not directly aggrieved by a cause or problem, are driven by different factors. Studies of altruism offer fascinating insights into the behavioral motivations of people who have selflessly assisted others, attributing explanatory power not to moral or ethical development, empathy, duty, cost-benefit calculations, or reason, but rather to a perception of a common humanity and a spontaneous or intuitive motivation to work together and help others (Monroe 1996, 2004). However, because the very definition of altruism involves disinterest and selflessness, the studies do not include individuals who are directly aggrieved, even if they may hold an altruistic worldview and try to help others in their aggrieved group. Applying this logic to the aftermath of violence, a study might be devoted exclusively to understanding the behavioral response of nonvictims.

Similarly, studies on the related topic of volunteerism ask "who cares" and "who helps," focusing on individuals not directly hit by tragedy (e.g., Wilson and Musick 1997). The motivations for helping oneself after victimization, or for victims helping other victims, is slightly outside the purview of the research question. Volunteers are implicitly nonvictims.

Studies of organizational justice are concerned with standards of fair treatment and motivations for the punishment of justice violators, such as the refusal to do business with an organization that violates moral and social norms or supporting fines for such organizations. These studies increasingly focus on third parties whose behavior cannot easily be explained by self-interest. Rather, moral identity, or the centrality of a person's moral character to his or her self-definition, drives third-party responses (O'Reilly et al. 2016). Of course, victims are first parties, not third parties, and their victim identity takes precedence over their moral identity in the definition assigned to them by researchers.

Studies of the aftermath of civil wars come closest to distinguishing explicitly between victims and nonvictims and analyzing post-violence behavioral similarities and differences. These studies show that victims of violence are significantly more likely than nonvictims to be members of community groups and attend community meetings (Bellows and Miguel 2006, 2009), vote and assume community leadership (Blattman 2009), and contribute to public goods (Gilligan et al. 2011). Victims experience "posttraumatic growth" (Blattman 2009) and adopt new pro-social norms (Gilligan et al. 2011). Few if any studies, however, go beyond civil wars to compare victim and nonvictim behavior in other post-violence contexts and, importantly, to compare victim and nonvictim motivations for that behavior.

As described above, variation among nonvictims in their personal and/or geographic proximity to the aggrieved population matters, and this variation may help bridge the study of victim and nonvictim populations. For volunteerism, personal identification with victims, and especially having friends or relatives among the victims, is a critical factor in explaining blood donation (Drake et al. 1982; Piliavin and Callero 1991), AIDS work (Omoto and Snyder 1995), and helping victims of terrorism and disaster (St. John and Fuchs 2002; Beyerlein and Sikkink 2008). Living close to a disaster site, such as Oklahoma City after the bombings or New York City after the September 11 terrorist attack, may also increase the probability of volunteerism (St. John and Fuchs 2002; Beyerlein and Sikkink 2008). For political participation, proximity to a grievance has also been found to be significant (Lyons and Lowery 1986; Verba et al. 1995). Issue salience heightens the salience of political action (Campbell 2003).

In terms of support for retaliatory violence, it is even more difficult to understand whether victims of violence and nonvictims should be studied jointly or independently. The literature on violence focuses less on individual-level motivations and more on factors that are contextual, structural, or institutional. For example, violence has been shown to vary with political order or chaos (Varshney 2010), social order or chaos (Horowitz 1985), socioeconomic factors such as aggregate levels of education and employment (Huntington 1968), the fight for resources (Olzak 1992; Kalyvas 2001, 2003), international factors such as interaction with international organizations or international social movement organizations (Keck and Sikkink 1998a, 1998b; Uvin 1998; Tsutsui 2004; Olzak 2006), and elite behavior (Laitin 1986; Olzak 1992; Lake and Rothchild 1996; Fearon and Laitin 2000:846; Brass 2003; Kalyvas 2001, 2003; Wilkinson 2004; Bhavnani 2006; North et al. 2009; Varshney 2010; Pearlman 2011). To the extent that studies of violence investigate individual-level factors promoting or discouraging retaliatory violence, they discuss selective incentives such as monetary offers or gains in looting or protection (Kalyvas 2001; Humphreys and Weinstein 2008), the perception that there is no other way out (Goodwin 2001; Politkovskaya 2007), or personality differences (Adorno et al. 1950; Milgram 1974).

Still, the unstated and unjustified assumption seems to be that these individual-level motivations for retaliatory violence apply to all members of a community or region. Few studies examine whether victims of violence and nonvictims should behave similarly or differently in terms of their desire to repay violence with further violence.

Because the existing literature for the most part has not differentiated and compared victims and nonvictims or even more generally aggrieved individuals and unaggrieved, it provides little guidance for theory building. This chapter thus addresses the empirical question and tests whether the findings in Part II about victim behavior also apply to nonvictims. Future theory-building remains necessary to understand why the behavior of directly and indirectly aggrieved individuals should be similar or different.

Applying Victim Models of Post-Violence Behavior to Nonvictims

Is peaceful political behavior best explained by a single model applied to both victims of violence and nonvictims? Or are the variables explaining victim behavior different from those explaining nonvictim behavior, or perhaps somewhere in between, with some variables accounting for political behavior regardless of proximity to the grievance and others depending critically on one's status as a victim or nonvictim? Should there be one model or more to explain support for retaliatory violence, one set of variables explaining support for violence regardless of level of victimization or separate models for victims and nonvictims?

Data to test these questions come from the two nonvictim surveys described in the introduction: the Beslan nonvictim survey, consisting of a random sample of 1,023 Beslan residents, and the Vladikavkaz nonvictim survey, consisting of a random sample of 1,020 residents of the North Ossetian capital, located roughly thirteen miles south of Beslan. Almost all of these people were not held hostage, but most Beslan residents knew some of the former hostages personally, and most Vladikavkaz residents were deeply affected by the violence, although perhaps less personally. Variation in the level of grievance therefore ranged from personal loss or injury to the insecurity of living in a region where such violence occurred and could occur again.

Nonvictim Political Participation

Table 12.1 shows that victims participated significantly more than nonvictims. Of the possible thirty-one concrete post-hostage-taking political activities, not a single activity generated more nonvictim participation than victim participation. Commonly, five or ten times as many victims participated as nonvictims. Among Beslan victims, at least 37.9 percent participated in one or more activities, as compared to 9 percent of Beslan nonvictims and 12.6 percent of Vladikavkaz nonvictims. If we impute missing data using the multiple imputation program in Stata, the differences are even starker, with 44.8 percent of Beslan victims

Table 12.1. Political Participation of Victims and Nonvictims: Number Reporting Participation (%)

	Beslan Victims	Beslan Nonvictims	Vladikavkaz Nonvictims
Attended some part of the trial against accused hostage taker Nurpashi Kulayev (inside the courtroom during proceedings) starting in May 2005	357 (32.5)	17 (1.7)	9 (.9)
Met with North Ossetian president Mamsurov since the tragedy	213 (19.4)	17 (1.7)	35 (3.4)
Wrote to a newspaper, called news show, or spoke to a reporter at any time since the tragedy	206 (18.8)	28 (2.7)	9 (.9)
Attended meeting with Russian Deputy Prosecutor General Shepel at the House of Culture on November 3, 2004	176 (16.0)	30 (3.0)	4 (.4)
Participated in rallies in Beslan right after the tragedy in early September 2004	122 (11.1)	48 (4.8)	28 (2.8)
Picketed the Rostov-Baku/Caucasus Federal Highway in January 2005	118 (10.7)	8 (.8)	2 (.2)
Signed the open letter to Putin and the parliamentary investigation committee in November 2004	117 (10.7)	7 (.7)	8 (.8)
Traveled to Vladikavkaz to participate in a rally since September 2004	93 (8.5)	10 (.9)	—
Supplied the picketers of the Rostov-Baku/Caucasus Federal Highway with food, bonfire wood, or other supplies in January 2005	93 (8.5)	14 (1.4)	6 (.6)
Met with other political official since the tragedy (besides those specifically named)	91 (8.3)	13 (1.3)	11 (1.1)

(continued)

Table 12.1. Continued

	Beslan Victims	Beslan Nonvictims	Vladikavkaz Nonvictims
Met with federal officials from the Federation Council and Duma who visited Beslan three weeks after the tragedy	88 (8.0)	13 (1.3)	9 (.9)
Wrote or signed a letter to any other political official since the tragedy (besides those specifically named)	88 (8.0)	23 (2.3)	7 (.7)
Attended meeting with new Deputy Prosecutor General Sydoruk at the House of Representatives on August 9, 2006	85 (7.7)	8 (.8)	4 (.4)
Protested outside the courtroom where accused hostage taker Kulayev was tried starting in May 2005	84 (7.7)	6 (.6)	14 (1.4)
Helped write the open letter to Putin and the parliamentary investigation committee in November 2004	82 (7.5)	4 (.4)	1 (.1)
Met with Deputies Prosecutor General Shepel or Kolesnikov or General Public Prosecutor Ustinov any other time since the tragedy	79 (7.2)	20 (2.0)	0 (.0)
Signed the letter to the international community fearing that authorities will not reveal truth and requesting asylum or immigration in August 2005	79 (7.2)	4 (.4)	4 (.4)
Participated in any other rallies or acts of protest in the two years since the tragedy (besides those specifically named)	74 (6.7)	16 (1.6)	45 (4.5)
Wrote a letter to federal officials such as Federation Council members or Duma deputies	72 (6.6)	7 (.7)	4 (.4)
Participated in a sit-in at the court where accused hostage taker Kulayev was tried in August 2005	63 (5.7)	6 (.6)	4 (.4)
Refused to leave the courtroom at any other time during accused hostage taker Kulayev's trial (besides the August 2005 sit-in)	59 (5.4)	3 (.3)	2 (.2)
Participated in rallies outside of Beslan such as Prigorodny or Vladikavkaz right after the tragedy in early September 2004	58 (5.3)	12 (1.2)	71 (7.1)
Supplied with food and water those sitting in the courtroom where accused hostage taker Kulayev was tried in August 2005	54 (4.9)	14 (1.4)	6 (.6)

(continued)

Table 12.1. Continued

	Beslan Victims	Beslan Nonvictims	Vladikavkaz Nonvictims
Participated in a hunger strike at the end of accused hostage taker Kulayev's trial	50 (4.6)	3 (.3)	2 (.3)
Met with Kozak any other time since the tragedy (besides February 2005)	41 (3.7)	10 (.9)	3 (.3)
Met with President Putin in Moscow in September 2005	38 (3.5)	2 (.2)	1 (.1)
Signed any other letters to Putin in the two years since the tragedy (besides the open letter in November 2004)	38 (3.5)	5 (.5)	4 (.4)
Picketed the Rostov-Baku/Caucasus Federal Highway in January 2005, for more than one day	33 (3.0)	4 (.3)	0 (.0)
Met with Putin's special envoy to South Federal District Kozak in Rostov-on-Don in February 2005	31 (2.8)	6 (.6)	2 (.2)
Called the special hotline to speak with federal officials such as Federation Council members or Duma deputies	29 (2.6)	4 (.4)	5 (.5)
Traveled to other town in North Ossetia to participate in a rally since September 2004	17 (1.5)	4 (.2)	17 (1.7)
[For Vladikavkaz residents] participated in a rally in Vladikavkaz concerning the events in Beslan?	—	—	82 (8.1)
[For Vladikavkaz residents] Since September 2004, have you traveled to Beslan to participate in a rally?	—	—	17 (1.7)
N	1,098	1,023	1,020

participating in one or more activities, compared to 9 percent and 15 percent of Beslan and Vladikavkaz nonvictims, respectively.

If victims of violence participate in politics at higher levels than nonvictims, is it because they are motivated by different factors or motivated by the same factors, which the victims happen to have in higher abundance? The results suggest it is mostly the former: only some findings about victims are generalizable to nonvictims.

Table 12.2 shows the results of a negative binomial model on the count variable of political participation for nonvictims based on hypotheses about victim behavior. The data show that, for nonvictims, severity of or proximity

Table 12.2. Explaining Nonvictim Responses to Violence

		Political Participation Negative Binomial Estimates, Coef. (SE)	Support for Retaliatory Violence Ordered Logit Estimates, Coef. (SE)
Severity of grievance	Hostage	2.34 (.58)***	−.09 (.49)
	Number of relatives affected	.07 (.02)***	.01 (.01)
Anger		.10 (.07)	.02 (.05)
Anxiety		−.05 (.05)	.08 (.04)
Enthusiasm		.03 (.05)	−.06 (.04)
Political alienation (decreased pride)		−.27 (.19)	.22 (.11)*
Blame toward and punishment of federal officials	Putin's guilt	.27 (.09)***	.02 (.06)
	Dissat. with punishment of officials	.01 (.11)	−.56 (.07)***
Social alienation		−.27 (.11)*	.09 (.07)
Blame toward Chechens		−.31 (.09)***	.55 (.06)***
Prejudice toward Ingush		.82 (.30)**	.69 (.17)***
Political efficacy	Politically informed	.18 (.13)	−.14 (.07)
	Perceived effectiveness of protest	.23 (.09)	.11 (.08)
Self-efficacy		−.14 (.12)	.12 (.08)
Optimism	Optimistic about future	−.11 (.12)	.02 (.07)
	Possible to solve Beslan's problems	.25 (.09)**	−.04 (.06)
Prior political activism	Prior voting	.20 (.07)***	.04 (.04)
	Prior nonvoting behavior	.25 (.08)***	.04 (.06)
Prior harm to relatives		.60 (.18)***	.23 (.15)
Perceived risk of political activism		.14 (.17)	.48 (.10)***
Trust in government		−.36 (.12)	−.10 (.07)

(continued)

Table 12.2. Continued

		Political Participation Negative Binomial Estimates, Coef. (SE)	Support for Retaliatory Violence Ordered Logit Estimates, Coef. (SE)
Demographics	Female	−.07 (.17)	−.14 (.10)
	Age	−.01 (.01)	−.01 (.004)
	Household income	−.10 (.05)	−.01 (.04)
	Education	.13 (.07)*	−.06 (.05)
Vladikavkaz		.56 (.19)***	−.20 (.12)
Constant		−2.65 (1.01)	—
Cutpoints	τ_1		.96 (.64)
	τ_2		2.46 (.64)
	τ_3		3.76 (.66)
N		2,037	2,037

See Table 11.4 for variable description and coding. $*p < .05; **p < .01; ***p < .005$.

to the grievance matters critically for political participation. In the victim sample, participation was unaffected by whether the individual was a hostage himself or herself, lost a child or children, lost a spouse, or had one or several relatives held hostage, because, by definition, all victims fit in one or more of these categories. They all were extremely proximate to the hostage taking. For the nonvictim samples, because they were randomly generated from city populations, a small number of former hostages ended up selected in proportion to the percentage of former hostages in the town (22 former hostages of 1,023 Beslan nonvictim respondents, or 2%, compared to roughly 1,226 former hostages of 36,000 Beslan residents, or 3%). Among nonvictims, being a former hostage is strongly correlated with political participation. Having friends or relatives among the hostages is also strongly correlated with political participation.

So far, these results might suggest the appropriateness of using random population samples in order to study political action and simply controlling for proximity to a grievance such as victimization by violence. The results might also suggest the appropriateness of random population samples to study support for retaliatory violence and the inconsequential nature of the decision to control or not control for proximity to the grievance. However, further investigation of other explanatory variables for political participation suggest that the story is not quite so simple. Victim and nonvictim responses to the hostage taking are driven by some similar factors but also some different factors, suggesting that victim-only or aggrieved-only samples may often be a helpful tool in understanding political participation and support for retaliatory violence.

As Table 12.2 shows, only four variables—prior physical harm to a family member or friend by someone of Ingush or Chechen descent, the perceived guilt of Vladimir Putin for causing the tragedy, and prior political activism as measured by prior voting and prior nonvoting behavior—are statistically significant for explaining peaceful political participation among both victims and nonvictims. The importance of the prior harm variable is again consistent with the argument that grievances matter: presumably, respondents who viewed the current violent incident as just one in a longer and very personal history of violent incidents were more aggrieved than respondents who had no personal past connection with victimization. The accumulation of grievances is politically mobilizing. The importance of assigning guilt to Putin for the hostage taking is also consistent with a story about grievances as well as the effects of political alienation on political action.

Otherwise, the coherent story explaining the political mobilization of victims after the hostage taking is not easily applied to nonvictims. Anger, political alienation, and political efficacy, which prove to be highly significant correlates of peaceful political activism among victims, are not significant for nonvictims. Most findings from the nonvictims do not directly contradict findings from the victims: for example, emotions such as anxiety and enthusiasm prove to be not significant for victims and nonvictims alike. A standard collective action variable, the perceived risk of political action, measured by a belief that participants will be punished or otherwise suffer, is also not significant for both victims and nonvictims. Even some of the findings that are significant for nonvictims but not for victims, such as social alienation and assigning guilt to Chechens for the hostage taking (both negatively related to participation among nonvictims) and prejudice toward Ingush and the belief that it is possible to solve the problems that led to the tragedy (both positively related), are not necessarily contradictory but are unexplained.

Apart from arguing for the importance of proximity to the grievance, including prior harm and thus the longstanding nature of a grievance, it is difficult to derive a theory inductively from the nonvictim data about the motivations of nonvictims to participate in politics. Even a deductive, standard resource theory finds little support in the nonvictim data. Education is positively significant for participation among nonvictims, but the relationship is neither strong nor robust, and age and household income have no significant effect.

Nonvictim Support for Retaliatory Violence

For support for retaliatory violence, there were no significant differences between victims and nonvictims in the distribution of attitudes (Table 12.3): 13.9 percent of victims fully or somewhat approved of killing the same number of Chechens as were killed in Beslan, compared to a slightly greater number of Beslan nonvictims (16.5 percent) and a slightly lesser number of Vladikavkaz nonvictims (11.3 percent), but the differences are not statistically significant.

Multivariate analysis supports this descriptive finding. Table 12.2 shows the results of an ordered logit model on the ordered categorical variable of support for retaliatory violence among nonvictims. As found among victims, the willingness of nonvictims to kill Chechens in response to the hostage taking was not affected by status as a former hostage or relative of former hostage(s). Where the severity of or proximity to the grievance of victimization was statistically significant for nonvictim political participation, it was not significant for nonvictim support for retaliatory violence.

Another common thread between victims and nonvictims is that dissatisfaction with the punishment of guilty federal officials has negative, statistically

Table 12.3. Support for Retaliatory Violence among Victims and Nonvictims: Number (%)

"I will now read some specific strategies that some people recommend to resolve problems in North Ossetia. For each one, please tell me whether you fully approve, somewhat approve, somewhat disapprove, or completely disapprove: *kill the same number of Chechens as were killed in Beslan.*"

	Beslan Victims	Beslan Nonvictims	Vladikavkaz Nonvictims
Fully approve	65 (5.9)	41 (4.0)	57 (5.6)
Somewhat approve	88 (8.0)	128 (12.5)	58 (5.7)
Somewhat disapprove	371 (33.8)	226 (22.1)	198 (19.4)
Completely disapprove	446 (40.6)	455 (44.5)	596 (58.4)
Difficult to answer	45 (4.1)	90 (8.8)	70 (6.9)
Refused to answer	83 (7.6)	83 (8.1)	41 (4.0)
N	1,098	1,023	1,020

significant effects on support for retaliatory violence. Among both groups, those who were satisfied with the treatment of guilty federal officials were more likely to support killing Chechens in retaliation. (Political alienation per se is positively significant for support for violence among nonvictims, but that finding is not especially strong or robust and cannot be replicated at the bivariate level.) The significance of (dis)satisfaction with punishment of federal officials is strong, robust, and consistent theoretically: few if any federal officials in Russia were punished in any meaningful way for their role in the hostage taking, so satisfaction with their punishment suggests a particularly positive mindset toward government. Individuals with such mindsets might search outside the political system in responding to the hostage taking, and the most obvious nongovernment targets might be innocent members of the ethnic group perceived as responsible for the violence.

Two other variables, prejudice toward Ingush and assigning guilt for the hostage takings to Chechens, are statistically significant for explaining support for retaliatory violence among both victims and nonvictims. The malevolence of prejudice is clear: disliking an ethnic group and blaming an ethnic group for the crimes of some of its members are related to seeking vengeance against that ethnic group. The finding holds, whether an individual was victimized or not.

The surprising finding for victims that anger is not significantly correlated with support for retaliatory violence is also found for the nonvictims. Although anger is widely disparaged for having dangerous behavioral implications, there is no empirical evidence supporting this relationship for either victims or nonvictims. Similarly, there is no statistically significant relationship between many demographic variables (age, income, and education) and support for retaliatory violence among victims, and the lack of relationship holds for nonvictims as well.

Otherwise, variables that were statistically significant in explaining victim support for retaliatory violence are not significant for nonvictims (lack of political alienation and presence of social alienation, self-efficacy, pessimism, prior nonvoting behavior, prior harm to relatives, and female sex), or the reverse, a variable that was not significant for victims is significant for nonvictims (perceived risk of political activism).[2] These different findings suggest that there may be differing motivations among victims and nonvictims for supporting retaliatory

---

[2] The significance of perceived risk of political activism for supporting retaliatory violence among nonvictims is unclear. One explanation involves scapegoating: if activism against government is feared, perhaps the less risky alternative is to target members of the rival ethnic group. However, if true, this logic should apply to victims as well as nonvictims. Another possible explanation involves the later date of the nonvictim surveys when substantial political activism had already occurred. Supporters of violence may have interpreted the question as an assessment not of the objective risk associated with activism but of their own feelings about activism. Among nonvictims, those who supported violence may have also supported punishment of activists. Such an interpretation is speculative.

violence and that modeling nonvictim support for retaliatory violence based on theories about victims may still be misguided.

Intercity Variation

The models in Table 12.2 control for the city of residence, a dichotomous variable for whether respondents reside in Vladikavkaz or Beslan. For political participation, the control variable is strongly and positively significant, confirming that, among nonvictims, political participation was higher in Vladikavkaz than Beslan. This outcome might seem surprising, given the above discussions about the importance of proximity to victims in motivating political behavior. However, other variables in the model are stronger proxies for this proximity and the severity of the grievance, such as being held hostage and having many relatives affected by the hostage taking, so the variable for city of residence is probably not capturing proximity to victims in a personal, emotional, or even geographic sense. Rather, the variable may be capturing proximity to decision-makers in Vladikavkaz, the more participatory or oppositional culture in the republic capital, or some other aspect of the city's community.

Whatever the reason, the significance of city of residence is problematic. It suggests that the models are missing important, generalizable factors for postviolence political participation by nonvictims. The omitted variables may be relevant only for some nonvictims, if there are context-specific causes of nonvictim behavior. The hypotheses derived to understand victim behavior are either incomplete or inappropriate for nonvictims.

For support for retaliatory violence, the control variable for city of residence is not statistically significant. Nonvictims in Vladikavkaz were no different from nonvictims in Beslan in their approval of killing Chechens. Some findings about retaliation may thus be generalizable across nonvictims and between victims and nonvictims, partly because victimization (severity of the grievance) may be less relevant for retaliation than for political participation.

Table 12.4 supports this assertion. The table shows the models for political participation and support for retaliatory violence with separate samples of Beslan and Vladikavkaz nonvictims. Among either population, the number of relatives held hostage in the school was not significantly related to support for retaliation.

Other results are common across samples. Harm to relatives prior to the hostage taking is statistically significant for the political participation of nonvictims in both city samples. Anger is not statistically significant for supporting retaliatory violence in either sample, again providing important evidence against the conventional wisdom holding anger accountable for interethnic violence.

Table 12.4. Comparing Beslan and Vladikavkaz Nonvictim Responses to Violence

		Political Participation Negative Binomial Estimates, Coef. (SE)		Support for Retaliatory Violence Ordered Logit Estimates, Coef. (SE)	
		Beslan	Vladikavkaz	Beslan	Vladikavkaz
Severity of grievance	Hostage	2.88 (.56)***	—	.31 (.60)	—
	Number of relatives affected	.06 (.02)***	.15 (.05)***	−.005 (.02)	.06 (.05)
Anger		.02 (.10)	.16 (.09)	.12 (.08)	−.01 (.07)
Anxiety		−.07 (.08)	.02 (.07)	.03 (.06)	.06 (.06)
Enthusiasm		.07 (.08)	.01 (.06)	−.0001 (.06)	−.09 (.05)
Political alienation (decreased pride)		−.05 (.32)	−.28 (20)	−.04 (.21)	.28 (.13)*
Blame toward and punishment of federal officials	Putin's guilt	.59 (.17)***	.03 (.11)	−.02 (.09)	.24 (.10)*
	Dissat. with punishment of officials	.07 (.18)	.11 (.15)	−.57 (.13)***	−.57 (.11)***
Social alienation		−.07 (.20)	−.26 (.14)	.40 (.12)***	−.26 (.11)*
Blame toward Chechens		−.54 (.13)***	−.22 (.11)	.59 (.09)***	.45 (.09)***
Prejudice toward Ingush		1.06 (.54)	.74 (.31)*	.49 (.30)	.78 (.28)**
Political efficacy	Politically informed	.09 (.18)	.13 (.17)	−.06 (.10)	−.09 (.13)
	Perceived effectiveness of protest	.29 (.18)	.33 (.10)***	.16 (.13)	.05 (.10)
Self-efficacy		−.17 (.20)	−.11 (.13)	.24 (.11)*	.03 (.13)
Optimism	Optimistic about future	−.42 (.16)**	.21 (.21)	.05 (.11)	−.12 (.13)
	Possible to solve Beslan's problems	.25 (.14)	.13 (.13)	−.05 (.09)	−.17 (.12)

(continued)

Table 12.4. Continued

		Political Participation Negative Binomial Estimates, Coef. (SE)		Support for Retaliatory Violence Ordered Logit Estimates, Coef. (SE)	
		Beslan	Vladikavkaz	Beslan	Vladikavkaz
Prior political activism	Prior voting	.34 (.13)*	.04 (.09)	.12 (.07)	.004 (.06)
	Prior nonvoting behavior	−.11 (.11)	.46 (.09)***	.20 (.14)	−.21 (.10)*
Prior harm to relatives		1.11 (.25)***	.45 (.22)*	.19 (.23)	.002 (.21)
Perceived risk of political activism		−.19 (.21)	.18 (.26)	.41 (.17)*	.50 (.14)***
Trust in government		−.43 (.18)*	.04 (.18)	−.07 (.12)	−.11 (.11)
Demographics	Female	−.25 (.27)	.05 (.23)	−.17 (.14)	−.10 (.16)
	Age	.01 (.01)	−.02 (.01)**	−.01 (.01)	−.01 (.01)
	Household income	.05 (.09)	−.23 (.07)***	−.04 (.05)	.01 (.05)
	Education	.26 (.13)	.02 (.09)	−.08 (.07)	−.05 (.08)
Constant		−3.67 (1.80)*	−2.12 (1.41)	—	—
Cutpoints	τ_1	—	—	1.89 (1.09)	−.10 (1.10)
	τ_2	—	—	3.44 (1.12)	1.40 (1.11)
	τ_3	—	—	5.20 (1.11)	2.35 (1.10)
N		1,020	1,017	1,020	1,017

See Table 11.4 for variable description and coding. *$p < .05$; **$p < .01$; ***$p < .005$.

Blaming Chechens, satisfaction with the punishment of officials, and the perceived risk of political activism are significant for violence in both samples.

However, the many differences between the two nonvictim samples are noteworthy. A nonvictim from Vladikavkaz is more likely to support retaliatory killing if the nonvictim is politically alienated, blames Putin, is prejudiced toward Ingush, and is not socially alienated or a longtime political activist. These findings contradict the findings from the Beslan nonvictims, for whom political alienation, blaming Putin, prejudice, and prior activism are not statistically significant, although prejudice comes close, and social alienation is significant but in the opposite direction. The findings from Vladikavkaz also contradict the findings from the victim survey: among victims, political alienation was nega-tively and powerfully related to support for violence, social alienation was posi-tive, and blaming Putin was not significant. Many Vladikavkaz findings are only modestly significant at $p < .05$ and not robust; nevertheless, the findings are dis-similar to those from Beslan.

Therefore, although some factors contributing to support for retaliatory vio-lence may be generalizable to nonvictims, the cross-city inconsistencies suggest large gaps in understanding. Modeling nonvictim support for retaliatory vio-lence based on theories about victims is inadequate.

Nonvictims in Vladikavkaz and Beslan also differ in the factors motivating their political participation (Table 12.4). Findings vary for blaming Putin, blaming Chechens, prejudice toward Ingush, perceived effectiveness of protest, optimism about the future, prior voting and nonvoting behavior, trust in govern-ment, age, and household income. To even begin making sense of such disparate findings, it would be essential to have some compelling hypotheses for why some factors influence participation among nonvictims in one city but not in another. Post hoc explanations may be interesting but not necessarily valid or reliable.

The extant literature unfortunately offers little help in interpreting these differences and understanding the potential dimensions of nonvictim varia-tion beyond proximity to victims and other measures of nonvictim grievances, such as prior harm to relatives. The significant variation between nonvictims in the nearby towns of Beslan and Vladikavkaz suggests not only that general-ization from victim to nonvictim political behavior may be ill-advised but that generalization from one nonvictim population to another might be ill-advised. Nonvictims are diverse, and greater theorizing is required to understand which segments merit inclusion in the nonvictim mobilization potential.

Conclusion

Victims participate in politics more than nonvictims, but victims and nonvictims are not significantly different in their support for retaliatory violence. For po-litical participation, these findings reinforce the importance of the grievance context. Former hostages and relatives of former hostages are the aggrieved population and represent the most likely pool of mobilizable individuals. Nonvictims are more likely to join the victims when they share some connection to the grievance, as when they or their family members suffered prior physical harm by someone of Ingush or Chechen descent.

Studies of political participation would thus benefit from defining and selecting populations of interest based on grievances, rather than random popu-lation samples or convenience samples. A study involving only sufferers of a par-ticular problem should have less "noise" and allow a more rigorous investigation into the behavioral reactions of the sufferers. Behavioral reactions of onlookers or other third parties to the suffering may be interesting, but they also may be the product of different factors.

Therefore, to the question of whether findings about victim political participation should be generalizable to nonvictims, the answer is mostly no. Studies of political participation should involve at least two sets of theories, one for the directly aggrieved and one or more for others in the population. For example, instead of studying population-wide motivations to mobilize on behalf of minority rights, researchers should explicitly theorize about whether members of ethnic majorities are mobilized on behalf of minority rights for the same reasons that members of ethnic minorities are mobilized (Nepstad 2007).

For retaliatory ethnic violence, direct grievances, such as victimization by violence, are less relevant, and some findings about victim support for violence may be appropriately generalized to nonvictims. For victims and nonvictims, blaming Chechens, feeling prejudice toward Ingush, and being satisfied with the punishment of guilty political officials are (mostly) significant and strong correlates. Pro-violence individuals seem to believe their country can do no wrong while their Muslim neighbors can do no right. Conversely, individuals who are more accepting of their neighbors and dissatisfied with their political officials hold better prospects for breaking the cycle of ethnic violence. A generalizable truism, therefore, is that prejudice is a destructive force.

Anger, however, never seems to be a destructive force. For victims and nonvictims, anger is not significantly related to support for retaliatory violence. Blaming government in some way, when the government played a role in victimizing its people or otherwise engendering grievance, is also rarely harmful and if anything might discourage further ethnic violence. Beyond this, generalizations about support for retaliatory violence from victims to nonvictims, or vice versa, may also be misguided.

Disparities between victims and nonvictims are not easily explained and spotlight gaps in our understanding of nonvictim behavioral motivations. These gaps need to be filled, because aggrieved populations typically benefit from allies among the non-aggrieved. Beyond proximity to victims, factors worthy of further study for political participation include the targeting of sympathetic nonvictims for mobilization (Oegema and Klandermans 1994; Brady et al. 1999), sorrowful identification with victims (Beyerlein and Sikkink 2008), and the perception of a common humanity that is so essential to altruism (Monroe 1996, 2004). Factors worthy of further study for retaliatory violence include the concentration of rival ethnic or religious groups and the frequency and modes of interaction between ethnic rivals (Disha et al. 2011), as well as collective or ingroup identification (Brewer 1999; Simon and Ruhs 2008).

13

Should Results Apply to Victims in Other Places and Times?

The North Caucasus is populated by a tiny percentage of humanity, and North Ossetians, Beslan residents, and Beslan victims comprise tinier percentages still. Beyond their small numbers, Beslan victims are also distinguished by unique religious, cultural, geographic, and historical characteristics. It is therefore tempting to treat their post-violence experiences as equally unique and to limit claims about external validity. Findings might apply only to post-communist contexts, Russia, the Caucasus, or some smaller geopolitical territory or to culturally similar victims who have endured similar conflicts or similar violence.

However, evidence from research in social psychology and political science suggests that the findings from Beslan victims should be reasonably generalizable to much broader victim populations. While all incidents of ethnic violence have their unique features, responses to violence are not necessarily dependent on those unique features. This chapter explores characteristics of the Beslan victim population that are unique and characteristics that are common across many victim populations to determine which inferences about post-violence retaliation and political participation might be broadly applicable. Reasonable generalizations include that anger and political alienation from unaccountable governments increase the probability of peaceful political responses to violence, whereas ethnic prejudice and pride in unaccountable governments increase the probability of violent responses.

Why Beslan and Its Victims Might Seem Unique

The school hostage taking in Beslan was in some ways a very specific context. Unique factors potentially include:

- the grievance
- the perceived source of the grievance and target of redress
- the type of violence committed
- the type of violence contemplated as revenge
- the religion and culture of the victims

After Violence. Debra Javeline, Oxford University Press. © Oxford University Press 2023.
DOI: 10.1093/oso/9780197683347.003.0014

- the religion and culture of the perpetrators
- the political system where victims and perpetrators reside
- the power position of Beslan victims relative to the state and other ethnic groups.

Beslan victims may thus seem different enough from other victims of violence to question whether lessons from their response to the hostage taking are broadly applicable. Here limitations to generalizability across victim communities are explored, followed by consideration of the many factors common across victims that suggest that findings from Beslan are indeed broadly applicable.

The grievance following the hostage taking could be characterized as an act of violence in a longstanding ethnic conflict. It could be characterized as an act of terrorism that devolved into a massacre. It could also be characterized as a botched government action or, more specifically, botched counterterrorism and an associated lack of government accountability. Whether ethnic violence, terrorism, or botched counterterrorism, the scope of the grievance was staggering. Given that one out of every 100 Beslan residents died, most every surviving Beslan resident knew someone held hostage, if not a murder victim, and some surviving residents knew almost everyone in the school, including all the deceased (Sands 2004b). This grievance context may seem relatively unique and may appear to differentiate Beslan victims from other victims of ethnic violence. For example, the grievance context of Ingush and Chechen victims of violence has involved demands for territory, sovereignty, and an end to state-sponsored terrorism.

Accordingly, the perceived source of the grievance and appropriate target for redressing the grievance may also differentiate victims in ways that limit generalizability. In Beslan, the source of grievance and appropriate target were subject to interpretation: it might be the terrorists, members of the terrorists' ethnic group, a seemingly uncaring and incompetent government, or some combination. Findings from Beslan might thus be limited to situations where the potential for culpability lies with different parties, some societal and some governmental, therefore opening the door to both retaliatory ethnic violence and political participation. In other post-violence contexts, especially where the state itself is the clear perpetrator of violence, there may be only a single target for redressing the grievance, that is, the state. Such victims may differ from Beslan victims when deliberating their peaceful or violent response, turning to violence especially when political channels are blocked and directing that violence against the state.

Findings might also seem limited to the specific situation of hostage taking, rather than all types of ethnic violence. Ethnic violence is heterogeneous, and the causes, consequences, mechanisms, and dynamics of riots, terrorism, state violence, and other forms may vary (Brubaker and Laitin 1998:446). A hostage taking, particularly of children and particularly when those children died, may provoke responses that are more emotional or otherwise different than responses to other acts of violence.

Similar distinctiveness may characterize the type of violence contemplated as revenge. Retaliatory ethnic violence is not necessarily directed at the perpetrator but at the perpetrator's co-ethnics. Findings from Beslan victims may thus seem generalizable only to victims who contemplate or perpetuate retaliation against historic ethnic rivals.

The cultural distinctiveness of Beslan, North Ossetia, and the Caucasus may also limit generalizability because revenge has a cultural component. Revenge depends on internalized social norms and perceptions of mistreatment, harm, threat, or violations of morality that can be place-specific and vary across cultures. What is offensive or hurtful in one context may be acceptable in another (Jackson et al. 2019:323–325). The appropriateness of retaliatory violence can also vary by culture, with entire societies sometimes labeled as "vengeful" and having "cultures of honor" that feature "virtuous violence." In such cases, retaliatory violence is not stigmatized and instead is accepted and even encouraged to restore honor, and failure to retaliate signals weakness or cowardice. At its most extreme, some cultures sanction blood revenge or honor killings, at times even through local legislatures (Souleimanov and Aliyev 2015:170; Jackson et al. 2019:328–332). Findings from Beslan victims may thus seem generalizable only to victims who come from similar cultures of honor and blood revenge, such as tribal Amazon societies (Chagnon 1988), modern-day Jordan, Turkey, Egypt, Tunisia, Libya, and Kuwait (Jackson et al. 2019:332), and the conflict-ridden societies of Albania, Yemen, Colombia, and even the Ossetian rival, Chechnya (Souleimanov and Aliyev 2015:158).

Beyond vengefulness, other cultural factors may mark Beslan victims as culturally unique. Religion played a notable role, especially in requiring a mourning period of forty days, which inhibited any rash response to the killings. Respect for authority and deference to age in the tightly knit Beslan community also factored meaningfully into post-violence response, as elder males reined in more volatile younger males who otherwise may have acted on their violent inclinations. Perhaps findings from Beslan are then limited only to other cultures that are religious enough or patient enough to withhold violence long enough for heads to cool.

Features of the Russian government may limit the generalizability of findings from Beslan victims to the extent that structural factors shape responses to violence (della Porta 1995). Beslan victims were less than fifteen years from their relatively repressive Soviet government, and their current Russian government offered a mid-level of police intimidation and other forms of repression and a mid-level of openness or closure of the political system to public participation: The government permitted some action within institutions and in the streets but simultaneously tried to limit participation to unthreatening levels. The macrolevel structural factors were thus quite specific and differed even from factors governing ethnic rivals living presumably under those same structures. Contemporary Chechens were subject to harsh state repression, including "systematic torture, forced eviction, extrajudicial killings, rape, and abductions all at the hands of Russian soldiers" (Reuter 2004:22) and a relatively closed political system and an absence of viable nonviolent alternatives for redressing grievances (Speckhard and Akhmedova 2006:483). While some Chechen villages escaped shelling and produced insurgents, indiscriminate artillery strikes quelled insurgency in many other villages (Lyall 2009). State repression and political opportunities may thus vary across ethnic groups, insurgent organizations, and other groups even within the same country (della Porta 1995; McAdam 1996; Lyall 2009:358), suggesting the need for caution when generalizing from findings about one victim group to another.

Finally, the power position of Beslan victims relative to their ethnic rivals might limit generalizability. For some forms of violence, the status of a group as advanced or backward matters. Deadly riots, for example, involve the targeting of advanced groups by backward groups (Horowitz 2001:179–180), as, for example, when violence was directed against Jews and Germans in Soviet Lithuania and Latvia (Petersen 2002). Ossetians are sometimes stereotyped as being more advanced than their Ingush and Chechen neighbors and, had they retaliated violently, would have been expected to execute the retaliation differently. Indeed, a hypothetical reversing of the ethnic groups in the school hostage taking—the "what if" scenario of Ossetian terrorists taking hostage Ingush and Chechen schoolchildren—seems unrealistic and therefore unhelpful for analysis.

For some forms of political participation, advanced groups may have more access or experience than backward groups, especially the oppressed (Halperin et al. 2011:287). The "what if" scenario of surviving Chechen mothers of murdered Chechen children calling for and being granted a meeting with President Putin seems equally unrealistic. To the extent that Beslan victims and their larger Ossetian community constitute an "advanced group" due to their privileged status relative to the ethnic groups of their attackers, findings from Beslan may apply only to victims of similar status.

Why Beslan and Its Victims Are Not Unique

The type of violence contemplated as revenge—ethnic retaliatory violence, or committing an-eye-for-an-eye murderous attacks on the co-ethnics of perpetrators—is the most distinguishing feature of the Beslan school hostage taking. Indeed, it is one of the two main questions about the aftermath of violence central to this study. Although findings may apply to other kinds of community grievances, it is reasonable to focus on the applicability of lessons from Beslan to the many ethnic conflicts around the world where retaliatory violence is an open question.

Within such ethnic conflicts and post-violence contexts, most other supposedly distinctive features of the Beslan hostage taking are actually common. And features of the hostage taking that are unique are often not central for influencing responses to the violence. Given the more consequential commonalities between the Beslan hostage taking and other acts of violence and between Beslan victims and other victims of violence, the major lessons from this case study should indeed apply to other victims.

The hostage taking was certainly unique in its multiple manifestations as ethnic violence, terrorism, botched counterterrorism, and massacre, as well as its scope in community deaths and resulting grievance framework. These grievances are critical in identifying Beslan as a permissive context for retaliatory violence or political participation. Beyond the permissive context, however, the specific grievances of individual victims do not play a significant role in post-violence response. Witnessing numerous deaths, suffering numerous losses, and coping with numerous injured loved ones surely takes a greater toll on a victim than suffering only a single tragic outcome. Nevertheless, as shown in Chapter 11, the severity of grievance has no significant effect on support for retaliatory violence or political participation. Grief and grievance accompany most forms of victimization by violence. The fact of devastating victimization, more than the nature or extent of that victimization, provides enough parallel motivation for retaliation and political action to make the Beslan story broadly relevant.

Victims likely experience a greater emotional impact from observing the torment and harm suffered by children, as in Beslan. Taking children hostage may generate greater response, violent or peaceful, than adult hostage takings, mass executions, or other forms of terrorism. If so, findings from Beslan victims may have greater applicability to other victims of violent acts involving children, but this does not disqualify the applicability of findings to victims of violence involving only adults. Indeed, as described in Chapter 4, Beslan victims at times coordinated their political action with victims of other terrorist acts in Russia, such as survivors of the 2002 Moscow theater hostage taking, who were predominantly adults (Buribayev 2005). Both groups saw parallels in their situations and learned from each other.

The Beslan scenario of multiple potential targets for retaliation is also relatively common. In situations of ethnic conflict, violence is typically directed not against government but against members of rival ethnic groups who are proxies for co-ethnic perpetrators (Horowitz 2001:8, 178). These targets of convenience may be longtime neighbors or, in cases where perpetrators live beyond reach, resident aliens or visiting foreigners (Horowitz 2001:178). Meanwhile, other targets may be governmental, especially if redress is sought through political processes, as in Beslan.

Even for victims of state-sponsored violence, where presumably there is a single potential target for redressing grievances, the findings from Beslan may still apply. Such victims may respond with a variety of state-directed actions, peaceful and violent, seeing both as valid and often complementary methods of contentious political action. But displaced aggression is also possible. Violent experiences in public life may lead to retaliatory violence in private life (Rule 1988), with ethnic rivals seen as reasonable proxy targets for the repressive state.

The type of violence committed, hostage taking, also does not seem to differentiate Beslan victims from other victims. Like the hostage taking, most ethnic riots are designed "to further ethnic polarization in an already polarized environment or to take advantage of a hostile mood" (Horowitz 2001:225). Like the hostage taking, state-sponsored terrorism leads to victim grievances that may provoke further violence or political activism. For example, Chechen victims of Russian state-sponsored terrorism have certainly been highly traumatized (Speckhard and Akhmedova 2006:429), and it is unclear why the killing of a Chechen child, or even a spouse, parent, or adult sibling in a non-hostage situation, should be categorized as an emotional experience entirely different from the killings in Beslan. In terms of political responses, many victims of other types of violence have been activated in ways similar to Beslan victims. For example, war violence in Sierra Leone is significantly related to higher voter turnout, community meeting attendance, and community group memberships per household (Keen 2005; Bellows and Miguel 2006). Victimization by war violence in Uganda also led to increased voter turnout (Blattman 2009), as did victimization by crime in five continents (Bateson 2012) and victimization by terrorism in fifty-one democracies (Robbins et al. 2013).

Even cultural distinctiveness does not preclude generalizations from Beslan victims to victims elsewhere. Vengeful behavior is not as place-specific as place reputations and conventional wisdom may suggest. It may be most common among collectivist cultures, or people with strong group identity who take personally the harm committed against a group member, but the concept of revenge is found in most societies (Henrich et al. 2006; Lennon 2013; Jackson et al. 2019:332). Vengeful behavior has a biological component and is within the experience of most humans (Jackson et al. 2019:322).

Furthermore, there is probably cross-cultural similarity in the response to the specific type of violence experienced in Beslan. The mass killing of children is one of the most likely acts to transcend cultural differences and to be perceived universally as immoral. Even smaller numbers of child deaths have inspired social movements, campaigns, legislation, and other action, as for example in the United States with Mothers Against Drunk Driving (MADD), Road Safe America, and America's Most Wanted. If revenge or activism were to be contemplated for any atrocity in any society, surely it would be this barbaric and deadly school hostage taking.

Perhaps more important, Beslan victims themselves reject the cultural characterization of their people as vengeful. As shown in Chapters 1 and 3, retaliatory violence may color much of the history of the Caucasus, but most Beslan victims do not embrace this history. Some, especially among the men, felt culturally obliged to retaliate, but many possessed a redefined, contemporary self-image that reflected righteous nonviolence. They saw themselves and their culture as having moved beyond their barbaric eye-for-an-eye past.

The self-identification of Ossetian victims of violence as not vengeful stands in stark contrast to the self-identification of Chechens. In interviews with former Chechen insurgents, many comfortably shared their need for blood revenge against Russian troops and their Chechen proxies (Souleimanov and Aliyev 2015:172–173). The different dispositions of Ossetian and Chechen victims could suggest limited generalizability only to nonvengeful cultures, but such an argument is post hoc, given that conventional wisdom and media reports categorize peoples of the Caucasus, including Ossetians, as vengeful. An equally if not more plausible interpretation is that victims tend to respond truthfully to questions about vengeance as a motivation for their people and themselves personally. Among both the self-proclaimed revenge-oriented Chechens and the self-proclaimed nonvengeful Ossetians, there is variation in support for retaliatory violence, suggesting again that cultural distinctions do not limit generalizations from Beslan findings.

Other cultural factors also do not limit generalizability. Authority dynamics in Beslan, while having their own distinctions, resemble those in many other conflict-ridden communities. Local leaders trying to manipulate aggrieved individuals to be peaceful or violent is a common phenomenon (Brass 2003; Varshney 2010). Religion may have dictated a relatively unique forty-day mourning period that prohibited retaliation when tempers were hottest, impulses hardest to control, and retaliatory violence most tempting. However, after the mourning, Beslan victims varied in their political participation and support for retaliatory violence, and lessons should still be applicable from this individual variation, with religion held relatively constant.

The type of political system may also not matter so much for victim responses. If Beslan's Soviet heritage were a factor, it should have discouraged political activism in Beslan and manifested in differences between older and younger victims in their post-violence behavior, but activism exploded, and age made no significant difference. As for the relevance of the current government, some macrolevel features may be unique, such as the precise repressiveness of the state and opportunities for political participation, and these features influence the aggregate level of political participation in a country. For example, broad social processes or dislocations such as war, industrialization, or demographic changes can restructure domestic power relations and raise or lower the likelihood of political protest (Jenkins and Perrow 1977; Piven and Cloward 1977; Oberschall 1996; McAdam 1996). However, it is unclear that these macrolevel factors influence relationships between individual-level variables, such as anger, prejudice, alienation, and efficacy, and behavioral outcomes. Findings from Beslan victims may even understate these relationships. Among violence victims living under more repressive governments that highly restrict civil society and political activism, perhaps the findings would be weaker, simply because the sample sizes of active citizens could be too low to detect relationships. Among victims living under less repressive governments, the findings might be more detectable and stronger.

Also, societies dealing with ethnic violence have important factors in common across political systems that make the Beslan experience highly relevant. All incidents of ethnic violence are manifestations of government failure. Even where governments do not cause or encourage the violence, they are implicated by their unwillingness or inability to prevent the violence or bring it to a halt once begun. Many victims, like those in Beslan, feel that government let them down in some way, and the disappointment and disillusionment likely inform the victim response.

The status of Ossetians is also not terribly problematic for applying findings from Beslan victims to other victims of violence. First, the description of Beslan victims as members of an advanced group does not seem very appropriate or relevant. The Ossetian nationality is "advanced" only relative to their Ingush and Chechen rivals and not elsewhere in the Russian Federation where they are sometimes seen as indistinguishable from these very same nationalities and other Caucasians. Ossetians have not been at war with Russians, but their political status and access could hardly be considered high. Ossetian political successes, including in-person meetings with top-level political officials all the way to President Putin and victory in the European Court of Human Rights, were predicted by no one. Claims that Ossetian political activism is possible but Ingush or Chechen political activism is impossible are post hoc and debatable.

More importantly, while advanced groups have not been found to engage in deadly riots, they have indeed been found to engage in other forms of violence (Horowitz 2001:179–180). The support of members of majority ethnic groups for repressing minorities is common. White Americans, for example, have long directed violence against black Americans (Olzak 1992), and many supported retaliatory ethnic violence or at least rights violations against Japanese Americans after the attack on Pearl Harbor. The propensity of so-called advanced groups to retaliate against the co-ethnics of terrorists even informs the strategy of the terrorists: Al-Qaeda, for example, attacked the United States on September 11, 2001, presumably with the goal of provoking an anti-Muslim backlash by the United States, much like the terrorists in Beslan attacked the school to provoke an anti-Muslim backlash. Advanced groups may also reject retaliatory violence, as did most Beslan victims. In the United States after the September 11 attacks, anti-Muslim violence occurred but, as in North Ossetia, not at the scale predicted. Findings from Beslan victims thus likely speak to a broad range of other victims, regardless of their status as "advanced" or "backward."

Reasonable Inferences and Generalizations

Given the sufficient similarities between victims of ethnic violence, findings from the study of Beslan victims should be relevant across victim communities. Political efficacy, prior political activism, and prior harm from ethnic violence unambiguously facilitate political participation. The significant role of these factors in Beslan is consistent with findings from ample research within the context of victimization by ethnic violence and outside that context. Prior political activism also unambiguously diminishes support for retaliatory violence. Self-efficacy, pessimism, and prior harm facilitate support for retaliatory violence, and while these factors are not central to most studies of ethnic violence, it seems reasonable that they should have significant effects beyond Beslan. For example, victims of violence outside of Beslan who feel empowered to take matters into their own hands should support retaliatory violence more than unempowered victims. The findings about pessimism and prior harm seem similarly generalizable.

Only a few findings merit caution in generalizing to other victim communities. Social alienation played a limited role in post-violence retaliation and participation in Beslan, but the social context of Beslan is specific enough to reserve judgment about the effects of social alienation more generally. For communities with similarly tight social networks but complicated feelings about social support from those networks, it seems reasonable to speculate that social alienation would play a similarly limited role in response to violence. For other communities, however, perhaps the dynamics of the social networks and social support systems work differently. Still, even in these less comparable contexts, more theorizing is required to understand why social alienation should matter, given that it sometimes is alleged to motivate action and sometimes inaction. Current theoretical ambiguity combined with findings from Beslan suggest that the weak role of social alienation may indeed be found in further studies.

Age, gender, education, and income did not factor prominently in responses to the Beslan school hostage taking, but these demographic characteristics have had significant enough effects on political participation and violence in other contexts and cultures as to reserve judgment about the role of demographics more generally.

Still other findings are not only generalizable but particularly novel and important. These are described in greater detail here.

Anger Is a Productive Emotion

Anger among Beslan victims did not increase support for retaliatory violence. If that finding is generalizable, it is reasonable to ask why other studies draw different conclusions and frequently attribute retaliatory violence to anger. The answer, the reason that the striking finding de-linking anger and violence is credible, lies in the rigor of the research design.

The Beslan study involved an indisputably aggrieved population experiencing genuine emotions and genuinely contemplating the pros and cons of retaliatory violence. Most other studies involve samples of people who are not necessarily aggrieved, whose emotions are purposefully evoked by an artificial problem or perhaps a real problem that may be remote from their daily concerns, and who may not have pondered aggressive responses until the very moment they are asked by a researcher. Evoking anger so indirectly and artificially is a poor proxy measure for actual anger and may distort research findings (Klimecki et al. 2018). By minimizing the hypothetical and speculative elements of the research design, the Beslan study reduces the potential for measurement error. Given that the grievance context is essential for understanding victim responses to violence (Part I), and given that nonvictim populations differ significantly from victim populations (Chapter 12), only victim studies can validly test the role of anger and other emotions in post-violence victim responses.

Some analysts argue that the emotion of anger is treated differently in different cultures. In some cultures, anger is avoided, and in others it is encouraged (Oatley 2000:97). This assertion is, perhaps surprisingly, controversial and not supported by evidence: studies conducted in thirty-seven countries show that emotional reactions to perceived injustice are similar across cultures (Mikula et al. 1998:781). Recent neuroimaging studies are even able to show that distinct parts of the brain are involved in angry feelings, on the one hand, and the regulation of aggressive responses or reactive punishment behaviors, on the other (Klimecki et al. 2018), a finding presumably relevant for all human brains, regardless of culture. Moreover, no prior studies have characterized Ossetian or Caucasian culture as anger-promoting or anger-averse, in the way that many studies *have* characterized these cultures as vengeful, so any attempt to label the culture and circumscribe generalizability only to cultures that are similarly inclined toward anger is both arbitrary and post hoc, for both Ossetians and those other cultures.

Most importantly, even if there are cross-cultural differences in the treatment of anger and other emotions, the within-culture findings from Beslan still stand: victims who are angriest after an episode of ethnic violence are no more or less likely to support retaliatory violence against the co-ethnics of the perpetrators than victims who are least angry. Anger-promoting and anger-averse cultures are populated by individuals who vary in their anger response to victimization, even if pushed by the culture to display or conceal anger. Findings from Beslan suggest that these varying emotional responses will not relay much information about the likelihood of victim support for retaliation and perpetuating the cycle of violence.

What the varying emotional responses will relay is information about activism. Anger among Beslan victims contributed to greater political engagement. Victims' anger may have been particularly widespread due to the extensive impact of the hostage taking on children, but the scope or aggregate level of community anger is less relevant for generalization than variation across individual victims: the angrier the victims, the more they participated in politics. That finding's broad applicability is corroborated by findings from studies of emotion and political participation in other populations and using other methodologies. For example, laboratory experiments in the United States suggest that causality runs from anger to political participation (e.g., Valentino et al. 2011), even if the participation itself in turn intensifies or otherwise influences anger.

The rigor of the research design in Beslan again provides strong justification for generalizations about the relationship between anger and political participation. As described in Chapter 5, the measurement of Beslan victims' emotions, especially anger, provided a level of validity not matched by many other studies of emotion and political participation and thus heightens confidence in the initial findings in Beslan itself. The internal validity is a prerequisite for external validity (Lucas 2003:248): only genuine measures of post-violence anger allow for genuine tests of the effects of that anger. It seems fair to conclude that anger after an episode of horrific violence, especially in the context of ongoing ethnic conflict and failed government response, is a productive emotion that encourages victims to demand political accountability.

Prejudice Is Deadly

The Beslan study confirms that dehumanization is at the heart of retaliatory ethnic violence (Bruneau and Kteily 2017). Anger, hate, and other emotions are beside the point. If it is unpalatable to share a meal, an education, or a family because of differences in ethnicity (or race, religion, or other ascriptive characteristics), the foundation is set for negative judgments of ethnic rivals that, in a time of tragedy and tension, could be exploited. The ethnic other is someone to be avoided at all costs. The ethnic other is someone who could justifiably be killed.

This simple finding demonstrates how the banal can become evil. After all, what could be so harmful in the commonplace desire to avoid dining with someone of another ethnicity or interethnic mingling in schools? And intermarriage? Many people in the world are uncomfortable seeing their relatives wed to ethnic others. The discomfort might be politically incorrect but hardly harmful. Yet, harmful it is. As the Beslan study shows, this ordinary prejudice is a seed of support for ethnic violence.

Just as interethnic prejudice is global (Monroe et al. 2000), so too is the link between prejudice and retaliatory ethnic violence, especially after victimization. For example, after terrorist attacks, people become less politically tolerant and less supportive of civil liberties for the co-ethnics of the terrorists (Skitka et al. 2004:743–744). Prejudice against African Americans, as evidenced by opposition to interracial dating and marriage, explains white supremacist advocacy of violence (Glaser et al. 2002). Dehumanization of Israelis by Palestinians and Palestinians by Israelis increases willingness to sacrifice out-group lives (Bruneau and Kteily 2017). A correlate of prejudice, strong in-group identification, has been shown to decrease tolerance toward rival ethnic groups and to obstruct forgiveness in conflict situations in twenty different countries (Van Tongeren et al. 2013) and to increase support for violence in eighteen countries (Chapman 2008:259).

Resolving ethnic conflicts thus typically depends on rectifying prejudice. Such efforts meet with great resistance, often due to elite provocateurs or political entrepreneurs who stand to gain personally from the continuation of both the prejudice and the conflict. Findings from Beslan suggest that victims who resist prejudice, particularly in highly charged atmospheres of longstanding antipathy and aggression, are consistently the least supportive of retaliatory violence. Again, the findings are globally relevant. Efforts to move beyond conflict resolution and achieve intergroup reconciliation in many parts of the world have involved changing the nature of formerly adversarial relations and fostering inclusion, empathy, trust, and respect (Kelman 2008; Nadler et al. 2008; Bakke et al. 2009:1014–1015). A perception of common identity, the antithesis of prejudice, is often critical to success (Nadler et al. 2008:8–9; Van Tongeren et al. 2013).

Political Alienation from Unaccountable Governments Can Be Productive; Pride in Unaccountable Governments Brings Harm

Beslan victims who felt less pride in their Russian citizenship after the hostage taking channeled that feeling away from retaliatory violence and into peaceful political activism. Beslan victims who felt the opposite and retained or increased their pride in Russia were more supportive of retaliatory violence and less politically active. The generalizability of these findings is relatively uncontested, mainly due to limited scholarly interest in recent years in the concept of political alienation. The rare examinations of political alienation and protest in Peru, West Germany, and New York City found the relationship to be positive, as it was in Beslan (Muller and Opp 1986; Muller et al. 1991). Given that political alienation was one of the only factors in the Beslan study to have effects on both responses to ethnic violence—to motivate a normatively desirable "politics not violence" response—renewed interest in the sentiment seems warranted.

While political alienation has fallen out of favor, a related concept, "system justification," has gained traction (e.g., Jost et al. 2004). System justification refers to the propensity to defend and support the current political order. Political systems are often unworthy of such defense, and system justification may be a "positive illusion," an adaptive form of self-deception, delusion, or false consciousness (Lerner 1980; Taylor and Brown 1988; Jost 1995:400). It is in some ways the opposite of political alienation, and it operates similarly: justifying the status quo, like political pride, makes individuals less sensitive to potential injustices and less willing to participate in system-challenging collective action (Cichocka and Jost 2014:11; Jost 2019:299). For example, American system justifiers are unlikely to support the "Black Lives Matter" social movement and more likely to support system-defensive ideas such as "all lives matter" (Osborne et al. 2019). Even among political activists, system justification can undermine the willingness to protest (Jost et al. 2012). Decreased system justification or outright system rejection, much like political alienation, occurs when individuals experience instability or threat from the status quo (Jost et al. 2010). In response, system questioners or rejectors are more likely to engage in political activism.

System justification is a global phenomenon. It is found in capitalist and post-communist societies in over twenty countries and has similar causes and consequences (Cichocka and Jost 2014). System justification, or the lack thereof, is related to political protest and support for collective action in the United States, United Kingdom, Greece, and New Zealand (Jost et al. 2012; Osborne et al. 2019). Within countries, individuals vary in their attitudes toward the existing political order, with some justifying and defending it, while others are more critical (Jost et al. 2010; Kay and Friesen 2011).

Given the cross-cultural pervasiveness of system justification, and given the similarities of the concept to political alienation, it seems reasonable to expect that findings from Beslan about the constructive role of political alienation in the aftermath of ethnic violence should travel to other contexts. Pride in a government that has acted unjustly and even violently, as happened in Beslan, may indeed be a positive illusion or false consciousness and should dampen political action. Alienation from that government should be politically mobilizing.

This is especially true for victim populations. Much of the literature on system justification is concerned with disadvantaged populations. Individuals who are disadvantaged by the system are sometimes its most ardent defenders (Jost et al. 2003; van der Toorn et al. 2015). Among victims of violence in Beslan and elsewhere are many who understandably justify the political system that governs their lives. When confronted with evidence of the system's unaccountability, even a personally devastating botched counterterrorism operation that took the lives, physical health, and mental health of relatives and neighbors, their unshakable pride in government deters them from acts that seem confrontational and even from attributing blame to representatives of the justified political system. Victims of violence who resist system justification and are politically alienated have other options: they blame government, hold officials accountable for outcomes, and channel that political alienation constructively into activism.

The constructive response of politically alienated victims is especially noteworthy because such victims are also less supportive of retaliatory violence. Politically proud victims in Beslan and many other contexts are more likely to perpetuate the cycle of violence. Pride in country manifests not just in benign do-nothingness in the political arena. Denied by their own sentiments the possibility of seeking redress with their government, politically proud victims may see members of the terrorists' ethnic group as their sole remaining targets, especially if the government they find so worthy seems to sanction retaliatory ethnic violence.

Evidence from ethnic riots supports the generalizability of these relationships. Support for violence by pro-government victims is common where governments sympathize with retaliatory ethnic violence or even legitimize or aid that violence (Horowitz 2001:344–362). This unfortunately describes many if not most governments historically and cross-nationally, which have at some point repressed ethnic minorities or looked the other way as ethnic majorities did the repressing. As found in Beslan, pride in such governments can have violent consequences. Alienation from such governments, despite the possibly negative connotations of the concept, can have peaceful and constructive consequences.

Conclusion

The aftermath of the Beslan school hostage taking is representative of other post-violence contexts around the world where victims contemplate peaceful or violent responses. While there are certain distinctive features of the hostage taking, its victims, perpetrators, and geopolitics, the main feature that potentially limits generalizability is the scope condition of the study: a situation of interethnic conflict where retaliatory violence against ethnic rivals was a possible outcome.

Other presumably unique features of Beslan are actually relatively common to post-violence contexts or, where uncommon, not highly relevant to the decisions to retaliate or take political action. Culture and the macropolitical context, for example, are less limiting than at first glance. In some cases, even the scope condition of interethnic conflict is not so limiting: victimization by violence with no ethnic dimension often leads to greater involvement in the political process, and that mobilization process may resemble the mobilization of Beslan victims.

Questions about Beslan victim behavior are not just relevant but critical for the numerous populations around the world who are victimized by violence and seek to redress their victimization. And the answers are broadly applicable: If the goal is for a peaceful response involving political participation and not retaliatory ethnic violence, anger helps. Prejudice hurts. Political alienation helps. Political pride hurts.

Conclusion

Peace after violence

By now, many people around the world have forgotten about Beslan, or perhaps they never heard of the town in the first place. This is a luxury afforded to humanity thanks to the victims of the hostage taking in School No. 1. After a massacre that upended their lives, permanently in many cases, they made choices that stopped the bloody situation from becoming bloodier.

They could have made different choices. Beslan could be a place everyone knows. It could have been the center of a global hot spot, with the hostage taking triggering "virtuous violence" sanctioned by the culture and norms of the region. As one atrocity paid back another, Beslan could have been remembered as the starting point of a seemingly endless cycle of ethnically motivated bloodbaths, yet another exasperating example of unresolvable ethnic and religious conflict. Indeed, retaliatory violence was the widespread expectation and often-stated prediction in September 2004. It was the pledge of some residents in Beslan itself. Graffiti on the remnant walls of School No. 1 read, "Through tears of grief, we say we will avenge this" (Chivers 2004).

Here is the realistic counterfactual, the quite possible alternative sequence of events pieced together from the many prognostications of reporters and other observers at the time and from firsthand testimony of the victims themselves:

It starts in Beslan, a small town in the Russian republic of North Ossetia, located in a heavily weaponized, high-conflict region just north of Georgia's disputed South Ossetia and just west of ethnic rival republic Ingushetia and war-torn Chechnya. Over 1,200 North Ossetians, mostly Orthodox Christian, get taken hostage by terrorists who are mostly ethnic Chechens and Ingush and religiously Muslim. The attack leaves over 360 dead, a majority of them children, and most remaining hostages physically injured, traumatized, or both. It devastates not only all survivors but their relatives, friends, neighbors, and the Ossetian people and nearby fellow Christian sympathizers. As widely predicted, ethnically motivated revenge attacks follow. Young volatile Ossetian men seize their readily accessible weapons and seek vengeance on conveniently located Ingush and Chechen people, first targeting the few remaining in North Ossetia and then crossing republic borders to find more. The Ingush and Chechens, having their own civilian populations now slaughtered

After Violence. Debra Javeline, Oxford University Press. © Oxford University Press 2023.
DOI: 10.1093/oso/9780197683347.003.0015

for the sins of co-ethnic terrorists, seek vengeance on civilian Ossetians, joined by opportunistic jihadists, Chechen nationalists, and pathological warlords, until the proverbial eye-for-an-eye retaliation erupts in regional blindness: full-scale ethnic violence across the many republics of the North Caucasus. Fighting is rekindled in the Prigorodny region and spreads into Dagestan to the east and Kabardino-Balkaria and other regions to the west. To quell the violence, the Russian government begins aerial bombing and sends troops. Like Grozny in the 1990s, whole towns are wiped out, anarchy reins, and human rights violations are rife. Responding to Russian military atrocities, terrorists launch new attacks on civilian ethnic Russians in European Russia, leaving those populations feeling vulnerable and increasing public support for still harsher measures. With untold deaths, a refugee crisis, and shattered local economies, the North Caucasus in the aftermath of the Beslan school hostage taking joins the list of places designated by the United Nations as critical hot spots of protracted conflict and humanitarian disaster, and to this day, no end is in sight.

That this tragic, grisly outcome did not happen is not to say that it was impossible or even unlikely. The school hostage taking in many ways looked like a classic "precipitant," a highly inciting act because it confirms the hostile behavior or intentions of ethnic rivals, the failure of the political process to handle the situation, and the futility of peaceful alternatives to retaliatory violence (Horowitz 2001: 268–269, 317–318). Acts of retaliation did occur after the hostage taking but not nearly with the frequency and intensity that journalists and students of the North Caucasus had forecast with such alarm. Support for retaliation also existed but, as the victims attest, at a lower level than predicted. One in seven victims surveyed expressed full or partial approval of killing the same number of Chechens as were killed in the school, an alarming statistic out of context but perhaps a comforting one in light of what might have been.

What the hostage taking did precipitate was arguably the most extensive and sustained political activism in modern Russian history. The constructive and peaceful organizing, demonstrating, petitioning, and meeting with political officials was unprecedented and unanticipated. Over 50 percent of victims surveyed participated in at least one political activity. Over 23 percent of victims became activists as evidenced by participation in at least four activities, and at least 7 percent became full-fledged activist leaders, participating in more than ten activities. Rallies with political demands proliferated, and this in a country increasingly labeled authoritarian or at best a "hybrid" regime not easily challenged by ordinary citizens, let alone faraway Ossetians who were led by women and lacked access to power—this in a country where anti-regime political action was historically low, especially against the newly re-elected and popular president (Javeline 2003a, 2003b).

Victim demands were blunt and courageous: not just complete and accurate lists of the names of victims and escaped terrorists, not just a full and honest accounting of how the tragedy transpired, but the resignation of powerful political officials whose corrupt, negligent, and irresponsible behavior they partly blamed for enabling the terrorist attack, the bungled rescue operation, and the uncertainty and chaos in the weeks that followed. Victims, sometimes at their peril, demanded accountability from a government determined to avoid that accountability.

The activism mattered. Had Beslan victims simply refrained from retaliation but taken no political action, the aftermath of the school hostage taking would have been noteworthy only for the avoided additional carnage. The prodigious political response adds to the noteworthiness. Political participation is what allows for rights to be defended, interests to be represented, and grievances to be addressed rather than ignored.

In Beslan, victims were largely cynical about the efficacy of their political endeavors. Both activists and nonactivists expressed futility in the time-consuming and emotion-draining efforts, and they pointed to government resistance, numerous defeats, and minimal tangible outcomes. For example, by the eighth anniversary of the hostage taking in 2012, victims had been involved in 127 legal actions involving 50 Russian judges, 38 of them North Ossetian, judges of the Supreme Court, and the Constitutional Court Chairman, all of whom ruled against the victims (Milashina 2012). While the victims' frustration is entirely understandable, without activism, here is the other realistic counterfactual of the aftermath of the hostage taking: victim rights, interests, and grievances most certainly would have been ignored.

With such activism and the steadfast commitment to raising voices, the government had no choice but to hear, not as loudly as the victims wanted and not with all the desired results, but the accomplishment should nevertheless not be diminished. The Russian government investigated when it preferred to sweep under the rug, forget, and move on. Government officials resigned, admitted to actions such as using flamethrowers, and granted audiences to victims after trying unsuccessfully to dodge them and their persistent questions. Even President Putin eventually capitulated and met with victim activists. The stamina of the victims was finally rewarded in April 2017 with a judgment by the European Court of Human Rights that condemned Russian counterterrorism procedures and awarded the victims almost three million euros. In this verdict, another gift was awarded to victims outside Beslan and to all humanity, because by pressing their case so relentlessly and persuasively, litigants in *Tagayeva and Others v. Russia* convinced the ECHR to set a global precedent: states must prioritize the human rights of hostages and other victims even when defending national security against terrorists (Galani 2019).

There is therefore much to be learned from the aftermath of the Beslan school hostage taking. The place-specific question is: Why did many Beslan victims focus on government violations, incompetence, and insensitivity over Chechen and Ingush community culpability, while some victims interpreted their grievances in ethnic terms? This specific question is a subset of the more general question: Why do some victims of ethnic violence respond by taking political action and some with retaliatory violence? The answers can help illuminate how vicious cycles of violence might end and how interest representation might be achieved.

Implications for Violence Reduction

To the degree that retaliatory violence was supported among Beslan victims, potential supporters seemed to think: I am as proud of Russia today as ever, I want nothing to do with Ingush and Chechen people, and I feel pessimistic about the future, but I feel personally empowered, and anger aside, I want revenge and would comfortably see Chechens killed.

Support for retaliatory violence was highest among those most prejudiced against their Muslim neighbors. Prejudice, independent of any emotions it might inspire, was a large and robust factor in support for retaliatory violence. Anger was not. Support for retaliatory violence was also higher among victims who felt political pride and had a relatively sympathetic attitude toward the Russian leadership; among those who felt self-efficacy and pessimism but not political efficacy; and among those whose relatives had experienced harm by someone of Ingush or Chechen descent prior to the hostage taking but who had no history of political activism.

Victims with these attributes are the potential perpetrators of the cycle of violence. By implication, trying to end the cycle involves changing the attributes, which is no small task. Manipulating the conditions that cause ethnic violence is a difficult and sometimes impossible proposition (Horowitz 2001:513). But difficult or not, with few alternatives to halt seemingly endless rounds of retaliation by longtime adversaries, changing the identified attributes may be the most promising path forward.

Reduce Prejudice

Beslan victims are humans with all the complexity humanity entails. This book has hopefully honored them by treating them as such, rather than portraying them as one-dimensional flawless characters transformed into saints by their victimhood. Some Beslan victims are altruistic, community-oriented, egalitarian, open-hearted, and open-minded. Others have some of these beneficent traits but not all. Some are spiteful, self-centered, and hostile, which is to say, human. There are all sorts of people in all societies, and treating Beslan victims as if they were of a type—even a "good" type—is insulting to them, both those who survived and those who were murdered. It is to deny them their humanity, including their prejudices.

And prejudiced most of them are. The Beslan tragedy exacerbated longstanding negative impressions of Ingush and Chechens. Not only were the majority of terrorists of Chechen and Ingush descent, but even ordinary Chechens and Ingush were suspected by victims of having advance knowledge of the siege, not warning their Ossetian neighbors, and secretly leaving North Ossetia the evening before (Dyupin 2004). The unbelievable cruelty of the terrorists—including denying the children food, water, and use of a restroom and executing twenty-one adult male hostages right before the children's eyes (Dunlop 2006)—reinforced ethnic stereotypes. It provided further evidence to those inclined to think in ethnic terms that Chechens and Ingush are barbaric people.

A majority of victims want nothing to do with people of Ingush or Chechen ethnicity. They object to routine interactions with Ingush. They prefer not to dine together, send their kids to the same schools, or intermarry (Chapter 6).

To the extent that retaliatory violence could have materialized in the North Caucasus, this prejudice, these seemingly benign sentiments, would have been the fuel. The more prejudiced the victim, the more likely he or she was to approve of killing Chechens as an-eye-for-an-eye retribution. Prejudice does not predict support for violence; prejudice toward Ingush and Chechens is widespread among victims, but approval of retaliatory killing is not widespread. Prejudice simply makes support for retaliatory violence much more likely. That support matters greatly should a political leader, "ethnic entrepreneur," or other elite try to exploit the volatile situation and provoke some victims to turn the support into actual retaliation. Importantly, the strong relationship between prejudice and support for violence is one of the few findings from Beslan victims that also applied to nonvictims (Chapter 12).

Most importantly, the *lack* of prejudice is very strongly correlated with disapproval of violence. A victim comfortable with interethnic dining, schooling, and marriage has little to no chance of supporting or being recruited to ethnic violence, even after a massacre that claimed the lives of their loved ones (Chapters 6 and 11). Such a victim is more likely to see the terrorists as individual criminals, thugs, or psychopaths rather than spokespeople and executors for ethnic rivals.

Violent individuals are sometimes excused for their violent acts with the rationale that some circumstance legitimately angered or frightened them. In the context of retaliatory ethnic violence, that excuse is weak. There is no evidence that every individual brought to some high emotional threshold would support retaliatory violence against co-ethnics of the perpetrators. Aversion to other individuals based on their ethnicity is dangerous in itself. The circumstance, while very real and legitimately anger-provoking, is nonetheless a pretext for violence based on prejudice.

Nor can prejudice be justified as legitimate or excusable based on the terrorism or other violence that caused the victimization. In Beslan, for example, the terrorist leader Khuchbarov, the mastermind warlord Basayev, and some other militant Ingush and Chechen hostage takers were cruel, sadistic, and pathological. Among them were wanted murderers, rapists, and thieves. However, the victims also knew of the complex circumstances that put many of the other hostage takers such as Nur-Pasha Kulayev in the school that day. Some of these desperate Ingush and Chechen people may have been coerced or even forced into militancy or felt sympathy for the Ossetian victims. When they expressed that sympathy by objecting to the targeting of children or by providing hostages with water, they paid for it with their lives. Generalizing from the psychopaths to entire ethnic groups and conveniently ignoring the more human and humane people in those ethnic groups, even among the militants, is a perspective colored by prejudice.

Acknowledging the humanity of victims and the reality of their prejudices is a step toward rectifying historical ethnic conflict. If prejudice is one of the most significant causes of individual support for retaliatory ethnic violence, solutions must involve addressing this reality. Prejudice reduction must precede violence reduction.

Reducing violence through the reduction in prejudice may be as tall an order as reducing violence directly. As discussed in Chapter 6, people may be socialized from childhood to dislike ethnic others. The socialization may come from parents, community narratives, or government provocateurs and may be reinforced by the true history of atrocities committed during past protracted ethnic conflict. An episode of violence like a school hostage taking may only reinforce these preconceptions and biases or even breed new prejudice (Skitka et al. 2004; Huddy et al. 2005:594). Changing these attitudes may take decades (Horowitz 2001:521).

Contact may help create a common identity and facilitate reconciliation, as shown in studies of integrated schools in Northern Ireland and individuals in Bosnia and Herzegovina, and in a meta-analysis of 515 studies (Pettigrew and Tropp 2006; Van Tongeren et al. 2013). However, the effects of contact vary, with racial or ethnic prejudice at times enduring despite contact (Paluck et al. 2019) or perhaps because of it (Bhavnani et al. 2014).

Findings from Beslan suggest that individual openness to contact matters. Feelings about contact—about interethnic dining, schooling, and marriage—were shown to influence support for retaliatory violence. Changing hearts and minds, rather than the objective fact of integration, is essential. Greater contact with ethnic rivals may reduce prejudice, but if not, other paths to prejudice reduction must be identified in order to end the cycle of retaliatory ethnic violence.

Curb Concern about Anger

Emotions, especially anger, are often portrayed as frightening states to be avoided or minimized. Emotions have even been described as the basis "for a common understanding that an ethnically distinct group is an enemy deserving some form of attack or punishment" (Petersen 2002:6–7). Findings from Beslan suggest that no emotion is required to see an ethnically distinct group as an enemy (Chapter 5). North Ossetians were killed by people who look, talk, and pray differently than they do. The killers' identities as Ingush and Chechen made the prejudiced among the victims see Ingush and Chechens as the enemy. The legitimate anger instigated by the hostage taking is beside the point. The angriest and least angry victims showed no difference in their support for retaliatory violence. As early studies of violence have shown, ordinary people in emotionless contexts are quite capable of supporting or committing grave atrocities (Arendt 1963; Milgram 1963).

To say that anger plays no role in retaliatory ethnic violence is not to say that victims of ethnic violence have little anger. Of course they are angry. The argument is simply that the violent among them are no angrier than the peaceful. To argue otherwise is pretty much to invite retaliation. It is the equivalent of saying, "If you are so angry, then why don't you prove it?!," as if the only proof of anger is murderous acts or intentions. Victims bent on revenge may be full of wrath, or not. Victims bent on stifling their urge to seek vengeance may be full or wrath, or not. The decision to commit or not commit retaliatory violence or to support such violence is orthogonal to anger—that is, violent inclinations occupy different brain pathways and should not be attributed to the quite legitimate anger that victims feel after victimization.

The abundant predictions of ethnic retaliatory violence after the hostage taking were unrealized, partly due to misunderstandings about the role of anger in violence. Anger has so long been accepted as the seed of violence in scholarship, media reports, and policy discussions that observers of the tragedy could be forgiven for calling attention to the massive outpouring of anger in Beslan and making erroneous inferences about its implications. Findings from Beslan show, however, that even pervasive, intense anger in the aftermath of violence should not be alarming. Anger is an appropriate, healthy, and potentially constructive emotion. Many factors warrant concern and attention in efforts to stop the cycle of retaliatory ethnic violence, but anger is not one of them.

Raise Concern about Pride in Country

Pride in country sounds desirable. Especially after an act of terrorism, pride in one's country could be comforting for both individuals and communities seeking positivity and support amidst all the anguish. Individual and collective trauma might heal more quickly with a sense of connectedness to government and its officials. The sense of connectedness seems most promising with an accountable government that is worthy of the pride.

But what if government actions were partly responsible for the trauma? In such cases, pride in country—especially, *increased* pride—requires a generous interpretation of those actions, ignoring or excusing the blunders of the counterterrorist operation, the lax security that preceded it, and the mistreatment of victims that followed. It requires portraying the incident of violence that ends in massacre as something other than government failure. Pride in country might require buying fully into the government narrative about the militants and the terrorist act, a narrative that is usually self-serving in casting blame away from government officials and exclusively onto the terrorists.

In such cases, the government need not explicitly encourage retaliatory ethnic violence or even hint that ethnic communities are responsible for the violence perpetrated by some of its members. Victims who are most proud of their country may infer the need for retaliation nevertheless from its compatibility with the government narrative. Or they may feel the independent need for some response to their victimization and, with government institutions and officials excluded as potential targets, see retaliatory ethnic violence as the lone and logical remaining option. The option is especially enticing where political authorities appear to greenlight violence against members of the rival ethnic group.

Pride in country in the aftermath of violence can thus be harmful. Victims of violence who believe their country can do no wrong—in the face of much evidence of wrongs—have the greatest potential to perpetuate the cycle of violence. In Beslan, the proudest victims were the most violence-accepting, seeing tit-for-tat murders of Chechens as a reasonable course of action (Chapter 7).

In contrast, politically alienated Beslan victims were the least likely to support retaliatory violence. Their political alienation has a downside: alienated victims of violence may miss the comfort and perceived care that accompanies a sense of pride in country. However, if political alienation is warranted by shameful actions of the state, it should raise no more alarm bells than anger. Like anger, political alienation seems an appropriate and even healthy sentiment in the context of government mishandling of a hostage crisis.

Political pride, however, does merit concern. It suggests a link between the least questioning victims, the most blindly accepting of government, and a willingness to kill. Violence reduction may be facilitated by reducing the blindness and encouraging inquisitiveness, expectations of government accountability, and a willingness to feel and express shame in government when government has acted shamefully.

Exercise Caution about Self-Efficacy

Victims of violence, by definition, have lost agency. If they were hostages, they were literally restricted in movement, told where to sit and whether they would be allowed food, water, or basic hygiene. If they were related to hostages, they were powerless to influence the course of events, literally standing by as loved ones were maimed and killed. After the violence, agency is often limited as well. Many injuries are permanent. Lives are forever changed. Efforts to obtain information and assistance, let alone accountability or retribution, may seem hopeless.

Actual agency aside, the perception of agency varies across victims. Some victims feel self-efficacy, or a sense of control over their lives and the situation that caused the victimization. In many ways, this feeling is helpful and healthy. Self-efficacy boosts victims' ability to cope and facilitates posttraumatic recovery (Gecas 1989; Luszczynska et al. 2009).

However, in the aftermath of violence, feeling in control is not always a peaceful sentiment. In Beslan, victims were asked whether they could do anything to help solve the problems that led to the tragedy, and those answering affirmatively were more likely than other victims to support retaliatory violence (Chapter 9). Pessimists among the victims—those who believe problems are unsolvable, independent of their personal agency—were also more likely to support retaliatory violence.

The implication for peace is that political efficacy is the far more important characteristic to cultivate. Political efficacy motivates political participation while having no effect on support for retaliatory violence, whereas self-efficacy could be channeled toward either outcome. Victims who feel personally effective after a violent episode but not politically effective, especially if they are pessimists, are among the most likely to support repaying violence with violence.

Foster Regular Political Engagement

Victims who, prior to experiencing victimization, are habituated to political engagement demonstrate the most promise for nonviolent, political outcomes. In Beslan, prior political activism was the only variable besides political alienation to have constructive effects on both post-violence responses: longtime activists were less likely to support retaliatory violence and more likely to continue activism in response to the hostage taking (Chapter 10).

Importantly, the effects of prior activism are independent of political efficacy (Chapter 11). Regardless of whether victims believe that activism works and that they personally are informed enough to participate meaningfully, the mere fact of the prior activism, the habit of engagement, creates tendencies to continue the habit after victimization and to steer away from retaliation.

Also noteworthy, there was no significant relationship in Beslan between post-violence political participation and support for retaliatory violence. Current political activism was influenced by prior activism, but current activism—political participation in response to the recent victimization and not born of a longstanding orientation to activism—did not work like prior activism to dampen support for retaliatory violence (Chapter 11). The pre-violence, pretrauma history of experience in the political process is what mattered. Victims with no experience in the political process, when newly aggrieved, are more likely to think of retaliation as a go-to response.

The implication for violence reduction is that habits of political participation are important to cultivate. When individuals are accustomed to seeing politics as a space for citizens to articulate grievances and engage with institutions and officials, they are more likely to return to that space after an incident of violence and less likely to consider perpetuating the cycle of violence.

Implications for Interest Representation

To the degree that Beslan victims addressed their grievances politically, activists seemed to think: I am incredibly angry, and my country has let me down, but I have engaged in the political process before and am quite capable of doing so now.

Angry and politically alienated Beslan victims were more likely to respond to the tragedy with constructive and peaceful political participation, as were victims who felt politically efficacious, had engaged in political activism prior to the hostage taking, and had relatives who experienced harm by an Ingush or Chechen prior to the hostage taking. Other variables played little to no role in post-violence political action in Beslan. Self-efficacy mattered for participation, but not as much as specifically political efficacy. Social alienation and optimism/pessimism might have both positive and negative effects on participation, counteracting themselves as both grievances and sources of perceived inefficacy, and thus were not significant mobilizers. Biographical availability and demographic characteristics such as gender, age, income, and education were also not critical in explaining political mobilization.

As for violence reduction, manipulating conditions for political participation and trying to change attributes of individuals—such as anger, political alienation, and political efficacy—is difficult but potentially fruitful. Findings from Beslan victims suggest that the following approaches are most likely to generate positive outcomes. The approaches go beyond simply avoiding making a bad situation worse. They involve increasing the probability of post-violence political action and in turn increasing the probability of interest representation.

Stoke, Don't Quench, Anger

Anger and hate sound undesirable and have often been treated as detrimental by scholars, journalists, and other observers of politics and violence. However, evidence from Beslan shows that anger and hate are reasonable and cathartic emotions that get channeled into peaceful political participation. Indeed, in the aftermath of violence, productive responses may depend on these awful feelings.

Angrier Beslan victims were more likely to participate in a range of activities, including signing petitions, writing to newspapers, attending rallies, meeting with political officials, blockading a highway, and staging a courtroom sit-in. The angriest were six to nine times more active than the less angry, and only a quarter participated in no activities, whereas nonparticipation was the norm for the majority of those who were rarely or never angry (Chapter 5).

Moreover, among Beslan victims, the positive relationship between hatred and political participation is one of the most robust. Conventional wisdom blames hatred for much of the world's ills, and indeed the label, "act of hatred," implicitly indicts hatred as an evil emotion that makes an already awful deed worthy of additional scorn and punishment. Data from Beslan victims show that support for killing is not at all correlated with hatred. Contrary to the conventional wisdom, these negative feelings somehow translate into positive, constructive action. An "act of hatred" may really be a peaceful demonstration.

By implication, then, the anger, hatred, or resentment of victims of violence is not something to be feared. Instead, these sentiments should be welcomed and encouraged. Let victims have a voice, and let them use that voice to express their outrage, because the odds are good that they will do so in the political arena in the name of interest representation.

This lesson from Beslan directly contradicts recommendations from prior scholarly research and conventional wisdom. Because anger has been long stigmatized as a source of violence, the general counsel has been to reduce it. Anger should be "quenched." Only then can conflicts supposedly terminate and reconciliation begin (Petersen and Zukerman 2009).

Evidence from Beslan victims shows, however, that quenching anger will not stop retaliatory ethnic violence but may very well stop political participation. And without political participation, victims of violence may continue to suffer. They are unlikely to receive adequate compensation for losses, assistance with ongoing health problems, and answers to important questions about the violent act that transformed their lives. These and other grievances associated with unaccountable government action in the aftermath of violence might be sustained indefinitely. Anger-induced political participation does not guarantee grievance satisfaction, but quenched anger seems a recipe for grievance perpetuation.

Quenched anger makes sense as a goal for victims, if quenching results from grievance satisfaction. In the case of Beslan, had the Russian government done a thorough, transparent, and truthful investigation and admitted its mistakes and failures in preventing the attack on the school and managing the counterterrorism operation, and had the Russian government treated the victims with greater sensitivity and compensated them appropriately for their pain and suffering, victims might have moved on. Their demands were concrete, finite, and reasonable. Truth often quenches anger (Petersen and Zukerman 2009).

But without such truth, government incompetence, insensitivity, or downright cruelty might continue. The Russian government commission, composed mainly of members of the ruling party, did not truly look into the root causes of terrorism and the failed rescue operation. Quenching or, more accurately, stifling anger in response to the false reports hardly serves justice. Stifling anger in response to the failure to investigate bribery of police at checkpoints and its enabling of the hostage taking also hardly serves justice. Indeed, without anger and the resulting activism that put the issue in the public eye, bribes and their violent ramifications are likely to repeat. More generally, stifling anger about the continued vulnerability of Russian citizens to government counterterrorism operations hardly serves justice. "Fearful relatives now worry about a storming more than anything during a hostage crisis, because they know they have terrible odds for seeing their loved ones emerge alive" ("Seeking Public Accountability" 2004). Had Beslan victims stifled their anger and done nothing to draw attention to this pattern of government behavior, future victims, not just in Russia but around the world, would be in a worse predicament.

Lack of anger or the attenuation of anger is demobilizing. As Bella, a female Beslan victim under thirty-five years old, explained, "As time goes on, a person gets smarter, realizes, analyzes. But in those days, everyone was in such a state.... There were lots of emotions. Maybe that was the reason why I took part in all the rallies. Now, I'm quite sure, I [*wouldn't take part*], not now."

As anger dies, so does the will to engage in politics. And with unengaged victims comes the diminishing possibility of a government taking interests and grievances seriously. Remembering that anger is healthy and productive should encourage its expression.

Value Justifiable Political Alienation

Victims who lose pride in their country face a double whammy in the initial victimization and in the detachment from their country at a time when they need that attachment more than ever. Victims typically need medical assistance from their country and often financial assistance for the medical care, lost work time, or new family care obligations. Victims also typically need emotional support, which can come from the government "doing right by victims" and perhaps allowing them to renew their pride in country. When that pride is lacking, the feeling of political alienation undoubtedly adds negativity to the posttraumatic context and may therefore seem unhelpful.

However, in terms of motivating political participation, evidence from Beslan shows that the relative advantages and disadvantages of political pride and political alienation are actually reversed. Despite its seeming disadvantages, political alienation is a productive response to victimization, allowing victims to raise their voices about injury and injustice. Political alienation is one of the only variables, besides prior activism, to have a significant positive effect on political participation and a significant negative effect on support for retaliatory violence. Conversely, despite its seeming advantages, political pride, much like system justification, is a hindrance to interest representation. Beslan victims who remained proud of Russia or even increased their pride in Russia after the hostage taking, especially those most ready to withhold blaming President Putin or other political officials, were least likely to become political activists and to challenge the government's interpretation of events. Indeed, none of the proudest victims could be labeled activists, as defined by participation in more than ten activities, whereas over a quarter of the most alienated victims could be labeled activists (Chapter 7).

A recommendation to stoke political alienation has a different feel than a recommendation to stoke anger, because the former could be misconstrued as disloyal or unpatriotic. Such a claim represents a misunderstanding of political alienation, as defined here. Loyalty and love of country are not at issue. A politically alienated victim of violence could be extremely loyal and patriotic. The loyalty and patriotism might even contribute to the diminished pride suffered after a traumatic event like the hostage taking that was grossly mishandled by government. The event may have violated previously high expectations about government concern for its citizens. In such cases, the diminished pride is warranted and serves to enhance the political engagement of victims. Political alienation serves to push the victims to demand greater accountability and responsiveness from their government, which is to be encouraged as the highest form of patriotism.

Nurture Political Efficacy and Habits of Political Activism

People who are historically committed to addressing grievances through the political process continue that activism when faced with new grievances. Accordingly, Beslan victims who participated in politics prior to the 2004 school hostage taking were more likely to continue that activism after the tragedy (Chapter 10). Also more likely to be active after the tragedy were victims who believed that demonstrating or protesting is an effective way to address dissatisfaction and who believed in their competence to participate in politics (Chapter 9).

These are relatively uncontroversial findings with relatively uncontroversial implications: nurturing political efficacy and habits of political activism, prior to tragedy striking, seems essential for interest representation. Active citizenship begets more active citizenship, and feeling efficacious about politics begets more active citizenship.

The positive feeling of efficacy in the political process may not be matched for long stretches of time with objective evidence of effectiveness. Demands may not be met. But they most certainly will not be met if victims prejudge and consider the task of political advocacy to be impossible. Beslan activists persevered in the face of stonewalling, sidestepping, denials, and dismissals. Somehow they found the fortitude to keep pushing. Political efficacy and habits of activism should be seen as ingredients for such fortitude.

Implications for Methodology: Studying Responses to Violence

Research on violence typically concentrates on the macrolevel story, emphasizing, for example, the role of leaders who sometimes provoke or fan the flames of violence. Equally important is the microlevel story of why the followers follow entrepreneurs of violence (Horowitz 1985:140) or pursue peaceful political alternatives. This study of the aftermath of the Beslan school hostage taking tells a microlevel story by investigating the motivations of individual victims. In doing so, it provides methodological lessons for future studies of individual motivations in the aftermath of violence.

Select Populations of Consequence

One methodological lesson from the study of the school hostage taking is in case selection. To understand responses to ethnic violence, cases must be drawn from the real world of ethnic conflict, with a focus on victims of the conflict, because they are the populations whose behavioral responses are most relevant for scholarship and policy. Grievances are the defining characteristic of the post-violence context, and only victims are incontrovertibly aggrieved (Introduction).

The role of grievances in violence has been downplayed in recent decades in favor of other variables that supposedly do more of the work in mobilizing individuals. Such arguments miss the point: in a context like a hostage taking or other instance of communal violence, grievances are so universal and severe that they do not vary enough to be the driver of varied behavior *within that context*. Violent and peaceful, activists and nonactivists, all victims suffer. But the limited individual-level variation does not make grievances unimportant. Grievances still matter tremendously. They should define the scope condition for studies of interethnic violence. Only with violence or the realistic threat of violence is there a real puzzle about the responses to violence. And only studies of victims can provide answers to that puzzle.

Bystanders, onlookers, third parties, sympathizers, and others who do not directly experience harm but might nevertheless be mobilized to commit retaliatory violence or participate in politics are interesting and worthy of study. Indeed, allies who are not directly aggrieved can be critical partners for helping aggrieved populations achieve their goals. But how to identify the mobilization pool of such outsiders—the theoretically justified and empirically relevant population from which political activists or violent retaliators might be drawn—is unclear. The study of nonvictim allies is thus fertile ground for future research.

Retaliatory violence is contextual. Protests and other political activities are contextual. Efforts to understand either response by assuming grievances, eliciting grievances, or even prompting grievances will generate findings of dubious value. If an issue is not truly salient to study subjects, there is little to be learned from analyzing their projected responses to the issue (Introduction and Chapter 12). Thus, studies of nonvictims have the greatest potential relevance and validity when they are based on random samples of general populations proximate to victims in terms of geography, identity, or some other factor, and they have the least potential relevance and validity when they are based on samples of students or other convenient populations in manufactured settings far removed from actual grievances.

Even at their most rigorous, however, studies of nonvictim allies should not be conflated with victim studies, because the lack of clarity in defining cases can render analysis meaningless and lead to erroneous inferences about the cycle of ethnic violence, how to end it, and how to address problems arising from it. For example, in Beslan, while individual-level variation in grievances had no significant effect on the behavior of victims, such variation did seem significant for nonvictims. But really, this finding simply reinforced that grievances matter as context: city populations were randomly sampled, and they happened to include some former hostages or relatives of former hostages who, because they were truly victims, participated in politics more than true nonvictims detached from the hostage taking (Chapter 12).

Other fundamental differences between victims and nonvictims could lead to more seriously erroneous inferences. Anger, political alienation, and political efficacy play powerful roles in explaining the political participation of victims in the aftermath of violence. A study of nonvictims would miss these important findings.

Of course, victims and nonvictims are not entirely different, and some findings about both populations may be the same. In Beslan and Vladikavkaz, anger played no role in support for retaliatory violence among either victims or nonvictims, while prejudice increased support for violence among both. Only the clear separation of victim and nonvictim populations as distinct cases for analysis can illuminate these similarities and help determine which findings are universal.

Study Nonviolence

To understand responses to ethnic violence, cases must also not be limited to outbreaks of violence, "positive" cases of retaliation, and so-called hot spots that remain hot. The aftermath of the Beslan school hostage taking is a "negative case," or an instance of nonviolence (Mahoney and Goertz 2004). Studies of negative cases are necessary, because without them, understanding of ethnic violence would be biased by reliance only on cases where violence is present.

To date, studies of negative cases of violence—nonviolence—are rare. One reason might be publication bias: social scientists tend to report only statistically significant findings, and they may anticipate that analysis of a negative case is unlikely to generate significant findings and that null results will not get accepted for publication (Franco et al. 2014). Another reason for the rarity of negative case studies might be because the negative case is often undefined and potentially so boundless as to include all of civil peace. Without boundaries, studies of nonviolence cannot advance understanding (Horowitz 2001:469–471).

Studying the aftermath of the hostage taking offers one solution. It is a "near miss strategy," where nonviolence occurs under conditions that are fertile for such violence. The aftermath is a plausible case of retaliatory violence that wasn't, and as such, it offers great potential for advancing understanding (Horowitz 2001:478, 509). Future studies of other negative cases have the potential to make further contributions.

Specify, Compare, and Contrast Types of Violence

The study of Beslan victims answers longstanding calls for precision in defining the type of violence under investigation (Fearon and Laitin 1996; Brubaker and Laitin 1998:426; Horowitz 2001:39). The aftermath of the school hostage taking is a negative case of retaliatory ethnic violence. Lessons from Beslan victims' disinclination to retaliate may be applicable to ethnic riots, terrorism, and other forms of violence, but generalizing across forms of violence depends on future theorizing and empirical tests.

For example, prior research on terrorism suggests that efficacy matters, but differently than for retaliatory ethnic violence. Terrorist violence is supposedly driven by the lack of political efficacy. Powerless against the state, terrorists have little recourse beyond violence (Tausch et al. 2011:143). It is possible that these two types of violence differ and that political efficacy has no effect on one, retaliatory violence, and a strongly negative effect on the other, terrorism. However, it is also possible that, if studies of terrorists applied findings from Beslan victims and parsed efficacy into self-efficacy and political efficacy, the analysis would produce similar nuanced insights—that even terrorists are driven to commit violence less by power and powerlessness in the political arena and more by a sense of personal empowerment to right perceived wrongs.

Use Realistic Measures of Political and Violent Responses

Beslan victims answered survey questions that were designed to produce valid measures of support for retaliatory violence, political participation, emotions, prejudice, political alienation, and a variety of other concepts. These careful measurement decisions in many cases represent important contributions to research design.

For political participation, survey questions were drawn from preexisting studies, and many new ones were designed to reflect participation in specific political events that occurred since the Beslan tragedy, including specific public demonstrations, public meetings attended by local and national political officials, the organization of Mothers of Beslan, and the written appeal from Beslan victims to President Putin (Chapter 4). The aggregate measure of political participation used to classify Beslan victims along a scale of activism included both institutional and extra-institutional forms of political action, since once-unconventional activities such as protest are now "a common part of the political repertoire in many nations" (Dalton et al. 2010:71). The specificity and detailed descriptions of political acts minimized response error in the study of Beslan victims.

In contrast, extant work on political participation often relies on survey questions about actions without first clarifying if a strong grievance exists and whether actions are a response to that genuine problem. Problems are often assumed or even manufactured. Also, survey questions are often phrased as hypotheticals, asking respondents if they "would" do something or if they "support" a particular action. The stated intention or support is treated as a valid proxy for actual behavior, despite evidence that people often profess intentions to participate and ultimately do not, perhaps due to routine obstacles such as unavailability or conflicting commitments. Going forward, future studies of individual motivations to respond to ethnic violence—and participate in politics in other contexts—would benefit from a similar measurement approach: asking questions about participation in specific, real actions.

For ethnic retaliatory violence, a survey question measuring support rather than the actual commission of violence may suffer similar limitations to the hypothetical questions about political participation. Measuring "support for violence" is justified, however, because it may be the only measure allowable given the ethical and methodological challenges of asking direct questions about individual acts of violence. With its limitations, the measure still has strong advantages. Understanding violent impulses is an important step toward understanding violence itself. Killers are almost always fewer in numbers than supporters of the killers and the killing, but without support, violence would be less frequent (Horowitz 2001:14). Violence is the extreme manifestation of the supporters' feelings and preferences (Horowitz 2001:14).

The measurement contribution from the study of Beslan victims comes again in the precision of the survey question about support for violence. Victims were asked if they approved of the retaliatory killing of Chechens in proportion to the number killed in the school hostage taking—a question reflecting the genuine approach to retaliation in a region of the world infamous for an-eye-for-an-eye justice (Chapter 3). If intention or support is measured in place of actual violent behavior, the survey question should serve to close the gap by bluntly and unambiguously capturing the extremeness of the potential violent act, retaliatory murder, that victims might support or oppose.

Use Distinct Measures of Emotion and Prejudice

Beslan victims were asked about the frequency of their feelings of anger, hatred, resentment, and other emotions (Chapter 5). The emotional response to the hostage taking is credible on its face and corroborated by all other evidence about the victims gathered from abundant media reports and discussions of victims in focus groups. The validity of measures of victims' emotions surpasses the validity of measures used in laboratory experiments where emotions are manufactured, manipulated, and likely transient in response to issues of questionable salience.

Beslan victims were asked separately about their approval of interethnic mingling in schools, in marriage, and at the dinner table (Chapter 6). These measures resemble frequently used and validated questions in the context of race relations in the United States. In the context of ethnic conflict, measuring prejudice with such simple, seemingly innocent questions represents an important contribution, partly due to their ability to elicit valid responses. From the perspective of victims and others living in zones of ethnic conflict, it seems reasonable to be asked such questions and provide honest answers.

Perhaps the most important measurement contribution is in delinking measures of emotion from measures of prejudice. The conceptual clarity improves upon prior studies of ethnic violence that bundle anger, hatred, or other emotions along with negative assessments of rival ethnic groups, thereby preventing analysis of the independent role of each factor. Only by measuring these factors separately and distinctly could analysis reveal the relationship between ordinary prejudice and support for retaliatory violence. Analysis of the distinct measures is also the only approach that clarifies that prejudice is dangerous with or without anger and other emotions and their accompanying volatility and drama.

Capitalize on the Advantages of Mixed Methods

This book is at once a single case study, a large-N quantitative analysis, and a small-N in-depth qualitative investigation. It combines insights from surveys of victims of ethnic violence, focus group interviews of victims, comprehensive analysis of media reports, and surveys of city populations proximate to the violence. It therefore avoids many of the deficiencies associated with each method in isolation, such as the overly descriptive nature of case studies that can make them inappropriate for testing hypotheses and the acontextual nature of large quantitative studies that can make them detached from reality (Demmers 2012:91). The simultaneous deployment of both quantitative and qualitative tools is a form of nested analysis for comparative research (Lieberman 2005).

Each component method has its advantages. This study not only capitalizes on the advantages, but tries to derive the greatest benefit from each by maximizing rigor. In particular, the victim surveys included 1,098 of 1,340 surviving adult hostages, parents of underage hostages, and next of kin of deceased hostages, a response rate of 82 percent (Introduction). With no sampling and therefore no sampling error, and with attention to measurement driving down response error as well, the statistical analysis produced results that have high internal validity. The focus groups and media reports filled any gaps in understanding with the precise words of the victims, while the large-N nonvictim surveys allowed tests of external validity. These tests helped show that generalizations are most appropriate across victim populations and that much work remains to understand post-violence behavior and attitudes of ally nonvictims (Chapter 12).

Such large-N analysis combined with interviews of individuals is increasingly common in sociology and psychology and is a pillar of medical research (Goertz 2017:17–21). This study of responses to the Beslan school hostage taking shows the great value of multimethod research for other areas of study, particularly those that are interdisciplinary or fall at the intersection of several subfields within a single discipline.

As the definitive history of the aftermath of the Beslan school hostage taking, this book contributes to the study of political history, Russian politics, and the politics of the Caucasus. It also makes contributions as a work of political science to the subfields of ethnic conflict, terrorism, political participation, social movements, contentious politics more generally, emotions and politics, and political psychology more generally. New insights for each of these subfields might be gained from future multimethod research approaches.

Final Thoughts on the Victims of Beslan

Telling the story of Beslan victims hopefully brings benefit to the survivors, other residents of North Ossetia and Russia, victims of violence around the world, and scholars and policymakers interested in understanding the emergence of peace after violence. Telling the story is "a consciousness-raising that allows the past to become a resource and sets the stage for action against repetition of trauma. . . . In this way, the survivors of violence can become the most powerful members of their societies" (Tedeschi 1999:334).

A victim community's most active citizens perform the tireless and often thankless tasks of investigations, meetings, organization, letter-writing, petition-writing, and media interviews. They are often unappreciated, resented, and harassed. They are sometimes charged with serving their own interests, which even if true, misses the larger point that their interests mainly coincide with those of the extended victim community. All stand to benefit when activists uncover new evidence, push for more thorough and truthful investigations, and litigate, especially when they win and establish legal precedent.

Victim activists deserve thanks and appreciation, as do all victims who manage to stifle inclinations to return violence with violence. To the victims of Beslan, this book was written with sincere condolences for your unimaginable losses and extreme gratitude for your considered response.

Chronology of Activities after the Beslan School Hostage Taking

Date	Activity
Days after siege	Mothers of Beslan (www.materibeslana.com) formed mostly by those who lost children or grandchildren; 150 members by August 2005.
Days after siege	Committee of Beslan Teachers formed to help those affected by hostage taking.
Days after siege	www.beslan.ru is established to solicit donations, post lists of victims, post offers to victims for rehabilitation vacations and material goods, and maintain news archives.
September 4, 2004	100 rally at Beslan school wreckage for two hours, demanding lists of victims, lists of terrorists, and resignation of North Ossetian president Dzasokhov and other officials.
September 4, 2004	300 rally at Beslan House of Culture for six hours, demanding lists of victims and terrorists and resignation of Dzasokhov and other officials.
September 4, 2004	Rally held at Beslan's central square for one hour with demands for lists of victims and terrorists and resignation of Dzasokhov and other officials.
September 4–5, 2004	Rally held in Prigorodny against Ingush.
September 5, 2004	North Ossetian minister of Internal Affairs Kazbek Dzantiyev resigns, saying, "After what happened in Beslan, I don't have the right to occupy this post as an officer and as a man."
September 6, 2004	Putin rejects possibility of public inquiry/federal investigation.
September 7, 2004	Rallies held in Beslan.
September 7, 2004	Rallies held in Vladikavkaz.
September 7, 2004	130,000 demonstrate in government-organized rally against terror in Moscow.
September 8, 2004	3,000 demonstrate at government headquarters in Vladikavkaz and accuse Dzasokhov and ministers of lying over the number of hostages, demand their resignation, and throw tins and bottles.

Date	Activity
September 9, 2004	6,000 rally in Vladikavkaz with most pro-Dzasokhov, although some demand his resignation.
September 9, 2004	Dzasokhov dissolves his Cabinet of Ministers but himself refuses to resign, citing Moscow's fears of domino effect in Caucasus.
September 10, 2004	Putin announces parliamentary commission to be created by Sergei Mironov, speaker of Federation Council, the upper house of Parliament, and investigation to be led by Deputy Speaker Alexander Torshin.
September 11, 2004	Russian government orders compensation to victims ranging from 15,000 to 100,000 rubles (~$525 to $3,500) based on injuries and deaths, plus 18,000 rubles ($630) for funeral expenses for each deceased person.
September 13, 2004	Putin removes from their posts North Ossetian minister of Internal Affairs Kazbek Dzantiyev and North Ossetian head of FSB Valery Andreyev. In early 2005, Putin makes Dzantiyev deputy commander of internal troops of Moscow Military District and Andreyev deputy head of FSB Academy of the Russian Federation.
September 14, 2004	Relatives of victims meet with Dzasokhov and establish public commission to monitor investigation into the hostage taking and make sure that responsible officials are named and punished.
September 16, 2004	Putin agrees to a second parliamentary inquiry by Duma, the lower house of Parliament, to focus on improved anti-terrorism legislation, and upper and lower houses then work together under Torshin.
September 2004	North Ossetian Parliament decides to conduct investigation independent of federal authorities and led by Stanislav Kesayev, deputy chairman of North Ossetian parliament.
September 20–27, 2004	Torshin Commission, composed of 12 Federation Council members and 10 Duma deputies, visits Beslan, meets with former hostages and local authorities, and receives hundreds of letters and 147 phone calls on special hotline.
September 21, 2004	Website www.beslan.ru reports to media that fate of 400 hostages is still unknown; website's numbers of injured, killed, or missing compiled by teachers from the school who studied the school registers and went door to door to all houses of former students and asked about children and their parents; www.beslan.ru numbers are much higher than those released by government; website also begins raising money for survivors, allowing donations to target specific victims by name.

Date	Activity
September 24, 2004	Putin establishes investigation by federal prosecutors led by Nikolai Shepel, new deputy prosecutor general for Southern Federal District, with oversight by Vladimir Kolesnikov, deputy prosecutor general.
September–December 2004	Head of Federal Centre of Disaster Psychiatry at Moscow's Serbsky State Centre of Social and Forensic Psychiatry installs Psychosomatic Division at Beslan's hospital, including 24-hour hotline and on-site psychologists.
October 8, 2004	Shepel opens criminal cases of negligence against officials in Pravoberezhny police headquarters of North Ossetia and Malgobek district of Ingushetia who should have been aware of militant training in their territory.
October 27, 2004	Shepel announces that three Beslan policemen would be charged with criminal negligence leading to siege but provides no details.
November 3, 2004	More than 1,000 Beslan residents attend angry town meeting at Beslan House of Culture held by Shepel and delegation of local authorities; accuse delegation of half-truths and force them to leave.
November 10, 2004	Rally held in Beslan with demands for international investigation of tragedy and the truth before the new year.
November 10, 2004	Rally held in Vladikavkaz to protest lack of publication of lists of dead and authorities concealing results of investigation and names of those to blame.
November 18, 2004	300+ Beslan residents sign open letter to Putin and parliamentary commission blaming "corruption, permissiveness, and incorrect national policy" for siege and demanding punishment of negligent local officials.
late November 2004	Victims receive payments from Fund for Aid to Victims of a Terrorist Act ranging from 350,000 rubles for minor injuries to 1 million rubles for loss of relative; religious sects arrive, presumably to exploit new influx of money; North Ossetia enacts "Law on Missionary Activity" requiring permission for such work.
December 2004	Families of deceased victims receive payments of 100,000 rubles (~$3,500) from compensation fund set up by Russian government in September; Deputy Prime Minister Alexander Zhukov announces new $49 million reconstruction project to finance schools, art institute, nursery school, hospital, and new apartment block.
December 17, 2004	100 victims and relatives rally at Beslan school wreckage, demanding "objective and transparent investigation of the tragedy."

Date	Activity
January 18, 2005	General Prosecutors deliver report on progress of their investigation but refuse to address question of which leaders are to blame.
January 20–22, 2005	Initially 50 and swelling to 400 blockade Rostov-Baku/Caucasus Federal Highway toward Vladikavkaz by building tents across highway in response to prosecutor's progress report; other residents supply picketers with bonfire wood and food; they demand Dzasokov's resignation, criminal investigation of Andreyev and Dzantiyev's actions during siege, more objective investigation of siege in general, international investigation, and securing North Ossetian border with Ingushetia; blockade ends when Dmitry Kozak, Putin's special envoy to South Federal District, telephones leaders of protest and promises meeting on February 1.
February 1, 2005	Victims meet with Kozak in Rostov-on-Don.
February 17, 2005	Mothers of Beslan go to Moscow with open letter to Putin demanding resignation of Dzasokhov and hold news conference calling for Dzasokhov's resignation.
February 22, 2005	Beslan residents discover human remains in dump a mile outside of town, and relatives of victims gather to search; Susanna Dudiyeva, spokesperson for Mothers of Beslan, calls local prosecutors, security officials, and journalists.
February 24, 2005	Vladimir Khodov, head of the North Ossetian administration, goes on television to address public outcry, deny involvement, and promise to find those responsible.
February 25, 2005	Mothers of Beslan officially created as public organization with approximately 200 members, although it had been operating unofficially since just days after siege.
March 3, 2005	Handful of people protest near North Ossetia's representative office in Moscow; organizer is detained by police.
March 8, 2005	1,000 rally in Vladikavkaz's central Square of Liberty in demonstration named "Mothers against Terror" and organized by Mothers of Beslan, who are stopped and checked many times on their way to Vladikavkaz and otherwise threatened and hindered in holding event.
May 12, 2005	North Ossetian Ministry of Internal Affairs suspends acceptance of applications for permission to hold rallies, meetings, and other events that attract large numbers of people, citing fears of terrorist attacks and inability to provide necessary security forces; Mothers of Beslan expressed outrage and accuse government of being afraid of a wave of popular anger.

Date	Activity
May 17, 2005	Relatives of victims shout down judge as trial begins against Nur-Pasha Kulayev, allegedly only surviving terrorist, and demand that they be allowed to punish Kulayev themselves and that officials responsible be put on trial; judge is forced to suspend trial.
May 17, 2005	Several dozen protest outside courtroom.
May 31, 2005	Dzasokhov resigns but does not respond to corruption charges.
May 31, 2005	FSB first deputy director and overseer of storming of School No. 1, Vladimir Pronichev, is promoted to rank of four-star general.
June 7, 2005	North Ossetian Parliament approves Putin's appointment of Taimuraz Mamsurov to replace Dzasokhov as president of North Ossetia; Mamsurov was speaker of Parliament and from Beslan, and his two children were held hostage in the school; he gained stature by turning down an offer to get his children out in one of the groups initially released by the terrorists, although opponents were critical of his business interests and close ties to Dzasokhov.
June 7–8, 2005	About 20 members of Mothers of Beslan protest in front of main government building in Vladikavkaz against appointment of Mamsurov as president of North Ossetia, with 9 protesters going on a hunger strike; they charge that Mamsurov never met Beslan survivors or made public statements about attack.
July 5, 2005	Mothers of Beslan issue statement expressing lack of confidence in Prosecutor General's office conducting investigation (Krivorotov and Shepel) and demand change in leadership.
July–August 2005	During Kulayev's trial, Mothers of Beslan find and submit to court several launch tubes from *Shmel* flamethrowers, forcing Shepel to admit in court, despite previous denials, that they were used during assault; Shepel still contends that incendiary explosives were not used that day, but Kesayev counters that napalm traces were found during medical investigations; Mothers also get authorities to admit during testimony that two T-72 tanks fired several cannon rounds into school.
August 2005	Mothers of Beslan shuffle through wreckage, meet daily at hair salon two blocks from the school, and organize bus to carry members 20 minutes to Vladikavkaz courthouse two mornings a week during Kulayev's trial.

Date	Activity
August 2005	Mothers of Beslan ask Putin not to attend upcoming one-year anniversary events.
Mid- to late August 2005	12 members of Mothers of Beslan protest to demand accountability of Putin and Nikolai Patrushev, chief of Federal Security Service (FSB).
August 23–24, 2005	15 mothers of children who died in the siege stage sit-in for 28 hours in Vladikavkaz court during Kulayev's trial, insist on meeting with Shepel, demand that Putin and other top officials be held responsible, and charge that witness testimony is being ignored; supporters gather outside courthouse and pass food and water to the women.
Late August 2005	Kesayev previews findings of regional parliament investigation and notes lack of radical changes in security in response to Beslan events, likelihood that terrorists bribed corrupt roadside guards and traveled under noses of security forces to reach Beslan, and lack of preparation by local authorities during siege and its aftermath.
Late August 2005	Putin invites 20 Beslan mothers to talk with him in Moscow during week of one-year memorial services, but invitation is met with mixed reaction because Mothers of Beslan had asked for such a meeting three times before with no response, and current invitation is considered insensitively timed.
August 31, 2005	Beslan teachers send letter to Putin expressing frustration that neither Dzasokhov or Mamsurov agreed to meet them, that they have been "accused of surviving," and that names of the guilty had not been revealed.
August 31, 2005	More than 30 families and hundreds of individuals sign letter to international community expressing lost hope in hearing the truth and asking for asylum or immigration status from foreign governments.
September 1, 2005	20+ Beslan mothers hold three-night vigil in burned-out gym covered only by light blankets at night.
September 1, 2005	10 victims and relatives meet with Kozak and Mamsorov behind closed doors in North Ossetian cabinet building for two hours and complain about Shepel and prosecutor's investigation and about Putin's absence during siege.
September 1, 2005	Hundreds of mourners carrying red roses gather at school to mark one year anniversary of siege.

Date	Activity
September 2, 2005	4 members of Mothers of Beslan, 3 fathers of deceased child hostages, and North Ossetian president Mamsurov meet with Putin in Moscow (remaining invitees want to stay in Beslan for memorial services and/or doubt utility of the meeting) and present documents to Putin, including information on lack of coordination and objectivity in protracted investigation and their perspective on what happened at the school; Putin promises to work for the truth.
September 2005	Grigory Grabovoi, self-proclaimed faith healer and miracle worker, promises he can resurrect deceased children for large sum of money, reportedly 1,000 euros ($1,195) per resurrected victim.
September 2, 2005	300 rally in Moscow calling for top officials to be held responsible
September 3, 2005	Putin sends Kolesnikov and other prosecutors to Beslan to conduct comprehensive additional review of entire body of information available about the case.
September 3, 2005	Mamsurov makes televised remarks: "With the involvement of the Russian president, the investigation has taken on a new impetus. . . . Dozens of victims from Beslan have been able to say what they have not been given the chance to over the past year."
September 3, 2005	7,000–25,000 join Nashi-led "silent rally" near Red Square in Moscow.
September 11, 2005	Some Beslan residents refuse to be interviewed by oversight prosecutors, complaining that local investigators are too attached to Prosecutor General's commission.
Mid-September 2005	Kesayev refuses to disclose findings of his independent commission to Kolesnikov, citing victim dissatisfaction with federal prosecutors' investigation.
September 11, 2005	Shepel comments to ITAR-TASS that hostage takers were international terrorists acting at joint instigation of Arab mercenary Abu Dzeit and radical Chechen field commander Shamil Basayev.
September 11, 2005	Ella Kesayeva of Mothers of Beslan replies on *Ekho Moskvy* that Shepel's words were "one more link in a chain of lies" showing that "the official investigation is desperately trying to cover up the crimes" that many believe were committed by Russian forces.

Date	Activity
September 12, 2005	Mothers of Beslan express outrage and desire for Shepel's dismissal.
Mid-September 2005	Igor Tkachov is announced as new prosecutor in charge of prosecutors' investigation; Mothers of Beslan point out that Tkachov investigated the case at the beginning, created chaos, and made a lot of mistakes, but that they intend to speak with him and not let things run their own course; Shepel says he did not resign, investigation team was just strengthened.
Mid-September 2005	Some Beslan residents begin to join local self-defense armed battalions that are forming around North Ossetia with approval of North Ossetian interior minister Sergei Arenin.
September 14, 2005	Anne Brasseur, member of Council of Europe's Parliamentary Assembly, meets with Mothers of Beslan and promises to help victims' families.
September 17, 2005	At least 11 Beslan mothers, including Mothers of Beslan leader Susanna Dudiyeva, meet with Grabovoi at Kosmos Hotel in Moscow.
September 25, 2005	Mothers of Beslan leader Ella Kesayeva leads group of Beslan residents to sign petition asking for criminal proceedings to be initiated against Grabovoi.
September 29, 2005	Victims and their attorney, Taimuraz Chedzhemov, demand of judge at Kulayev's trial that Shepel be replaced, with Dudiyeva charging that Shepel's conclusions were predetermined and attorney charging that Shepel refused to question senior officials and therefore failed to investigate siege and its consequences properly.
October 2, 2005	Voice of Beslan (www.golosbeslana.ru) is created as splinter group from Mothers of Beslan; groups differ over utility of meeting with Putin in early September and over Grabovoi, with some Mothers of Beslan supporting him and willing to listen and Voice of Beslan members believing him to be a charlatan, con artist, and cult leader who served to discredit the cause of Beslan victims by making them appear gullible; Ella Kesayeva becomes spokesperson for new group.
October 3, 2005	Mothers of Beslan gather at school wreckage and unexpectedly meet Kolesnikov and criticize prosecutors' investigation; Kolesnikov promises "high profile trials" of "bungling bureaucrats" in Beslan.

Date	Activity
October 4, 2005	Judge of Supreme Court of North Ossetia refuses request to replace Shepel.
October 20, 2005	Kolesnikov reports at press conference in Vladikavkaz that general prosecutors' investigation is completed and that he agrees with Shepel on all points discovered so far and refutes almost every claim made by victims' families about faulty actions of officials, except that security agencies of North Ossetia and Ingushetia had been warned in advance of impending terrorist acts and that several agencies failed to take appropriate measures.
October 25, 2005	Relatives of victims team with survivors and relatives of Moscow theater hostage taking, demand from Putin a fair investigation into both attacks, form new nongovernmental organization, Nord Ost, and issue appeal to Putin at news conference to take another look at biased official Beslan investigation and to admit his own responsibility.
October 27, 2005	5 women and 2 men who lost children at Beslan or Moscow theater picket Russian Prosecutor General's office in Moscow to protest choice of Kolesnikov as top investigator and are arrested.
November 11, 2005	Judge Vitaly Besolov says that three Beslan police officers accused of criminal negligence would go on trial in the Pravobrerezhny District Court on November 15, 2005.
November 25, 2005	Voice of Beslan officially created as public organization.
November 29, 2005	At parliamentary session in Vladikavkaz, Kesayev gives oral summary presentation of report of North Ossetian Parliament's independent investigation, which blames insufficient measures taken by law enforcement agencies but denies that North Ossetian Interior Ministry or FSB had advance warning of attack and has few answers on issues such as tanks, flamethrowers, and explosion at school; written copies are not available, even to deputies, but copy is leaked and is more critical of federal authorities than Kesayev's oral summary; victims call report evasive and are disappointed.
November 30, 2005	Voice of Beslan issues statement asking United States and European Union to help investigate the attack.

Date	Activity
Mid-December 2005	Head of North Ossetia's Federal Security Service Valery Andreyev testifies at Kulayev's trial, refuses to say why authorities had initially released an erroneously low hostage count, and accuses North Ossetia's Emergency Situations minister Boris Dzgoyev of negligence, especially in having firefighters arrive at scene late and with empty water tanks; Dzgoyev then testifies, blames Andreyev for firefighting delay, and claims that fire occurred after the rescue operation when all hostages were dead; survivors and victims' relatives in the courtroom accuse both men of lying and shout angry words.
December 27, 2005	Federal prosecutors post their 92-page report (dated December 25) on Prosecutor General Offices' website and find no fault with authorities, claiming that tanks did not open fire on school until evening of September 3 when rescue operation was complete, FSB's Alpha and Vympl units did not use flamethrowing *Shmel* projectiles or conventional rocket-propelled projectiles until no hostages remained alive, and federal sniper did not fire at bomb-laden gym; report runs contrary to statements by Beslan residents.
December 27, 2005	30 members of Mothers of Beslan and Voice of Beslan protest prosecutors' report by refusing to leave courtroom of Kulayev's ongoing trial and demanding that judge summon three deputy directors of FSB to testify and hopefully contradict official version of events.
December 28, 2005	Parliament releases its report led by Torshin based on interviews with over 1,000 people and which blames no federal officials but harshly criticizes local and regional authorities said to have ignored warnings sent by federal authorities and blundered in assault on school; Beslan residents generally welcome tone and thrust of report despite its whitewashing of mistakes of high-ranking officials.
January 12, 2006	Dzasokhov testifies for four hours at Kulayev's trial, claims he had general warnings of possible attacks in North Ossetia but no advance warning of possible attack on a school, underreporting of hostage count was not deliberate but caused by chaos, and removal of five road traffic police checkpoints from Beslan was not to allow the police to accompany him on a trip to Nalchik since he never planned to go to Nalchik on that day; survivors and victims' relatives try to pull Dsazokhov's bodyguards from their seats, shout at Dzasokhov, blame him for not offering to exchange himself for child hostages, and pin a handwritten poster to the courtroom wall saying "Dzasokhov, you are a coward."

Date	Activity
January 13, 2006	Hearing begins for trial of three Beslan police officers accused of negligence in allowing terrorists to cross through a checkpoint, including former head of Pravoberezhny District Regional Interior Ministry Miroslav Aydarov, deputy Taimuraz Martazov, and chief of staff Guram Dryayev; Mothers of Beslan demand that journalists be allowed in courtroom and petition for trial to be linked with Kulayev's trial, since testimony of Dzasokhov and others at Kulayev's trial would be relevant to police officer trial; Voice of Beslan petitions to suspend trial until scheduled March conclusion of main investigation.
January 24, 2006	Victims and relatives refuse to leave courtroom of Kulayev's trial after Judge Tamerlan Aguzarov announces that all information had been gathered and trial would wrap up soon; Kesayeva leads protest and demands more witnesses, especially high-ranking federal officials, and submits petition to Supreme Court of North Ossetia-Alania for disqualification of Judge Aguzarov in Kulayev's trial.
February 2, 2006	Kesayeva submits petition to court to question presidential advisor Aslanbek Aslakhanov and Ingush president Murat Zyazikov on why they did not turn up in Beslan on time and why talks were broken off; victims' public representative Taymuraz Chedzhemov disagrees with need to question Zyazikov because he was not a witness to events; judge rejects Kesayeva's petition; Kesayeva then petitions to wind up trial so that she could appeal based on objections to judge and prosecution team; judge rejects this petition as well; Dudiyeva and other victims do not support Kesayeva and focus more on getting witness testimony from former Ingushetian president Ruslan Aushev, pediatrician and hostage negotiator Dr. Leonid Roshal, and Russian FSB special forces commander General Aleksandr Tikhonov; Dudiyeva says complaints are with prosecutor's office not court; Kesayeva charges that Chedzhemov is taking position of prosecutor and working on victims to do the same.
February 7, 2006	Roshal arrives in Vladikavkaz at request of Kesayeva and is questioned by Shepel; Kesayeva and two other members of Voice of Beslan accuse Roshal of lying to waiting families during siege about how long children could live; Roshal and Kesayeva threaten to sue each other.
February 7, 2006	Judge announces that last witness was questioned and court investigation/questioning process of Kulayev's trial is closed.

Date	Activity
February 9, 2006	Judge signals for beginning presentation of arguments; Kesayeva demands that investigation not be closed until all proper witnesses are questioned, especially former Ingushetian president Ruslan Aushev who agrees to come to court on February 16; judge refuses this request.
February 9, 2006	15 relatives of Beslan victims announce their intention to begin hunger strike to protest trial being "neither objective nor thorough" and true culprits not being named
February 9, 2006	Mothers of Beslan voice support of prosecution's demand for death penalty for Kulayev while still demanding punishment for all guilty parties including officials; Voice of Beslan opposes death penalty.
February 9–19, 2006	7 members of Voice of Beslan go on hunger strike and demand new investigation with independent experts who would interrogate all witnesses, with 6 continuing the strike for 11 days; Mothers of Beslan do not support hunger strike and focus on restoring death penalty; regional newspapers are apparently told not to cover hunger strike, phone turned off in office building where hunger strike takes place, and eviction threatened.
February 14, 2006	Mothers of Beslan call for restoration of death penalty in Russia.
February 16, 2006	Trial concludes of Nur-Pasha Kulayev.
February 22, 2006	Voice of Beslan members meet with UN High Commissioner for Human Rights Louise Arbour in Vladikavkaz and hand her letter calling on UN to help with Beslan investigation.
March 3, 2006	Mothers of Beslan submit petition to Russian General Prosecutor's office demanding that Dzasokhov and other officials be tried for criminal negligence and incompetence during hostage rescue operation.
March 7, 2006	Voice of Beslan issues statement supporting continued moratorium on death penalty and opposing use of death penalty against Kulayev, which would mean becoming "barbarians in response to barbarity."
March 2006	Garry Kasparov's top aide and editor of website *Pravda Beslana*, Marina Litvinovich, is savagely beaten by unidentified assailants in Moscow but not robbed; attack is widely assumed to be related to her Beslan investigation.
March 13, 2006	Voice of Beslan speaks out against new Russian anti-terror law which they say permitted the authorities to commit absolute, unlimited, and anti-constitutional arbitrariness.

Date	Activity
March 16, 2006	Trial begins for three Beslan police officers accused of criminal negligence for allowing truck full of heavily armed attackers to cross unimpeded through many police checkpoints into Beslan.
April 2006	Federal prosecutors claim that in late August 2004 Beslan police department received written order from region's Interior Ministry to increase security around roads and schools, warning of possible terrorist attack; defendants claim that order warning of attack was created after the fact and then backdated and point out that police colleagues lost close relatives in school, which is inconsistent with knowing about attack in advance; many witnesses testify that guilt of national leadership is higher than guilt of local police.
April 2006	Grabovoi arrested and indicted on fraudulently obtaining money from parents of victims; some claim he is being used by government to discredit Mothers of Beslan.
April 15, 2006	Five former members of Voice of Beslan and their relatives show up at organization's office and force the one woman present to hand over keys and vacate premises; group supports third term for President Putin and objects to Voice of Beslan's criticism of Putin and demands for his accountability in attack; building's owner decides not to continue renting to either party.
May 1, 2006	1,000 Beslan residents, including survivors and victims' relatives, protest armed raid on home of Cossack leader Khariton Yedziyev, demanding end to arbitrary behavior of law enforcement agencies, illegal security sweeps, and persecution of Cossacks for fulfilling their obligation to guard administrative border.
May 16, 2006	Kulayev is found guilty on all eight charges of murder and terrorism; judge begins to read entire verdict over next few days; prosecution demands death penalty despite Russia's moratorium on capital punishment; Voice of Beslan argues that officials still need to be held accountable and that Kulayev should be kept alive as valuable resource who could continue to provide evidence and keep case alive; Mothers of Beslan continue to push for public execution.
May 23, 2006	Victims and relatives meet with Kozak, who promises to organize meeting between them and General Public Prosecutor Vladimir Ustinov.
May 24, 2006	20 women protest outside courtroom demanding objective investigation and conviction of the guilty.
May 26, 2006	Victims and relatives pack courtroom for Kulayev's formal sentencing to life in prison.

Date	Activity
May 31, 2006	Voice of Beslan appeals to Russian Supreme Court through North Ossetian Supreme Court, protesting that Kulayev trial was one-sided and a cover-up and did not reflect victims' testimonies regarding actions of authorities; they do not argue with guilty verdict or life sentence, but rather that no one else is punished.
June 1, 2006	Five male Beslan residents are supposed to meet with General Public Prosecutor Vladimir Ustinov and meet instead with Deputy Prosecutors General Shepel and Kolesnikov; share information that differs from official version of events, including that at least four terrorists fled from scene.
June 2, 2006	General Public Prosecutor Vladimir Ustinov resigns.
June 2006	Members of the federal Parliament's commission under Torshin vote 17 to 2 to endorse final version of commission's investigation report.
July 10, 2006	Supposed mastermind of siege and notorious warlord Shamil Basayev is killed by an explosion of controversial origin.
August 9, 2006	Russia's new prosecutor Yuri Chaika fires Shepel and replaces him with Ivan Sydoruk as new deputy prosecutor general for southern Russia; Sydoruk promises victims and their relatives to extend investigation until January; Voice of Beslan expresses pessimism that anything will change.
August 17, 2006	12 relatives block authorities' attempt to recreate Beslan rescue operation claiming that re-creation was part of larger cover-up.
August 28, 2006	Yuri Savelyev, explosives and firearms specialist (leading expert on the physics of combustion and explosions), former rector of Baltic State Technical University, Motherland faction Duma deputy, and member of Torshin's parliamentary commission investigation, releases his dissenting report, "Beslan: The Hostages' Truth"; claims that reliable information about terrorist attack in Beslan was available at least three hours before siege, two blasts that triggered fire in gymnasium were caused by grenades fired from outside, likely by Russian security forces, commandos fired machine guns, grenade throwers, and tanks while hostages were still being held, officials waited more than two hours to send firefighters into blazing school as hostages burned alive, and hostage takers numbered 60–68, or twice as many as official estimates, meaning that half escaped; Mothers of Beslan and Voice of Beslan voice support for Savelyev's report.

Date	Activity
Late August 2006	Newly appointed Deputy Prosecutor General Sydoruk conducts experiment with Voice of Beslan that showed that 32 or more terrorists plus explosives, grenade launchers, machine guns, and assault rifles could not possibly all have been transported in single relatively small GAZ-66 truck on extremely poor roads from Psedakha, Ingushetia, to Beslan as Kulayev testified in his trial and as official version of events maintained; they conclude that only some terrorists and only some weapons were in the truck; experiment lends support to claim of police officer Fatima Dudiyeva that some terrorists were already in school prior to siege and of Dr. Larisa Mamitova and other former hostages that number of terrorists was much larger than 32.
August 31, 2006	Human rights group applies to hold picket on September 3 to commemorate second anniversary of Beslan but is denied permission.
September 1, 2006	Voice of Beslan submits 200-page appeal to Russian Supreme Court as extension of their May 31 appeal and argues that verdict in Kulayev's trial is incompatible with testimony about reactions of authorities and that court never established who was in command, origin of earliest blasts, and heavy hardware used; if Supreme Court rejects the appeal, Voice of Beslan announces it will sue Russia in European Court of Human Rights.
Early September 2006	Mothers of Beslan ask Russian officials not to attend anniversary events, citing anger with authorities for hiding the truth.
September 3, 2006	At least 10 protesters are detained by Moscow police and special riot forces for unauthorized action; about 80 protesters remain near Lubyanskaya Square.
September 2, 2006	Authorities confiscate 100–300 printed copies of Savelyev's dissenting report, "Beslan: The Hostages' Truth," at Vladikavkaz airport that arrived from Moscow in a courier's bag.
September 15, 2006	Federation Council Speaker Sergei Mironov announces that Torshin commission will delay releasing its final report until end of year in order to refute Savelyev's claims.
September 21, 2006	Torshin announces that his commission will continue its work due to pressure from *Novaya Gazeta*, www.pravdabeslana. ru, and Savelyev; Torshin intends to carry out further expert analysis and refute Savelyev's claims; *Pravda Beslana* website publishes draft version of Torshin's report so people can later compare whether commission addressed Savelyev's findings.
October 7, 2006	Anna Politkovskaya, well-known journalist, book author, and specialist on Chechnya, is assassinated in Moscow.

Date	Activity
Mid-October 2006	Savelyev publishes seventh part of his report and claims that 56–78 terrorists took part and came in five vehicles (three cars and two GAZ-66 trucks).
December 22, 2006	Parliamentary commission report led by Torshin is presented to Federation Council and State Duma without circulating the 240-page document in advance and with only 15 minutes allotted for discussion; Duma votes 333–91 to accept report and consider commission's work complete.
December 26, 2006	Russia's Supreme Court denies the appeal submitted on May 31 (and extended on September 1) asking for a retrial of Kulayev and upholds his life sentence; Kesayeva and other survivors and victims' relatives score minor victories in being granted their request to add findings of Savelyev's alternative investigation to Kulayev's case file and in having a special ruling against Shepel for violations committed during his investigation, specifically his unlawful seeking of death penalty; they score minor defeats in having their request denied to bring Kulayev to courtroom or link to it via video and in seeing no real consequences for Shepel who has already been sent into retirement.
January 4, 2007	Ella Kesayeva tells radio station *Ekho Moskvy* that victims intend to demand proof from government agencies that Kulayev is still alive and to ask for meeting with him.
January 5, 2007	Spokesman from Federal Penal Service tells RIA-Novosti that Kulayev is alive in a remand center and has not yet moved to place where he will serve his life sentence.
January 18, 2007	101 victims sign open letter to North Ossetian Parliament requesting them to invite Savelyev to present his report in victims' presence; Parliament says they will consider hearing Savelyev's report after criminal investigation is complete.
February 5, 2007	Communist Duma deputy Yuri Ivanov issues statement against government's version of events and accuses Putin of ordering special security forces to fire grenades at school in effort to prevent rebel leader Aslan Maskhadov from negotiating with militants as planned and thus allowing Putin to save face.
February 27, 2007	Voice of Beslan members meet with Thomas Hammarberg, Council of Europe's Human Rights Commissioner, in unplanned meeting during Hammarberg's visit to Beslan.

Date	Activity
March 6, 2007	Voice of Beslan publishes statement demanding that Putin, Chaika, and Sydoruk press criminal charges against heads of security forces and other government officials who oversaw hostage release operation, including former head of North Ossetia's Federal Security Service Andreyev, head of the special operations center of Russian Federal Security Service Aleksei Tikhonov, and Dzasokhov; authors of statement claim to have new evidence to convince government of need for prosecution.
March 19, 2007	80 victims sign complaint filed by Voice of Beslan in Vladikavkaz at Leninsky District Court of North Ossetia-Alania about illegal actions or inaction of officials and violations of victims' rights to access to justice.
April 3, 2007	Leninsky District Court ruled that regional prosecutors acted illegally in refusing demand of victims' relatives to initiate criminal investigation into how officials such as Dzasokhov, Andreyev, and Tikhonov responded during crisis; through the ruling, court effectively orders local Prosecutor General's Office to begin appropriate investigation, but prosecutors appeal decision to North Ossetian Supreme Court.
May 2, 2007	Supreme Court of North Ossetia overturns April decision of Leninsky District Court; members of Mothers of Beslan and Voice of Beslan refuse to leave Supreme Court building in hopes of meeting court chairman and head judge Tamerlan Aguzarov and remain there overnight.
May 3, 2007	Judge Aguzarov meets with Mothers of Beslan and Voice of Beslan members, explains that reversal of Leninsky court ruling resulted from procedural violations, promises that there will be fair hearing into possible misconduct of officials overseeing Beslan siege operation, and says case will be sent back to lower court to consider the appeal; while pleased with meeting with Aguzarov, Kesayeva says, "We think there will always be a way to stall our pleas. . . . We think the prosecutor's office will not open a criminal case because it would require summoning high ranking officials to court as witnesses, and the prosecutor's office is acting in the interests of the Kremlin, which is not interested in digging into the Beslan tragedy."

Date	Activity
May 10, 2007	At court hearing for three Beslan police officers accused of negligence that allowed the school siege, amnesty becomes possibility when defendants petition to stop trial based on September 22, 2006, Duma decision, "On the Announcement of Amnesty Concerning the Persons Who Committed Crimes in the Process of Counterterrorist Operation in the South Federal District"; 30–40 members of Voice of Beslan and Mothers of Beslan attend the hearing but leave in protest, claiming that amnesty would be violation of their constitutional rights to justice and that amnesty is designed to shut mouths of law enforcement officers and avoid summoning high-ranking witnesses; Judge Vitaly Beselov adjourns court to speak with the different sides, and some Mothers of Beslan members angrily stay in courtroom until they are persuaded to leave after three hours; some Beslan mothers march in Vladikavkaz from Friendship Square to Public Prosecutor's Office holding signs reading, "The Beslan tragedy is beyond amnesty!"; "Terrorists' helpers are terrorists themselves"; and "The FSB and Ministry of Internal Affairs are responsible for the act of terror"; and lodging a complaint with Public Prosecutor of North Ossetia Herman Shtadler demanding that police officers first be declared guilty in court before amnesty can be considered.
May 12, 2007	Supreme Court of Kabardino-Balkaria in Nalchik holds preliminary hearing in trial of Malgobek (Ingushetia) police chief Mukhazhira Yevloyev and his deputy Akhmed Kotiyev for negligence in failing to prevent gathering of gangsters from Ingushetia and Chechnya in their territory, ultimately leading to school siege; Beslan victims had insisted that preliminary hearings be held in "neutral" Kabardino-Balkaria and here petition for trial to take place in North Ossetia due to difficulty of injured victims traveling to another republic and security issues in Ingushetia, but Judge Issa Gazdiyev rules to examine case at site of alleged crime, meaning Ingushetia and its Supreme Court, and to select jury from Ingushetia while still using physical space of Supreme Court of Kabardino-Balkaria; victims frustrated with decision to use jury from Ingushetia, which they believe makes "not guilty" verdict foregone conclusion.

Date	Activity
May 29, 2007	Three Beslan police officers accused of failing to stop militants from seizing the school are granted amnesty at Pravoberezhny Court in Beslan; approximately 50 victims gather at 10 a.m. in the courtroom and begin to shout, bang, and clap in opposition to proclaiming the decision without defendants being present and cause Judge Beselov to stop; judge resumes reading verdict at 4 p.m., but victim Elvira Tuaeva breaks through and tries to take file from judge's hands, causing him to leave room; approximately 25 women respond by smashing courtroom windows, overturning furniture, and tearing down blinds and Russian flag; judge pronounces verdict in empty room with only state prosecutor, secretary, bailiff, and two video cameras present.
May 29, 2007	Mothers of Beslan mark 1,000 days since siege with event at Beslan memorial cemetery called "1,000 Nights Without Children" and light candles on every grave and ask residents of North Ossetia to place candles in their windows.
May 30, 2007	Supreme Court of Kabardino-Balkaria finishes forming jury for trial of two Ingushetian police officers.
June 6, 2007	Victims' families file appeal with Supreme Court of North Ossetia against ruling in Pravoberezhny Court that granted amnesty to three accused Beslan police officers and argue that amnesty can be applied only to those found guilty of a crime, so defendants need to be questioned and court must provide assessment of evidence of their guilt.
June 6, 2007	Leninsky District Court upholds legality of prosecutor's office's decision to refuse victims' demands to initiate criminal proceedings against officials who oversaw Beslan hostage rescue operation, thereby overturning its initial verdict against prosecutors and instead following Supreme Court's May 2 ruling in favor of prosecutors.
June 9, 2007	Rita Techiyeva, Mziya Kochishvili, and Zalina Guburova, three Beslan mothers who were injured in siege and lost children and who participated in ransacking of Pravoberezhny Court on May 29, 2007, are charged under Article 20.1 of Code of Administrative Offenses of Russian Federation with "petty hooliganism"; court police officers who failed to keep order are also charged.

Date	Activity
Mid-June 2007	Pravda Beslana and media outlets report that on August 18, 2004, North Ossetian deputy interior minister Batrbek Dzutsev sent teletype messages to police chiefs throughout North Ossetia warning of gunmen moving from Chechnya and Ingushetia to North Ossetia, their plans to seize a civilian target and take hostages and demand federal troop withdrawal from Chechnya, the rebels' locations, the need to ensure that dirt roads between North Ossetia and Ingushetia were unsuitable for vehicles, and the need to close borders and increase security at schools on first day.
June 26, 2007	89 relatives of victims file 50-page joint complaint in European Court of Human Rights in Strasbourg accusing Russian government of failing to investigate properly and arguing that their rights to life, objective investigation, and efficient legal defense were violated.
June 27, 2007	Two Ingushetian police officers Yevloyev and Kotiyev are officially charged in Supreme Court of Kabardino-Balkaria with negligence and plead innocent.
July 13, 2007	Mothers of Beslan members meet with Kozak and Sydoruk in Nalchik at latter's initiation and with condition that no outsiders attend, especially radical Voice of Beslan members; meeting is dominated by familiar complaints, official silences, and general sense that there will never be thorough, objective investigation.
July 20, 2007	Mothers of Beslan activists Techiyeva, Kochishvili, and Guburova are fined 1,000 rubles each for ransacking Pravoberezhny Court on May 29, 2007, despite the fact that other mothers had also participated in incident; the three women become the only people besides Kulayev to be convicted of a crime related to the terrorist attack.
July 26, 2007	Mothers of Beslan release on their website new video sent anonymously to them by mail showing evidence contradicting official version of events, including weapons being fired from outside building and leading to initial explosions, army officers concluding that there was no explosion inside the building and that grenade launchers had been used, and children running from building before two loud blasts were heard from outside gymnasium; about 40 survivors watch showing of the video at Beslan's Palace of Culture.

Date	Activity
August 28, 2007	Judge Panaiotidi at Leninsky Court in Vladikavkaz rules that Voice of Beslan be terminated in its present composition, have its leaders changed to Ruslan Tebieva, Viktor Alikov, and Marina Melikova who were less critical of Kremlin, and then re-register; Ella Kesayeva says that Melikova had been kicked out of group 1½ years earlier for trying to disrupt group and now had forged signatures on documents allegedly showing that she was elected to head the group; Kesayeva says she had witnesses to back up these claims, but witnesses were not allowed to testify, and she believes that Melikova was being used by North Ossetian registration office to undermine Voice of Beslan; Novaya Gazeta points out that neither Tebieva, Alikov, nor Melikova had been involved in any of many prior petitions and activities of Voice of Beslan, casting further doubt on legitimacy of their leadership claims.
Late August 2007	Beslan mothers write to Putin, his wife, and Moscow government, demanding to know of Mrs. Putin why she as a mother had not visited Beslan or expressed sympathy for mothers of victims, and saying to Putin, "Two years have passed since our meeting with you. . . . Two years of useless waiting and illusions. We hoped that we would bring home to you the truth, of which perhaps you were not fully aware. But over time we realized how naïve we are."
September 1, 2007	Victim lawyer Taimuraz Chedzhemov pulls out of lawsuit to prosecute Russian officials for negligence after receiving death threat to his family.
September 1, 2007	Many Beslan mothers travel from North Ossetia to Moscow to demonstrate in city center on Remembrance Day but find center blocked off due to City Day activities and hold rally in Boltnaya Square instead, with a few hundred in attendance, including United Civic Front leader Garri Kasparov, Union of Right Forces leader Nikita Belykh, Moscow Helsinki Group chair Lyudmila Alekseyeva, and State Duma deputy and author of "Beslan: The Hostages Truth" Yuri Savelyev; after a moment of silence, Beslan mothers then speak out and make many accusations against government authorities.

Date	Activity
September 1, 2007	To mark third anniversary of tragedy, delegation led by Duma Speaker Boris Gryzlov visit Beslan along with Kozak, Duma security committee head Vladimir Vasilyev, and other officials; victims' relatives set up photo exhibit in school gym showing children shot and burned in siege and with messages underneath such as "The Federal Security Service and the Internal Affairs Ministry bear responsibility for terrorism"; "There is no forgiveness for the authorities who allowed Beslan"; and "President Putin! We demand an objective investigation into Beslan and punishment for all the guilty!"; but delegation officials do not look at photos or approach graves or look at stuffed animals and children's portraits when they visit Beslan's cemetery; delegation meets with Mothers of Beslan who ask why investigation had not found anything yet, why no punishments had been handed out, and why video evidence about storming operation on school by authorities was not accepted, and authorities answer evasively that investigation was continuing and that Mothers were free to appeal court decision granting amnesty to police officers.
September 3, 2007	Beslan mothers officially release documentary film that had already made its way to Internet and that they say proves that federal troops fired into school and greatly contributed to death toll; film includes Kulayev's testimony, holes in wall of the school, and voice of bomb expert explaining that holes could not have been caused by an explosive as official reports claim.
October 5, 2007	Police chief of Malgobek district interior agency Muzahir Yevloyev and his deputy Ahmed Kotiyev are acquitted of charges of dereliction of duty in allowing armed gang to set up camp and move unhampered over Malgobek district and cross into North Ossetia to seize school; Ingushetia's Supreme Court declares them not guilty on basis of jury decision that guilt of police had not been proved.
October 26, 2007	Some relatives of Beslan victims join crowd of several hundred on steps of Dubrovka theater in Moscow to commemorate 2002 terrorist attack.
October 26, 2007	Supreme Court rules that Kulayev's life sentence is lawful, rejecting applications to review sentence filed by Voice of Beslan and Kulayev.
November 1, 2007	Victims file claim against Ministry of Internal Affairs with Leninsky Court of Republic of North Ossetia-Alania, Vladikavkaz, seeking compensation for damages caused by terrorist act.

Date	Activity
Late November 2007	Some Beslan mothers participate in election campaign against Putin's party, United Russia, linking it with school tragedy, hanging street signs that say "Putin's course" with arrows pointing to school (a play on first syllable of Putin's name, which means "course" in Russian), and reminding voters that Putin refused to negotiate with terrorists to save Beslan's children, failed to carry out fair investigation, and failed to keep promise to Beslan mothers to punish defenders; although some say they will vote for United Russia due to fears of losing jobs, getting poor grades, or uncertainties of a new government, many plan to vote for Savelyev's Patriots of Russia Party because Savelyev is the only Duma deputy to conduct independent investigation.
November 28, 2007	Court date set in Beslan district court for case against Ella Kesayeva, who is charged with "arbitrary behavior and improper use of roadside areas" (articles 19.1 and 11.21 of the Code of Administrative Violations) for putting up "Putin's course" street signs, but judge defers hearing indefinitely after more than 50 people arrive to support Kesayeva.
November 30, 2007	To protest upcoming December 2, 2007, elections, Mothers of Beslan hang sign outside their office stating that Mothers would not forgive authorities for tragedy and placed framed pictures of burned bodies and human remains.
December 2, 2007	Mothers of Beslan explicitly decide not to protest on election day to avoid interpretation of their actions as political, when their goal is for nobody to forget what happened three years ago in Beslan.
December 19, 2007	Supreme Court of North Ossetia orders Voice of Beslan to disband, upholding lower court ruling that Kesayeva was not group's leader and prohibiting Voice of Beslan to change its status from North Ossetian organization to Russian organization to get around court decision.
December 20, 2007	Kesayeva and three other Voice of Beslan members begin hunger strike and picket outside North Ossetian Supreme Court to protest 19 December decision and make their voices heard; they also send appeal to Supreme Court of North Ossetia.
January 5, 2008	Kesayeva tells *Ekho Moskvy* radio that Voice of Beslan intended to file appeal to Prosecutor General's Office calling for removal of investigator Aleksandr Solzhenitsyn for impeding investigation into school siege by not reacting to complaints, questioning hostages, or generally looking to make progress.

Date	Activity
January 2008	Voice of Beslan is charged by Nazran Prosecutor's Office with "extremism" over their November 2005 appeals to European Parliament and United States, which allegedly slander Putin by calling him "accomplice of terrorism" and saying he bears responsibility for botched rescue and deaths.
January 11, 2008	Voice of Beslan members send appeal to Putin requesting that authorities stop pressuring group and labeling their statements extremist.
January 13, 2008	Voice of Beslan sends telegram to Nazran court saying they will not attend trial without an independent expert assessing charges.
January 15, 2008	Voice of Beslan requests that hearing of case be moved from Nazran to Vladikavkaz, and court grants request, as well as the petition for expert review to examine appeal and determine whether Voice of Beslan statements were extremist, while denying their request to dismiss case.
January 24, 2008	Supreme Court of North Ossetia rules that Pravoberezhny District Court in Beslan must hear claim filed in November 2007 by Voice of Beslan activists and 60 parents of Beslan victims demanding that "the government pay all parents who lost children monthly pensions to compensate for the loss of potential breadwinners and the resultant inability to provide for themselves."
January 30, 2008	Voice of Beslan receives reply from Putin to their letter asking to end extremism proceedings, with Putin saying that this was not within his power and forwarding the letter to Russian Prosecutor General's office who also thinks this is not within his power; Kesayeva says, "All our illusions ended today"; Voice of Beslan also receives letter from Sydoruk saying he cannot solve issues related to legal actions of Nazran's prosecutor.
February 7, 2008	Ella Kesayeva and other Voice of Beslan members appear in Pravoberezhny District Court; Voice of Beslan forced officially to change name to Voice of Beslan All-Russian Public Organization of Terror Act Victims; members express dissatisfaction with Judge Zaurbek Tavitov's decisions, and organization does not re-register under new name; another group registered under Marina Melikova uses original Voice of Beslan name, making her the technical defendant in lawsuit against Voice of Beslan for organization's alleged extremist statements in November 2005 appeals, despite that she did not author or sign these appeals; activists of unregistered organization who in fact authored and signed appeals are not admitted to subsequent hearings.

Date	Activity
February 8, 2008	Investigator of Office of the Federal Bailiff Service (UFSSP) appears at home of Voice of Beslan chair Emma Tagayeva-Betrozova, which also serves as VOB office, and tells Ella Kesayeva to write explanatory note about supposed beating that she and other VOB members gave to seven bailiffs and judge.
February 11, 2008	Ella Kesayeva, Svetlana Margiyeva, and Emilia Bzarova summoned to appear in Office of Federal Bailiff Service in Vladikavkaz; women accused of assaulting seven officers and Judge Tavitov; Kesayeva charged with violating Articles 115 (deliberately inflicting minor bodily harm), 116 (beatings), 129 (slander), and 130 (insult) of Russia's Criminal Code.
February 15, 2008	Criminal case opened against Voice of Beslan members Kesayeva, Margiyeva, and Bzarova; Kesayeva says source of accusations is unclear, submits written denial of accusations, and is told by inspector of Investigatory Committee at Beslan City Prosecutor's Office Aslan Badtiev that case is forejudged; accuser later revealed to be Melikova, who fraudulently took over original Voice of Beslan.
February 16, 2008	Dozens of people participate in unauthorized rally in Beslan in response to criminal proceedings initiated against Voice of Beslan members and to show their support; Kesayeva says case was fabricated, created out of nothing.
February 18, 2008	Approximately 60 female Voice of Beslan members protest outside police headquarters/prosecutor's office, expressing their anger with criminal proceedings launched previous week.
March 6, 2008	Russia's Supreme Court dismisses appeal from over 200 victims and separate appeal filed by prosecutors and upholds not guilty verdict for Ingushetian police officers Yevloyev and Kotiyev; victims claim verdict was biased and unlawful because jury included defendants' relatives.
March 13, 2008	Extremism charges against Voice of Beslan are heard in Beslan court with absence of Ella Kesayeva and presence of members of new "official" Voice of Beslan who are more sympathetic to Kremlin and did not actually write letter that is considered in court.
March 30–31, 2008	Pravoberezhny District Court hears administrative cases against Kesayeva, Margiyeva, and Bzarova; Court closes administrative cases for lack of evidence but keeps open Kesayeva's criminal case that charges her with deliberate light bodily harm, assault, slander, and insult.

Date	Activity
April 7, 2008	Pravoberezhny District Court closes criminal case against Kesayeva; according to Voice of Beslan, many victims were ready to point out false medical examinations of main prosecutorial witness K. F. Tekhov in relation to hostages' causes of death; demand to summon Tekhov to court leads prosecution to ask for amicable settlement; Kesayeva agrees, as does Melikova, who would have faced counter lawsuits for libel and insult by Kesayeva and Voice of Beslan.
April 10, 2008	Deputy Prosecutor of North Ossetia appeals March 31 ruling against Kesayeva, Martiyeva, and Bzarova.
April 24, 2008	Pravoberezhny District Court upholds its original decision to close the administrative cases against Kesayeva, Margiyeva, and Bzarova.
May 2008	New president Medvedev appoints former prosecutor general Vladimir Ustinov as his representative in Southern Federal District, much to dismay of Beslan victims who believe that Ustinov was one of authorities who failed them by conveying misinformation to Putin.
May 4, 2008	Russian deputy prosecutor general Sydoruk submits supervisory petition to Russian Supreme Court asking to set aside acquittal of two Ingushetian police officers, Yevloyev and Kotiev, and claiming that victims' rights had been denied in first trial and their arguments ignored in appeal.
May 22, 2008	Pravoberezhny District Court orders victims' civil case against Ministry of Internal Affairs to be transferred to Leninsky District Court.
June 4, 2008	Voice of Beslan files criminal charges against Putin for violations of 11 articles of the Russian Criminal Code including negligence, intended bodily harm, dereliction of duty, and murder, arguing that, according to federal law on defense, president must have given order for armed forces to be used for something other than their intended purpose.
June 30, 2008	Kesayeva is elected one of five co-chairs of fifth All-Russian Civic Conference.
July 7, 2008	Self-proclaimed healer Grabovoi is found guilty of fraud and sentenced to 11 years in prison.
September 1–3, 2008	Victims and relatives commemorate siege anniversary with three-day mourning period including poetry reading, moment of silence, reading of victims' names, requiem and concert, and releasing of 334 white balloons; more than 2,000 people appear in front of school by 1 p.m. on September 3; off to the side, Voice of Beslan conducts signature campaign calling for international investigation.

Date	Activity
September 3, 2008	Hundreds gather around Moscow to commemorate Beslan siege; approximately 100 attend rally organized by Garry Kasparov's oppositional Other Russia party, some with signs saying "We need the truth!" and "No more lies! No more blood! No More Putin."
September 26, 2008	Leninsky District Court orders victims' civil case against Ministry of Internal Affairs to be transferred to Zamoskvoretskii District Court of Moscow near the Ministry.
October 21, 2008	North Ossetia Supreme Court, following appeal by victims, quashes ruling by Zamoskvoretskii District Court and remits victims' civil case against Ministry of Internal Affairs to Leninsky District Court.
December 10, 2008	Leninsky Court dismisses victims' civil action against Ministry of Internal Affairs, claiming that Suppression of Terrorism Act does not provide for compensation for non-pecuniary damage by State body participating in counter-terrorism operation.
December 17, 2008	Victims file cassation appeal with Supreme Court of Republic of North Ossetia-Alania against December 10, 2008, decision of Leninsky Court.
February 24, 2009	North Ossetia Supreme Court rejects appeal by victims against December 2008 Leninsky Court decision; subsequent attempts by victims to obtain supervisory review of these decisions fail.
Early April 2009	Approximately 30 parents of children who survived the siege receive notice that they must pay taxes and penalties in range of 20,000–70,000 rubles per family on money they allegedly paid for their children to attend boarding school in Korallovo, Moscow Province, intended for orphans and children of parents affected by catastrophic events and educating these Beslan children free of charge; family members are mostly unemployed and unable to pay, despite threats that tax authorities could take them to court and place liens on their properties, so they contact Beslan tax authorities many times who say it is not their doing but Moscow's; Kesayeva speculates that these actions resulted from school's funding by former Yukos CEO Mikhail Khodorkovsky and Voice of Beslan's recent labeling of Putin as "abettor to terrorists" in 2008 published statement and their subsequently being accused of extremism.

Date	Activity
August 9, 2009	Voice of Beslan members try to meet with Medvedev in Vladikavkaz, where he is visiting to commemorate the anniversary of the 2008 war in South Ossetia and hope to discuss how they continue to be affected on daily basis by tragedy and complain about poor handling of investigation; women go around tightly cordoned off 58th Army headquarters and try to deliver letter to Medvedev requesting meeting but are asked for passports, threatened with use of firearms, blocked from walking, have their posters torn and arms grabbed, and are left in tears as they drive out of Vladikavkaz, only to be stopped by road police inspectors and chief of section for countering extremism who writes down details of driver.
August 15, 2009	Voice of Beslan writes letter to Medvedev pointing out that they tried to meet with him on August 9 and asking for meaningful negotiations and compliance with constitution.
August 18, 2009	Voice of Beslan writes letter to North Ossetian Parliament asking that they appeal to Medvedev to pass federal law on victims of terrorist acts.
September 1, 2009	People gather to commemorate fifth anniversary of attack, including round-the-clock vigil, photo display of victims on gym walls, and visits to school and nearby cemetery.
September 1, 2009	Mothers of Beslan send statement to Medvedev pointing out that investigation has been extended 31 times, political considerations have become primary, and members of the crisis task force have not been held accountable for lies and incompetence and even got promotions after siege; Mothers of Beslan activist Aneta Gadiyeva points out need for ongoing medical or psychological assistance for children and insists that government pass law defining status of victims of terrorists acts in place of currently humiliating process of needing repeated extensions of their disability status.
September 2, 2009	Mothers of Beslan lodge three complaints with European Court of Human Rights accusing local authorities of violating hostages' rights to live and have case investigated completely and objectively, and specifically accusing former North Ossetian interior minister Dzantiyev of failing to take proper security measures before attack despite warnings and Malgobek police department heads of negligence in allowing terror group to form in forest under their control.

Date	Activity
September 3, 2009	Over 5,000 people attend service in Beslan to remember those who were killed, hold moment of silence, release 335 balloons, one for each of the dead, and then move to cemetery where names of the dead are read aloud.
September 28, 2009	Three Voice of Beslan members meet with deputy plenipotentiary presidential envoy for the Southern Federal District, Nikolai Fedoryak, about investigation, law on victims of terror, rehabilitation for victims, and other federal issues.
October 15, 2009	Pravoberezhny Court of Beslan bans text of Voice of Beslan's November 30, 2005, appeal to European Union, European Parliament, U.S. president, and Congress, "To all who sympathize with the victims of Beslan terrorist attack" as "extremist" under Suppression of Extremism Act; puts appeal on federal list of extremist material, making it an offense to disseminate by any means; banning does not receive much publicity.
November 18, 2009	Kesayeva announces creation of new public movement called "For the Status of Victims of Acts of Terrorism" to push for law guaranteeing social support for victims of terrorism who often need continuous rehabilitation, psychological services, or medical treatment; Federation Council previously discussed need for the law, and North Ossetian senator Aleksandr Dzasokhov asked for working group between Federation Council and Duma to draft legislation.
April 22, 2010	October 2009 banning of Voice of Beslan's appeal as "extremist" becomes more widely known when text is included into new version of Federal List of Extremist Materials on Ministry of Justice website.
May 21, 2010	Convicted "healer" Grabovoi is released from jail on parole.
August 31, 2010	Delegation of approximately 60 Alfa and Vympel members (special operations counterterrorist and counter-sabotage units who suffered casualties at the school) fly into Beslan to make quick trip to school and cemetery, as they have every year on anniversary of siege, with apparently no contact with civilian victims who are unaware of this tradition.
September 1–3, 2010	Usual memorial events take place for sixth anniversary of siege, only with fewer and fewer participants; Mamsurov speaks; South Ossetian president Kokoity visits for events, but his motorcade blocks highway and interferes with others driving to cemetery.

Date	Activity
September 1–3, 2010	Delegation of European Parliament members headed by Heidi Hautala arrive at invitation of Voice of Beslan's Kesayeva and first meet with deputy speaker of North Ossetian Parliament Kesayev who seems to be rewriting his well-known report of local parliamentary investigative commission, telling Hautala that there is no need for an international inquiry and bypassing critical issues in his report; European Parliament deputies then eat at Ella Kesayeva's house.
September 1–3, 2010	Voice of Beslan sends another request to Medvedev for meeting about investigation and adoption of law to support terror victims.
September 5, 2010	Voice of Beslan members and other victims protest in Vladikavkaz, angry at not receiving expression of sympathy from president on anniversary of attack and demanding objective investigation and law on status of terrorist victims.
September 12, 2010	Approximately 250 people, including some Mothers of Beslan, participate in unauthorized protest near house of government in Vladikavkaz three days after suicide car bombing killed 17 people in Vladikavkaz marketplace, demanding meeting with President Mamsurov to answer how car with 40 kilograms of explosives could drive undetected from Ingushetia to North Ossetia.
September 13, 2010	Voice of Belsan members, along with other public figures and Dagestan's Mothers for Human Rights, sign statement expressing solidarity with Memorial Human Rights Center director Oleg Orlov, who faces trial for allegedly slandering Chechen president Ramzan Kadyrov when he said Kadyrov could have been linked to murder of one of his center's employees in Grozny.
September 15, 2010	Approximately 1,000 rally in central square in Vladikavkaz to protest against terrorist acts and demand increased security measures; Mothers of Beslan activist Marina Pak addresses group and expresses displeasure that many young people were deterred from participating due to warnings from their educational institutions and that extra class time was intentionally added to their schedules.
November 13, 2010	Approximately 60 people participate in picket organized by Voice of Beslan in center of Vladikavkaz to demand investigation of all terrorist attacks in North Ossetia and adoption of law on status of terror victims that would allow victims to receive assistance from the state.

Date	Activity
December 15–30, 2010	Kesayeva and three other Voice of Beslan members receive decision from Beslan judge that they have violated Administrative Legal Code and Penal Code and are threatened with detention and meet investigators at bailiff's office.
January 25, 2011	Voice of Beslan, Nord-Ost organization, and Volga-Don organization co-sign statement calling for speedy adoption of law to protect status of victims of terror.
February 19, 2011	Voice of Beslan and other organizations hold anti-terrorism rally in Vladikavkaz; participants sign petition to Medvedev to comply with constitution and investigate terrorism objectively.
February 22, 2011	Elvira Tuayeva and Mziya Kokoity meet unexpectedly with Medvedev who arrives at Beslan airport unannounced, heads to the City of Angels cemetery, lays flowers at Tree of Sorrow memorial, and then responds to them when they call out to him; Medvedev claims not to have received a single one of their messages, promises to organize a meeting with mothers through North Ossetian leadership, and later mentions Beslan a few times in his speech in Vladikavkaz; women plead for objective investigation.
March 25, 2011	117 victims sign an appeal sent to Medvedev to comply with the constitution and investigate terrorist acts objectively; appeal explains Voice of Beslan's contributions to defense of victims' interest and reminds Medvedev of promise to meet.
March 31, 2011	Voice of Beslan members hold authorized picket in Vladikavkaz, get approached by police who try to detain them, but members get on tram and go home; 34 picketers send signed statement to Medvedev, Khloponin, and Mamsurov to help resolve victims' problems.
May 5, 2011	Mothers of Beslan members Susanna Dudiyeva and Elvira Tuayeva fly to Moscow for promised meeting with Medvedev, but Medvedev cancels at last minute; Voice of Beslan members not invited; journalists and others speculate about difficult public relations for Medvedev in meeting with victims, especially those strongly critical of Putin.
May 8, 2011	250+ victims meet in school courtyard, convened by Voice of Beslan, and sign appeal to Medvedev about adoption of law on status of victims of terror and provision of social assistance to victims.
May 10, 2011	Appeal to Medvedev, signed by 258 victims who attended school courtyard meeting, is sent and posted on Voice of Beslan website.

Date	Activity
May 16, 2011	Five Voice of Beslan members meet in Vladikavkaz with Thomas Hammarberg, Council of Europe's commissioner for human rights, to discuss dissatisfaction with investigation and combating terrorism.
June 1, 2011	Dudiyeva and Tuayeva meet for 1½ hours with Medvedev, who promises to reinvigorate investigation and consider victims' proposals on law on status of victims of terror acts and provision of social assistance to victims.
March 2, 2012	Ella Kesayeva and other Voice of Beslan members denied request to serve as poll observers during presidential election.
April 2012	European Court of Human Rights accepts complaints filed by Beslan victims (officially 447 petitioners), noting its recent consideration of the Nord-Ost case and award of unprecedented 1.3 million euros to those 64 applicants; ECHR sends questions to Russian government with answers due in 2–3 months.
November 2012	Russian government still has not responded to ECHR; North Ossetian news website reports that victims accuse Russian government of dragging its feet.
December 18, 2012	Beslan residents gather in school gymnasium to light candles in memory of victims of school shooting in Newtown, Connecticut.
June 25, 2013	European Court of Human Rights holds hearing on admissibility and merits and invites parties to respond in writing to list of questions.
September 2, 2013	North Ossetian State University holds conference on "Children, Victims of Terror in Recent History," organized by Russian Jewish Congress and Holocaust Foundation, with goal of including Beslan events in school curriculum.
September 4, 2013	Mothers of Beslan send open letter to U.S. president Barack Obama, urging him not to use force in Syria.
September–October 2013	Russian government and victims respond to questions of European Court of Human Rights.
October 24, 2013	Leaders of Voice of Beslan, Ella Kesayeva, and Mothers of Beslan, Aneta Gadiyeva, urge Duma to consider bill on improving social support for victims of terror.
February 2014	Susanna Dudiyeva interviewed in school gymnasium about security concerns at Sochi Olympics.

Date	Activity
September 1–3, 2014	Tenth anniversary is commemorated with tradition of families sleeping in school gym on hard benches, 334 candles laid on ground near school, 334 white balloons released into sky, bell ringing twice at 1:05 p.m. to mark time of explosions, and procession to City of Angels cemetery for another memorial event.
Early September 2014	Hearing scheduled for European Court of Human Rights to hear comments on *Tagayeva and Others v. Russia*.
October 14, 2014	ECHR public hearing held in Human Rights Building in Strasbourg.
June 5, 2015	North Ossetian president Mamsurov replaced by former North Ossetian Supreme Court chairman Tamerlan Aguzarov, who presided over Kulayev trial to victims' dissatisfaction and had been serving as Duma deputy; Aguzarov serves only months before dying on February 19, 2016.
July 2, 2015	ECHR declares victims' complaints admissible
September 1, 2016	Six Voice of Beslan members arrested after wearing T-shirts stating "Putin—Beslan executioner" at commemorative service for victims.
September 2, 2016	Pravoberezhny District Court finds six Voice of Beslan members guilty of administrative offense and sentences them to either 20 hours of labor or €260 fine.
October 20, 2016	On appeal, Pravoberezhny District Court reclassifies Ella Kesayeva's administrative offense to lesser violation of "established procedure of public action" with €150 fine instead of 20 hours of labor.
April 13, 2017	Thirteen years after the violence, victims win case; ECHR orders Russia to pay unprecedented €2,955,000 in damages to 409 victims and €88,000 in legal costs and validates victims' claims that Russian state failed in planning and control of rescue operation, minimizing recourse to lethal force, and conducting effective and independent investigation.
September 2017	After appealing ruling, Russia agrees to comply.
March 28, 2018	Kaspolat Ramonov, caretaker for City of Angels memorial in Beslan, posts on Facebook that City of Angels has not received financial support from government in two years, memorial's accounts have been frozen, and he is using his own resources to pay workers, keep grounds clean, and restore monuments.

Date	Activity
July 29, 2018	*Pravda Beslana* forced to remove text of Basayev's note from site by Federal Service for Supervision of Communications, Information Technology, and Mass Media (Roskomnadzor); note was handed to former Ingushetia president Ruslan Aushev during hostage taking and contained list of demands; Roskomnadzor considers note extremist, whereas maintainers of *Pravda Beslana* consider it public historical document because it was read aloud in open trial.
December 6, 2018	Presidential envoy to North Caucasus Federal District Alexander Matovnikov admits (for first time by official) that storming of school in Beslan was planned by authorities in advance and that school was fired upon by tank but still maintains there were no live hostages in building by then.
September 1, 2019	Memorial service held for 15th anniversary of school hostage taking.
September 1, 2019	Mothers of Beslan hold press conference with victims of terrorist attacks in Moscow, St. Petersburg, Volgodonsk, Dagestan, and Kabardino-Balkaria and sign agreement to unite in All-Russian Association of Victims of Terrorist Attacks and lobby for law on status of victims of terrorist attacks; Mothers of Beslan appeal to presidential envoy Matovnikov to take personal control of investigation of terrorist attack.
September 2, 2019	Video blogger Yuri Dud publishes three-hour documentary about hostage taking; by end of 2020 has over 22 million views and 129,000 comments.
September 2019	Russian Justice Ministry claims that all but one victim has received ECHR-awarded payout.
April 24, 2020	President Putin signs law marking end of World War II on September 3, a day later than most other countries and overlapping with Day of Solidarity in Fight against Terrorism to honor victims of Beslan hostage taking; victims object to forgetting school tragedy and plan to appeal.

Note: Given the unprecedented extensive activism of Beslan victims after the hostage taking, this chronology undoubtedly omits activities and events but captures the most notable.

Survey and Focus Group Methodologies

This study is based on findings from (1) a survey of 1,098 victims of the 2004 siege on School No. 1 in Beslan, North Ossetia, (2) a survey of 1,023 nonvictim residents of Beslan and 1,020 nonvictim residents of the North Ossetian capital of Vladikavkaz, and (3) six focus groups of activist and nonactivist Beslan victims. Survey and focus group methodologies were designed by Debra Javeline and Vanessa Baird and implemented by the Institute for Comparative Social Research (CESSI) under the leadership of CESSI's Director of Social Research, Dr. Anna Andreenkova.

Beslan Victim Survey ($N = 1,098$)

A questionnaire for Beslan victims was drafted based on a prior survey instrument for victims of the 2002 Moscow theater hostage taking (Javeline and Baird 2007). Two workshops were then conducted to review and refine the questionnaire with political science faculty and graduate students at the University of Colorado and the University of Notre Dame. The questionnaire was pretested on residents of North Ossetia in order to get feedback from respondents who were similar to the target population, and it was revised accordingly. The victim survey was then conducted with approval from Notre Dame's Institutional Review Board. (English translation of the victim questionnaire available on request.)

Information on the victim survey population and sample can be found in the Introduction.

Survey Administration

Face-to-face interviews were conducted in respondents' homes in May, June, July, and August 2007 (213, 649, 163, and 73 respondents, respectively). Thirty-nine interviewers participated in the survey, with an average of twenty-eight interviews per interviewer. All interviewers were female; most were between thirty and forty-nine years old, with four interviewers in their twenties and two in their fifties; and most were ethnic Ossetians with a few Russians and Ukrainians.

Interviewers were Beslan residents who underwent extensive training sessions conducted by CESSI's Moscow field supervisor, Inna Chuslyaeva, and two field managers from Vladikavkaz. The initial two-day training session consisted of general rules of conducting interviews, ethical considerations, language issues, line-by-line review of the Beslan victim questionnaire, field manager demonstration of interviews, and mock interviews among the interviewer trainees. After careful observation of two interviews with real (but nonvictim) respondents, Chuslyaeva selected those interviewers most competent to work on this project. Chuslyaeva also worked directly with interviewers for two weeks in May–June and another two weeks in July–August. For quality control, a Beslan field manager reviewed each completed questionnaire for thoroughness and problems, and the field manager personally visited at least 10 percent of each interviewer's respondents to verify the authenticity of the completed questionnaires. Of the 1,098 respondents, 174 were subject to quality control by a follow-up visit from a manager. Quality control also included visual checks of all questionnaires by three field managers in Moscow, manual checking of missing data and the logic of the questionnaire by the supervisor of CESSI's Data Coding Group, Marina Stulova, and checking the logic of the data during the data-cleaning stage by Anna Medvedeva.

Locating respondents was relatively easy, since the vast majority of targeted respondents continue to live compactly in the small city of Beslan with its tight-knit community. The high willingness to participate could be attributed to three factors. First, respondents appeared comfortable with their local, Beslan-based interviewers who seemed to inspire greater trust than strangers, even those coming from the nearby Ossetian capital of Vladikavkaz. Second, respondents were offered a food pack of coffee, tea, and other products as incentive to participate. The food pack represented a familiarity with the Ossetian cultural tradition of guests bringing gifts to a host's home and also met a true need for people with scarce resources. Third, time had elapsed between the tragedy and the interviews, making it easier for victims to talk and sometimes even glad to keep the memory of the tragedy alive.

Challenges for this survey involved the length of interview time (96 minutes on average), formal nature of the standardized interview, and difficulty understanding some response scales, which pushed the attention limits of some respondents. Also, although the elapsed time since the tragedy made discussion easier relative to 2004, discussion of the event was still painful for many respondents, some of whom cried during the interview. Although it is possible that the above challenges affected the data, the effects were probably random and did not systematically bias conclusions.

Translation

Survey questions were written in English by Javeline and Baird in consultation with CESSI. The questions were translated into Russian and Ossetian, and respondents were offered the choice of whichever language they preferred. The vast majority of interviewers were bilingual.

The Russian translation was prepared by CESSI and checked by Javeline. Since bilingual English and Ossetian translators are rare, and since functional equivalency between Russian and Ossetian questionnaires was the paramount concern, the Russian translation was then used as the source questionnaire to translate to Ossetian. Two translators translated the survey independently (one based in North Ossetia, and the other in Moscow), and CESSI's translation team compared the translations and noted the differences. CESSI then conducted three joint sessions of the original Moscow-based translator, the original Ossetia-based translator via telephone, a third professional translator uninvolved in the original translation, and CESSI's translation team, with each session lasting four hours. CESSI prepared a final Ossetian-language version of the questionnaire and sent to the three translators for final review. In the end, 814 (74 percent) victim respondents completed the survey in Russian, and 284 (26 percent) completed the survey in Ossetian. Although offering the option to interview in Ossetian may have been unnecessary from a linguistic perspective, the offer signified respect to prospective respondents and may have consequently encouraged participation, even among some who chose to interview in Russian.

Data Processing and Weighting

The data were coded and entered into SPSS by CESSI's data-processing group (consisting of the data-coding and data-entry subgroups). Twenty percent of the work of each data-entry person was also entered by another data-entry person for double checking. The final data cleaning and data processing were done in SPSS Win 11. All questions were checked for correct values, skip patterns, logical flow, and other common concerns.

Nonvictim Survey in Beslan ($N = 1{,}023$) and Vladikavkaz ($N = 1{,}020$)

A questionnaire specifically tailored to nonvictim residents of Beslan and Vladikavkaz was drafted based on the victim survey instrument. Questions that were irrelevant to nonvictims, such as information about injuries sustained during the hostage taking, were deleted; names of political officials were updated (for example, President Putin was replaced by President Medvedev), and adjustments were made for the passage of time by substituting "four years since the hostage-taking" for "two years." (English translation of the nonvictim questionnaire available on request.)

Information on the nonvictim survey populations and samples can be found in the introduction.

Survey Sampling

Given its small size and lack of administrative divisions, Beslan required no stratification as part of the sampling procedure. Vladikavkaz, however, was divided into five strata based on its administrative divisions (city *rayoni*). The number of interviews assigned to each stratum was proportionate to the population in that stratum.

Primary sampling units (PSUs) and sampling points were electoral districts. PSUs were selected by the method of probability proportionate to size. In total, 100 electoral districts were selected within each city.

Households in each district were selected by an area sample approach of targeting the Nth household in each district for a target sample of 15–16 respondents in each of the 100 electoral districts in Beslan and 16–17 respondents in each of the 100 electoral districts in Vladikavkaz and an anticipated 64 and 60 percent response rate, respectively, in order to achieve approximately 10 interviews per district. Four field managers in Beslan and six field managers in Vladikavkaz selected the households (residential addresses) using a random route approach, compiled the lists, and then provided them to interviewers. Individuals within households were selected randomly based on the most recent birthday. No substitutions of households or individuals were allowed. All members of the household who were 18 years or older were listed, and the individual with the most recent birthday was selected. To maximize the chance that the selected individual would participate, at least three call-backs were attempted on different days of the week and different times of the day.

Survey Administration

Face-to-face interviews were conducted in respondent homes in December 2008, and January 2009 (837 and 186, respectively, in Beslan; 736 and 284, respectively, in Vladikavkaz). One hundred interviewers participated in the surveys, with an average of 20 interviews per interviewer; 97 interviewers were female, and 3 were male; 46 were 18–25 years old, 19 were 26–35 years old, 30 were 36–50 years old, and 5 were over 50; and most (92) were ethnic Ossetians, with six Russians, one Georgian, and one Kabardinian.

As with the victim survey, interviewers participated in extensive training sessions conducted by CESSI's Moscow field supervisor, Inna Chuslyaeva, and two field managers, one from Beslan and one from Vladikavkaz. Training for Beslan interviewers was conducted in Beslan; training for Vladikavkaz interviewers was conducted in Vladikavkaz. The substance of the training sessions was similar to the victim survey training sessions, as were the requirements for interviewers to participate in the actual survey.

Quality-control procedures were also similar to the victim survey. A field manager selected at random at least 10 percent of each interviewer's respondents to verify the authenticity of the completed questionnaires. Of the 2,043 respondents, 586 were subject to quality control by a follow-up visit (236 respondents) or follow-up phone call (350 respondents). Unfortunately, the quality control led to the dismissal of seven interviewers during the nonvictim surveys, mostly for violations of the selection procedure (finding no one at home at the designated household and making unauthorized substitutions of the household next door) and occasionally for violation of the interview method (leaving the questionnaire for self-completion rather than face-to-face interview). None of the work of dismissed interviewers was included in the final data set, and the interviewers were replaced. Quality control also included visual checks of all questionnaires by three field managers in Moscow, manual checking of missing data and the logic of the questionnaire by the supervisor of CESSI's Data Coding Group, Marina Stulova, and checking the logic of the data during the data-cleaning stage by Anna Medvedeva.

Translation

Since the vast majority of questions for nonvictims were taken from the victim survey, the translated questions were almost all readily available. For the few instances where a new question was introduced, the same procedure was used of multiple Russian-Ossetian independent translators, who then met in joint sessions to discuss and resolve areas of disagreement.

Data Processing and Weighting

The data were coded and entered into SPSS by CESSI's data-processing group (consisting of the data-coding and data-entry subgroups). Twenty percent of the work

Table B.1. Age, Gender, and Education: Nonvictim Survey and Census Comparisons

	Beslan				Vladikavkaz			
	Survey (%)		Census (%)		Survey (%)		Census (%)	
Age	Male	Female	Male	Female	Male	Female	Male	Female
18–29	10	10	11	12	11	11	14	13
30–44	15	19	14	16	14	18	13	16
45–54	9	11	7	8	9	9	7	9
55–64	6	8	5	7	8	8	6	7
65+	5	7	7	12	5	7	6	10
Education								
Secondary and lower	48		53		43		39	
Special technical	32		26		31		27	
Incomplete higher	3		4		5		6	
Higher	17		17		21		28	

of each data-entry person was also entered by another data-entry person for double checking. The final data cleaning and data processing were done in SPSS Win 11. All questions were checked for correct values, skip patterns, logical flow, and other common concerns.

The resulting sample closely resembles the demographic profile of the Beslan and Vladikavkaz populations, according to the 2002 Census (Table B.1). Nevertheless, it could be argued that the sample slightly overrepresents middle-aged residents while underrepresenting those under 30 and over 64 years of age and that there are some differences between the populations and samples in education distribution, such as the underrepresentation of college-educated individuals in Vladikavkaz. To ensure that the resulting data represent the populations, the data were weighted by age, gender, and education for each city according to the recent census information.

Difficulties Comparing Victim and Nonvictim Surveys

A year and a half elapsed between the time the victim and nonvictim surveys were conducted, largely due to funding issues. Several events occurred during the interval between surveys that should urge caution about drawing comparisons across surveys.

First, attitudes toward the Russian government were probably influenced by Russia's military actions in South Ossetia in August–September 2008, on behalf of South Ossetians against Georgians. North Ossetians likely interpreted Russian's actions as supportive of their people and thus looked upon the Russian government with greater appreciation and favor than two years earlier. The increased favorability may have made many North Ossetians more forgiving of the perceived past mistakes and misbehavior of the Russian government in Beslan and elsewhere in North Ossetia, and likely influenced responses to related questions in the nonvictim survey.

Second, since the victim survey, the Russian economy performed relatively well, leading on average to a higher standard of living, increased income and state pensions, and decreased unemployment. Then in October 2008, Russia's economic crisis began and lasted through the fieldwork period of the nonvictim surveys. While these events are important, it is difficult to hypothesize how they may have influenced survey responses and whether the upward economic trend or the sudden crisis was more influential. At the very least, caution should be exercised when using the household income variable in analysis, and income should not be compared across surveys.

Third, Dmitry Medvedev was elected president in March 2004, to succeed Vladimir Putin, who himself became prime minister and official leader of the United Russia Party. New parties, Spravedlivaya Rossiya (A Just Russia) and Pravoe Delo (Right Cause), also emerged on the scene. These events may have influenced responses to questions about trust in and performance of various political institutions and individuals.

Fourth, if the Beslan hostage taking had started to recede from public memory by the time of the nonvictim surveys, memory of the older tragedy of the 2002 hostage taking in the Moscow theater had become even more distant. Respondents in the nonvictim surveys may have forgotten the details of both the theater hostage taking and the legal aftermath, again suggesting caution when comparing survey results.

Focus Groups (6 Groups with 49 Total Participants)

All questions asked during the focus groups were similar if not identical to the questions already asked on the closed-ended questionnaire. Participants in the focus groups discussed their personal opinions on what differentiates active Beslan victims from inactive victims, hostile victims capable of retaliatory ethnic violence from peaceful and even tolerant victims, and severely depressed and incapacitated victims from more resilient victims. Other topics included details on the origins of the activist organizations, Mothers of Beslan and Voice of Beslan, and each of their demonstrations, sit-ins, meetings with politicians, and other major activities, attitudes toward Ingush, and attitudes toward leaders in Moscow, Vladikavkaz, Beslan, and the rest of the region. (English translations of focus group moderator guides available on request.)

Information on focus group participant selection and recruitment can be found in the introduction.

Focus Group Participant Selection: Additional Information

The concepts of activist versus nonactivist are less complicated in theory than in reality. Respondents who were labeled "nonactivists" all indicated on the nonvictim survey that they participated in none of the actions listed in question 23, but focus group discussions often revealed some participation. Supposed nonactivists offered comments such as "when I was on the square during the demonstration . . ." and "when a woman came and asked to sign a letter and I agreed. . . ." In their minds, some nonactivists differentiated between listening or being present at an activity from participating, meaning that the category of nonactivist is not as straightforward as the label may suggest. Still, for the purposes of this study, (1) the modest participation of even nonactivists supports the premise that violence in Beslan gave rise to a tremendous amount of peaceful political activism, and (2) those who participated modestly while self-describing as nonparticipants are still qualitatively different from respondents who indicate participation in four or more activities in question 23.

Focus Group Participant Recruitment

After victims were selected at random, five local CESSI recruiters in Beslan, under the supervision of local field manager Elam Sedakova, invited the selected people to participate in the focus group. All recruiters had been interviewers for the victim survey, and Sedakova had been field manager. After locating a potential focus group participant, the recruiter explained the purposes of the focus group in detail, provided comprehensive information about CESSI (the organization conducting the research), including organizational description, address, website, and telephone numbers, and then asked the person to respond to a short screening questionnaire to confirm that they would be allocated into the appropriate "activist" or "nonactivist" group. Questions in the screening questionnaire were identical to the questions used in the victim questionnaire and served only as a check. The recruiter then explained the focus group procedure and invited the person to participate, offering the name and phone number of CESSI's field manager if the person would like to learn more about the focus groups.

Participants were paid 600 rubles (approximately $20) as incentive for their participation and a token of gratitude for their time. In Beslan, this amount was considered large enough to demonstrate respect for someone's time and to match appropriately the requested task but not so large as to arouse suspicion that participants were being paid for something more than the stated research goal. Wages and pensions are small in Beslan, and many potential participants may be unemployed or stay-at-home moms, so although the monetary incentive did not appear to be the primary motivation for participating in the research, it seemed a welcome benefit. It also seemed useful in defining the focus group exercise as an equal partnership in information gathering, rather than a special favor.

Recruitment for focus group participation was difficult, as is reflected in Table B.2. Victims hesitated to agree to talk in front of other people about the tragedy. Some said they were fed up with the topic and/or found it too painful to dig up bad memories. Some were tired of being treated as "laboratory rats" because too many journalists and state commissions interviewed them, but no one actually helped. Some who work in state organizations such as the government, police, or schools do not like to talk publicly about their political activism.

The biggest difficulty was recruiting for "Group 3: male activists of thirty-five years and younger." Some male victims promised to participate and then did not show; some arrived, looked at the other participants, and departed with no explanation. When reasons were offered for not participating, they included the inability to deal publicly with feelings about the tragedy. (Some started crying and could not stop.) Also, by Ossetian tradition, young men should not express their personal opinion publicly but should listen to their elders. The separate group created for young males mitigated this problem somewhat but not entirely. After three attempts and three very strong efforts, the group of young male activists was finally convened and was the least talkative of the six groups.

Table B.2. Focus Group Participant Recruitment

Group	Contacted	Agreed to Participate	Arrived	Departed before Group Began	Departed during First Half	Participated for Duration of Focus Group
1. Female activists of 35 years and younger	32	15[a]	2 then 9[b]	2 then 0	0	9
2. Female activists older than 35 years	37	14	10	1[c]	0	9
3. Male activists of 35 years and younger	18	10	1 then 3 then 10[d]	0 then 0 then 2	0	8
4. Male activists older than 35 years	42	15	12	4	2	6
5. Female nonactivists	28	15	12	3	0	9
6. Male nonactivists	48	15	10	2	0	8

[a] Many victims in this group refused to participate due to lack of time. Many have small children and/or study and work.

[b] The first time this focus group convened, only two people showed up, and even those two then said they did not want to talk about their political activities in front of other people. The second time the group convened, fifteen people promised to come the evening before, and only nine showed up.

[c] One woman arrived and would agree to participate only if someone could get her daughter admitted to the hospital. This was beyond the powers of the focus group administrators, so she left.

[d] The first time this focus group convened, only one person showed up of the ten who promised. The second time, three people showed up, and the third time, with great effort, ten people showed up. The number of respondents to the victim survey who fall in this category of young male activist is very small, and many of them were not currently in Beslan (moved, studying in Vladikavkaz or another city, etc.).

The difficulty in getting victims to agree to participate in focus groups should remind us that the information gathered from these groups must be treated as anecdotal descriptive support for the survey data, not as a substitute for data. It should be noted that *all* of the victims who refused to participate in the focus groups had earlier agreed to participate in the face-to-face individual standardized survey interviews. The refusers have thus shown that they are not opposed across the board to sharing opinions and past behavior, only to doing so in groups of strangers.

Focus Group Administration

Focus groups were conducted in Beslan in December 2008, by CESSI's Olga Karetnikova, a Moscow-based moderator with twenty years of experience conducting focus groups and in-depth interviews on social issues including civic participation, political participation, and attitudes toward such sensitive topics as corruption. CESSI consulted with various specialists on ethnic relations and politics in Beslan and concluded that a local moderator might be suspected of having a political or economic agenda or might elicit less complete conversations due to the assumption that the local moderator already knows certain details and perspectives. Bringing the moderator from outside Beslan or Vladikavkaz gave her the legitimate status of an outsider with clear, research-based interests who would require thorough answers that began at square one.[1] Karetnikova also supervised the recruitment process.

The moderator explained to focus group participants all the rules and procedures to be used during discussions and what to expect, including the topics for discussion, confidentiality procedures, use of audio and video recording, the purely analytical purposes for recording, and procedures for ultimately destroying the recording. She also explained that there is no right answer to any question and that each opinion and statement is valued.

Focus groups took place in the building of the Labor Recruiting Agency in Beslan. This building had the following advantages: (1) its location is familiar and easily accessible for Beslan residents; (2) it is unrelated to the hostage taking; (3) it is unrelated to the government; (4) it is unrelated to a political party, NGO, or any other institution that might make invited participants misinterpret the goal of the focus group invitation; (5) it is respected by Beslan residents for its role in helping people find employment in a region where unemployment is a huge problem; and (6) it has an attractive room large enough for a big table and chairs, which is relatively rare in Beslan.

All focus groups were conducted in Russian, rather than Ossetian, for the following reasons: (1) the victim survey showed that a majority of victims are very fluent in Russian, sometimes better than in Ossetian, and they chose Russian language as their survey language when given the option; (2) most public discussions and debates on public issues in North Ossetia are conducted in Russian; (3) schools, universities, and the media in North Ossetia use Russian as their primary language; (4) all public events in which Beslan residents participated (demonstrations, open letters to public officials, etc.) were conducted in Russian; (5) back translations of the focus groups from Russian to English is relatively easy and therefore minimizes translation errors, whereas it is practically impossible to find a skilled translator for Ossetian to English, causing an intermediary translation stage to Russian that could introduce additional errors and misinterpretations; (6) some potential focus group participants were not ethnic Ossetians, leaving Russian as the only common language; (7) it is difficult if not impossible to find an Ossetian-speaking moderator as skilled and experienced as Karetnikova.

Focus group discussions were audio- and video-recorded, transcribed into Russian, and translated into English, with both the Russian and English transcripts made available to Javeline and Baird.

---

[1] Note then that the requirements for survey interviewers and the focus group moderator were different. For home-based private discussions, respondents felt comfortable letting local interviewers into their homes. For public group discussions, focus group participants felt comfortable with the outsider as moderator, although local people played a great role in focus group recruitment.

Risks and Benefits of Participation in Surveys and Focus Groups in North Ossetia

Survey respondents and focus group participants did not encounter any risks from this research. Respondents readily participated in the surveys without worry, as evidenced by the high response rate (82 percent, in the case of the Beslan victims), whereas they expressed greater hesitancy to participate in focus groups, usually for reasons besides risk, such as discomfort in sharing feelings in a public group. Although Western media frequently report about the increasingly authoritarian tendencies within contemporary Russia, the Russian government at the time of this research was extraordinarily popular at home and in most cases seemed unbothered by public opinion polling and other types of information-gathering research.

For the victim survey, many respondents were eager to share their opinions, were grateful for the interest, and even felt some catharsis from the opportunity to discuss these issues at length. Residents in areas hit by tragedy can over time feel forgotten, similar to "Katrina fatigue" in the United States, and there is some psychological benefit to being told that outsiders still care.

In addition to this psychological benefit, victim respondents received a small food pack and focus group participants received a monetary benefit of 600 rubles ($20) as gratitude for their time and participation.

Confidentiality and Sensitivity

Survey Confidentiality Procedures

The survey interviews were not videotaped or recorded in any way. Responses were not attributed to individual respondents; they were used in aggregate statistical analyses only.

The collaborating survey firm (CESSI) is well regarded and used by many scholars and U.S. government agencies. The firm's continued good reputation depends on their being scrupulous with the confidentiality of responses.

For the victim survey, the list of respondents was kept separately from completed questionnaires. There was no identifying information on the questionnaire, only an identification number. Information connecting identification numbers on the questionnaire and the contact details of respondents was possessed by only two people: Inna Chuslyaeva, CESSI's chief field manager, and Anna Andreenkova, CESSI's project manager.

With the victim survey, precise individuals who had been in the school at the time of the hostage taking needed to be identified. For the nonvictim surveys, there was no list of respondents, because the sampling procedure did not require knowing respondents' names. There was no identifying information on the questionnaire, only an identification number. Information connecting identification numbers on the questionnaire and the sampling procedure was again possessed by only two people, Chuslyaeva and Andreenkova.

CESSI collected completed questionnaires from interviewers every two days, so interviewers never had more than two or three completed questionnaires in hand. The data-processing group had access only to the completed questionnaires and did not have access to any identifying information.

The CESSI office is secured by a security guard twenty-four hours a day, seven days a week. Even if someone had gained access to the office, he or she would have been able to find only completed questionnaires but would not be able to access any identifying information, which was kept in a password-protected electronic form on a CD in a locked security box. Identifying information was never stored on any computer. The identifying information on the CD was taken out only when absolutely necessary for project purposes by either Andreenkova or Chuslyaeva and was restored immediately in the locked security box. It was never left open in the office.

In Russia, the laws prevent government agencies from requiring access to any information collected by a survey company. CESSI did not provide the Principal Investigators (Javeline and Baird) with any information about respondents' identification. CESSI physically destroyed the CD with the identifying information after the completion of the focus groups. The physical questionnaires were destroyed one year after project completion.

Focus Group Confidentiality Procedures

Using responses to questions in the surveys of Beslan victims, Javeline and Baird identified 257 victims who could be considered "activists" and 548 victims who could be considered "nonactivists." No names or other identifying information about these victims were provided, only CESSI's assigned case numbers (ID) in the datafile. Anna Andreenkova of CESSI was the only one who had record of IDs in the data file and contact details for respondents, and this information was kept separately and securely in a password-protected CD in a locked security box for which only she had the key and which was in her fully secured office, guarded twenty-four hours a day, seven days a week. Identifying information was never stored on any computer. The password-protected CD was taken out only when absolutely necessary for project purposes by Andreenkova and then restored immediately in the locked security box. It was never left open in the office. CESSI destroyed the password-protected CD in 2010.

Andreenkova extracted only the contact details for each respondent (name, address, and telephone number) along with their gender and age (information required for allocating respondents into groups). She sent only this information to recruiters in Beslan. Recruiters had no other identifying information about potential focus group participants and no information about their previous responses to survey questions.

During focus group discussions, every effort was made to treat participants with respect and sensitivity. The moderator expressed sympathy and deep interest in the problems faced by people in the group but no sympathy to any particular opinion, and she facilitated debate and discussion.

Video and audio recordings were kept securely among a very limited number of CESSI personnel and were never seen or heard by the principal investigators, Javeline and Baird, nor by any other person outside of the assigned CESSI employees. A single technical assistant installed the equipment and conducted the recordings, and the tapes were taken immediately by the moderator, Karetnikova. She kept them with her during her stay in Beslan and transported the records personally from Beslan to Moscow, not relying on any postal or delivery services. She never carried any list of participant names while the recordings were in her possession.

Back in Moscow, after completion of the focus groups, the audio recordings were assigned to a professional transcribing company for transcription. These transcribers heard only voices but had no access to faces, names, or contact information. Transcribers were obliged to return the audiotapes to CESSI without copying them. They signed a contract with CESSI that included this requirement, details about strict confidentiality, and the transcribers' obligation to destroy all records after they completed their work.

After transcription, the original moderator, Karetnikova, used the video recording in CESSI's office in order to attribute each statement in the transcription. No one besides Karentikova was involved in this process, and therefore no one besides Karetnikova ever saw records of who said what. Attributions were made to first names only. If surnames, children's names, specific places of employment, or other identifying information was accidentally used during the focus group discussions, this information was deleted from the transcripts. Neither Javeline nor Baird nor anyone besides Karetnikova and Andreenkova had any possibility at any time of connecting statements to identified individuals.

The recordings were kept in a locked security box in CESSI's office in Moscow, which is guarded by security personnel twenty-four hours a day, seven days a week. Anna Andreenkova is the only individual with access to the security box. Four months after the transcripts were complete, translated into English, and reviewed by Javeline and Baird, CESSI destroyed the audio and video recordings.

In Russia, the laws prevent government agencies from requiring access to any information collected by a survey company. CESSI does not provide the Principal Investigators (Javeline and Baird) with any information about respondents' identification.

References

"1,000 Protest in Southern Russia After Armed Raid on Cossack Leader's House." 2006. *Associated Press Worldstream*, May 1.

"A Welcome Russian Inquiry." 2004. *New York Times*, September 11.

Abbas, Hassan. 2008. "Assassination of Vladikavkaz Mayor: Business or Politics?" *The Jamestown Foundation, North Caucasus Weekly*, 9, no. 46 (December 5).

Abdullaev, Nabi. 2004. "Duma to Hear Beslan Findings," *Moscow Times*, September 28.

Abdullaev, Nabi, and Yana Voitova. 2004. "Ossetia Ministers Fired after Angry Protest." *Moscow Times*, September 9.

Abdullaev, Nabi, and Oksana Yablokova. 2006. "Chaika Sacks 6 of His Deputies." *Moscow Times*, July 6.

Abramson, Paul R., and William Claggett. 2001. "Recruitment and Political Participation." *Political Research Quarterly* 54, no. 4 (December): 905–916.

Adams, James, Jay Dow, and Samuel Merrill, III. 2006. "The Political Consequences of Abstention from Alienation and Abstention from Indifference: Applications to Presidential Elections." *Political Behavior* 28: 65–86.

Adorno, Theodore W., Else Frenkel-Brunswik, Daniel Levinson, and Nevitt Sanford. 1950. *The Authoritarian Personality*. New York: Harper and Row.

Allenova, Olga. 2005a. "Godovshcina Beslana. Traurnyi karaul" [Anniversary of Beslan. Mourning watch]. *Kommersant*, no. 163 (September 1): 1.

Allenova, Olga. 2005b. "Godovshchina Beslana. Polpred podstavilsya na mesto prezidenta" [Anniversary of Beslan. Envoy in the president's place]. *Kommersant*, no. 164 (September 2).

Allenova, Olga. 2005c. "Materei Beslana raskololo tselitelsvo" [Healing split Mothers of Beslan]. *Kommersant*, no. 180 (September 26): 7.

Allenova, Olga. 2006. "Beslanskii terakt doshel do Evropy" [Beslan attack came to Europe]. *Kommersant*, no. 243 (December 27): 4.

Allenova, Olga, and Zaur Farniyev. 2007. "Beslan slovam ne verit" [Beslan does not believe words]. *Kommersant*, no. 158 (September 3): 4.

Allenova, Olga, and Fedor Maksimov. 2006. "Beslan To Be Counted In; Mathematicians Will Check Conclusions of the Parliamentary Panel." *Kommersant*, no. 177 (September 22): 1, 4.

Allison, Paul D. 2002. *Missing Data*. Thousand Oaks, CA: Sage University, Paper No. 136.

"An Empire's Fraying Edge." 2005. *The Economist* 374, no. 8413 (February 12): 23–25.

Anderson, Craig A., and L. Rowell Huesmann. 2003. "Human Aggression: A Social-Cognitive View." In M. A. Hogg and J. Cooper, eds., *Handbook of Social Psychology*. London: Sage Publications, pp. 296–323.

Apter, David. 1997. "Political Violence in Analytical Perspective." In David Apter, ed., *The Legitimization of Violence*. New York: New York University Press, pp. 1–32.

Arendt, Hannah. 1963. *Eichmann in Jerusalem: A Report on the Banality of Evil*. New York: Penguin Books.

Arutunyan, Anna. 2008. "Four Years On, Beslan Remembered." *Moscow News*, no. 35 (September 5).

"'As if They Fell from the Sky': Counterinsurgency, Rights Violations, and Rampant Impunity in Ingushetia." 2008. Human Rights Watch.

Averill, James R. 1983. "Studies on Anger and Aggression: Implications for Theories of Emotion." *The American Psychologist* 38: 1145–1160.

Baev, Pavel K. 2006. "The Russian Military Campaign in the North Caucasus: Is a Victory in Sight?" *The Jamestown Foundation*, September 14.

Baker, Jean A. 1998. "Are We Missing the Forest for the Trees? Considering the Social Context of School Violence." *Journal of School Psychology* 36, no. 1 (Spring): 29–44.

Bakhvalova, Milena. 2005. "Back to Beslan." *Russkii Kurier*, January 24, p. 2; retrieved through *What the Papers Say: Part B (Russia)*, January 24, 2005.

Bakke, Kristin M., John O'Loughlin, and Michael D. Ward. 2009. "Reconciliation in Conflict-Affected Societies: Multilevel Modeling of Individual and Contextual Factors in the North Caucasus of Russia." *Annals of the Association of American Geographers* 99, no. 5: 1012–1021.

Balch, George I. 1974. "Multiple Indicators in Survey Research: The Concept 'Sense of Political Efficacy.'" *Political Methodology* 1, no. 2 (Spring): 1–43.

Bandura, Albert. 1973. *Aggression: A Social Learning Analysis*. Englewood Cliffs, NJ: Prentice-Hall.

Bandura, Albert. 1977. "Self-Efficacy: Toward a Unifying Theory of Behavioral Change." *Psychological Review* 84: 191–215.

Bandura, Albert. 1982. "Self-Efficacy Mechanism in Human Agency." *American Psychologist* 37, no. 2: 122–147.

Bandura, Albert. 1986. *Social Foundations of Thought and Action: A Social Cognitive Theory*. Englewood Cliffs, NJ: Prentice Hall.

Bandura, Albert, ed. 1995. *Self-Efficacy in Changing Societies*. Cambridge: Cambridge University Press.

Bandura, Albert. 1997. *Self-Efficacy: The Exercise of Control*. New York: W. H. Freeman.

Barchia, Kirstin, and Kay Bussey. 2011. "Individual and Collective Social Cognitive Influences on Peer Aggression: Exploring the Contribution of Aggression Efficacy, Moral Disengagement, and Collective Efficacy." *Aggressive Behavior* 37: 107–120.

Barnes, Samuel H., et al. 1979. *Political Action: Mass Participation in Five Western Democracies*. Beverly Hills, CA: Sage Publications.

Bassiouni, M. Cherif. 2006. "International Recognition of Victims' Rights." *Human Rights Law Review* 6, no. 2: 203–279.

Bateson, Regina. 2012. "Crime Victimization and Political Participation." *American Political Science Review* 106, no. 3 (August): 570–587.

Baumeister, Roy F., Laura Smart, and Joseph M. Boden. 1996. "Relation of Threatened Egotism to Violence and Aggression: The Dark Side of High Self-Esteem." *Psychological Review* 103: 5–33.

Becker, Julia C., Nicole Tausch, and Ullrich Wagner. 2011. "Emotional Consequences of Collective Action Participation: Differentiating Self-Directed and Outgroup-Directed Emotions." *Personality and Social Psychology Bulletin* 37, no. 12: 1587–1598.

Beissinger, Mark R. 1998. "Nationalist Violence and the State: Political Authority and Contentious Repertoires in the Former USSR." *Comparative Politics* 30, no. 4 (July): 401–422.

Bellows, John, and Edward Miguel. 2006. "War and Institutions: New Evidence from Sierra Leone." *The American Economic Review* 96, no. 2 (May): 394–399.

Bellows, John, and Edward Miguel. 2009. "War and Local Collective Action in Sierra Leone." *Journal of Public Economics* 93: 1144–1157.

Berkowitz, Leonard. 1993. *Aggression: Its Causes, Consequences, and Control*. Philadelphia, PA: Temple University Press.

Berman, Sheri. 1997. "Civil Society and the Collapse of the Weimar Republic." *World Politics* 49, no. 3: 401–429.

Berseneva, Anastasia. 2005. "Beslan na grani nervnogo sryva" [Beslan on the verge of a nervous breakdown]. *Noviye Izvestia*, no. 164 (September 12): 6.

"Beslan Activists Arrested for Picketing Russian Prosecutor-General's Office." 2005. *BBC Monitoring International Reports*, October 27.

"Beslan Committee Ready to Sue Russia over School Seizure Verdict." 2006. *BBC Monitoring Trans Caucasus Unit: BBC Worldwide Monitoring*, September 4.

"Beslan Court Rejects Victims' Demand to Replace Prosecutor." 2005. *Mosnews.com*, October 4.

"Beslan Families Demand Prosecution of Russian Officials." 2007. *Ekho Moskvy Radio*, March 12.

"Beslan Kidnapper Jailed for Life." 2006. *The Times (UK)*, May 27.

"Beslan Kids Still Haunted by 2004 Bloodbath." 2007. *RT*, September 5.

"Beslan Locals Call on Putin to Punish 'Corrupt Officials' Guilty of Hostage Tragedy." 2004. *Agence France Presse*, November 19.

"Beslan Mothers Ask US, EU to Help Investigate School Siege." 2005. *Mosnews.com*, November 30.

"Beslan Mothers Expect European Court to Deal with Their Complaint Next Year." 2009. *Russia & CIS General Newswire*, September 2.

"Beslan Mothers Given Explanation Why Operative HQ Members Not Taken to Court." 2007. *RIA Novosti*, retrieved through *BBC Worldwide Monitoring*, May 3.

"Beslan Mothers Lash Out at Putin." 2005. *BBC News*, August 24.

"Beslan Mothers Protest as Verdict Reading Winds Down." 2006. *Agence France Presse*, May 24.

"Beslan Mothers Report Aquittal of Russian Officers Accused of Negligence." 2007. *Ekho Moskvy Radio*, retrieved through *BBC Worldwide Monitoring*, May 10.

"Beslan Mothers Stay in Court All Night." 2007. *Moscow Times*, May 4.

"Beslan Protesters Not Letting Russian Prosecutors Leave Courtroom." 2006. *Ekho Moskvy Radio*, retrieved through *BBC Worldwide Monitoring*, January 24.

"Beslan Siege: Russia 'Will Comply' with Critical Ruling." 2017. *BBC News*, September 20.

"Beslan Teachers Send Letter to Putin One Year after School Siege Looking for Truth." 2005. *Pravda.Ru*, September 1.

"Beslan Teachers Write to Putin as Last Resort." 2005. *MosNews*, August 31.

"Beslan Victims Back Russian MP's Alternative Probe Report." 2006. *BBC Monitoring International Reports*, September 4.

"Beslan Victims Demand Action from Russian Authorities." 2010. *BBC Monitoring Former Soviet Union: Political, Ekho Moskvy Radio*, September 3.

"Beslan Victims Denounce Russian Antiterror Law." 2006. *BBC Worldwide Monitoring: Trans Caucasus Unit*, March 16.

"Beslan Victims' Mothers Said Threatened, Barred from Meeting Russian President." 2009. *BBC Monitoring Former Soviet Union: Political, Ekho Moskvy Radio*, August 10.

"Beslan Victims' Relatives Block Authorities Attempt to Recreate Bungled Rescue Effort." 2006. *Associated Press Worldstream*, August 17.

"Beslan Women Continue Hunger Strike Demanding New School Siege Probe." 2006. *Mosnews.com*, February 13.

"Beslan Women End Hunger Strike." 2006. *Russia & CIS General Newswire*, Interfax News Agency, February 20.

Beyerlein, Kraig, and John R. Hipp. 2006. "A Two-Stage Model for a Two-Stage Process: How Biographical Availability Matters for Social Movement Mobilization." *Mobilization* 11: 219–240.

Beyerlein, Kraig, and David Sikkink. 2008. "Sorrow and Solidarity: Why Americans Volunteered for 9/11 Relief Efforts." *Social Problems* 55, no. 2: 190–215.

Bhavnani, Ravi. 2006. "Ethnic Norms and Interethnic Violence: Accounting for Mass Participation in the Rwandan Genocide." *Journal of Peace Research* 43, no. 6: 651–669.

Bhavnani, Ravi, Karsten Donnay, Dan Miodownik, Maayan Mor, and Dirk Helbing. 2014. "Group Segregation and Urban Violence." *American Journal of Political Science* 58, no. 1: 226–245.

Bhui, Kamaldeep, Brian Everitt, and Edgar Jones. 2014. "Might Depression, Psychosocial Adversity, and Limited Social Assets Explain Vulnerability to and Resistance against Violent Radicalisation?" *PLoS ONE* 9, no. 9: e105918. doi: 10.1371/journal. pone.0105918.

Biernat, Monica, and Christian S. Crandall. 1999. "Racial Attitudes." In John P. Robinson, Phillip R. Shaver, and Lawrence S. Wrightsman, eds., *Measures of Political Attitudes*. San Diego: Academic Press, pp. 297–411.

Bigg, Claire. 2005. "Russia: Bereaved Beslan Mothers Give Up Protest, But Not Fight." *Radio Free Europe/Radio Liberty*, August 24.

Billiet, Jaak, and Hans de Witte. 1995. "Attitudinal Dispositions to Vote for a 'New' Extreme Right Party: The Case of the 'Vlaams Blok.'" *European Journal of Political Research* 27, no. 2 (February): 181–202.

Birch, Julian. 1995. "Ossetia: A Caucasian Bosnia in Microcosm." *Central Asian Survey* 14, no. 1: 43–74.

Blalock, Hubert M., Jr. 1967. *Towards a Theory of Minority Group Relations*. New York: John Wiley & Sons.

Blattman, Christopher. 2009. "From Violence to Voting: War and Political Participation in Uganda." *American Political Science Review* 103, no. 2 (May): 231–247.

Bobo, Lawrence, and Franklin D. Gilliam, Jr. 1990. "Race, Sociopolitical Participation, and Empowerment." *American Political Science Review* 84, no. 2: 377–393.

Bobrova, Olga. 2011. "Materei Beslana perenesli na 'posle prasnikov' " [Mothers of Beslan moved to 'after the holidays']. *Novaya gazeta*, no. 48 (May 6).

Bobrova, Olga, and Elena Milashina. 2005. "Sensatsionnoe zayavlenie predstavitelya prokuratury: tanki i ognemety premenyalis pri shtormye" [Sensational statement by representatives of the procuracy: tanks and flamethrowers were used during the storm]. *Novaya gazeta*, no. 25 (April 7).

Bondarenko, Maria. 2005. "Kozak gotov k otstavkye Dzasokhova" [Kozak is ready for Dzasokhov's dismissal]. *Nezavisimaya Gazeta*, no. 19 (February 2): 1.

Borisov, Timofei. 2006a. "Tainy Beslana ne raskryty" [Secrets of Beslan are not disclosed]. *Rossiiskaya gazeta*, no. 190 (August 29): 6.

Borisov, Timofei. 2006b. "First Explosion Was Recorded." *Rossiskaya gazeta*, September 1, pp. 1, 3.

Brader, Ted, Eric W. Groenendyk, and Nicholas A. Valentino. 2011. "Fight or Flight? When Political Threats Arouse Public Anger and Fear." Unpublished manuscript.

Brady, Henry. 1999. "Political Participation." In John P. Robinson, Phillip R. Shaver, and Lawrence S. Wrightsman, eds., *Measures of Political Attitudes*. San Diego, CA: Academic Press, pp. 737–801.

Brady, Henry E., Kay Lehman Schlozman, and Sidney Verba. 1999. "Prospecting for Participants: Rational Expectations and the Recruitment of Political Activists." *American Political Science Review* 93 (March): 153–198.

Brass, Paul. 1996. *Riots and Pogroms*. New York: New York University Press.

Brass, Paul R. 2003. *The Production of Hindu-Muslim Violence in Contemporary India*. Seattle: University of Washington Press.

Brehm, John, and Wendy Rahn. 1997. "Individual-Level Evidence for the Causes and Consequences of Social Capital." *American Journal of Political Science* 41 (July): 999–1023.

Brewer, John D., and Bernadette C. Hayes. 2013. "Victimhood Status and Public Attitudes Towards Post-conflict Agreements: Northern Ireland as a Case Study." *Political Studies* 61: 442–461.

Brewer, John D., and Bernadette C. Hayes. 2014. "Victimisation and Attitudes Towards Former Political Prisoners in Northern Ireland." *Terrorism and Political Violence* 27, no. 4: 741–761.

Brewer, Marilynn B. 1999. "The Psychology of Prejudice: Ingroup Love or Outgroup Hate?" *Journal of Social Issues* 55, no. 3: 429–444.

Brewer, Marilynn B. 2001. "Ingroup Identification and Intergroup Conflict: When Does Ingroup Love Become Outgroup Hate?" In Richard Ashmore et al., eds., *Social Identity, Intergroup Conflict, and Conflict Reduction*. Oxford: Oxford University Press, pp. 17–41.

Brockett, Charles D. 2005. *Political Movements and Violence in Central America*. New York: Cambridge University Press.

Brubaker, Rogers, and David D. Laitin. 1998. "Ethnic and Nationalist Violence." *Annual Review of Sociology* 24: 423–452.

Bruneau, Emile, and Nour Kteily. 2017. "The Enemy as Animal: Symmetric Dehumanization during Asymmetric Warfare." *PLoS ONE* 12, no. 7: e0181422.

Buribayev, Aidar. 2005. "Relatives of Terror Attack Victims Sent a Letter to President Putin." *Gazeta*, no. 203 (October 26): 6.

Buse, Uwe, Ullrich Fichtner, Mario Kaiser, Uwe Klussmann, Walter Mayr, and Christian Neef. 2004. "Putin's Ground Zero." *Der Spiegel*, no. 53 (December 27): 65–101.

Butorina, Yekaterina, and Marina Lepina. 2012. "Strasburg sprosit pro Beslan" [Strasbourg inquires about Beslan]. *Moskovskiye Novosti*, no. 271 (May 4).

Campbell, Andrea Louise. 2003. "Participatory Reactions to Policy Threats: Senior Citizens and the Defense of Social Security and Medicare." *Political Behavior* 25, no. 1 (March): 29–49.

Campbell, Angus, Gerald Gurin, and Warren Miller. 1954. *The Voter Decides*. Evanston, IL: Row, Peterson.

"Captured Ingush Insurgency Commander Unrepentant in Court." 2013. *Radio Free Europe/Radio Liberty*, June 28.

Carmines, Edward G., Paul M. Sniderman, and Beth C. Easter. 2011. "On the Meaning, Measurement, and Implications of Racial Resentment." *Annals of the American Academy of Political and Social Science* 634 (March): 98–116.

Carver, Charles S., and Eddie Harmon-Jones. 2009. "Anger Is an Approach-Related Affect: Evidence and Implications." *Psychological Bulletin* 135, no. 2: 183–204.

Case of Tagayeva and Others v. Russia. 2017. European Court of Human Rights, Application no. 26562/07 and 6 other applications, Judgment, April 13, September 18, final.

Chagnon, Napoleon A. 1988. "Life Histories, Blood Revenge, and Warfare in a Tribal Population." *Science* 239 (February 26): 985–992.

Chapman, Terrence L. 2008. "Unraveling the Ties between Civic Institutions and Attitudes toward Political Violence." *International Studies Quarterly* 52, no. 3 (September): 515–532.

Chenoweth, Erica, and Maria J. Stephan. 2011. *Why Civil Resistance Works: The Strategic Logic of Nonviolent Conflict.* New York: Columbia University Press.

Chivers, C. J. 2004. "Mourning and Anger at School Caught Up in Terrorism," *New York Times*, October 13, p. 3.

Chivers, C. J. 2005a. "Russia: Beslan Protest over Siege Inquiry." *New York Times*, January 22, p. A2.

Chivers, C. J. 2005b. "For Russians, Wounds Linger in School Siege." *New York Times*, August 26, p. 1.

Chivers, C. J. 2005c. "11 Months Later, Russian School Siege Claims New Victim." *New York Times*, August 4, p. A4.

Chivers, C. J. 2006. "Survivors Put Kremlin on Trial in Russian School Siege." *New York Times*, April 25, p. A3.

Chivers, C. J. 2007. "The School." *Esquire*, March 14.

Chong, Dennis. 1991. *Collective Action and the Civil Rights Movement.* Chicago: University of Chicago Press.

Chong, Dennis, and Reuel Rogers. 2005. "Racial Solidarity and Political Participation," *Political Behavior* 27, no. 4 (December): 347–374.

Church, Michael. 2006. "Life after the Horror of Beslan." *The Independent*, March 30.

"Chuzhoye gorye" [Someone else's grief]. 2007. *Vedomosti*, September 3, pp. 1, 4.

Cichocka, Aleksandra, and John T. Jost. 2014. "Stripped of Illusions? Exploring System Justification Processes in Capitalist and Post-Communist Societies." *International Journal of Psychology* 49, no. 1 (February): 6–29.

Citrin, Jack. 1974. "Comment: The Political Relevance of Trust in Government." *American Political Science Review* 68: 973–988.

Citrin, Jack. 1977. "Political Alienation as a Social Indicator: Attitudes and Action." *Social Indicators Research* 4, no. 1: 381–419.

Citrin, Jack, Herbert McClosky, J. Merrill Shanks, and Paul M. Sniderman. 1975. "Personal and Political Sources of Political Alienation." *British Journal of Political Science* 5, no. 1 (January): 1–31.

Clore, Gerald L., and Karen Gasper. 2000. "Feeling Is Believing: Some Affective Influences on Belief." In Nico H. Frijda, Antony S.R. Manstead, and Sacha Bem, eds., *Emotions and Beliefs: How Feelings Influence Thoughts.* Cambridge: Cambridge University Press, pp. 10–44.

Cockburn, Cynthia. 2007. *From Where We Stand: War, Women's Activism, and Feminist Analysis.* New York: Zed Books.

Coffé, Hilde, Bruno Heyndels, and Jan Vermier. 2007. "Fertile Grounds for Extreme Rightwing Parties: Explaining the Vlaams Blok's Electoral Success." *Electoral Studies* 26, no. 1 (March): 142–155.

Cole, Elizabeth R., Alyssa N. Zucker, and Joan M. Ostrove. 1998. "Political Participation and Feminist Consciousness among Women Activists of the 1960s." *Political Psychology* 19, no. 2 (June): 349–371.

Collier, David. 2000. "Doing Well Out of War: An Economic Perspective." In Mats Berdal and David M. Malone, eds., *Greed and Grievance: Economic Agendas in Civil Wars.* Boulder: Lynne Rienner, pp. 91–111.

Collins, Randall. 2008. *Violence: A Micro-Sociological Theory.* Princeton, NJ: Princeton University Press.

Corner, Emily, and Paul Gill. 2015. "A False Dichotomy? Mental Illness and Lone-actor Terrorism." *Law and Human Behavior* 39, no. 1: 23–34.

Cornell, Svante E. 1998. "Conflicts in the North Caucasus." *Central Asian Survey* 17, no. 3: 409–441.

Corrigall-Brown, Catherine, David A. Snow, Kelly Smith, and Theron Quist. 2009. "Explaining the Puzzle of Homeless Mobilization: An Examination of Differential Participation." *Sociological Perspectives* 52: 309–35.

Cortner, Richard. 1968. "Strategies and Tactics of Litigants in Constitutional Cases." *Journal of Public Law* 17: 287–307.

"Court Orders Beslan Mothers to Disband." 2007. *Moscow Times,* December 21: 3.

"Court Rules on Beslan Investigation." 2007. *Moscow Times,* April 26.

"Courtroom Chaos as Beslan Siege Trial Begins." 2005. *The Australian,* May 19.

Cozens, Claire. 2004. "Editor Fired over Siege Coverage." *The Guardian,* September 6.

Craig, Stephen C., and Kenneth D. Wald. 1985. "Whose Ox to Gore? A Comment on the Relationship between Political Discontent and Political Violence." *The Western Political Quarterly* 38, no. 4 (December): 652–662.

Cramer, Christopher. 2006. *Civil War Is Not a Stupid Thing: Accounting for Violence in Developing Countries.* London: Hurst.

Cress, Daniel M., and David A. Snow. 1996. "Mobilization at the Margins: Resources, Benefactors, and the Viability of Homeless Social Movement Organizations." *American Sociological Review* 61, no. 6 (December): 1089–1109.

"Criminal Cases Opened against VOB activists." 2008. *Russia & CIS General Newswire,* Interfax News Agency, February 15.

Cullison, Alan. 2005. "In Beslan, Distrust of Authority Fosters Pity for a Terrorist." *Wall Street Journal,* August 2, p. A1.

Cunningham, Kathleen Gallagher. 2013. "Understanding Strategic Choice: The Determinants of Civil War and Nonviolent Campaign in Self-Determination Disputes." *Journal of Peace Research* 50, no. 3: 291–304.

Dadasheva, Diana, Zaur Farniyev, and Sergei Mashkin. 2008. "Genprokuratura vspomnila o pravakh poterpevshikh ot Beslana" [Prosecutor General's Office remembers Beslan victims' rights]. *Kommersant,* no. 75 (May 5): 5.

Dahl, Robert A. 1961. *Who Governs? Democracy and Power in an American City.* New Haven, CT: Yale University Press.

Dalton, Russell, Alix Van Sickle, and Steven Weldon. 2010. "The Individual-Institutional Nexus of Protest Behavior." *British Journal of Political Science* 40, no. 1 (January): 51–73.

Daly, Martin, and Margo Wilson. 1985. "Competitiveness, Risk-Taking and Violence: The Young Male Syndrome." *Ethology and Sociobiology* 6: 59–73.

Daly, Martin, and Margo Wilson. 1989. "Homicide and Cultural Evolution." *Ethology and Sociobiology* 10: 99–110.

de Figueiredo, Rui J. P., and Barry Weingast. 1999. "The Rationality of Fear: Political Opportunism and Ethnic Conflict." In Barbara F Walter and Jack Snyder, eds., *Civil Wars, Insecurity, and Intervention*. New York: Columbia University Press, pp. 261–302.

DeLisi, Lynn E., Andrea Maurizio, Marla Yost, Carey E Papparozzi, Cindy Fulchino, Craig L. Katz, Josh Altesman, Mathew Biel, Jennifer Lee, and Pilar Stevens. 2003. "A Survey of New Yorkers after the September 11, 2001, Terrorist Attacks." *American Journal of Psychiatry* 160: 780–783.

della Porta, Donatella. 1995. *Social Movements, Political Violence and the State*. New York: Cambridge University Press.

della Porta, Donatella, and Sidney Tarrow. 1986. "Unwanted Children: Political Violence and the Cycle of Protest in Italy, 1966–1973." *European Journal of Political Research* 14, no. 6: 607–632.

"Delo obvinyayemogo v terrorizme Ali Taziyeva vskore budet napravleno v sud, utverzhdayet ego advokat" [The case of the accused terrorist Ali Taziev will soon be sent to court, his lawyer asserts]. 2012. *Kavkazskii Uzel*, February 8.

Demmers, Jolle. 2012. *Theories of Violent Conflict: An Introduction*. New York: Routledge.

Detges, Adrien. 2017. "Droughts, State-Citizen Relations and Support for Political Violence in Sub-Saharan Africa: A Micro-Level Analysis." *Political Geography* 61: 88–98.

Disha, Ilir, James C. Cavendish, and Ryan D. King. 2011. "Historical Events and Spaces of Hate: Hate Crimes against Arabs and Muslims in Post-9/11 America." *Social Problems* 58, no. 1 (February): 21–46.

Dollard, John, Leonard W. Doob, Neal E. Miller, O. H. Mowrer, and Robert R. Sears. 1939. *Frustration and Aggression*. New Haven, CT: Yale University Press.

Dorius, Cassandra R., and John D. McCarthy. 2011. "Understanding Activist Leadership Effort in the Movement Opposing Drinking and Driving." *Social Forces* 90, no. 2 (December): 453–473.

Drake, Alvin W., Stan N. Finkelstein, and Harvey M. Sapolsky. 1982. *The American Blood Supply*. Cambridge, MA: MIT Press.

Dudouet, Veronique. 2013. "Dynamics and Factors of Transition from Armed Struggle to Nonviolent Resistance." *Journal of Peace Research* 50, no. 3: 401–413.

Dunlop, John B. 2006. *The 2002 Dubrovka and 2004 Beslan Hostage Crises: A Critique of Russian Counter-Terrorism*. Stuttgart: ibidem-Verlag.

Dunlop, John B. 2009. "The September 2004 Beslan Terrorist Incident: New Findings." Center on Democracy Development, and The Rule of Law. Working Paper Number 115, July.

Dunning, Thad. 2011. "Fighting and Voting: Violent Conflict and Electoral Politics." *Journal of Conflict Resolution* 55, no. 3 (June): 327–339.

Dyupin, Sergei. 2004. "Ossetian Police Search for Provocateurs." *Kommersant*, no. 169/P (3008) (September 13): 5.

"Dzasokhov vstretilis s zhenshchinami, poteryavshimi blizkikh v Beslane" [Dzasokhov met with women who lost relatives in Beslan]. 2004. *RIA Novosti*, September 14.

Dzutsev, Khasan V. 2011. "The Republic of North Ossetia-Alania after the Terrorist Act of 9 September 2010 in Vladikavkaz." *Anthropology & Archeology of Eurasia* 49, no. 4 (Spring): 40–53.

Dzutsev, Valery. 2004. "In the Wake of Beslan, Open Debate is Key." *Moscow Times*, October 13.

Dzutsev, Valery. 2009. "Government of Ingushetia Tries to Resolve Ossetian-Ingush Conflict." *The Jamestown Foundation* 6, no. 180 (October 1).

Eckel, Mike. 2005. "Mothers of Beslan Massacre Seek Answers." *Associated Press*, June 27.

Elder, Miriam. 2010. "Moscow Seizes Islamic Terror Chief Amid Fears for 2014 Winter Olympics." *The Guardian*, June 12.

Elster, Jon. 1998. "Emotions and Economic Theory." *Journal of Economic Literature* 36 (March): 47–74.

Elster, Jon. 1999. *Alchemies of the Mind: Rationality and the Emotions.* Cambridge: Cambridge University Press.

Ennis, James G., and Richard Schreuer. 1987. "Mobilizing Weak Support for Social Movements: The Role of Grievance, Efficacy, and Cost." *Social Forces* 66, no. 2 (December): 390–409.

Ernst, J. M., and J. T. Cacioppo. 1999. "Lonely Hearts: Psychological Perspectives on Loneliness." *Applied and Preventive Psychology* 8, no. 1: 1–22.

Evangelista, Matthew. 2002. *The Chechen Wars: Will Russia Go the Way of the Soviet Union?* Washington, DC: Brookings Institution Press.

Eysenck, Michael W. 2000. "Anxiety, Cognitive Biases, and Beliefs." In Nico H. Frijda, Antony S. R. Manstead, and Sacha Bem, eds. *Emotions and Beliefs: How Feelings Influence Thoughts.* Cambridge: Cambridge University Press, pp. 171–184.

Farniyev, Zaur. 2004. "Ossetia on the March." *Kommersant-vlast*, no. 36 (589) (September 13).

Farniyev, Zaur. 2005a. "Dyelo Kulayeva. 'Po nam terroristy voobshche ne streliali' " [The case of Kulayev. 'The terrorists did not shoot at us at all']. *Kommersant*, no. 107 (June 15): 3.

Farniyev, Zaur. 2005b. "Scandal: 'Mothers of Beslan' Power Split." *Kommersant* (October 3).

Farniyev, Zaur. 2006a. "Yuriyu Chaike napomnyat o Beslane" [Yuri Chaika is reminded of Beslan]. *Kommersant*, no. 119 (July 4): 6.

Farniyev, Zaur. 2006b. "Zamgenprokurora provedet materinskoye rassledovaniye" [Deputy Prosecutor General will conduct the mothers' investigation]. *Kommersant*, no. 146 (August 10): 4.

Farniyev, Zaur. 2007a. " 'Golos Beslana' zagovoril s prezidentom" ['Voice of Beslan' spoke with the president]. *Kommersant*, no. 38 (March 12): 5.

Farniyev, Zaur. 2007b. "Militseiskuyu khalatnost v Beslanye rassudyat prisyazhnye" [Jury will judge police negligence in Beslan]. *Kommersant*, no. 80 (no. 3656) (May 12).

Farniyev, Zaur. 2007c. "Yesli ne khotyat nas slushat po-khoroshemu, budyet po-plokhomu" [If they do not want to listen to us the good way, then it will be the bad way]. *Kommersant*, no. 92 (May 30): 5.

Farniyev, Zaur. 2007d. "Obzhaluyut amnistiyu militsionerov" [Amnesty of police officers is appealed]. *Kommersant*, no. 93 (May 31): 7.

Farniyev, Zaur. 2007e. "Beslanskikh materei priznali melkimi khuliganami" [Beslan mothers recognized as petty holligans]. *Kommersant*, no.128 (July 21): 4.

Farniyev, Zaur. 2007f. " 'Golos Beslana' otkazalsya ot yedy" ['Voice of Beslan' refused food]. *Kommersant*, no. 235 (December 20): 5.

Farniyev, Zaur. 2009. "V Beslane pomyanuli pogibshikh" [In Beslan, victims are remembered]. *Kommersant*, no. 161 (September 2): 3.

Farniyev, Zaur. 2011a. "Aleksandr Khloponin nashel vremya dlya beslanskikh materei" [Alexander Khloponin found time for Beslan mothers]. *Kommersant* (March 25).

Farniyev, Zaur. 2011b. "Prezident vzyal na zametku Beslanskii terakt" [The President took note of the Beslan terrorist act]. *Komersant*, no. 98 (June 2): 2.

Farniyev, Zaur, and Olga Allenova. 2006. "Beslanskiye muzhchini poshli po prokuroram." *Kommersant*, no. 98 (June 2): 5.

Farniyev, Zaur, and Nataliya Gorodetskaya. 2004. "Dmitrii Rogozin podskazal, gdye iskat terroristov" [Dmitry Rogozin suggested where to look for terrorists]. *Kommersant*, no. 208 (November 5): 3.

Farniyev, Zaur, and Oleg Kashin. 2005. "North Ossetia Is Asked Not to Demonstrate." *Kommersant* (May 13): 8.

Farniyev, Zaur, and Nikolai Sergeyev. 2014. "Beslan doshel do Yevropy" [Beslan came to Europe]. *Kommersant*, no. 187 (October 15): 3.

Fearon, James, and David Laitin. 1996. "Explaining Interethnic Cooperation." *American Political Science Review* 90, no. 4 (December): 715–735.

Fearon, James, and David Laitin. 2000. "Violence and the Social Construction of Ethnic Identity." *International Organization* 54, no. 4 (Autumn): 845–877.

Fearon, James, and David Laitin. 2003. "Ethnicity, Insurgency, and Civil War." *American Political Science Review* 97, no. 1: 75–90.

Finkel, Steven E. 1985. "Reciprocal Effects of Participation and Political Efficacy: A Panel Analysis." *American Journal of Political Science* 29, no. 4: 891–913.

Finkel, Steven E. 1987. "The Effects of Participation on Political Efficacy and Political Support: Evidence from a West German Panel." *The Journal of Politics* 49, no. 2 (May): 441–464.

Finkel, Steven E., Edward N. Muller, and Karl-Dieter Opp. 1989. "Personal Influence, Collective Rationality, and Mass Political Action." *American Political Science Review* 83, no. 3: 885–903.

Finn, Peter. 2005a. "New Report Puts Blame on Local Officials in Beslan Siege." *Washington Post*, December 29.

Finn, Peter. 2005b. "School Is Symbol of Death for Haunted Children of Beslan." *Washington Post*, August 28.

Finn, Peter. 2006. "Blame Assigned in Siege at Beslan." *Washington Post*, May 17.

Fireman, Bruce, and William A. Gamson. 1988. "Utilitarian Logic in the Resource Mobilization Perspective." In Mayer Zald and John D. McCarthy, eds., *The Dynamics of Social Movements: Resource Mobilization, Social Control, and Tactics*. New York: University Press of America, pp. 8–44.

Fischhoff, B., R. M. Gonzalez, D. A. Small, and J. S. Lerer. 2003. "Judged Terror Risk and Proximity to the World Trade Center." *Journal of Risk and Uncertainty* 26, no. 2–3: 137–151.

Fisher, Agneta H., and Ira J. Roseman. 2007. "Beat Them or Ban Them: The Characteristics and Social Functions of Anger and Contempt." *Journal of Personality and Social Psychology* 93, no. 1: 103–115.

"Former Vladikavkaz Mayor Assassinated in His Car." 2008. *RIA Novosti*, December 31.

Foster, Mindi D., and Kimberly Matheson. 1999. "Perceiving and Responding to the Personal/Group Discrimination Discrepancy." *Personality and Social Psychology Bulletin* 25, no. 10 (October): 1319–1329.

Franchetti, Mark. 2004. "Beslan Turns Hate on School Director." *The Sunday Times*, October 17.

Franchetti, Mark. 2005. "Wounds of Beslan Still Raw." *The Australian*, August 29.

Franchetti, Mark. 2009. "The Aftermath of the Beslan School Massacre." *The Sunday Times*, August 9.

Franchetti, Mark, and Matthew Campbell. 2004. "How a Repressed Village Misfit Became the Butcher of Beslan." *The Sunday Times*, September 12.

Franco, Annie, Neil Malhotra, and Gabor Simonovits. 2014. "Publication Bias in the Social Sciences: Unlocking the File Drawer." *Science* 345, no. 6203: 1502–1505.

Fredrickson, Barbara L., Michele M. Tugade, Christian E. Waugh, and Gregory R. Larkin. 2003. "What Good Are Positive Emotions in Crises? A Prospective Study of Resilience and Emotions Following the Terrorist Attacks on the United States on September 11th, 2001." *Journal of Personality and Social Psychology* 84, no. 2: 365–76.

Freeman, Jo. 1979. "Resource Mobilization and Strategy: A Model for Analyzing Social Movement Organization Actions." In Mayer N. Zald and John D. McCarthy, eds., *The Dynamics of Social Movements*. Cambridge, MA: Winthrop, pp. 167–189.

Frijda, Nico H. 1994. "The Lex Talionis: On Vengeance." In Stephanie H. van Goozen, Nanne E. Van de Poll, and Joseph A. Sergeant, eds., *Emotions: Essays on Emotion Theory*. Hillsdale, NJ: Lawrence Erlbaum Associates, pp. 263–289.

Frijda, Nico, and Batja Mesquita. 2000. "Beliefs Through Emotions." In Nico H. Frijda, Antony S. R. Manstead, and Sacha Bem, eds., *Emotions and Beliefs: How Feelings Influence Thoughts*. Cambridge: Cambridge University Press, pp. 45–77.

Frijda, Nico H., Antony S.R. Manstead, and Sacha Bem, eds. 2000. *Emotions and Beliefs: How Feelings Influence Thoughts*. Cambridge: Cambridge University Press.

Fuller, Liz. 2004. "Ingushetian Parliamentarians Appeal to North Ossetian Colleagues." *Radio Free Europe/Radio Liberty Newsline* 8, no. 194 (October 13).

Fuller, Liz. 2005. "Deputy Prosecutor Criticized for Beslan Comments." *Radio Free Europe/Radio Liberty Newsline* 9, no.172 (September 12).

Fuller, Liz. 2007. "Federal Official Suggests Ingush Abductions Are Revenge for Beslan." *Radio Free Europe/Radio Liberty Newsline*, July 17.

Fuller, Liz. 2015. "The End of an Era in North Ossetia." *Radio Free Europe/Radio Liberty Newsline*, June 11.

Galani, Sofia. 2019. "Terrorist Hostage-Taking and Human Rights: Protecting Victims of Terrorism under the European Convention on Human Rights." *Human Rights Law Review* 19: 149–171.

Galea, Sandro, Jennifer Ahern, Heidi Resnick, Dean Kilpatrick, Michael Bucuvalas, Joel Gold, and David Vlahov. 2002. "Psychological Sequelae of the September 11 Terrorist Attacks in New York City." *New England Journal of Medicine* 346, no. 13 (March 28): 982–987.

Galea, Sandro, Adam Karpati, and Bruce Kennedy. 2002. "Social Capital and Violence in the United States, 1974–1993." *Social Science & Medicine* 55: 1373–1383.

Gamson, William A. 1968. *Power and Discontent*. Homewood, IL: Dorsey Press.

Gamson, William A. 1975 (1990). *The Strategy of Social Protest*. 2nd ed. Belmont, CA: Wadsworth.

Gamson, William A., Bruce Fireman, and Steven Rytina. 1982. *Encounters with Unjust Authority*. Homewood, IL: Dorsey.

Gamson, William A., and David S. Meyer. 1996. "Framing Political Opportunity." In Doug McAdam, John D. McCarthy, and Mayer N. Zald, eds., *Comparative Perspectives on Social Movements: Political Opportunities, Mobilizing Structures, and Cultural Framings*. Cambridge: Cambridge University Press, pp. 275–290.

Gatsoyeva, Nataliya. 2005. "Kolesnikov opravdal Shepelya [Kolesnikov excused Shepel]," *Izvestiya*, no. 191m (October 21): 3.

Gecas, Viktor. 1989. "The Social Psychology of Self-Efficacy." *Annual Review of Sociology* 15: 291–316.

Gibson, James L., and Marc Morje Howard. 2007. "Russian Anti-Semitism and the Scapegoating of Jews." *British Journal of Political Science* 37, no. 2 (April): 193–223.

Giles, Michael W., Douglas S. Gatlin, and Everett F. Cataldo. 1976. "Racial and Class Prejudice: Their Relative Effects on Protest against School Desegregation." *American Sociological Review* 41 (April): 280–288.

Gilens, Martin. 1995. "Racial Attitudes and Opposition to Welfare." *The Journal of Politics* 57, no. 4 (November): 994–1014.

Gilens, Martin. 1996. "'Race Coding' and White Opposition to Welfare." *American Political Science Review* 90, no. 3 (September): 593–604.

Gilliam, Franklin D., Jr., and Karen M. Kaufman. 1998. "Is There an Empowerment Life Cycle? Long-Term Black Empowerment and Its Influence on Voter Participation." *Urban Affairs Review* 33, no. 6: 741–766.

Gilligan, Michael J., Benjamin J. Pasquale, and Cyrus D. Samii. 2011. "Civil War and Social Capital: Behavioral-Game Evidence from Nepal." New York University. Unpublished manuscript.

"Give Us a Gun, Say Mothers as First Beslan Trial Begins." 2005. *The Times*, May 18.

Glaser, Jack, Jay Dixit, and Donald P. Green. 2002. "Studying Hate Crime with the Internet: What Makes Racists Advocate Racial Violence?" *Journal of Social Issues* 58, no. 1: 177–193.

Goertz, Gary. 2017. *Multimethod Research, Causal Mechanisms, and Case Studies: An Integrated Approach.* Princeton, NJ: Princeton University Press.

Goldstone, Jack A. 2001. "Demography, Environment, and Security: An Overview." In Myron Weiner and Sharon Stanton Russell, eds., *Demography and National Security.* New York: Berghahn Books, pp. 38–61.

Goodwin, Jeff. 2001. *No Other Way Out: States and Revolutionary Movements, 1945–1991.* Cambridge: University of Cambridge Press.

Goodwin, Jeff, and James M. Jasper. 2006. "Emotions and Social Movements." In Jan E. Stets and Jonathan H. Turner, eds., *Handbook of the Sociology of Emotions.* New York: Springer, pp. 611–635.

Graham, Hugh Davis, and Ted Robert Gurr. 1969. *Violence in America: Historical and Comparative Perspectives.* New York: Bantam Books.

Granik, Irina, and Zaur Farniyev. 2011. "Uroven terroristicheskoi ugrozy povyshen do presidentskovo" [Terrorism threat elevates to the presidential level]. *Kommersant*, no. 32 (February 24): 3.

Green, Donald P., Laurence H. McFalls, and Jennifer K. Smith. 2001. "Hate Crime: An Emergent Research Agenda." *Annual Review of Sociology* 27: 479–504.

Gritchin, Nikolai. 2005. "Sledstviye po Beslanu proverit Generalnaya prokuratura" [Prosecutor General's office will review Beslan investigation]. *Izvestia*, September 6, p. 1.

Grodnenskii, Nikolai. 2007. *Pervaya chechenskaya: Istoriya vooruzhenogo konflikta.* Minsk: FUAinform.

Gurin, Charles. 2004. "Ex-North Ossetian Law-Enforcer Describes Endemic Corruption." Jamestown Foundation's *Eurasian Daily Monitor* 1 (September 13): 95.

Gurr, Ted Robert. 1970. *Why Men Rebel.* Princeton, NJ: Princeton University Press.

Hale, Henry E. 2010. "Eurasian Polities as Hybrid Regimes: The Case of Putin's Russia," *Journal of Eurasian Studies* 1, no. 1 (January): 33–41.

Halperin, Eran, Alexandra G. Russell, Carol S. Dweck, and James J. Gross. 2011. "Anger, Hatred, and the Quest for Peace: Anger Can Be Constructive in the Absence of Hatred." *Journal of Conflict Resolution* 55, no. 2: 274–291.

Hamlin, Alan, and Colin Jennings. 2004. "Group Formation and Political Conflict: Instrumental and Expressive Approaches." *Public Choice* 118, no. 3–4 (March): 413–435.

Hamlin, Alan, and Colin Jennings. 2011. "Expressive Political Behaviour: Foundations, Scope and Implications." *British Journal of Political Science* 41, no. 3: 645–670.

Hammarberg, Thomas. 2011. *Report of the Commissioner for Human Rights of the Council of Europe, Following His Visit to the Russian Federation from 12 to 21 May.* Strasbourg: Commissioner for Human Rights.

Hansen-Nord, Nete Sloth, Mette Skar, Finn Kjaerulf, Juan Almendarez, Sergio Bähr, Óscar Sosa, Julio Castro, Anne-Marie Nybo Andersen, and Jens Modvig. 2014. "Social Capital and Violence in Poor Urban Areas of Honduras." *Aggression and Violent Behavior* 19: 643–648.

Haraszti, Miklos. 2004. "Report on Russian Media Coverage of the Beslan Tragedy: Access to Information and Journalists' Working Conditions." *Organization for Security and Co-operation in Europe*, September 16.

Harding, Sue-Ann. 2012. *Beslan: Six Stories of the Siege.* New York: Manchester University Press.

Harmon-Jones, Eddie. 2000. "A Cognitive Dissonance Theory Perspective on the Role of Emotion in the Maintenance and Change of Beliefs and Attitudes." In Nico H. Frijda, Antony S. R. Manstead, and Sacha Bem, eds., *Emotions and Beliefs: How Feelings Influence Thoughts*. Cambridge: Cambridge University Press, pp. 185–211.

Harmon-Jones, Eddie, and Jonathan Sigelman. 2001. "State Anger and Prefrontal Brain Activity: Evidence That Insult-Related Relative Left-Prefrontal Activation Is Associated with Experienced Anger and Aggression." *Journal of Personality and Social Psychology* 80, no. 5: 797–803.

Hayes, Andrew F., Dietram A. Scheufele, and Michael E. Huge. 2006. "Nonparticipation as Self-Censorship: Publicly Observable Political Activity in a Polarized Opinion Climate." *Political Behavior* 28, no. 3 (September): 259–283.

Heath, Anthony, Jean Martin, and Thees Spreckelsen. 2009. "Cross-National Comparability of Survey Attitude Measures." *International Journal of Public Opinion Research* 21: 293–331.

Heinrich, L. M., and E. Gullone. 2006. "The Clinical Significance of Loneliness: A Literature Review." *Clinical Psychology Review* 26, no. 6: 695–718.

Hemment, Julie. 2009. "Soviet-Style Neoliberalism? Nashi, Youth Voluntarism, and the Restructuring of Social Welfare in Russia." *Problems of Post-Communism* 56, no. 6 (November–December): 36–50.

Henrich, Joseph, Richard McElreath, Abigail Barr, Jean Ensminger, Clark Barrett, Alexander Bolyanatz, Juan Camilo Cardenas, Michael Gurven, Edwins Gwako, Natalie Henrich, Carolyn Lesorogol, Frank Marlowe, David Tracer, and John Ziker. 2006. "Costly Punishment across Human Societies." *Science* 312: 1767–1770.

Herman, Burt. 2004. "Row after Row of Freshly Dug Graves." *Associated Press*, September 6.

Herring, Cedric. 1989. "Acquiescence or Activism? Political Behavior among the Politically Alienated." *Political Psychology* 10, no. 1 (March): 135–153.

Herrmann, Richard K., Philip E. Tetlock, and Penny S. Visser. 1999. "Mass Public Decisions to Go to War: A Cognitive-Interactionist Framework." *American Political Science Review* 93, no. 3: 553–573.

Herzog, A. Regula, and Jerald G. Bachman. 1981. "Effects of Questionnaire Length on Response Quality." *Public Opinion Quarterly* 45, no. 4 (Winter): 549–559.

Hjerm, Mikael. 2005. "What the Future May Bring: Xenophobia among Swedish Adolescents." *Acta Sociologica* 48, no. 4 (December): 292–307.

"High-Ranking Security Officer Killed in Ingushetia." 2007. *Itar-Tass*, September 18.

Hirsch, Jameson K., Karen Wolford, Steven M. LaLonde, Lisa Brunk, and Amanda Parker-Morris. 2009. "Optimistic Explanatory Style as a Moderator of the Association between Negative Life Events and Suicide Ideation." *Crisis: The Journal of Crisis Intervention and Suicide Prevention* 30, no. 1: 48–53.

Hochschild A. R. 1975. "The Sociology of Feeling and Emotion: Selected Possibilities." In M. Millman and R. Moss Kanter, eds., *Another Voice: Feminist Perspectives on Social Life and Social Science*. Garden City, NY: Anchor/Doubleday, pp. 280–307.

Holmes, Mary. 2004. "Feeling beyond Rules: Politicizing the Sociology of Emotion and Anger in Feminist Politics." *European Journal of Social Theory* 7, no. 2 (May): 209–227.

Horowitz, Donald. 1985. *Ethnic Groups in Conflict*. Berkeley: University of California Press.

Horowitz, Donald L. 2001. *The Deadly Ethnic Riot*. Berkeley: University of California Press.

Huddy, Leonie, Stanley Feldman, and Erin Cassese. 2007. "On the Distinct Political Effects of Anxiety and Anger." In W. R. Neuman, G. E. Marcus, A. Crigler, and M. B. MacKuen, eds., *The Affect Effect: Dynamics of Emotion in Thinking and Behavior*. Chicago: University of Chicago Press, pp. 202–230.

Huddy, Leonie, Stanley Feldman, Charles Taber, and Gallya Lahav. 2005. "Threat, Anxiety, and Support for Antiterrorism Policies." *American Journal of Political Science* 49, no. 3: 593–608.

Humphreys, Macartan. 2005. "Natural Resources, Conflict, and Conflict Resolution." *The Journal of Conflict Resolution* 49, no. 4 (August): 508–537.

Humphreys, Macartan, and Jeremy M. Weinstein. 2008. "Who Fights? The Determinants of Participation in Civil War." *American Journal of Political Science* 52, no. 2 (April): 436–455.

"Hundreds Still Missing in Beslan." 2004. *BBC News*, September 21.

Huntington, Samuel P. 1968. *Political Order in Changing Societies*. New Haven, CT: Yale University Press.

Ifeagwazi, Chuka Mike, John Bosco, Chika Chukwuorji, and Endurance Avah Zacchaeus. 2015. "Alienation and Psychological Wellbeing: Moderation by Resilience." *Social Indicators Research* 120, no. 2: 525–544.

"In Northern Ossetia the Number of Victims of Beslan Has Increased up to 334." 2006. *15-I Region [North Ossetian Information Portal 15th Region]*, December 8.

Inglehart, Ronald. 1990. *Culture Shift in Advanced Industrial Society*. Princeton, NJ: Princeton University Press.

Inglehart, Ronald, and Christian Welzel. 2005. *Modernization, Cultural Change and Democracy: The Human Development Sequence*. New York: Cambridge University Press.

Isaenko, Anatoly V., and Peter W. Petschauer. 1999. "Traditional Civilization in the North Caucasus: Insiders and Outsiders." In Kathleen Nader, Nancy Dubrow, and B. Hudnall Stamm, eds., *Honoring Differences: Cultural Issues in the Treatment of Trauma and Loss*. Philadelphia: Brunner/Mazel.

Iyengar, Shanto. 1989. "How Citizens Think about National Issues: A Matter of Responsibility." *American Journal of Political Science* 33 (November): 878–897.

Iyengar, Shanto. 1991. *Is Anyone Responsible? How Television Frames Political Issues.* Chicago: University of Chicago Press.

JAC. 2005. "Resurrection of Beslan Children Delayed until Next Year." *Radio Free Europe/ Radio Liberty Newsline: Russia* 9, no. 148 (October 20).

Jack, Andrew. 2004. *Inside Putin's Russia: Can There Be Reform without Democracy.* New York: Oxford University Press.

Jackson, John S. 1973. "Alienation and Black Political Participation." *The Journal of Politics* 35, no. 4 (November): 849–885.

Jackson, Joshua Conrad, Virginia K. Choi, and Michele J. Gelfand. 2019. "Revenge: A Multilevel Review and Synthesis." *Annual Review of Psychology* 70: 319–345.

Jacoby, Susan. 1983. *Wild Justice: The Evolution of Revenge.* New York: Harper & Row.

Jasper, James M. 2011. "Emotions and Social Movements: Twenty Years of Theory and Research." *Annual Review of Sociology* 37: 285–303.

Javeline, Debra. 1999. "Response Effects in Polite Cultures: A Test of Acquiescence in Kazakhstan." *Public Opinion Quarterly* 63, no. 1 (Spring): 1–28.

Javeline, Debra. 2003a. *Protest and the Politics of Blame: The Russian Response to Unpaid Wages.* Ann Arbor: University of Michigan Press.

Javeline, Debra. 2003b. "The Role of Blame in Collective Action: Evidence from Russia." *American Political Science Review* 97, no. 1 (February): 107–121.

Javeline, Debra, and Vanessa A. Baird. 2007. "Who Sues Government? Evidence from the Moscow Theater Hostage Case." *Comparative Political Studies* 40, no. 7 (July): 858–885.

Javeline, Debra, and Vanessa A. Baird. 2011. "The Surprisingly Nonviolent Aftermath of the Beslan School Hostage Taking." *Problems of Post-Communism* 58, no. 4–5 (July/ August–September/October): 3–22.

Javeline, Debra, and Vanessa A. Baird. 2012. "Victim and Non-Victim Behavioral Responses to Ethnic Violence." Paper presented at the Annual Meeting of the American Political Science Association, New Orleans.

Jenkins, J. Craig, and Charles Perrow. 1977. "Insurgency of the Powerless: Farm Worker Movements (1946–1972)." *American Sociological Review* 42 (April): 249–268.

Jersild, Austin. 2002. *Orientalism and Empire: North Caucasus Mountain Peoples and the Georgian Frontier, 1845–1917.* Montreal: McGill-Queen's University Press.

Johnson, Janet Elise, and Aino Saarinen. 2011. "Assessing Civil Society in Putin's Russia: The Plight of Women's Crisis Centers." *Communist and Post-Communist Studies* 44, no. 1 (March): 41–52.

Joiner, T. E. 2005. *Why People Die by Suicide.* Cambridge, MA: Harvard University Press.

Jones, Michael P. 1996. "Indicator and Stratification Methods for Missing Explanatory Variables in Multiple Linear Regression." *Journal of the American Statistical Association* 91 (March): 222–230.

Jost, John T. 1995. "Negative Illusions: Conceptual Clarification and Psychological Evidence Concerning False Consciousness." *Political Psychology* 16: 397–424.

Jost, John T. 2019. "A Quarter Century of System Justification Theory: Questions, Answers, Criticisms, and Societal Applications." *British Journal of Social Psychology* 58: 263–314.

Jost, John T., Banaji, M. R., & Nosek, B. A. 2004. "A Decade of System Justification Theory: Accumulated Evidence of Conscious and Unconscious Bolstering of the Status Quo." *Political Psychology* 25: 881–919.

Jost, John T., B. W. Pelham, O. Sheldon, and B. N. Sullivan. 2003. "Social Inequality and the Reduction of Ideological Dissonance on Behalf of the System: Evidence of Enhanced

System Justification among the Disadvantaged." *European Journal of Social Psychology* 33: 13–36.

Jost, John T., I. Liviatan, J. Van der Toorn, A. Ledgerwood, A. Mandisodza, and B. Nosek. 2010. "System Justification: How Do We Know It's Motivated?" In D. R. Bobocel, A. C. Kay, M. P. Zanna, and J. M. Olson, eds., *The Psychology of Justice and Legitimacy: The Ontario Symposium.* Hillsdale, NJ: Lawrence Erlbaum Associates, vol. 11, pp. 173–203.

Jost, John T., Vagelis Chaikalis-Petritsis, Dominic Abrams, Jim Sidanius, Jojanneke van der Toorn, and Christopher Bratt. 2012. "Why Men (and Women) Do and Don't Rebel: Effects of System Justification on Willingness to Protest." *Personality and Social Psychology Bulletin* 38, no. 2: 197–208.

Justice, Nicole Marie. 2018. "Development and Validation of a Measure of Social Alienation for Student Veterans." University of Northern Colorado, Dissertations. 534.

Kaboyev, Murat. 2005. "Vladimir Kolesnikov: My priyekhali, shtoby nachat robatat" [Vladimir Kolesnikov: we came to start working]. *Novaya gazeta*, no. 67 (September 12).

Kalyvas, Stathis N. 1998. "Wanton and Senseless? The Logic of Massacres in Algeria." *Rationality and Society* 11, no. 3: 243–285.

Kalyvas, Stathis N. 2001. "'New' and 'Old' Civil Wars: A Valid Distinction?" *World Politics* 54 (October): 99–118.

Kalyvas, Stathis N. 2003. "The Ontology of 'Political Violence': Action and Identity in Civil Wars." *Perspectives on Politics* 1, no. 3: 475–494.

Kalyvas, Stathis N. 2006. *The Logic of Violence in Civil War.* New York: Cambridge University Press.

Kalyvas, Stathis N., and Matt Kocher. 2007. "How Free Is 'Free Riding' in Civil Wars? Violence, Insurgency, and the Collective Action Problem." *World Politics* 59, no. 2: 177–216.

Karacheva, Yekaterina. 2006a. "Priglashenie na kazn [Invitation to an execution]," *Vremya novostei*, no. 23 (February 10): 1.

Karacheva, Yekaterina. 2006b. "We Are Ashamed." *Vremya novostei*, no. 22 (February 9): 1–2.

Kaufman, Stuart J. 2001. *Modern Hatreds: The Symbolic Politics of Ethnic War.* Ithaca, NY: Cornell University Press.

Kaufman, Stuart J. 2006. "Symbolic Politics or Rational Choice? Testing Theories of Extreme Ethnic Violence." *International Security* 30, no. 4 (Spring): 45–86.

Kay, A. C., and J. Friesen. 2011. "On Social Stability and Social Change: Understanding When System Justification Does and Does Not Occur." *Current Directions in Psychological Science* 20: 360–364.

Keck, Margaret E., and Kathryn Sikkink. 1998a. *Activists beyond Borders: Advocacy Networks in International Politics.* Ithaca, NY: Cornell University Press.

Keck, Margaret E., and Kathryn Sikkink. 1998b. "Transnational Advocacy Networks in the Movement Society." In David S. Meyer and Sidney Tarrow, eds., *The Social Movement Society: Contentious Politics for a New Century.* New York: Rowman & Littlefield, pp. 217–238.

Keen, David. 2005. *Conflict and Collusion in Sierra Leone.* London: James Currey.

Kelly, Catriona. 2007. *Children's World: Growing up in Russia 1890–1991.* New Haven, CT: Yale University Press.

Kelman, Herbert C. 2008. "Reconciliation From a Social-Psychological Perspective." In Arie Nadler, Thomas E. Malloy, and Jeffrey D. Fisher, eds., *The Social Psychology of Intergroup Reconciliation.* New York: Oxford University Press, pp. 15–32.

Keltner, Dacher, Phoebe C. Ellsworth, and Kari Edwards. 1993. "Beyond Simple Pessimism: Effects of Sadness and Anger on Social Perception." *Journal of Personality and Social Psychology* 64, no. 5 (May): 740–752.

Keniston, Kenneth. 1968. *Young Radicals: Notes on Committed Youth*. New York: Harcourt, Brace, and World.

Khinshtein, Aleksandr. 2004. "Pozor. Prigovoreny k svobode" [Shame. Sentenced to freedom]. *Moskovskii komsomolets*, no. 239 (October 21).

"Khronika zakhvata zalozhnikov v shkole nomer 1 g. Beslan" [Chronicla of the hostage taking in school number 1 in Beslan]. 2009. *RIA Novosti*, September 1.

Kinder, Donald R., and David O. Sears. 1981. "Prejudice and Politics: Symbolic Racism versus Racial Threats to the Good Life." *Journal of Personality and Social Psychology* 40, no. 3: 414–431.

King, Charles. 2008. *The Ghost of Freedom: A History of the Caucasus*. New York: Oxford University Press.

Kiselyev, Ilya. 2006. "Beslan: Pravda, vymysel ili spekulyatsii?" [Beslan: truth, fiction or speculation?]. *Izvestiya*, September 21.

Klandermans, Bert. 1979. "Werklozen en de werklozenbeweging." *Mens en Maatschappij* 54: 5–33.

Klandermans, Bert. 1984. "Mobilization and Participation: Social-Psychological Expansions of Resource Mobilization Theory." *American Sociological Review* 49, no. 5 (October): 583–600.

Klandermans, Bert. 1997. *The Social Psychology of Protest*. Oxford: Wiley-Blackwell.

Klandermans, Bert. 2003. "Collective Political Action." In David O. Sears, Leonie Huddy, and Robert Jervis, eds., *The Oxford Handbook of Political Psychology*. New York: Oxford University Press, pp. 670–709.

Klandermans, Bert, and Dirk Oegema. 1987. "Potentials, Networks, Motivations, and Barriers: Steps Towards Participation in Social Movements." *American Sociological Review* 52, no. 4 (August): 519–531.

Klar, Malte, and Tim Kasser. 2009. "Some Benefits of Being an Activist: Measuring Activism and Its Role in Psychological Well-Being." *Political Psychology* 30, no. 5 (October): 766–777.

Klimecki, Olga M., David Sander, and Patrik Vuilleumier. 2018. "Distinct Brain Areas Involved in Anger versus Punishment during Social Interactions." *Nature* 8: 10556.

Knudsen, Hannah K., Paul M. Roman, J. Aaron Johnson, and Lori J. Ducharme. 2005. "A Changed America? The Effects of September 11th on Depressive Symptoms and Alcohol Consumption." *Journal of Health and Social Behavior* 46, no. 3 (September): 260–273.

Kornhauser, William. 1959. *The Politics of Mass Society*. New York: Macmillan.

Kozenko, Andrei, and Zaur Farniyev. 2009. "Beslanskim detyam vmenili nalog" [Taxes levied on children of Beslan]. *Kommersant*, no. 64 (April 10): 4.

Kuran, Timur. 1998. "Ethnic Dissimilation and Its International Diffusion." In David A. Lake and Donald Rothchild, eds., *The International Spread of Ethnic Conflict: Fear, Diffusion, and Escalation*. Princeton, NJ: Princeton University Press, pp. 35–60.

Kusov, Oleg. 2012. "'Ni odnogo golosa Beslan ne dolzhen otdat Putinu [Not a single vote in Beslan should go to Putin]." *Ekho Kavkaza*, March 2.

Lago, Ignacio, and Jose Ramon Montero. 2006. "The 2004 Election in Spain: Terrorism, Accountability and Voting." *Taiwan Journal of Democracy* 2, no. 1: 13–36.

Laitin, David. 1986. *Hegemony and Culture: Politics and Religious Change among the Yoruba*. Chicago: University of Chicago Press.

Lake, David, and Donald Rothchild. 1996. "Containing Fear: The Origins and Management of Ethnic Conflict." *International Security* 21, no. 2 (Autumn): 41–75.

Lake, David, and Donald Rothchild, eds. 1998. *The International Spread of Ethnic Conflict: Fear, Diffusion, and Escalation*. Princeton, NJ: Princeton University Press.

Lambert, Alan J., Laura D. Scherer, John Paul Schott, Kristina R. Olson, Rick K. Andrews, Thomas C. O'Brien, and Alison R. Zisser. 2010. "Rally Effects, Threat, and Attitude Change: An Integrative Approach to Understanding the Role of Emotion." *Journal of Personality and Social Psychology* 98, no. 6: 886–903.

Lane, E. J., and T.K. Daugherty. 1999. "Correlates of Social Alienation among College Students." *College Student Journal* 33, no. 1: 7–9.

Lansford, Lynn Milburn. 2006. *Beslan: Shattered Innocence*. BookSurge.

Latynina, Yulia. 2010. "Beslan's Main Terrorist Finally Caught." *Moscow Times*, June 16.

Lau, Richard. 1985. "Two Explanations for Negativity Effects in Political Behavior." *American Journal of Political Science* 29: 119–138.

Laufer, Avital, and Zahava Solomon. 2006. "Posttraumatic Symptoms and Posttraumatic Growth among Israeli Youth Exposed to Terror Incidents." *Journal of Social and Clinical Psychology* 25, no. 4: 429–447.

Lavelle, Peter. 2004. "Feature: Beslan's Call for Help." *United Press International*, September 22.

"Lawyer of Russian School Siege Victims Quits Following Threats." 2007. *BBC Monitoring Trans Caucasus Unit*, from Regnum News Agency, September 1.

"Lawyers for Beslan School Siege Victims Dissatisfied with ECHR Ruling." 2017. *Tass*, April 13.

Leahy, Peter, and Allen Mazur. 1978. "A Comparison of Movements Opposed to Nuclear Power, Fluoridation and Abortion." In Louis Kriesberg, ed., *Research in Social Movements, Conflicts and Change*, vol. 1. Greenwich, CT: JAI.

Lee, Alexander. 2011. "Who Becomes a Terrorist? Poverty, Education, and the Origins of Political Violence." *World Politics* 63, no. 2 (April): 203–245.

Leighley, Jan E. 1995. "Opportunities and Incentives: A Field Essay on Political Participation." *Political Research Quarterly* 48, no. 1 (March): 181–209.

Lemaitre, Roemer. 2006. "The Rollback of Democracy in Russia after Beslan." *Review of Central and East European Law* 31: 369–411.

Lemish, Dafna. 2000. "'Four Mothers': The Womb in the Public Sphere." *European Journal of Communication* 15, no. 2: 147–169.

Lenta.ru. 2005. "V zakhvate beslanskoi shkoly uchastvoval saudovskii nayemnik" [Saudi Mercenary participated in the capture of the Beslan school]. *Lentra.ru*, September 1.

Lennon, Rachelle Evelyn. 2013. "A Meta-Analysis of Cultural Differences in Revenge and Forgiveness." University of North Florida, Master's thesis.

Lerner, M. J. 1980. *The Belief in a Just World: A Fundamental Delusion*. New York: Plenum Press.

Levine, Adeline. 1982. *Love Canal: Science, Politics, and People*. Lexington, MA: Lexington Books.

Lichbach, Mark. 1998. *The Rebel's Dilemma*. Ann Arbor: University of Michigan Press.

Lieberman, Evan S. 2005. "Nested Analysis as a Mixed-Method Strategy for Comparative Research." *American Political Science Review* 99, no. 3 (August): 435–452.

Lind, Edgar Allan, and Tom R. Tyler. 1988. *The Social Psychology of Procedural Justice*. New York: Plenum.

Linke, Andrew M., Sebastian Schutte, and Halvard Buhaug. 2015. "Population Attitudes and the Spread of Political Violence in Sub-Saharan Africa." *International Studies Review* 17, no. 1 (March): 26–45.

Linley, P. Alex, and Stephen Joseph. 2004. "Positive Change Following Trauma and Adversity: A Review." *Journal of Traumatic Stress* 17, no. 1 (February): 11–21.

Lipset, Seymour Martin. 1971. "Youth and Politics." In Robert K. Merton and Robert Nisbet, eds., *Contemporary Social Problems*, 3rd ed. New York, Harcourt Brace Jovanovich, pp. 743–791.

Litvinovich, Marina. 2005. "The Truth about Beslan." *Pravda Beslana*. http://www.pravda beslana.ru/truth.htm.

Litvinovich, Marina. 2008. "Dobro pozhalovat v absurdistan, ili troye zhenshchin I vosem muzhchin" [Welcome to Absurdistan, or three women and eight men]. *Yezhednevny zhurnal*, February 11.

Lucas, Jeffrey W. 2003. "Theory-Testing, Generalization, and the Problem of External Validity." *Sociological Theory* 21, no. 3: 236–253.

Luszczynska, Aleksandra, Charles C. Benight, and Roman Cieslak. 2009. "Self-Efficacy and Health-Related Outcomes of Collective Trauma." *European Psychologist* 14, no. 1: 51–62.

Lyall, Jason. 2009. "Does Indiscriminate Violence Incite Insurgent Attacks? Evidence from Chechnya." *Journal of Conflict Resolution* 53, no. 3 (June): 331–362.

Lyons, William E., and David Lowery. 1986. "The Organization of Political Space and Citizen Responses to Dissatisfaction in Urban Communities: An Integrative Model." *The Journal of Politics* 48, no. 2 (May): 321–346.

Mahoney, James, and Gary Goertz. 2004. "The Possibility Principle: Choosing Negative Cases in Comparative Research." *American Political Science Review* 98, no. 4 (November): 653–669.

Mainville, Michael. 2005a. "Beslan Mothers Abandon Protest." *Toronto Star (Canada)*, August 25, p. A10.

Mainville, Michael. 2005b. "Terrorism Response Still Weak, Report Says." *Washington Times*, August 31.

Mainville, Michael. 2005c. "We Have to Take Extreme Measures." *Toronto Star (Canada)*, August 24, p. A04.

Mainville, Michael. 2005d. "Beslan Survivors Beg for Asylum Outside Russia." *Toronto Star (Canada)*, August 31, p. A03.

Mansbridge, Jane, and Aldon Morris, eds. 2001. *Oppositional Consciousness: The Subjective Roots of Social Protest*. Chicago: University of Chicago Press.

Marcus, George E., Michael MacKuen, Jennifer Wolak, and Luke Keele. 2006. "The Measure and Mismeasure of Emotion." In David Redlawsk, ed., *Feeling Politics: Emotion in Political Information Processing*. New York: Palgrave Macmillan, pp. 31–45.

Marcus, George E., W. Russell Neuman, and Michael MacKuen. 2000. *Affective Intelligence and Political Judgment*. Chicago: University of Chicago Press.

Marcus, George E., John L. Sullivan, Elizabeth Theiss-Morse, and Sandra L. Wood. 1995. *With Malice Toward Some: How People Make Civil Liberties Judgments*. Cambridge: Cambridge University Press.

Marzoyeva, Emma. 2009. "Members of 'Voice of Beslan' Complain to Fedoryak of Inspector's Threats." *Caucasian Knot*, September 28.

Marzoyeva, Emma. 2011. "Victims of Beslan Terror Act Tell Khloponin about Drawbacks of Inquiry." *Caucasian Knot*, March 25.

McAdam, Doug. 1982. *Political Process and the Development of Black Insurgency, 1930–1970*. Chicago: University of Chicago Press.

McAdam, Doug. 1986. "Recruitment to High-Risk Activism: The Case of Freedom Summer." *American Journal of Sociology* 92, no. 1 (July): 64–90.

McAdam, Doug. 1989. "The Biographical Consequences of Activism." *American Sociological Review* 54 (October): 744–760.

McAdam, Doug. 1996. "Conceptual Origins, Current Problems, Future Directions." In Doug McAdam, John D. McCarthy, and Mayer N. Zald, eds., *Comparative Perspectives on Social Movements: Political Opportunities, Mobilizing Structures, and Cultural Framings*. Cambridge: Cambridge University Press, pp. 23–40.

McAllister, J. F. O., and Paul Quinn-Judge. 2004. "Defenseless Targets." *Time*, September 5.

McCarthy, John, and Mayer Zald. 1973. *The Trend of Social Movements in America: Professionalization and Resource Mobilization*. Morristown, NJ: General Learning Press.

McCarthy, John, and Mayer Zald. 1977. "Resource Mobilization and Social Movements: A Partial Theory." *American Journal of Sociology* 82, no. 6: 1212–1241.

McCullough, M. E., R. Kurzban, and B. A. Tabak. 2010. "Evolved Mechanisms for Revenge and Forgiveness." In P. R. Shaver and M. Mikulincer, eds., *Understanding and Reducing Aggression, Violence, and Their Consequences*. Washington, DC: American Psychological Association, pp. 221–239.

McDoom, Omar Shahabudin. 2013. "Who Killed in Rwanda's Genocide? Micro-space, Social Influence and Individual Participation in Intergroup Violence." *Journal of Peace Research* 50, no. 4: 453–467.

Medetsky, Anatoly, and Yana Voitova. 2005. "A Reversal over Beslan Only Fuels Speculation." *Moscow Times*, July 21.

Melander, Erik. 2005. "Political Gender Equality and State Human Rights Abuse." *Journal of Peace Research* 42, no. 2: 149–166.

Mereu, Francesca. 2005. "Beslan Witnesses Accused of Falsehoods." *Moscow Times*, September 14: 3.

Mereu, Francesca. 2007. "Beslan Mothers an Island of Opposition." *Moscow Times*, November 30: 1.

Meteleva, Svetlana. 2005a. "Sovershenno sekretno. Beslan bez grifov." *Moskovskii komsolets*, no. 113 (May 25).

Meteleva, Svetlana. 2005b. "Sovershenno sekretno. Beslan bez grifov." *Moskovskii komsolets*, no. 114 (May 26).

Migalin, Sergei. 2005. "Kesayev myagko upreknul silovikov v nedorabotkakh" [Kesayev mildly rebuked law enforcement agencies]. *Nezavisimaya Gazeta*, no. 260 (November 30).

Migalin Sergei, and Aleksandra Samarina. 2005. "Dzasokhov Says Good-bye, but He Hasn't Left Politics." *Nezavisimaya Gazeta*, no. 114 (June 8): 4.

Mikula, Gerold, Klaus R. Scherer, and Ursula Athenstaedt. 1998. "The Role of Injustice in the Elicitation of Differential Emotional Reactions." *Personality and Social Psychology Bulletin* 24, no. 7 (July): 769–783.

Mikulincer, Mario. 1988. "Reactance and Helplessness Following Exposure to Unsolvable Problems: The Effects of Attributional Style." *Journal of Personality and Social Psychology* 54: 679–686.

Milashina, Elena. 2004a. "Sentiyabr 2004. Okno s vidom na shturm" [September 2004. Window overlooking the storm]. *N ovaya gazeta*, no. 66 (September 9).

Milashina, Elena. 2004b. "Kak shturmovali shkolu" [How the school was stormed]. *Novaya gazeta*, no. 74 (October 7).

Milashina, Elena. 2004c. "Ochevidtsy: Krysha zagorelas, kogda po nei stali strelyat kakumi-to snaryadami" [Eyewitnesses: The roof burned when they started to shoot some kind of missiles at it]. *Novaya gazeta*, no. 74 (October 7).

Milashina, Elena. 2005a. "Rassledovaniya: Polety shmelei" [Investigations: Flights of 'the Shmel']. *Novaya gazeta*, no. 51 (July 18).

Milashina, Elena. 2005b. "Den neznaniya" [Day of ignorance]. *Novaya gazeta*, no. 64 (September 1).

Milashina, Elena. 2005c. "Politika/Rassledovaiya. Kogda strelyali tanki" [Politics/ Investigations. When the tanks fired]. *Novaya gazeta*, no. 89 (November 28).

Milashina, Elena. 2006a. "Korpunkt v Beslane. Peregovorshchik" [News bureau in Beslan: The negotiator]. *Novaya gazeta*, no. 6 (January 30).

Milashina, Elena. 2006b. "Politika/Rassledovaniya. Sud ustal. [Politics/Investigations. The Court is tired]," *Novaya gazeta*, no. 11 (February 16): 6.

Milashina, Elena. 2006c. "Ostalis printsipalnye doprosy [Principal interrogations remain]," *Novaya gazeta*, no. 13 (February 20): 7.

Milashina, Elena. 2006d. "Beslan. Rezultaty Rassledovaniya: Fakty, svidetelstva, khronologiya. Yest lyui, kotorym izvestno vsye" [Beslan. Results of the investigation: There are people who know everything]. *Novaya gazeta*, no. 65 (August 28).

Milashina, Elena. 2006e. "Beslan. Rezultaty Rassledovaniya: 13.03 03.09.2004. Pravda o pervykh vzryvakh" [Belsan. Results of the investigation: 13.03 03.09.2004. The truth about the first explosions]. *Novaya gazeta*, no. 65 (August 28).

Milashina, Elena. 2007a. "Zdes bolshe nekogo sudit [There's no one else here to try]," *Novaya gazeta*, no. 40 (May 31): 5.

Milashina, Elena. 2007b. "Kogda strelyal tank n.325?" [When did tank no.325 fire?]. *Novaya gazeta*, no. 55 (July 23).

Milashina, Elena. 2007c. "Shkolu vzorvali ne terroristy" [It wasn't terrorists who blew up the school]. *Novaya gazeta*, no. 57 (August 1).

Milashina, Elena. 2007d. "Ne zhenskoye dyelo" [Not women's business]. *Novaya gazeta*, no. 65 (August 27): 4.

Milashina, Elena. 2010. "Two Beslans." *Novaya gazeta* (September 3).

Milashina, Elena. 2012. "Strasburgskaya zhaloba po delu Beslana vesit 43 kilogramma" [Strasbourg complaint in the Beslan case weighs 43 kilograms]. *Novaya gazeta*, no. 98 (August 31).

Milashina, Elena. 2014. "Chtoby grazhdanye Rossii uslyshali i ponyali" [So the citizens of Russia would hear and understand]. *Novaya gazeta*, no. 117 (October 17).

Milgram, Stanley. 1963. "Behavioral Study of Obedience." *Journal of Abnormal and Social Psychology* 67, no. 4: 371–378.

Milgram, Stanley. 1974. *Obedience to Authority: An Experimental View.* New York: Harper & Row.

Miller, Arthur H. 1974. "Rejoinder to 'Comment' by Jack Citrin: Political Discontent or Ritualism." *The American Political Science Review* 68, no. 3 (September): 989–1001.

Miller, Dale T. 2001. "Disrespect and the Experience of Injustice." *Annual Review of Psychology* 52, no. 1: 527–553.

Mirowsky, John, and Catherine E. Ross. 1989. *Social Causes of Psychological Distress.* New York: Aldine de Gruyter.

Mirowsky, John, and Catherine E. Ross. 2002. "Depression, Parenthood, and Age at First Birth." *Social Science and Medicine* 54 (April): 1281–1288.

Mishtein, Ilya. 2006. "Podryvnaya literature. Pravda zalozhnikov" [Subversive literature. The truth of the hostages]. *Novaya vremya*, no. 036 (September 10): 10–11.

Mite, Valentinas. 2004. "Russia: Mourning Period Ends for Beslan Tragedy Amid Fears of Interethnic Violence." *Radio Free Europe/Radio Liberty*, October 13.

Moghaddam, F. M. 2005. "The Staircase to Terrorism: A Psychological Exploration." *American Psychologist* 60: 161–169. doi: 10.1037/0003-066X.60.2.161.

Molotch, Harvey. 1970. "Oil in Santa Barbara and Power in America." *Sociological Inquiry* 40: 131–144.

Monroe, Kristen Renwick. 1996. *The Heart of Altruism: Perceptions of a Common Humanity*. Princeton, NJ: Princeton University Press.

Monroe, Kristen Renwick. 2004. *The Hand of Compassion: Portraits of Moral Choice during the Holocaust*. Princeton, NJ: Princeton University Press.

Monroe, Kristen Renwick, James Hankin, and Renée Bukovchik Van Vechten. 2000. "The Psychological Foundations of Identity Politics." *Annual Review of Political Science* 3 (June): 419–447.

Moore, Robert S. 1975. "Religion as a Source of Variation in Working-Class Images of Society." In Martin Bulmer, ed., *Working Class Images of Society*. London: Routledge and Kegan Paul, pp. 35–55.

Morris, Aldon. 1981. "Black Southern Student Sit-in Movements: An Analysis of Internal Organization." *American Sociological Review* 46: 744–767.

Morris, Aldon D. 1984. *The Origins of the Civil Rights Movement: Black Communities Organizing for Change*. New York: The Free Press.

"Moscow Police Break Up Rally Mourning Beslan School Tragedy." 2006. *MosNews.com*, September 3.

Moshkin, Mikhail, and Maria Bondarenko. 2006. "Not a Period but a Comma: Final Report from the Parliament's Beslan Commission Left More Questions than Answers." *Nezavisimaya gazeta*, December 25, p. 3.

Moskalenko, Sophia, and Clark McCauley. 2009. "Measuring Political Mobilization: The Distinction between Activism and Radicalism." *Terrorism and Political Violence* 21: 239–260.

Muller, Edward N. 1972. "A Partial Test of a Theory of Potential for Political Violence." *American Political Science Review* 66 (September): 928–959.

Muller, Edward N. 1982. "An Explanatory Model for Differing Types of Participation." *European Journal of Political Research* 10: 1–16.

Muller, Edward N., Henry A. Dietz, and Steven E. Finkel. 1991. "Discontent and the Expected Utility of Rebellion: The Case of Peru." *American Political Science Review* 85, no. 4 (December): 1262–1282.

Muller, Edward N., and R. Kenneth Godwin. 1984. "Democratic and Aggressive Political Participation: Estimation of a Nonrecursive Model." *Political Behavior* 6, no. 2: 129–146.

Muller, Edward N., Thomas O. Jukam, and Mitchell A. Seligson. 1982. "Diffuse Political Support and Antisystem Political Behavior: A Comparative Analysis." *American Journal of Political Science* 26, no. 2 (May): 240–264.

Muller, Edward N., and Karl-Dieter Opp. 1986. "Rational Choice and Rebellious Collective Action." *American Political Science Review* 80, no. 2 (June): 471–487.

Murphy, Shirley A., L. Clark Johnson, and Janet Lohan. 2002. "The Aftermath of the Violent Death of a Child: An Integration of the Assessments of Parents' Mental Distress and PTSD during the First 5 Years of Bereavement." *Journal of Loss and Trauma* 7: 203–222.

Mydans, Seth. 2004a. "For Some Beslan Families, Hope Itself Dies Agonizingly." *New York Times*, September 17, p. A3.

Mydans, Seth. 2004b. "In Ethnic Tinderbox, Fear of Revenge for School Killings." *New York Times*, September 20, p. A3.

Myers, Steven Lee. 2006a. "Death Penalty Asked for Beslan Raider, Reviving a Debate." *New York Times*, February 10, p. A12.

Myers, Steven Lee. 2006b. "World Briefing | Europe: Russia: Chechnya School Siege Toll Up to 334." *New York Times*, December 9, p. A10.

Nadler, Arie, Thomas E. Malloy, and Jeffrey D. Fisher, eds. 2008. *The Social Psychology of Intergroup Reconciliation*. New York: Oxford University Press.

Naidenov, Igor. 2005a. "Beslanskii sindrom. Chast No. 1 Zavist" [Beslan syndrome. Part 1. Envy]. *Izvestia*, August 28, reprinted in English in Rebecca Kalisher, ed., *Journalism as an Act of Conscience*. Kostroma: Kostroma Publishers, pp. 80–85.

Naidenov, Igor. 2005b. "Beslanskii sindrom. Chast No. 2" [Beslan syndrome. Part 2. Obsession]. *Izvestia*, August 29, reprinted in English in Rebecca Kalisher, ed., *Journalism as an Act of Conscience*. Kostroma: Kostroma Publishers, pp. 86–92.

Naidenov, Igor. 2005c. "Beslanskii sindrom. Chast No. 3" [Beslan syndrome. Part 3. Hatred]. *Izvestia*, August 30, reprinted in English in Rebecca Kalisher, ed., *Journalism as an Act of Conscience*. Kostroma: Kostroma Publishers, pp. 92–98.

"Negligence Trial of Beslan Police Is Adjourned." 2006. *Agence France Presse*, January 13.

Nepstad, Sharon Erickson. 2007. "Oppositional Consciousness among the Privileged: Remaking Religion in the Central America Solidarity Movement." *Critical Sociology* 33: 661–688.

Nichol, Jim. 2010. "Stability in Russia's Chechnya and Other Regions of the North Caucasus: Recent Developments." Congressional Research Service, December 13.

Nilson, Douglas C., and Linda Burzotta Nilson. 1980. "Trust in Elites and Protest Orientation: An Integrative Approach." *Political Behavior* 2, no. 4: 385–404.

Niven, David. 2000. "The Other Side of Optimism: High Expectations and the Rejection of Status Quo Politics." *Political Behavior* 22, no. 1 (March): 71–88.

Norris, Pippa. 2002. *Democratic Phoenix: Reinventing Political Activism*. New York: Cambridge University Press.

North, Douglass C., John Joseph Wallis, and Barry R. Weingast. 2009. *Violence and Social Orders: A Conceptual Framework for Interpreting Recorded Human History*. New York: Cambridge University Press.

"Notorious North Caucasus Militant Gets Life Sentence." 2013. *RIA Novosti*, as reprinted in *Moscow Times*, October 17.

Nowak, David. 2008. "Marshals Say Group Beat Them." *Moscow Times*, February 12.

Oatley, Keith. 2000. "The Sentiments and Beliefs of Distributed Cognition." In Nico H. Frijda, Antony S. R. Manstead, and Sacha Bem, eds., *Emotions and Beliefs: How Feelings Influence Thoughts*. Cambridge: Cambridge University Press, pp. 78–107.

Oberschall, Anthony. 1973. *Social Conflict and Social Movements*. Englewood Cliffs, NJ: Prentice-Hall, Inc.

Oberschall, Anthony. 1996. "Opportunities and Framing in the East European Revolts of 1989." In Doug McAdam, John D. McCarthy, and Mayer N. Zald, eds., *Comparative Perspectives on Social Movements: Political Opportunities, Mobilizing Structures, and Cultural Framings*. Cambridge: Cambridge University Press, pp. 93–121.

O'Donnell, D. A., M. E. Schwab-Stone, and V. Ruchkin. 2006. "The Mediating Role of Alienation in the Development of Maladjustment in Youth Exposed to Community Violence." *Development and Psychopathology* 18, no. 1: 215–232.

Odynova, Alexandra. 2011. "Medvedev Snubbing Beslan Mothers Talks." *Moscow Times,* May 6.

Oegema, Dirk, and Bert Klandermans. 1994. "Why Social Movement Sympathizers Don't Participate: Erosion and Nonconversion of Support." *American Sociological Review* 59, no. 5 (October): 703–722.

Official Kremlin International News Broadcast. 2005. "Press Conference on the Way Funds Raised in the US for the Children of Beslan Has Been Used with Producer Georgy Vasilyev and Doctor Leonid Roshal." *RIA Novosti,* August 29.

Olisayeva, Albina. 2004. "Postradavshiye v Beslane proveli vo dvore shkoly miting" [Victims of Beslan terrorist act hold rally]. *RIA Novosti,* December 17.

O'Loughlin, John, and Frank D. W. Witmer. 2011. "The Localized Geographies of Violence in the North Caucasus of Russia, 1999–2007." *Annals of the Association of American Geographers* 101, no. 1 (January): 178–201.

O'Loughlin, John, and Frank D. W. Witmer. 2012. "The Diffusion of Violence in the North Caucasus of Russia, 1999–2010." *Environment & Planning A* 44, no. 10 (October): 2379–2396.

Olson, Mancur. 1965. *The Logic of Collective Action: Public Goods and the Theory of Groups.* Cambridge, MA: Harvard University Press.

Olzak, Susan. 1992. *The Dynamics of Ethnic Competition and Conflict.* Stanford, CA: Stanford University Press.

Olzak, Susan, 2006. *The Global Dynamics of Racial and Ethnic Mobilization.* Stanford, CA: Stanford University Press.

Omoto, Allen M., and Mark Snyder. 1995. "Sustained Helping Without Obligation: Motivation, Longevity of Service, and Perceived Attitude Change among AIDS Volunteers." *Journal of Personality and Social Psychology* 68: 671–686.

"Only One Beslan Victim Has Yet to Receive ECHR-Awarded Payout: Justice Ministry." 2019. *Interfax,* September 3.

Opp, Karl-Dieter. 1988. "Grievances and Participation in Social Movements." *American Sociological Review* 53, no. 6 (December): 853–864.

O'Regan, Davin. 2018. "Civil Society and Civil War Onset: What Is the Relationship?" Center for Internationa & Security Studies at Maryland Working Paper, December.

O'Reilly, Jane, Karl Aquino, and Daniel Skarlicki. 2016. "The Lives of Others: Third Parties' Responses to Others' Injustice." *Journal of Applied Psychology* 101, no. 2: 171–189.

Osadchuk, Svetlana. 2008. "Beslan Group Is Called Extremist." *Moscow Times,* January 14: 2.

Osborn, Andrew. 2004a. "Russian Tells American to Mind Its Own Business after Democracy Lecture." *The New Zealand Herald,* September 16.

Osborn, Andrew. 2004b. "Beslan Hostage-Takers Were on Drugs." *The Independent,* October 18.

Osborn, Andrew. 2004c. "Flame-throwers Used at Beslan Seige." *The Independent,* October 24.

Osborne, D., J. T. Jost, J. C. Becker, V. Badaan, and C. G. Sibley. 2019. "Protesting to Challenge or Defend the System? A System Justification Perspective on Collective Action." *European Journal of Social Psychology* 49, no. 2 (March): 244–269.

Osgood, D. Wayne, and Jeff M. Chambers. 2000. "Social Disorganization Outside the Metropolis: An Analysis of Rural Youth Violence." *Criminology* 38, no. 1 (February): 81–116.

"Ossetian Official Freed in Chechnya." 1997. *Moscow Times*, July 5.

"Ossetian Revenge Killer Honoured," 2008. *Institute for War & Peace Reporting*, February 6.

"Over 5,000 Attend Remembrance Ceremony for Beslan Victims." 2009. *RIA Novosti*, September 3.

Page, Jeremy. 2005a. "Beslan Hostage-taker's Trial Fails to Satisfy the Grieving Families." *The Times (UK)*, August 27.

Page, Jeremy. 2005b. "Putin Overture Angers Beslan Mothers." *The Times (UK)*, August 30.

Page, Jeremy. 2005c. "Victims of Beslan Siege Found in a Rubbish Dump." *The Times*, February 26.

Page, Jeremy. 2005d. "We Do Not Wish to Live in a Country Where a Human Life Means Nothing." *The Times (UK)*, September 2, p. 39.

Paluck, Elizabeth Levy, Seth A. Green, and Donald P. Green. 2019. "The Contact Hypothesis Re-evaluated." *Behavioural Public Policy* 3, no. 2: 129–158.

Panyushkin, Valery. 2006a. "Beslan zabyvayetsya" [Beslan is being forgotten]. *Kommersant*, no. 163 (September 2): 3.

Panyushkin, Valery. 2006b. "Beslan chuvstvuyet sebya obmanutym" [Beslan feels cheated]. *Kommersant*, no. 163 (September 4).

Parfitt, Tom. 2004. "How Beslan's Children Are Learning to Cope." *Lancet* 364, no. 9450 (December 4): 2009–2010.

Parfitt, Tom. 2006. "Beslan Militant 'Lived to Kill Again.'" *The Guardian*, May 21.

Parfitt, Tom. 2008. "Relatives of Victims of Beslan Siege Go on Trial." *The Guardian*, January 14.

Parfitt, Tom. 2011. "The Secret History of Beslan." *Foreign Policy*, March 1.

Paris, Roland. 2004. *At War's End: Building Peace after Civil Conflict*. Cambridge: Cambridge University Press.

"Parliament to Investigate." 2004. *Reuters*, September 16.

Paxton, Pamela, Sheri Kunovich, and Melanie M. Hughes. 2007. "Gender in Politics." *Annual Review of Sociology* 33: 263–284.

Pearlman, Wendy. 2011. *Violence, Nonviolence, and the Palestinian National Movement*. Cambridge: Cambridge University Press.

Petersen, Roger D. 2002. *Understanding Ethnic Violence: Fear, Hatred, and Resentment in Twentieth-Century Eastern Europe*. Cambridge: Cambridge University Press.

Petersen, Roger, and Sarah Zukerman. 2009. "Anger, Violence, and Political Science." In M. Potegal, G. Stemmler, and C. Spielberger, eds., *A Handbook of Anger: Constituent and Concomitant Biological, Psychological, and Social Processes*. New York: Springer, pp. 561–581.

Pettigrew, Thomas F., and Linda R. Tropp. 2006. "A Meta-Analytic Test of Intergroup Contact Theory." *Journal of Personality and Social Psychology* 90: 751–783.

Phillips, Timothy. 2007. *Beslan: The Tragedy of School No. 1*. London: Granta UK.

Pierce, John C., and Addison Carey, Jr. 1971. "Efficacy and Participation: A Study of Black Political Behavior." *Journal of Black Studies* 2, no. 2: 201–223.

Piliavin, Jane Allyn, and Peter L. Callero. 1991. *Giving Blood: The Development of an Altruistic Identity*. Baltimore, MD: John Hopkins University Press.

Piotrowski, Przemyslaw. 2004. "Soccer Hooliganism in Poland: Its Extent, Dynamism and Psycho-Social Conditions." In Richard Jackson, ed., *(Re)Constructing Cultures of Violence and Peace.* Amsterdam: Rodopi, pp. 79–89.

Piston, Spencer. 2010. "How Explicit Racial Prejudice Hurt Obama in the 2008 Election." *Political Behavior* 32, no. 4 (December): 431–451.

Piven, Frances Fox, and Richard Cloward. 1977. *Poor People's Movements: How They Succeed, Why They Fail.* New York: Vintage.

Plotnikova, Rita, and Midea Mitrophanova. 2006. "The Beslan Tragedy: All Are Welcome in the Russian Red Cross Rehabilitation Center." August 30. Red Cross Operations Update.

Plutzer, Eric. 2002. "Becoming a Habitual Voter: Inertia, Resources, and Growth in Young Adulthood." *American Political Science Review* 96, no. 1 (March): 41–56.

"Police Charged over Beslan Siege." 2004. *BBC News*, October 27.

Politkovskaya, Anna. 2001. *A Dirty War.* London: The Harvill Press.

Politkovskaya, Anna. 2003. *A Small Corner of Hell: Dispatches from Chechnya.* Chicago: University of Chicago Press.

Politkovskaya, Anna. 2006. "Beslan. Rezultaty rassledovaniya: Dokumenty dlya vnutrennego polzovaniya" [Beslan. Results of the investigation: Documents for internal use]. *Novaya gazeta*, no. 65 (August 28): 6–7.

Politkovskaya, Anna. 2007. *A Russian Diary: A Journalist's Final Account of Life, Corruption, and Death in Putin's Russia.* London: Harvill Secker.

Popova, Nadezhda. 2004. "Obmana ne budyet" [There'll be no lies]. *Nezavisimaya gazeta*, no. 190 (September 6): 1.

"Poterpevshiye Beslana vstretilis s novym zamgenprokurorom v YuFO" [Beslan victims met with the new deputy prosecutor general in the Southern Federal District]. 2006. *15th Region: North Ossetian Information Portal*, August 9.

"Power Agents from Beslan Can Be Amnestied." 2007. *Caucasian Knot: North Osetia–Alania, South Federal District / Power organs, Crime*, May 11.

"Psychological Aid Center Opened in Beslan." 2005. *RIA Novosti*, May 15.

"Psychologists Provide Help to 5,000 Beslan Victims." 2005. *ITAR-TASS*, January 19.

Racheva, Elena. 2005a. "Mesto sobytii. Protest korotyi ne slushali" [Scene. The protest that was not attended]. *Novaya gazeta*, no. 1917 (March 10): 4.

Racheva, Elena. 2005b. "Korpunkt v Beslane. Zhivaya ploshchad" [News Bureau in Beslan. Living Area]. *Novaya gazeta*, no. 1918 (March 14): 9.

Radloff, Lenore S. 1977. "The CES-D Scale: A Self-Report Depression Scale for Research in the General Population." *Applied Psychological Measurement* 1 (Summer): 385–401.

Ransford, H. Edward 1968. "Isolation, Powerlessness, and Violence: A Study of Attidues and Participation in the Watts Riot." *American Journal of Sociology* 73, no. 5 (March): 581–591.

Ratiani, Natalia. 2005. "Materi Beslana doverilis Putinu [Beslan mothers put their trust in Putin]," *Izvestia*, September 5, p. 3.

Rechkalov, Vadim. 2006. "Voina. Terakt o trekh golovakh" [War. The terrorist act according to three heads]. *Moskovskii komsomolets*, no. 194 (August 30): 1, 4.

Reef, Mary Jo, and David Knoke. 1999. "Political Alienation and Efficacy." In John P. Robinson, Phillip R. Shaver, and Lawrence S. Wrightsman, eds., *Measures of Political Attitudes.* San Diego, CA: Academic Press, pp. 413–464.

Reuter, John. 2004. *Chechnya's Suicide Bombers: Desperate, Devout, or Deceived?* Washington, DC: American Committee for Peace in Chechnya, August 23.

Revazova, Regina, and Madina Teziyeva. 2005. "Prokurorskaya peretasovka" [Prosecutorial reshuffle]. *Noviye Izvestia*, no. 167 (September 15): 6.

"Rights Activists Outraged at Slander Charges Filed against Memorial Center Head." 2010. *Russia & CIS General Newswire*, September 13.

Robbins, Joseph, Lance Hunter, and Gregg R. Murray. 2013. "Voters Versus Terrorists: Analyzing the Effect of Terrorist Events on Voter Turnout." *Journal of Peace Research* 50, no. 4: 495–508.

Robertson, Graeme B. 2009. "Managing Society: Protest, Civil Society, and Regime in Putin's Russia." *Slavic Review* 68, no. 3: 528–547.

Robertson, Graeme B. 2011. *The Politics of Protest in Hybrid Regimes: Managing Dissent in Post-Communist Russia*. New York: Cambridge University Press.

Rodriguez, Alex. 2004a. "The Russian School Tragedy; Grieving City Seethes with Talk of Revenge." *The Chicago Tribune*, September 6.

Rodriguez, Alex. 2004b. "Terror Lingers in Russia's Caucasus Region." *The Chicago Tribune*, October 12.

Roefs, Marlene, Bert Klandermans, and Johan Olivier. 1998. "Protest Intentions on the Eve of South Afrida's First Nonracial Elections: Optimists Look Beyond Injustice." *Mobilization: An International Journal* 3, no. 1: 51–68.

Rosenstone, Steven J., and John Mark Hansen. 1993. *Mobilization, Participation, and Democracy in America*. New York: Longman.

Ross, Marc Howard. 1993. *The Culture of Conflict: Interpretations and Interests in a Comparative Perspective*. New Haven, CT: Yale University Press.

Rossiter, J. R. 2002. "The C-OAR-SE Procedure to Scale Development in Marketing." *International Journal of Research in Marketing* 19: 305–335.

Royston, Patrick. 2005. "Multiple Imputation of Missing Values: Update of Ice." *Stata Journal* 5: 527–36.

Rubin, Donald B. 1987. *Multiple Imputation for Nonresponse in Surveys*. New York: Wiley.

Rüdig, Wolfgang, and Georgios Karyotis. 2014. "Who Protests in Greece? Mass Opposition to Austerity." *British Journal of Political Science* 44, no. 3 (July): 487–513.

Rule, James B. 1988. *Theories of Civil Violence*. Berkeley: University of California Press.

"Russia: Beslan Families Appeal against Amnesty for Local Police Chiefs." 2007. *ITAR-TASS*, retrieved through *BBC Worldwide Monitoring*, June 6.

"Russia: Beslan Marks 1,000 Days since Tragedy." 2007. *Ekho Moskvy*, May 30, retrieved through *BBC Worldwide Monitoring*.

"Russia: Beslan Mothers Demand Law to Protect Victims of Terror." 2009. *Interfax News Agency*, retrieved through *BBC Monitoring Former Soviet Union – Political*, September 2.

"Russia: Beslan Teachers Say 400 Hostages Unaccounted For." 2004. *BBC Monitoring International Reports*, September 21.

"Russia: Beslan Terror Victims Demand More Attention, Assistance from State." 2010. *Ekho Moskvy Radio*, retrieved through *BBC Monitoring Former Soviet Union – Political*, November 13.

"Russia: Beslan Victims Appeal Against Court Verdict." 2006. *BBC Worldwide Monitoring (Trans Caucasus Unit)*, June 3.

"Russia: Beslan Victims' Families Complain to European Court of Human Rights." 2007. *ITAR-TASS*, retrieved through *BBC Worldwide Monitoring*, June 26.

"Russia: NGO Leader Denies Extremism Charges by Ingush Court." 2008. *Kavkazkiy Uzel* website, retrieved through *BBC Worldwide Monitoring*, January 16.

"Russia: Prosecutor Says Beslan Victims to Be Able to See Case Materials." 2004. *Moscow ITAR-TASS*, November 11.

Russia: The Ingush-Ossetian Conflict in the Prigorodnyi Region. 1996. New York: Human Rights Watch/Helsinki.

"Russia: Trial of Police Accused of Negligence over Beslan Begins." 2006. *Russian Channel One TV*, retrieved through *BBC Worldwide Monitoring*, January 13.

"Russian Campaign Group Want Proof Beslan Hostage-Taker Still Alive." 2007. *BBC Worldwide Monitoring*, January 4.

"Russian Court Amnesties Beslan Policemen Despite Protests." 2007. *RIA Novosti*, retrieved through *BBC Worldwide Monitoring*, May 29.

"Russian Court Charges District Police Officials in Connection with 2004 Beslan School Seizure." 2007. *The Associated Press*, June 27.

"Russian Court Overrules Move to Put Officials in the Dock over Beslan Siege." 2007. *Interfax News Agency*, retrieved through *BBC Monitoring*, May 2.

"Russian Federation: Beslan—One Year On. Rehabilitation for a Scarred Town." 2005. UNICEF, available at www.unicef.org/ceecis/2709.html.

"Russian NGO Calls for Removal of Beslan School Attack Investigator." 2008. *Ekho Moskvy Radio*, retrieved through *BBC Monitoring Former Soviet Union – Political*, January 5.

"Russian NGO Disappointed in Putin's Reaction to Appeal," 2008. *BBC Monitoring Trans Caucasus Unit*, January 31.

"Russian Red Cross Comm Assigns 178 Mln Rbls to Beslan Victims." 2005. *ITAR-TASS*, August 31.

"Russian Rights Activists Seek Meeting with UN Commissioner." 2006. *Russia & CIS General Newswires, Interfax News Agency*, February 22.

"Russia Supreme Court Upholds Acquittal of Beslan Police." 2008. *RIA Novosti*, March 6.

Sageyeva, Madina. 2006a. "Prosecutor Promises to Eliminate Beslan Case Shortcomings, if Any." *ITAR-TASS News Agency*, August 9.

Sageyeva, Madina. 2006b. "Beslan to Mourn Terror Victims Two Years after Siege." *Itar-Tass Weekly News*, August 30.

Sageyeva, Madina. 2013. "'Materi Beslana' prizyvayut prezidenta SShA ne preimenyat silu protiv Sirii" ['Mothers of Beslan' call on the president of the USA not to use force against Syria]. *Itar-Tass*, September 4.

Sageyeva, Madina, and Zarina Khubezhova. 2005. "Beslan Mothers to Bring Action against Cult Leader." *ITAR-TASS*, September 25.

Samoipova, Tatyana. 2006. "Beslan: Two Years since the Tragedy." *Izvestiya*, September 14.

Sands, David R. 2004a. "Ethnic, Religious Rivalries Blamed." *Washington Times*, September 9.

Sands, David R. 2004b. "Horror, Frozen in Time: For Beslan, Grief Is Inconsolable." *Washington Times*, December 6, p. A01.

Saradzhyan, Simon. 2005. "Beslan Panel Clears Authorities." *Moscow Times*, December 28.

Sasson-Levy, Orna, Yagil Levy, and Edna Lomsky-Feder. 2011. "Women Breaking the Silence: Military Service, Gender, and Antiwar Protest." *Gender & Society* 25, no. 6 (December): 740–763.

Satterfield, Jason, and Martin Seligman. 1994. "Military Aggression and Risk Predicted by Explanatory Style." *Psychological Science* 5: 77–82.

Savina, Yekaterina, Zaur Farniyev, Maria Plyusnina, and Yevgenia Pastukhova. 2008. "Vlastyam pripomnili zhertv Beslana" [Authorities get reminded of Beslan victims]. *Kommersant*, no. 158 (September 4): 5.

Savina, Yekaterina, and Tamila Dzhodzhua. 2008. "Vladimira Putina obvinili v prestupnoi khalatnosti" [Vladimir Putin accused of criminal negligence]. *Kommersant*, no. 96 (June 5): 6.

Savva, Mihail V., and Valerii A. Tishkov. 2012. "Civil Society Institutions and Peacemaking." *Russian Social Science Review* 53, no. 3: 60–87.

Schaefer, Robert W. 2011. *The Insurgency in Chechnya and the North Caucasus: From Gazavat to Jihad*. Santa Barbara, CA: Praeger Security International.

Schepp, Matthias. 2009. "Russia's Sept. 11: Five Years On, Beslan's Survivors Feel Forsaken." *Spiegel Online International*, August 24.

Scheppele, Kim, and Jack Walker. 1991. "The Litigation Strategies of Interest Groups." In Jack Walker, ed., *Mobilizing Interest Groups in America*. Ann Arbor: University of Michigan Press, pp. 335–372.

Schirmer, Jennifer G. 1989. "'Those Who Die for Life Cannot Be Called Dead': Women and Human Rights Protest in Latin America." *Feminist Review* 32 (Summer): 3–29.

Schlenger, William E., Juesta M. Caddell, Lori Ebert, B. Kathleen Jordan, Kathryn M. Rourke, David Wilson, Lisa Thalji, J. Michael Dennis, John A. Fairbank, and Richard A. Kulka. 2002. "Psychological Reactions to Terrorist Attacks: Findings from the National Study of Americans' Reactions to September 11." *Journal of the American Medical Association* 288, no. 5 (August 7): 581–588.

Schlozman, Kay Lehman, Nancy Elizabeth Burns, and Sidney Verba. 1994. "Gender and the Pathways to Participation: The Role of Resources." *The Journal of Politics* 56: 963–990.

Schlozman, Kay Lehman, Sidney Verba, and Henry E. Brady. 1995. "Participation's Not a Paradox: The View from American Activists." *British Journal of Political Science* 25 (January): 1–36.

Schreck, Carl. 2006a. "Assailants Beat Kasparov's Aide." *Moscow Times*, March 22.

Schreck, Carl. 2006b. "Fight over Putin Splits Beslan Group." *Moscow Times*, April 20.

Schröder, Ingo W., and Bettina Schmidt. 2001. "Violent Imaginaries and Violent Practices." In Bettina Schmidt and Ingo W. Schröder, eds., *Anthropology of Violence and Conflict*. New York: Routledge, pp. 1–25.

Schuessler, Alexander A. 2000. "Expressive Voting." *Rationality and Society* 12, no. 1: 87–119.

Schuman, Howard, Charlotte Steeh, Lawrence D. Bobo, and Maria Krysan. 1997. *Racial Attitudes in America: Trends and Interpretations*. Cambridge, MA: Harvard University Press.

Schuman, Howard, and Stanley Presser. 1996. *Questions and Answers in Attitude Surveys: Experiments on Question Form, Wording, and Context*. Thousand Oaks, CA: Sage.

Schuster, Mark A., Bradley D. Stein, Lisa H. Jaycox, Rebecca L. Collins, Grant N. Marshall, Marc N. Elliott, Annie J. Zhou, David E. Kanouse, Janina L. Morrison, and Sandra H. Berry. 2001. "A National Survey of Stress Reactions after the September 11, 2001, Terrorist Attacks." *New England Journal of Medicine* 345, no. 20 (November 15): 1507–1512.

Schwartz, David C. 1976. "Political Alienation." *Society* 13, no. 5 (July–August): 27–29.

"Seeking Public Accountability for Beslan." 2004. *Radio Free Europe/Radio Liberty Analytical Reports* 5, no. 16 (October 5).

Seeman, Melvin. 1959. "On the Meaning of Alienation." *American Sociological Review* 24, no. 6 (December): 783–791.

Seeman, Melvin. 1975. "Alienation Studies." *Annual Review of Sociology* 1: 91–123.

Seidman, Gay W. 2000. "Blurred Lines: Nonviolence in South Africa." *PS: Political Science and Politics* 33, no. 2 (June): 161–167.

Seligman, Martin E. P. 1975. *Helplessness: On Depression. Development. and Death*. San Francisco, CA: Freeman.

Seligman, Martin E. P. 1998. *Learned Optimism: How to Change Your Mind and Your Life*. New York: Pocket Books.

Seltzer, Judith A., and Debra Kalmuss. 1988. "Socialization and Stress Explanations for Spouse Abuse." *Social Forces* 67, no. 2 (December): 473–491.

Semyenova, Oksana. 2005. "The Charlatan." *Noviye Izvestia*, no. 174 (September 25): 1.

Sergeyev, Nikolai. 2006. "Alternativenyi Beslan" [Alternative Beslan]. *Kommersant*, no. 159 (August 29): 1.

Shapovalov, Alexander. 2005. "Kozak raschishchayet dorogi" [Kozak clears the roads]. *Nezavisimaya gazeta*, no. 11 (January 24): 3.

Shavlokhova, Madina. 2005a. "Chairman of Mothers of Beslan Susanna Dudiyeva: "Resurrection Is in the Bible, but It Is a Realistic with Grabovoi." *Izvestiya*, no. 178 (October 4): 1.

Shavlokhova, Madina. 2005b. "Kolesnikov poobeshchal materyam Beslana gromkie protsessy nad 'chinumami'" [Kolesnikov promises Beslan mothers high-profile trials of 'bungling bureaucrats']. *Izvestia*, no. 178 (October 4): 1.

Shavlokhova, Madina, Olga Allenova, and Alek Akhundov. 2004. "Beslan izgnal prokurora" [Beslan banished the prosecutor]. *Kommersant*, no. 208 (November 5): 1, 3; reprinted as "Beslan Sends Prosecutor Packing—Relatives of the Deceased Accuse Investigators of Lying." *The Current Digest of the Post Soviet Press* 56, no. 44 (December 1).

Shavlokhova, Madina, and Dmitry Balburov. 2007. "Victims Need No Money." *Gazeta*, no. 114, p. 4; retrieved through *RusData Dialine: Russian Press Digest*, June 29.

Shavlokhova, Madina, and Dmitry Sokolov-Mitrich. 2005. "Materi protiv Gravoboi" [Mothers against Grabovoi]. *Izvestia*, September 26, p. 1.

Shaw, Todd, Louis DeSipio, Dianne Pinderhughes, and Toni-Michelle C. Travis. 2015. *Uneven Roads: An Introduction to U.S. Racial and Ethnic Politics*. Thousand Oaks, CA: CQ Press.

Sidorov, Semyen. 2004. "Tragediya v Beslane: Neofitsialnye Spiski Zalozhnikov" [Tragedy in Beslan: Unofficial Lists of Hostages]. *Utro*, September 17.

Silver, Roxane Cohen, E. Allison Holman, Daniel N. McIntosh, Michael Poulin, and Virginia Gil-Rivas. 2002. "Nationwide Longitudinal Study of Psychological Responses to September 11." *JAMA: Journal of the American Medical Association* 288, no. 10: 1235–1244.

Simon, Bernd, Michael Lowey, Stefan Sturmer, Ulrike Weber, Peter Freytag, Corinna Habig, Claudia Kampmeier, and Peter Spahlinger. 1998. "Collective Identification and Social Movement Participation." *Journal of Personality and Social Psychology* 74, no. 3: 646–658.

Simon, Bernd, and Daniela Ruhs. 2008. "Identity and Politicization among Turkish Migrants in Germany: The Role of Dual Identification." *Journal of Personality and Social Psychology* 95, no. 6: 1354–1366.

Singh, Amardeep. 2002. "'We Are Not the Enemy': Hate Crimes against Arabs, Muslims, and Those Perceived to Be Arab or Muslim after September 11." *Human Rights Watch* 14, no. 6 (November, G).

Skitka, Linda J., Christopher W. Bauman, and Elizabeth Mullen. 2004. "Political Tolerance and Coming to Psychological Closure Following the September 11, 2001, Terrorist Attacks: An Integrative Approach," *Personality and Social Psychology Bulletin* 30, 6: 743–756.

Skitka, Linda J., Christopher W. Bauman, Nicholas P. Aramovich, and G. Scott Morgan. 2006. "Confrontational and Preventative Policy Responses to Terrorism: Anger Wants a Fight and Fear Wants 'Them' to Go Away." *Basic and Applied Social Psychology* 28, no. 4: 375–384.

"Slushaniye po delu materei Beslana v ESPCh zaplanirovano na seredinu oktyabrya" [A hearing on the Beslan mothers' case in the ECHR is scheduled for mid-October]. 2014. *Itar-Tass*, September 1.

Small, Deborah A., Jennifer S. Lerner, and Baruch Fischhoff. 2006. "Emotion Priming and Attributions for Terrorism: American's Reactions in a National Field Experiment," *Political Psychology* 27, no. 2 (April): 289–298.

Smirnov, Andrei. 2005. "Beslan Mothers Trust Putin, Demand Dzasokhov's Head." *Eurasia Daily Monitor* 2, no. 38 (February 24).

Smith, Christian. 1991. *The Emergence of Liberation Theology: Radical Religion and Social Movement Theory*. Chicago: University of Chicago Press.

Smith, Craig A., and Phoebe Ellsworth. 1985. "Patterns of Cognitive Appraisal in Emotion." *Journal of Personality and Social Psychology* 48: 813–838.

Smith, Tom W. 1984. "The Polls: Gender and Attitudes Toward Violence." *The Public Opinion Quarterly* 48, no. 1 (Spring): 384–396.

Snow, David A. E., Burke Rochford, Jr., Steven K. Worden, and Robert D. Benford. 1986. "Frame Alignment Processes, Micromobilization, and Movement Participation." *American Sociological Review* 51 (August): 464–481.

Sokirianskaia, Ekaterina. 2007. "'Reliable' and 'Unreliable' Peoples: The Ingush-Ossetian Conflict and Prospects for Post-Beslan Reconciliation." In Pamela Kilpadi, ed., *Islam and Tolerance in Wider Europe*. New York: Open Society Institute/Central European University Press, pp. 45–61.

Sokolov-Mitrich, Dmitry. 2004. "Beslan Seized by Sectarians and Swindlers." *Izvestia*, November 26, p. 1.

Solomon, Robert C. 1994. "Sympathy and Vengeance: The Role of the Emotions in Justice." In Stephanie H. van Goozen, Nanne E. Van de Poll, and Joseph A. Sergeant, eds., *Emotions: Essays on Emotion Theory*. Hillsdale, NJ: Lawrence Erlbaum Associates, pp. 291–311.

Souleimanov, Emil Aslan, and Huseyn Aliyev. 2015. "Blood Revenge and Violent Mobilization: Evidence from the Chechen Wars." *International Security* 40, no. 2: 158–180.

Speckhard, Anne, and Khapta Akhmedova. 2006. "The Making of a Martyr: Chechen Suicide Terrorism." *Studies in Conflict & Terrorism* 29, no. 5: 429–492.

Sperling, Valerie. 1999. *Organizing Women in Contemporary Russia: Engendering Transition*. New York: Cambridge University Press.

St. John, Craig, and Jesse Fuchs. 2002. "The Heartland Responds to Terror: Volunteering after the Bombing of the Murrah Federal Building." *Social Science Quarterly* 83: 397–415.

Staub, Ervin, and Daniel Bar-Tal. 2003. "Genocide, Mass Killing, and Intractable Conflict: Roots, Evolution, Prevention, and Reconciliation." In David O. Sears, Leonie Huddy, and Robert Jervis, eds., *Oxford Handbook of Political Psychology*. Oxford: Oxford University Press, pp. 710–751.

Stephen, Chris. 2005a. "Belsan Siege Inquiry Has Dodged Big Questions," *The Irish Times*, September 1.

Stephen, Chris. 2005b. "Beslan Victims Remembered as Families Allege Official Cover-Up." *The Irish Times*, September 2.

Struch, Naomi, and Shalom H. Schwartz. 1989. "Intergroup Aggression: Its Predictors and Distinctiveness from In-Group Bias." *Journal of Personality and Social Psychology* 56, no. 3: 364–73.

Sukhov, Ivan. 2004. "Dzasokhov Sacrifices Ministers." *Vremya Novostei*, no. 164, September 10.

"Survivors of School Siege in Southern Russia Set Up Movement to Support Victims." 2009. *Interfax News Agency*, retrieved through *BBC Monitoring Former Soviet Union – Political*, November 20.

Tagayeva, Emma Lazarovna, and Others against Russia. 2012. European Court of Human Rights, Application no. 26562/07, April 10.

Taratuta, Yulia. 2007. "Ubistvo detei v Rossii ne povod dlya pokayaniya" [Killing children is not grounds for repentance in Russia]. *Kommersant*, no. 158 (September 3): 4.

Tarrow, Sidney. 1998. *Power in Movement: Social Movements and Contentious Politics*, 2nd ed. Cambridge: Cambridge University Press.

Tate, Katherine. 2003. *Black Faces in the Mirror: African Americans and Their Representatives in the U.S. Congress*. Princeton, NJ: Princeton University Press.

Tausch, Nicole, Julia C. Becker, Russell Spears, Oliver Christ, Rim Saab, Purnima Singh, and Roomana N. Siddiqui. 2011. "Explaining Radical Group Behavior: Developing Emotion and Efficacy Routes to Normative and Nonnormative Collective Action." *Journal of Personality and Social Psychology* 101, no. 1: 129–148.

Taylor, S. E., and J. D. Brown. 1988. "Illusion and Wellbeing: A Social Psychological Perspective on Mental Health." *Psychological Bulletin* 2: 193–210.

Tedeschi, Richard G. 1999. "Violence Transformed: Posttraumatic Growth in Survivors and Their Societies." *Aggression and Violent Behavior* 4, no. 3: 319–341.

Tedeschi, Richard G., and Lawrence G. Calhoun. 1996. "The Posttraumatic Growth Inventory." *Journal of Traumatic Stress* 9: 455–471.

Tessler, Mark, and Ina Warriner. 1997. "Gender, Feminism, and Attitudes toward International Conflict: Exploring Relationships with Survey Data from the Middle East." *World Politics* 49, no. 2 (January): 250–281.

"The European Court Came to the Slowness of Russia on the Question of the Beslan Terrorist Act." 2012. *15-I Region*, November 20.

Tilly, Charles. 1978. *From Mobilization to Revolution*. Reading, MA: Addison-Wesley.

Tilly, Charles, and Sidney Tarrow. 2007. *Contentious Politics*. Boulder, CO: Paradigm Press.

"Timeline: the Beslan School Seige." 2004. *The Guardian*, September 6.

Tishkov, Valery. 1997. *Ethnicity, Nationalism and Conflict in and After the Soviet Union: The Mind Aflame*. Thousand Oaks, CA: Sage Publications.

Tlisova, Fatima. 2006a. "New Federal Prosecutor Vows More Investigation into Beslan Terror Attack." *Associated Press International*, August 11.

Tlisova, Fatima. 2006b. "Remembering the Dead in Beslan." *Moscow Times*, September 4.

Tokhsyrov, Vadim. 2004. "Pisma vlasti: Materi pogibshikh v Beslane gotovyat pismo prezidentu" [Letters to the authorities: Mothers of the dead in Beslan are preparing a letter to the president]. *Kommersant*, no. 217 (3056) (November 19): 8.

Tokhsyrov, Vadim. 2005. "Beslantsam nadoyelo zhdat pravdy" [Beslan residents are tired of waiting for truth]. *Kommersant*, no. 9 (January 21): 3.

Tokhsyrov, Vadim. 2007a. "Osetinskikh militsionerov prigovoryat k amnistii [Ossetian police officers sentenced to amnesty]," *Kommersant*, no. 79 (3655) (May 11).

Tokhsyrov, Vadim. 2007b. "Ikh naznachat nevinovnymi" [They will be found not guilty]. *Gazeta.ru*, May 31.

Tomkins, Silvan S. 1991. *Affect, Imagery, Consciousness: III. The Negative Affects: Anger and Fear*. New York: Springer.

Traugott, M., Ted Brader, D. Coral, R. Curtin, D. Featherman, R. Groves, et al. 2002. "How Americans Responded: A Study of Public Reactions to 9/11/01." *PS.: Political Science and Politics* 35, no. 3: 511–516.

Tskhurbayev, Alan. 2005. "News. Vladikavkaz." *Nezavisimaya Gazeta*, no. 115 (June 9): 4.

Tskhurbayev, Alan. 2006. "Beslan Controversy Won't Go Away." *Institute for War & Peace Reporting*, issue 356, September 16.

Tskhurbayev, Alan. 2007a. "Novy Beslanskii sud" [New Beslan trial]. *Gazeta.ru*, June 26.

Tskhurbayev (also spelled Tsukurbayev), Alan. 2007b. "The Hole in the Wall Is Not from That Explosion." *Gazeta.ru*, July 27.

Tskhurbayev, Alan, and Sergei Migalin. 2006. "Dzasokhov Haunt." *Nezavisimaya Gazeta*, March 16.

Tsugaeva, Bela. 2006. "A Rehabilitation Centre for Families Is Opened in Beslan." *UNICEF: Russian Federation*, March 29.

Tsutsui, Kiyoteru. 2004. "Global Civil Society and Ethnic Social Movements in the Contemporary World." *Sociological Forum* 19, no. 1 (March): 63–87.

Tuathail, Gearoid O. 2009. "Placing Blame: Making Sense of Beslan." *Political Geography* 28: 4–15.

Tufekci, Zeynep, and Christopher Wilson. 2012. "Social Media and the Decision to Participate in Political Protest: Observations From Tahrir Square." *Journal of Communication* 62, no. 2 (April): 363–379.

Turner, Jonathan H. 2011. *The Problem of Emotions in Societies*. New York: Routledge.

Turner, Jonathan H., and Jan E. Stets. 2006. "Sociological Theories of Human Emotions." *Annual Review of Sociology* 32: 25–52.

Tyler, Tom R., Robert J. Boeckmann, Heather J. Smith, and Yuen J. Huo. 1997. *Social Justice in a Diverse Society*. Boulder, CO: Westview Press.

Urdal, Henrik . 2006. "A Clash of Generations? Youth Bulges and Political Violence." *International Studies Quarterly* 50, no. 3 (September): 607–629.

Useem, Bert. 1980. "Solidarity Model, Breakdown Model, and the Boston Anti-Busing Movement." *American Sociological Review* 45: 357–369.

Uvin, Peter. 1998. *Aiding Violence: The Development Enterprise in Rwanda*. West Hartford, CT: Kumarian.

Uzzell, Lawrence. 2004. "Official Statements on Beslan: A Study in Obfuscation." *The Jamestown Foundation North Caucasus Analysis* 5, issue 35.

Valentino, Nicholas A., Krysha Gregorowicz, and Eric W. Gorenendyk. 2009. "Efficacy, Emotions and the Habit of Participation." *Political Behavior* 31: 307–330.

Valentino, Nicholas A., Ted Brader, Eric W. Groenendyk, Krysha Gregorowicz, and Vincent L. Hutchings. 2011. "Election Night's Alright for Fighting: The Role of Emotions in Political Participation." *The Journal of Politics* 73, no. 1 (January): 156–170.

Valenzuela, Sebastian, Arturo Arriagada, and Andres Scherman. 2012. "The Social Media Basis of Youth Protest Behavior: The Case of Chile." *Journal of Communication* 62, no. 2 (April): 299–314.

Valieva, Rita. 2012. "In Beslan, the Memory of Children Killed in the US Is Honored." *15-I region*, December 18.

van der Toorn, Jojanneke, Matthew Feinberg, John T. Jost, Aaron C. Kay, Tom R. Tyler, Robb Willer, and Caroline Wilmuth. 2015. "A Sense of Powerlessness Fosters System Justification: Implications for the Legitimation of Authority, Hierarchy, and Government." *Political Psychology* 36, no. 1 (February): 93–110.

Van Orden, K. A., T. K. Witte, L. M. James, Y. Castro, K. H. Gordon, S. R. Braithwaite, and T. E. Joiner. 2008. "Suicidal Ideation in College Students Varies across Semesters: The Mediating Role of Belongingness." *Suicide and Life-Threatening Behavior* 38, no. 4: 427–435.

Van Tongeren, Daryl R., Jeni L. Burnette, Ernest O'Boyle, Everett L. Worthington Jr., and Donelson R. Forsyth. 2013. "A Meta-Analysis of Intergroup Forgiveness." *The Journal of Positive Psychology* 9, no. 1: 81–95.

van Zomeren, Martijn, Russell Spears, Agneta H. Fischer, and Colin Wayne Leach. 2004. "Put Your Money Where Your Mouth Is! Explaining Collective Action Tendencies Through Group-Based Anger and Group Efficacy." *Journal of Personality and Social Psychology* 87, no. 5: 649–664.

Varese, Federico, and Meir Yaish. 2000. "The Importance of Being Asked: The Rescue of Jews in Nazi Europe." *Rationality and Society* 12: 307–334.

Varshney, Ashutosh. 2002. *Ethnic Conflict and Civic Life: Hindus and Muslims in India.* New Haven, CT: Yale University Press.

Varshney, Ashutosh, ed. 2010. *Collective Violence in Indonesia.* Boulder, CO: Lynne Rienner.

Veenema, Tener Goodwin, and Kathryn Schroeder-Bruce. 2002. "The Aftermath of Violence: Children, Disaster, and Posttraumatic Stress Disorder." *Journal of Pediatric Health Care* 16, no. 5 (September–October): 235–244.

Verba, Sidney, and Norman H. Nie. 1972. *Participation in America: Political Democracy and Equality.* New York: Harper and Row.

Verba, Sidney, Kay Lehman Schlozman, and Henry E. Brady. 1995. *Voice and Equality: Civic Voluntarism in American Politics.* Cambridge, MA: Harvard University Press.

Verba, Sidney, Nancy Burns, and Kay Lehman Schlozman. 1997. "Knowing and Caring about Politics: Gender and Political Engagement." *The Journal of Politics* 59, no. 4 (November): 1051–1072.

"Victims File Appeal Against Russian School Seizure Verdict," 2006. *Associated Press International*, May 31.

Vlasova, Irina. 2004a. "Vsye commissii peressorilis [All commissions are quarreling]," *Novye Izvestiya*, no. 171 (September 20).

Vlasova, Irina. 2004b. "Beslan Aftermath." *Pravda*, September 27.

"Voice of Beslan against Bringing Back Death Penalty." 2006. *Russia & CIS General Newswire, Interfax News Agency*, March 9.

"Voice of Beslan Appeal Found Extremist." 2010. *SOVA Center for Information and Analysis*, April 23.

"Voice of Beslan Members Meet with UN Commissioner." 2006. *Russia & CIS General Newswires, Interfax News Agency*, February 22.

"Voice of Beslan NGO Appeals to Russian President about 'Persecution.'" 2008. *BBC Monitoring Former Soviet Union – Political*, January 11.

Voitova, Yana. 2005. "Beslan Relatives Quiz FSB Official." *Moscow Times*, December 16: 1.

Voitova, Yana. 2006a. "Dzasokhov Testifies to Jeers and Sobs." *Moscow Times*, January 13.

Voitova, Yana. 2006b. "Beslan Tries to Cope, 2 Years On." *Moscow Times*, September 1.

Voronov, Vladimir. 2006. "Glavnaya taina Beslana" [The main mystery of Beslan]. *Novoe Vremya*, no. 36 (September 8): 6–9.

Vose, Clement E. 1959. *Caucasians Only*. Berkeley: University of California Press.

Walsh, Edward J. 1981. "Resource Mobilization and Citizen Protest in Communities around Three Mile Island." *Social Problems* 29, no. 1 (October): 1–21.

Walsh, Nick Paton. 2004a. "Frantic Search for Missing as Beslan Begins to Bury Its Dead." *The Guardian*, September 6.

Walsh, Nick Paton. 2004b. "Grieving Beslan Residents Suspect Death Toll Cover-Up." *The Guardian*, September 20.

Walsh, Nick Paton. 2005. "Mystery Still Shrouds Beslan Six Months On." *The Guardian*, February 15.

Walter, Barbara F. 2004. "Does Conflict Beget Conflict? Explaining Recurring Civil War." *Journal of Peace Research* 41, no. 3 (May): 371–388.

Weaver, Kent R. 1986. "The Politics of Blame Avoidance." *Journal of Public Policy* 6: 371–398.

Weir, Fred. 2004. "In Beslan, a Tense Bid for Calm." *The Christian Science Monitor* 96, no. 224 (October 14): 6.

Weir, Fred. 2005a. "Beslan Mothers: Putin Is Culpable." *The Christian Science Monitor* 97, no. 193 (August 29): 6.

Weir, Fred. 2005b. "Russia Struggles to Keep Grip in Caucasus." *The Christian Science Monitor*, no. 203 (September 13): 6.

Weissman, M. M., D. Scholomskas, M. Pottenger, B. A. Prusoff, and B. Z. Locke. 1977. "Assessing Depressive Symptoms in Five Psychiatric Populations: a Validation Study." *American Journal of Epidemiology* 106: 203–214.

Wexler, Martha. 2005. "Mothers of Beslan Become Political Force." *National Public Radio*, July 22.

White, Ian R., Patrick Royston, and Angela M. Wood. 2011. "Multiple Imputation Using Chained Equations: Issues and Guidance for Practice." *Statistics in Medicine* 30 (November 4): 377–399.

Wilkinson, Steven I. 2004. *Votes and Violence: Electoral Competition and Ethnic Riots in India*. Cambridge: Cambridge University Press.

Wilson, John, and Marc Musick. 1997. "Who Cares? Toward an Integrated Theory of Volunteer Work." *American Sociological Review* 62: 694–713.

Wolfinger, Raymond E., and Steven J. Rosenstone. 1980. *Who Votes?* New Haven, CT: Yale University Press.

Wood, Elisabeth J. 2003. *Insurgent Collective Action and Civil War in El Salvador*. New York: Cambridge University Press.

Yasmann, Victor. 2004. "Beslan Commission Head Blames Lack of Leadership." *Radio Free Europe/Radio Liberty Newsline* 8, no. 240, part I (December 23).

Yasmann, Victor. 2006. "Russia: Corruption Scandal Could Shake Kremlin." *Radio Free Europe/Radio Liberty*, September 26.

"Zhenshchiny iz 'Golosa Beslana' obyavili golodovku" [Women from Voice of Beslan announced a hunger strike]. 2006. *Nezavisimaya gazeta*, February 9.

"Zhiteli Beslana vstretyatsya s genprokurorom Ustinovym" [Beslan Residents Meet with Prosecutor General Ustinov]. 2006. *Nezavisimaya gazeta*, June 1.

Zimprich, Daniel, and Anna Mascherek. 2012. "Measurement Invariance and Age-related Differences of Trait Anger Aaross the Adult Lifespan." *Personality and Individual Differences* 52 (February): 334–339.

Zurcher, Christoph. 2009. *The Post-Soviet Wars: Rebellion, Ethnic Conflict, and Nationhood in the Caucasus*. New York: New York University Press.

Index

For the benefit of digital users, indexed terms that span two pages (e.g., 52–53) may, on occasion, appear on only one of those pages.

Tables and figures are indicated by *t* and *f* following the page number

Besolov, Valery, 157–58, 164, 165–66
Betrozov, Ruslan, 47, 47n.2, 56, 105n.15
biases
    acquiescence bias, 186, 212, 305–6
    recall bias, 13, 176, 177, 178, 184, 302–4
    response bias, 15, 19–20, 122, 358–59
    sampling bias, 19
    social desirability bias, 123, 176, 177–78,
        258, 259
Bilan, Dima, 274–75
biography
    age and, 381–83, 383t
    applicability of findings to other places and
        times and, 453–54
    biographical availability, 389–93
    demographics and, 380–89, 383t
    education and, 383t, 387–89
    gender and, 383–87, 383t
    income and, 383t, 387–89
    interviews on, 375, 377, 382, 385, 386–87,
        390–93
    overview of, 373–74
    political action and, 375–81, 376t, 379t, 382–
        83, 383t, 386–87, 388–89, 390–92
    portrait of activists and retaliators and, 412,
        419, 421
    previous research on, 384, 386, 387–88
    prior harm as predictor, 374–77, 376t
    prior political activism as predictor, 377–80,
        379t
    retaliatory violence and, 375, 376–77, 376t,
        380–82, 383–86, 383t, 387–88, 389–90,
        392–93
blame. See also accountability for attack
    anger and, 209, 217–18, 219–20, 221t, 222,
        313
    attribution of, 209, 211, 217–18, 222, 278,
        291, 292–93, 297, 299–301, 306, 313, 396–
        97, 458
    avoidance of, 278, 279, 282, 301
    blame game, 291–92
    causal responsibility and, 278
    conditionality of, 313–14, 314t, 315t
    conspiracy theories and, 293–95
    corruption and, 290
    counterterrorism operation and, 291–92
    difficulty of assigning, 278, 291–93
    efficacy and, 313–14, 314t, 315t, 362–63
    elusiveness of, 291–93
    emotions and, 211
    ethnic prejudice and, 264–65, 265t, 266t
    firefighters and, 292
    incompetence and, 290

interviews on, 280–90, 293–94, 300–1
limitations to measurement of, 305–7
local authorities singled out for, 286–90
measurement and, 302–7, 303t
mobilizing frame of, 278–80
overview of, 269
political action and, 300–1, 310, 312t, 362–63
portrait of activists and retaliators and,
    419–21
Putin singled out for, 280–86, 306
responses to violence and, 278–95
retaliatory violence and, 296–97, 307–10,
    309t, 362–63, 419–21
scapegoating and, 95, 210, 215, 293–95
variation in, 284–86, 288–90
victim data on, 303t, 307–10, 309t, 312t
blockade, 8, 59, 87, 139, 154–55, 227, 299, 329–
    30, 351, 355, 365
blood feuds, 11, 114
Boloyev, Ruslan, 103–4
Brady, Henry, 13, 176–77, 184
Brasseur, Anne, 142–43
bribery, 65–66, 70, 290, 471. See also corruption
Budennovsk hospital hostage taking (1995),
    43, 55, 67
Bzarova, Emilia, 143, 155–56, 170

cafeteria of school, 49, 63–64
casualties of attack, 81–83, 82t
Caucasus Refugee Council, 15
causal responsibility, 278
causation, 26, 203, 207–9, 363–67, 371, 413
cemetery (Beslan City of Angels Cemetery), 59,
    137–38, 142, 232, 385
census surveys, 15
Chaika, Yuri, 140–41, 145, 168
chain of command issues, 75–77
Chechen-Ossetian conflict
    Beslan attack in context of, 43
    Chechen Wars and, 41–42
    history of, 41–43
    hostage situations in, 42
    nationalist dimensions of, 41–42
    Prigorodny region and, 41
    terrorist attacks in, 42–43
Chechen War (1994-1996), 35, 41–42, 55, 123
Chechen War (1999-2009), 35, 42, 55, 123
checkpoints, 64–66, 92–93, 163, 471
Chedzhemov, Taimuraz, 106, 159–60, 162,
    165–66
Churkin, Vitaly, 275–76
City of Angels Cemetery. See cemetery (Beslan
    City of Angels Cemetery)